ALGEBRA 1
for Christian Schools®

Bob Jones University Press, Greenville, South Carolina 29614
Textbook Division

NOTE:

The fact that materials produced by other publishers are referred to in this volume does not constitute an endorsement by Bob Jones University Press of the content or theological position of materials produced by such publishers. The position of the Bob Jones University Press, and the University itself, is well known. Any references and ancillary materials are listed as an aid to the student or the teacher and in an attempt to maintain the accepted academic standards of the publishing industry.

ALGEBRA 1 for Christian Schools®

Kathy Diane Pilger, Ed.D

Produced in cooperation with the Bob Jones University Department of Mathematics of the College of Arts and Science, the School of Education, and Bob Jones Academy.

for Christian Schools is a registered trademark of Bob Jones University Press.

ISBN 0-89084-227-2

15   14   13   12   11   10   9   8   7

CONTENTS

INTRODUCTION

Welcome to Algebra I. Your goal this year in this course should be to increase your mathematical knowledge and to expand your mathematical intellect. The Bible says in Proverbs 1:5, "A wise man will hear, and will increase learning; and a man of understanding shall attain unto wise counsels." You should strive not only to learn how to do the skills taught in this course but also to understand why the skills you learn work to produce the correct answer.

Just as our spiritual lives must be built upon the strong foundation of Jesus Christ—"For other foundation can no man lay than that is laid, which is Jesus Christ" (I Cor. 3:11)—mathematics must be built upon a strong foundation of arithmetic. You have had arithmetic in all of your previous math classes. Now you will be able to apply to algebra what you have learned about arithmetic. If you learn each principle each day, you will successfully and logically build mathematical principles. You need to develop logical thinking to guide you through life. You must also be able to take biblical principles and reason to true conclusions. Likewise, by applying mathematical rules, your answers to problems will be correct. God is true and orderly: "He is the Rock, his work is perfect: for all his ways are judgment: a God of truth and without iniquity, just and right is he" (Deut. 32:4). Mathematics, which comes directly from our study of God's created universe, is also true and orderly.

This book starts with a review of basic computations in the first chapter; then it introduces algebra and continues to more advanced topics in algebra. Do not let the term *algebra* frighten you. Here are a few suggestions to help you become successful in algebra.

1. Listen carefully to all instructions and examples your teacher gives in class. Write down examples to study later.

2. Read each section of the book and study examples carefully.

3. Study in the same place and at the same time each day. Study in a quiet place.

4. Don't put off your work until later. Get the work done; then relax.

5. Make diagrams and pictures of problems when possible.

6. If you have questions while studying, write them down so you won't forget them.

7. Practice mentally what you have learned. Go through the process from memory.

8. Do all work neatly. You can avoid much confusion by working neatly.

Throughout this book you will gain a firm mathematical foundation on which to build in future math classes, science classes, and everyday life; and you will gain logical reasoning concepts to be used even in biblical studies. Algebra takes characteristics of the physical world, analyzes these characteristics through the use of symbols, and then relates this analysis to our physical world. You should see the orderliness of God through your study of algebra, and the reflection of God in algebra should help you become more Christ-like.

You are about to embark on a new endeavor, so have a good time. Remember the Bible says, "And whatsoever ye do, do it heartily, as to the Lord, and not unto men" (Col. 3:23). This admonition includes algebra. Have fun as you increase your knowledge.

CHAPTER 1

NUMBERS AND THEIR OPERATIONS

Why do we study numbers and their operations? How do we use numbers? How do your parents use numbers when they write checks or pay bills? Of what use are numbers to scientists and computer programmers?

A number is an idea, an abstraction that represents that which is concrete. Numerals are symbols or letters used to denote numbers. We can refer to the number of wheels on a car by either the word *four* or the symbol 4, an Arabic numeral that stands for a certain number. When God created the world, He counted the days. Through the ages, civilizations have developed various systems of enumeration. For example, one hundred may be represented in Arabic numerals as 100, in Roman numerals as C, in ancient Egyptian numerals as $\mathcal{9}$, and in Greek numerals as ρ.

Look at the following mathematical representations.

- 5,382
- 5.382×10^3
- $\overline{\text{V}}$CCCLXXXII
- ⲢⲢⲢⲢⲢ999∩∩∩∩∩∩∩II
- $1010100000110_{(2)}$

Do all of them mean 5,382 to you? Certainly not, but a person familiar with each system can easily determine the number represented by such symbols. Although the symbolic representations of the number differ, the number itself is a specific, absolute number that God has established, and that number remains fixed.

What does π or e mean? What does 32K mean when you see it in a computer advertisement? What does 4.39×10^{-13} mean when you see it in a scientific magazine? How can you work with a problem that uses 25%? What is a 94.5-inch telescope? What kind of number is 94.5? What does 50 million electron volts mean? Does -14 have any meaning to you? What does it mean for bacteria to grow at a rate of 2^n?

Numbers of various shapes and forms are found in every field of study. It is important that you learn what these numbers mean and how to use them. Because you need to be acquainted with many of the number systems that are commonly used in today's technological society, this chapter will familiarize you with different types of numbers and review the four basic operations using these numbers.

KINDS OF NUMBERS

Our Number System

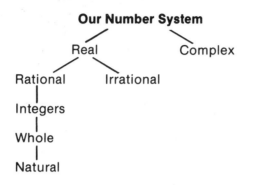

Can you remember when you learned to count? Slowly and deliberately you probably learned to count to ten: 1, 2, 3, 4, 5, 6, 7, 8, 9, 10. But you soon learned to count beyond ten. The numbers you used are called the *natural numbers*, or *counting numbers*, because they are numbers that describe what people see in nature. The natural numbers begin with 1 and continue infinitely.

Another group of numbers is the *whole numbers*, which have only one more number than the natural numbers. What one number is a whole number but not a natural number?

The numbers 0, 1, 2, 3, and so forth, are whole numbers. Sometimes the symbol . . . is used for "and so forth." Thus you could write "The whole numbers are 0, 1, 2, 3, ..." Whole numbers are the stepping stones for our entire number system.

The next group in the number system is the integers. The word *integer* comes from the Latin word that means "entire." *Integers* are whole numbers and their opposites.

$$\ldots, -4, -3, -2, -1, 0, 1, 2, 3, 4, \ldots$$

Notice that the integers have no smallest number and no largest number. Integers smaller than 0 are preceded by a negative sign.

Data Base

Johann Widman published a book in 1489 that used the + and - symbols for the first time. These symbols were not really used at that time to indicate the operations of addition and subtraction but rather to indicate excess and deficiency. By 1514, + and - were being used to indicate operations and were used quite often by Vander Hoecke, a mathematician from the Netherlands. The plus sign probably originated from the Latin word *et*, meaning "and," a word often used to indicate addition. The minus sign may have come from the symbol $\overline{m}$, meaning minus.

Mr. Weber, the football coach at East Park High School, wants his players to gain the most yardage possible in the weekly scrimmage games. Each time a scrimmage team gains yards, the coach records a positive number. For example, if the team gains 5 yards, the coach records a +5. When the team loses yardage, Coach Weber records a negative number. At the end of the scrimmage, Mr. Weber totals the yardage to find the amount gained or lost. If the team gains at least 30 yards, the members do not have to run two miles after practice. Do you think the boys on the teams learned to work with integers?

Notice that numbers that look like fractions have not yet appeared in our number system. Many of you would probably like to stop right here because you don't like fractions. But fractions are very important. If there were no fractions, how could you buy half a pound of candy?

In home economics class, the girls are learning to sew a new pattern. For her dress, each girl must purchase $\frac{3}{4}$ of a yard of $\frac{5}{8}$-inch wide elastic. Do you think it is important to know the difference between $\frac{3}{4}$ of a yard and $\frac{1}{4}$ of a yard? Could the girls finish their dresses if they got $\frac{1}{4}$ of a yard of elastic?

All numbers presented so far are rational numbers. The word *rational* comes from the word meaning "ratio." *Rational numbers* are numbers that can be written as a ratio. All fractions produced by placing one integer over a nonzero integer are rational numbers. Because any integer can be written over 1, integers are also rational numbers. Numbers that cannot be expressed in fractional form are called *irrational numbers*. Look up *rational* and *irrational* in the dictionary. Do their dictionary meanings coincide with their algebraic meanings? God has created some irrational numbers such as π, $\sqrt{3}$, and $\sqrt{5}$. These numbers can only be approximated in decimal form. The decimal approximation of an irrational number is a nonterminating, nonrepeating decimal.

Natural numbers, whole numbers, integers, rational numbers, and irrational numbers make up the big group of numbers called *real numbers*. Algebra I will deal primarily with numbers in the real number system. You should realize, however, that there are other numbers besides real numbers. Complex and imaginary numbers are not part of the real number system illustrated here.

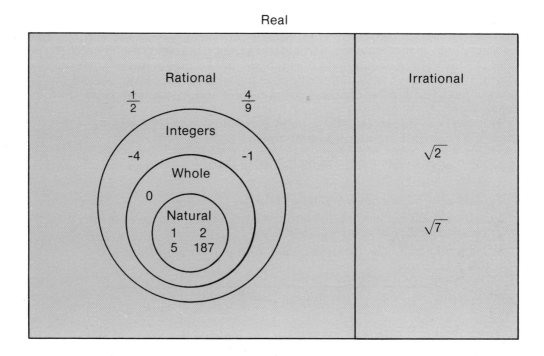

Real

Exercises

On your paper draw a chart like the one above. Label the number systems. Then place each real number below in the innermost position possible.

1. -6

2. 3

3. 4.868668666 . . .

4. $\frac{3}{2}$

5. 0.5

6. 0.313131 . . .

7. $\frac{4}{11}$

8. -100

9. 20

10. 0.721721172111 . . .

11. 0

12. $\sqrt{5}$

13. $\frac{3}{1}$

14. $\frac{-1}{4}$

15. Does the real number system have a smallest number? a largest number?

16. Does the whole number system have a smallest number? A largest number?

17. Does the natural number system have a smallest number? a largest number?

LOCATING NUMBERS ON A NUMBER LINE

Many times in mathematics, particularly algebra, graphs and number lines will aid your understanding of algebraic ideas. Later in this chapter you will review how to use number lines to perform the four basic operations of integers. In other chapters you will learn about graphs and how to use them.

Numbers can be represented in picture or model form. The picture form of a number is shown on a number line.

You can construct a number line by following these four steps.

1. Draw a line.

2. Mark an arbitrary point and label it 0.

3. Mark a point to the right of 0 and label it 1. (The distance from 0 to 1 determines a unit on the number line.)

4. Mark off equal units (as determined in step 3) on both sides of 0.

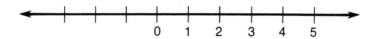

The arrows at the ends of the number line indicate that the number line extends without limit in both directions. Can you think of anything else that has no end? Does eternity end? Will everyone live forever? Yes, even you will live forever somewhere. Will it be in heaven or in hell?

Since the line continues, what would the mark after 5 be? The arrow indicates 6, 7, 8, and so on. What system of numbers is pictured on the number line above? Notice that the numbers increase in value as they go from left to right. All numbers to the right of 0 are called *positive numbers*.

What number would be on the left of 0? Draw a number line on your paper and label the units to the left and right of 0. What kind of numbers are pictured now? On this graph, the numbers to the left of 0 are called *negative numbers*. The arrow on the left end of the number line, indicating the continuation of the number line in that direction, includes numbers less than the last number you put on the

...THAT **INTEGERS** CONTINUE WITHOUT LIMIT IN BOTH DIRECTIONS... I KNOW...

line. Is -6 less than -5? Is 6 degress below 0 colder than 5 degrees below 0? On the number line, any number to the left of a given number is less than the given number.

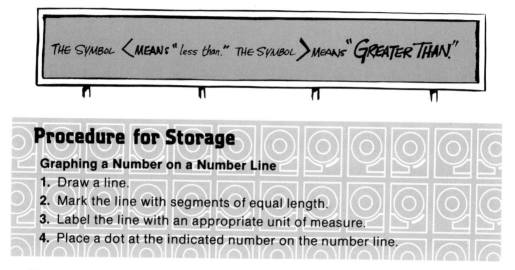

THE SYMBOL < MEANS "less than." THE SYMBOL > MEANS "GREATER THAN."

Procedure for Storage

Graphing a Number on a Number Line
1. Draw a line.
2. Mark the line with segments of equal length.
3. Label the line with an appropriate unit of measure.
4. Place a dot at the indicated number on the number line.

The dot on the number line is called the graph of the number while the number is called the coordinate of the graph.

EXAMPLES

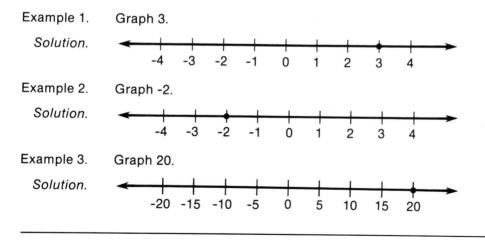

Example 1. Graph 3.

Solution.

Example 2. Graph -2.

Solution.

Example 3. Graph 20.

Solution.

The number line does not always have to be partitioned into units of one. It can be partitioned into units greater than one or into units smaller than one, which will be fractions. You will usually graph on a horizontal number line, but you could also graph on a vertical number line.

EXAMPLE

Example 4.   Graph -22.

Solution.

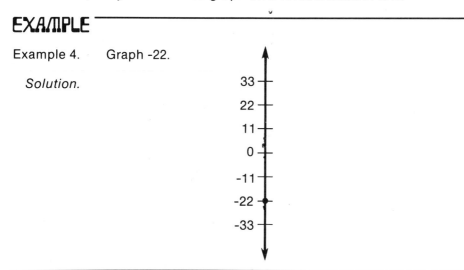

On a horizontal number line, positive is always to the right, negative to the left. On a vertical number line, positive is always up, negative down.

Exercises

Locate each integer on a horizontal number line.

1. 4   **2.** -3   **3.** -24   **4.** 80   **5.** -1

Locate each integer on a vertical number line.

6. -4   **7.** 9   **8.** -25   **9.** 100   **10.** -144

What integer is indicated by the dot on each number line?

11.

12.

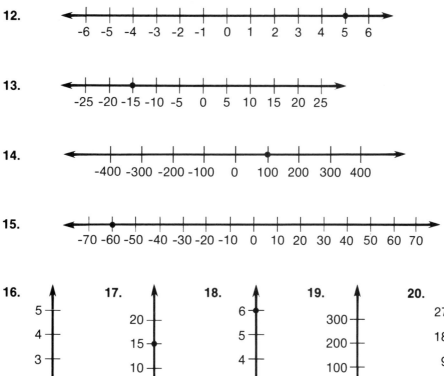

13.

14.

15.

16. **17.** **18.** **19.** **20.**

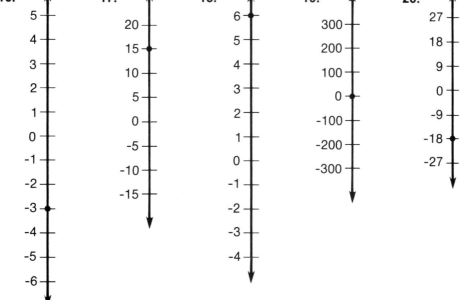

OPPOSITES AND ABSOLUTE VALUE

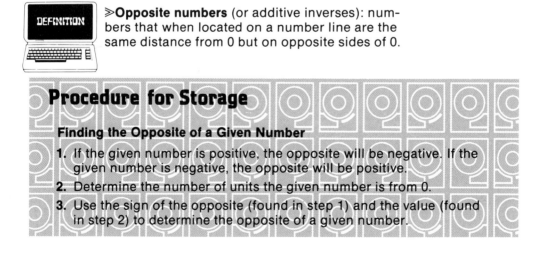

You can locate any integer on a number line. When you graph the integer 5, notice that the dot is five units to the right of 0.

```
←—+——+——+——+——+——+——+——+——+——+——+——+——+——+——+——+→
  -7  -6  -5  -4  -3  -2  -1   0   1   2   3   4   5   6   7   8
```

What number is five units to the left of 0? The numbers 5 and -5 are opposite numbers. What is the opposite of 3? 100? If the opposite of -4 is 4, what is the opposite of -10? -23?

DEFINITION ≫**Opposite numbers** (or additive inverses): numbers that when located on a number line are the same distance from 0 but on opposite sides of 0.

Procedure for Storage

Finding the Opposite of a Given Number

1. If the given number is positive, the opposite will be negative. If the given number is negative, the opposite will be positive.
2. Determine the number of units the given number is from 0.
3. Use the sign of the opposite (found in step 1) and the value (found in step 2) to determine the opposite of a given number.

Opposites are easy to find.

The opposite of 3 is -3.

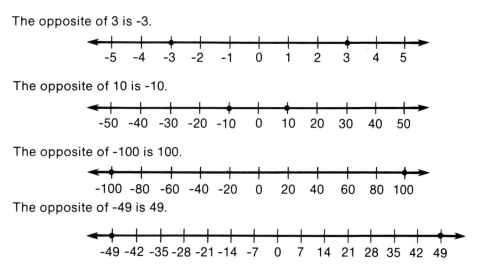

The opposite of 10 is -10.

The opposite of -100 is 100.

The opposite of -49 is 49.

Can you think of any opposites that are not numbers but are things you see each day? Can you think of any spiritual opposites? Can you find some Scripture references of opposites in the Bible?

Before you can become proficient in algebra, you must become very skilled in performing the basic operations of addition, subtraction, multiplication, and division. If you can perform these calculations quickly and accurately, you will have an advantage later in the course. A thorough knowledge of number lines and absolute value will aid you in your operations with numbers.

At this point the definition of absolute value is not a formal definition but an adequate and understandable one. In Chapter 3 you will see a more formal definition of absolute value.

 DEFINITION

≫**Absolute value of an integer:** the number of units between the integer and 0 on the number line.

The absolute value of an integer *a* is denoted by vertical parallel bars, |*a*|. This symbol is read "the absolute value of *a*."

Find |4|. How far is 4 from 0 on the number line? By counting the units, you find out that 4 is four units from 0.

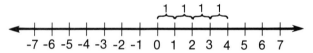

So |4| = 4

Find |-7|. How far is -7 from 0 on the number line? To find out, count seven units from 0.

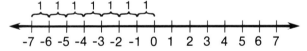

So |-7| = 7.

Notice that the negative sign does not influence the absolute value of 7 or -7 because both numbers are seven units from 0.

Exercises

Find the opposite of each integer.

1. 38	**3.** 42	**5.** 134	**7.** -412	**9.** -5
2. -14	**4.** -56	**6.** -368	**8.** -3247	**10.** 34,892

Find the absolute value of each integer.

11. |8|

12. |-17|

13. |-382|

14. |-147|

15. |0|

16. |123|

17. |84|

18. |-234|

19. |74|

20. |-132|

21. |4|

22. |-4|

23. |-307|

24. |307|

Perform the indicated operation.

25. |341 - 26|

26. |18 + 27|

27. |1246 - 389|

28. |367 - 366|

29. |64 - 32|

30. |-12| + |3|

31. |-9| + |-4|

32. |18| - |-6|

33. |-3| + |-9|

34. |26| + |-100|

35. |-86| - |23|

36. |-9| + |10|

37. |86| - |-10|

38. |4| + |27|

39. |-56| + |-29|

40. |-25| + |30|

41. What is true about the absolute values of a number and its opposite?

ADDING INTEGERS

The first operation you ever performed on numbers was probably addition. Adding is very easy. When you add two nonzero numbers, watch for the following two conditions.

EXAMPLES

Condition 1—Both numbers (addends) have the same sign.

Example 1.   (+3) + (+2) = ?

Solution.

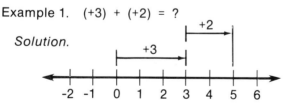

1. Start at 0.

2. Move right three units.

3. Move right two more units.

4. The final resting place, 5, is your answer.

Therefore (+3) + (+2) = +5

ple 2.   (-1) + (-3) = ?

Solution.

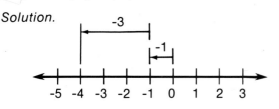

1. Start at 0.
2. Move left one unit.
3. Move left three more units.
4. The final resting place, -4, is your answer.

Therefore (-1) + (-3) = -4

Condition 2—One addend is positive and the other is negative.

Example 3.   (+3) + (-2) = ?

Solution.

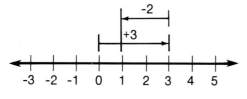

1. Start at 0.
2. Move right three units.
3. From 3, go in the negative direction (left) two units.
4. The final resting place, 1, is your answer.

Therefore (+3) + (-2) = +1

Example 4.   (-5) + (+7) = ?

Solution.

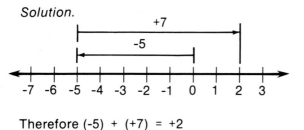

1. Start at 0.
2. Move left five units.
3. From -5, go in the positive direction (right) seven units.
4. The final resting place, 2, is your answer.

Therefore (-5) + (+7) = +2

Adding integers on number lines is often awkward and time consuming, especially if you are working with very large or very small numbers. Instead of always adding on the number line, you can add by using the following procedures.

Procedure for Storage

Adding Integers

Condition 1	Condition 2
Like-signed addends	Unlike-signed addends

Condition 1 — Like-signed addends

1. Add the absolute value of the addends.
2. Give the sum the sign of the two addends.

Condition 2 — Unlike-signed addends

1. Determine the absolute value of the addends.
2. Subtract the smaller absolute value from the larger.
3. Give the difference the sign of the addend with the greater absolute value. The result is the sum.

EXAMPLES

Example 5. $(-1) + (-3) = ?$

Solution. $|-1| + |-3| = 1 + 3 = 4$ **1.** Add absolute values.

$(-1) + (-3) = -4$ **2.** The sign of the sum must be negative. Why?

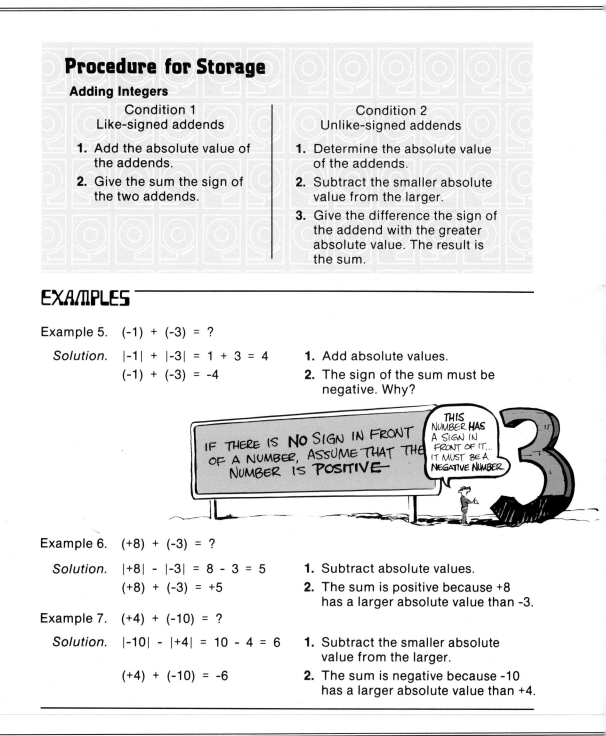

IF THERE IS NO SIGN IN FRONT OF A NUMBER, ASSUME THAT THE NUMBER IS POSITIVE

THIS NUMBER HAS A SIGN IN FRONT OF IT... IT MUST BE A NEGATIVE NUMBER

Example 6. $(+8) + (-3) = ?$

Solution. $|+8| - |-3| = 8 - 3 = 5$ **1.** Subtract absolute values.

$(+8) + (-3) = +5$ **2.** The sum is positive because +8 has a larger absolute value than -3.

Example 7. $(+4) + (-10) = ?$

Solution. $|-10| - |+4| = 10 - 4 = 6$ **1.** Subtract the smaller absolute value from the larger.

$(+4) + (-10) = -6$ **2.** The sum is negative because -10 has a larger absolute value than +4.

Just for Practice

1. 12 + (-3)
2. 5 + 9
3. (-2) + (-4)
4. (17) + (-5)
5. (-8) + (-3)

6. (7) + (8)
7. (-9) + (-7)
8. (4) + (-8)
9. (7) + (4)
10. (-8) + (-2)

You have learned in previous math classes that numbers have some special properties. These properties have been given special names so that mathematicians can talk about them without confusion. Here are several properties related to addition.

DEFINITION

➤**Mathematical property:** an equation or statement that is true for any value of the variable. Properties are sometimes called identities.

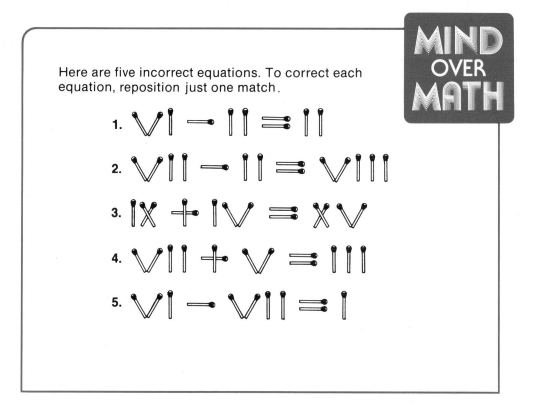

MIND OVER MATH

Here are five incorrect equations. To correct each equation, reposition just one match.

Properties of Numbers

1. What happens if you add two numbers together in different orders?

$$3 + 5 = ?$$
$$5 + 3 = ?$$

Since both expressions equal 8, the following is also true:

$$3 + 5 = 5 + 3$$

This example describes the *commutative property of addition*, which, formally stated, says that for every integer a and for every integer b,

$$a + b = b + a.$$

2. What happens if you group the numbers differently before you add these integers together?

$$2 + (9 + 4) = ?$$
$$(2 + 9) + 4 = ?$$

Since both expressions equal 15, the following is also true:

$$2 + (9 + 4) = (2 + 9) + 4$$

The way you group integers before adding them makes no difference in the sum. Formally stated, the *associative property of addition* says that for integers a, b, and c,

$$a + (b + c) = (a + b) + c$$

3. What happens if you add 0 to any integer?

$$(-10) + 0 = ?$$

Whenever you add 0, you will always get the original number; adding zero does not affect the sum. This example describes the *identity property of zero.* Zero is called the *additive identity element.* Formally stated, this property says that for every integer a, there is an integer 0, such that

$$a + 0 = a.$$

4. What happens if you add an integer and its opposite?

$$(+3) + (-3) = ?$$

The sum of any integer and its opposite is always 0, the additive identity element. Since by definition a and $-a$ are opposites, each may be called the *additive inverse* of the other. Formally stated, the *additive inverse property* says that for any integer a,

$$a + (-a) = 0.$$

Exercises

Find each sum.

1. (+3) + (+21)
2. (-13) + (+32)
3. (+26) + (-28)
4. (-7) + (-8)
5. (-126) + (+35)
6. (+781) + (+243)
7. (+7) + (-3)

8. (-14) + (-7)
9. (+36) + (+19)
10. (-7) + (+37)
11. (+384) + (-24)
12. (+6) + (-6)
13. (-10) + (10)
14. (4) + (0)

15. (-14) + (0)
16. (342) + (-463)
17. (141) + (891)
18. (-147) + (-684)
19. (-4897) + (+387)
20. (-426) + (-741)

21. Give the steps in thinking when solving (-349) + (+684).
22. What property does (-3) + 0 = -3 describe?
23. What property does (27) + (-27) = 0 describe?
24. If the temperature on a cold January day is 0° F at 7:00 A.M., increases 14° by noon, and then decreases 20° from noon to 10 P.M., what is the temperature at 10 P.M.?
25. A motorboat travels an average speed of 17 knots in still water. Set up an integer equation and solve to find the actual speed the motorboat is traveling if it is traveling against a current of 5 knots.

SUBTRACTING INTEGERS

Subtraction is simply addition of the opposite. For all integers *a* and *b*, $a - b = a + (-b)$. Since you already know how to add integers, you also know how to subtract integers.

EXAMPLES

Example 1.   (+7) - (+3) = ?

In addition, this problem would be (+7) + (-3) = (?). In subtraction, we must find the direction and distance from the subtrahend to the minuend. Look at this problem on the number line.

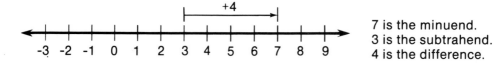

7 is the minuend.
3 is the subtrahend.
4 is the difference.

The distance from the subtrahend 3 to the minuend 7 is four units, moving from left to right, which is the positive direction. Thus the answer is +4.

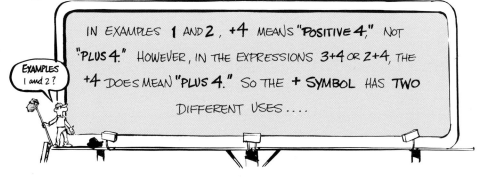

Example 2.   (+4) − (−2) = ?
Find the direction and distance from −2 to +4.

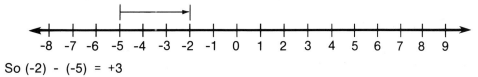

How many units are covered from −2 to 4? What direction does the arrow indicate? Thus (+4) − (−2) = +6

Example 3.   (−2) − (−5) = ?
What is the subtrahend in this example? the minuend? What is the distance and direction from the subtrahend to the minuend?

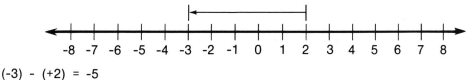

So (−2) − (−5) = +3

Example 4.   (−3) − (+2) = ?
Tell the steps of thought for solving this subtraction problem.

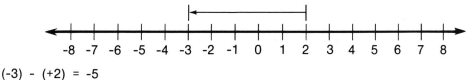

(−3) − (+2) = −5

Now that you understand the number line process of subtraction, you are ready to see a more sophisticated approach to subtraction. Look at these examples and compare them with examples 1-4.

EXAMPLES

Example 5. (+7) + (-3) = +4   Example 7. (-2) + (+5) = +3
Example 6. (+4) + (+2) = +6   Example 8. (-3) + (-2) = -5

How do the answers to examples 1-4 compare to the answers for examples 5-8? What is the difference between examples 1 and 5? First notice that example 1 is a subtraction problem but example 5 is an addition problem. Is there any other difference in the problem? Did you notice that the second integer in example 5 is the opposite of the second integer in example 1? You are now ready for the subtraction rule.

Procedure for Storage

Subtracting Integers

To subtract integers, change the subtrahend to its opposite and add the two integers.

TO SUBTRACT A NUMBER, ADD ITS OPPOSITE.

for example:
(+14) - (-6) = (+14) + (+6) = 20
(-12) - (-3) = (-12) + (+3) = -9

Exercises

Find the difference.

1. (+3) - (-2)
2. (+4) - (+5)
3. (+7) - (-3)
4. (+4) - (-9)
5. (+6) - (+8)
6. (-8) - (-2)
7. (-247) - (+82)
8. (-313) - (-629)
9. (-12) - (+5)

10. (+34) - (-241)
11. (-29) - (-5)
12. (-16) - (-31)
13. (-83) - (+47)
14. (+392) - (-78)
15. (-27) - (-41)
16. (+1324) - (+571)
17. (+387) - (-27)
18. (-12) - (-3)

19. Show on a number line the subtraction of (+5) - (-1).
20. World War I started in 1914 and World War II started in 1939. How many years apart did these two wars begin?

MULTIPLYING INTEGERS

In grade school you learned that multiplication is repeated addition.

$$3 \cdot 5 = 5 + 5 + 5 = 15$$

Since algebra uses letters so extensively, especially x for any unknown quantity, you might have difficulty distinguishing when x means "multiply" and when it is an unknown. So from now on you will use a small dot in the middle of the line to indicate multiplication. Also, when no sign is shown, as in $3x$ or $3(2 + 5)$, multiplication is intended. So $3x$ means $3 \cdot x$, and $3(2 + 5)$ means $3 \cdot (2 + 5)$.

Data Base

About 1700, Gottfried Leibniz of Leipzig, Germany, introduced the · to indicate multiplication. Leibniz was one of the inventors of calculus, an advanced mathematics. He also invented many symbols used in higher mathematics.

Properties of Numbers

1. Do you remember that $3 \cdot 5 = 5 \cdot 3$? What property describes this truth? You're right if you said the commutative property of multiplication. The factors of a multiplication problem can be arranged in any order without affecting the product. The *commutative property of multiplication* says that if *a* and *b* are integers,

$$a \cdot b = b \cdot a.$$

2. The associative property of multiplication works on the same regrouping principle as the associative property of addition. The *associative property of multiplication* simply states that you can multiply integers in different groups without changing the product.

$$2(5 \cdot 3) = (2 \cdot 5)3$$

Formally stated, the associative property says that for any integers *a*, *b*, and *c*,

$$a(bc) = (ab)c.$$

3. Do you remember what the distributive property of multiplication over addition or subtraction is? The *distributive property* can be shown with the following example.

$$3(6 + 7) = (3 \cdot 6) + (3 \cdot 7)$$
$$3(13) = 18 + 21$$
$$39 = 39$$

If *a*, *b*, and *c* are integers,

$$a(b + c) = ab + ac$$
$$\text{or}$$
$$a(b - c) = ab - ac.$$

4. What happens when you multiply an integer by 0?

$$4 \cdot 0 = ?$$

Whenever an integer is multiplied by 0, the product will always be 0. The *zero property of multiplication* states that for any integer *a*,

$$a \cdot 0 = 0.$$

5. Do you know what the identity number for multiplication is? For example, what number can you multiply with 3 and still have 3? That's right, 1. So the *multiplicative identity element* is 1. The *multiplicative identity property* states that for any integer *a*,

$$a \cdot 1 = a.$$

Factors, like addends, minuends, and subtrahends, can be positive or negative. Look at the following illustrations of multiplication as repeated addition. Watch carefully the signs of the factors and the resulting products.

$$3 \cdot 5$$
$$5 + 5 + 5 = 15$$

$$3 \cdot -5$$
$$(-5) + (-5) + (-5) = -15$$

Notice that in the first example both factors are positive and the product is also positive. In the second example, one factor is positive and the other is negative. The product is negative.

If we apply the commutative property of multiplication to the second example, we have $3 \cdot -5 = -5 \cdot 3$. Thus we know that if one factor of a multiplication problem is negative the resulting product is also negative.

Do you know what will happen if both factors are negative? Look at the following and observe the pattern in the products.

$$(-5) \cdot (3) = -15$$
$$(-5) \cdot (2) = -10$$
$$(-5) \cdot (1) = -5$$
$$(-5) \cdot (0) = 0$$
$$(-5) \cdot (-1) = ?$$
$$(-5) \cdot (-2) = ?$$
$$(-5) \cdot (-3) = ?$$

As the second factor decreases by one, by how much does the product increase? What will the missing products be?

Notice that the product of a negative factor and a positive factor is negative, but if both factors are negative, the product is positive.

Procedure for Storage

Multiplying Integers

1. If the factors are both positive or both negative, the product is positive.
   a. For $a > 0$ and $b > 0$, $ab = |a| \cdot |b|$.
   b. For $a < 0$ and $b < 0$, $ab = |a| \cdot |b|$.
2. If one factor is positive and one factor is negative, the product is negative.
   a. For $a > 0$ and $b < 0$, $ab = - |a| \cdot |b|$.
   b. For $a < 0$ and $b > 0$, $ab = - |a| \cdot |b|$.

EXAMPLES

Example 1. (-2) · (+9)

Solution.

Since -2 < 0 and +9 > 0, condition **2b** applies.

So -|-2| · |9| = -(2 · 9) = -18.

Example 2. (-4) · (-6)

Solution.

Since -4 < 0 and -6 < 0, condition **1b** applies.

So +|-4| · |-6| = +(4 · 6) = +24.

Exercises

Multiply.

1. (+3) · (-2)

2. (+7) · (+8)

3. (-4) · (-6)

4. (-8) · (+6)

5. (-3) · (-1)

6. (+3) · (-7)

7. (+4) · (+9)

8. (-32) · (+3)

9. (-41) · (-7)

10. (+79) · (-8)

11. (-25) · (-5)

12. (-182) · (+3)

13. (+471) · (-34)

14. (-964) · (-81)

15. (+372) · (-46)

16. (+1234) · (+369)

17. (-374) · (-941)

18. (-76) · (-423)

19. (-10) · (+3892)

20. (+462) · (-491)

21. Jim earns $8 a week from his paper route. If he goes on vacation for 3 weeks, how much money will he lose?

22. If Mr. Hendrick invests $85 in a savings account each month, how much will he have invested in a year?

DIVIDING INTEGERS

Subtraction is the inverse operation of addition. Division is the inverse operation of multiplication. Every multiplication problem has two corresponding division problems, and every division problem has a corresponding multiplication problem.

$$9 · 2 = 18 \quad \text{so} \quad 18 ÷ 2 = 9 \quad \text{and} \quad 18 ÷ 9 = 2.$$
$$6 · 4 = 24 \quad \text{so} \quad 24 ÷ 6 = 4 \quad \text{and} \quad 24 ÷ 4 = 6.$$
$$-5 · 3 = -15 \quad \text{so} \quad -15 ÷ -5 = 3 \quad \text{and} \quad -15 ÷ 3 = -5.$$

Because division and multiplication are inverse operations, the sign rules for division correspond to the sign rules for multiplication.

Procedure for Storage

Dividing Integers

1. If the divisor and the dividend have like signs, the quotient will be positive.
   a. For $a > 0$ and $b > 0$, $a \div b = |a| \div |b|$.
   b. For $a < 0$ and $b < 0$, $a \div b = |a| \div |b|$.

2. If the divisor and the dividend have unlike signs, the quotient will be negative.
   a. For $a > 0$ and $b < 0$, $a \div b = -|a| \div |b|$.
   b. For $a < 0$ and $b > 0$, $a \div b = -|a| \div |b|$.

EXAMPLES

Example 1. $+14 \div +2 = +7$

Example 2. $-72 \div +9 = -8$

Example 3. $+105 \div -21 = -5$

Example 4. $-864 \div -36 = +24$

A good way to check your division is to multiply the quotient by the divisor. The answer should be the same as your dividend.

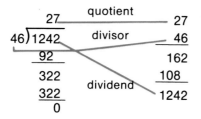

Now here's a division problem for you.

$$18 \div 0 = ?$$

Change it to a multiplication problem.

$$0 \cdot ? = 18$$

What number can you multiply by 0 to get 18? According to the zero property of multiplication, the product of any number and 0 is always 0. Therefore, there is no number that can be multiplied with 0 to equal 18. Consequently, division by 0 is not possible and is, therefore, undefined.

Exercises

Divide.

1. $27 \div 3$
2. $-56 \div 8$
3. $36 \div 0$
4. $-20 \div -4$
5. $54 \div -6$
6. $-2352 \div -56$
7. $-1953 \div 31$

8. $588 \div -84$
9. $3403 \div 41$
10. $-1768 \div -52$
11. $-48 \div 6$
12. $1075 \div -25$
13. $-516 \div 86$
14. $6584 \div 823$

15. $\frac{-124}{0}$
16. $\frac{-732}{-61}$
17. $\frac{198}{-22}$
18. $\frac{0}{-37}$
19. $\frac{-3136}{56}$

20. The product of two numbers is 7904 and the absolute value of one of the numbers is 247. Find two possible solutions to this problem.

EXTRA WORK WITH INTEGERS

Look at the chart below and review the properties of integers. You should be able to identify and use all of these properties. Then do the exercises.

Property	of Addition	of Multiplication
commutative	$3 + 4 = 4 + 3$ $7 = 7$	$4 \cdot 2 = 2 \cdot 4$ $8 = 8$
associative	$2 + (3 + 4) = (2 + 3) + 4$ $2 + 7 = 5 + 4$ $9 = 9$	$5 \cdot (3 \cdot 2) = (5 \cdot 3) \cdot 2$ $5(6) = 15(2)$ $30 = 30$
identity	$3 + 0 = 3$	$5 \cdot 1 = 5$
inverse	$3 + (-3) = 0$	
zero		$6 \cdot 0 = 0$
distributive		over addition and subtraction $4(3 + 2) = (4 \cdot 3) + (4 \cdot 2)$ $4 \cdot 5 = 12 + 8$ $20 = 20$

Exercises

Compute.

1. 37 - 85
2. 126 + 395
3. 27(-82)
4. 3 · 5 · -18
5. -389 + -27
6. 23 + -82
7. -146 + -29 + 35
8. -135 ÷ 5
9. -83 · -24
10. 34 + 25 - 84
11. 689 · -4
12. -27 ÷ 3
13. 142 + 386 - 1024
14. 82 - 79 - 38 + 124
15. 6 · -3 · -18 · 4
16. -1863 ÷ -3
17. 25 + 38 - 472 + 6
18. 34 · -27 · -3
19. 126 + 14 - 86 + 39
20. -47 + 39 - 142 + 64

21. 87 + 98 - 378
22. 48(-5)7
23. 387 - 873 - 278
24. -75 + 78 + 98
25. 16 - 14 - 32 + 87
26. (-8)(-4)(-27)
27. 3 + 4 - 9 + 6 - 28
28. 4500 ÷ -36
29. -8978 ÷ -67
30. -129 - 35 - 69 - 72
31. 42 + 38 - 147 + 25
32. 12(-15) · 3(10)
33. -176,295 ÷ 69
34. -56 + 29 + 186
35. 192 - 35 - 81
36. 685 + 892 - 147
37. 3(-42)(-5)
38. 51 + 38 - 29 + 16
39. 1,405,184 ÷ -256
40. 187 + 35 - 26 + 195

41. Using integers, write an example of each of the properties mentioned in the summary chart.

EXPONENTS

Do you know a short way to write 6 · 6 · 6 or 5 · 5? To save time and writing space, you could use the exponential form. *Exponential form* is a shorter way to write repeated multiplication just as multiplication is a shorter way to write repeated addition. In exponential form, 6 · 6 · 6 equals 6^3. The 3 is the *exponent*, and the 6 is the *base*. The expression 6^3 is read "six to the third power" or "six cubed."

DEFINITION

≫**Exponential form:** a simplified form of writing repeated multiplication.

Can you use exponents to simplify problems? Here are a few examples.

EXAMPLES

Example 1. Write $2 \cdot 2 \cdot 2 \cdot 2$ in exponential form.

The base is 2, which is multiplied by itself four times.

$$2 \cdot 2 \cdot 2 \cdot 2 = 2^4$$

Example 2. Write $4 \cdot 4 \cdot 4 \cdot 4 \cdot 4$ in exponential form.

$$4 \cdot 4 \cdot 4 \cdot 4 \cdot 4 = 4^5$$

Now we can expand and evaluate exponential forms. "To evaluate" means to change from exponential form to a number. For example, the evaluation of 2^2 is 4.

EXAMPLES

Example 3. Evaluate 5^3.

$$5 \cdot 5 \cdot 5 = 125$$

Example 4. Evaluate 8^4.

$$8 \cdot 8 \cdot 8 \cdot 8 = 4096$$

Example 5. Evaluate $(-3)^2$.

$$-3 \cdot -3 = 9$$

Example 6. Evaluate $(-7)^3$.

$$-7 \cdot -7 \cdot -7 = -343$$

Data Base

François Viète (1540-1603) indicated powers such as x, x^2, x^3, as A, A quadratum, A cubum. You can imagine how long it would take to write an expression such as $5x^3y^2z^5$. René Descartes (1596-1650) improved Viète's notation by introducing our present system.

What happens when you multiply like bases?

$$5^2 \cdot 5^3 = (5 \cdot 5) \cdot (5 \cdot 5 \cdot 5) = 5^{2+3} = 5^5$$

Notice that both bases are 5 and the operation is multiplication. Can you see a shorter method to solve this problem?

What happens when you divide like bases?

$$8^5 \div 8^2 = \frac{8^5}{8^2} = \frac{8 \cdot 8 \cdot 8 \cdot 8 \cdot 8}{8 \cdot 8} = 8^{5-2} = 8^3$$

Both bases are 8, and the operation is division. Do you see a shortcut for dividing like bases?

What happens when you raise an exponential expression to a power?

$$(3^2)^4 = 3^2 \cdot 3^2 \cdot 3^2 \cdot 3^2 = (3 \cdot 3)(3 \cdot 3)(3 \cdot 3)(3 \cdot 3) = 3^8$$

What shortcut do you see for raising a power to a power?

Procedure for Storage

Properties of Exponents

1. To multiply like bases, add the exponents.

For integers x, a, and b,

$$x^a \cdot x^b = x^{a+b}.$$

2. To divide like bases, subtract the exponents.

For integers x, a, and b, with $x \neq 0$,

$$\frac{x^a}{x^b} = x^{a-b}.$$

3. To raise a power to a power, multiply the exponents.

For integers x, a, and b,

$$(x^a)^b = x^{ab}.$$

For any base $a \neq 0$, $a^0 = 1$. This definition follows the properties of exponents.

$$5^0 = 1 \qquad (-5)^0 = 1$$
$$10^0 = 1 \qquad 14^0 = 1$$

Since $\dfrac{3^4}{3^4} = 3^{4-4} = 3^0$

and $\dfrac{3^4}{3^4} = \dfrac{3 \cdot 3 \cdot 3 \cdot 3}{3 \cdot 3 \cdot 3 \cdot 3} = 1$

then $3^0 = 1$.

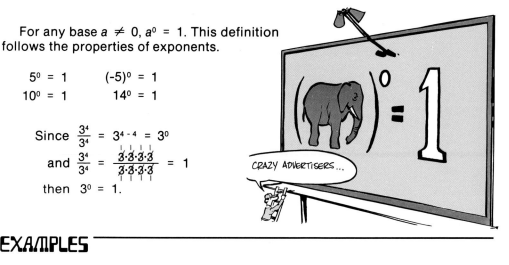

CRAZY ADVERTISERS...

EXAMPLES

Example 7. Simplify.
- a. $5^2 \cdot 5^{10} = 5^{12}$
- b. $3^2 \cdot 3^4 \cdot 3^9 = 3^{15}$
- c. $2^4 \div 2 = 2^3$
- d. $10^5 \div 10^3 = 10^2$
- e. $(5^3)^6 = 5^{18}$

Example 8. Simplify.
- a. $3^2 \cdot 3^5 \cdot 2^4 \cdot 2^6 = 3^7 \cdot 2^{10}$
- b. $4^3 \cdot 4^5 \cdot 4 \cdot 5^3 = 4^9 \cdot 5^3$

YOU CAN COMBINE ONLY LIKE BASES

Exercises

Expand and evaluate.
1. 4^3
2. 3^2
3. 5^3
4. 16^2
5. $(-2)^4$
6. $(-3)^5$
7. 1^4
8. 2314^0
9. 6^4
10. $(-11)^2$

Place in exponential form.
11. $7 \cdot 7 \cdot 7 \cdot 7$
12. $(-1) \cdot (-1) \cdot (-1)$
13. $5 \cdot 5 \cdot 5 \cdot 5 \cdot 5 \cdot 5$
14. $(-4) \cdot (-4)$
15. $127 \cdot 127 \cdot 127$

Simplify, leaving the answer in exponential notation.

16. $3^2 \cdot 3^3$

17. $7^2 \cdot 7^9$

18. $10^{12} \cdot 10^3$

19. $8^7 \div 8^3$

20. $17^{81} \div 17^{12}$

21. $3^{148} \div 3^{140}$

22. $(7^2)^3$

23. $(28^4)^2$

24. $5^3 \cdot 5^2 \cdot 5^{10}$

25. $2^3 \div 2$

26. $(8^3)^5$

27. $12^2 \cdot 12^7$

28. $4^{16} \div 4^{12}$

29. $(10^{10})^5$

30. $(3^{11})^0$

31. $2^2 \cdot 2^3 \cdot 3^4 \cdot 5^2 \cdot 5$

32. $10^2 \cdot 10^4 \cdot (-2)^3 \cdot (-2)^6$

33. Will $(-2)^3$ be positive or negative?

34. Will $(-2)^4$ be positive or negative?

35. Will $(-3)^2$ be positive or negative?

36. Will $(-3)^5$ be positive or negative?

37. If you raise a negative number to an odd power, is the answer positive or negative?

38. If you raise a negative number to an even power, is the answer positive or negative?

FACTORING AND PRIME NUMBERS

What is factoring? Two integers multiplied together are called *factors* of the product. For example, to factor 12, you must think what numbers multiplied together equal 12. There are several: -4 and -3 are factors of 12, because $-4 \cdot -3 = 12$; 6 and 2 are factors of 12; 1 and 12 are factors of 12. In fact, ± 1, ± 2, ± 3, ± 4, ± 6, and ± 12 are all factors of 12. (The symbol $\pm$ means "positive or negative.") What are the factors of 8? The factors of 8 are ± 1, ± 2, ± 4, and ± 8. Give all the integral factors of 10.

In order to find the prime factorization of a number, you need to know what a prime number is.

 DEFINITION ≫**Prime number:** an integer greater than 1 whose only positive factors are 1 and itself.

Can you think of a prime number? What is the first prime number? The first prime number is 2, because the only positive factors of 2 are 1 and 2.

DEFINITION

≫**Composite number:** a nonprime positive integer greater than 1.

By definition 0 and 1 are neither prime nor composite.

Data Base

Eratosthenes found an interesting way to find prime numbers. It is called the sieve of Eratosthenes. To find the primes from 1 to 100 according to his method, list the numbers. Here are 1-30.

1	2	3	4	5	6	7	8	9	10
11	12	13	14	15	16	17	18	19	20
21	22	23	24	25	26	27	28	29	30

Mark the first prime number, which is 2. Now cross out every second number; it is not prime. How do you know? Move to the next unmarked number, which is 3. How many factors does 3 have? Since 3 and 1 are the only factors, 3 is the next prime. Cross out every third number. Some will already be crossed out. Move to the next unmarked number. Since it is prime, mark it; then cross out all multiples of 5. When you finish crossing out multiples of 5, you will have all ten prime numbers between 1 and 30.

1	②　③	⨉	⑤	⨉	7	⨉	⨉	⨉
11	⨉	13	⨉	⨉	⨉	17	⨉	19	⨉
⨉	⨉	23	⨉	⨉	⨉	⨉	⨉	29	⨉

Now you finish marking your chart. Use the sieve of Eratosthenes to find all prime numbers between 30 and 100.

Twin primes are prime numbers that differ in value by 2. For example, 11 and 13 are twin primes. What is another pair of twin primes? Find all twin primes between 1 and 100.

Every natural number greater than 1 can be factored uniquely into a product of primes. Remember, if you have a factorization of a number, the product of the factors will give the original number. When all factors of a given number are prime numbers, we say the number has been factored to its prime factors.

EXAMPLES

Example 1.   Find the prime factors of 12.

First try 6 and 2. Notice that 2 is prime, but 6 is not. Continue factoring until all factors are prime. Factors of 6 are 3 and 2. Since 3 and 2 are primes, the prime factorization of 12 is $3 \cdot 2 \cdot 2$ or $3 \cdot 2^2$.

What happens if you start the factorization with 3 and 4? Are the results the same?

Example 2.   Find the prime factors of 36 three ways.

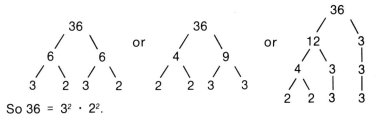

So $36 = 3^2 \cdot 2^2$.

Example 3.   Find the prime factors of 86.

The prime factors of 86 are 43 and 2.

You should be able to find the prime factors of any composite number.

Here is a large number to factor into primes.

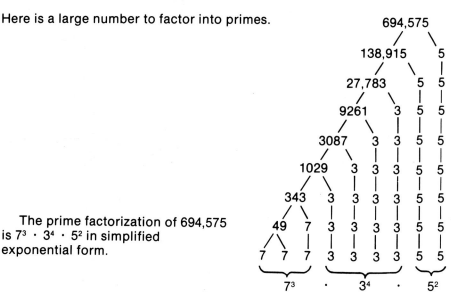

The prime factorization of 694,575 is $7^3 \cdot 3^4 \cdot 5^2$ in simplified exponential form.

The method of factoring illustrated above is the tree method. Another method for factoring a number to its prime factors is called the ladder method, or successive division. The following ladder illustrates the prime factorization of 18.

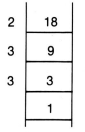

In this method you divide by prime numbers until the quotient is 1, writing the prime numbers on the outside of the ladder. These are the prime factors. So $18 = 2 \cdot 3^2$.

Exercises

Use either method to factor each number to its prime factors. Give answers in exponential form.

1. 48
2. 158
3. 873
4. 840
5. 820

6. 14,553
7. 1384
8. 978
9. 94
10. 89

11. 27,783
12. 6048
13. 20,160
14. 11,664
15. 2688

GREATEST COMMON DIVISOR AND LEAST COMMON MULTIPLE

Once you have factored numbers into primes, you can easily find the greatest common divisor (GCD) and the least common multiple (LCM) of the two numbers. The GCD is used to simplify fractions. To rename a fraction in lowest terms, you simply divide the numerator and the denominator by the GCD of the two numbers.

UPPER LEVEL ▲

COMMON DENOMINATORS

▼ LOWER LEVEL

LOWEST COMMON DENOMINATORS

DEFINITION ≫**Greatest common divisor** (GCD): the largest positive integer that divides evenly into two numbers.

The greatest common divisor (GCD) of two numbers is the product of the prime factors that the numbers have in common.

EXAMPLE

Example 1.   Find the GCD of 18 and 56.

Solution.

1. Find the prime factors of 18 and 56.

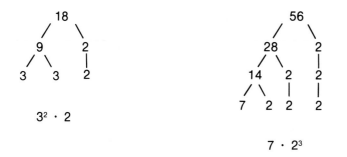

$$3^2 \cdot 2$$

$$7 \cdot 2^3$$

2. Determine the prime factors common to both numbers. Here 2 is the common factor.

3. The GCD of 18 and 56 is the highest power of 2 common to both numbers. Although 2 is a factor of 56 three times, it is a factor of 18 only once. Therefore, the GCD of these numbers is 2.

Procedure for Storage

Finding the Greatest Common Divisor (GCD)

1. Factor both numbers into primes and write in exponential form.
2. Circle each factor common to both numbers and determine the highest common power of each factor.
3. Find the product of the factors found in step 2.

EXAMPLE

Example 2.   Find the GCD of 720 and 840.

Solution.

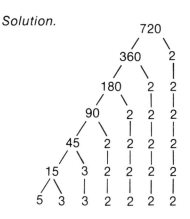

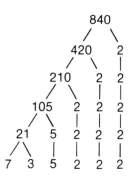

The prime factors of 720 are 5, 3^2, and 2^4.

The prime factors of 840 are 7, 3, 5, and 2^3.

These two numbers have several common factors: 5, 3, and 2. Since the factors 2 and 3 have different exponents, we choose the factors with the largest exponent common to both numbers. The GCD is the product of these common primes.

$$5 \cdot 3 \cdot 2^3 = 120$$

The largest integer that will divide evenly into both 720 and 840 is 120.

TWO NUMBERS ARE CALLED **RELATIVELY PRIME** IF THEIR <u>GREATEST COMMON DIVISOR</u> IS **1** (LIKE 8 and 15)

Data Base

Another interesting method for finding the GCD of two numbers is Euclid's algorithm. Who was Euclid? And what is an algorithm? Euclid was a third-century A.D. Greek mathematician. An algorithm is a set of rules or a formula for finding the correct solution. Euclid's algorithm is a method for finding the GCD of two numbers.

Consider example 1 again.

Find the GCD of 18 and 56.

Solution.

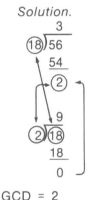

1. Divide the larger number by the smaller.

2. Divide again, using the divisor as the dividend and the remainder as the divisor.

GCD = 2

3. Continue in this way until the remainder is 0. The last nonzero remainder is the GCD.

Now use Euclid's algorithm to find the GCD of 720 and 840.

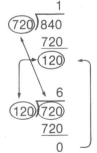

The GCD of 720 and 840 is 120.

Can you find the GCD of 324 and 1050?

The least common multiple (LCM) is frequently used in arithmetic and in algebra when adding or subtracting fractions or rational expressions because it is the lowest common denominator.

 >**Least common multiple** (LCM): the smallest positive integer that is a multiple of two numbers.

EXAMPLES

Example 3.   Find the LCM of 12 and 42.

Solution.

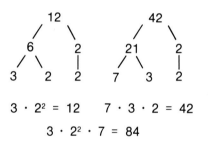

$3 \cdot 2^2 = 12$ $7 \cdot 3 \cdot 2 = 42$

$3 \cdot 2^2 \cdot 7 = 84$

1. Prime factor each number and write the factorizations in exponential form.

2. Multiply the largest exponential form of each factor.

The product of these factors is 84, the smallest number that both 12 and 42 will divide into evenly.

Example 4.   Find the LCM of 63 and 82.

Solution.

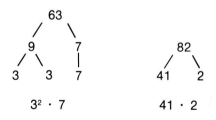

$3^2 \cdot 7$ $41 \cdot 2$

The LCM of 63 and 82 is $3^2 \cdot 7 \cdot 41 \cdot 2 = 5166$.

Procedure for Storage

Finding the Least Common Multiple (LCM)

1. Factor both numbers into primes written in exponential form.

2. Circle the highest power of each prime factor.

3. Find the product of all circled factors.

Exercises

Find the GCD.

1. 34 and 784

2. 358 and 934

3. 792 and 392

4. 5760 and 34,560

5. 3780 and 420

6. 4725 and 378

Find the LCM

7. 140 and 34

8. 82 and 54

9. 38 and 95

10. 924 and 36

11. 504 and 352

12. 92 and 38

ADDING AND SUBTRACTING RATIONALS

If Bill needs $\frac{1}{2}$ gallon of paint for the bathroom and $\frac{3}{4}$ gallon for the bedroom, how much paint would he buy?

To solve his problem, Bill will have to know how to work with rational numbers. What are rational numbers? Rational numbers are better known as fractions.

DEFINITION

≫**Rational number:** a number that can be expressed as a ratio of two integers when the denominator is not equal to 0.

Sometimes a rational number may not look like the usual ratio. The decimal 1.3 equals $\frac{13}{10}$, so 1.3 is a rational number. The whole number 8 equals $\frac{8}{1}$, so 8 is a rational number too. What does a rational expression like $\frac{6}{7}$ actually mean? It means that something is divided into seven parts and six parts are represented. Therefore, $\frac{6}{7}$ is 6 times $\frac{1}{7}$ of the objects, or $6 \cdot \frac{1}{7}$. In general, a rational number can be expressed $\frac{a}{b}$ where a and b are integers and $b \neq 0$. Therefore, for any rational number

$$\frac{a}{b} = a \cdot \frac{1}{b}$$

where $\frac{1}{b}$ is the multiplicative inverse of b.

When working with rational numbers, you should always state the rational number in its lowest form. For example, if you come up with $\frac{6}{21}$ as a solution to a computation, you would simplify, or reduce, the fraction to $\frac{2}{7}$ instead of $\frac{6}{21}$. To simplify a fraction, you cancel the common factor (in this case 3) from both the numerator and the denominator. What common factor is in $\frac{8}{28}$? What is the simplified form of $\frac{8}{28}$?

Before you can add or subtract rational numbers, you must express each rational as a larger equivalent fraction with the same denominator as each other fraction in the problem. To rename $\frac{2}{3}$ as a larger equivalent fraction, you simply multiply the fraction by 1, the identity element of multiplication, in the form of any rational number.

$$\frac{2}{3} \cdot \frac{2}{2} = \frac{4}{6}$$

$$\frac{2}{3} \cdot \frac{3}{3} = \frac{6}{9}$$

$$\frac{2}{3} \cdot \frac{4}{4} = \frac{8}{12}$$

As you can see, $\frac{4}{6}$, $\frac{6}{9}$, and $\frac{8}{12}$ are equivalent to $\frac{2}{3}$.

Suppose the denominator of the equivalent fraction is given. To rename the fraction, first determine the factor used to produce the given denominator. Then to produce the numerator of the equivalent fraction, multiply the numerator of the original fraction by the same factor.

The simplifying and expanding procedures use the *fundamental principle of fractions,* which states

if a is an integer, and b and c are nonzero integers,

$$\frac{a}{b} = \frac{ac}{bc} .$$

Here is the principle applied to simplifying. Substituting 6 for a, 21 for b, and $\frac{1}{3}$ for c, you get

$$\frac{6}{21} = \frac{6 \cdot \frac{1}{3}}{21 \cdot \frac{1}{3}} = \frac{\frac{6}{3}}{\frac{21}{3}} = \frac{2}{7}$$

Here is the principle applied to renaming. Substituting 2 for a, 3 for b, and 6 for c, you get

$$\frac{2}{3} = \frac{2 \cdot 6}{3 \cdot 6} = \frac{12}{18}.$$

To add or subtract rationals with different denominators, you must first rename the fractions to equivalent fractions that have the same denominator.

EXAMPLE

Example 1. Solve $\frac{3}{7} + \frac{2}{7}$.

Since the denominator of both rationals is the same, add the numerators. The resulting rational number cannot be reduced.

$$\frac{3}{7} + \frac{2}{7} = \frac{5}{7}$$

Why does $\frac{3}{7} + \frac{2}{7} = \frac{5}{7}$? All computations follow basic principles set down in mathematics. Each step of a mathematical computation works for a reason. Here is the reasoning behind this computation.

$$\frac{3}{7} + \frac{2}{7} = 3\left(\frac{1}{7}\right) + 2\left(\frac{1}{7}\right) \qquad \frac{a}{b} = a \cdot \frac{1}{b}$$
$$= (3 + 2)\left(\frac{1}{7}\right) \qquad \text{distributive property}$$
$$= 5\left(\frac{1}{7}\right) \qquad a \cdot \frac{1}{b} = \frac{a}{b}$$
$$= \frac{5}{7}$$

EXAMPLES

Example 2.   Solve $\frac{3}{4} + \frac{2}{3}$.

Solution.

$4 = 2^2 \qquad 3 = 3$

$\text{LCM} = 2^2 \cdot 3 = 12$

$$\frac{3}{4} \cdot \frac{3}{3} = \frac{9}{12}$$

$$\frac{2}{3} \cdot \frac{2^2}{2^2} = \frac{2}{3} \cdot \frac{4}{4} = \frac{8}{12}$$

$$\frac{9}{12} + \frac{8}{12} = \frac{17}{12}$$

This rational number cannot be reduced. So $\dfrac{3}{4} + \dfrac{2}{3} = \dfrac{17}{12}$.

1. Prime factor the denominators.
2. Find the LCM.
3. Rename the fractions as equivalent fractions with the same denominators, using the fundamental principle of fractions.
4. Add the numerators.
5. Simplify if possible.

Example 3. Solve $\dfrac{4}{7} - \dfrac{5}{28}$.

Solution.

$7 = 7 \qquad 28 = 7 \cdot 2^2$

$\text{LCM} = 7 \cdot 2^2 = 28$

$$\frac{4}{7} \cdot \frac{4}{4} = \frac{16}{28}$$

$$\frac{16}{28} - \frac{5}{28} = \frac{11}{28}$$

This rational cannot be reduced.

Thus $\dfrac{4}{7} - \dfrac{5}{28} = \dfrac{11}{28}$.

Example 4. Solve $\dfrac{3}{32} - \dfrac{5}{8}$.

Solution.

$32 = 2^5 \qquad 8 = 2^3$

$\text{LCM} = 2^5 = 32$

$$\frac{5}{8} \cdot \frac{2^2}{2^2} = \frac{5}{8} \cdot \frac{4}{4} = \frac{20}{32}$$

$$\frac{3}{32} - \frac{20}{32} = \frac{-17}{32}$$

This rational cannot be reduced.

$$\frac{3}{32} - \frac{5}{8} = \frac{-17}{32}$$

Procedure for Storage

Adding and Subtracting Rationals

1. Factor each denominator into primes.
2. Find the LCM of the two denominators and use it for the common denominator.
3. Change each rational number to an equivalent fraction having the LCM as the denominator. Do this by multiplying both the numerator and the denominator of the rational number by the factor that will make the denominator equal to the common denominator.
4. Add (or subtract) the renamed numerators. Place the sum (or difference) over the LCM.
5. If possible, reduce the rational expression.

Do you remember how to add and subtract rationals in decimal form? Look at these examples.

EXAMPLES

Example 5.   Solve 2.39 + 14.682.

Solution.

$$\begin{array}{r} 2.390 \\ \underline{14.682} \\ 17.072 \end{array}$$

Write the addends in vertical form, lining up decimal points. Add.

2.39 + 14.682 = 17.072

Example 6.   Solve 39.27 - 112.6.

Solution.   39.27 - 112.6   When subtracting, add the opposite.
                   39.27 + (-112.6)
                   -73.33

Exercises

Simplify.

1. $\frac{10}{14}$ **2.** $\frac{3}{6}$ **3.** $\frac{12}{36}$ **4.** $\frac{8}{32}$ **5.** $\frac{15}{25}$

Change these rational numbers to equivalent fractions having the given denominator.

6. $\frac{2}{3} = \frac{?}{9}$ **9.** $\frac{2}{5} = \frac{?}{105}$

7. $\frac{5}{7} = \frac{?}{56}$ **10.** $\frac{8}{3} = \frac{?}{24}$

8. $\frac{1}{6} = \frac{?}{30}$

Change the following fractions so that the denominator equals 48.

11. $\frac{1}{2}$ **12.** $\frac{5}{12}$ **13.** $\frac{3}{8}$ **14.** $\frac{11}{16}$ **15.** $\frac{7}{6}$

Perform the indicated operations.

16. $\frac{2}{9} + \frac{5}{9}$ **21.** $\frac{12}{21} + \frac{10}{3}$

17. $\frac{4}{7} - \frac{11}{7}$ **22.** $\frac{3}{4} - \frac{8}{9}$

18. $\frac{14}{9} + 4$ **23.** $\frac{1}{7} + \frac{14}{5}$

19. $\frac{7}{12} + \frac{1}{4}$ **24.** $\frac{2}{11} - \frac{3}{8}$

20. $\frac{3}{5} - \frac{7}{2}$ **25.** $\frac{4}{27} - \frac{8}{21}$

26. 3.896 + 11.42

27. 1876.31 - 1026.48

28. 621.4 - .23

29. 527.69 + 89.41

30. Sue is making a dress for school chorus. She needs $\frac{3}{8}$ yard of lace for the cuffs and $\frac{1}{4}$ yard of the same lace for the decoration on the front of her dress. How much lace should she buy?

HISTORY OF COMPUTERS

From the beginning of time man has counted. In fact, God counted the days of Creation and rested on the seventh day (cf. Gen. 2:2). Throughout history, man has tried to find quicker, more accurate, and more reliable ways to count and calculate. The abacus is one of the oldest known calculating devices. Though its origin is unknown, Chinese history records its use as early as the sixth century B.C.

In 1642 Blaise Pascal made one of the first mechanical calculators. Pascal was only eighteen years old when he invented an adding machine run by gears. Each gear in Pascal's calculator represented a different number. Pascal invented this machine because his father, a superintendent of taxes in Paris, France, needed help with his calculations.

Almost a hundred years later a Frenchman named Jacquard invented a weaving loom controlled by punched cards similar to the modern computer cards. These punched cards helped him to control the loom and to make a design in his fabric. Punched cards were first used for numerical purposes in 1886. In 1890 Herman Hollerith developed a machine that used punched cards to store data. The U.S. government used Hollerith's machine in taking the 1890 census.

Charles Babbage designed the forerunner of our modern-day computer in 1812. He wanted a machine that would do sequences of mathematical operations. In 1822 he invented the difference engine, and in 1833, the analytical engine. With these machines he could compute simple polynomials like $x^2 + x + 25$. Though he worked on his projects for nearly fifty years, Babbage could not complete them because he could not secure the precision mechanical parts that he needed.

Babbage's ideas and inventions were about a hundred years ahead of their time. It was not until 1937 that Howard Aiken of

Integrator and Calculator). Weighing thirty tons, it contained over 16,000 vacuum tubes. This speedy computer could do 5000 additions in one second. Since electronic devices work more quickly than mechanical parts, ENIAC with its vacuum tubes was a landmark in computer design. Soon after ENIAC was developed, Hungarian-born mathematician John von Neumann developed the basic ideas of modern

transistors in TRADIC eliminated the need for vacuum tubes and proved that smaller, quicker, and much more dependable computers could be produced. By 1963 transistorized computers could perform a million calculations per second.

Recent decades have produced computers that are faster, more compact, and more reliable than their predecessors. Modern computers, controlled by

Harvard University designed the first large-scale automatic digital computer. This machine was actually a calculator that followed a sequence of instructions stored on paper tape. In 1944 IBM built this computer and named it Mark I.

In 1945, one year after Aiken's invention, John Mauchly and J. Eckert designed the first large electronic digital computer. This was a secret wartime project called ENIAC (Electrical-Numerical

computer design. His goal was to store the computer program electronically in the machine's memory. Many scientists worked on this idea, and by 1950 computers could perform several thousand calculations per second.

The circuits of these first electronic computers contained bulky vacuum tubes. Scientists at Bell Laboratories developed transistors in 1947, and in 1954 they built TRADIC, the first transistorized computer. The 800

microscopic electronic chips, can perform hundreds of millions of numerical computations per second. Complete processing units on single computer chips made possible the growing flood of home computers and pocket-sized programmable calculators. What will the next improvements be? That remains to be seen. Perhaps after you gain your education, you will help to make some new steps in computer technology.

MULTIPLYING AND DIVIDING RATIONALS

Chip's bucket contains $2\frac{1}{2}$ gallons of water. He is to give $\frac{2}{3}$ of the water to his horse, Byte. How many gallons of water will the horse get?

To solve this problem, you must be able to multiply rationals. Do you need a common denominator for multiplying or dividing rationals? No, you can simply multiply the numerators and then the denominators.

$$\frac{3}{4} \cdot \frac{7}{8} = \frac{3 \cdot 7}{4 \cdot 8} = \frac{21}{32}$$

Why does $\frac{3}{4} \cdot \frac{7}{8} = \frac{21}{32}$?

$$\frac{3}{4} \cdot \frac{7}{8} = 3 \left(\frac{1}{4} \right) \cdot 7 \left(\frac{1}{8} \right) \qquad \frac{a}{b} = a \cdot \frac{1}{b}$$

$$= (3 \cdot 7) \left(\frac{1}{4} \cdot \frac{1}{8} \right) \qquad \text{commutative and associative}$$
$$\text{properties of multiplication}$$

$$= 21 \cdot \left(\frac{1}{32} \right) \qquad a \cdot \frac{1}{b} = \frac{a}{b}$$

$$= \frac{21}{32}$$

When you multiply rational numbers in fractional form, you can reduce the terms either before you multiply or after.

$$\frac{12}{7} \cdot \frac{14}{3} = \left(\frac{2^2 \cdot \cancel{3}}{\cancel{7}} \right) \left(\frac{2 \cdot \cancel{7}}{\cancel{3}} \right) = \frac{2^3}{1} = \frac{8}{1} = 8$$

$$\frac{12}{7} \cdot \frac{14}{3} = \frac{168}{21} = \frac{2^3 \cdot \cancel{3} \cdot \cancel{7}}{\cancel{3} \cdot \cancel{7}} = \frac{2^3}{1} = \frac{8}{1} = 8$$

Procedure for Storage

Multiplying Rationals

1. Place the product of the numerators over the product of the denominators.

2. Factor the products to prime numbers.

3. Reduce to lowest terms.

or

1. Factor numerators and denominators into prime factors.

2. Reduce to lowest terms.

3. Place the product of the reduced numerators over the product of the reduced denominators.

EXAMPLES

Example 1. Solve $\dfrac{3}{4} \cdot \dfrac{18}{7}$.

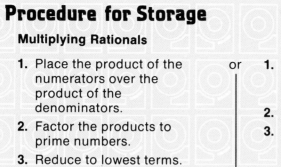

Solution. $\dfrac{3}{4} \cdot \dfrac{18}{7} = \dfrac{54}{28} = \dfrac{3^3 \cdot \overset{1}{\cancel{2}}}{\underset{\underset{1}{2}}{\cancel{2^2}} \cdot 7} = \dfrac{27}{14}$

or

$\dfrac{3}{4} \cdot \dfrac{18}{7} = \dfrac{3}{\underset{\underset{1}{2}}{\cancel{2^2}}} \cdot \dfrac{3^2 \cdot \overset{1}{\cancel{2}}}{7} = \dfrac{3^3}{2 \cdot 7} = \dfrac{27}{14}$

Example 2. Solve $\dfrac{12}{35} \cdot \dfrac{42}{27}$.

Solution. $\left(\dfrac{2^2 \cdot \overset{1}{\cancel{3}}}{5 \cdot \underset{1}{\cancel{7}}} \right) \left(\dfrac{\overset{1}{\cancel{3}} \cdot 2 \cdot \overset{1}{\cancel{7}}}{\underset{\underset{1}{3}}{\cancel{3^3}}} \right) = \dfrac{2^2 \cdot 2}{5 \cdot 3} = \dfrac{2^3}{15} = \dfrac{8}{15}$

Since division is the inverse operation of multiplication, each division problem can be restated as a multiplication problem. You can easily recognize that multiplication is the inverse of division. Division with rational numbers can be changed to multiplication by using the reciprocal of the divisor.

EXAMPLE

Example 3. Solve $\dfrac{4}{5} \div \dfrac{9}{10}$.

Solution. $\dfrac{4}{5} \div \dfrac{9}{10} = \dfrac{4}{5} \cdot \dfrac{10}{9}$

$= \dfrac{40}{45} = \dfrac{8}{9}$

Example 4. Solve $\dfrac{5}{7} \div 5$.

Solution. $\dfrac{5}{7} \div 5 = \dfrac{5}{7} \cdot \dfrac{1}{5}$

$= \dfrac{\overset{1}{\cancel{5}}}{7} \cdot \dfrac{1}{\underset{1}{\cancel{5}}} = \dfrac{1}{7}$

≫**Reciprocals:** two numbers whose product is 1.

Procedure for Storage

Dividing Rationals

To divide rational numbers, multiply by the reciprocal (multiplicative inverse) of the divisor.

EXAMPLES

Example 5. Solve $\dfrac{2}{3} \div \dfrac{8}{7}$.

Solution.
$$\dfrac{2}{3} \div \dfrac{8}{7} = \dfrac{2}{3} \cdot \dfrac{7}{8}$$
$$= \dfrac{2}{3} \cdot \dfrac{7}{2^3_{2^2}}$$
$$= \dfrac{7}{3 \cdot 2^2} = \dfrac{7}{12}$$

Example 6. Solve $\dfrac{12}{19} \div \dfrac{-5}{38}$.

Solution.
$$\dfrac{12}{19} \div \dfrac{-5}{38} = \dfrac{12}{19} \cdot \dfrac{-38}{5}$$
$$= \dfrac{2^2 \cdot 3}{19} \cdot \dfrac{19 \cdot -2}{5}$$
$$= \dfrac{-2^3 \cdot 3}{5} = \dfrac{-24}{5}$$

Do you remember how to multiply and divide decimals? These examples may remind you. Be sure you know how to perform these operations.

EXAMPLES

Example 7. Solve $4.28 \cdot 5.31$.

```
  4.28
  5.31
   428
 1284
 2140
22.7268
```

The total number of decimal places in the factors equals the total number in the product.

AW, COME ON...

Example 8. Solve 1.26 ÷ 0.3.

$$0.3\overline{)1.2\,6} \begin{array}{r} 4.2 \\ \underline{12} \\ 6 \\ \underline{6} \\ 0 \end{array}$$

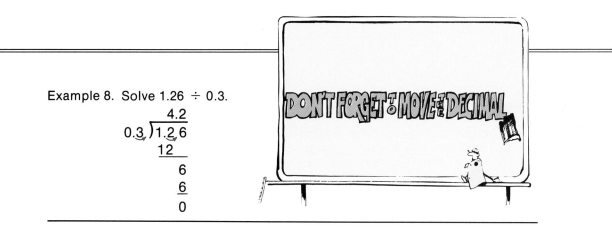

Exercises

Perform the indicated operations.

1. $\frac{4}{7} \cdot \frac{5}{12}$

2. $\frac{34}{9} \cdot \frac{3}{17}$

3. $\frac{21}{8} \cdot \frac{7}{3}$

4. $\frac{1}{6} \cdot \frac{18}{19}$

5. $\frac{3}{7} \cdot \frac{84}{15}$

6. $\frac{4}{9} \div \frac{8}{11}$

7. $\frac{1}{4} \div \frac{9}{16}$

8. $\frac{5}{11} \div \frac{3}{22}$

9. $\frac{2}{17} \div 8$

10. $\frac{54}{19} \div \frac{18}{7}$

11. $14.1 \cdot 5.6$

12. $3.9 \cdot 8.42$

13. $56.4 \div 0.2$

14. $61 \div 12.2$

15. $6.09 \div 7$

16. Chip's bucket contains $2\frac{1}{2}$ gallons of water. If he gives his horse, Byte, $\frac{2}{3}$ of the water, how much water does Byte get?

17. Bonnie, Brad, and Ben picked $1\frac{1}{2}$ gallons of blackberries and divided them evenly among themselves. How many gallons of blackberries did each child get?

18. If one side of a square is $\frac{3}{8}$ inches, what is the perimeter of the square?

19. What is the product of a number and its reciprocal? What property of multiplication does the number represent?

20. Does the zero property of multiplication hold true for all rational numbers?

SUMMARY OF PROPERTIES OF REAL NUMBERS

Biblical truths and principles that God has established and revealed in His Word must guide your life. To become more Christ-like, you must understand biblical principles and build new principles upon established principles.

Do you know what the terms *Rapture* and *Millennium* mean? These terms do not appear in the Bible; however, they do refer to specific events that are discussed in the Bible. The terms were derived from the actual truths. The names make it easier for Christians to quickly know what is meant when they talk about Christ's "snatching out" His bride, the church, and about His 1000-year reign of peace. The names are a shorter way of describing the biblical truth.

In mathematics several truths have been given special names. These names help you remember the properties, which simply classify long-known properties of numbers.

Procedure for Storage

Properties of Real Numbers

property	of addition	of multiplication
commutative	$2 + 5 = 5 + 2$	$2 \cdot 5 = 5 \cdot 2$
associative	$3 + (2 + 4) = (3 + 2) + 4$	$3 \cdot (2 \cdot 4) = (3 \cdot 2) \cdot 4$
identity	$8 + 0 = 8$	$8 \cdot 1 = 8$
inverse	$3 + (-3) = 0$	$5 \cdot \frac{1}{5} = 1$
zero		$4 \cdot 0 = 0$
distributive		over addition and subtraction $3(5 + 2) = (3 \cdot 5) + (3 \cdot 2)$ $3(5 - 2) = (3 \cdot 5) - (3 \cdot 2)$

Exercises

True statements are given below. Identify the property each one illustrates. Do not solve.

1. $6 \cdot 1 = 6$

2. $3(2 + 4) = (3 \cdot 2) + (3 \cdot 4)$

3. $5 + 9 = 9 + 5$

4. $-2 \cdot (3 \cdot -6) = (-2 \cdot 3) \cdot -6$

5. $8 \cdot 2 = 2 \cdot 8$

6. $(3 - 2) 10 = (3 \cdot 10) - (2 \cdot 10)$

7. $7 + 0 = 7$

8. $5 \cdot \frac{1}{5} = 1$

9. $(2 \cdot 3) \cdot 7 = 7 \cdot (2 \cdot 3)$

10. $27 + (-27) = 0$

11. $(2 \cdot 24) + (8 \cdot 7) = (8 \cdot 7) + (2 \cdot 24)$

12. $3 + (2 + 9) = (3 + 2) + 9$

13. Give an example from the real number system of each of the ten properties.

SQUARE ROOTS AND RADICALS

If Nancy has a square flower garden encompassing an area of 16 square feet, what are the dimensions of the garden?

Do you remember how to find the area of a square? To find the area of any rectangle, multiply the length by the width. To find the dimensions of Nancy's garden, you must find equal factors whose product is 16. Why do the factors have to be equal? What are the dimensions of the flower garden? The process needed to find the answer to this problem is called finding the square root.

DEFINITION ≫**Square root:** one of a number's two equal factors.

Since $3 \cdot 3 = 3^2 = 9$, the square root of 9 is 3. Since $-3 \cdot -3 = (-3)^2 = 9$, the square root of 9 is -3 too. A positive number always has two square roots: one positive and one negative. You should use the positive square root (principal square root) unless you are instructed to use the negative root. The number whose square root you are trying to find is called the *radicand*. For example, in $\sqrt{9}$, 9 is the radicand.

Data Base

The radical sign $\sqrt{}$ is the symbol for the principal (positive) square root. It probably originated from the use of the letter *r*, an abbreviation for the Latin word *radix*, meaning "root."

EXAMPLES

Example 1. $\sqrt{25} = \sqrt{5^2} = 5$ since $5 \cdot 5 = 25$

Example 2. $\sqrt{36} = \sqrt{6^2} = 6$

Example 3. $\sqrt{4} = \sqrt{2^2} = 2$

Example 4. $-\sqrt{16} = -\sqrt{4^2} = -4$ Notice that the negative sign is outside the radical. Therefore the negative square root is asked for.

Don't confuse taking the square root of a number with squaring a number. Finding the square root is the inverse of squaring.

The radical is used to indicate other roots as well as the square root.

$\sqrt{}$ denotes square root

$\sqrt[3]{}$ denotes cube root

$\sqrt[4]{}$ denotes fourth root

$\sqrt[5]{}$ denotes fifth root

The small number above the radical sign is called the *index*. It indicates the root to be taken. What do you think the index of $\sqrt{}$ is?

DEFINITION

≫**Cube root:** one of a number's three equal factors.

You can extend this definition for all indices.

EXAMPLES

Example 5. $\sqrt[3]{27} = \sqrt[3]{3^3} = 3$ since $3 \cdot 3 \cdot 3 = 27$

Example 6. $\sqrt[3]{8} = \sqrt[3]{2^3} = 2$

Example 7. $\sqrt[4]{16} = \sqrt[4]{2^4} = 2$ since $2 \cdot 2 \cdot 2 \cdot 2 = 16$

Example 8. $\sqrt[5]{3125} = \sqrt[5]{5^5} = 5$

Example 9. $\sqrt{\dfrac{4}{9}} = \sqrt{\dfrac{2^2}{3^2}} = \dfrac{2}{3}$

Example 10. $\sqrt[3]{\dfrac{27}{125}} = \sqrt[3]{\dfrac{3^3}{5^3}} = \dfrac{3}{5}$

Some radicals, such as $\sqrt{5}$, do not have whole number square roots. These numbers are called irrational numbers. You will learn more about them later.

Exercises

Memorize the squares of the numbers 1-20.

Find the indicated roots.

1. $\sqrt{49}$

2. $-\sqrt{36}$

3. $\sqrt{81}$

4. $-\sqrt{121}$

5. $\sqrt{1}$

6. $\sqrt{\dfrac{49}{16}}$

7. $\sqrt{\dfrac{81}{25}}$

8. $\sqrt{100}$

9. $\sqrt{\dfrac{9}{16}}$

10. $\sqrt{\dfrac{144}{9}}$

11. $-\sqrt{225}$

12. $-\sqrt{196}$

13. $\sqrt{361}$

14. $\sqrt{\dfrac{400}{100}}$

15. $\sqrt[3]{216}$

16. $\sqrt[4]{1}$

17. $\sqrt[3]{-27}$

18. $-\sqrt[4]{256}$

19. $-\sqrt[3]{-343}$

20. $\sqrt[3]{\dfrac{27}{125}}$

SETS, INTERSECTION, AND UNION

Calvary Christian Academy Class Schedule				
	English I	Biology	Bible	Algebra I
Beth	x		x	x
Julie	x	x	x	
Kevin	x		x	
Martin	x	x	x	x
Frank		x	x	x
Sara	x	x	x	

The principal wants to know how many students are taking both Bible and Algebra I. The group of students taking Bible are Beth, Julie, Kevin, Martin, Frank, and Sara. Those taking Algebra I are Beth, Martin, and Frank. How many are taking both Bible and Algebra I?

 DEFINITION ≫**Set:** a collection of objects.

In algebra you will usually deal with sets of numbers. For example, the number systems discussed at the beginning of the chapter are sets of numbers. Using set notation, you can describe the natural numbers as follows: {1, 2, 3, 4, . . . }.

The { } are called *set braces* and are read "the set of." The *ellipsis* (. . .) means that the numbers continue in the same pattern. The numbers 1, 2, 3, 4, and so forth, in the set above are called *elements,* or *members,* of the set. If the set has a fixed number of elements, the set is called a *finite set.* An *infinite set* is a set that does not have a fixed number of elements. A set that has no elements is called the *null set* or *empty set.* It is denoted by { } or ∅ . The empty set is considered a finite set. Sets are denoted by capital letters.

$$A = \{1, 3, 7, 9, 10\}$$

$$B = \{1, 6, 4, 10\}$$

Are A and B finite or infinite sets? If you put the elements from A and B together into one set, you would get the set $\{1, 3, 4, 6, 7, 9, 10\}$. This set is called the union of A and B and is denoted $A \cup B$.

$$A \cup B = \{1, 3, 4, 6, 7, 9, 10\}$$

If you identify the elements that A and B have in common (1 and 10), you recognize the intersection of A and B, denoted $A \cap B$.

$$A \cap B = \{1, 10\}$$

DEFINITIONS

≫**Union of sets:** the set of all the elements that appear in any of the sets.

≫**Intersection of sets:** the set of all elements that appear in all of the sets.

Procedure for Storage

Union and Intersection of Sets

To find the union of two or more sets, place into one set all elements of the sets.

To find the intersection of two or more sets, place into one set all elements common to the sets.

MIND OVER MATH

Unscramble the letters to find terms you learned in Chapter 1. Some terms are more than one word.

1. ets

2. bemrsem

3. craftos

4. sabe

5. pahrg

6. temsleen

7. gritsnee

8. nixed

9. poxenten

10. tarniloa

11. orequators

12. pstoreripe

13. stirconneite

14. acidrand

15. obeatvaselulu

16. mattecommuneillslop

Sets are often represented in picture form. From the diagram you can easily determine the elements in the union and in the intersection of the sets.

$C = \{1, 2, 3, 4, 5, 6\}$ $D = \{2, 4, 6, 8, 10\}$

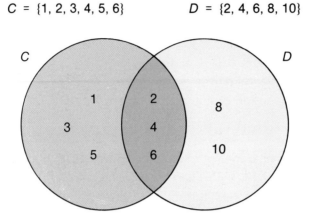

$C \cup D = \{1, 2, 3, 4, 5, 6, 8, 10\}$ Numbers in either circle C or D are in the union of the sets.

$C \cap D = \{2, 4, 6\}$ Numbers in the overlapping area of the circles C and D are in the intersection of the sets.

Exercises

$A = \{1, 2, 3, 4, 5, \ldots\}$

$B = \{-2, -1, 1, 3\}$

$C = \{-1, 2, 5, 6\}$

Identify these sets, using set notation.

1. $A \cap B$
2. $C \cup A$
3. $B \cap C$
4. $(A \cup B) \cap C$
5. $(B \cap C) \cup C$

D = {all states of the U.S. that border the Mississippi River}

E = {all states of the U.S. that begin with the letter M}

F = {all states of the U.S. that border the Gulf of Mexico}

6. $D \cup E$

7. $D \cup F$

8. $E \cup F$

9. $D \cap E$

10. $E \cap F$

11. $(D \cup E) \cap F$

12. $(D \cap E) \cap F$

13. Write in set notation the set of whole numbers.

14. Write in set notation the set of integers.

15. Draw a diagram to represent the following sets.

$$A = \{-5, -3, -1, 0, 1, 2, 3\} \qquad B = \{0, 2, 4, 6, 8, 10\}$$

16. Give an example of a finite set.

17. Give an example of an infinite set.

MEMORY RECALL

Identify.

absolute value	index
additive identity element	infinite set
additive inverse	integers
associative property of addition	intersection
associative property of multiplication	irrational numbers
	least common multiple (LCM)
base	members
commutative property of addition	multiplicative identity element
	multiplicative inverse
commutative property of multiplication	natural numbers
	null set
distributive property	number line
elements	opposite numbers
empty set	prime numbers
exponent	radical sign
exponential form	radicand
factors	rational numbers
fundamental principle of fractions	real numbers
	set
graph	square root
greatest common divisor (GCD)	twin primes
	union
identity	whole numbers
identity property of zero	zero property of multiplication

You should now be able to do the following:

1. Locate numbers on a number line.

2. Give the opposite of any number.

3. Give the absolute value of any number.

4. Add, subtract, multiply, and divide any integers.

5. Use the laws of exponents.

6. Add, subtract, multiply, and divide rational expressions.

7. Find the specified root of certain numbers.

8. Identify properties of real numbers and how these properties work.

9. Describe how to find the intersection and the union of sets.

You should be able to do these problems.

1. Name five different kinds of numbers in our real number system and give an example of each.

2. Graph these integers on separate vertical number lines.

   a. 5   **b.** -2   **c.** 0

3. Graph these integers on separate horizontal number lines.

   a. -3   **b.** 1   **c.** 24

4. Identify the opposite of each number.

   a. 29   **b.** -10   **c.** 3024

5. Identify the absolute value of each number.

   a. |-13| **b.** |6| **c.** |-249|

6. Evaluate each expression.

   a. 12 - 42   **c.** 14 + (-18)   **e.** $(-2)^3$
   b. 13 + 39   **d.** 15^0 **f.** $(9^0)^4$

7. Perform the indicated operation.

   a. -5 + 3   **i.** (-37) (-12)
   b. -2 + -4   **j.** (3) (61)
   c. +8 + -4   **k.** 182 + -2
   d. -2 - -6   **l.** $\frac{1}{2} + \frac{-5}{2}$
   e. 3 - -182   **m.** (0.4) (-0.31)
   f. 7 - 18   **n.** -144 ÷ -12
   g. 32 - 12   **o.** 32 ÷ 8
   h. (-14) (2)

8. Perform the indicated operation and leave in exponent form.

   a. $5^3 \cdot 5^4$ **e.** $4^5 \cdot 4^8 \div 4^2$
   b. $8^9 \cdot 8^6$ **f.** $(10^{2^3})^2$
   c. $(3^4)^3$ **g.** $6^5 \div 6^2$
   d. $3^2 \cdot 4^3 \cdot 3^5$

9. Give the prime factorization of these numbers.

   a. 75
   b. 210
   c. 118

10. Find the LCM.

    a. 9 and 24

    b. 18 and 27

    c. 6 and 16

11. Find the GCD.

    a. 216 and 308

    b. 270 and 330

12. Perform the indicated operations. Reduce if possible.

    a. $\frac{1}{8} + \frac{3}{8}$ **e.** $\frac{1}{4} \cdot 7$

    b. $\frac{5}{7} - \frac{2}{7}$ **f.** $\frac{1}{9} \cdot \frac{4}{5}$

    c. $\frac{2}{9} + \frac{3}{21}$ **g.** $\frac{4}{7} \div \frac{3}{8}$

    d. $\frac{5}{8} - \frac{7}{9}$ **h.** $\frac{2}{3} \div \frac{1}{3}$

13. Find the indicated root.

    a. $\sqrt{169}$

    b. $\sqrt{36}$

    c. $\sqrt{\frac{4}{16}}$

    d. $\sqrt[3]{-8}$

14. Give an example of each of the ten properties listed below.

    a. commutative property of addition

    b. associative property of multiplication

    c. commutative property of multiplication

    d. distributive property of multiplication

    e. identity property of addition

    f. associative property of addition

    g. zero property of multiplication

    h. identity property of multiplication

    i. additive inverse property

    j. multiplicative inverse property

15. $A = \{2, 4, 6, 8, 10\}$
$B = \{0, 1, 2, 3, 4, 5\}$
$C = \{2, 8, 14, 20, \ldots\}$

Find.
   a. $A \cup C$
   b. $B \cap C$
   c. $A \cap B$
   d. $A \cap C$
   e. $A \cup B$
   f. $B \cup C$

Which sets a through f are infinite? Which ones are finite?

CHAPTER 2

THE LANGUAGE OF ALGEBRA

Cheryl works for the Bea Quilting Company, making quilt patterns from which the company manufactures quilts. Most of Cheryl's designs incorporate pieces of material cut into geometric shapes, usually regular polygons. Some designs utilize triangular pieces; others incorporate squares, pentagons, hexagons, and other polygons.

Cheryl is designing a quilt that will be made from hexagonal pieces of material. The quilt must be 72 inches wide for a twin bed and have a minimum length of 108 inches. Cheryl must figure out how many quilt pieces she should cut for this pattern. A quilt piece will have the dimensions illustrated after it is sewn into a quilt. The formula to find the area of a regular polygon is $A = \frac{1}{2}ap$, where A represents the area of the polygon, a represents the length of the apothem (the radius of the inscribed circle in the polygon) and p represents the perimeter of the regular polygon.

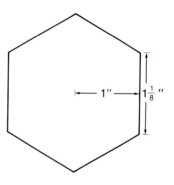

How many square inches must the area of the quilt be to cover a twin bed? How many square inches does each hexagonal piece of quilt cover? Since Cheryl is making the pattern for the quilt, she must know how many hexagonal pieces should be cut for a twin-size quilt. How many pieces should she put in her pattern? How many pieces should she cut for a quilt for a full-size bed if the quilt must cover 9720 square inches?

Cheryl needs to decide which formulas to use, how to apply the formulas to the problem, and how to solve the problem. You will learn to do all of these things in this chapter.

ORDER OF OPERATIONS

Solve this problem.

$$3 + 2 \cdot 4 - 6 \div 3$$

What is your answer? Did you get $\frac{14}{3}$? $\frac{5}{3}$? $\frac{-1}{3}$? 9? 18? confused? If you got confused, you have good reason to be confused because all of those numbers are possible answers; but only one of them is the correct answer.

If you think a math problem with more than one solution is confusing, what do you suppose a life without purpose or direction is like? Perhaps you wonder, "How do I know what is right and what is wrong? How do I determine which answer is right?" God did not put man on earth and leave him without directions. He gave man a rule book, the Bible. In it He tells sinful man that he needs a Saviour. Then He tells the saved man how to live like Christ. God established absolute truths that never change. His Word is truth (cf. John 17:17) and will never pass away (cf. Matt. 24:35). You do not have to wonder what the purpose of life is, for you can turn to God's Book and find the answers. You must follow God's rules.

In mathematics we are not left to wonder which answer is correct. Certain guidelines have been established so that you can correctly solve a problem such as the one above. You need only learn the order of operations.

Procedure for Storage

Order of Operations

If the numerical expression contains no grouping symbols, evaluate it as follows:

1. Evaluate all exponential expressions.
2. Perform all multiplication and division from left to right.
3. Perform all addition and subtraction from left to right.

Once you have the rules, you can easily solve the introductory problem correctly. Try it again. Since this problem has no grouping symbols and no exponential expressions, you perform the multiplication and division first.

$$3 + 2 \cdot 4 - 6 \div 3$$

Multiply 2 and 4. Then divide 6 by 3.
Now your problem looks like this:

$$3 + 8 - 2$$

Performing the addition and subtraction from left to right, you get 11 - 2.
Now you know the correct answer to this problem is 9.

EXAMPLES

Example 1.   Evaluate $2 + 3^2 - 4 \div 2 \cdot 3$.

> *Solution.* Since there are no grouping symbols, look for exponential expressions.

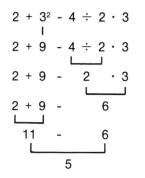

1. The exponential expression 3^2 equals 9.

2. Find the first multiplication or division left to right and follow with any other multiplication or division.

3. Add 2 and 9. Then subtract 6 from the sum. The answer is 5.

Example 2.   Evaluate $4 \cdot 5 - 3 \cdot 2 + 8 \div 4$.

> *Solution.*

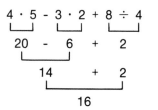

1. Multiply and divide left to right.

2. Add and subtract left to right.

Example 3. Evaluate $2^3 - 1^2 + 5 \cdot 4 - 3^2 + 9 \div 3$.

Solution.

$2^3 - 1^2 + 5 \cdot 4 - 3^2 + 9 \div 3$ **1.** Evaluate exponential expressions.

$8 - 1 + 5 \cdot 4 - 9 + 9 \div 3$ **2.** Multiply and divide left to right.

$8 - 1 + 20 - 9 + 3$ **3.** Add and subtract left to right.

$7 + 20 - 9 + 3$

$27 - 9 + 3$

$18 + 3$

21

Exercises

Evaluate.

1. $3 \cdot 4 + 5$

2. $8 - 3 \cdot 2 + 10 \div 2$

3. $10 + 7 - 3 \cdot 2$

4. $8 + 10 \div 5$

5. $1 + 9 \div 3 \cdot 2$

6. $10 - 2 \cdot 4 \div 4 + 3$

7. $4 + 6 \cdot 2 \cdot 3 \div 9$

8. $3 \div 1 \cdot 3 + 7$

9. $2 - 1 + 4 \cdot 1$

10. $8 + 2 \div 2 + 6$

11. $2^3 \div 4 + 7$

12. $1 + 7^2 \cdot 2 - 50$

13. $27 - 3^2 + 8 \div 2$

14. $17 + 4 \cdot 8 \div 2$

15. $22 - 11 \cdot 2$

16. $81 + 14 \cdot 3 \div 1 \cdot 2$

17. $3 + 4 - 2 + 6 \cdot 3$

18. $2 \div 2 + 4 - 2 + 7$

19. $6 \cdot 2 + 10 \div 5$

20. $7 - 3^2 - 1 + 4^3 \div 2$

SYMBOLS FOR GROUPING

Sometimes you may want to perform a sequence of operations in an order different from the one prescribed by the order of operations. For instance, you may want to add two numbers before you divide. If so, you must have some way to indicate the revised order. Grouping symbols let you indicate which operation to perform first.

Remember this problem?

$$3 + 2 \cdot 4 - 6 \div 3$$

If we wanted to add the 3 and the 2 and subtract the 6 from the 4 first, we would have to write the problem like this.

$$(3 + 2) \cdot (4 - 6) \div 3$$

Is the answer still 9? No. It is $\frac{-10}{3}$. Why? The parentheses are a grouping symbol. They say to do what is inside them first. Then you can follow the usual order of operations.

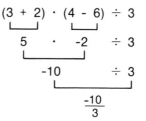

Now let's try that problem another way and see what answer we get.

[(3 + 2) · 4] − 6 ÷ 3

[(5)   · 4] − 6 ÷ 3

20   − 6 ÷ 3

20   −   2

18

This problem has two sets of grouping symbols. Again, do what is in the parentheses first. Then finish the operations in the brackets. Once those operations are performed, follow the usual order of operations.

There are three grouping symbols that you will see in mathematical expressions. They are parentheses ( ), brackets [ ], and braces { }. These grouping symbols indicate that the operations enclosed by grouping symbols are to be performed prior to any other operations.

Procedure for Storage

Using Grouping Symbols

1. Find the innermost set of grouping symbols.
2. Perform operations inside these grouping symbols according to the order of operations.
3. If there are any more grouping symbols in the expression, go back to step 1.
4. When all grouping symbols are removed, evaluate the expression by following the order of operations.

EXAMPLES

Example 1. Evaluate 2 + 3 · (5 + 7) ÷ 2.

Solution.

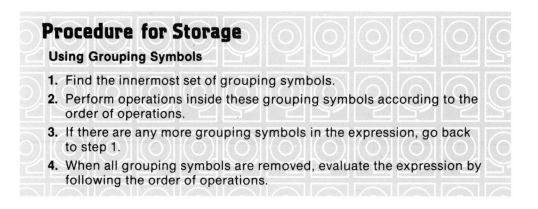

2 + 3 · (5 + 7) ÷ 2

2 + 3 ·   12   ÷ 2

2 +   36   ÷ 2

2 +   18

     20

First remove the parentheses by performing the operation within them. Then evaluate by following the order of operations.

Example 2. Evaluate 9 - 3 [2 + 7 · 8(3 + 5)] - 4.

Solution.

9 - 3 [2 + 7 · 8(3 + 5)] - 4

9 - 3 [2 + 7 · 8 · 8]   - 4

9 - 3 [2 + 56   · 8]   - 4

9 - 3 [2 +   448]   - 4

9 - 3 ·   450   - 4

9 -   1350   - 4

 -1341   - 4

     -1345

Compute inside parentheses first and remove them. Compute inside brackets and remove them. Evaluate by order of operations.

Now that you know how to solve problems containing grouping symbols, you can also insert grouping symbols to produce a specific value. Look at this problem.

$$24 \div 4 + 8 \cdot 3 - 10$$

Because there are no grouping symbols, the solution is 20. Suppose, however, that you know the value is -50. How can the terms be grouped to equal -50? You must try several ways. Since the order of operations says that multiplication and division should be performed first, insert grouping symbols so that addition or subtraction can be performed first.

$24 \div (4 + 8) \cdot 3 - 10$	
$24 \div \quad 12 \quad \cdot 3 - 10$	$24 \div (4 + 8) \cdot (3 - 10)$
$2 \quad \cdot \quad 3 - 10$	$24 \div \quad 12 \quad \cdot \quad - 7$
$6 \quad - 10$	$2 \quad \cdot \quad - 7$
$-4 \quad$ (not -50)	$-14 \quad$ (not -50)
$(24 \div 4 + 8) \cdot 3 - 10$	$24 \div 4 + 8 \cdot (3 - 10)$
$(6 + 8) \quad \cdot 3 - 10$	$6 + 8 \cdot -7$
$14 \quad \cdot \quad 3 - 10$	$6 + -56$
$42 \quad - 10$	-50
$32 \quad$ (not -50)	

Exercises

Evaluate step by step. Show all your work.

1. 5 + 4 · (3 + 7)

2. 3 · 2 + 4(5 + 8) · 2

3. 4 + 5 + [(8 + 2 · 4) - 5] · 6

4. 6 · 3 ÷ (5 + 4) + 1 - 6

5. 8 · 4 + 3(1 + 6) ÷ 2 · 9

6. 3 + {[(4 · 8 - 2) + 2 + 7 · 4] - 7 · 2} - 8

7. 9 - [(4 · 2 + 6) - 9] + (4 + 2 · 6)

8. 4 - {3 + [2 · (8 + 9) ÷ 4] + 9} · 2

9. {1 · 3 + 2[5 + 7 · 2(3 + 9)] · 4} + 2

10. 10 + 3 - [4 · 8 - (7 - 8) · 6] · 9

11. 7 - 5 + {[6 + 2 - (3 - 4) · 6] + 5} + 9

12. 8 ÷ 2 + (3 - 6) · (8 + 2) - (3 + 1) · 4

13. 6 + (2 - 5) · 8 - [3 + (4 - 7) · 3] + 6

14. 4 + (2 - 3) · 6 + 8 - 9(3 + 2)

15. 1 + 3(4 + 2) - 6 + (3 - 5) - 8 + 6

Insert grouping symbols so that each expression will have the given value.

16. 2 + 4 · 7 ÷ 2 = 21

17. 3 + 9 · 2 - 6 = -33

18. 4 + 7 · 2 - 8 + 4 = 6

19. 5 · 6 - 1 + 3 ÷ 20 = 2

20. 14 + 5 - 10 ÷ 2 · 7 - 2 - 3 = 15

VARIABLES

The ninth-grade class is planning to have a fall cookout. The food committee decided to shop for the best buy in canned soft drinks. Here is what the committee found.

Soft Drinks	Price per can p
Ryan's Root Beer	20 ¢
Cross Cola	25 ¢
Kwik Zip	18 ¢

The class president told the committee to find the cost of each brand if the committee bought one can for each of the sixty-two members of the class. So the committee multiplied each p value by 62.

Brand	Price per can p	Total Price $62p$
Ryan's	$0.20	$62(0.20) = 12.40
Cross	$0.25	$62(0.25) = 15.50
Kwik	$0.18	$62(0.18) = 11.16

62p = 62·p

OK WISEGUY! PUT MY LADDER BACK!!

If symbols are written next to each other with no operational sign between them, multiply them.

On the chart above, p represents three different values: $0.20, $0.25, $0.18. We say p is a variable because its value varies. A variable is usually denoted by a letter that stands for any member of a set with at least two elements. This set of replacement values is called the domain of the variable. Variables are used extensively in algebra to indicate an unknown quantity and to work out general solutions. Frequently a mathematical expression will contain a constant, a number or letter whose value does not change. The Greek letter pi (π) represents a constant approximately equal to 3.14. What is the constant in the chart above?

DEFINITIONS

≫**Variable:** a symbol used to represent any number of a given set of numbers called the domain.

≫**Constant:** a symbol that represents a fixed number.

Is God variable or constant? Does He do what He says He will do? Read James 1:17, Hebrews 13:8, and Malachi 3:6. Can God make the answer any plainer? When you get discouraged, you can rest in God, knowing that He is always the same. Man is changeable and doesn't always keep his promises. But God is always the same. Write down other verses that tell of God's steadfastness.

To become proficient in algebra, you must learn how to read a word phrase and convert it into an algebraic expression containing variables.

DEFINITION

≫**Algebraic expression:** a string of one or more variables and constants connected with + and - signs.

EXAMPLES

Example 1.   If *c* represents the cost of one pencil, what is the cost of ten pencils?

Solution. Let *T* = the total cost (in cents) of ten pencils
c = the cost (in cents) of one pencil

Then *T* = 10*c*.

If the replacement set for *c* is {5, 10, 17}, what is the cost of the pencils?

If *c* = 5, then 10*c* = 10 · 5.
10 · 5 = 50 cents
If *c* = 10, then 10*c* = 10 · 10.
10 · 10 = 100 cents
If *c* = 17, then 10*c* = 10 · 17.
10 · 17 = 170 cents

Example 2.   Write an equation showing the sum of 5 and any real number represented by *n*.

Solution. Let *n* = any real number
s = the sum

Then *s* = *n* + 5

Example 3.   If the domain of *x* is $\{3, 2, \frac{1}{2}, -5\}$, what is the value of *x* + 9?

Solution. If *x* = 3, then *x* + 9 = 3 + 9 = 12.

If *x* = 2, then *x* + 9 = 2 + 9 = 11.

If $x = \frac{1}{2}$, then $x + 9 = \frac{1}{2} + 9 = 9\frac{1}{2}$.

If *x* = -5, then *x* + 9 = -5 + 9 = 4.

Exercises

Write an algebraic expression for each word phrase.

1. The product of 8 and any number x.
2. The perimeter of a rectangle 24 units long and w units wide.
3. The number of spider legs in a box containing s spiders.
4. The number of points a basketball player gets in one game when he makes x baskets and four free throws.
5. The calories Joe consumes eating n sweet rolls when one sweet roll has 325 calories.
6. Sue's score and Jim's score if Sue got six more points on the test than Mark and Jim got ten fewer than Mark. Mark's score was m.
7. A number that is four more than five times another number.
8. Joy's typing speed if Joy types twice as fast as Lynn.
9. The amount Evelyn makes the week she gives x haircuts at $5 each and y permanents at $25 each.
10. The number of history books the bookstore has if it has four more than three times the number of math books.

The domain of the variable is $\{-4, 3, 1, 8\}$. Evaluate each expression and give all possible solutions.

11. $x - 4$
12. $y + 6$
13. $3z$
14. $a + 4$

Name the variables and constants in each expression.

15. $3x + 6$
16. $\dfrac{ab}{3}$
17. $c + d - 5$
18. $\dfrac{t}{4} + 6$

State the properties described.

19. $x + y = y + x$
20. $a(b + c) = ab + ac$
21. $t(sq) = (ts)q$

NEGATIVE EXPONENTS

In Chapter 1, you learned how to write in a shorter form a number multiplied by itself several times. Instead of writing $4 \cdot 4 \cdot 4$, you learned to write 4^3. Notice the phrase "a number" in the first sentence. If you substitute the variable n for 4, you can write n^3. Do you remember what this shorter form is called? What would n^3 be in expanded form? Since the base is now a variable, the exact value of the expression is unknown until the value of n is established.

EXAMPLES

Example 1. Write $aaabb$ in exponential form.
$$a^3b^2$$

Example 2. Write x^4yz^5 in expanded form.
$$xxxxyzzzzz$$

The properties of exponents that you learned in Chapter 1 apply to variables as well as to known values. Here are those properties again, with variables and numbers.

$$x^a \cdot x^b = x^{a+b} \qquad\qquad 2^4 \cdot 2^2 = 2^{4+2}$$

$$x^a \div x^b = x^{a-b} \qquad\qquad 2^5 \div 2^3 = 2^{5-3}$$

$$(x^a)^b = x^{ab} \qquad\qquad (2^2)^3 = 2^{2\cdot3}$$

$$x^0 = 1, \text{ if } x \neq 0 \qquad\qquad 321^0 = 1$$

Following the above laws, simplify the next division problem by subtracting exponents.
$$5^2 \div 5^3 = 5^{2-3} = 5^{-1}$$

As you know, a division problem can be written as a fraction. If this fraction is expanded and simplified, the following fraction results.

$$5^2 \div 5^3 = \frac{5^2}{5^3}$$

$$\frac{5^2}{5^3} = \frac{5\cdot5}{5\cdot5\cdot5} = \frac{1}{5}$$

From these computations you can conclude that $5^{-1} = \frac{1}{5}$.

$$5^2 \div 5^3 = 5^{-1} \quad \text{and} \quad 5^2 \div 5^3 = \frac{5^2}{5^3} = \frac{1}{5}$$

$$\text{so} \quad 5^{-1} = \frac{1}{5}$$

A fractional expression such as $\frac{1}{8}$ can be expressed in exponential form as $\frac{1}{2^3}$. You can also express this fraction in exponential form as a whole number with a negative exponent.

$$\frac{1}{8} = \frac{1}{2^3} = 2^{-3}$$

By following the properties of exponents, you can understand this general reasoning.

$$\frac{1}{x^a} = \frac{x^0}{x^a} = x^{0-a} = x^{-a}$$

So $\frac{1}{x^a} = x^{-a}$

Procedure for Storage

Negative Exponents

$x^{-a} = \frac{1}{x^a}$, if a is any real number and $x \neq 0$.

When you multiply, divide, or raise the power of exponential expressions with negative exponents, use the same rules that you used when working with positive exponents.

EXAMPLES

Example 3.
Simplify $\frac{1}{2^2} \cdot \frac{1}{2^3}$.

Solution.
$$\frac{1}{2^2} \cdot \frac{1}{2^3} = 2^{-2} \cdot 2^{-3}$$
$$= 2^{(-2 + -3)}$$
$$= 2^{-5}$$
$$= \frac{1}{2^5}.$$

Example 4.
Simplify $\frac{1}{4^2} \div \frac{1}{4^3}$.

Solution.
$$\frac{1}{4^2} \div \frac{1}{4^3} = 4^{-2} \div 4^{-3}$$
$$= 4^{(-2 - -3)}$$
$$= 4^1$$
$$= 4$$

Example 5.
Simplify $\left(\frac{1}{5^3}\right)^4$.

Solution.
$$\left(\frac{1}{5^3}\right)^4 = (5^{-3})^4$$
$$= 5^{-3 \cdot 4}$$
$$= 5^{-12}$$
$$= \frac{1}{5^{12}}$$

Example 6.
Simplify $\left(\frac{1}{3^9}\right)^0$.

Solution.
$$\left(\frac{1}{3^9}\right)^0 = (3^{-9})^0$$
$$= 3^{-9 \cdot 0}$$
$$= 3^0$$
$$= 1$$

Exercises

Write in exponential form.

1. aaa
2. xx
3. kk
4. $qqqqq$
5. $ddpppp$
6. $uuvw$
7. $vvvvvvv$
8. $mnoo$
9. $ruaa$
10. $zzzzzzzzzz$

Write in expanded form.

11. x^5
12. n^2b^7
13. c^3
14. jo^4
15. t^6

Write each expression with positive exponents.

16. 3^{-2}
17. x^{-5}
18. 4^{-8}
19. y^{-2}
20. $x^{(-3)}y^{(-4)}$
21. 4^{-3}

Write each expression with negative exponents.

22. $\dfrac{1}{4^3}$
23. $\dfrac{1}{8^2}$
24. $\dfrac{1}{x^4}$
25. $\dfrac{1}{x^2y^9}$
26. $\dfrac{1}{3^2x^3}$
27. $\dfrac{1}{x^2yz^3}$

Compute, leaving the answers in positive exponential form.

28. $\dfrac{1}{3^2} \cdot \dfrac{1}{3^3}$
29. $4^{-2} \div 4^{-9}$
30. $\left(\dfrac{1}{7^3} \right)^4$
31. $\dfrac{1}{9^2} \div \dfrac{1}{9^4}$
32. $(3^{-6})^0$
33. $4^{-5} \div \dfrac{1}{4^2}$
34. $8^{-3} \cdot \dfrac{1}{8^5}$
35. $\dfrac{1}{3^{-2}} \cdot \dfrac{1}{3^2}$
36. $x^{-5} \cdot x^3$
37. $y^{-4} \div y^{-2}$
38. $z^4 \cdot z^6$
39. $x^2 \cdot x^5 \cdot x^3$
40. $(x^4)^{-3}$

EVALUATING ALGEBRAIC EXPRESSIONS

What does the noun *value* mean? What does *evaluate* mean? Since you probably know but can't quite say the definitions, look up the words in a dictionary. Does your dictionary give special mathematical definitions for these words? If so, what are they?

Does your life have any value? For many people the answer is "no," because they have not accepted Jesus Christ as their Saviour. The Christian, however, recognizes that his life does have value and seeks to live to glorify God. But he must evaluate his life every day to see if he is living up to God's standard. How does he do this? Does he look at others around him and assume that he is as good if not better than the next person? Definitely not! The Bible is the Christian's mirror to reflect God's standard and to reveal man's sins (cf. James 1:23-25). The Christian must read and study God's Word every day so that he can become more like Jesus Christ, the only standard by which he should evaluate his life.

Can you find the value of $x + 10$ when $x = 5$? If you replace x with its value of 5, the expression becomes $5 + 10$, which has the value of 15.

 DEFINITION ≫**Evaluation:** the process of calculating the numerical value of an expression.

EXAMPLES

Example 1.   Evaluate x^2 when $x = 3$.

   Solution. $x^2 = 3^2 = 3 \cdot 3 = 9$

Example 2.   Evaluate $x + y + z^2$ when $x = 4$, $y = 9$, and $z = 2$.

   Solution.
$$x + y + z^2$$
$$4 + 9 + 2^2$$
$$4 + 9 + 2 \cdot 2$$
$$4 + 9 + 4$$
$$13 + 4$$
$$17$$

Example 3. Evaluate $3a^2 - b + c^3$ when $a = 1$, $b = 4$, and $c = 3$.

Solution.
$$3a^2 - b + c^3$$
$$3 \cdot 1^2 - 4 + 3^3$$
$$3 \cdot 1 - 4 + 27$$
$$3 \quad\; - 4 + 27$$
$$-1 + 27$$
$$26$$

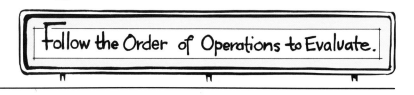

Follow the Order of Operations to Evaluate.

DEFINITION ≫**Substitution:** the process of replacing a variable with a value or an algebraic expression.

Procedure for Storage

Evaluating Expressions

1. Substitute the given values for the variables.
2. Evaluate by following the order of operations.

Exercises

1. Evaluate with $x = 4$, $y = -2$, $z = 3$, and $h = -1$.

a. x^2y

b. $x + yz$

c. $\dfrac{x + y}{h}$

d. $x^2 + h - 3$

e. $\dfrac{x}{y} + \dfrac{z}{h}$

f. $(x + y) \cdot (x - y)$

g. $x^3 - z^3$

h. $h(x + z)$

i. $h^2 + y^2 - x^3$

j. $\dfrac{3x^2y - z}{5}$

2. Evaluate a through j again with $x = \frac{1}{2}$, $y = \frac{-1}{4}$, $z = 1$, and $h = \frac{1}{3}$.

USING FORMULAS

When Bill goes swimming, he likes to dive to the bottom of the pool. At the bottom of the deep end, he feels a great amount of pressure on his ears. In shallow water, he feels less pressure. Underwater the amount of pressure (p) in pounds per square inch (psi) depends upon the height (h), or depth, of the water. The relationship is shown in the formula $p = 0.433h$. If Bill is in 10 feet of water, what amount of pressure does he feel? If he is in 3 feet of water, what amount of pressure does he feel?

$p = 0.433h \quad h = 10$ $p = 0.433h \quad h = 3$

$p = 0.433(10)$ $p = 0.433(3)$

$p = 4.33$ psi $p = 1.299$ psi

DEFINITION

≫**Formula:** an equation that describes a principle of nature or numbers.

The metric system is used more frequently in today's scientific world than the English measurements used here. Instead of measuring in pounds per square inch, a scientist measures in newtons per square meter, which is called a pascal (Pa). The formula for converting pounds per square inch (psi) to pascals (Pa) is

pressure in Pa = 6894 × pressure in psi.

What is the number of pascals in each example above?

In chemistry class Sara found that the temperature of the chemicals in her experiment registered 35° C. She was to make sure the chemicals reached at least 100° F. She had to use the formula $F = \frac{9}{5}C + 32°$ to convert Celsius readings to Fahrenheit equivalents. Had the chemicals reached the desired temperature yet? Should she continue to heat the chemicals?

$F = \left(\frac{9}{5}\right)C + 32°$

$F = \left(\frac{9}{5}\right)35° + 32°$

$F = 63° + 32°$

$F = 95°$

The Fahrenheit temperature is 95°, so the chemicals have not reached the desired temperature. Sara must continue to heat them.

Formulas are used extensively in science, business, engineering, carpentry, and many other professions. You use formulas every day. Make a list of some formulas that you or someone you know uses.

Where should a Christian find the formula for success in his life? Will a good job and lots of money bring success? No, nothing this world offers can bring happiness and success. The Bible, God's holy Word, provides the formula for the Christian's success (cf. Josh. 1:8; Ps. 1:1-3).

Procedure for Storage

Using Formulas

1. Write the correct formula.
2. Substitute given values for the variables in the formula.
3. Evaluate the expression.

Exercises

1. Brandon plans to cut a piece of plastic to go around the outer edge of a circular table. To find out how long he needs to cut the plastic, Brandon must use the formula $c = 2\pi r$, which gives the circumference of a circle. If the radius of Brandon's table is 2 feet and the constant π is approximately 3.14, how long should Brandon cut the plastic?

2. The amount of simple interest that Shanda receives on the money she saves from babysitting is expressed by $i = prt$.

   In this formula, i is simple interest, p is the principal (or amount invested), r is the percentage rate of the investment, and t is the time or length of the investment in years. If Shanda invests $150 at 5% interest, how much interest will she gain in one year?

WHEN USING PERCENT, CHANGE THE PERCENT TO DECIMAL

for example, 4% means:

A. 4 PER HUNDRED,

B. $\frac{4}{100}$, or

C. .04

I'D SAY ALL OF THE ABOVE

3. Mr. Denton wants to put a fence around his rectangular garden, but first he needs to know the distance around the outside of the garden. The formula for finding the perimeter of a rectangle is $p = 2l + 2w$. If his garden is 60 feet long and 30 feet wide, how many feet of fencing does he need?

4. The formula $d = rt$ gives the distance as the rate multiplied by the time. If a bus carrying spectators to a soccer game travels 47 mph for 2 hours, how far does the bus travel?

5. Chris plans to paint a cylinder that will hold gasoline. After Chris finds out the number of square feet of surface area on the cylinder by using the formula $A = 2\pi rh + 2\pi r^2$, he can compute the amount of paint needed. If the height of the cylinder is 5 feet and the radius is 2 feet, what is the total surface area of the cylinder?

6. The formula for normal weight is $w = \dfrac{11(h - 40)}{2}$. The variable h is the height in inches. If Ben is 5'2" tall and weighs 154 pounds, what is his normal weight? Should he lose or gain weight to be at his normal weight? How much?

7. The volume of a rectangular box can be found with the formula $V = lwh$. Find the volume of boxes having the following dimensions.

   a. $l = 4''$
   $w = 2''$
   $h = 5''$

   b. $l = 10''$
   $w = 3''$
   $h = 2''$

   c. $l = 8''$
   $w = 7''$
   $h = 6''$

You've always wanted to know the answer to a question before you know the question, haven't you? Well, here's your chance. The answer is 1089.

MIND OVER MATH

1. Choose any three-digit number with three different digits.
2. Reverse the number you choose.
3. Subtract the smaller number from the larger number.
4. If the difference is less than 100, multiply by 2. If it is greater than 100, go on to step 5.
5. Reverse the last answer.
6. Add the last answer and the reverse of the last answer.
7. Your sum is 1089.

WHAT IS A COMPUTER?

A computer is any device that man uses to help him perform mathematical calculations and organize information. Today we use two basic types of computers: analog computers and digital computers. Analog computers find results by using variable quantities such as voltages and currents. The speedometer on a car is an analog computer. It measures the rotational speed of the moving drive shaft and translates it into the approximate speed of the car. A digital computer performs operations with numbers. It may be able to work with words or even to draw pictures, but it does so by converting into numbers all information it is given. A small electronic calculator is a simple digital computer that does only arithmetic.

Programmers and people who operate computers use two terms to describe what they work with. *Hardware* refers to the physical equipment in the computer system. *Software* refers to the program that gives the computer its instructions.

The hardware of the computer includes four major components. They are the input unit, the processing unit, the output unit, and the auxiliary storage unit. The input unit is the device used to load the computer with data and programs. Information can be input through a keyboard, card reader, or laser scanner. The most common input device today is the keyboard. The computer can also receive input from auxiliary storage devices such as cassette tapes or disk drives.

The processing unit is composed of two parts: the computer's central processing unit (CPU) and the main memory. The CPU, made up of electronic parts, has two major functions. One of its functions is to control the traffic of input and output. Another is to interpret the program instructions, perform all arithmetic operations, and make all logical decisions. The computer's main memory consists of electronic components that store the letters, numbers, and special codes that make up a program and data.

For people to use the data generated by the computer, it must be output in an organized manner. There are several forms of output devices. Permanent output is usually in the form of a print-out, which comes from the computer through a printer. Another common (cathode-ray tube) screen. Output can also be sent to an auxiliary storage device.

An auxiliary storage device is a piece of computer equipment that stores data or programs for later use. Often these devices can be removed from the actual computer and used on a different computer in another location. Some common auxiliary storage devices are magnetic (cassette) tapes, floppy disks, and hard disks. Any

of a computer. Programs are called software because the programmer can change them easily by typing in a new series of instructions.

What is a computer? It is a complex machine that works very quickly to help people solve problems. Yet it is only a helper. A computer's memory can hold and

use millions of pieces of information, but some person must put the information in the memory to start with. Even if in the near future scientists design computers that can decide for themselves how to solve problems, the machines will still be serving human beings—as man's most useful electronic friend.

program or data stored on an auxiliary storage system must be read into the computer's main memory before the computer can use it.

Using a set of instructions called a program, the CPU controls the processes

COMBINING LIKE TERMS

"Simplicity is truth's most becoming garb." The man who made that statement realized that God's truth is never complicated. In II Corinthians 11:3, Paul warns the Corinthian Christians not to believe anyone (or anything) who would turn their minds "from the simplicity that is in Christ." God's plan of salvation is that one simply believe. The gospel— that Christ died, was buried, and rose again—could be no simpler. But Satan corrupts that simplicity and says there are other things to do besides believe. Christians need to guard themselves against Satan's complications by trusting fully in the simplicity of Jesus Christ.

Mathematical expressions are written as simply as possible. When you speak of a group of 50 apples, you would not speak of 30 apples plus 20 apples, or 25 apples doubled, or of 17 apples plus 36 apples minus 3 apples. You would simply say 50 apples. These phrases can be written as algebraic expressions.

$$30 + 20 \qquad 2(25) \qquad 17 + 36 - 3$$

Although in like terms, each expression is not in its simplest form. To simplify an expression, you need to combine like terms by performing the indicated operations. In algebra, as in all math work, always express your final answer in its simplest form.

>**Term:** A variable, number, or product or quotient of numbers and variables separated by + or - signs in an algebraic expression.

>**Like terms:** terms that have the same variable (or variables) with the same exponent.

The expression $3x + 4y + 5x$ has three terms: $3x$, $4y$, and $5x$. There are only two variables: x and y. So the terms $3x$ and $5x$ are like terms. Like terms can be combined into a simpler form, but unlike terms cannot be combined. This expression in its simplest form is $8x + 4y$.

>**Numerical coefficient** (coefficient): the numerical factor accompanying the variables in a term.

The coefficient of $3x$ is 3. If there is no expressed coefficient of a variable, the coefficient is 1. When you combine like terms, you are actually applying the distributive property $ab + ac. = a(b + c)$

EXAMPLES

Example 1.   Combine $3x + 5x$.
  Solution. $3x + 5x = (3 + 5)x = 8x$

Example 2.   Simplify $3x + 4y - 5x$.

Solution.
$$3x + 4y - 5x$$
$$3x - 5x + 4y$$
$$(3 - 5)x + 4y$$
$$-2x + 4y$$

1. Rearrange the terms.
2. Apply the distributive property.
3. Perform the operations. Since $-2x$ and $4y$ are unlike terms, they cannot be combined. The expression is now in its simplest form.

Example 3.   Simplify $7x^2 + 8x - 4x^2 + 10x$

Solution.
$$7x^2 + 8x - 4x^2 + 10x$$
$$7x^2 - 4x^2 + 8x + 10x$$
$$3x^2 + 18x$$

Although the variable is x, x^2 and x are unlike terms because the exponents of x are different.

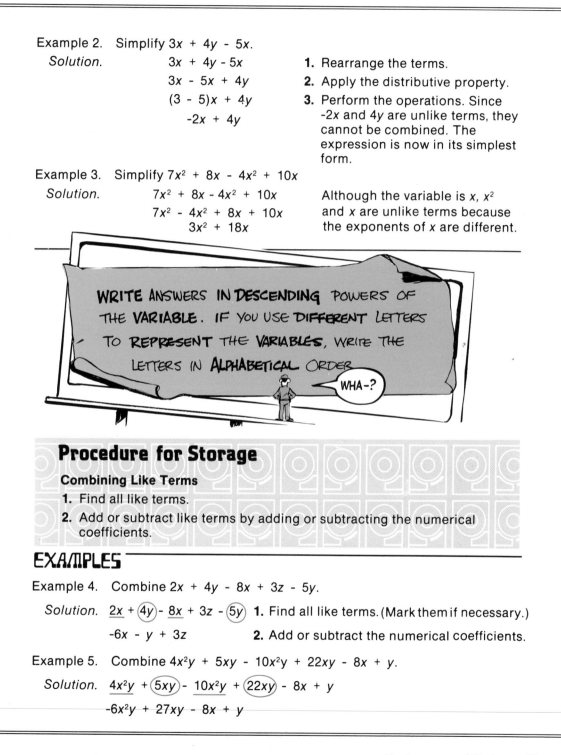

WRITE ANSWERS IN DESCENDING POWERS OF THE VARIABLE. IF YOU USE DIFFERENT LETTERS TO REPRESENT THE VARIABLES, WRITE THE LETTERS IN ALPHABETICAL ORDER

WHA-?

Procedure for Storage

Combining Like Terms

1. Find all like terms.
2. Add or subtract like terms by adding or subtracting the numerical coefficients.

EXAMPLES

Example 4.   Combine $2x + 4y - 8x + 3z - 5y$.

Solution. $\underline{2x} + (4y) - \underline{8x} + 3z - (5y)$
$$-6x - y + 3z$$

1. Find all like terms. (Mark them if necessary.)
2. Add or subtract the numerical coefficients.

Example 5.   Combine $4x^2y + 5xy - 10x^2y + 22xy - 8x + y$.

Solution. $\underline{4x^2y} + (5xy) - \underline{10x^2y} + (22xy) - 8x + y$
$$-6x^2y + 27xy - 8x + y$$

Example 6.   Combine $8x^3 - x^2 + x^3 + 4x^3 - x^2 + 6x^3$.

   Solution. $\underline{8x^3} - \boxed{x^2} + \underline{x^3} + \underline{4x^3} - \boxed{x^2} + \underline{6x^3}$

   $19x^3 - 2x^2$

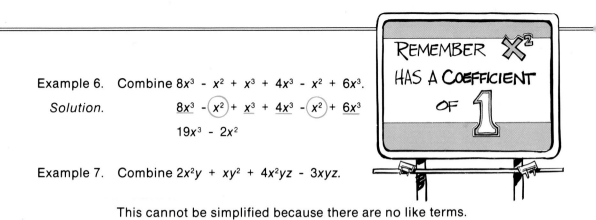

REMEMBER X^2 HAS A COEFFICIENT OF 1

Example 7.   Combine $2x^2y + xy^2 + 4x^2yz - 3xyz$.

   This cannot be simplified because there are no like terms.

Exercises

For each algebraic expression, tell which terms are like terms. Then give each numerical coefficient.

1. $3x + 4x - 5y$

2. $8x^2 + 3x + 6x^2$

3. $xy - 2xy - 9xy$

4. $x^2yz - xy^2z + 3x^2yz$

5. $2x^3 - 17x + 5x^3$

Simplify by combining like terms.

6. $3a + 7a$

7. $19k - 13k$

8. $12xy + 4xy$

9. $21b - 2b$

10. $2x^2 + 3x + 5x$

11. $d - 4d + 3f + 7f$

12. $\frac{1}{2x} + \frac{3}{2x}$

13. $2.46m + 1.6n - 8.4m$

14. $6x^2 + 3x^2y - 4x + 8x^2$

15. $12ab + 9ab - 7ab$

16. $21c^2 + 3d - 5cd + 6c^2 + 8cd$

17. $y - 9y + 3y^2$

18. $8x^2 - 6x^2y + 2xy + 7x^2y + xy$

Find the terms that should be added or subtracted to obtain the indicated expression.

19. $3a^2 + ? = 2a^2 + 3a + 4$

20. $x^2 + x + 7 + ? = 5x^2 + 3x - 8$

Simplify and evaluate with $x = 2, y = -3$.

21. $4x + 3y - x + 6y - 8y$

22. $x^2 + 2x - 7x + 4$

23. $xy - 3x + y^2$

24. $3y - x^3 + 1^{10} - y$

25. $(4x)^0 + xy^2 + x$

REMOVING PARENTHESES

An algebraic expression enclosed in parentheses, braces, or brackets is treated as one term. For example, $(2x + 5)$ is considered one term that contains two terms. The term $(2x + 5)$ should be read "the quantity $2x$ plus 5." If a number precedes the parentheses, you can remove the parentheses by applying the distributive property. Remember that the sign preceding a number can be considered part of the number.

Observe how parentheses are removed from each expression.

EXAMPLES

Example 1. $2(3x^2 + 4x + 5)$

   Solution. $2(3x^2 + 4x + 5)$ Apply the distributive property.
   $6x^2 + 8x + 10$ Notice that the signs do not change because the 2 is positive.

Example 2. $-4(a + 3ab)$

   Solution. $-4(a + 3ab)$ Notice that the signs inside the parentheses change when the parentheses are removed. Why?
   $-4a - 12ab$

Example 3. $2(3x^2 + 4x) - 8(x^2 + 2x)$

   Solution. $2(3x^2 + 4x) - 8(x^2 + 2x)$ The terms in this expression are $2(3x^2 + 4x)$ and $8(x^2 + 2x)$. Apply the distributive property and combine like terms.
   $6x^2 + 8x - 8x^2 - 16x$
   $-2x^2 - 8x$

Example 4. $(5x - 7) - (x - 6)$

   Solution. $(5x - 7) - (x - 6)$ Since subtracting a negative is the same as adding a positive, $-(-6)$ becomes $+6$.
   $5x - 7 + -x + 6$
   $5x - 7 - x + 6$
   $4x - 1$

Example 5. $(2x + 5) + (3x - 9)$

   Solution. $(2x + 5) + (3x - 9)$
   $2x + 5 + 3x - 9$
   $5x - 4$

Procedure for Storage

Removing Parentheses

1. If the parentheses are preceded by a plus sign, remove the parentheses without changing any signs within them.
2. If the parentheses are preceded by a minus sign, remove the parentheses and change all signs within them as well as the minus sign preceding them.
3. Combine like terms.

or

1. Remove parentheses by applying the distributive property.
2. Simplify by combining like terms.

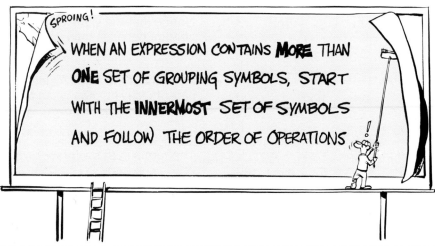

SPROING!

WHEN AN EXPRESSION CONTAINS **MORE** THAN **ONE** SET OF GROUPING SYMBOLS, START WITH THE **INNERMOST** SET OF SYMBOLS AND FOLLOW THE ORDER OF OPERATIONS

EXAMPLES

Example 6.   Remove grouping symbols and simplify the expression.

Solution.

$7x^2 - [3x + 4y(2x - 8y) - 4x] + 5xy$

1. Apply the distributive property and remove parentheses.

$7x^2 - [3x + 8xy - 32y^2 - 4x] + 5xy$

2. Combine like terms.

$7x^2 - [-x + 8xy - 32y^2] + 5xy$

3. Remove brackets, changing signs.

$7x^2 + x - 8xy + 32y^2 + 5xy$
$7x^2 + x - 3xy + 32y^2$

4. Combine like terms.

Example 7.   Remove parentheses and simplify the expression.

Solution.

$3k(k + 2) - k(k - 1)$ **1.** Apply the distributive property and remove parentheses.

$3k^2 + 6k - k^2 + k$ **2.** Combine like terms.
$2k^2 + 7k$

Exercises

Simplify. Show all work.

1. $4a + (2a + 9)$

2. $(7b - 8c) - (3b + 2c)$

3. $4(x + 2y)$

4. $-2(3z + 7)$

5. $5 - (2x - 18)$

6. $2x - (8y + x)$

7. $-5a - (3a + b) + (2a - 7b)$

8. $3x + 2y + (5x - 7y)$

9. $(2a - b) - (3a + 4b) + (6a + b)$

10. $9m + 11n + (3n - m)$

11. $7b - 3(2b + 6)$

12. $-4(x + 3) + 5(x - 7)$

13. $10(2x^2 - 3x + 4) - 5(x^2 + 2x - 9)$

14. $4a - (2a^2 + 3z) + 7(a^2 - 2a + 8)$

15. $2x(x - 4) + 3x(x + 2)$

16. $6(m^2 - 2m + 4) - m(m + 3)$

17. $4 - 3p - 6(p + 5) + 9$

18. $2r^2 + 5r + 3r - r(6r + 2)$

19. $a + 6a + 2 - a(a + 4) + 5 - 2$

20. $u^2 + 3(u^2 + 4) - 5(u + 4u + 6)$

PROPERTIES OF EQUALITY

What does *equality* mean? *Equality* means the condition of being equal. Are all men equal in man's eyes? Read James 2:1-10. Do you have "respect of persons"? Are all men equal in God's eyes? Are all men sinners? Read Romans 3. Yes, we are all sinners, for "there is none righteous, no, not one" (Rom. 3:10). God gives everyone an equal chance to be saved. "Whosoever" in Romans 10:13 means anyone. Any person can have heaven for his home if he will accept Jesus Christ as his personal Saviour.

In algebra you will spend most of your time solving mathematical equalities. An equality contains an equal sign and two expressions, one on each side of the equal sign. When two expressions represent the same number, the expressions are said to be equal. For example, 4^2, 2^4, $12 + 4$, $22 - 6$, and 16 all have the same numerical value. Therefore, $4^2 = 12 + 4$ is an equation. Read the equal sign (=) "is," "equals," or "is equal to."

DEFINITION

≫**Equation:** a mathematical sentence stating that two expressions are equal.

One of your main objectives in algebra is to learn to solve algebraic equations that involve variables. To do this effectively, you must have a complete understanding of the four properties of equality. These properties will give you a method for solving equations.

PROPERTIES OF EQUALITY			
Operation	Used to Solve	Example	Symbolization
Addition	$x - 29 = -58$	$5 = 3 + 2$ $5 + 4 = 3 + 2 + 4$ $9 = 9$	If $a = b$, and c is a real number, then $a + c = b + c$.
Subtraction	$x + 18 = 122$	$7 = 4 + 3$ $7 - 3 = 4 + 3 - 3$ $4 = 4$	If $a = b$, and c is a real number, then $a - c = b - c$.
Multiplication	$\dfrac{x}{8} = -34$	$4 = 1 + 3$ $2(4) = 2(1 + 3)$ $8 = 2 + 6$ $8 = 8$	If $a = b$, and c is a real number, then $ac = bc$.
Division	$4x = 62$	$8 = 2 + 6$ $\dfrac{8}{2} = \dfrac{(2 + 6)}{2}$ $\dfrac{8}{2} = \dfrac{2}{2} + \dfrac{6}{2}$ $4 = 1 + 3$ $4 = 4$	If $a = b$, and c is a real number not equal to zero, then $\dfrac{a}{c} = \dfrac{b}{c}$.

Exercises

In each problem below, the left side of the equation has been changed.
What must you do to the right side of the equation to maintain balance?

1. $3 = 1 + 2$
$3 + 5 =$

2. $x + 7 = 15$
$x + 7 - 7 =$

3. $8 - 2 = 6$
$8 - 2 + 2 =$

4. $x - 3 = 24$
$x - 3 + 3 =$

5. $5 = 2 + 3$
$2 \cdot 5 =$

6. $8 + 4 = 12$
$3(8 + 4) =$

7. $24 = 12 \cdot 2$
$\frac{24}{2} =$

8. $20 = 4x$
$\frac{20}{4} =$

9. $5x = 75$
$\frac{5x}{5} =$

10. $\frac{x}{2} = 8$
$2 \left(\frac{x}{2} \right) =$

11. Give a numerical example of each of the four properties of equality.

Read John 3:16. What word tells us that we all have an equal opportunity to be saved?

Read Revelation 3:20. Do you have the same opportunity as anyone else in the class to open this door and know Jesus Christ as Saviour? What is the key word that tells us that we are all equal in God's eyes?

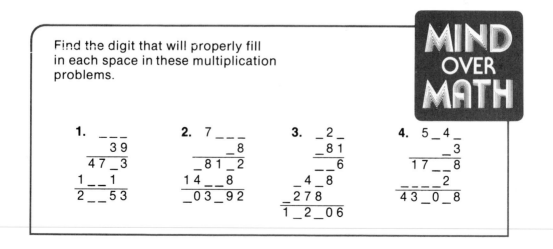

MIND OVER MATH

Find the digit that will properly fill in each space in these multiplication problems.

1.
```
    _ _ _
      3 9
  ———————
  4 7 _ 3
  1 _ _ 1
  ———————
  2 _ _ 5 3
```

2.
```
  7 _ _ _
      _ 8
  —————————
  _ 8 1 _ 2
  1 4 _ _ 8
  —————————
  _ 0 3 _ 9 2
```

3.
```
    _ 2 _
    _ 8 1
  ———————
    _ _ 6
  _ 4 _ 8
  _ 2 7 8
  ———————
  1 _ 2 _ 0 6
```

4.
```
  5 _ 4 _
        3
  ———————
  1 7 _ _ 8
  _ _ _ _ 2
  ———————
  4 3 _ 0 _ 8
```

TRANSLATING WORD PHRASES INTO ALGEBRAIC PHRASES

As a student of algebra, you must be able to take information from our God-created universe and translate it into algebraic language. After you have symbolized the problem, you can solve it and relate it back to the physical world. In this section you should be concerned with changing the verbal problem into algebraic symbols. Look for words that indicate certain operations. What operations do the following words make you think of?

difference	add
less	subtract
times	product
quotient	divided by
sum	increased by
decreased by	diminished
twice	double

Symbolize the following.

EXAMPLES

Example 1. The sum of n and 4

$$n + 4$$

Example 2. The difference between a number and 5

$$n - 5$$

Example 3. One-third of a number

$$\frac{1}{3}(n)$$

Example 4. A number divided by 6

$$\frac{n}{6}$$

Example 5. 8 more than 3 times a number

$$3n + 8$$

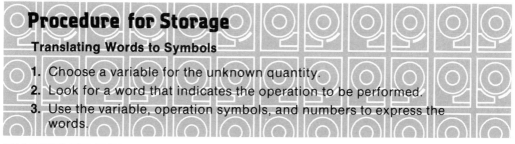

Procedure for Storage

Translating Words to Symbols

1. Choose a variable for the unknown quantity.
2. Look for a word that indicates the operation to be performed.
3. Use the variable, operation symbols, and numbers to express the words.

EXAMPLES

Example 6. Symbolize the sum of 3 and 8 times a number.

Solution.

1. Let x stand for the number.
2. Since the operational word *sum* means addition and the operational word *times* means multiplication, the phrase in symbols is $3 + 8x$.

Example 7. The quotient of the difference of a number and 8, and 2 times the number.

$$\frac{n - 8}{2n}$$

Exercises

Express in algebraic form.

1. A number decreased by 17
2. The product of a number and 4
3. The sum of twice a number and 6
4. n less 10
5. x increased by y
6. A number cubed plus the number squared
7. 24 greater than a number
8. The quotient of twice a number, and the sum of the number and 7
9. 126 diminished by the product of a number and 1 less than the number
10. The difference between a number and twice the number
11. The sum of a number and 82 times the number
12. Three less than the product of a number and 2 more than the number

Write a word phrase to describe each algebraic expression.

13. $x + 4$

14. $2a + 5$

15. $a - 9$

16. $3(x + 2)$

17. $\dfrac{4}{x}$

18. $\dfrac{5(x)}{y}$

19. $(a + b) - 8$

20. $6(a - 9)$

21. What are some key words that describe the operations of addition, subtraction, multiplication, and division? List at least 5 for each operation.

TRANSLATING WORD PROBLEMS INTO EQUATIONS

The sum of a number and 5 is 23. Find the number.

How can you translate this word problem into a numerical equation? First, analyze it very carefully. Find out what the phrase *the sum* indicates. What does *of a number and 5* tell you? What letter are you going to use as a variable? The last word in the problem, *is*, is a very important word. The word *is* means *equals*. Whenever you see *is*, put = in your algebraic sentence. The final number, 23, is the sum. The statement *find the number* tells that the variable will stand for the number.

After you have read and analyzed a word problem systematically and methodically, you should be able to come up with an equation that symbolizes the word problem. What is the equation form of this word problem?

EXAMPLES

Example 1. The difference of a number and 10 is 37. Find the number.

Solution.   Analyze: Let x = the number

                 difference   -

                 is   =

         Equation: $x - 10 = 37$

Example 2.   If 23 is added to 4 times a number, the result is 143. What is the number?

Solution.   Analyze: Let n = the number

added to   +

times   ·

is   =

Equation: $23 + 4n = 143$

Example 3.   Six subtracted from three times a certain number equals thirty-six decreased by four times the number. Find the number.

Solution.   Analyze: Let x = the number

subtracted from   -

times   ·

equals   =

decreased by   -

times   ·

Equation: $3x - 6 = 36 - 4x$

If you learn to analyze problems carefully, you will have no difficulty setting up algebraic equations.

Procedure for Storage

Translating Words to Equations

1. Read the problem carefully.
2. Analyze the problem.
3. Substitute algebraic symbols for words.
4. Write the equation.

EXAMPLES

Example 4. The sum of two consecutive integers is 49. Find the two integers.

> *Solution.* Analyze: Let x = the first integer
>
> $x + 1$ = the second integer
>
> sum   +
>
> is   =
>
> Equation: $x + (x + 1) = 49$ Combine like terms.
>
> $2x + 1 = 49$

Example 5. One number is 6 more than 3 times another number. The difference of the numbers is 34. What are the two numbers?

> *Solution.* Analyze: Let x = the first number
>
> $6 + 3x$ = the second number
>
> more   +
>
> times   ·
>
> difference   -
>
> is   =
>
> Equation: $(6 + 3x) - x = 34$ Simplify.
>
> $6 + 3x - x = 34$
>
> $6 + 2x = 34$

Now that you can translate words into equations, you need to learn how to solve these equations. Solving equations is the topic of the next chapter. For now, concentrate on getting the equation from the words.

Exercises

Analyze each word problem. Write the equation you would use to solve the problem, but do not solve it.

1. The product of a number and 12 is 780. Find the number.

2. Four times a number plus 8 is 28. What is the number?

3. The quotient of 3 times a number and 16 is 12. Find the number.

4. Jim and Bill share a bookshelf in their room. Jim has 4 more than twice as many books as Bill. There are 22 books on the shelf. How many of the books belong to Jim and how many belong to Bill?

5. The number of girls in Mrs. Conn's math class is 2 less than 3 times the number of boys. She has 26 students in her class. How many boys are in the class?

6. Sue bought two new dresses, paying $60.00 for the pair. One of the dresses cost $12.00 more than the other. How much did each dress cost?

7. The sum of two numbers is 85, and their difference is 29. Find the two numbers.

8. The total attendance for Sunday's services was 266. If there were 18 more people at the morning service than at the evening service, how many attended each service?

9. Find two consecutive integers whose sum is 175.

10. The sum of three numbers is 40. The first number is four more than the product of 6 and the second number. The third number is 9 less than twice the second number. Find the three numbers.

11. Mr. Collins is going to enclose his rectangular garden with 74 feet of fencing. The length is 7 feet longer than the width. What are the dimensions of Mr. Collins's garden?

12. Find two consecutive even integers whose sum is 178. (If x is the first even integer, how do you represent the next even integer?)

13. The sum of the angles of a triangle is 180°. Angle A is 3 times as large as angle B, and angle C is 120° more than angle B. What is the measure of each angle?

14. In a basketball game, 96 points were scored. The winners scored twice as many as the losers. How many points did each team score?

15. Kenny is 7 years older than his sister. The sum of their ages is 31. Find the age of each child.

MEMORY RECALL

Identify.

coefficient	numerical coefficient
constant	order of operations
domain	substitution
equation	term
evaluating	variable
like terms	

You should now be able to do the following:

1. Evaluate any string of numbers.
2. Evaluate a numerical expression that has grouping symbols.
3. Evaluate expressions containing variables.
4. Solve exponential expressions and use negative exponents.
5. Use formulas.
6. Combine like terms.
7. Give examples of the properties of equality.
8. Change word problems to algebraic expressions and equations.

You should be able to do the following problems:

1. Evaluate.

   a. $2 \cdot 3 + 9$

   b. $4 + 6 \cdot 8 \div 2 - 14$

   c. $3 + 8 - 5 \cdot 4 + 6$

   d. $4^2 - 1 \cdot 8 + 3 - 7 + 10 \div 2$

   e. $12 \cdot 3 + 6 - 8 \cdot 2 \div 4$

   f. $3 + 6^2 - 7 - 2 \cdot 4 - 9$

   g. $3 + 9 \cdot (2 - 6) \cdot 8 + 4$

   h. $6 - 2 \cdot (9 \div 3 + 8) - 6 \cdot 4$

   i. $8 + 2 \cdot [4 \cdot (3 + 9) - 7] - 15 + 3 \cdot 6$

   j. $5 + 3 \cdot (2 - 6 \cdot 2) - 4 + 6$

   k. $2 + \{[3 - 6 \cdot (2 - 9) + 4 \cdot (6 + 3)] -8\} \cdot 4$

   l. $3^2 + (8 - 2) + 5 \cdot (9 - 6) + 2 \cdot (1 + 4)$

2. Write the following in algebraic form using a variable.

   a. The product of any number y and the sum of the number y and 5.

   b. The total number of legs in a barnyard of n cows.

3. Using the domain $\{2, 3, 8, -4\}$, evaluate each expression, giving all possible solutions.

   a. $x - 8$

   b. $y^2 + 4$

   c. $z + 4z - 2$

   d. $w^2 + w - 3$

4. What are the variables and the constants in the following expressions?

   a. $3x - 4$

   b. $\dfrac{5ab}{c}$

   c. $2x^2 + y$

   d. $\dfrac{x}{8} - 4$

   e. $4a^2 + 3a - 7$

   f. $2xy - z^2$

5. Write with positive exponents.

   a. 5^{-3}

   b. 2^{-7}

   c. x^{-8}

   d. 1^{-4}

6. Write with negative exponents.

   a. $\dfrac{1}{3^2}$

   b. $\dfrac{1}{8^3}$

   c. $\dfrac{1}{x^4}$

   d. $\dfrac{1}{x^2y}$

7. Compute, leaving answers in positive exponential form.

   a. $3^{-2} \cdot 3^{-8}$ **d.** $4^2 \div 4^{-3}$

   b. $5^3 \cdot 5^{-3}$ **e.** $2^8 \cdot 2^{-4}$

   c. $7^2 \div 7^8$ **f.** $8^3 \div 8^5$

8. Evaluate, if $x = 3$, $y = -4$, and $z = 2$.

   a. $4x^3y$

   b. $3xy^2$

   c. $2x + 3y - 6z$

   d. $x^2 + yz$

   e. $2x - 3y + z^3$

   f. $5x^2 + 2x + 7$

9. The formula for finding the volume of a cube is $V = e^3$, where e is the length of one side. If the edge of the cube is 4 inches, what is the volume of the cube?

10. Combine like terms.

   a. $4x^2 + 3x - 8x^2$

   b. $2a - 4a + 3b$

   c. $8a^2 + 3a^2 - 4b$

   d. $x + 2y - 4x - 6x + y$

   e. $2a - 3b + 4a - 6b$

   f. $2x^2 + 3x - 8 + 4x^2 - 5x + 2$

11. Simplify.

   a. $3x + (2x - 5y)$

   b. $2a - (4a + 3b) - 6a$

   c. $8 - [3x + (2y - 4) - (8y + 3)]$

   d. $3x^2 + (2x + 7) - (5x + 6)$

   e. $(a^2 + 2a + 5) + (3a^2 + 4a - 9)$

   f. $x + 3y - [(4x + 2y) - (8x - 9y)]$

12. Give an example for each of the four properties of equality.

13. Give one spiritual lesson that you learned in this chapter.

14. Express in algebraic form.

   a. A number increased by 8

   b. The sum of three times a number and the number squared.

   c. The quotient of a number and 27.

   d. The difference of a number and 5 times the number.

15. Place in equation form. Do not solve the equations.

    a. The sum of twice a number and 8 is 24.

    b. In a football game the total score for one team was 20 points, which included 2 extra points after touchdowns. How many touchdowns did the team score if it made no field goals or safeties?

    c. Brent is 3 years older than Jan. The sum of their ages is 59. Find each of their ages.

CHAPTER 3

SOLVING EQUATIONS

Three rocket engines that run on liquid fuel provide the power to lift the space shuttle against gravity into an earth orbit. During every minute of flight, each engine uses 64,000 gallons of fuel that is 86% oxygen and 14% hydrogen. Together the three engines use 192,000 gallons of fuel each minute in order to provide 1,410,000 pounds of thrust. This may seem like a lot of thrust to us, but it is not enough to take the space shuttle into orbit. During the first few minutes of takeoff, two additional booster rockets provide the necessary impetus to push the shuttle away from the earth's gravitational pull.

The three main engines used at blastoff are powered by a mixture of liquid oxygen and liquid hydrogen. These two fuels are held in the large external tank that the shuttle is attached to at blastoff. This tank is 154 feet long and about 27 feet in diameter. The upper third contains liquid oxygen; the lower portion, liquid hydrogen. The external tank holds a total of 520,000 gallons of fuel. When the oxygen and hydrogen combine and a spark is ignited, the two fuels combust to produce energy that pushes against the atmosphere and makes the shuttle rise into orbit. After combustion the hydrogen and oxygen form water, creating the white billow of steam seen at liftoff.

NASA engineers must be precise in mixing the liquid fuels in the correct percentages so that the shuttle will blast off with the proper power. Mixture problems are crucial for NASA researchers. In this chapter you will learn methods for solving mixture problems as well as other types of practical word problems. The section on solving word problems is probably the most important part of this chapter, because the word problems are similar to problems you will encounter in your future work.

How many gallons of liquid oxygen and liquid hydrogen should be stored in the external tank of the space shuttle to make the 520,000 gallons of fuel necessary for blastoff? Do you think the shuttle would get off the ground with your calculations? Do you trust them? Would the astronauts in the shuttle be safe if you were responsible for the calculations?

USING PROPERTIES OF EQUALITY

$x + 10 = 142$ $\qquad$ $x - 17 = -35$ $\qquad$ $3x = 9$ $\qquad$ $\frac{x}{5} = 21$

Can you find the number that should replace x to make each of the above examples true? Each number is called the solution of the equation.

Which operation is the opposite of addition? Which one is the opposite of division? Observe how opposite operations work.

a. $3 + 2 - 2 = 3$

b. $7 + 8 - 8 = 7$

c. $x + 4 - 4 = x$

d. $-3 - 2 + 2 = -3$

e. $10 - 1 + 1 = 10$

f. $x - 4 + 4 = x$

g. $4 \cdot 2 \div 2 = 4$

h. $7 \cdot 5 \div 5 = 7$

i. $x \cdot 4 \div 4 = x$

j. $14 \div 7 \cdot 7 = 14$

k. $21 \div 3 \cdot 3 = 21$

l. $x \div 4 \cdot 4 = x$

Review the properties of equality on page 92. Remember that these properties show that if you perform an operation on one side of an equation you must perform that same operation on the other side of the equation to keep the equation true. You know that $4 + 2 = 6$. If you subtract 2 from the left side only, then $4 + 2 - 2 = 6$, or $4 = 6$. Since 4 is not equal to 6, the statement is now false; thus it is not a balanced equation. To keep the equation balanced, you must subtract 2 from both sides.

$$4 + 2 - 2 = 6 - 2$$
$$4 = 4$$

To solve an equation like $x + 10 = 142$, first notice the variable x. What is being done to x? Ten is being added to it. The opposite of adding 10 is subtracting 10.

TO SOLVE AN EQUATION, FIND WHAT IS HAPPENING TO THE VARIABLE. THEN DO THE OPPOSITE TO BOTH SIDES OF THE EQUATION.

EXAMPLES

Example 1. Solve $x + 10 = 142$.

Solution. $x + 10 = 142$

1. Since 10 is added to x, subtract 10 from both sides.

$x + 10 - 10 = 142 - 10$

2. Simplify both sides.

$x + 0 = 132$

$x = 132$

Check. Does $132 + 10 = 142$?

3. Check your solution by substituting it for the variable. If the resulting equation is true, the solution is correct.

Example 2. Solve $x - 17 = -35$.

Solution. $x - 17 = -35$

1. What is happening to the variable? Seventeen is being subtracted from it. What is the opposite of subtracting 17?

$x - 17 + 17 = -35 + 17$

2. Add 17 to both sides of the equation and simplify.

$x = -18$

Check. $-18 - 17 = -35$

$-35 = -35$

Example 3. Solve $3x = 9$.

Solution. $3x = 9$

1. What is happening to the variable? What is the opposite of multiplying by 3?

$\frac{3x}{3} = \frac{9}{3}$

$x = 3$

2. Divide both sides of the equation by 3 and simplify. (What is $\frac{3}{3}$?)

Example 4.　　$\dfrac{x}{5} = 21$ Solve for x.

Solution.　　$\dfrac{x}{5} = 21$

$\dfrac{x}{5} \cdot 5 = 21 \cdot 5$

1. What is happening to the variable? What is the opposite of dividing? Multiply both sides of the equation by 5.

$x = 105$

2. Simplify.

Check.　　Does $\dfrac{105}{5} = 21$?

Procedure for Storage

Solving Equations

1. Determine the operation performed on the variable in the equation.
2. Perform the opposite operation on both sides of the equation.
3. Simplify both sides of the equation.
4. Check your answer.

Sometimes an equation will have other letters in it besides the variable. This type of equation is called a literal equation. You solve a literal equation exactly as you solve a numerical equation.

EXAMPLE

Example 5.　Solve $x + m = n$ for x.

Solution.　　　$x + m = n$
$x + m - m = n - m$
$x = n - m$

Check.　Does $(n - m) + m = n$?

Exercises

Solve each equation. Show all steps on your paper. Check your answers.

1. $x + 3 = 12$

2. $x - 4 = -23$

3. $a + 7 = -3$

4. $\dfrac{y}{5} = 24$

5. $2x = 16$

6. $b - 14 = 62$

7. $\frac{y}{2} = -28$

8. $\frac{c}{-9} = -8$

9. $4x = 164$

10. $x + \frac{1}{2} = \frac{3}{4}$

11. $m - 20 = 14$

12. $18 = y + 27$

13. $\frac{z}{4} = -7$

14. $8x = -56$

15. $y + 12 = 2$

16. $\frac{n}{-21} = -46$

17. $x + 0.93 = 1.42$

18. $y - 3.89 = 0.49$

19. $2z = \frac{1}{2}$

20. $3z = 12$

21. $b + 14 = 36$

22. $\frac{m}{2} = -146$

23. $15n = 1020$

24. $82 = x - 24$

25. $40 = 5x$

26. $3 + x = 9$

27. $\frac{a}{13} = 1.24$

28. $32x = 160$

29. $\frac{b}{2} = 14$

30. $9 = 3a$

31. $x + 0 = 21$

32. $0.8x = 0.24$

33. $\frac{1}{2} + y = 1$

34. $9n = 9$

35. $\frac{x}{4} = 1$

36. $\frac{y}{10} = 20$

37. $a - 127 = -2$

38. $0.3x = 0.96$

39. $\frac{x}{12} = 4.69$

40. $y + 17 = -24$

Solve for x.

41. $x + a = c$

42. $x - b = d$

43. $rx = d$

44. $a = bx$

An Apple a Day . . .

Isaac Newton
(1642-1727)

Like many children of modern times, Isaac Newton cared little for school studies. Isaac entertained numerous ideas of "modern inventions" in his active child's mind. He found more enjoyment in inventing things like a water clock, a windmill, a sundial, and even a self-propelled carriage than he did in studying. He neglected his studies so much that others considered him a poor student.

Isaac was born on Christmas, 1642 (the same year Galileo, another great scientist, died). Isaac's father died several months before Isaac was born.

Isaac's mother, Hannah, thus had to assume the care of the family farm in addition to caring for Isaac, a sickly child. When he was only three, his mother remarried, leaving him in the care of his grandmother. He attended several schools, most of them lacking in educational quality. Between the ages of twelve and fourteen, he was in grammar school at Grantham. Soon after leaving grammar school, he went to work on his mother's farm. Unsuited for farm work because he spent more time reading books than working, Newton was sent back to school. In spite of such an unpromising

childhood, he soon became one of the greatest names in the history of mathematics.

In 1661 Newton entered Trinity College at Cambridge University with no outstanding aptitude for mathematics. There he mastered Descartes's work in analytical geometry. Under the tutelage of Dr. Isaac Barrow, Newton made several mathematical discoveries, including the binomial theorem, or the expansion of $(x + y)^n$, where n is a natural number. This aided in the development of calculus and other higher mathematics. In fact,

Newton is credited as being one of the founders of calculus.

Newton's scientific discoveries included a study of the effects of gravity upon objects as diverse as an apple and the moon. These studies led him to the development of his three laws of motion. Because Newton was extremely sensitive to the criticisms of others and sought to avoid controversy at any cost, he was unwilling to publish his findings for public scrutiny. Contemporaries discovered that Newton had proof that their own conjectures were accurate and persuaded him to publish his works for the benefit of all mankind.

Through Edmund Halley's financial assistance, Newton's three books entitled *Mathematical Principles of Natural Philosophy* (or *Principia*) appeared in 1687. This work was the first to discuss relationships between celestial bodies and earthly objects; consequently, it greatly changed man's attitude toward himself and his world. Newton also developed a 6″ reflecting telescope (the forerunner of Mount Palomar's 200″ telescope), with which he viewed Jupiter's satellites. By the time he was thirty, Newton had been elected to

the famed Royal Society, the oldest scientific society in England. In 1669 Newton became a professor of mathematics at Cambridge, where he remained until 1689. During his time at Cambridge he made most of his contributions to mathematical science.

In 1701 Newton was elected to Parliament. Two years later he became President of the Royal Society and was reelected each year until his death. One of the last honors of his life came in 1705 when he was knighted by Queen Anne and given the title Sir Isaac Newton. He died on March 20, 1727, and was buried in Westminster Abbey, burial place for illustrious Englishmen.

HOW TO ATTACK WORD PROBLEMS

When a problem arises in your life, how do you solve it? Do you hide your head in the sand like an ostrich and hope the problem will go away? Do you consider it unimportant? Do you worry and fret about it? Or do you plan a solution to the problem and attempt to put it into action?

A Christian must always be prepared, especially against the craftiness of the Devil. Read Ephesians 6:10-18. This passage tells the Christian how to prepare himself to overcome the problems he will encounter. The Christian must put on armor before he goes into battle. He cannot defeat the enemy unless he is prepared.

In mathematics you must also be prepared and have a plan of attack. With a good basic knowledge of math facts and the ability to read, you should be able to solve most word problems without being afraid of them. Simply follow the procedures below, practice on many different problems, and finish the job. If you quit part way through a problem, you will never get the answer. One key to success is hard work and perseverance.

Procedure for Storage

Solving Word Problems

1. Carefully read the problem several times, looking for operational words.
2. If possible, draw a picture to represent the problem.
3. Determine the unknown quantity or quantities. If there is one unknown, assign a variable to it. If there are two or more unknowns, assign a variable to one of them and express other unknowns in terms of the one.
4. Using operational words as clues, find two expressions that are equal and form an equation.
5. Solve the equation.
6. If there is more than one unknown, find the others by substituting the found value in the expression for the variable.
7. Check your solution(s). Make sure that you have answered all the questions in the problem.

EXAMPLES

Example 1.   The sum of five times a number and two times the number is 161.

Solution.

   1. Read the problem carefully, noting the operational words *sum, times,* and *is.*

   2. You cannot draw a picture for this problem.

   3. The unknown quantity is a number, so let the variable x represent this number.

   4. The equal expressions are $5x + 2x$ and 161. They form the equation $5x + 2x = 161$.

   5. Solve.

$$5x + 2x = 161 \qquad \text{Combine like terms.}$$
$$7x = 161$$

$$\frac{7x}{7} = \frac{161}{7} \qquad \text{Using properties of equality, divide both sides by 7.}$$

$$x = 23$$

The number is 23.

   6. There is only one unknown.

   7. There is only one question, and it has been answered.

Check.
$$5 \cdot 23 + 2 \cdot 23 = 161$$
$$115 + 46 = 161$$
$$161 = 161$$

Example 2.   In 14 years Joe will be 42. How old is Joe now?

Solution.

   1. Read carefully. What operation does "in 14 years" indicate?

   2. No picture representation is needed.

   3. What is the unknown quantity? Let n = Joe's age now.

   4. What are two equivalent expressions? How do you express "in 14 years"?

   5. Solve.
$$n + 14 = 42$$
$$n + 14 - 14 = 42 - 14$$
$$n = 28$$

Joe's age is 28.

   6. There is only one unknown.

Check.   Does $28 + 14 = 42$? The question in the problem has been answered.

Example 3.   One number is twelve times another number.
             The difference of the two numbers is 99.
             Find the two numbers.

Solution.   Let x = one number
                   $12x$ = the other number

             $12x - x = 99$

                 $11x = 99$

             $\dfrac{11x}{11} = \dfrac{99}{11}$

                   $x = 9$ $12x = 12 \cdot 9 = 108$

One number is 9; the other number is 108.

Check. $12 \cdot 9 - 9 = 99$
              $108 - 9 = 99$
                   $99 = 99$

Exercises

Solve, using the procedures for solving word problems. Show all your work.

1. A number added to 27 is -14. Find the number.

2. On vacation last year the Hill family traveled 300 miles each day. How many days did they travel if they went a total of 1800 miles?

3. The difference of a number and 72 is 12. Find the number.

4. A number multiplied by 12 is 60. Find the number.

5. How many feet of fencing should be added to the 24 yards that the school owns to enclose a field that has a perimeter of 89 feet?

6. When Laura is six times as old as she is now, she will be 84. How old is she now?

7. In triangle *ABC*, side *AB* is 9" and side *BC* is 5". How large is *AC* if the perimeter is 21"?

8. Dorothy canned 24 quarts of green beans, which was four times as many as Lou Ann canned. How many quarts of green beans did Lou Ann can?

9. Kent has three times as many stamps in his collection as Joan has in her collection. If Kent has 243 stamps, how many stamps does Joan have?

10. A train going 80 miles per hour moves ten times faster than I move on my bicycle. How fast can I ride my bicycle?

11. The difference of a number and -9 is -74. Find the number.

12. The elephant at the circus weighs 5075 pounds, which is twenty-five times Mr. Lee's weight. How much does Mr. Lee weigh?

13. I can buy a candy bar for 35¢, which is seven times the amount I pay for a piece of hard candy. What is the price of a piece of hard candy?

14. One number is four times another, and the sum of the two numbers is 155. What are the two numbers?

15. If you subtract seven times a number from eight times a number, you get 13. What is the number?

16. First hour Miss Miller teaches three times as many students as she does third hour. Her second-hour class has two times as many as her third-hour class. If she has a total of 72 people in her three morning classes, how many does she have in each class?

EQUATIONS OF THE FORM
$ax + b = c$

$$2x + 6 = 21 \qquad 4y - 36 = 16$$

These two examples are in the form $ax + b = c$ in which the letters *a*, *b*, and *c* represent real numbers and *x* is an unknown variable. There is nothing new about this type of equation; it is just a combination of two operations on a variable instead of one.

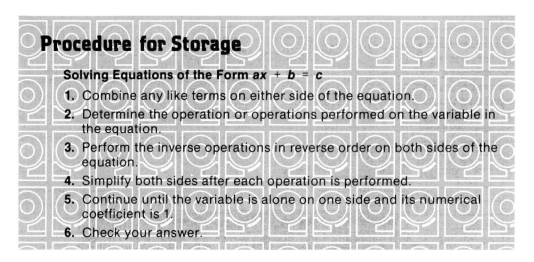

Procedure for Storage

Solving Equations of the Form $ax + b = c$

1. Combine any like terms on either side of the equation.
2. Determine the operation or operations performed on the variable in the equation.
3. Perform the inverse operations in reverse order on both sides of the equation.
4. Simplify both sides after each operation is performed.
5. Continue until the variable is alone on one side and its numerical coefficient is 1.
6. Check your answer.

EXAMPLES

Example 1.   Solve $2x + 6 = 21$.

Solution.

$$2x + 6 = 21$$

1. There are no like terms to combine.

$$2x + 6 - 6 = 21 - 6$$

$$2x = 15$$

$$\frac{2x}{2} = \frac{15}{2}$$

$$x = \frac{15}{2}$$

2. First, x is multiplied by 2; then 6 is added to the product. Division and subtraction are the inverse operations. Perform these in reverse order.

Check.

$$2 \cdot \frac{15}{2} + 6 = 21$$

$$15 + 6 = 21$$

$$21 = 21$$

 <!-- INVERSE OPERATIONS banner with character -->

Example 2.   Solve $4y - 36 = 16$.

Solution. $4y - 36 = 16$

1. y is multiplied by 4, and 36 is subtracted from the product.

$4y - 36 + 36 = 16 + 36$

2. Division and addition are the inverse operations; perform these in reverse order and simplify.

$$4y = 52$$

$$\frac{4y}{4} = \frac{52}{4}$$

$$y = 13$$

Check. $4 \cdot 13 - 36 = 16$

$52 - 36 = 16$

$16 = 16$

Example 3.   Solve $-2x + 5x + 9 = 87$.

Solution. $-2x + 5x + 9 = 87$

1. Combine like terms.

$3x + 9 = 87$

2. x is multiplied by 3, and 9 is added to the product.

$3x + 9 - 9 = 87 - 9$

3. Perform the inverse operations in reverse order.

$$3x = 78$$

$$\frac{3x}{3} = \frac{78}{3}$$

4. Simplify

$$x = 26$$

Check. $-2 \cdot 26 + 5 \cdot 26 + 9 = 87$

$-52 + 130 + 9 = 87$

$87 = 87$

Exercises

Solve for the variable.

1. $3x - 10 = 14$

2. $5x + 24 = -36$

3. $17 = 3x + 2$

4. $12 = 2x - 28$

5. $4x - 8x + 9 = 41$

6. $9x + 17 = 71$

7. $\frac{x}{5} - 13 = -84$

8. $4 + \frac{x}{6} = 9$

9. $12b - 18 = 474$

10. $3x + 4 - 5x + 9 = 15$

11. $2x + 24 = 52$

12. $\frac{n}{7} + 12 = -27$

13. $162 = 24m - 86$

14. $\frac{p}{4} - 7 = 10$

15. $\frac{2n}{5} = 14$

Solve each word problem. Show all work.

16. If 47 is added to three times a certain number, the result is 68. What is the number?

17. Sue receives a salary of $64.00 a week plus a commission of $2.00 for every piece of furniture she sells. How many pieces of furniture must she sell to make $110.00 per week?

18. One number is 4 more than another, and their sum is 120. Find the two numbers.

19. If Bill's salary is $15.00 and he gets a 20¢ commission on every newspaper he sells, how many newspapers must he sell in order to make $37.00?

20. How many quarters must be added to $1.89 to make a total of $2.64?

MORE WORK WITH EQUATIONS

The foundation on which a structure is built is the most important part of the construction. If the foundation is weak, the house will be weak. Read Matthew 7:24-27. Why did one house stand through the storms and the other house fall? Who is the Rock that must be the Christian's foundation? Remember, the foundation is the most important part of your life.

Equations are the foundations upon which algebra is built. To be successful in algebra and higher math, you must have a thorough and strong foundation in solving equations. Look back to page 108 and review the procedure for solving equations.

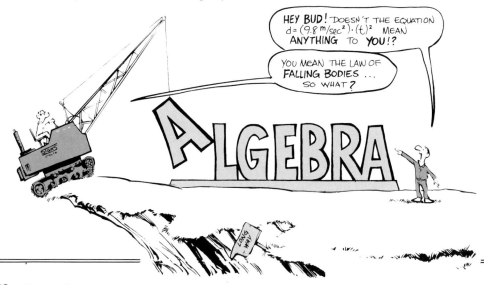

EXAMPLES

Example 1. Solve $2x + 7 - 8x + 12 = 73$.

Solution.

$$2x + 7 - 8x + 12 = 73$$
$$-6x + 19 = 73$$
$$-6x = 54$$
$$x = -9$$

1. Combine like terms.
2. Solve.

Check.
$$2(-9) + 7 - 8(-9) + 12 = 73$$
$$-18 + 7 + 72 + 12 = 73$$
$$73 = 73$$

Example 2. Solve $3x + 2 + 5x - 7 = 28$.

Solution.

$$3x + 2 + 5x - 7 = 28$$
$$8x - 5 = 28$$
$$8x - 5 + 5 = 28 + 5$$
$$8x = 33$$
$$\frac{8x}{8} = \frac{33}{8}$$
$$x = \frac{33}{8}$$

1. Combine like terms.
2. Solve.

Check.
$$3 \cdot \frac{33}{8} + 2 + 5 \cdot \frac{33}{8} - 7 = 28$$
$$\frac{99}{8} + 2 + \frac{165}{8} - 7 = 28$$
$$\frac{99}{8} + \frac{16}{8} + \frac{165}{8} - \frac{56}{8} = 28$$
$$\frac{224}{8} = 28$$
$$28 = 28$$

If parentheses appear in the equation, remove the parentheses before solving the equation.

EXAMPLE

Example 3. Solve $4(x + 5) - 3x = 24$.

Solution.

$$4(x + 5) - 3x = 24$$
$$4x + 20 - 3x = 24$$
$$x + 20 = 24$$
$$x + 20 - 20 = 24 - 20$$
$$x = 4$$

1. Remove parentheses by applying the distributive property.
2. Combine like terms.
3. Solve.

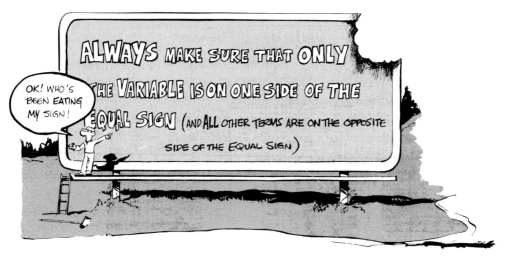

EXAMPLE

Example 4. John's mother is four times as old as John, and John's brother is two times as old as John. If you find the sum of their ages and add 3, you get 80. What is the age of all three people?

Solution. Read the problem carefully to find the unknowns.

Let x = John's age
$4x$ = John's mother's age
$2x$ = John's brother's age

Then set up the equation.

$$4x + 2x + x + 3 = 80$$
$$7x + 3 = 80$$
$$7x + 3 - 3 = 80 - 3$$
$$7x = 77$$
$$\frac{7x}{7} = \frac{77}{7}$$
$$x = 11 \qquad 4x = 44 \qquad 2x = 22$$

So John is 11, Mother is 44, and John's brother is 22.

Check. $4 \cdot 11 + 2 \cdot 11 + 11 + 3 = 80$
$44 + 22 + 11 + 3 = 80$
$80 = 80$

Exercises

Solve for x.

1. $4x + 8x = 12$
2. $3x + (2 + 4x) = 23$
3. $2(9x + 3) - 4x = 34$
4. $5x - (3 + 2x) = 9$
5. $(x + 3) + 2(x + 5) = 34$
6. $5x + 9x - 4 - 6x = 12$
7. $3x - 4(x + 5) = -17$
8. $4(x - 7) = 8$
9. $-8x - 4x = 24$
10. $3(x + 2) = 66$

11. $2x - 4(x - 3) = 26$
12. $6 - 2(x + 4) = 108$
13. $-7(x + 3) = 77$
14. $3x + 9x + (12 - 2x) = 2$
15. $-2(x - 1) + 3(x + 4) = 8$
16. $3.2x + 4(x + .7) = 38.8$
17. $4x + 9x = 26$
18. $nx + n(x - n) = mn$
19. $ax + b + a(x + b) = b$
20. $a(x + c) + b(x + d) - ax = e$

Set up an equation and solve.

21. In the freshman class there are 11 more girls than boys. There are 63 students in the freshman class. How many of each is in the class?

22. One number is 23 more than another number. The sum of the two numbers is 83. Find the two numbers.

23. A calculator costs $12.00 less than a camera. Both together cost $87.00. What is the cost of each?

24. The difference of two numbers is 12, and the sum of the two numbers is 40. What are the two numbers?

25. Sue wants to make a rectangular flower garden. She has 34 feet of fencing to put around the perimeter of the flower garden. She wants the length to be 5 feet more than the width. How wide and how long should she make the flower garden?

EQUATIONS OF THE FORM
$ax + b = cx + d$

$2x + 5 = x - 2$ $\qquad$ $3(x - 4) = 4(x - 6)$ $\qquad$ $5x + 3x - 4 = x + 2$

Why are these equations different from the ones in the last two sections? The only difference between these and the others is that these equations have variables on both sides of the equal sign.

If there are any parentheses in the equation, remove them first. After removing parentheses, you must move all the variables to one side of the equation and all other terms to the other side.

EXAMPLE

Example 1. Solve $2x + 5 = x - 2$.

Solution. To place all the variables on the left, you must eliminate the x on the right. What is the sign in front of the x? There is none, so the term is positive. To eliminate x from the right side, subtract x (since subtraction is the inverse operation of addition). If you subtract x from the right side, you must also subtract x from the left side.

$$2x + 5 - x = x - 2 - x$$
$$x + 5 = -2$$
$$x = -2 - 5$$
$$x = -7$$

Simplify.
Notice that all the variables are now on the left. The equation is in a form you can solve.

Check.
$$2 \cdot -7 + 5 = -7 - 2$$
$$-14 + 5 = -7 - 2$$
$$-9 = -9$$

Procedure for Storage

Solving Equations of the Form
ax + b = cx + d

1. Remove any parentheses in the equation and combine like terms.
2. Choose the side on which to place the variables.
3. Use inverse operations to move the variables to the desired side of the equation.
4. Solve the equation according to procedures on page 108.

EXAMPLES

Example 2. Solve $3(x - 4) = 4(x - 6)$.

Solution.

$$3(x - 4) = 4(x - 6)$$ **1.** Remove parentheses.

$$3x - 12 = 4x - 24$$ **2.** Move the variables to the right.

$$3x - 12 - 3x = 4x - 24 - 3x$$ **3.** Subtract 3x from both sides.

$$-12 = x - 24$$ Solve.

$$-12 + 24 = x$$

$$12 = x$$

Will you get the same answer by moving the variables to the left?

$$3(x - 4) = 4(x - 6)$$

$$3x - 12 = 4x - 24$$

$$3x - 12 - 4x = 4x - 24 - 4x$$ **1.** Subtract 4x from both sides.

$$-x - 12 = -24$$ **2.** Solve.

$$-x = -24 + 12$$

$$-x = -12$$

$$\frac{-x}{-1} = \frac{-12}{-1}$$

$$x = 12$$

Yes, you will get the same answer regardless of the side you put the variables on.

Example 3. Solve $5x + 3x - 4 = x + 2$.

Solution.

$$5x + 3x - 4 = x + 2$$ You can provide the reasons.

$$8x - 4 = x + 2$$ Check your answer.

$$8x - 4 - x = x + 2 - x$$

$$7x - 4 = 2$$

$$7x = 2 + 4$$

$$7x = 6$$ Can you follow this procedure without the step $\frac{7x}{7} = \frac{6}{7}$?

$$x = \frac{6}{7}$$

Does getting the correct answer give you a wonderful sense of satisfaction? You can find true satisfaction only in Jesus Christ. He supplies your needs and hears your prayers. Is Jesus satisfied with what you are doing with your life?

Exercises

Solve. Show all work.

1. $3x + 5 = 8x - 5$
2. $7x - 20 = 2x + 25$
3. $3(x + 1) = 8x - 12$
4. $7(x - 9) = 3(x - 2) - 1$
5. $3x = 5x - 2$
6. $11x - 8 = 12x + 9$
7. $4(x - 9) = 3x - 8x$
8. $6x - 1 = x + 4$
9. $82b - 3b + 7 = 71b + 19$
10. $4(m - 6) - m(3 + 4) = 8m - 2$

11. $7n - 13 = 4n - 9$
12. $.25x - 3.09 = .75x + 8$
13. $3x = 9x$
14. $4 - 9a + 10 = 3a - 10$
15. $5(x - 4) + 4x = 3x - 14$
16. $8(2x + 1) - (x - 9) = -52 - 8x$
17. $y + 9 = 2y - 4$
18. $3x - 7 = 2x$
19. $8a = 4(a - 9)$
20. $5(y + 2) - 4y = 8y - (2 + y)$

Solve for x.

21. $mx + n = 2mx - n$
22. $a(x + c) = 2ax + d$

23. Find two consecutive even numbers such that four times the smaller is equal to 4 more than three times the larger.
24. Eight times a number equals the number increased by 504. Find the number.
25. Find two consecutive integers such that twice the smaller is 10 more than eight times the larger.
26. The length of a rectangle is three times the width. The perimeter of the rectangle is equal to the perimeter of a triangle that has one side equal to the length of the rectangle. The sum of the other two sides of the triangle equals 85. What is the length and width of the rectangle?
27. If 3 subtracted from two times a number is equal to 31 more than three times the number, what is the number?

ABSOLUTE VALUE EQUATIONS

Do you remember the definition of *absolute value*? Look back to page 12 if you need to refresh your memory.

$$|6| = 6 \qquad\qquad\qquad |-6| = 6$$
$$|8| = 8 \qquad\qquad\qquad |-8| = 8$$

What is $|25| = ?$ $|-25| = ?$

If x is a positive number (e.g., 6), then $|x| = x$, or $|6| = 6$.

If x is a negative number (e.g., -6), then $|x| = -x$, or $|-6| = --6 = 6$.

 DEFINITION ≫**Absolute value:** $|y| = \begin{cases} y, & \text{if } y \geq 0 \\ -y, & \text{if } y < 0 \end{cases}$

Look at the equation $|x| = 4$. It has two possible solutions. What are they? Since $|4|$ equals 4 and $|-4|$ also equals 4, the two solutions are the numbers 4 and -4.

$$|x| = 4$$
Therefore, $x = 4$, or $x = -4$.

The formal solution to this equation, following the absolute value definition, is this:

Consider the possible cases involving x.

$$|x| = 4$$

If $x \geq 0$, then $|x| = x$.   If $x < 0$, then $|x| = -x$.
       So $|x| = x = 4$ So $|x| = -x = 4$
                                                $x = -4$

Again we see that the two solutions to the equation $|x| = 4$ are $x = \pm 4$. The symbol $\pm$ indicates two solutions, in this case both +4 and -4.

What are the two solutions to $|x| = 15$? Notice that the solution is always both the positive and the negative values of the number that the absolute value equals.

$$|x| = 3, \quad \begin{matrix} \text{so } x = 3, \\ \text{or } x = -3 \end{matrix}$$

To graph these solutions on a number line, place a dot on both answers.

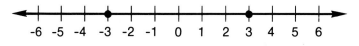

EXAMPLE

Example 1.   Solve $| 2x + 5 | = 11$.

Solution. Set the quantity in the absolute value sign equal to the positive value and the negative value of the number on the other side of the equation. In other words, you will solve for x in two different equations.

$$
\begin{array}{lll}
2x + 5 = 11 & \text{or} & 2x + 5 = -11 \\
2x = 11 - 5 & & 2x = -11 - 5 \\
2x = 6 & & 2x = -16 \\
\dfrac{2x}{2} = \dfrac{6}{2} & & \dfrac{2x}{2} = \dfrac{-16}{2} \\
x = 3 & & x = -8
\end{array}
$$

Check.
$$
\begin{array}{ll}
| 2 \cdot 3 + 5 | = 11 & | 2 \cdot -8 + 5 | = 11 \\
| 6 + 5 | = 11 & | -16 + 5 | = 11 \\
| 11 | = 11 & | -11 | = 11 \\
11 = 11 & 11 = 11
\end{array}
$$

The two solutions are $x = 3$ or $x = -8$.

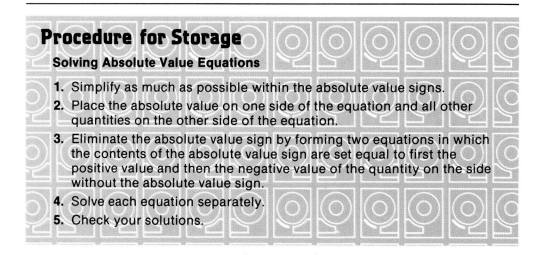

Procedure for Storage

Solving Absolute Value Equations

1. Simplify as much as possible within the absolute value signs.
2. Place the absolute value on one side of the equation and all other quantities on the other side of the equation.
3. Eliminate the absolute value sign by forming two equations in which the contents of the absolute value sign are set equal to first the positive value and then the negative value of the quantity on the side without the absolute value sign.
4. Solve each equation separately.
5. Check your solutions.

EXAMPLE

Example 2. $| 2y + 4 - 5y | = 16$

Solution. $| 2y + 4 - 5y | = 16$ Simplify.

$| -3y + 4 | = 16$

$-3y + 4 = 16$ or $-3y + 4 = -16$

$-3y = 16 - 4$ $-3y = -16 - 4$

$-3y = 12$ $-3y = -20$

$y = \dfrac{12}{-3}$ $y = \dfrac{-20}{-3}$

$y = -4$ $y = \dfrac{20}{3}$

Check.

$| 2 \cdot -4 + 4 - 5 \cdot -4 | = 16$ $\left| 2\left(\dfrac{20}{3}\right) + 4 - 5\left(\dfrac{20}{3}\right) \right| = 16$

$| -8 + 4 + 20 | = 16$ $\left| \dfrac{40}{3} + \dfrac{12}{3} - \dfrac{100}{3} \right| = 16$

$| 16 | = 16$ $\left| \dfrac{-48}{3} \right| = 16$

$16 = 16$ $| -16 | = 16$

$16 = 16$

Exercises

Give the solutions to each equation.

1. $| x | = 16$

2. $| y | = 129$

3. $| x + 2 | = 37$

4. $| x - 8 | = 14$

5. $| 2x - 3 | = 2$

6. $| 5y + 12 | = 24$

7. $| 3z + 4 - z | = 16$

8. $| 7x + 9 | = 51$

9. $19 = | 12x - 5 |$

10. $26 = | 3y + 4 - 6y |$

11. $| 7x - 4 | = 9$

12. $| 2x + 4 - 5x | + 3 = 17$

13. $| 2y - 5 | - 9 = 24$

14. $| 3z - 10 + 4z | = 18$

15. $172 = | 12x - 5 | + 82$

MINICOMPUTERS AND MAINFRAMES

"All right, everybody, let's quiet down," Mr. Jackson said. Mr. Jackson was Paul's math teacher. The whole class was excited because Mr. Jackson had arranged a tour of the local university's computer center.

While Mr. Jackson went to find the tour guide, Paul peered through the big glass window at the long

rows of cabinets standing like soldiers at attention. He had been interested in computers for a long time, but he had never before seen a big computer up close.

Just then Mr. Jackson returned with the guide.

"Students, I want you to meet Miss Wolff. She will show us through the computer center. I want you all to stay close together. And DON'T push any buttons!"

Miss Wolff, a pleasant-looking young woman, shepherded Paul and his classmates into a large air-conditioned room. When everyone was finally inside, she began the tour.

"Computers come in many different sizes and shapes. Some of you probably even have your own computers. We have two different types of computers here at the computer center. One kind is called a

mainframe, and the other kind is called a minicomputer. Each kind of computer handles its own special tasks.

"The really big computer before you is a mainframe. We use the mainframe to manipulate large quantities of information very quickly. Our particular mainframe performs nearly 15 million calculations per second. That is, it takes only about a second for the computer to count from 1 to 15,000,000. How many of you can do that?"

"Paul can," piped up a small, freckle-faced, red-headed girl at the front of the group. "He's a brain." The class groaned.

"It's nice that we all have brains," Miss Wolff replied. Then she continued the tour.

"Another advantage of a mainframe," she continued, "is that it has a large main memory. The computer's memory can hold nearly 16 million characters of information at once. This allows us to perform many different programs on the computer at the same time.

"The cabinet you see on the left side of the computer connects with other computers and with terminals in many different places. As you can see, this room could hold very few people. Yet right now approximately 200 people are using this computer from terminals connected through that cabinet.

"Mainframes also connect to other pieces of

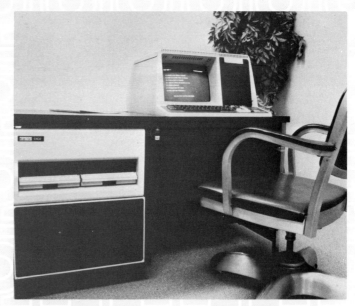

computer equipment such as disk drives and tape drives. I am sure that Mr. Jackson has already taught you about those parts of the computer. Are there any questions before we go on to the minicomputer?"

As Miss Wolff answered questions, Paul stared at the sleek machines. He jumped when a tape drive near him whirred to life without warning. When Miss Wolff finished answering all the questions, she guided the group to another computer.

"Now I need a helper. Do I have a volunteer?"

Paul and several others shot their hands into the air. "I see 'the Brain' has his hand up. Well, let's see

what kind of brain you have, Paul." Paul grinned as pretty Miss Wolff seated him at a terminal near the computer.

"Paul, I want you to type the word *who* on the keyboard and then tap the key marked 'return.'" Paul typed the word and tapped "return." Almost immediately bright green characters filled the screen.

"These are the names of all the people who are presently using this computer. As you can see, there are only about 25 users because minicomputers do not perform calculations quite as quickly as mainframes usually do. Therefore, not as many people can use the computer at the same time.

"The largest number of characters of information we can store in this minicomputer's main memory is

only 8 million—half that of the mainframe. Also, this minicomputer can perform only 1.5 million calculations per second.

"We use the minicomputer for those tasks that do not require large numbers of numerical calculations, such as word processing and keeping track of the university's grade records.

"The main advantage of a minicomputer over a mainframe is that it costs much less. Most businesses could not buy a computer like our mainframe; mainframes cost too much. These same businesses, however, could probably afford a minicomputer.

"Are there any more questions?" Miss Wolff asked. "If not, that concludes our tour of the computer center. I hope you all had a good time and found the tour interesting."

CLEARING EQUATIONS OF FRACTIONS

Tom is marking off a field for a new game the coach is going to introduce in physical education class. The field is to be rectangular with the width being $\frac{1}{3}$ of the length. The perimeter of the field is 280 feet. What length and width should Tom mark off?

To solve this problem and others like it, you must be able to work with equations containing fractions.

Let x = the length of the field
$\frac{1}{3}x$ = the width of the field

$$x + x + \frac{1}{3}x + \frac{1}{3}x = 280$$

First you need to clear the equation of fractions by multiplying both sides of the equation by the common denominator of the fractions, which in this equation is 3.

$$3(x + x + \frac{1}{3}x + \frac{1}{3}x) = 280 \cdot 3$$
$$3x + 3x + x + x = 840$$
$$8x = 840$$
$$\frac{8x}{8} = \frac{840}{8}$$
$$x = 105$$
$$\frac{1}{3}x = 35$$

The length of the field is 105 feet, and the width is 35 feet. So Tom must mark off a field that is 105 feet long by 35 feet wide.

EXAMPLES

Example 1. Solve $\frac{x}{4} + x - \frac{1}{3} = 3$.

Solution. To solve for x in this equation, find the common denominator. Since the common denominator of 4 and 3 is 12, multiply both sides of the equation by 12. Then use the distributive property to remove parentheses.

$$\frac{x}{4} + x - \frac{1}{3} = 3$$
$$12\left(\frac{x}{4} + x - \frac{1}{3}\right) = 3 \cdot 12$$
$$3x + 12x - 4 = 36$$
$$15x - 4 = 36$$
$$15x = 40$$
$$x = \frac{40}{15} = \frac{8}{3}$$

Example 2. Solve $\left(\frac{x+2}{6}\right) - \left(\frac{x-1}{3}\right) = \frac{1}{9}$.

Solution. $\left(\frac{x+2}{6}\right) - \left(\frac{x-1}{3}\right) = \frac{1}{9}$

The common denominator of 6, 3, and 9 is 18.

$$18\left(\frac{x+2}{6} - \frac{x-1}{3}\right) = \frac{1}{9}(18)$$
$$18\left(\frac{x+2}{6}\right) - 18\left(\frac{x-1}{3}\right) = \frac{1}{9}(18)$$
$$3(x+2) - 6(x-1) = 2$$
$$3x + 6 - 6x + 6 = 2$$
$$-3x + 12 = 2$$
$$-3x = 2 - 12$$
$$-3x = -10$$
$$x = \frac{-10}{-3} = \frac{10}{3}$$

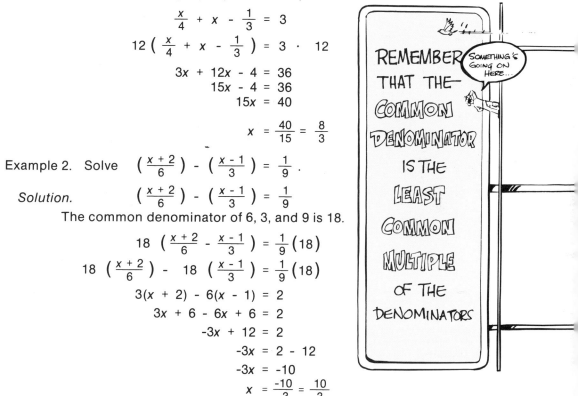

REMEMBER THAT THE COMMON DENOMINATOR IS THE LEAST COMMON MULTIPLE OF THE DENOMINATORS

SOMETHING'S GOING ON HERE...

Procedure for Storage
Solving Equations Containing Fractions

1. Find the common denominator in the equation.
2. Eliminate fractions by multiplying both sides by the common denominator.
3. Solve the resulting equation.
4. Check the solution in the original equation.

Exercises

Solve.

1. $\dfrac{x}{4} = \dfrac{1}{2}$

2. $\dfrac{x}{3} + \dfrac{x}{8} = \dfrac{11}{24}$

3. $\dfrac{2x}{9} + \dfrac{1}{3} = 5$

4. $\dfrac{x}{6} - \dfrac{3x}{2} = \dfrac{16}{3}$

5. $\dfrac{y}{2} - \dfrac{2y}{7} = \dfrac{25}{7}$

6. $a + \dfrac{3a}{2} = \dfrac{15}{2}$

7. $\dfrac{b}{3} - \dfrac{8b}{7} = \dfrac{68}{21}$

8. $9m - \dfrac{3m}{8} = \dfrac{345}{8}$

9. $\dfrac{x}{3} - \dfrac{x}{4} = 1$

10. $y = \dfrac{3y}{5} + 12$

11. $\left(\dfrac{x + 2}{9} \right) - \dfrac{x}{3} = 10$

12. $\left(\dfrac{4y - 4}{8} \right) + \dfrac{26}{2} = \dfrac{1}{4}$

13. $\left(\dfrac{a - 3}{2} \right) - \left(\dfrac{a + 3}{4} \right) + \dfrac{a}{8} = 6$

14. $3k + \left(\dfrac{k - 4}{9} \right) = \dfrac{1}{3}$

15. $\dfrac{107}{6} = \dfrac{7m}{2} - \left(\dfrac{3m - 1}{3} \right)$

16. $0.5x = 0.3x + 9$

17. $1.4y + 0.09y = 1.49$

18. $0.67a + 3.06 = 0.84a$

19. $2b - 8 = 0.4b$

20. $0.8(x + 4) - 0.3x = 1.7$

MOTION PROBLEMS

A jet leaves O'Hare Airport in Chicago at 7:00 A.M. and flies south towards Atlanta, 606 air miles away, at a rate of 420 mph. An hour later a jet leaves Atlanta and flies toward Chicago at a rate of 500 mph. Because of an error in calculations, the jets are flying at the same altitude and on the same route towards each other. How much time do the controllers have to change direction or altitude of the jets before they collide?

This is a motion problem. To solve it, you need to use the formula $rt = d$, in which d stands for distance, r for rate, and t for time.

How far will a car travel if it goes 50 mph for 3 hours?

$$d = rt$$
$$d = 50 \cdot 3$$
$$d = 150 \text{ miles}$$

How far will a car travel if it goes 50 mph for x hours?

$$d = rt$$
$$d = 50x \text{ miles}$$

At what rate is a car traveling if it goes 225 miles in 5 hours?

$$d = rt$$
$$225 = r \cdot 5$$
$$\frac{225}{5} = r$$
$$45 = r \quad 45 \text{ mph}$$

Often you can simplify motion problems if you make a diagram and a chart and fill in the known quantities.

rate	·	time	=	distance
50		3		150
50		x		50x
r		5		5r

When you have two quantities in any horizontal row, find the third quantity by using the formula $rt = d$.

EXAMPLES

Example 1.   Jim rides his bicycle at a rate of 8 mph for t hours. How far does he ride?

Solution.   1. Let d = the distance he rides.
2. Make a chart.

r	·	t	=	d
8		t		8t

So he rides 8t miles.

Example 2. The junior high and high school Sunday school classes are going on a hike. The junior high class leaves the church and travels east at 3 miles per hour. The high school class leaves an hour later traveling at 5 miles per hour on the same route. How much time will pass before the high school class catches up with the junior high class?

Solution.

1. Determine what to look for in the problem (the time that passes before the high school class catches up). Let *x* = the amount of time the high school class hikes.

2. Draw a picture to represent the problem; then make a chart. What is the variable? Fill in the box that represents the unknown. The junior high class traveled one hour longer, so they traveled *x* + 1 hours.

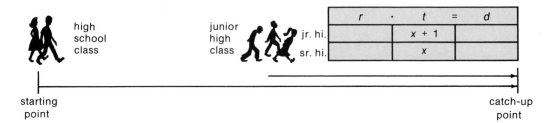

high school class   junior high class   jr. hi.   sr. hi.

r	·	t	=	d
		x + 1		
		x		

starting point   catch-up point

3. Since the rate for each group is also given, fill in the rate column.

	r	·	t	=	d
junior high	3		x + 1		
senior high	5		x		

4. Since two columns of the chart are complete, fill in the third column using *rt = d* without looking at the problem.

	r	·	t	=	d
junior high	3		x + 1		3(x + 1)
senior high	5		x		5x

5. Now that the chart is complete, look back at the problem to find information about the column filled in last, which was the distance column. The problem states that the high school class will catch up with the junior high class. When they catch up, they have gone the same distance. At that point the distances will be equal. So the equation is $3(x + 1) = 5x$.

6. Solve the equation.

$$3(x + 1) = 5x$$
$$3x + 3 = 5x$$
$$3 = 5x - 3x$$
$$3 = 2x$$
$$\frac{3}{2} = x$$

7. In $1\frac{1}{2}$ hours the high school class will catch up with the junior high class.

Procedure for Storage

Solving Motion Problems

1. Read the problem carefully. Find the unknown in the problem and let the variable stand for this unknown.

2. Draw a picture to represent the problem and make a chart, placing the variable in the appropriate column.

3. Find other information from the problem to complete two columns of the chart.

4. After substituting values from the two columns into the formula $rt = d$, perform the necessary operation to fill in the third column.

5. Look back at the problem for information about the last column you filled in. Set up an equation using this information.

6. Solve the equation.

7. Relate the answer to the problem.

EXAMPLE

Example 3.   Two trains leave Mattoon at the same time. The
northbound train travels 5 mph faster than the southbound
train. What is the rate of each train if after 3 hours they are
333 miles apart?

Solution.

1.   Let x = the rate of the southbound train
$x + 5$ = the rate of the northbound train

2. Make a sketch.

S   N

	r $\cdot$	t	=	d
northbound	$x + 5$	3		
southbound	x	3		

3. Fill in two
columns.

	r $\cdot$	t	=	d
northbound	$x + 5$	3		$3(x + 5)$
southbound	x	3		$3x$

4. Fill in the third column; use $r \cdot t = d$.

5. Since d was the last column completed, determine what the problem
says about the distance. After three hours the trains are 333 miles
apart, the total distance the two trains have traveled. So
$$3(x + 5) + 3x = 333.$$

6. Solve the equations.

$$3(x + 5) + 3x = 333$$
$$3x + 15 + 3x = 333$$
$$6x + 15 = 333$$
$$6x = 333 - 15$$
$$6x = 318$$
$$\frac{6x}{6} = \frac{318}{6}$$
$$x = 53 \qquad x + 5 = 58$$

7. The southbound train travels 53 mph, and the northbound train
travels 58 mph.

Exercises
Fill in the following chart.

1.

	r	· t	= d
a.	3	18	
b.		2	132
c.	x		19
d.	52	x	

	r	· t	= d
e.	35	x + 2	
f.		16	16x
g.	x + 12		4(x + 12)
h.	a	7b	

2. A train is traveling 62 mph and has to go 372 miles. How long will it take the train to make the trip?

3. A jet travels the 2800 miles from New York to Los Angeles in 4 hours. What is the average speed of the jet?

4. Steve, a cyclist, leaves the corner of First and Maple on his bicycle and travels 9 mph. Two hours later his brother leaves from First and Maple and comes after him on a moped traveling 27 mph. How long will it take him to catch up with Steve?

5. A passenger train leaves Charleston heading east at the same time a loaded coal train leaves Charleston heading west. The passenger train travels 23 mph faster than the coal train, and in 4 hours the two trains are 412 miles apart. What is the speed of each train?

6. Brandon and Shanda walk to Grandma's house at a rate of 4 mph. They ride their bicycles back home at a rate of 8 mph over the same route that they walked. It takes one hour longer to walk than ride. How long did it take them to walk to Grandma's?

7. Sue leaves Lewistown for Clarksville 388 miles away and drives 52 miles per hour. Monica leaves Clarksville for Lewistown at the same time and travels 45 miles per hour. How soon will the two meet?

8. Mr. Thomas drove his old truck to the city at a speed of 20 mph and drove back home at a rate of 40 mph. The total trip took 6 hours. How far is Mr. Thomas's house from the city?

9. A fishing boat leaves Tampa Bay at 7:00 A.M. and travels at 12 knots. At 10:00 A.M. a second boat leaves the same dock for the same destination and travels at 15 knots. How long will it take the second boat to catch the first?

10. Brent rides a moped down the country road in front of his house. Brent's wife, Jan and her two sons ride bicycles in the opposite direction on the same road. If they leave at the same time and Brent travels 25 mph and Jan, and the boys travel 8 mph, how much time will pass before they are $24\frac{3}{4}$ miles apart?

11. A roller coaster train goes up the first grade eight times more slowly than it goes down the other side. If the distance down the hill is 100 feet more than the distance up the hill and if it takes 70 seconds to go up and 10 seconds to go down, what is the speed in feet per second of the roller coaster train when it goes up the hill and when it goes down the hill?

12. In 5 hours, how far can a car go and return if the average speed going is 48 mph and the average speed returning is 52 mph?

13. A freight train leaves Centralia for Chicago at the same time a passenger train leaves Chicago for Centralia. The freight train moves at a speed of 45 mph, and the passenger train travels at a speed of 64 mph. If Chicago and Centralia are 218 miles apart, how long will it take for the two trains to meet?

14. At the auto race one car travels 180 mph while another car travels 195 mph. How long will it take the faster car to gain two laps on the slower car if the speedway track is $2\frac{1}{2}$ miles long?

15. John and Jay run the 220-yard dash, and Jay wins the race by 10 yards. If Jay runs the race in 30 seconds, what is the rate of each boy in yards per second? How long would it take John to run the 220-yard dash?

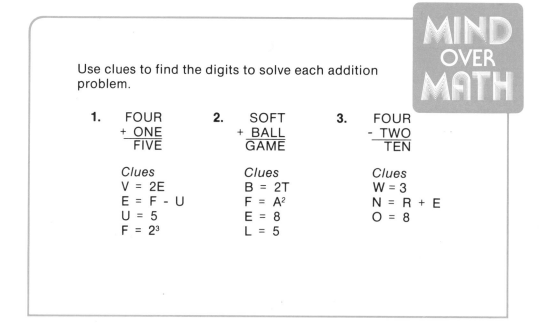

MIND OVER MATH

Use clues to find the digits to solve each addition problem.

1.
```
  FOUR
+ ONE
  FIVE
```
Clues
V = 2E
E = F - U
U = 5
F = 2³

2.
```
  SOFT
+ BALL
  GAME
```
Clues
B = 2T
F = A²
E = 8
L = 5

3.
```
  FOUR
- TWO
  TEN
```
Clues
W = 3
N = R + E
O = 8

MIXTURE PROBLEMS

Mixture problems involve the combination of different substances. For instance, a doctor wants to know how much sodium-o-phenylphenate to mix with water to get a 0.4% phenate solution for cleaning instruments. Perhaps the local health-food store plans to sell a mixture of sesame seeds and toasted pumpkin seeds. How much should the mixture cost?

To solve problems such as these, you should draw diagrams and make charts just as you did with motion problems. Read the following problem and collect all the necessary facts.

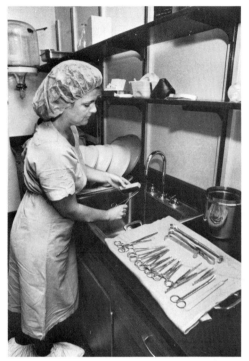

EXAMPLES

Example 1.   A feed-store owner wants to mix corn and barley to make 150 bushels of silage additive for cattle feed. If corn costs $2.40 a bushel and barley costs $2.20 a bushel, how many bushels of each grain should he mix to yield an additive worth $2.34 a bushel?

Solution.

1. Read carefully to find the unknown quantity.

We want to know how many bushels of corn and of barley should be combined to yield 150 bushels. So we'll let x = the number of bushels of corn; then 150-x = the number of bushels of barley.

2. Make a chart and fill in two columns. After two columns are filled in, do not look at the problem. Instead fill in the third column of the chart by multiplying the number of bushels by the price per bushel to get the total price.

	number of bushels	price per bushel	total price
corn	x	2.40	2.40x
barley	150 - x	2.20	2.20(150 - x)
mix	150	2.34	351

3. The total price of the corn plus the total price of the barley equals the total price of the mix.

$$2.4x + 2.2(150 - x) = 351$$

4. Solve.
$$24x + 22(150 - x) = 3510$$
$$24x + 3300 - 22x = 3510$$
$$2x + 3300 = 3510$$
$$2x = 3510 - 3300$$
$$2x = 210$$
$$x = 105$$
$$150 - x = 45$$

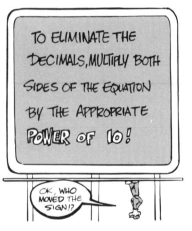

TO ELIMINATE THE DECIMALS, MULTIPLY BOTH SIDES OF THE EQUATION BY THE APPROPRIATE POWER OF 10!

OK, WHO MOVED THE SIGN!?

5. The additive should contain 105 bushels of corn and 45 bushels of barley.

Example 2. Nickel silver, often used for coating tableware, is an alloy containing 15% nickel along with copper and zinc. How much pure nickel must be melted with 70 pounds of nickel silver to make an alloy that is 20% nickel?

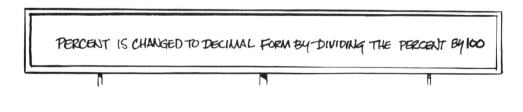

PERCENT IS CHANGED TO DECIMAL FORM BY DIVIDING THE PERCENT BY 100

Solution. Let x = pounds of pure nickel

	pounds of alloy	% of nickel	pounds of nickel
nickel silver	70	0.15	
pure nickel	x	1.0	
mix	70 + x	0.20	

Study this chart to find out how the columns were filled in. Notice that the percent is changed to decimal form.

Using the fact that the pounds of metal multiplied by the percent of nickel produce the pounds of nickel, fill in the third column.

	pounds of alloy	% of nickel	pounds of nickel
nickel silver	70	0.15	70(0.15)
pure nickel	x	1.0	1(x)
mix	70 + x	0.20	0.20(70 + x)

Now form an equation from the column you just completed. The pounds of nickel in nickel silver plus the pounds of nickel in pure nickel will equal the pounds of nickel in the whole mix.

$$70(0.15) + 1x = 0.20(70 + x)$$ To eliminate decimals, multiply both sides by 100.
$$70(15) + 100x = 20(70 + x)$$
$$1050 + 100x = 1400 + 20x$$
$$1050 + 100x - 20x = 1400$$
$$1050 + 80x = 1400$$
$$80x = 1400 - 1050$$
$$80x = 350$$
$$x = 4.375$$

The amount of pure nickel that must be melted with the nickel silver is 4.375 pounds.

Procedure for Storage

Solving Mixture Problems

1. Read the problem carefully to find the unknown quantities and to assign them variables.
2. Make a sketch and a chart to correspond to the problem.
3. After filling in two columns, complete the last column without looking back at the problem.
4. Set up an equation using the information just recorded in the last column filled in.
5. Solve the equation.
6. Relate the solution to the problem.

Exercises

Solve.

1. A chemist has 2 liters of solution that is 20% hydrochloric acid, and he wants a solution that is 25% hydrochloric acid. How much pure hydrochloric acid must be added to the solution?

2. Mr. Harper, the candy store manager, wants to mix butterscotch candies and cinnamon balls to make a deluxe mix to sell for $2.10 a pound. Butterscotch sells for $2.90 a pound while cinnamon balls sell for $1.90 a pound. How many pounds of each should Mr. Harper use to make 20 pounds of the mix?

3. How many gallons of cream that is 30% butterfat must be mixed with skim milk that is 10% butterfat to make 45 gallons of milk that is 22% butterfat?

4. The grocer wants to make an exotic blend of tea. He has two brands to mix. One brand is a Brazilian tea that sells for $3.25 per pound. The other is a Colombian tea that sells for $4.00 per pound. If he wants a mix of 35 pounds that will sell for $3.70 a pound, how many pounds of each tea should he mix?

5. Chris has 3 gallons of a solution that is 30% antifreeze that he wants to use to winterize his car. How much pure antifreeze should he add to this solution so that the new solution will be 65% antifreeze?

6. How many gallons of pure water must be added to 10 gallons of 30% salt water to make a solution that is 25% salt water?

7. Babbitt metal, named for its developer, Isaac Babbitt, who first made the metal in 1839, is used primarily for machine gearings. This metal alloy is composed of 90% tin, 7% antimony, and 3% copper. How many ounces of pure tin must be added to the alloy to make 6 ounces of a metal that is 94% tin?

8. One 1700-pound load of feed mixture contains 25% corn, 40% bran, and roughage. How many pounds of corn should be added to a load of feed mixture to make the feed 40% corn?

9. How many gallons of pure alcohol must be added to 25 gallons of 28% alcohol solution to obtain a solution that is 40% alcohol?

10. A nurse wants 4 liters of an iodine solution that is 5% iodine. She already has 3 liters of 3% iodine solution. What percentage of iodine should the additional liter contain?

11. A butcher is making a meat mixture for meat loaf. He is mixing hamburger, that sells for $1.39 per pound and sausage, that sells for $0.99 per pound. How many pounds of each should he mix if he is to make 30 pounds of mix and sell it for $1.23 per pound?

12. Sue is making a fruit salad of grapefruit and pineapple. Grapefruit costs 50¢ per 12 ounce can, and pineapple costs 85¢ per 12 ounce can. How many cans of each should she mix to obtain 84 ounces of a mixture that will cost 70¢ for every 12 ounces?

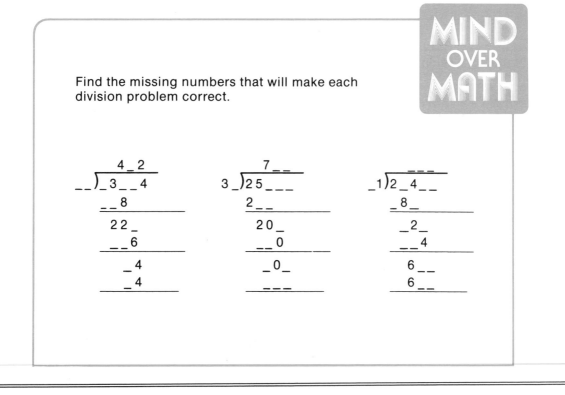

MIND OVER MATH

Find the missing numbers that will make each division problem correct.

COIN AND AGE PROBLEMS

Do you know a small child or have a younger brother or sister? What do you think would happen if you offered a young child a choice between one quarter and five pennies? Which do you think he would choose? He would probably choose the five pennies because he doesn't know the value of the coins.

How many coins do you have in your pocket or purse? Find the total value. If you have five dimes in your pocket, what is their value in cents? To answer this, you must multiply the number of dimes (5) by the value of a dime (10 cents). Your five dimes have a total value of 50 cents. How many cents do you have if you have 3 nickels, 4 quarters, and 6 pennies? To find out, you must multiply the value of each coin by the number of coins of that type, and then find the sum of these totals to find the worth of all the coins.

	number of coins	¢ value of coin	total value
nickels	3	5	15
quarters	4	25	100
pennies	6	1	6

So the total value of all the coins is 15 + 100 + 6 = 121 cents or $1.21.

In elementary school you learned to count coins and figure up their value. These coin problems are somewhat more difficult in that they state a total value and the type of coins but ask you to compute the number of coins. Charts similar to those you used for motion and mixture problems will help you with these problems too.

EXAMPLE

Example 1. Chris has 17 coins in his pocket, and they are all dimes and quarters. If he has a total of $2.45, how many of each coin does he have in his pocket?

Solution.

Let x = quarters
17 - x = dimes

1. You need to find out how many quarters and how many dimes Chris has. Since he has 17 coins, x can equal one value and 17 - x the other.

2. Make a chart and fill it in.

	number of coins	¢ value of coin	total value
quarters	x	25	$25x$
dimes	$17 - x$	10	$10(17 - x)$

$25x + 10(17 - x) = 245$

3. Since you know that the total value of the coins is $2.45, set up an equation using the last column of the chart.

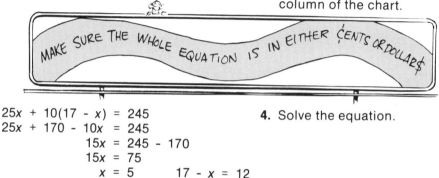

MAKE SURE THE WHOLE EQUATION IS IN EITHER CENTS OR DOLLARS

4. Solve the equation.

$$25x + 10(17 - x) = 245$$
$$25x + 170 - 10x = 245$$
$$15x = 245 - 170$$
$$15x = 75$$
$$x = 5 \qquad 17 - x = 12$$

Chris has five quarters and twelve dimes.

Procedure for Storage

Solving Coin Problems

1. Read the problem, carefully looking for the unknown values. Assign a variable to each unknown.
2. Make a chart indicating the number of coins, the value of each coin, and the total value.
3. Set up an equation using the information in the total value column and any other necessary information from the problem.
4. Solve the equation and relate the information to the problem.

Age problems often relate the present age of people to their ages sometime in the future or perhaps the past. Set up a chart with each person's name, his present age, and his "adjusted" age. Fill in the known facts, and then set up an equation. After you find the equation, you can easily solve it.

Example 2. Emily is 5 years older than Rebecca. In 10 years, three times Emily's age will equal four times Rebecca's age. How old are they now?

Solution. Let x = Rebecca's age
$x + 5$ = Emily's age   Do you know why?

1. Make a chart. Complete the chart and set up an equation.

	age now	age in 10 years
Rebecca	x	$x + 10$
Emily	$x + 5$	$(x + 5) + 10$

2. Solve.

$$3(x + 15) = 4(x + 10)$$
$$3x + 45 = 4x + 40$$
$$45 - 40 = 4x - 3x$$
$$5 = x \qquad x + 5 = 10$$

Rebecca is 5, and Emily is 10.

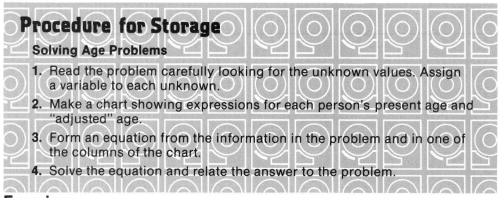

Procedure for Storage

Solving Age Problems

1. Read the problem carefully looking for the unknown values. Assign a variable to each unknown.
2. Make a chart showing expressions for each person's present age and "adjusted" age.
3. Form an equation from the information in the problem and in one of the columns of the chart.
4. Solve the equation and relate the answer to the problem.

Exercises

Solve.

1. Jill has $5.46 in nickels, pennies, and half dollars in her bank. If she has 12 more pennies than nickels and 5 less half dollars than nickels, how many of each coin does she have?

2. One Saturday afternoon Bill collected from his newspaper customers twice as many quarters as dimes and one less nickel than dimes. If Bill collected $2.55, how many quarters, nickels, and dimes did he get?

3. Linda has $8.58 in quarters and pennies in her purse. If she has eight times as many pennies as quarters, how many of each are in her purse?

4. Jim has a jar of dimes, nickels, and pennies in his room. In it he has one dime more than five times the number of nickels and four times as many pennies as nickels. How many of each coin are in the jar if the total value is $7.77?

5. A bank teller knows that she received 34 dimes and nickels from a customer. If the change totaled $2.05, how many dimes and nickels did the teller receive?

6. In his pocket Chip has 4 more dimes than quarters. If the quarters and dimes total $2.85, how many quarters and dimes does Chip have?

7. The value of the 189 pennies and nickels in Judy's piggy bank was $6.45. How many of each coin did the bank contain?

8. Mike said, "Guess how many coins I have in my pocket. Their value is $9.40, and I have three times as many dimes as half dollars and half as many quarters as dimes. How many of each coin do I have?"

9. Josh has seven times as many nickels as quarters. If the coins total $2.40, how many of each does he have?

10. The age difference between Bill and his younger sister, Suzie, is 3 years; in 8 years their combined ages will be 33. How old are they now?

11. The Harwoods have three children. The youngest is 7 years younger than the oldest, and the oldest is 2 years older than the middle child. In 12 years the children's combined ages will be 57. What is each child's age now?

12. Stephen is $\frac{1}{5}$ the age of his father. In 9 years he will be $\frac{1}{3}$ his father's age. What are Stephen's age and his father's age?

13. Emily is three years older than Jack. If Emily's and Jack's combined ages six years ago were 11, what are their ages now?

14. Kelly's age now is twice Judy's age. Four years ago Kelly was three times as old as Judy. How old is each girl now?

15. Jill is twice as old as Beth. In six years Beth's age will be $\frac{3}{5}$ Jill's age. What is each girl's age now?

16. Mr. Biehler is three times as old as his daughter Jeannette. Fourteen years ago he was seven times as old as Jeannette. How old are each now?

17. Jan is 30, and her daughter Shanda is 6. In how many years will Jan be twice as old as Shanda?

18. Grandma Wessel is 75 years old, and she has a grandson who is 32 years old. How many years ago was her age one year greater than seven times her grandson's age?

MEMORY RECALL

Identify.
  absolute value
  literal equation

You should now be able to solve the following:
1. Simple one-step equations.
2. Simple word problems by following a specific strategy.
3. Equations of the form $ax + b = c$
4. Equations of the form $ax + b = cx + d$
5. Absolute value equations.
6. Equations containing fractions.
7. Motion problems.
8. Mixture problems.
9. Coin and age problems.

You should be able to solve the following problems.

1. $x - 5 = 126$

2. $4x = 32$

3. $\frac{x}{8} = 19$

4. $x + 8 = 87$

5. $2x - 16 = 74$

6. $\frac{x}{5} - 6 = 84$

7. $6x + 21 = 165$

8. $\frac{x}{9} + 3 = 14$

9. $\frac{y}{-2} = 7 + 3y$

10. $4a = 7 - 4a + 6$

11. $3x + 9 = 10x + 16$

12. $\frac{4k}{9} = 2$

13. $-6(x - 8) = 12$

14. $3(x + 2) = 4(x - 6) + 2(x + 5)$

15. $8x + 4x = 12$

16. $89x + 17 + 6x = 5x - 19$

17. $3y - 10 = 10y$

18. $4(a + 10) - 6(2a + 9) = 146$

19. $5b + (b - 8) = 28$

20. $4c - 2(c + 9) + 10 = -14$

21. $|5x + 9| = 9$

22. $|3x| = 18$

23. $23 = |5x| - 2$

24. $\frac{x}{2} + \frac{4x}{3} = \frac{22}{3}$

25. $\frac{x}{5} + \frac{3x}{10} = \frac{5}{2}$

26. $2x + b = 3c$ Solve for x.

27. $x + 5x - 14 = 3y - 12$ Solve for x.

28. $\frac{ab}{x} = b$ Solve for x.

29. $Rx = H$ Solve for x.

30. $x(a + 2b) = 4(ac + b)$ Solve for x.

31. Bill has 9 more pencils than Jim. If Jim's and Bill's pencils total 3 more than three times the number of Jim's pencils, how many pencils does each boy have?

32. Mr. Gonzales is a salesman at the J.N. Car Sales and Service. His salary is $128 per week plus $47 per car that he sells. How many cars must he sell in one week to make $504?

33. The sum of two numbers is 111, and their difference is 63. What are the two numbers?

34. Find two consecutive integers such that the sum of five times the smaller and three times the larger is 67.

35. Julie drives the 120 miles from Greenup to Newton at 46 mph while Betty drives from Newton to Greenup at 34 mph. How long will it take for Julie and Betty to meet each other if they leave at the same time?

36. A coffee merchant wants to make a mixture of 50 pounds of Colombian and Brazilian coffee that will cost $3.19 per pound. If Colombian coffee sells for $3.35 per pound and Brazilian coffee sells for $2.95 per pound, how much of each type of coffee should the merchant mix?

37. Angie is 4 years older than Barb. If in 6 years the girls' combined ages will be 40, what are their ages now?

38. Craig has a bank that contains only half dollars and nickels. How many of each does he have if he has 126 coins worth $47.25?

CHAPTER 4

SOLVING INEQUALITIES

The First National Bank of Newtown is holding its annual board meeting. Mr. Lee is the bank president, and he must go before the board and explain the annual report to the members of the board. One of Mr. Lee's jobs is to make wise investments of the bank's funds so that the bank and eventually the stockholders will make a profit. Bank investments are made from money that is invested in the bank by individuals of the community. While the bank pays these individuals interest for the use of their money, the institution itself makes a profit by lending the money to other people at a higher interest rate or by investing it in government or municipal bonds or in other investments that return a high rate of interest. The profit the bank obtains from these investments is then divided among the stockholders as dividends. You can see, therefore, the importance of Mr. Lee's making wise investments for the bank.

The stockholders have great interest in what Mr. Lee has to say at their annual board meeting today. He knows that he must gain their confidence in his plans for future investments for their money. While making the report, he summarizes his plans for investments from which the bank will earn $55,000 in the coming year. He needs to know how much money he must invest in municipal bonds that yield 25% annually so that the total interest income for the bank will be at least $75,000. Also, if there are 13 stockholders and each stockholder gets equal shares, how much will each stockholder get from the interest income in one year?

When Mr. Lee solves these important business problems algebraically, he must work with inequalities. Can you find the solution to the bank president's problem? Do you think it is important that Mr. Lee know how to solve these problems accurately? Where do you think Mr. Lee first learned the principles for solving these problems?

You should feel confident about working with equations now, and you can be successful at solving inequalities. If you are unable to solve these problems now, by the time you finish this chapter you should be able to do so easily.

INEQUALITIES

You have learned that *equality* means the condition of having the same value. Scripture reminds us that all men are equal in that all have sinned and all must be saved. God has provided salvation equally for all. Scripture also reminds us of things that are not equal, called inequalities. The great conflict of the ages, the fight between God and Satan, is actually Satan's attempt to make an inequality equal. In Isaiah 14:14, Lucifer says, "I will be like the most High." In Genesis 3:5, the serpent Satan told Eve the great lie that she could be like, or equal to, God. Humanism is Satan's way of continuing that lie. Humanism says that man is his own God. Many Scripture passages such as Deuteronomy 4:39 tell us that there is only one God. No matter how hard man tries, he cannot make himself equal to God. The only way man can make himself acceptable to God is to accept the free gift of salvation.

Read John 10:27-30. Here Jesus says that He will give eternal life to His sheep. How can He do that? Because of an equality. What is Jesus equal to? He is equal to God the Father. Jesus also tells us that no one can pluck God's sheep out of God's hands. How can He say that? Because of an inequality. God the Father is greater than all. He is not equal to any man. He is not less than any man.

Now read I John 4:4. The "little children" refers to all Christians. Whom does "he that is in you" refer to? Who is He greater than? What does this verse mean to Christians?

The phrases *greater than, is not equal to,* and *less than* are phrases that often appear in mathematical inequalities. Symbols, however, are usually used to represent these and other important inequality phrases. See the chart.

symbol	meaning	example
$<$	is less than	$4 < 6$
$>$	is greater than	$5 > 3$
$\neq$	is not equal to	$2 \neq 4$
$\leq$	is less than or equal to	$3 \leq 3$
$\geq$	is greater than or equal to	$9 \geq 7$

NOTICE: THE SYMBOLS $<$ and $>$ POINT TO THE SMALLER NUMBER

You already know that $3x + 5 = 10$ is an equation. The equal sign (=) is the sign of an equality. How many solutions does an equation have?

A mathematical sentence such as $3x + 5 < 10$ is an inequality.

 DEFINITION ≫**Inequality:** a mathematical sentence stating that two numbers or expressions are not always equal.

Consider the inequality $x < 5$. How many values can x have? Does $x = -2$ make the inequality true? How about $x = -10$? $\frac{1}{2}$? $1\frac{1}{2}$? 2? any negative number? any positive number? An inequality has an infinite number of solutions, all of which can be indicated on a number line. Since 5 is the smallest whole number that is not a solution, place a circle over 5 on the number line and draw a line with an arrow pointing to the left of 5. You have just indicated that all numbers less than 5 are solutions to the inequality $x < 5$.

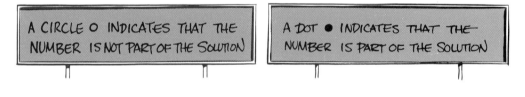

A CIRCLE O INDICATES THAT THE NUMBER IS NOT PART OF THE SOLUTION

A DOT ● INDICATES THAT THE NUMBER IS PART OF THE SOLUTION

EXAMPLES

Example 1.   Graph $x \geq -3$.

Solution.

1. Draw a number line and label it.
2. Decide if -3 should be included in the solution. Since the symbol means "greater than or equal to," x could equal -3. Therefore, -3 is part of the solution.
3. Put a dot over -3; then draw a line to indicate all numbers greater than (to the right of) -3.

Example 2. Graph x ≠ 2.

Solution.

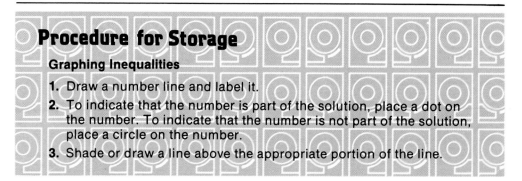

1. This inequality is not as specific as the others. We know only that x does not equal 2. So x could be greater than or less than 2.

$$x > 2 \text{ or } x < 2$$

Therefore, the solutions for this inequality include any number except 2.

2. Draw a circle over 2. Draw one line with an arrow pointing to the left and another line with an arrow pointing to the right.

Procedure for Storage

Graphing Inequalities

1. Draw a number line and label it.
2. To indicate that the number is part of the solution, place a dot on the number. To indicate that the number is not part of the solution, place a circle on the number.
3. Shade or draw a line above the appropriate portion of the line.

Exercises

Look up each reference. Then write the correct symbols for the equalities and inequalities.

1. Job 33:12   God   man

2. John 13:16   the servant   his lord

3. Isaiah 55:8   God's thoughts   man's thoughts

4. Matthew 12:42   one (Jesus)   Solomon

5. John 5:18   Jesus   God

6. Exodus 18:11   the Lord   all gods

7. Ephesians 3:8   Paul   least of all saints

8. I John 3:20   God   our heart

9. Luke 7:28   those born   John the   least in the
                          of woman   Baptist   kingdom of God

10. Revelation 21:16 length   breadth   height
                          of city   of city   of city

Graph each inequality on a separate number line.

11. $x < 4$ **16.** $x > 3$ **21.** $x \neq -4$

12. $x \geq -2$ **17.** $x < 6$ **22.** $x > 7$

13. $x \neq 5$ **18.** $x \leq -8$ **23.** $x \leq 0$

14. $x > -1$ **19.** $x < 2$ **24.** $x \geq 18$

15. $x \leq 22$ **20.** $x \geq 100$ **25.** $x < -52$

Graph each pair of inequalities on the same number line.

26. $x > 6$ **27.** $x \leq 1$ **28.** $x \leq 2$ **29.** $x > -3$ **30.** $x < 4$
    $x < 2$ $x > 5$ $x < 4$ $x \geq 4$ $x \geq 0$

FFFFWHOOOMP!

CLASS, SEE HOW EASY THIS IS !?

MIND OVER MATH

Mr. Jenkins, the chemistry teacher, discovered that it took his students only 90 minutes to conduct a certain experiment properly if he wore a blue shirt to class and a whole hour and a half for the same experiment if he wore a white shirt. Can you explain why?

COMPUTERS IN BUSINESS

When you walk into almost any grocery store today, you can see evidence of computers everywhere. At the checkout counter electronic cash registers connected to computers whir and buzz and spit out the customer's bill. Many boxes and cans carry on their sides a computer-readable bar code, called the universal product code. Specially equipped cash registers with light scanners can read this code; an attached computer rings up the price on the register, records the sale for inventory, orders a replacement item, and notifies store personnel when the shelves need to be restocked.

Manufacturers may use computers at many different stages of production. For instance, an engineer can describe a machine part to a computer through a special graphics terminal. The computer shows him a picture of the part as soon as he finishes his description. Then the engineer can instruct the computer to simulate the stresses the part must withstand. Once the part has passed this test, the computer produces a program to control the machines that will make the part. Many automobile factories use computers to operate robots that weld automobile frames and assemble other parts.

The influence of computers in business does not stop at the end of the production line. Quality-control engineers use computers to check the quality of the product. Computers also tell manufacturers when to order more raw materials and even help warehouse managers keep track of the parts they have on hand.

Secretaries use computers to type and proofread letters. Accountants use computers to do bookkeeping and print payroll checks. Company executives and sales managers may use computers to analyze how the company is doing. Using this information, they can then schedule new projects or adjust the product prices to account for higher costs.

Banks are almost completely run by computers. They use computers to keep track of daily transactions, to cancel checks, to post debits and credits, and to print monthly statements. At electronic automatic-teller stations, a customer can deposit or withdraw money and make payments without ever seeing a bank employee—and sometimes

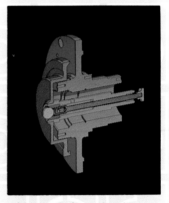

without seeing a bank.

Computers have become an indispensable part of modern business. As businesses depend more and more on computers, consumers will need to know more and more about computers to deal with business. Before long, you may be able to order groceries, do your banking, and run your "office" from your computer terminal, without ever leaving your home!

PROPERTIES OF INEQUALITY:
ADDITION AND SUBTRACTION

The addition and subtraction properties for inequalities are very similar to those for equalities. Observe these examples.

EXAMPLES

Example 1. $5 < 7$ **Addition**

$5 + 2 < 7 + 2$

$7 < 9$ If 2 is added to both sides, the statement is still true.

Example 2. $2 \geq -4$

$2 + 5 \geq -4 + 5$

$7 \geq 1$ If 5 is added to both sides, the statement is still true.

Example 3. $6 \neq -2$

$6 + 3 \neq -2 + 3$

$9 \neq 1$ If 3 is added to both sides, the statement is still true.

Example 4. $-9 \leq -3$ **Subtraction**

$-9 - 4 \leq -3 - 4$ If 4 is subtracted from both sides, the

$-13 \leq -7$ statement is still true.

Example 5. $2 > 0$

$2 - 9 > 0 - 9$ If 9 is subtracted from both sides, the

$-7 > -9$ statement is still true.

Procedure for Storage

Addition and Subtraction Properties of Inequality

Addition Property of Inequality

If a and b are two real numbers or expressions such that $a < b$ and c is any real number or expression, then
$$a + c < b + c.$$

Subtraction Property of Inequality

If a and b are two real numbers or expressions such that $a < b$ and c is any real number or expression, then
$$a - c < b - c.$$

Any inequality symbol could replace the symbol $<$ in these properties without changing the truth of the property.

Use these properties to solve inequalities exactly as you would use them to solve equations. Just think of the inequality as an equation. Solve, keeping the inequality symbol in place.

EXAMPLES

Example 6. Solve $x + 7 < 8$.

  Solution. $x + 7 < 8$

            $x + 7 - 7 < 8 - 7$ Subtract 7 from both sides.

                   $x < 1$

Example 7. Solve $y - 5 \neq 32$.

  Solution. $y - 5 \neq 32$

          $y - 5 + 5 \neq 32 + 5$

               $y \neq 37$ Since $y \neq 37$, $y > 37$ or $y < 37$.

Example 8. Solve $x - 6 \geq 12$.

  Solution. $x - 6 \geq 12$

              $x \geq 12 + 6$

              $x \geq 18$

Exercises

Do All

Solve each inequality. Graph 1 to 5 on number lines.

graph

1. $x + 8 > -4$
2. $x - 2 \leq 3$
3. $y - 10 > 2$
4. $z + 1 \neq -2$
5. $x - 3 > 9$
6. $x + 18 \leq 7$
7. $y - 26 > 82$
8. $z + 5 < -1$

9. $y + 4 \neq 12$
10. $x - 10 \geq 21$
11. $x - 8 < 2$
12. $y + 15 \neq 29$
13. $x - 26 \geq 129$
14. $y + 87 < 62$
15. $z - 193 > -149$

PROPERTIES OF INEQUALITY: MULTIPLICATION AND DIVISION

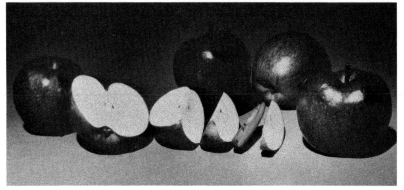

Have you ever done an experiment? What is an experiment? An experiment is a test to illustrate a known truth or to examine a hypothesis. Most experiments are limited to science class but can be performed in other classes as well, like algebra. Here are some experiments to see if inequalities are always solved like equations.

Experiment 1.

Is this statement true?	$3 < 5$
Now multiply both sides of this inequality by 2.	$3 \cdot 2 < 5 \cdot 2$
Is this statement true?	$6 < 10$

This experiment shows that if you multiply both sides of an inequality by a number, the inequality is still true. Before you accept that conclusion as a true statement, look at experiment 2.

Experiment 2.

Is this statement true?	$4 < 6$
Multiply both sides by -3. Is the inequality still true? No!	$4 \cdot -3 < 6 \cdot -3$ $-12 < -18$
How could you make this final statement true? If you change the inequality sign to $>$, will the statement then be true?	$-12 > -18$

Experiment 1 shows that if you multiply both sides of an inequality by a positive number the inequality remains the same. But if you multiply both sides of an inequality by a negative number, the inequality sign must be reversed.

Procedure for Storage

Multiplication Property of Inequality

If a, b, and c are real numbers or expressions and

1. $c > 0$, then $a < b$ implies $ac < bc$, and $a > b$ implies $ac > bc$.

2. $c < 0$, then $a < b$ implies $ac > bc$, and $a > b$ implies $ac < bc$.

Now experiment with division.

Experiment 3.

Is this statement true?	$10 > 6$
Now divide both sides by 2.	$\dfrac{10}{2} > \dfrac{6}{2}$
Is the statement still true?	$5 > 3$
Yes, but before we draw any conclusions, let's experiment with a negative number.	

Experiment 4.

Is this statement true?	$18 > 9$
Divide both sides by -3.	$\dfrac{18}{-3} > \dfrac{9}{-3}$
Is this statement true? How can you make the statement true?	$-6 > -3$
Is this statement true?	$-6 < -3$

Procedure for Storage

Division Property of Inequality

If a, b, and c are real numbers or expressions with $c \neq 0$ and

1. $c > 0$, then $a < b$ implies $\dfrac{a}{c} < \dfrac{b}{c}$, and $a > b$ implies $\dfrac{a}{c} > \dfrac{b}{c}$.

2. $c < 0$, then $a < b$ implies $\dfrac{a}{c} > \dfrac{b}{c}$, and $a > b$ implies $\dfrac{a}{c} < \dfrac{b}{c}$.

By performing these simple experiments, you have found that multiplying or dividing both sides of an inequality by a negative number changes the inequality sign, but multiplying or dividing both sides by a positive number does not change the inequality sign.

EXAMPLES

Example 1. $\frac{x}{-2} > -7$

Solution. $(-2)\,\frac{x}{-2} < (-2)(-7)$ Multiply both sides by
                                              -2 and reverse the
$x < 14$ inequality sign.

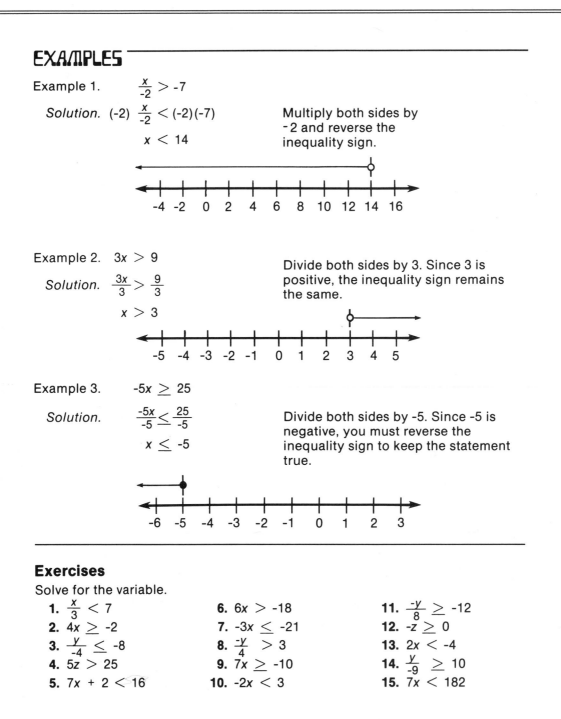

Example 2. $3x > 9$

Solution. $\frac{3x}{3} > \frac{9}{3}$ Divide both sides by 3. Since 3 is
                                          positive, the inequality sign remains
$x > 3$ the same.

Example 3. $-5x \geq 25$

Solution. $\frac{-5x}{-5} \leq \frac{25}{-5}$ Divide both sides by -5. Since -5 is
                                               negative, you must reverse the
$x \leq -5$ inequality sign to keep the statement
                                               true.

Exercises

Solve for the variable.

1. $\frac{x}{3} < 7$

2. $4x \geq -2$

3. $\frac{y}{-4} \leq -8$

4. $5z > 25$

5. $7x + 2 < 16$

6. $6x > -18$

7. $-3x \leq -21$

8. $\frac{-y}{4} > 3$

9. $7x \geq -10$

10. $-2x < 3$

11. $\frac{-y}{8} \geq -12$

12. $-z \geq 0$

13. $2x < -4$

14. $\frac{y}{-9} \geq 10$

15. $7x < 182$

SOLVING INEQUALITIES

$3x < 9$
$x < 3$

These two inequalities are called equivalent inequalities. If you graph the solution to each of these inequalities, you get this:

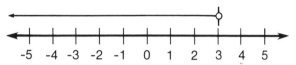

-5 -4 -3 -2 -1 0 1 2 3 4 5

 DEFINITION

≫**Equivalent inequalities:** inequalities that have the same solution set.

How many solutions does an inequality have? To solve an inequality, think of it as an equation and solve for the variable, making sure you reverse the inequality sign when multiplying or dividing by a negative number.

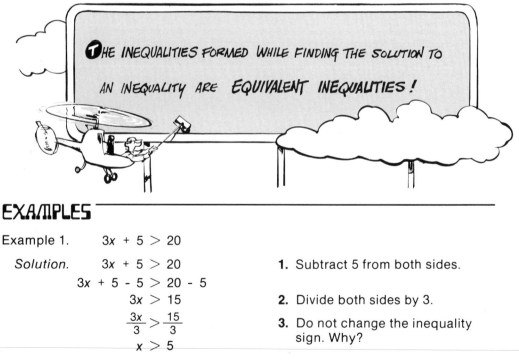

THE INEQUALITIES FORMED WHILE FINDING THE SOLUTION TO AN INEQUALITY ARE *EQUIVALENT INEQUALITIES!*

EXAMPLES

Example 1. $3x + 5 > 20$

Solution. $3x + 5 > 20$
$3x + 5 - 5 > 20 - 5$
$3x > 15$
$\frac{3x}{3} > \frac{15}{3}$
$x > 5$

1. Subtract 5 from both sides.

2. Divide both sides by 3.

3. Do not change the inequality sign. Why?

Example 2. $-4x - 6 \leq 18$

Solution. $-4x - 6 \leq 18$

$-4x - 6 + 6 \leq 18 + 6$

$-4x \leq 24$

$\dfrac{-4x}{-4} \geq \dfrac{24}{-4}$

$x \geq -6$

When dividing by a negative number, reverse the inequality sign.

Example 3. $\dfrac{z}{-3} + 8 \geq 12$

Solution. $\dfrac{z}{-3} + 8 \geq 12$

$-3(\dfrac{z}{-3} + 8) \leq 12 \cdot -3$

$z - 24 \leq -36$

$z \leq -36 + 24$

$z \leq -12$

Since this is a fractional inequality, multiply by the common denominator -3 to clear the inequality of fractions and reverse the inequality sign. Why?

Exercises

Solve for the variable. Graph 1 to 5 on number lines.

1. $-5x + 3 \geq 13$

2. $8y - 7 > 17$

3. $\dfrac{z}{-2} - 4 \geq 2$

4. $4x - 6 - 6x > 10$

5. $-3y + 10 < 31$

6. $\dfrac{-x}{4} - 6 + x \neq 9$

7. $\dfrac{x}{6} + 3 \leq -5$

8. $4x + 5 \geq 9x - 2$

9. $-8x + 4x + 6 < 3x + 6$

10. $6y - 3 + 2y \geq 9y - 7$

11. $\dfrac{-8z}{3} + 2z - 6 \leq 3z + 2$

12. $x - 5 + 3x \neq 2x - 4$

13. $4z - 12 < 3z - 142$

14. $-5x - 2x + 6 \geq -6x + 3$

15. $2z - 9 < 3z + 9$

CONJUNCTIONS

$x = 4$ and $x < 6$ $\quad$ $x > 2$ and $x \leq 4$ $\quad$ $x < -3$ and $x > 7$
$x < 3$ or $x \leq -5$ $\quad$ $x > -1$ or $x < 8$ $\quad$ $x \neq 5$ or $x < 9$

These mathematical expressions are compound sentences. The three containing the word *and* are called *conjunctions.* The three containing the word *or* are called *disjunctions,* which will be covered in the next section.

DEFINITION

≫**Conjunction:** a compound sentence consisting of mathematical sentences connected by the word *and,* meaning intersection, and symbolized by $\wedge$.

The solution to a conjunction is the intersection of the solutions to the separate sentences in the compound statement. If the intersection is $\varnothing$, the solution set is empty; hence there is no solution. When you solve conjunctions, graph each separate sentence and then find the intersection of the graphs.

EXAMPLES

Example 1. Solve $x > 2$ and $x \leq 4$.

Solution. $x > 2 \quad \wedge \quad x \leq 4$

1. Graph each sentence on the same number line.

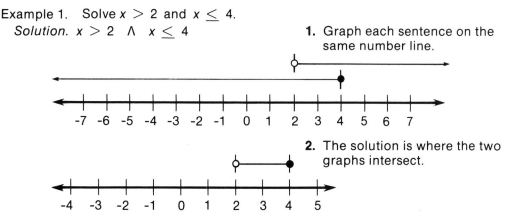

2. The solution is where the two graphs intersect.

Any numbers between 2 and 4, including 4, are solutions of this compound sentence. The solution is written $2 < x \leq 4$. To check, choose any number in the solution and substitute it in both statements. The key word here is *both.* Since 3 is in the solution, try $x = 3$.

Check. By substituting 3 for x, you get $3 > 2$ and $3 \leq 4$. Both statements are true; therefore, the conjunction is true.

Example 2. Solve $x = 4$ and $x < 6$.

Solution. $x = 4 \quad \wedge \quad x < 6$

1. Graph $x = 4$ on a number line.
2. Graph $x < 6$ on the same number line.

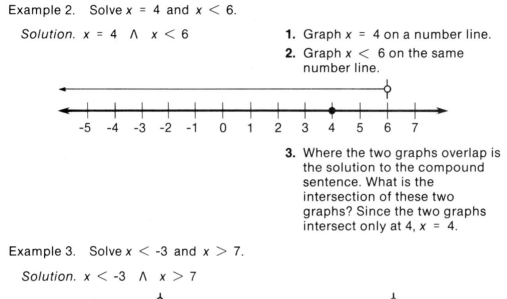

3. Where the two graphs overlap is the solution to the compound sentence. What is the intersection of these two graphs? Since the two graphs intersect only at 4, $x = 4$.

Example 3. Solve $x < -3$ and $x > 7$.

Solution. $x < -3 \quad \wedge \quad x > 7$

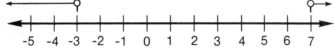

Do these graphs intersect? Do they overlap at any point? No, they don't; therefore, the solution is the empty set, $\varnothing$.

Example 4. Solve $x \leq 5$ and $x < 0$.

Solution. $x \leq 5 \quad \wedge \quad x < 0$

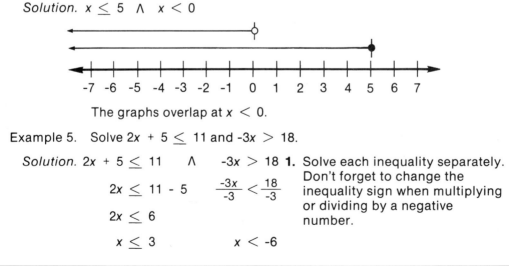

The graphs overlap at $x < 0$.

Example 5. Solve $2x + 5 \leq 11$ and $-3x > 18$.

Solution. $2x + 5 \leq 11 \qquad \wedge \qquad -3x > 18$

$2x \leq 11 - 5 \qquad \dfrac{-3x}{-3} < \dfrac{18}{-3}$

$2x \leq 6$

$x \leq 3 \qquad\qquad x < -6$

1. Solve each inequality separately. Don't forget to change the inequality sign when multiplying or dividing by a negative number.

$x \leq 3 \; \wedge \; x < \text{-}6$

2. Graph the solutions on the same number line to find the solution for the compound sentence.

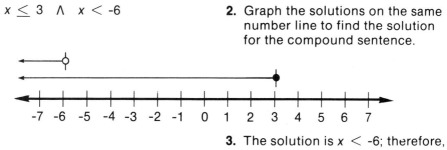

3. The solution is $x < \text{-}6$; therefore, any number less than -6 will make both inequalities true.

Procedure for Storage

Solving Conjunctions

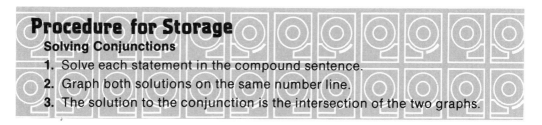

1. Solve each statement in the compound sentence.

2. Graph both solutions on the same number line.

3. The solution to the conjunction is the intersection of the two graphs.

Exercises

Solve.

1. $x > 4$ and $x \geq 2$

2. $x \leq 3$ and $x < 6$

3. $2x > \text{-}6$ and $x \leq 1$

4. $4x + 6 \leq 26$ and $3x \neq 12$

5. $8x - 12 > 4$ and $2x \geq 14$

6. $x - 3 \leq 4x$ and $2x + 6 < 18$

7. $\text{-}5x + 13 > \text{-}7$ and $4x - 6 \leq 10$

8. $3x + 4 - 2x \leq 12$ and $2x + 6 \neq 8$

9. $4x - 2 - 5x > 10$ and $3x - 6 \leq 12$

10. $8x - 14 + x - 6 \leq 7$ and $x - 16 \geq 0$

11. $x \geq 5$ and $4x < 32$

12. $5x + 3 < 28$ and $6x < 12$

13. $2x - 7 \geq 5$ and $\text{-}7x < \text{-}49$

14. $9x + 2 < \text{-}7$ and $\text{-}2x - 8 \leq 12$

DISJUNCTIONS

 ≫**Disjunction:** a compound sentence consisting of mathematical sentences connected by the word *or*, meaning union, and symbolized by V.

As stated in Chapter 1, the union of two sets is the set of elements contained in either set. It is a combination of the two sets. To solve a disjunction, simply graph both statements on a number line and find the union of the two solutions. Everything that is shaded will be the solution to the disjunction since a shaded portion will be a solution to one sentence or the other.

EXAMPLES

Example 1. $x < 4$ or $x \leq 2$

   Solution. $x < 4$ V $x \leq 2$ Graph each sentence on the same number line.

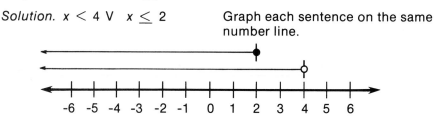

The solution to the disjunction is the union of the two solutions, not the intersection. The solution to this disjunction is $x < 4$.

Example 2. $x > -1$ or $x < -4$

   Solution. $x > -1$ V $x < -4$ Graph each sentence. The solution is $x > -1$ or $x < -4$.

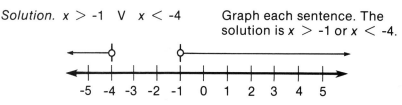

   Check.

        Try some number in the solution. Zero is in the solution. Is $0 > -1$ true? Is $0 < -4$ true? To make the disjunction true, either statement must be true. Is either statement true? Yes, $0 > -1$ is true; therefore, 0 is a solution.

Example 3. $x \neq 5$ or $x < 2$

Solution. $x \neq 5$ ∨ $x < 2$
$x > 5$ ∨ $x < 5$ ∨ $x < 2$

Graph each inequality on one number line. The solution is the union of all the graphs. Thus any number except 5 is a solution.

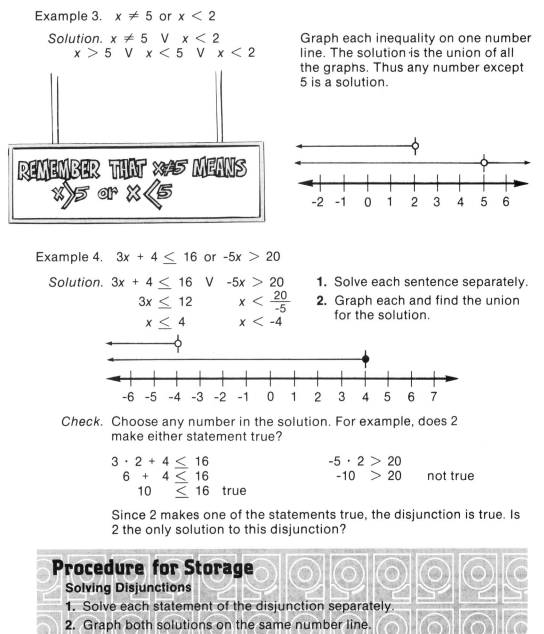

REMEMBER THAT x≠5 MEANS x>5 or x<5

Example 4. $3x + 4 \leq 16$ or $-5x > 20$

Solution. $3x + 4 \leq 16$ ∨ $-5x > 20$
$3x \leq 12$ $x < \dfrac{20}{-5}$
$x \leq 4$ $x < -4$

1. Solve each sentence separately.
2. Graph each and find the union for the solution.

Check. Choose any number in the solution. For example, does 2 make either statement true?

$3 \cdot 2 + 4 \leq 16$ $\qquad$ $-5 \cdot 2 > 20$
$6 + 4 \leq 16$ $\qquad$ $-10 > 20$ $\qquad$ not true
$10 \leq 16$ true

Since 2 makes one of the statements true, the disjunction is true. Is 2 the only solution to this disjunction?

Procedure for Storage
Solving Disjunctions
1. Solve each statement of the disjunction separately.
2. Graph both solutions on the same number line.
3. The solution to the disjunction is the union of the two graphs.

Example 5. $3x - 6 \leq 12$ or $5x > -25$

Solution. $3x - 6 \leq 12$ $\quad$V$\quad$ $5x > -25$

$\qquad\qquad 3x \leq 18 \qquad\quad x > -5$

$\qquad\qquad\quad x \leq 6$

The union of the two solutions is the entire number line. Any number you choose would make at least one of the statements true.

Exercises

Solve.

1. $x < 5$ or $x \geq 2$

2. $x \leq -1$ or $x > 4$

3. $x \neq 6$ or $x > 3$

4. $2x + 5 > 17$ or $x + 2 \leq 8$

5. $x - 6 \leq -6$ or $3x - 5 > 10$

6. $3x + 5 > 2x$ or $6x - 3x + 4 \geq 16$

7. $2x - 6 \geq 14$ or $8x + 2x - 3 > 27$

8. $x - 7 > 0$ or $2x + 16 \leq 2$

9. $3x + 6 \leq -9$ or $x < 6$

10. $2x - 7 > -21$ or $4x + 6 \neq 22$

ABSOLUTE VALUE INEQUALITIES

Do you remember the definition of absolute value? Here it is again to refresh your memory.

$$|x| = \begin{cases} x, \text{ if } x \geq 0. \\ -x, \text{ if } x < 0. \end{cases}$$

Let $\quad x = 4.$

Then $|x| = |4|$

Since $4 \geq 0$, use the first part of the definition.

$|x| = x$, so $|4| = 4$

Let $\quad x = -4$

Then $|x| = |-4|$

Since $-4 < 0$, use the second part of the definition.

$|x| = -x$, so $|-4| = --4 = 4$

You have learned how to solve absolute value equations. Now you will learn how to solve absolute value inequalities. Here is a simple example to start with.

EXAMPLES

Example 1. Solve $|x| < 3$.

 Solution. What values will make this inequality true?

5?	$\|5\| < 3$	no
2?	$\|2\| < 3$	yes
0?	$\|0\| < 3$	yes
-2?	$\|-2\| < 3$	yes
-5?	$\|-5\| < 3$	no

Here is the solution on a number line.

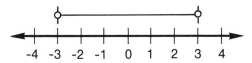

It is written as the conjunction $x < 3$ and $x > -3$.

If we take a close look at the definition of absolute value, we can solve these absolute value inequalities algebraically. In the problem $|x| < 3$, there are two possible situations that can occur according to the definition of absolute value.

1. If $x \geq 0$, then by definition
$|x| = x$.
Therefore, $|x| = x < 3$.

2. If $x < 0$, then by definition
$|x| = -x$.
Therefore, $|x| = -x < 3$.
$= x > -3$

The two possible solutions are $x < 3$ and $x > -3$. If the inequality sign in an absolute value inequality is $<$, the solution is less than ($<$) the number and greater than ($>$) the opposite of the number.

Example 2. Solve |x| < 5.

　　Solution.　x < 5 and x > -5　　Since the inequality sign is < , only
　　　　　　　　　　　　　　　　numbers in the conjunction x < 5
　　　　　　　　　　　　　　　　and x > -5 make the inequality true.

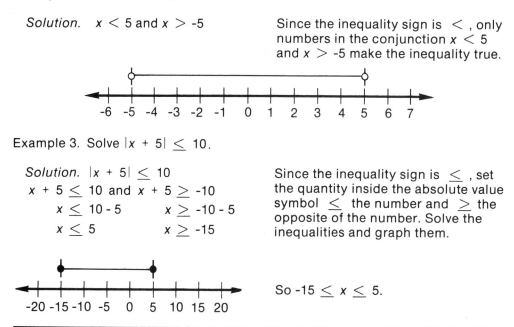

Example 3. Solve |x + 5| ≤ 10.

　　Solution. |x + 5| ≤ 10　　　　Since the inequality sign is ≤ , set
　　x + 5 ≤ 10 and x + 5 ≥ -10　　the quantity inside the absolute value
　　　x ≤ 10 - 5　　　x ≥ -10 - 5　symbol ≤ the number and ≥ the
　　　x ≤ 5　　　　　x ≥ -15　　　opposite of the number. Solve the
　　　　　　　　　　　　　　　　inequalities and graph them.

So -15 ≤ x ≤ 5.

　　　So far the solutions have been conjunctions. Whenever the sign in an absolute value inequality is < , you can expect the solution to be a conjunction.
　　　If the sign is > , what type of compound sentence do you suppose the answer will be?

EXAMPLE

Example 4. Solve |x| > 1.

　　Solution. What values will make this inequality true?

　　　　　0?　|0| > 1　no
　　　　　4?　|4| > 1　yes
　　　　　6?　|6| > 1　yes　　　　　How many solutions are there?
　　　　-3?　|-3| > 1　yes　　　　Graph the inequality.

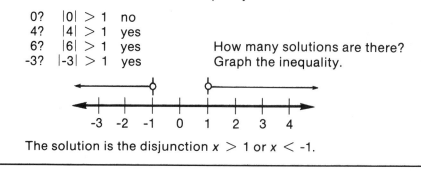

The solution is the disjunction x > 1 or x < -1.

If the inequality sign in an absolute value inequality is $>$, the solution is greater than ($>$) the number or less than ($<$) the opposite of the number.

How does the definition of absolute value apply to this example? Again, according to the definition, two possible situations can occur.

1. If $x \geq 0$, then by definition
   $|x| = x$.
   Therefore $|x| = x > 1$.

2. If $x < 0$, then by definition
   $|x| = -x$.
   Therefore $|x| = -x > 1$
   $\qquad\qquad x < -1$

The two possible solutions are $x > 1$ or $x < -1$.

EXAMPLES

Example 5. Solve $|x| > 6$.

  Solution. $x > 6$ ∨ $x < -6$ Since the symbol is $>$, the solution will be a disjunction. So set the quantity inside the absolute value symbol $>$ the number and $<$ the opposite of the number.

Example 6. Solve $|-3x + 6| > 18$.

  Solution. Since the symbol is $>$, set the quantity $>$ the number and $<$ the opposite of the number. Solve the inequalities and find their union.

$$|-3x + 6| > 18$$

$-3x + 6 > 18$	∨	$-3x + 6 < -18$
$-3x > 18 - 6$		$-3x < -18 - 6$
$-3x > 12$		$-3x < -24$
$x < -4$		$x > 8$

The solution is $x < -4$
or $x > 8$.

Procedure for Storage

Solving Absolute Value Inequalities

1. If the inequality is $<$, the problem becomes a conjunction. Set the quantity in the absolute value symbol $<$ the number and $>$ the opposite of the number.

2. If the inequality is $>$, the problem becomes a disjunction. Set the quantity in the absolute value symbol $>$ the number and $<$ the opposite of the number.

3. Solve the conjunction or disjunction.
   Note: The signs $<$ and $\leq$ and the signs $>$ and $\geq$ follow the same rules.

Exercises

Solve for x.

1. $|x - 3| < 10$

2. $|x + 6| \geq 5$

3. $|x + 4| \leq 2$

4. $|2x + 6| \geq 14$

5. $|3x - 10| < 9$

6. $|4x + 17| > 7$

7. $|\frac{2x}{3} - 7| \leq 4$

8. $|\frac{5x}{9} + 6| > 5$

9. $|2x - 8| < 10$

10. $|4x - 7| \geq 29$

11. $|-4x - 8| > 4$

12. $|3x + 2| \leq 6$

13. $|7x + 9 - 6x| > 8$

14. $|2x - 6 + 5x| < 10$

15. $|4x - 6| < 24$

WORD PROBLEMS USING INEQUALITIES

When God repeats something, you should be sure to take notice, for God does not repeat His promises or warnings without a purpose. For example, salvation through the blood of Jesus Christ, the primary theme of the Bible, is repeated from Genesis to Revelation. Read Ephesians 1:7. Can you think of at least four other Scripture passages that refer to salvation through the blood of Jesus Christ? God wants everyone to be saved (cf. I Timothy 2:4). He repeats His plan of salvation often so that man will be without excuse. We should never grow tired of or ignore God's reminders.

Frequently in your studies, you must spend time reviewing what you have learned. During review time you shouldn't say, "Oh, I already know all that," or even, "Oh, no, not that again." Instead you should use the time to assure yourself that you do know what you are supposed to know. Then you won't have to make silly excuses for failing to do the work correctly. Right now take time to review the steps for solving word problems.

1. Read the problem carefully, looking for important words.
2. Whenever possible, make a drawing.
3. Identify the unknowns and assign variables.
4. Using operational words as clues, find two expressions that form an inequality.
5. Solve the inequality.
6. If there is more than one unknown, find each unknown by substituting the found value in the expression for the other variable.
7. Check your solutions.

important words	meanings
more than; greater than	$>$
less than	$<$
at least	$\geq$
at most	$\leq$

Write an operational sign in each box to indicate which mathematical operation must be performed to arrive at the answer given.

1. 9 ☐ 3 = 3
2. 9 ☐ 8 ☐ 4 = 13
3. 5 ☐ 7 ☐ 4 = 31
4. 8 ☐ 2 ☐ 6 ☐ 4 = 28
5. 6 ☐ 3 ☐ 4 ☐ 3 ☐ 8 = 2

EXAMPLES

Example 1. How much money must be invested at 7% a year to produce a yearly income of at least $875?

Solution.

1. Read the problem carefully, noting the words *at least*.
2. No drawing is needed.
3. The unknown is the amount to invest, the principal *p*. Let *x* = the amount invested.
4. Since *at least* means $\geq$, the product of the rate *r*, the time *t*, and the principal *p* must be larger than or equal to the interest produced. By substitution you get the inequality $x(0.07)(1) \geq 875$.
5. Solve $0.07x \geq 875$.

$$0.07x \geq 875$$
$$7x \geq 87,500$$
$$x \geq 12,500$$

6. Only one variable is used.

Check.

7. Is $12,500 (0.07) (1) \geq $875?
   Since $12,500 at 7% produces exactly $875, any amount larger than 12,500 will produce a larger amount that will also satisfy the inequality.

Example 2. The difference between a number and 25 is less than 82. What could the number be?

Solution. Let *x* = the number.

$$x - 25 < 82$$
$$x < 107$$

Thus *x* represents any number less than 107.

Exercises

1. The sum of two numbers is more than 20, and one number is 4 more than the other number. What are the numbers?

2. Find the least positive integer such that 4 more than seven times the number is greater than 95.

3. Peggy wants to buy three times as many cans of green beans, which cost 42¢ per can, as cans of peas, which cost 37¢ per can. If she has no more than $4.89 to spend, what is the maximum number of cans of peas she can buy?

4. Find the largest integer such that 8 more than six times the integer is less than -42.

5. The president of the First National Bank is responsible for making wise investments of the bank's funds. He has already made some investments from which the bank will earn $55,000. If he can buy some municipal bonds that yield 25% interest annually, how much money must he invest so that the total interest income for the bank will be at least $75,000?

6. Shirley is shopping at Crossroads Mall. She has $42.00 cash in her purse, and she refuses to write a check or use a credit card today. She finds a dress costing $21.95 and a pair of earrings costing $3.24. There is also a 5% sales tax to add to the total. How much more can she spend and stay within the limits of her cash?

7. For Mr. Rogers to pay his monthly bills he must make at least $675 each month. He sells cars and makes a guaranteed salary of $450 per month plus $75 commission on each car he sells. What is the least number of cars he can sell each month to meet his obligations for the month?

8. A certain number times 23 and added to 15 is greater than 429. What is the number?

9. Paul Bermudez earns twice as much per week as his sister Naomi. If she makes $30 per week more than her brother John and the sum of the children's salaries is at most $290, what range can their salaries take each week?

10. Each ounce of whole milk contains twice as many calories as an ounce of skim milk. A mixture of 4 ounces of whole milk and 2 ounces of skim milk contains at least 100 calories. What is the minimum number of calories in each ounce of whole and skim milk?

MEMORY RECALL

Identify.

  addition property of inequality
  compound sentence
  conjunction
  disjunction
  division property of inequality
  inequality
  multiplication property of inequality
  subtraction property of inequality

You should now be able to do the following:

1. Graph inequalities on a number line.
2. Solve inequalities using the properties of inequality.
3. Describe the properties of inequality and give an example of each.
4. Identify equivalent inequalities.
5. Solve conjunctions.
6. Solve disjunctions.
7. Solve absolute value inequalities.
8. Find solutions to word problems involving inequalities.

You should be able to do the following problems.

1. Graph each inequality on a separate number line.

 a. $x \leq 10$ **c.** $a \neq 7$
 b. $y > 4$ **d.** $c < 0$

2. Solve each inequality and graph the solution.

 a. $x + 3 \geq 5$ **d.** $\frac{x}{5} > 2$ **g.** $2y + 3 \neq 5$
 b. $y - 9 < -6$ **e.** $-6x < -30$ **h.** $7 - 3a \geq 21$
 c. $3x \leq 18$ **f.** $4x - 7 > 5$ **i.** $\frac{2b}{7} + 1 > 3$

3. Solve each compound sentence and graph the solution.

    a. $x > 2$ and $x \leq 5$

    b. $y < -3$ or $y > 2$

    c. $5x \geq 10$ and $3 + x \leq 8$

    d. $2x + 7 < 9$ and $-3x \leq 6$

    e. $12x - 6 \geq 6 \lor x < 5$

    f. $-3x + 1 \neq 3 \land 4x + 12 \geq 6$

4. Solve for the variable.

    a. $|x| > 5$

    b. $|x-6| \leq 8$

    c. $|3x-7| > 11$

    d. $|\frac{2x}{5} - 4| < 9$

5. The product of 7 and a number is more than the sum of 7 and the number. What is the number? What is the smallest integer that could be a solution for the number?

6. Bill has scores of 95, 78, and 93 on his English exams. If he wants to get an A on his report card, he must have an average of at least 90. What is the lowest score he can get on his next exam and still get an A?

CHAPTER 5

RELATIONS, FUNCTIONS, AND GRAPHS

Mark ran in the front door, yelling, "Mom, Mom!"

His mother came out of the kitchen to meet him. "What is it? What are you so excited about?"

Mark breathlessly told her about the announcement that Mr. Johnson had made in history class that day. Mr. Johnson told the class that he was going to take an archeological trip to Egypt during the summer to help in an excavation. He was going to take with him five students who could raise the money for their transportation and who had their parents' permission. They would earn room and board while they were there in exchange for work they would do at the excavation site. Since history was Mark's favorite class, he wanted to go.

After Mark discussed the matter with his parents, they decided that he could go on this summer trip and that they would pay half of the transportation costs if Mark could earn the other half. Mark was so excited about the trip that he saved every penny he earned. In his free time before the trip he got archeology books from the library and began his own digging.

He discovered that preparing the excavation site for the actual digging was very similar to graphing, something he had learned in his algebra class. First, a reference point is selected, and a white x with a circle around it is painted on this point. All other measurements are made and locations are found from this point, called the datum point. The archeologist then marks off the dig area with a grid formed by parallel lines, which run both north and south and east and west. The intervals between the lines vary from ten to twenty feet. The archeologists then mark the site by driving stakes at the intersections of the lines and stretching tape tautly along each grid line. All this is done so that digging areas can be easily identified. If Mark were told to go to 3E/2N to work in the dig, he would know exactly where to work. The section of grid would be identified by the intersection stake at the square's southwest corner. When the actual grid of the site is completely laid out, it is plotted on a piece of graph paper and labeled with the appropriate scale. Mark also learned that when an artifact is uncovered, its position in the dig must be recorded accurately according to the grid location.

Finally the day to leave arrived. As Mark waited at the airport to depart for Egypt, he thought of all the things he had learned about archeology. He had learned many other things too, like how to earn money and save it and how to read graphs and plot points. Now he was eager to apply what he had learned.

COORDINATES IN A PLANE

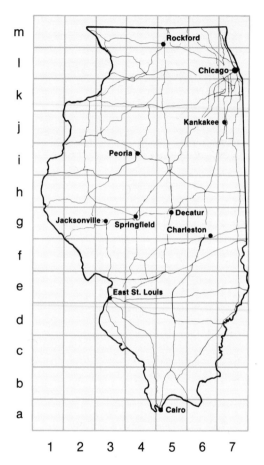

Have you ever looked at a road map? Sometimes when you try to find a certain town on a map, you first have to look at the index to find out what general region the town is in. Look at the map below and find the towns indicated in the index.

Index

Decatur	5g
East St. Louis	3e
Chicago	7l
Cairo	5a
Charleston	6g
Rockford	5m

On this map a number and a letter indicate a region where you would find these cities. The number shows the horizontal distance. The letter shows the vertical distance.

Give the location of the following Illinois cities. Use the map above. Be sure to state the number first, then the letter.

Springfield

Kankakee

Jacksonville

Peoria

In the index, the symbols that represent the location of the towns are actually ordered pairs.

DEFINITION ≫**Ordered pair:** A pair of symbols whose order has meaning

For each city the first element is a number from 1 to 7. The second element is a letter from *a* to *m*. You have now located ten cities, indicated by ordered pairs. But Illinois has many more than ten cities. All possible locations on the map can be represented by ordered pairs. The set of all possible ordered pairs is known as the Cartesian product. The *Cartesian product* is the set of all ordered pairs produced by arranging the elements of set *A* and the elements of set *B* such that the first element of the ordered pair comes from set *A* and the second element of the ordered pair comes from set *B*. Therefore, the sets are arranged as follows:

A = {1, 2, 3, 4, 5, 6, 7} the numbers in the index
B = {a, b, c, d, e, f, g, h, i, j, k, l, m} the letters in the index

Thus the Cartesian product of these two sets, indicated by the symbol X, would be this.

A X B = {(1, a), (1, b), (1, c), (1, d), (1, e), (1, f), (1, g),
(1, h), (1, i), (1, j), (1, k), (1, l), (1, m),
(2, a), (2, b), (2, c), (2, d), (2, e), (2, f), (2, g),
(2, h), (2, i), (2, j), (2, k), (2, l), (2, m),
(3, a), (3, b), (3, c), (3, d), (3, e), (3, f), (3, g),
(3, h), (3, i), (3, j), (3, k), (3, l), (3, m),
(4, a), (4, b), (4, c), (4, d), (4, e), (4, f), (4, g),
(4, h), (4, i), (4, j), (4, k), (4, l), (4, m),
(5, a), (5, b), (5, c), (5, d), (5, e), (5, f), (5, g),
(5, h), (5, i), (5, j), (5, k), (5, l), (5, m),
(6, a), (6, b), (6, c), (6, d), (6, e), (6, f), (6, g),
(6, h), (6, i), (6, j), (6, k), (6, l), (6, m),
(7, a), (7, b), (7, c), (7, d), (7, e), (7, f), (7, g),
(7, h), (7, i), (7, j) (7, k), (7, l), (7, m)}

This set includes all possible locations on the map. Note that these locations are regions, not points.

In this chapter you will be working with a special Cartesian product described by ℝ X ℝ, which simply means the set of all ordered pairs formed when the first element is taken from ℝ (the set of real numbers) and the second element is taken from ℝ. In algebra we use the plane to describe ℝ X ℝ. The plane formed by ℝ X ℝ is called the *Cartesian plane* for its inventor, René Descartes. He was the first to see the connection between lines in a plane and algebraic equations.

≫**Plane:** A flat surface that extends infinitely and has an infinite number of points.

Two perpendicular lines (one horizontal, the other vertical) divide the plane into four sections called *quadrants*. These quadrants are numbered counterclockwise with roman numerals. See the illustration below. The origin is usually labeled *O*.

≫*X*-**axis:** the horizontal reference line in a plane.
≫*Y*-**axis:** the vertical reference line in a plane.
≫**Origin:** the point at which the axes cross.

When the plane is marked off into squares to form a grid (or graph), points represented by ordered pairs can be identified on the plane. The process of locating points in a plane is called plotting points or graphing the ordered pair.

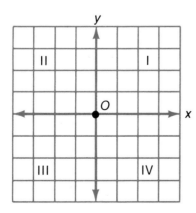

Look again at the map of Illinois on page 182. Remember that the horizontal distance was given first. Then the vertical distance was given. The order of the elements in an ordered pair is very important.

Example 1. Graph the ordered pair (2, 1).

Solution. **1.** Locate the origin.
2. Move right two units.
3. Move up one unit.
4. Place a dot at this point.
5. Label the point (2, 1).

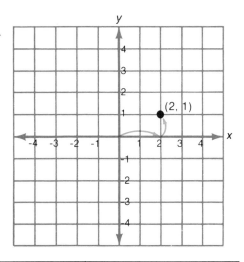

The *x*-axis is similar to a horizontal number line: positive is right, negative left. The *y*-axis is similar to the vertical number line: positive is up, negative down.

Example 2. Graph the ordered pair (-3, 4).

Solution. **1.** Locate the origin.
2. Move left three units.
3. Move up four units.
4. Label the point (-3, 4).

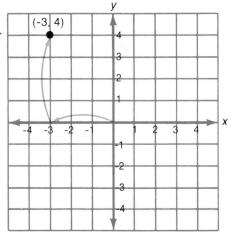

An ordered pair with unknown elements is usually expressed *(x, y)*.
The horizontal distance *(x)* along the *x*-axis is always given first.

≫**Abscissa** (*x*-coordinate): The first element of an ordered pair.

≫**Ordinate** (*y*-coordinate): The second element of an ordered pair.

The abscissa is always given first, and the ordinate is always given second in an ordered pair. The two elements together are the coordinates of the point.

EXAMPLES

Example 3. Graph the ordered pair (0, -7).

Solution. **1.** Locate the origin.
2. Since the *x*-coordinate is 0, do not move left or right.
3. Move down seven units.
4. Label the point (0, -7).

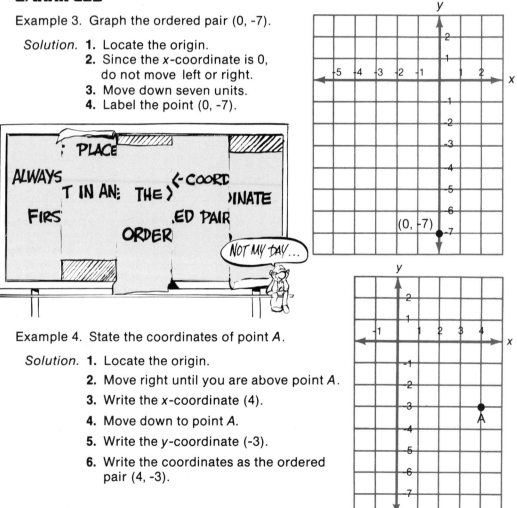

PLACE

ALWAYS

T IN AN: THE ⟩⟨-COORD

FIRS   ,ED PAIR   )INATE

ORDER

NOT MY DAY...

(0, -7)

Example 4. State the coordinates of point *A*.

Solution. **1.** Locate the origin.
2. Move right until you are above point *A*.
3. Write the *x*-coordinate (4).
4. Move down to point *A*.
5. Write the *y*-coordinate (-3).
6. Write the coordinates as the ordered pair (4, -3).

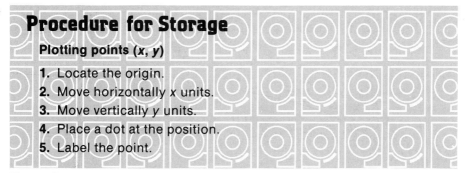

Procedure for Storage

Plotting points (x, y)

1. Locate the origin.
2. Move horizontally x units.
3. Move vertically y units.
4. Place a dot at the position.
5. Label the point.

Exercises

1. State the coordinates of each point.

A.
B.
C.
D.
E.
F.
G.
H.
I.
J.

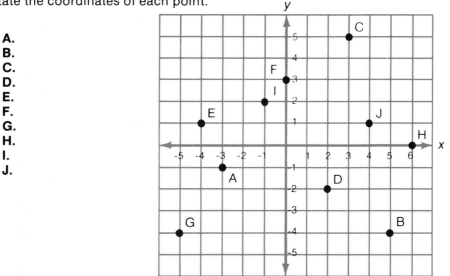

On graph paper draw a set of axes; label the axes and the origin. Then plot the following points and label them.

2. (2, 4)	**6.** (2, -9)	**10.** (-1, 3)
3. (-2, -5)	**7.** (-2, -6)	**11.** (-6, 0)
4. (5, -4)	**8.** (-4, 1)	**12.** (1, 5)
5. (3, 8)	**9.** (0, -4)	**13.** (-3, -3)

14. What are the coordinates of the origin?

15. What is true about the signs of the x- and y-coordinates for all points in quadrant I? quadrant II? quadrant III? quadrant IV?

16. What is true about all points that have the same ordinate (y-coordinate)?

Fun With Ordered Pairs

On graph paper draw a pair of axes and label them. Then label the origin. Plot the following points and read your answer.

(1, 5)	(-3, -1)	(7, 3)	(6, -1)	$(1\frac{1}{2}, 4)$
(-5, -1)	(5, -1)	(-1, 5)	(1, -3)	(-9, 1)
(-5, 1)	(6, 1)	(-1, -3)	(-7, -4)	(-8, 5)
(-5, -3)	(0, 5)	(4, -3)	(-5, 5)	(-2, 1)
(-2, -1)	(0, 4)	(-5, 3)	(3, -3)	(-2, -3)
(3, 1)	(-9, 4)	(-2, 2)	(4, -1)	(5, -5)
(-7, -2)	(-10, 1)	(6, -4)	(-4, 1)	(-4, -1)
(-2, 5)	(6, 2)	(5, 5)	(6, -3)	(2, -5)
(0, 3)	(-9, -4)	(-9, 3)	$(2\frac{1}{2}, 2)$	(7, 1)
(2, 3)	(0, -1)	(4, -5)	(1, -4)	(-5, 2)
(-8, -5)	(-5, -5)	(3, -4)	$(3\frac{1}{2}, 2)$	(-2, 3)
(3, -2)	(5, -3)	(0, -5)	(-5, -4)	(8, 1)
(4, 3)	(6, 4)	(6, -5)	(-6, -1)	(-9, -5)
(0, 2)	(6, 5)	(-4, -3)	$(4\frac{1}{2}, 4)$	(-9, 5)
(-1, 1)	(-7, -3)	(-2, -5)	(1, -2)	(3, -5)
(-7, -5)	(-5, -2)	(0, 1)	(4, -2)	(-9, 2)
(-1, -1)	(-4, -5)	(7, 5)	(-5, 4)	(-2, -2)
(1, -5)	(-8, -1)	(-2, 4)	(0, -4)	(-3, -5)
(3, -1)	(-1, -5)	(6, 3)	(1, -1)	(-8, 1)
(8, 5)	(0, -3)	(-7, -1)	(-10, 5)	(-3, 1)

RELATIONS AND FUNCTIONS

Do you know what a relation is? Look up the word *relation* in a dictionary and read the definitions. How many definitions does your dictionary give? Notice that a relation is sometimes called a relative. How many relatives do you have?

Can you think of another relation that you have with people who are not your blood relations? If you are a Christian, you are related to all other Christians through salvation in the blood of Jesus Christ. Throughout the New Testament, Christians are commanded to love and care for their Christian brothers. Think of some Scripture verses that command you to care for brothers in Christ. Then name some people who are your Christian relations and pray for them today.

In mathematics, too, *relation* means an association between two or more things. Specifically applied, a relation is any set of ordered pairs.

DEFINITION

≫**Relation:** any set of ordered pairs.

Look at the following relations. Can you tell how each pair is related?

EXAMPLES

Example 1.   {(stripes, red), (stripes, white), (stars, white)}

Example 2.   {(puppy, dog), (kitten, cat)}

Example 3.   {(Dover, Delaware), (Phoenix, Arizona), (Madison, Wisconsin)}

A common relation that exists is the relation in a grocery store between prices and items. If $A = \{x|\ x$ is all the prices in the store}, and $B = \{y|\ y$ is all the different items in the store}, a relation exists between A and B. The symbolism $\{x|\ x$ is . . . } means "the set of all x such that x is . . . ." The table below shows some of the relations that exist if $x = 30¢$.

x	y
30¢	gum
30¢	apple
30¢	yogurt

Here is a relation given in three different forms: (1) as a set of ordered pairs, (2) as a table, and (3) as a graph. A graph of a relation is the set of points in the plane that corresponds to the ordered pairs of the relation.

1. {(2, 4), (-3, 5), (2, 2), (4, -1)}

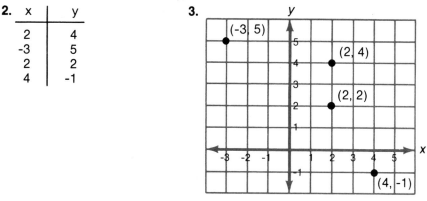

2.

x	y
2	4
-3	5
2	2
4	-1

3.

The set of first elements (*x*-coordinates) of the ordered pairs is called the domain of the relation. The domain of {(2, 4), (-3, 5), (2, 2), (4, -1)} is {2, -3, 4}. The set of second elements (*y*-coordinates) is called the range. The range of {(2, 4), (-3, 5), (2, 2), (4, -1)} is {4, 5, 2, -1}. The domain and range of a relation can be illustrated as follows.

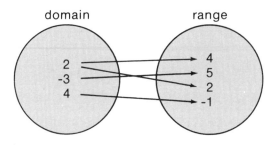

≫**Domain of a relation:** the set of first elements of the ordered pairs of a relation.

≫**Range of a relation:** the set of second elements of the ordered pairs of a relation.

This is an illustration of the relation {(2, 4), (-3, 5), (2, 2), (4, -1)}. The lines show the relation between a number in the domain and a number in the range. Notice that the 2 in the domain is mapped to the 4 and the 2 in the range. In this relation two ordered pairs have the same first element.

There is a special type of relation called a function. A function cannot have two or more of the same first elements in its ordered pairs. Every first element has to have a unique second element. *Unique* means one and only one, the only one of its kind.

≫**Function:** a relation in which each *x*-coordinate is paired with one and only one *y*-coordinate.

Our relation to Jesus Christ is unique. He is the only way of salvation (John 14:6; Acts 4:12). The only way one can get to heaven is through the blood of Jesus Christ.

A function, because it is a relation, also has a domain and a range. Furthermore, a function is graphed just like a relation. Remember, all functions are relations, but not all relations are functions.

Here are two different models of the same relation. One is a Cartesian graph; the other is a circle model showing the correspondence of the elements. They both represent the same relation. Is the relation {(3, 7), (2, 8), (1, 9)} a function? How can you tell?

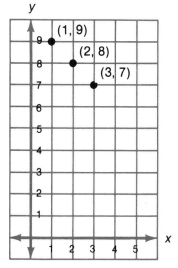

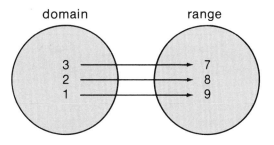

This relation is a function because each element of the domain relates to a unique element of the range.

Now look at the relation {(2, 4), (5, -2), (2, 5)}. Is it a function? How can you tell?

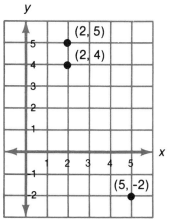

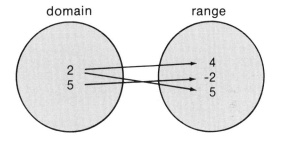

This relation is not a function because each element of the domain does not relate to a unique element of the range. In the circle model, the arrows show that 2 is paired with both 4 and 5. On the Cartesian graph, the plotted points (2, 4) and (2, 5) are on a vertical line. Whenever you see plotted points on a vertical line, you immediately know the relation is not a function because the graph reveals that two ordered pairs have the same x-coordinate.

Here is another relation to look at. Is {(3, 8), (2, 1), (4, 1)} a function? Look at the Cartesian graph. Do you see any points on a vertical line?

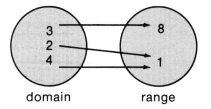

domain   range

This relation is a function because each element of the domain relates to only one element of the range. Besides, there are no points on a vertical line on the Cartesian graph.

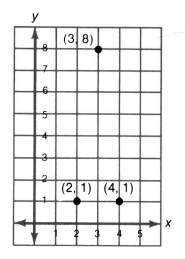

EXAMPLE

Example 4.

The local grocery store is having a sale on potato chips. One bag regularly sells for $1, but the sale price is 3 bags for $2. Plot the set of ordered pairs on a Cartesian plane. Are these ordered pairs a relation? What is the domain? What is the range? Are these ordered pairs a function?

x number of bags	cost in $ for x bags
0	0
1	1
2	2
3	2
4	3
5	4
6	4
7	5
8	6
9	6
10	7
11	8
12	8

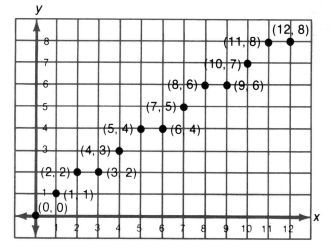

Yes, these ordered pairs are a relation since any set of ordered pairs is a relation. The domain is {0, 1, 2, 3, . . . , 11, 12} and the range is {0, 1, 2, . . . , 7, 8}. Each element of the domain relates to a unique element of the range, and there are no points on a vertical line; therefore, the relation is also a function.

Exercises

Tell which of the following are relations. Give the domain and the range of each relation. Then tell whether the relation is also a function. Make a circle model of each relation.

1. {(2, 4), (5, 9), (8, 2)}

2. {3, 7, 4, 9}

3. {(1, 6), (4, 9), (1, 3), (6, 1)}

4. {(-3, 2), (-3, 4), (7, 1), (6, 8)}

5. {(3, 7), (-4, 7), (-2, 5)}

6. {(-5, 2), (-5, 1), (2, 8), (5, 6)}

7. {(1, 3), (4, 7), (2, 3), (8, 1)}

Let A = {3, 4} and B = {1, 6, 9}.

8. Make a relation in which the domain is A and the range is B. List it in set form. Then make a circle model.

9. Make two functions in which the domain is A and the range is a subset of B. List each function in set form. Then make a circle model and map the elements.

10. There is a function called the greatest integer function symbolized by [x]. For any real number x, [x] is the largest integer less than or equal to x. Complete the following chart. Then make a circle model of this function.

x	$4\frac{1}{2}$	5	$5\frac{1}{4}$	$6\frac{3}{4}$	$-\frac{1}{2}$	$-2\frac{1}{2}$	$-5\frac{3}{4}$	$\frac{1}{3}$	$-\frac{1}{4}$
[x]	4	5		6	-1				

GRAPHING RELATIONS AND FUNCTIONS

Read Galatians 4:1-7. Paul tells the Galatian Christians that they have a special relation with Jesus Christ. Because Christ came, they are no longer under the law of sin. They are God's sons and His heirs. A Christian today has that same special relation. He is a son, and that makes him an heir.

What is your relation with Jesus Christ? Is He your personal Saviour? Does He have full control over your life—the domain and the range of it? If so, then you too are an heir, and you have a special function to perform: to show to others that you are like Christ. Because of this relationship with God, you should do what Paul says in Philippians 4:4: "Rejoice in the Lord alway: and again I say, Rejoice."

State the domain and the range of the relation {(1, 3), (1, 4), (2, 3), (2, 4)}. On a Cartesian plane plot the points indicated by each ordered pair.

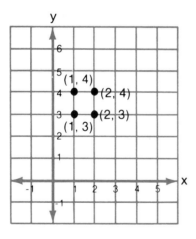

Is this relation a function? One way to tell before you graph the relation is to look at the first element of each ordered pair. If any element of the domain is used more than once, the relation is not a function. After you have graphed the relation, you can quickly tell by using the vertical line test: if any plotted points are on the same vertical line, the relation is not a function.

Procedure for Storage

Vertical Line Test for Functions

1. Imagine a vertical line at the left of the graph.
2. Move the vertical line to the right.
3. If the vertical line intersects the graph in more than one point, the relation is not a function.
4. If the vertical line does not intersect the graph in more than one point, the relation is a function.

Look at the graph on page 194, moving an imaginary vertical line across the plane from left to right. The line intersects two points when it gets to the x-coordinate 1. Immediately you know that this relation is not a function.

EXAMPLE

Example 1.   Graph $\{(x, y)\mid 1 \leq x \leq 5 \text{ and } x \text{ is an integer}, y = 3\}$.
Read this, "The set of ordered pairs (x, y) such that x is any integer from 1 to 5, including 1 and 5, and y is equal to 3."

This set is $\{(1, 3), (2, 3), (3, 3), (4, 3), (5, 3)\}$. Here is the graph for this relation.

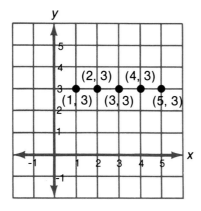

Is this relation a function? After checking by the vertical line test, you can definitely say, "Yes!"

What would happen to the graph in example 1 if the restriction about *x* as an integer were left out? If there is no restriction on *x*, you must consider *x* to be any real number. So if example 1 were stated $\{(x, y)|$ $1 \le x \le 5, y = 3\}$, the graph must contain all possible real numbers from 1 to 5. It would then look like this:

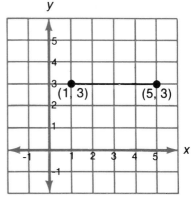

This graph indicates that every ordered pair with *x* equal to any real number from 1 to 5 and *y* equal to 3 has been graphed. The result is a line segment from 1 to 5 with an ordinate of 3.

Relations often can be described in terms of equations or inequalities.

EXAMPLES

Example 2.   Graph $\{(x, y)|y = x + 2; x = 1, 2, 3, 4\}$. Make a table of ordered pairs. Then graph the pairs.

Solution.

x	*y* = *x* + 2
1	3 = 1 + 2
2	4 = 2 + 2
3	5 = 3 + 2
4	6 = 4 + 2

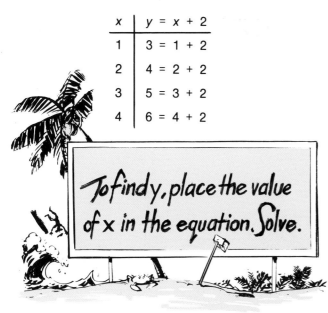

To find *y*, place the value of *x* in the equation. Solve.

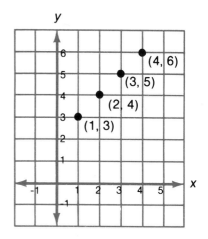

Is this relation a function?

Example 3. Graph $\{(x, y) | y = \pm \sqrt{x} \; ; \; x = 1, 4, 9\}$. Is this relation a function?

Solution.

1. Make a table to find ordered pairs. To find the y values, substitute the x values from the domain in the equation $y = \pm \sqrt{x}$. For each value of x you should find two values for y.

x	y
1	1
1	-1
4	2
4	-2
9	3
9	-3

2. Graph the set of ordered pairs $\{(1, 1), (1, -1), (4, 2), (4, -2), (9, 3), (9, -3)\}$.

3. This relation is not a function. How can you tell?

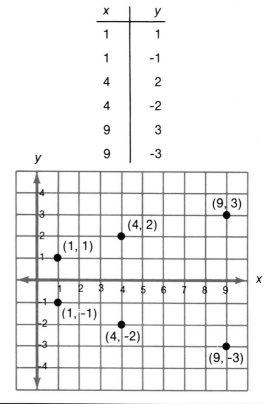

Exercises

Identify the functions.

1.
2.
3.

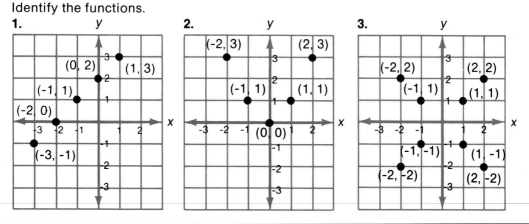

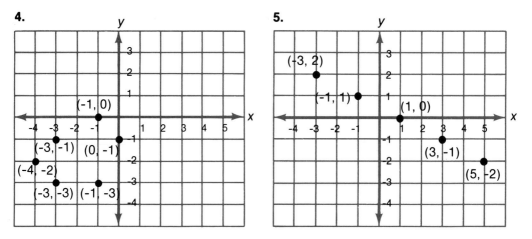

4.

5.

Make a table and graph each relation. Tell if each relation is a function.

6. $\{(x, y)|y = 3x; x = 0, 1, 3\}$

7. $\{(x, y)|y = x^2; x = -1, 0, 1, 2\}$

8. $\{(x, y)|y = x + 3; x = 0, 1, 2, 9\}$

9. $\{(x, y)|y = x^2 - 2; x = -2, 0, 2\}$

10. $\{(x, y)| x = 2; -1 \leq y \leq 3\}$

11. $\{(x, y)|0 \leq x \leq 4, -3 \leq y \leq 2, \text{ and } x \text{ is an integer}\}$

12. $\{(x, y)|y = x\}$

13. $\{(x, y)|y = 2x + 3\}$

14. $\{(x, y)|y = -x - 4\}$

15. $\{(x, y)|y = 3x\}$

LINEAR EQUATIONS AND THEIR GRAPHS

Many relations and functions can be described in terms of an equation. One such equation is the linear equation. Why is the equation called a linear equation? What does *linear* mean? *Linear* means in a line. Thus the equation is called a *linear equation* because when it is graphed all the points that satisfy the equation are in a straight line. The standard form of a linear equation is *ax + by = c, and a, b*, and *c* are any real numbers.

EXAMPLE

Example 1.   Graph $\{(x, y)\,|\,y = x + 5\}$. Label the graph with the standard form of the equation.

Solution.

1. Make a table of at least three ordered pairs. Choose any value for *x*. Then substitute the *x* value into the equation to find the corresponding value for *y*.

x	y = x + 5
0	5 = 0 + 5
1	6 = 1 + 5
2	7 = 2 + 5
-1	4 = -1 + 5

2. Plot the points.

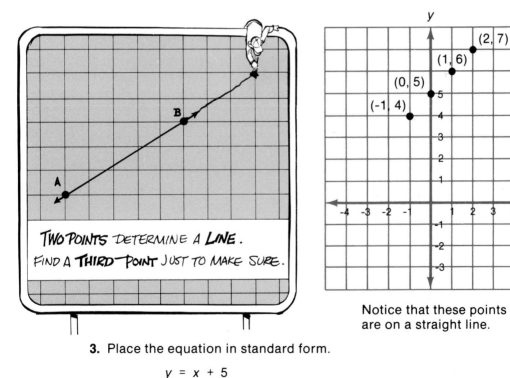

TWO POINTS DETERMINE A **LINE**.
FIND A **THIRD** POINT JUST TO MAKE SURE.

Notice that these points are on a straight line.

3. Place the equation in standard form.

$$y = x + 5$$
$$y - x = 5$$
$$-x + y = 5$$
$$x - y = -5$$

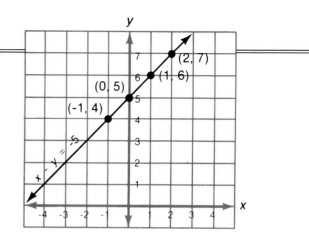

4. Connect the points on the graph to form a straight line. Label the line with the standard form of the equation.

In the graph: points labeled (-1, 4), (0, 5), (1, 6), (2, 7), line labeled $x - y = -5$

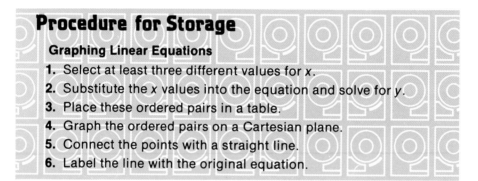

Procedure for Storage

Graphing Linear Equations

1. Select at least three different values for x.
2. Substitute the x values into the equation and solve for y.
3. Place these ordered pairs in a table.
4. Graph the ordered pairs on a Cartesian plane.
5. Connect the points with a straight line.
6. Label the line with the original equation.

EXAMPLE

Example 2.   Graph $x + 3y = 4$.

Solution.

1. Solve the equation for y.

$$x + 3y = 4$$
$$3y = -x + 4$$
$$y = \frac{-x + 4}{3}$$

2. Make a table of ordered pairs.

x	$y = \dfrac{-x + 4}{3}$
0	$\dfrac{4}{3} = \dfrac{0 + 4}{3}$
4	$0 = \dfrac{-4 + 4}{3}$
1	$1 = \dfrac{-1 + 4}{3}$

3. Graph these ordered pairs, connect them with a straight line, and label the line with the standard form of the equation.

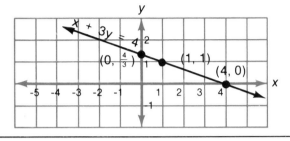

≫**Y-intercept:** The point where the line crosses, or intersects, the *y*-axis.

What is the *y*-intercept in Example 2? What is the *x* value of every *y*-intercept? How could you find the *y*-intercept if you were given the equation of the line?

Exercises

For each equation make a table of at least three ordered pairs. Then graph the equation on its own set of axes. Give the *y*-intercept for each of these graphs.

1. $2x + y = 5$

2. $x - y = 6$

3. $3x + 2y = -2$

4. $x = 6y$

5. $x - 3y = 9$

6. $4x + y = 1$

7. $x - 2y = 18$

8. $5x + 2y = 10$

9. $x + y = 8$

10. $2x - 4y = 16$

Graph each set of equations on the same set of axes. Label each line with the standard form of the linear equation.

11. $y = 3x + 2$
    $y = 3x - 6$

12. $y = -2x - 1$
    $y = -2x$

13. $y = 4x + 2$
    $y = \frac{1}{4}x - 3$

14. $y = x + 4$
    $y = -x - 5$

15. $y = x + 1$
    $y = 2x + 1$
    $y = -2x + 1$
    $y = -\frac{1}{2}x + 1$

What do the equations in exercise 15 have in common?

Swiss Family Bernoulli

The Bernoulli Family

The Bernoulli family of Switzerland (who escaped from Belgium under religious persecution from the Catholics) contributed greatly to the field of mathematics. In three generations the family produced eight mathematicians. Two of these mathematicians, Jakob and Johann Bernoulli, made calculus practical for the common man.

Although his father intended for him to study theology, Jakob Bernoulli (I) (1654 - 1705)

favored mathematics and astronomy. At age twenty, Jakob took the chair of math at the University of Basel, which he held until his death in 1705. His accomplishments included the development of differential and integral calculus, discovery of the isochrone, implementation of polar coordinates, the Bernoulli distribution, and the Bernoulli theorem. Jakob's work in differential and integral calculus is applied today in electrical engineering, and the Bernoulli theorem is widely used in statistics and insurance studies.

Johann Bernoulli (I) (1667 - 1748), like his brother, did not follow his father's plan for him to run the family business but sought instead a degree in medicine. After obtaining his M.A. degree, he left medicine to study mathematics. At age thirty, Johann took his first post as professor at Groningen University, leaving eight years later to succeed his brother at Basel. Johann wrote on various mathematical topics, including optical phenomena, analytical trigonometry, and exponential calculus. In 1696 he compiled the first calculus textbook.

Nikolaus Bernoulli (I) (1687 - 1759), a nephew of Jakob (I) and Johann (I), worked mainly in the fields of probability theory and infinite series. Encouraging Nikolaus to study mathematics were his friends Isaac Newton, Edmund Halley, and Gottfried Leibniz.

Besides his expertise in mathematics, Nikolaus was a lawyer. From 1722 to 1731 he was a professor of logic, and in 1731 he changed to a professorship in law.

Like their father, the sons of Johann (I) all became famous mathematicians and scientists. Nikolaus (II) (1695-1726) wrote about curves, differential equations, and probability. Daniel Bernoulli (1700-82),

the most famous son, is well known for his work in probability, astronomy, physics, hydrodynamics, and calculus. Johann (II) (1710-90), who originally studied law, spent his later years as a professor of mathematics at the University of Basel. He received the distinguished Paris Prize three times for his outstanding work in physics. Johann (II)'s sons, Johann (III) (1744-1807) and Jakob (II) (1759-89), also were great mathematicians.

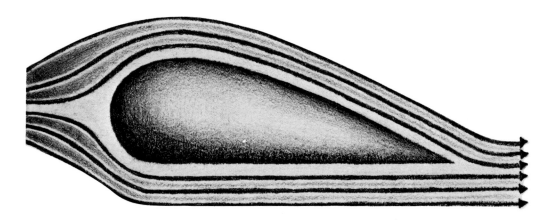

INTERCEPTS AND SLOPE OF A LINE

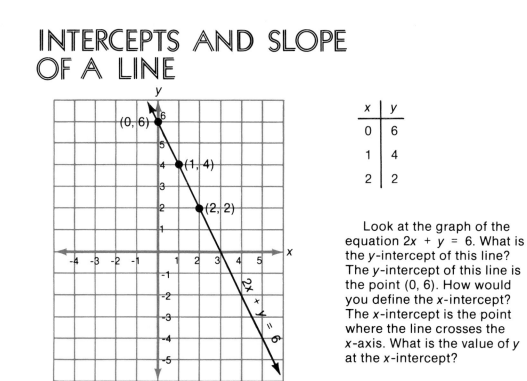

x	y
0	6
1	4
2	2

Look at the graph of the equation $2x + y = 6$. What is the y-intercept of this line? The y-intercept of this line is the point (0, 6). How would you define the x-intercept? The x-intercept is the point where the line crosses the x-axis. What is the value of y at the x-intercept?

REMEMBER THE **Y-INTERCEPT** IS THE POINT WHERE THE LINE CROSSES THE **Y-AXIS**

EXAMPLE

Example 1. Find the x-intercept of the line described by the equation $2x + y = 6$.

Solution. Since the value of y must be 0 at the x-intercept, simply substitute 0 for y and solve for x.

$$2x + y = 6$$
$$2x + 0 = 6$$
$$2x = 6$$
$$x = 3$$

So the x-intercept is the point (3, 0).

When you hear the word *slope*, what do
you think of? If you are like most people, you
probably think of a hill especially for skiing. If
you are a snow skier, you know that the slope
of a hill affects how fast you go down the hill.
The steeper the slope, the faster your
descent.

Actually, slope is any variation from the
horizontal. In math any line other than a
vertical line will have slope.

How is the slope of a ski run measured?
Let's try a beginner hill. The top of the hill, *A*,
is 2 units high. When you get to *B*, your
vertical change will be -2. Your horizontal
change will be +12. To find the slope, divide
the vertical change (-2) by the horizontal
change (+12).

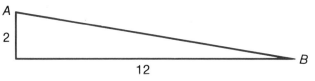

$$\frac{\text{vertical change}}{\text{horizontal change}} = \frac{-2}{12} = \frac{-1}{6}$$

DEFINITION ≫**Slope of a line:** the change in *y* values of two
points divided by the change in *x* values of those
two points, i.e., the vertical change divided by the
horizontal change.

In the following formula for finding the slope of a line going through two
points (x_1, y_1) and (x_2, y_2), the slope is indicated by *m*.

$$m = \frac{y_2 - y_1}{x_2 - x_1} \quad \text{if } x_2 - x_1 \neq 0.$$

EXAMPLE

Example 2.   Find the slope of the line that passes through (1, 4) and (2, 2).

Solution.

1. Find the vertical change (change in *y*) between the two points. Notice that if you start at (1, 4) and move to (2, 2) you move down two units. So the vertical change is -2.

2. Find the horizontal change (change in *x*). The horizontal change is one unit to the right. So the horizontal change is 1.

3. Therefore, the slope of the line is

$$\frac{\text{vertical change (rise)}}{\text{horizontal change (run)}} = \frac{-2}{+1} = -2$$

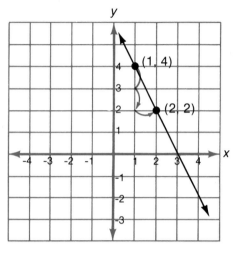

If you had started with the point (2, 2) and moved to (1, 4) to find the slope, the vertical change would have been two units up and the horizontal change would have been one unit left.
So

$$\frac{\text{vertical change}}{\text{horizontal change}} = \frac{2}{-1} = -2$$

The slope is the same. The slope between any two points on a given line will always be the same.

Different notations for slope	
m	$\dfrac{y_2 - y_1}{x_2 - x_1}$
$\dfrac{\text{vertical change}}{\text{horizontal change}}$	$\dfrac{\triangle y}{\triangle x}$
$\dfrac{\text{change in } y}{\text{change in } x}$	$\dfrac{\text{rise}}{\text{run}}$

Sometimes you will have to look at the graph of a line to find the slope. You should also be able to determine the slope of a line if you do not have a graph but are given two points on the line.

EXAMPLES

Example 3.   Find the slope of the line passing through (4, 1) and (2, -3).

Solution.
1. Label the points $(x_1, y_1) = (4, 1)$ and $(x_2, y_2) = (2, -3)$.
2. Substitute values into the equation.
3. Solve.

$$m = \frac{y_2 - y_1}{x_2 - x_1} = \frac{-3 - 1}{2 - 4} = \frac{-4}{-2} = 2$$

So the slope of this line is 2.

Example 4.   Find the slope of the line passing through (3, 4) and (-1, 5).

Solution.
$$(x_1, y_1) = (3, 4) \qquad (x_2, y_2) = (-1, 5)$$

$$m = \frac{y_2 - y_1}{x_2 - x_1} = \frac{5 - 4}{-1 - 3} = \frac{1}{-4} = \frac{-1}{4}$$

USE **X** VALUES IN THE DENOMINATOR IN THE SAME ORDER THAT **Y** VALUES ARE USED IN THE NUMERATOR.

A RATHER OUT OF THE WAY SIGN, EH?

Finding the Slope of a Line

If you are given two points, label them point (x_1, y_1) and point (x_2, y_2). Then find the slope by using

$$m = \frac{y_2 - y_1}{x_2 - x_1}$$

if $x_2 - x_1 \neq 0$.

or

If you are given the graph of a linear equation, count the vertical change and the horizontal change. Then divide the vertical change by the horizontal change.

In all these examples the lines have been diagonal. Can you think of any lines that are not diagonal? There are two types of lines: the horizontal line and the vertical line. What is the slope of these lines?

EXAMPLES

Example 5.   Given the two points (2, 4) and (7, 4), determine the slope.

Solution.

$$m = \frac{y_2 - y_1}{x_2 - x_1} = \frac{4 - 4}{7 - 2} = \frac{0}{5} = 0$$

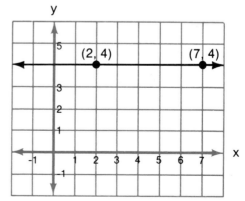

So the slope is 0. The slope of a horizontal line is always 0 because there is no variation from the horizontal. Now, does a vertical line have slope?

Example 6.   Given points (3, -2) and (3, 4), determine the slope.

Solution.

$$m = \frac{y_2 - y_1}{x_2 - x_1} = \frac{4 - (-2)}{3 - 3} = \frac{6}{0}$$

Hold it! Division by 0 is undefined; therefore, the slope of a vertical line is undefined. Thus, vertical lines have no slope.

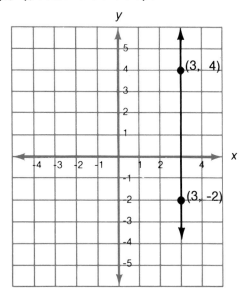

Exercises

Find the slope and *y*-intercept of each graph.

1.

2.

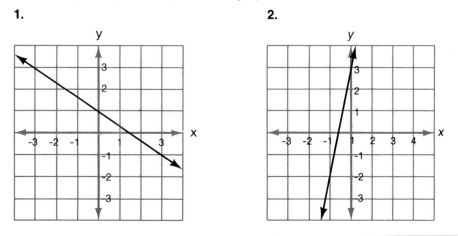

3.

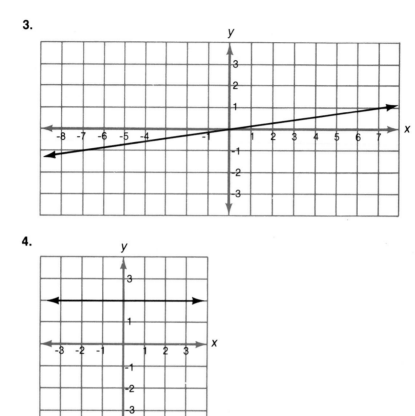

4.

Find the slope of the line going through the given points.

5. (2, 5) (3, 9)

6. (-1, 8) (3, 4)

7. (-2, -5) (1, 0)

8. (3, 6) (-4, -1)

9. (2, 7) (3, 7)

10. (-4, -6) (-3, -2)

11. (2, 5) (2, -3)

12. (5, 7) (1, -3)

13. (-2, 4) (-5, -2)

14. (3, 6) (1, 9)

15. (-4, -1) (-1, 7)

16. What is the slope of a vertical line?

SLOPE-INTERCEPT FORM OF A LINEAR EQUATION

The Bible tells us that the Devil takes many forms to deceive us. Satan appeared in Genesis as a beautiful serpent to tempt Eve. Other parts of the Bible describe the Devil as a shining angel (e.g., Isa. 14:12-15). What other forms of Satan does the Bible record? Give references that describe these forms. What forms does Satan assume when he comes to tempt you to sin?

Equations also have different forms that you must learn to recognize. You have already learned one form of a linear equation: $ax + by = c$. In this lesson you will learn how to change a linear equation into another form, called the *slope-intercept form*. It is the same equation; only its form has been changed by rearranging the terms in order to isolate y on the left side of the equals sign. In the slope-intercept form of the equation, which is $y = mx + b$, m is the slope of the line, and b is the y value of the y-intercept of the line. Do you remember what the y-intercept is?

EXAMPLES

Example 1. Write $2x + y = 4$ in slope-intercept form. Identify m and b.

Solution.
$2x + y = 4$	**1.** State the original equation.
$2x - 2x + y = 4 - 2x$	**2.** To solve for y, subtract $2x$ from both sides.
$y = 4 - 2x$ $y = -2x + 4$	**3.** Rearrange the right side so that the equation will be in the slope-intercept form $y = mx + b$.
$y = mx + b$ $m = -2$ $b = 4$	**4.** Compare the equation to the general form and identify the values of m and b.

Example 2. Write $3x + 2y = 6$ in slope-intercept form.

Solution.
$3x + 2y = 6$ $2y = 6 - 3x$	**1.** Subtract $3x$ from both sides to solve for y.
$2y = -3x + 6$	**2.** Rearrange the right side so that the term with x is first.
$\dfrac{2y}{2} = \dfrac{-3x}{2} + \dfrac{6}{2}$	**3.** Divide both sides by 2 so y is alone.
$y = \dfrac{-3x}{2} + 3$ $m = \dfrac{-3}{2}$ $b = 3$	**4.** Compare this equation with $y = mx + b$ to find m and b.

Example 3. Write $5x - y = 7$ in slope-intercept form. Identify the values of m and b. Make a table of at least three ordered pair solutions. Then graph the equation.

Solution.

$$5x - y = 7$$

$$-y = 7 - 5x$$

$$-y = -5x + 7$$

$$\frac{-y}{-1} = \frac{-5x}{-1} + \frac{7}{-1}$$

$$y = 5x - 7$$

$$m = 5$$

$$b = -7$$

x	y
0	-7
1	-2
2	3

1. Write the equation in slope-intercept form by solving for y.

2. Notice that b is negative here. Do you know why?

3. Make a table of solutions for $y = 5x - 7$.

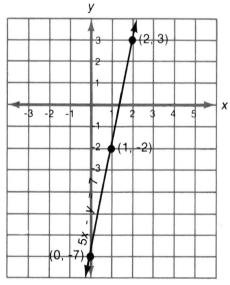

4. Graph the equation.

ALWAYS LABEL THE GRAPH WITH THE GIVEN EQUATION

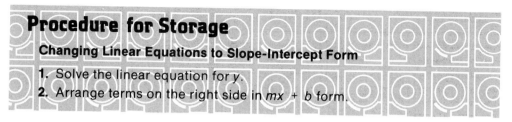

Procedure for Storage
Changing Linear Equations to Slope-Intercept Form
1. Solve the linear equation for y.
2. Arrange terms on the right side in $mx + b$ form.

EXAMPLE

Example 4. Write $y = 3$ in slope-intercept form. Identify m and b. Graph the equation. Does this equation describe a function?

Solution. **1.** This equation is already in slope-intercept form because it is solved for y.

2. If you compare $y = 3$ with $y = mx + b$, you notice that there is no x variable in the equation $y = 3$. We could rewrite $y = 3$ as $y = 0 \cdot x + 3$. So $m = 0$ and $b = 3$.

3. Make a table so you can graph $y = 3$. No matter what x is equal to, y is always equal to 3. This equation $y = 3$ is called a constant equation, because the value of y is constantly 3.

x	y
0	3
1	3
2	3

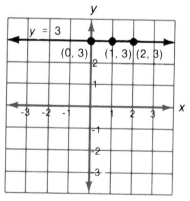

Now graph these points, connect them to form a line, and label the line. (0,3) (1,3) (2, 3)

4. Use the vertical line test to tell if this equation describes a function. Since the vertical line touches the graph of $y = 3$ at only one point at a time, the relation is a function.

Exercises

Write each equation in slope-intercept form. Give the values of *m* and *b*. Make a table, graph the equation, and label the line. State whether the equation describes a function.

1. $3x + y = 5$

2. $x - y = -6$

3. $2x + y = -2$

4. $x + y = 0$

5. $x = 4$

6. $x = -3$

7. $4x + 2y = 9$

8. $y = -2$

9. $y = 4$

10. $2x - 3y = 12$

11. $x + y = 8$

12. $3(x + 2) + y = 8$

13. $2x - y = 9$

14. $3x + 9y = 18$

15. $x + 2y = 6$

16. $3x + 7y = 21$

17. $x + 5y = -25$

18. $2x - y = 12$

19. $x + 7y = 14$

20. $8x - 3y = 9$

21. $x + y = 4$

22. $5x + y = 2$

23. $28x - 7y = -77$

24. $18x + 6y = 3$

25. $6(x - 10) + 4y = -20$

USING SLOPE-INTERCEPT FORM TO GRAPH A LINEAR EQUATION

You have already learned how to graph a linear equation by first making a table of ordered pairs, then plotting the points, and finally connecting these points to form a line. In this section you will learn how to use the slope-intercept form of an equation to quickly and easily graph the line. Since the equation $y = mx + b$ gives the *y* value of the *y*-intercept (*b*), you can immediately plot the point (0, *b*). Then you can use the slope *m* to find a second point.

EXAMPLE

Example 1.   Graph $y = \frac{1}{2}x + 4$.

Solution.

1. Locate the *y*-intercept. Since *b* = 4, the *y*-intercept is (0, 4).
2. Using the slope $\frac{1}{2}$, find another point on the line.
   a. From (0, 4), the *y*-intercept, move up one unit.
   b. From this point move right two units.
   c. Place a dot at this point.
   d. Label the point (2, 5).

REMEMBER THAT **SLOPE** IS $\dfrac{\text{VERTICAL CHANGE}}{\text{HORIZONTAL CHANGE}}$

PLEASE... DON'T ASK

3. Connect the points and label the line with the equation.

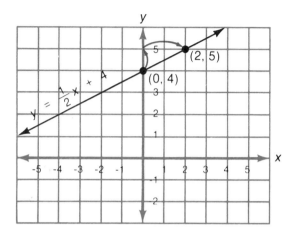

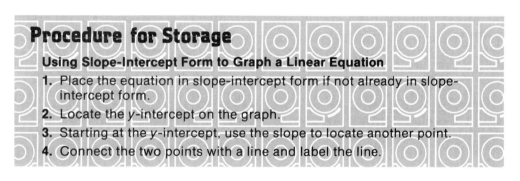

Procedure for Storage

Using Slope-Intercept Form to Graph a Linear Equation

1. Place the equation in slope-intercept form if not already in slope-intercept form.
2. Locate the y-intercept on the graph.
3. Starting at the y-intercept, use the slope to locate another point.
4. Connect the two points with a line and label the line.

EXAMPLES

Example 2. Graph $2x + y = -3$.

Solution.

1. Write the equation in slope-intercept form.
$$2x + y = -3$$
$$y = -3 - 2x$$
$$y = -2x - 3$$

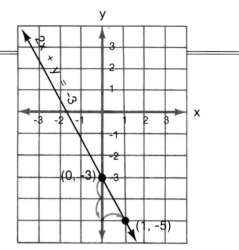

2. Locate the y-intercept (0, -3).

3. The slope is -2, or $\frac{-2}{1}$. Starting at the y-intercept, move down two units and right one unit. (Do you know why?)

4. Connect the points and label the line.

Example 3. Graph $2x + 3y = 6$.

Solution.
$$2x + 3y = 6$$
$$3y = -2x + 6$$
$$y = \frac{-2}{3}x + 2$$
$$m = \frac{-2}{3}$$
$$b = 2$$

The y-intercept is (0, 2). Beginning at (0, 2), find another point using the slope.

Exercises

Graph each linear equation by using its slope-intercept form.

1. $y = 3x + 4$

2. $y = \frac{-1}{3}x - 2$

3. $y = -x + 1$

4. $2x + y = 5$

5. $x - 3y = -6$

6. $3x + 2y = 8$

7. $x + y = 12$

8. $3x - y = -9$

9. $2x + y = 8$

10. $\frac{1}{2}y = x - 3$

11. $3x - 4y = -16$

12. $x + 5y = -20$

13. $6x - y = 12$

14. $y = 4x - 7$

15. $7x + 2y = 16$

16. $3x + y - 8 = 0$

17. $8x + y + 10 = 0$

18. $y = 4$

19. $y = \frac{-1}{4}x + 5$

20. $5x - 2y = 10$

Unscramble the mathematical words in the list below. Then write each word in the blank before the numbered phrase to which it is "loosely" connected.

xesa	rweop
rufaoml	thesynpuoe
sotor	tsrme
fifticoence	ebcu
luerr	bumrne
edegr	gtavenie
ngsi	sttbiteues
nepla	

MIND OVER MATH

_____ **1.** The effect that the dentist desires when he paralyzes the gums

_____ **2.** What a man gets when he graduates from college

_____ **3.** To work together effectively

_____ **4.** Sugar

_____ **5.** A board that gives guidance along the road

____ _____ **6.** Tall coffee pot and a rope used by a hangman

_____ **7.** Baby's bottle food

_____ **8.** No

_____ **9.** A machine with propellers

_____ **10.** Cutting tools that have sharp heads

_____ **11.** Queen or king

_____ **12.** The conditions of an agreement

_____ **13.** Saccharine

_____ **14.** An exponent

_____ **15.** The underground portion of a plant

FINDING THE EQUATION OF A LINE GIVEN A POINT AND THE SLOPE

In previous sections of this chapter, you learned how to graph linear equations. Beginning with this lesson, you will be given certain "facts" from which you must determine the equation of a line. You should be able to find the equation of a line if you know

1. the slope and *y*-intercept of the line,

2. the slope and a point of the line, or

3. two points of the line.

Using the slope and *y*-intercept to find the equation of the line is quite simple. Just substitute the given values for the appropriate variables in the slope-intercept form of the equation.

EXAMPLES

Example 1. Find the equation of the line with slope $\frac{2}{3}$ and *y*-intercept (0, 5).

Solution. Since $m = \frac{2}{3}$ and $b = 5$, simply insert these values into the equation $y = mx + b$. The slope-intercept form of the equation is $y = \frac{2}{3}x + 5$.

Example 2. Write the equation of the line with slope 3 and *y*-intercept (0, -2).

Solution. $y = 3x - 2$ Why is this correct?

So you see that determining the equation of a line from the slope and the *y*-intercept is simply a matter of substitution. You can also determine an equation of a line if you are given the slope and any point on the line.

EXAMPLE

Example 3. Find the equation of the line that passes through the point (1, 5) and has slope 3.

Solution.

1. Let some arbitrary point (x, y) be the second point and $(1, 5)$ be the first point. Substitute 1 for x_1 and 5 for y_1 in the slope formula.

$$m = \frac{y_2 - y_1}{x_2 - x_1}$$

$$m = \frac{y - 5}{x - 1}$$

Since the slope m is 3, substitute 3 in the equation too.

$$3 = \frac{y - 5}{x - 1}$$

2. Now clear the fraction from the equation. Do you remember how to clear an equation of fractions? Multiply both sides of the equation by the common denominator, which is $x - 1$ for this equation. Then rearrange the terms to slope-intercept form of the equation.

$$\frac{y - 5}{x - 1} = 3$$

$$\frac{y - 5}{x - 1}(x - 1) = 3(x - 1)$$

$$y - 5 = 3x - 3$$

$$y = 3x + 2$$

3. The slope-intercept form of the equation of the line going through (1, 5) with slope 3 is

$$y = 3x + 2.$$

Another way to write the equation of the line given a point and the y-intercept is by using the point-slope form of the equation. The point-slope form of the equation is $y - y_1 = m(x - x_1)$. The slope is m, and the coordinates of the given point are (x_1, y_1).

Look again at example 3. Substitute the values for m and (x_1, y_1) in the point-slope form of the equation to get $y - 5 = 3(x - 1)$. Now change this equation to slope-intercept form.

$$y - 5 = 3x - 3$$
$$y = 3x + 2$$

EXAMPLES

Example 4. Find the equation of the line that has slope -3 and goes through the point (2, 7).

Solution. $m = -3$
$(x_1, y_1) = (2, 7)$
$y - y_1 = m(x - x_1)$
$y - 7 = -3(x - 2)$
$y - 7 = -3x + 6$
$y = -3x + 13$

Example 5. Write the equation of the line that has slope $\frac{1}{2}$ and goes through the point (-3, 2).

Solution. $y - y_1 = m(x - x_1)$

$y - 2 = \frac{1}{2}[x - (-3)]$

$y - 2 = \frac{1}{2}(x + 3)$

$y - 2 = \frac{1}{2}x + \frac{3}{2}$

$y = \frac{1}{2}x + \frac{7}{2}$

Example 6. Write the equation of the line that has slope 0 and goes through the point (-1, 6).

Solution. $y - y_1 = m(x - x_1)$
$y - 6 = 0[x - (-1)]$
$y - 6 = 0$
$y = 6$ This is a horizontal line.

Procedure for Storage

Writing an Equation from Given Information

1. Given the slope and the y-intercept, substitute the appropriate values in the equation $y = mx + b$.
2. Given the slope and a point, substitute the appropriate values in the equation $y - y_1 = m(x - x_1)$. Then simplify to the slope-intercept form of the equation.

Exercises

Write the equation of the line given the slope and the y-intercept.

1. $m = 3,\ b = \frac{1}{4}$

2. $m = \frac{-1}{3},\ b = 3$

3. $m = -5,\ b = 10$

4. $m = 6,\ b = \frac{-1}{2}$

5. $m = 0,\ b = 7$

6. $m = 3,\ b = 2$

7. $m = 9,\ b = \frac{-2}{3}$

8. $m = 4,\ b = -9$

9. $m = \frac{1}{4},\ b = 8$

10. $m = \frac{-3}{2},\ b = -4$

Write the equation of the line given the slope and a point through which the line passes.

11. $\frac{-1}{4}$, (1,6)

12. 8, (-3,2)

13. $\frac{3}{5}$, (0,4)

14. -3, (2,-5)

15. $\frac{-1}{8}$, (-9,0)

16. $\frac{1}{4}$, (3,7)

17. -4, (-4,1)

18. $\frac{5}{3}$, (-3,-1)

19. $\frac{4}{5}$, (-5,2)

20. $\frac{9}{4}$, (3,0)

FINDING THE EQUATION OF A LINE GIVEN TWO POINTS

Now that you know how to determine a linear equation by using (1) the slope and the y-intercept of a line and (2) the slope and a point on the line, you will learn how to determine an equation given any two points on the line.

If you know that a line passes through the points (1, 3) and (4, -2), can you find the equation of this line? Is there any way you can simplify this problem so that you know the slope and a point? First, determine the slope of the line containing the two points by using the equation for determining slope. Then you can use the point-slope equation to find the equation of the line.

$$m = \frac{y_2 - y_1}{x_2 - x_1}$$

$$y - y_1 = m(x - x_1)$$

EXAMPLE

Example 1.   Write the equation of the line that passes through the points (1, 3) and (4, -2).

Solution.

1. First find the slope of the line.

$$m = \frac{y_2 - y_1}{x_2 - x_1}$$

$$m = \frac{-2 - 3}{4 - 1}$$

$$m = \frac{-5}{3}$$

2. By using the point-slope form of the equation and the point (1,3), you can now find the equation of this line. Substitute values for the point and for m in the point-slope form of the equation. Solve.

$$y - y_1 = m(x - x_1)$$

$$y - 3 = \frac{-5}{3}(x - 1)$$

$$y - 3 = \frac{-5}{3}x + \frac{5}{3}$$

$$y = \frac{-5}{3}x + \frac{14}{3}$$

Now do the same procedure, but use the point (4, -2). Do you get the same equation? One method of checking your work is by substituting values for the unused ordered pair and evaluating the expression. If the resulting equation is true, the linear equation is probably correct.

EXAMPLE

Example 2. Write the equation of the line passing through (-5, 2) and (3, -4). What is the y-intercept?

Solution.

1. Find the slope.

$$m = \frac{y_2 - y_1}{x_2 - x_1}$$

$$m = \frac{-4 - 2}{3 - (-5)}$$

$$m = \frac{-6}{8}$$

$$m = \frac{-3}{4}$$

2. Choose one of the given points and use the point-slope form of the equation to determine the slope-intercept form of the equation.

$$y - y_1 = m(x - x_1)$$

$$y + 4 = \frac{-3}{4}(x - 3)$$

$$y + 4 = \frac{-3}{4}x + \frac{9}{4}$$

Check. $$y = \frac{-3}{4}x - \frac{7}{4}$$

3. To check, substitute (-5, 2) into the equation and see if a true statement occurs.

$$2 = \left(\frac{-3}{4}\right)(-5) - \frac{7}{4}$$

$$2 = \frac{15}{4} - \frac{7}{4}$$

$$2 = \frac{8}{4}$$

$$2 = 2$$

4. The y-intercept is $(0, \frac{-7}{4})$.

Example 3. Write the equation of the line passing through (7, 4) and (7, 2).

Solution.

$$m = \frac{y_2 - y_1}{x_2 - x_1}$$

$$m = \frac{4 - 2}{7 - 7}$$

$$m = \frac{2}{0}$$

The slope is undefined. Therefore, the line must be a vertical line. To write the equation of a vertical line, set x equal to the x value of the ordered pairs. So the equation of this line is $x = 7$.

Procedure for Storage

Writing an Equation from Given Information

1. Given two points through which a line passes, find the slope of the line.
2. Substitute values in the point-slope form of the equation.
3. State the resulting equation in slope-intercept form.

Exercises

Write each equation and give the y-intercept for the line that passes through the given points.

1. (2,8) (-3,1)   **6.** (1,3) (-3,6)   **11.** (2,7) (1,8)

2. (0,4) (2,7)   **7.** (-4,2) (7,3)   **12.** (-3,4) (2,1)

3. (-1,-9) (4,4)   **8.** (1,3) (2,5)   **13.** (-5,-4) (3,-4)

4. (3,-1) (-10,-8)   **9.** (-3,2) (10,-6)   **14.** (2,0) (6,-5)

5. (1,4) (0,0)   **10.** (13,9) (-1,16)   **15.** (1,3) (-4,-9)

Write the equation of the line with the given information.

16. $m = 3$; $b = 8$

17. $m = \frac{1}{4}$; point (5,7)

18. $m = \frac{2}{5}$; point (-1,-3)

19. points (4,2) and (-3,9)

20. points (2,-8) and (-6,-1)

Fill in the grid with the number that answers each statement or expression.

ACROSS

1. 36 plus days in nine regular years

5. cups in 82 gallons

9. digits > 5

10. White House street number

11. 2^9

13. date the *Eagle* landed on the moon

14. date Lincoln was shot

18. Fahrenheit temperature at which water boils

20. square inches in a square yard

23. feet in $\frac{3}{4}$ mile

26. sum of all primes < 100

27. pounds in a ton

DOWN

1. degrees in a circle

2. normal body temperature on Celsius scale

3. days in a lunar month

4. middle year of the twentieth century

5. 37^2 minus minutes in four hours

6. inches in a yard

7. base of decimal system

8. America's age in 1976

12. 31 in the binary system

15. 1020 subtracted from feet in a mile

16. UCDB on the telephone

17. product of two primes < 40 whose difference is 34

19. centimeters in a meter

21. years in two decades

22. eight dozen

24. degrees in a right angle

25. seconds in a minute

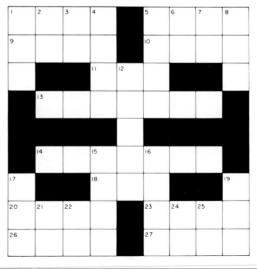

COMPUTERS IN SCIENCE

At one time computers were solely the dominion of scientists because they were so complex that only scientists understood how to use them. Though some of today's computers are simple enough for a child to operate, scientists still use computers to control experiments, analyze data, and perform multitudes of calculations.

Manned spacecraft carry many computers that control almost every function of the craft. Computers monitor both the inside and the outside of the ship. If the temperature of the cabin rises too high, a computer increases the airflow to lower it. If the oxygen content of the cabin's atmosphere drops too low, a computer increases the oxygen flow so that the astronauts will not suffocate. When a rocket engine is fired or a satellite is deployed, a computer gives directions to the equipment.

Scientists also use computers to interpret information from satellites. Satellites send information about the earth and other planets back to bases on earth. By processing and analyzing this information with computers, scientists have found such things as dry riverbeds under the shifting sands of the Sahara Desert. Computers analyze information from weather satellites to help meteorologists predict the weather. In addition, computers aboard space probes, such as *Mariner* or *Voyager*, have sent back to earth photographs of the surfaces of several planets.

Scientists use computers to control very precise conditions in experiments. At Lawrence Livermore Laboratories in Berkely, California, scientists use many computers to control an experimental laser-fusion device called SHIVA. A computer-controlled mechanism fires a small glass pellet that contains certain special gases into the blue chamber shown in the model on page 227. Once the pellet is on its way, another computer fires a very powerful laser. Computers control the journey of the light beam on its way to the blue chamber. At the chamber, the computers focus the beam of light on the pellet. This immense amount of energy causes the gas atoms to collide with such force that they fuse together, producing energy, new substances, and important information for scientists to use.

Computers also help scientists test their theories. A scientist builds a mathematical model of a physical process and then uses the computer to see how closely this model agrees with the data he gathers. For example, he may try to simulate the effects of volcanic dust on the weather.

Computer simulations can represent situations of any size. Weather problems may require simulating conditions over the entire planet. At the other extreme, scientists simulate collisions between the building blocks of matter, called fundamental particles. Using the information they gain from simulations, scientists can more accurately control these interactions in experiments. By helping to explore the nature of matter, computers may eventually provide us with solutions to some of our pressing energy problems.

DIRECT VARIATION

In our spiritual lives we should strive to be constant, like Jesus Christ. Hebrews 13:8 says, "Jesus Christ the same yesterday, and to day, and for ever." Read Hebrews 13:9 and Ephesians 4:14. What do these verses tell us about our Christian lives?

Look at the following table. What value for y should come next?

x	y
0	0
1	3
2	6
3	9
4	

This table might represent the amount of commission earned when you make $3 on each item sold. If you sell three items, you earn $9 commission. What equation decribes this relation? Since the y value in the table is three times the x value, x and y vary directly. The equation would be $y = 3x$. This equation is a special form of the slope-intercept equation in which b equals 0. Whenever one variable is a multiple of another variable, we say the variables are in direct variation to each other.

DEFINITION ≫**Direct variation:** a linear function in which one variable is a multiple of the other variable.

The general equation of a direct variation is $y = kx$, where k is the *constant of variation.* Don't forget! A direct variation must be in the form $y = mx$. So $y = 2x + 4$ is not a direct variation. Why?

Another example of direct variation is the perimeter of a square. It varies directly with (is directly proportional to) the length of one side of the square.

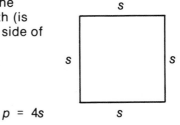

$p = 4s$

EXAMPLES

Example 1. Read the table. Is y a multiple of x? What is the constant of variation? Write an equation expressing the relation.

Solution. Yes, y is a multiple of x since each y is seven times the x value. The constant of variation is 7. The equation is $y = 7x$.

x	y
0	0
1	7
2	14
3	21

Example 2. Find k if y varies directly with x, and $y = 6$ when $x = 3$. Write the equation that expresses the variation.

Solution. Write the general form $y = kx$. Substitute the values of x and y.

$$6 = 3k$$
$$\frac{6}{3} = k$$
$$2 = k$$

The direct variation then is $y = 2x$.

Example 3. If y varies directly with x, and $y = 8$ when $x = \frac{4}{5}$, find y when $x = 3$.

Solution. **1.** Find the constant of variation.

$$y = kx$$
$$8 = k \left(\frac{4}{5} \right)$$
$$\frac{5}{4} (8) = k$$
$$10 = k$$

2. To find y when $x = 3$, substitute the values for k and x into the equation.

$$y = kx$$
$$y = 10 \cdot 3$$
$$y = 30$$

Exercises

Write the equation that describes the variation indicated by each table. Graph the equation on a Cartesian plane.

1.

x	y
0	0
1	6
2	12
3	18

2.

x	y
0	0
1	10
2	20
3	30

3.

x	y
0	0
1	2
2	4
3	6

4.

x	y
0	0
1	0.5
2	1
3	1.5

5. The formula for pressure under water is $p = 0.433h$. Is this a direct variation? If it is, what is the constant of variation? Make a table of at least 3 values.

6. The formula for the circumference of a circle is $c = \pi d$. What is the constant of variation in this formula?

If y varies directly with x, find the value of k when x and y have the value given. Then write the equation that expresses the variation.

7. $x = 9$ $y = 18$

8. $x = 5$ $y = 1/2$

9. $x = 7$ $y = 4$

10. $x = 12$ $y = 2$

11. If y varies directly with x, and $y = 16$ when $x = 4$, find y when $x = 10$.

12. If y varies directly with x, and $y = 3$ when $x = 2$, find y when $x = 7$.

13. If y varies directly with x, and $y = 5$ when $x = 1$, find y when $x = 20$.

14. Write a formula expressing the relationship of the distance *(d)* a car travels at the rate of 52 mph if the distance varies directly with the time *(t)* in hours.

GRAPHING LINEAR INEQUALITIES

 DEFINITION

≫**Linear inequality:** a mathematical sentence that is not an equation.

Since you know how to graph linear equations, you should find that graphing linear inequalities is quite simple. Linear inequalities are used extensively in solving linear programming problems, which you will learn to solve in the next chapter. Remember, an inequality uses the symbols $<$, $>$, $\leq$, or $\geq$. How many solutions did you have when you solved an inequality with one variable? You will have many solutions for inequalities with two variables.

EXAMPLE

Example 1. Graph $2x + y > 3$.

Solution. $2x + y > 3$

$y > 3 - 2x$

$y > -2x + 3$

1. Solve the inequality for y just as you would an equation. The inequality is now in a form similar to the slope-intercept form of an equation.

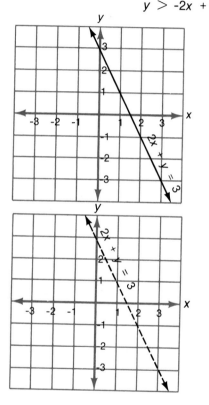

2. Using the slope and the y-intercept, graph the inequality as though it were an equation.

$$m = -2$$
$$b = 3$$

3. Since $y > -2x + 3$ is an inequality, not an equation, you must make some adjustments.

   a. The solution set does not include the points on the line; therefore, the line should be dotted, not solid.

   b. Since the points on the line are not part of the solution set, you need to find out which side of the line the solution set is on.

   (1) Choose a point on either side of the line.

   (2) Substitute the x and y values of the point in the inequality.

   (3) Solve the inequality. If the point you choose makes the inequality true, all points on that side of the line will also make the inequality true.

   c. Substitute $(0, 0)$ in the inequality. Does a true statement result?

$$2x + y > 3$$
$$2 \cdot 0 + 0 > 3$$
$$0 > 3$$

Since the inequality is not true, $(0, 0)$ is not a solution; neither is any value below the dotted line. Consequently, the points above the dotted line must be solutions.

4. Now use a value above the dotted line, say (3,4), to check the work.

$$2x + y > 3$$
$$2 \cdot 3 + 4 > 3$$
$$6 + 4 > 3$$
$$10 > 3 \quad \text{So (3,4) is a solution.}$$

In fact, all points above the dotted line are solutions to this inequality.

5. To indicate all the solutions, shade the area above the dotted line.

There are an infinite number of solutions.

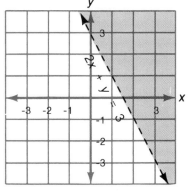

Procedure for Storage

Graphing Inequalities

1. Graph the corresponding equality. If the inequality is $<$ or $>$, use a dotted line. If the inequality is $\leq$ or $\geq$, use a solid line.

2. Choose any point not on the line and substitute it in the inequality. If the inequality is true, shade the side where the point is. If the inequality is false, shade the other side.

USE THE POINT (0,0) TO CHECK THE INEQUALITY **UNLESS** THE LINE PASSES THROUGH (0,0) . . . . .

EXAMPLE

Example 2.   Graph $6x - 2y \geq 10$.

Solution.

1. Write the inequality $6x - 2y \geq 10$ in slope-intercept form.

$$6x - 2y \geq 10$$
$$-2y \geq 10 - 6x$$
$$-2y \geq -6x + 10$$
$$y \leq \frac{-6x}{-2} + \frac{10}{-2}$$

Notice that the inequality sign changed. Why?

$$y \leq 3x - 5$$

Since the inequality sign is $\leq$, graph a solid line.

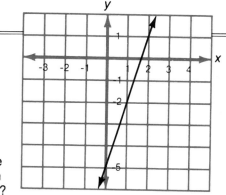

2. Substitute the point $(0,0)$ into the original inequality.

$$6x - 2y \geq 10$$
$$6 \cdot 0 - 2 \cdot 0 \geq 10$$
$$0 - 0 \geq 10$$
$$0 \geq 10$$

Since $(0, 0)$ makes the inequality false, the solution set lies either on the line or on the right side of the line.

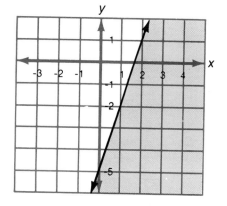

3. Try some points in this shaded portion to check the inequality. Do they make the inequality true?

DON'T FORGET TO CHANGE THE INEQUALITY SIGN WHEN MULTIPLYING OR DIVIDING BY A NEGATIVE NUMBER

Exercises

Graph each of the following inequalities on separate sets of axes.

1. $y > 3x + 2$

2. $y \leq -5x + 7$

3. $y \geq 2x - 6$

4. $3x + y > 12$

5. $2x - y \leq 4$

6. $3x - 2y \geq 6$

7. $x + y > -2$

8. $2x - y > -9$

9. $x + 3y \leq 12$

10. $x - 4y \geq 16$

11. How many solutions are there to a linear inequality?

MEMORY RECALL

Identify.

abscissa	plane
Cartesian plane	point-slope form
Cartesian product	quadrant
constant of variation	range
coordinates	relation
direct variation	slope
domain	slope-intercept form
function	standard form
linear equation	vertical line test
linear inequality	x-axis
linear programming	x-intercept
ordered pair	y-axis
origin	y-intercept
ordinate	

You should be able to do the following:

1. Plot points on a Cartesian plane.

2. Give examples of relations and functions.

3. Graph any given relation and function.

4. Perform the vertical line test.

5. Identify ordered pairs.

6. Graph linear equations.

7. Determine the slope of a line given the graph of the line or two points on the line.

8. Write equations in standard form or slope-intercept form.

9. Graph linear equations using the slope-intercept form of the equation.

10. Find the equation of a line given certain information.

11. Solve direct variation problems.

12. Graph linear inequalities.

Solve.

1. On a sheet of graph paper, graph the ordered pairs and label each point. Then tell which quadrant the point is in.

   a. (3,-5)

   b. (-6,7)

   c. (2,9)

   d. (-3,-1)

   e. (0, 5)

   f. (-7, 0)

2. State which are relations. Give their domain and range. Then tell if the relation is also a function.

   a. (3,7) (-2,4) (1,8)

   b. (2,8) (9,4) (2,7)

   c. (-1,4) (3,4) (7,4)

3. Graph these relations. Then state whether they are functions.

   a. $y = \frac{x}{3}$ with $x \in \{-3,0,9,27\}$

   b. $y = x + 4$ with $-4 \leq x \leq 6$

   c. $y = x - 5$ with $3 \leq x \leq 8$ and x is an integer

4. Make a graph to represent these equations.

   a. $x + y = 7$

   b. $2x - y = 8$

   c. $3x + y = 6$

   d. $x + 3y = 27$

   e. $5x + y = 9$

   f. $9x - 3y = 12$

5. Find the slope of the line passing through the given points.

   a. (2,5) (3,-7)

   b. (1,0) (2,-8)

   c. (3,-4) (-2,-5)

   d. (5, 7) (-3, -4)

   e. (-8, -2) (4, -6)

6. Place each equation in slope-intercept form. Then give the slope and y-intercept of the line. Make a graph to represent each equation.

   a. $x - y = 16$

   b. $3x + 2y = 8$

   c. $5x + y = 9$

   d. $2x - y = 7$

   e. $12x + 4y = 16$

7. Graph each linear equation.

    a. $4x - 6y = 11$

    b. $x - 2y = 12$

    c. $4x + 3y = 15$

    d. $6x + y = 9$

    e. $-2x - y = 8$

8. Find the equation of the line.

    a. with $m = 3$ and $b = \frac{-1}{5}$

    b. with $m = \frac{1}{2}$ and passing through (10,3).

    c. passing through (2,9) and (-1,4).

    d. passing through (11,2) and (11,-3).

    e. passing through (7, 8) and (0, 3)

9. Find the value of the constant of variation when y varies directly with x.

    a. $x = 6$
       $y = 3$

    b. $x = 2$
       $y = 10$

    c. $x = 7$
       $y = 21$

10. If y varies directly with x, and $y = 12$ when $x = -3$, find y when $x = 15$.

11. Graph.

    a. $y \leq x + 7$

    b. $6x + 2y < 18$

    c. $y > 3x + 4$

    d. $y \geq 5x - 1$

CHAPTER 6

SYSTEMS OF EQUATIONS AND INEQUALITIES

Behind the scenes of every manufacturing plant is a group of accountants and analysts who make decisions that affect the entire production process. Each product has a break-even point, which shows the number of items that should be manufactured and sold for the business to break-even (make income equal production cost). Since one goal of any company is to make a profit, the company will want to make and sell more items than the break-even number in order to make a profit.

Mr. Fitzgerald is planning to go into a business that makes hot-air balloons. He determines that his manufacturing costs will be $30,000 per month (light bill, cleaning of the plant, rent of the manufacturing facilities, and so forth) plus $7500 per item manufactured. He decides to sell each balloon for $13,500. How many balloons should he make and sell to break even?

What is Mr. Fitzgerald actually looking for in this problem? He really wants to know the number of items to make. So let x = the number of items to make and sell.

In a business problem like this, the cost and the profit are the two main ideas to consider. The cost equation can be expressed by $C = 30,000 + 7500x$: $30,000 for fixed costs plus $7500 per item made. Since each balloon sells for $13,500, the income equation is $I = 13,500x$.

Business and other fields require a knowledge of solving systems of equations. In this chapter you will learn methods of solving systems of equations. By the end of the chapter you should be able to easily solve the above problem. As you continue your study of mathematics as it applies to business, you will learn advanced methods of solving systems such as matrices and determinants. This study leads to a study of advanced linear programming and the solution to many business problems.

SYSTEMS OF LINEAR EQUATIONS

Up to this point all of your work in algebra has consisted of working one equation at a time. First you worked with one equation in one variable, or unknown *(x)*. Then you learned to work equations in two variables, or two unknowns *(x* and *y)*. Now you will learn to find the solution to two equations in two unknowns.

EXAMPLE

The sum of two numbers is -4, and their difference is 10. Find the two numbers.

Solution. First ask yourself, "What am I looking for in this problem?" The last statement of the problem asks you to find two numbers. Let variables stand for the two numbers you are trying to find.

Let x = the first number
y = the second number

Now you can write two equations: one for the sum, the other for the difference.

$$x + y = -4 \qquad x - y = 10$$

To find the answer to this problem, you must find an ordered pair solution that satisfies both equations simultaneously (at the same time). You could work the above problem by using one variable as you did in Chapter 3, and you would get the correct answer. Some problems, however, are easier to solve using the two-variable method, which you will learn in this chapter.

Can you think of any biblical event that happened at the same time as another event? In Isaiah 65:24, God says He will hear our prayers while we are still praying them. Matthew 27:35-54 records the simultaneous action that showed man that he could have access to God. Before Christ died, only one man (the high priest) entered the presence of God once a year by lifting the veil of the temple and entering the Holy of Holies. The veil was a symbol of separation between man and God. But at the same time that Jesus "yielded up the ghost," something happened to the veil to end that separation. Read Matthew 27:51 to learn what the simultaneous action was. When Jesus died, "the veil of the temple was rent in twain from the top to the bottom." This action, simultaneous with the death of Jesus Christ, was God's way of saying that man now had direct access to God. Man didn't have to rely on someone else to represent him before God. Hebrews 4:15-16 reminds us that we have a high priest (Jesus) that we can come to directly no matter what the time or the problem.

What other examples of simultaneous solutions can you find? When the Lord rose from the dead, were there any simultaneous actions?

Simultaneous equations can be solved several different ways. You will learn some of these ways in this chapter. Some methods will be reserved for advanced mathematical studies.

SOLVING SYSTEMS OF EQUATIONS BY GRAPHING

Reconsider the system of equations given in the example on page 240.

$$x + y = -4 \qquad x - y = 10$$

One way you could find the solution to this system of equations is by trying to think of all the ordered pairs that make the first equation true and then to see which one of them would also make the second equation true. How many ordered pairs make one equation true? How many of these ordered pairs make both equations true? This method is too time consuming and tedious. A more appropriate method would be to graph each equation on the same set of axes. The solution to the system is the coordinates of the point at which the two lines intersect.

EXAMPLES

Example 1. Solve $x + y = -4$
$x - y = 10$

Solution. $x + y = -4$
$y = -x - 4$

$x - y = 10$
$-y = -x + 10$
$y = x - 10$

1. Change each equation to slope-intercept form.

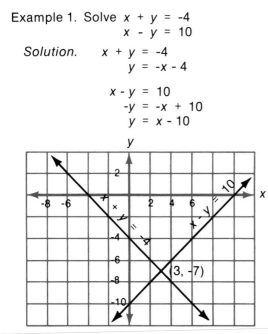

2. Graph both equations.
3. Determine the coordinates of the point of intersection.

These two lines intersect at the point (3, -7). Substitute 3 for x and -7 for y in the two equations and see if they make both equations true.

Check. $x + y = -4$
$3 + -7 = -4$
$-4 = -4$

$x - y = 10$
$3 - -7 = 10$
$3 + 7 = 10$
$10 = 10$

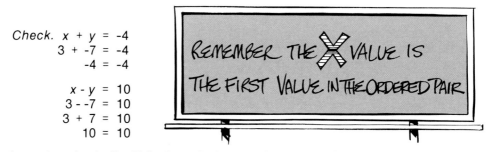

REMEMBER THE X VALUE IS THE FIRST VALUE IN THE ORDERED PAIR

So the ordered pair (3, -7) is the solution to this system of equations.

Example 2. Solve $x + y = 5$
$3x + y = 7$

Solution.

1. Graph each equation on the same set of axes.
$x + y = 5$
$y = -x + 5$

$3x + y = 7$
$y = -3x + 7$

2. Find the coordinates of the point of intersection.

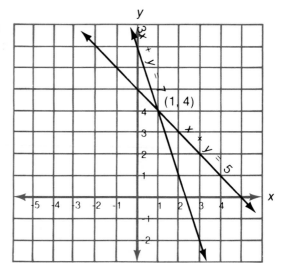

(1, 4)

According to the graph, the solution to the system is (1, 4). To check, substitute the values in both equations.

Check. $x + y = 5$ $3x + y = 7$
$1 + 4 = 5$ $3(1) + 4 = 7$
$5 = 5$ $7 = 7$

Procedure for Storage

Solving a System of Linear Equations by Graphing

1. Graph each equation on the same set of axes and label each line.

2. Find the coordinates of the point of intersection of the two lines.

3. Check the solution in all the original equations.

EXAMPLE

Example 3. Solve $2x + y = 14$.
$x - y = -2$

Solution. Graph both equations and label the lines.

$2x + y = 14$
$y = -2x + 14$

$x - y = -2$
$-y = -x - 2$
$y = x + 2$

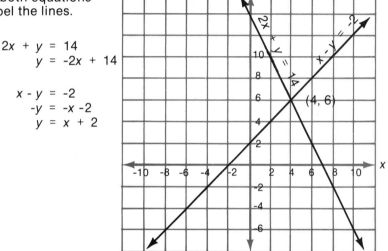

The point of intersection is (4, 6). Check the solution in both equations.

$2x + y = 14$	$x - y = -2$
$2(4) + 6 = 14$	$4 - 6 = -2$
$8 + 6 = 14$	$-2 = -2$
$14 = 14$	

Exercises

Graph each system of linear equations to find its solution.

1. $x + y = 5$
   $x - y = 1$

2. $x - y = -2$
   $4x - y = 4$

3. $6x + y = 7$
   $y = 1$

4. $x + 2y = 10$
   $9x + 2y = -6$

5. $8x - 3y = -12$
   $4x - y = -8$

6. $4x + y = 7$
   $x - 3y = 18$

7. $x + y = 9$
   $11x + y = 19$

8. $9x - y = -5$
   $12x - y = -8$

9. $x - 5y = -30$
   $2x - y = 3$

10. $7x - 4y = -32$
    $x - 2y = -6$

11. $7x - 4y = 16$
    $x - y = 1$

12. $x - y = -1$
    $2x - 3y = 0$

13. $16x - 7y = 42$
    $x - y = -3$

14. $3x + 8y = 16$
    $5x + 8y = 32$

15. $6x - y = -5$
    $5x + y = -6$

16. $y = 4x$
    $y = -3x$

17. $3x - 5y = -15$
    $3x + 5y = 45$

18. $x + y = -4$
    $y = -7$

19. $6x - y = -2$
    $2x - y = 2$

20. $x + 5y = 5$
    $x - y = -7$

POSSIBLE SOLUTIONS TO SYSTEMS OF LINEAR EQUATIONS

If you draw two lines on a piece of paper, one of the following possibilities will result.

The three types of lines just illustrated represent three systems of linear equations. So far, the two-equation problems you have graphed have produced a pair of intersecting lines. The coordinates of the point of intersection identify the only solution to both equations. But if the lines are parallel, you will not get a solution, for two parallel lines have no point in common.

EXAMPLE

Example 1. Solve $x + y = 3$
$\qquad\qquad\quad x + y = 7$

Solution. Graph each equation. After graphing the two equations, you notice that there is no point of intersection. The two lines are parallel. Because there is no solution, these lines represent an inconsistent system of linear equations. All systems without solutions are inconsistent systems.

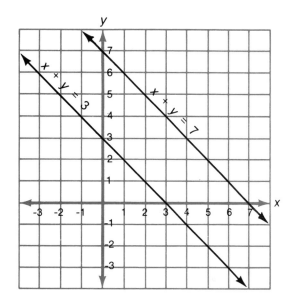

If a system has a solution, it is called a consistent system. The solution of a consistent system is either a point or a line.

EXAMPLES

Example 2. Solve $2x + y = -4$.
$\qquad\qquad\qquad x - 3y = -9$

Solution. $2x + y = -4$
$\qquad\qquad y = -2x - 4$

$\qquad x - 3y = -9$
$\qquad -3y = -x - 9$
$\qquad\quad y = \frac{1}{3}x + 3$

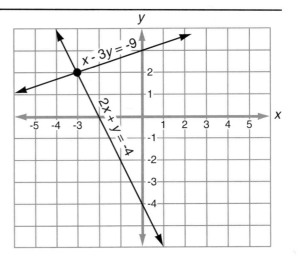

The solution is one point, (-3, 2). The system is consistent and independent. Any system of equations that produces lines that intersect in one point is called consistent and independent.

Example 3. Solve $x + y = 3$.
$\qquad\qquad\qquad 2x + 2y = 6$

Solution. $x + y = 3$
$\qquad\qquad y = -x + 3$

$\qquad 2x + 2y = 6$
$\qquad 2y = -2x + 6$
$\qquad\, y = -x + 3$

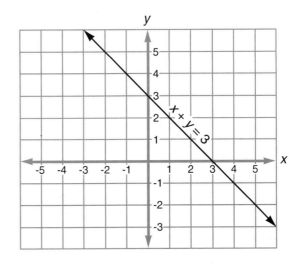

The graphs of these two equations coincide. The solution, the line described by the equation $y = -x + 3$, contains an infinite number of points. Any system of equations that produces an infinite number of solutions (a line) is called consistent and dependent.

DEFINITIONS

≫**Consistent system of equations:** a system that has a solution.
≫**Inconsistent system of equations:** a system that has no solution.
≫**Independent system of equations:** a consistent system that has only one solution.
≫**Dependent system of equations:** a consistent system that has an infinite number of solutions.

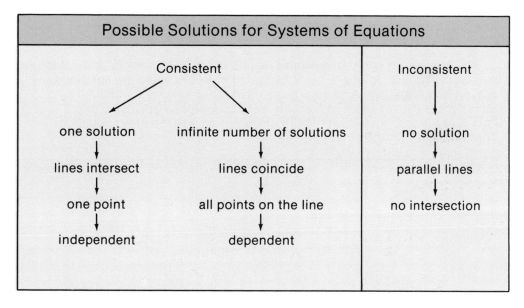

Possible Solutions for Systems of Equations	
Consistent	Inconsistent

Consistent:
- one solution → lines intersect → one point → independent
- infinite number of solutions → lines coincide → all points on the line → dependent

Inconsistent:
- no solution → parallel lines → no intersection

Exercises

Graph each system and tell whether it is consistent or inconsistent. If the system is consistent, tell whether it is dependent or independent.

1. $x + y = 4$
$5x + y = 8$

2. $x - y = 3$
$4x - y = 15$

3. $2x + y = 8$
$4x + 2y = 16$

4. $3x + y = 5$
$y = 3x - 4$

5. $x + 2y - 10 = 0$
$3x + 2y = 14$

6. $3x + y = 5$
$4x + 3y = 15$

7. $x - 2y = 4$
$3x + 2y = -12$

8. $x + 2y = 8$
$y = \frac{-x}{2} + 4$

9. $x - 3y = -15$
$y = 4$

10. $x - y = 6$
$5x - 5y = 30$

11. $5x - 3y = -12$
$2x + 3y = -9$

12. $2x - 7y = 21$
$3x + 7y = 14$

13. $3x + 4y = 20$
$x + 2y = 8$

14. $x - y = -4$
$x + 3y = 24$

15. $3x + 4y = 4$
$x - 2y = 8$

SOLVING SYSTEMS OF EQUATIONS BY SUBSTITUTION

Substitution means the putting of one thing in the place of another. As sinful mankind, we are condemned to die. But Jesus took our sin and paid sin's penalty for us through His death and shed blood at Calvary. (Read II Cor. 5:14-15.) If you are saved, thank God continually for providing a substitute for you so that you do not have to face the wrath and judgment of God. If you are not saved, accept the substitutionary death of Jesus and His shed blood as your hope of eternal life in heaven.

The graphing method of solving systems of equations works well if the solutions are small integers, but it becomes awkward when the solutions are large or fractional. A more precise method for solving simultaneous equations is the *substitution method.* With this method you solve one equation for one variable, substitute the solution into the other equation, and then solve for the other variable.

EXAMPLES

Example 1. Solve $x + y = -4$
$x - y = 10$

Solution.

$x + y = -4$
$x = -4 - y$

1. Solve the first equation for x in terms of y.

$x - y = 10$
$(-4 - y) - y = 10$
$-4 - y - y = 10$
$-4 - 2y = 10$
$-2y = 10 + 4$
$-2y = 14$
$y = -7$

2. The equation says that x equals $-4 - y$. You can now substitute $-4 - y$ wherever you see x. So substitute $-4 - y$ for x in the second equation and solve for y.

$x + y = -4$
$x = -4 - y$
$x = -4 - (-7)$
$x = -4 + 7$
$x = 3$

3. Now that you know $y = -7$, you can find the corresponding value of x by substituting -7 for y in either equation and solving again for x. Substitute $y = -7$ in the first equation.

Check. $x + y = -4$
            Does $3 + (-7) = -4$?

            $x - y = 10$
            Does $3 - (-7) = 10$?

4. The values then are $x = 3$ and
$y = -7$. These values represent
the ordered pair solution $(3, -7)$.

Notice that this is the same solution found by the graphing method on page 241.

Example 2. Solve $x + y = 5$
                   $3x + y = 7$

Solution. $3x + y = 7$
                    $y = 7 - 3x$

1. Solve the second equation for y in terms of x.

                $x + y = 5$
           $x + (7 - 3x) = 5$
            $x + 7 - 3x = 5$
               $7 - 2x = 5$
                  $-2x = -2$
                    $x = 1$

2. Substitute $7 - 3x$ for y in the first equation and solve for x.

            $3x + y = 7$
               $y = 7 - 3x$
               $y = 7 - 3(1)$
               $y = 7 - 3$
               $y = 4$

3. Find y by substituting this value of x in the second equation.

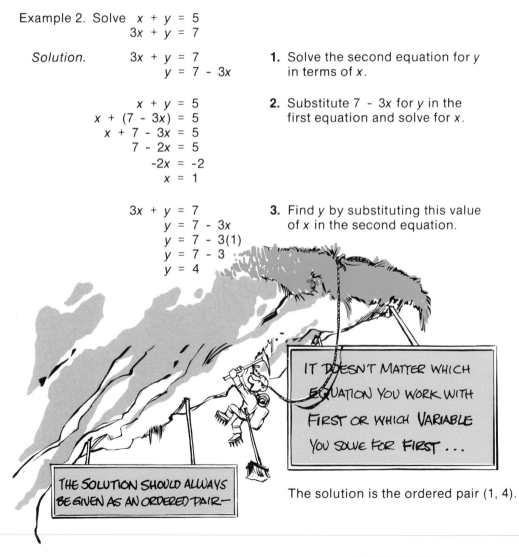

IT DOESN'T MATTER WHICH EQUATION YOU WORK WITH FIRST OR WHICH VARIABLE YOU SOLVE FOR FIRST ...

THE SOLUTION SHOULD ALWAYS BE GIVEN AS AN ORDERED PAIR—

The solution is the ordered pair $(1, 4)$.

Example 3. Solve by substitution.
$$x = 4y$$
$$3x + 2y = 8$$

Solution.

$3x + 2y = 8$	**1.** The first equation is already solved for x in terms of y. Substitute $4y$ for x in the second equation.
$3(4y) + 2y = 8$	
$12y + 2y = 8$	
$14y = 8$	
$y = \dfrac{8}{14} = \dfrac{4}{7}$	

$x = 4y$	**2.** Find x by substituting $\frac{4}{7}$ for y in the first equation.
$x = 4\left(\dfrac{4}{7}\right)$	
$x = \dfrac{16}{7}$	

The solution is the ordered pair $\left(\dfrac{16}{7}, \dfrac{4}{7}\right)$.

Procedure for Storage

Solving a System of Equations by the Substitution Method

1. Solve one equation for one variable in terms of the other.
2. Substituting this quantity for the variable into the other equation, solve the equation to obtain a numerical value for the second variable.
3. Substituting the value of the second variable into the original equation, solve for the numerical value of the original variable.
4. Write the values in ordered pair form.
5. Check the solution in all original equations.

Exercises

Solve each system by substitution. Be sure to give your solution as an ordered pair.

1. $3x + y = 12$
$x + y = 20$

2. $x + y = 5$
$x - y = 3$

3. $x + y = 10$
$y = 2x$

4. $x + 2y = 9$
$x + y = 28$

5. $2x - y = -4$
$x + y = -6$

6. $7x + 3y = 35$
$x - 2y = 5$

7. $2x + 3y = 25$
$x - y = -5$

8. $3x + y = 10$
$x - y = -6$

9. $x - 3y = -5$
$2x - 5y = -9$

10. $3x + 5y = 13$
$x + 8y = 36$

11. $2x - 3y = 16$
$5x + 9y = -59$

12. $x + 4y = 30$
$2x + 5y = 36$

13. $2x + 4y = 10$
$3x - y = 18$

14. $x - 5y = 17$
$2x - 7y = 22$

15. $x + 3y = 14$
$x = 2y$

16. $x - y = 1$
$x - 3y = 9$

17. $x + 8y = 23$
$x + 3y = 8$

18. $x - y = 2$
$x + y = 6$

19. $5x - y = 6$
$6x - y = 9$

20. $13x + 7y = 88$
$x + 8y = -38$

AN EXTENSION OF THE SUBSTITUTION METHOD

When you graphed a system of equations, how did you determine that it was consistent or inconsistent? When you used the algebraic method, how could you tell if a system were consistent or inconsistent? Watch what happens when you solve this inconsistent system algebraically by substitution.

$$x + y = 5$$
$$x + y = 7$$

$x + y = 5$ $y = 5 - x$	Solve the first equation for y and substitute the derived expression in the second equation.
$x + y = 7$ $x + (5 - x) = 7$ $5 = 7$	Solving the second equation, you find that the resulting equation is false.

Whenever you solve a system algebraically and get a false statement as a solution, the system is inconsistent. It has no solution.

Now look at a consistent, but dependent, system.

$$x + y = 2$$
$$3x + 3y = 6$$

$x + y = 2$ $y = 2 - x$	Solve this system by substitution.
$3x + 3y = 6$ $3x + 3(2 - x) = 6$ $3x + 6 - 3x = 6$ $6 = 6$	Substitute this expression into the second equation. The resulting equation is a true statement with no variables. The system is consistent and dependent and has an infinite number of ordered pairs as solutions.

EXAMPLE

Example 1.   Solve $2x + 3y = 16$
$4x + 5y = 28$

Solution.

$$2x + 3y = 16$$
$$2x = 16 - 3y$$
$$x = \frac{16 - 3y}{2}$$

1. Solve one of the equations for one of the variables. Here solve the first equation for x.

$$4x + 5y = 28$$
$$4\left(\frac{16 - 3y}{2}\right) + 5y = 28$$
$$2(16 - 3y) + 5y = 28$$

2. Now substitute this quantity for x in the second equation.

$$32 - 6y + 5y = 28$$
$$-y = -4$$
$$y = 4$$

$$x = \frac{16 - 3(4)}{2}$$
$$= \frac{16 - 12}{2}$$
$$= \frac{4}{2}$$
$$= 2$$

3. Substitute 4 for y in $x = \frac{16 - 3y}{2}$.

Since $x = 2$ and $y = 4$, the solution is $(2, 4)$.

So far all the systems of equations you have studied in this chapter have been linear systems of equations. Some systems of equations are not linear equations but can still be solved by the substitution method. The next example shows the solution of a nonlinear system.

EXAMPLE

Example 2. Solve $x^2 = y$
$$x^2 + 3y = 64$$

Solution.

1. Substitute so that you will get a linear equation with one unknown. Since $x^2 = y$, substitute y for x^2 in the second equation.

2. Solve for y.
$$x^2 + 3y = 64$$
$$y + 3y = 64$$
$$4y = 64$$
$$y = 16$$

3. Now find the value of x by substituting 16 for y in the first equation.
$$x^2 = y$$
$$x^2 = 16$$
$$x = \pm \sqrt{16}$$
$$x = \pm 4$$

4. Thus there are two possible solutions to this problem: (4, 16) and (-4, 16).

Exercises

Solve each system of equations by the substitution method. Tell whether each system is inconsistent or consistent. If the system is consistent, tell whether it is independent or dependent.

1. $x + y = 14$
$3x + 2(y - 5) = 21$

2. $y = x^2 + 3$
$x^2 + 3 = 28$

3. $x + 6y = -9$
$4x - 7y = -5$

4. $2x - y = 11$
$6x - 3y = -24$

5. $(x + y)^2 = 36$
$x + y = 6$

6. $2x - 3y = -13$
$x - 11y = 3$

7. $2x - 8y = 7$
$3x + y = -2$

8. $x + 3y = 18$
$3x - y = -6$

9. $5x + 7y = 38$
$9x + y = 80$

10. $4x + 3y = 9$
$x - 5y = 6$

11. $2(x + y) - 5(x + 1) = 3$
$-3x + 2y = 8$

12. $y^2 = x + 9$
$4x + y^2 = 209$

13. $x - 3y = -9$
$x - y = 1$

14. $5x - 4y = 11$
$3x - y = 1$

15. $3x + 5y = 8$
$2x - 4y = 7$

16. The sum of two numbers is 63, and their difference is 13. Find the two numbers.

17. The sum of two numbers is 996. The difference of the larger and twice the smaller is 33. Find the two numbers.

SOLVING SYSTEMS OF EQUATIONS BY THE ADDITION METHOD

So far you have learned to solve systems of equations by graphing and by substituting. In this lesson you will learn another method. First review the substitution method.

EXAMPLE

Example 1.   Solve. $3x + 2y = 7$
$4x + 3y = 10$

Solution. $3x + 2y = 7$
$2y = 7 - 3x$
$y = \dfrac{7}{2} - \dfrac{3x}{2}$

1. Solve the first equation for y.

$4x + 3y = 10$

$4x + 3\left(\dfrac{7}{2} - \dfrac{3x}{2}\right) = 10$

$4x + \dfrac{21}{2} - \dfrac{9x}{2} = 10$

$\dfrac{8x}{2} + \dfrac{21}{2} - \dfrac{9x}{2} = 10$

$2\left(\dfrac{21}{2} - \dfrac{x}{2}\right) = (10)2$

$21 - x = 20$

$-x = -1$

$x = 1$

2. Substitute into the second equation $\dfrac{7}{2} - \dfrac{3x}{2}$ for y and solve for x.

$3x + 2y = 7$
$3 \cdot 1 + 2y = 7$
$2y = 4$
$y = \dfrac{4}{2}$
$y = 2$

3. Returning to the first equation, substitute 1 for x and solve for y.

4. Thus $x = 1$ and $y = 2$. So the solution is (1, 2).

This solution is correct, but another method of solving systems of linear equations, called the *addition method,* avoids much of the fractional work. With this method you combine the two equations by either adding or subtracting them to eliminate one of the variables. Then you can solve the resulting linear equation for the remaining unknown variable.

EXAMPLE

Example 2.   Solve $x + y = 4$
$x - y = 10$

Solution.

$$\begin{array}{r} x + y = 4 \\ +\ \ x - y = 10 \\ \hline 2x\ = 14 \end{array}$$

1. Notice that the *y* variable has opposite signs and the same coefficient; consequently, adding the two equations will eliminate the *y* term. If you add the left sides, you must also add the right sides.

$$2x = 14$$
$$x = 7$$

2. Now solve the resulting equation.

$$x + y = 4$$
$$7 + y = 4$$
$$y = -3$$

3. To find the value of *y*, substitute 7 for *x* in **either** of the original equations. Then solve for *y*.

4. The values are $x = 7$ and $y = -3$. The solution to this system is $(7, -3)$.

Check.

$$x + y = 4 \qquad\qquad x - y = 10$$
Does $7 + -3 = 4$? $\qquad$ Does $7 - (-3) = 10$?

This system is quite easy to solve by the addition method. Other systems may be slightly harder to solve than this one, but any system can be solved by the addition method.

EXAMPLE

Example 3.   Solve
$$3x + 2y = 8$$
$$3x + 5y = 14$$

Solution. In some systems of equations such as this one, you can eliminate a variable by subtracting the two equations rather than adding them. Remember, subtraction is simply adding the opposite. If you subtract these two equations, the *x* variable will be eliminated.

$$
\begin{array}{r}
3x + 2y = 8 \\
- \quad 3x + 5y = 14 \\
\hline
-3y = -6 \\
y = 2
\end{array}
$$

1. Because the signs in front of the *x* terms are the same and the coefficients are the same, subtract the equations and solve for *y*. Be sure to subtract each term.

$$
\begin{aligned}
3x + 2y &= 8 \\
3x + 2(2) &= 8 \\
3x + 4 &= 8 \\
3x &= 4 \\
x &= \frac{4}{3}
\end{aligned}
$$

2. Find the value of *x* by substituting 2 for *y* in either of the original equations and solving for *x*.

3. The solution is $(\frac{4}{3}, 2)$.

Check.

$$
\begin{aligned}
3x + 2y &= 8 \\
3(\tfrac{4}{3}) + 2(2) &= 8 \\
4 + 4 &= 8 \\
8 &= 8
\end{aligned}
\qquad
\begin{aligned}
3x + 5y &= 14 \\
3(\tfrac{4}{3}) + 5(2) &= 14 \\
4 + 10 &= 14 \\
14 &= 14
\end{aligned}
$$

Procedure for Storage

Solving a System of Equations by the Addition Method

1. Add or subtract the equations to eliminate one variable.
   a. If the signs preceding the variable to be eliminated are different, add the equations.
   b. If the signs preceding the variable to be eliminated are the same, subtract the equations.
2. Solve the resulting linear equation for the remaining variable.
3. Substitute the value for the variable into either of the original equations and solve for the other variable.
4. To determine the solution, place the values in ordered pair form.
5. Check the solution in all original equations.

EXAMPLE

Example 4. Solve $4x - 2y = 13$
$8x + 2y = 23$

Solution.

$$4x - 2y = 13$$
$$+\ 8x + 2y = 23$$
$$\overline{12x = 36}$$

1. Because the *y* variables have the same coefficient and different signs, add the equations to eliminate *y*.

$$x = 3$$

2. Solve for *x*.

$$4x - 2y = 13$$
$$4(3) - 2y = 13$$
$$12 - 2y = 13$$
$$-2y = 1$$

3. Substitute and solve for *y*.

$$y = \frac{-1}{2}$$

4. The solution is $(3, \frac{-1}{2})$.

Check.

$$8x + 2y = 23$$
$$8(3) + 2(\tfrac{-1}{2}) = 23$$
$$24 + -1 = 23$$
$$23 = 23$$

$$4x - 2y = 13$$
$$4(3) - 2(\tfrac{-1}{2}) = 13$$
$$12 + 1 = 13$$
$$13 = 13$$

Exercises

Using the addition method, solve each system of equations.

1. $x + y = 5$
   $x - y = -3$

2. $7x + y = 35$
   $x + y = 5$

3. $2x + y = 9$
   $-2x - 3y = 13$

4. $x + 2y = 13$
   $x + 6y = 45$

5. $2x + 6y = 5$
   $2x - 3y = -4$

6. $x + 3y = 8$
   $x - 3y = 10$

7. $x - y = -2$
   $6x + y = -19$

8. $x + y = -3$
   $x = 1$

9. $x + 2y = 9$
   $3x - 2y = 7$

10. $2x + 3y = 19$
    $2x + 7y = 47$

11. $5x + y = 17$
    $3x + y = 12$

12. $2x + 9y = 30$
    $2x + y = -2$

13. $9x - 4y = -66$
    $x + 4y = 6$

14. $2x - 7y = 26$
    $x - 7y = 18$

15. $4x - 5y = 23$
    $3x + 5y = 18$

AN EXTENSION OF THE ADDITION METHOD

You just learned to eliminate one variable by adding or subtracting two linear equations. However, the addition method works only when the coefficients of one of the variables are the same. If the coefficients are different, you must make them the same by applying one of the basic properties of equations.

EXAMPLE

Example 1.   Solve $\quad x + y = 8$
$$3x + 2y = 22$$

Solution. $x + y = 8$
$3x + 2y = 22$

1. In this system, the coefficients of the x variables and y variables are not the same. If you add or subtract these equations, none of the variables will be eliminated. But if you multiply each term in the first equation by 2, the result is an equivalent equation. Then coefficients for the y terms are the same in both equations.

$x + y = 8$
$2(x + y) = 2 \cdot 8$
$2x + 2y = 16$

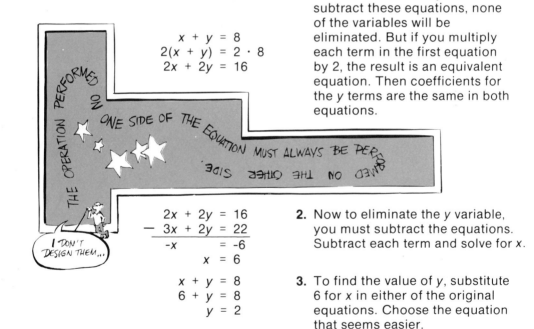

THE OPERATION PERFORMED ON ONE SIDE OF THE EQUATION MUST ALWAYS BE PERFORMED ON THE OTHER SIDE.

I DON'T DESIGN THEM...

$$\begin{array}{r} 2x + 2y = 16 \\ - \quad 3x + 2y = 22 \\ \hline -x \qquad = -6 \\ x = 6 \end{array}$$

2. Now to eliminate the y variable, you must subtract the equations. Subtract each term and solve for x.

$x + y = 8$
$6 + y = 8$
$y = 2$

3. To find the value of y, substitute 6 for x in either of the original equations. Choose the equation that seems easier.

The solution is the ordered pair (6, 2). Remember, the ordered pair represents the coordinates of the point where the two lines will intersect when you graph them.

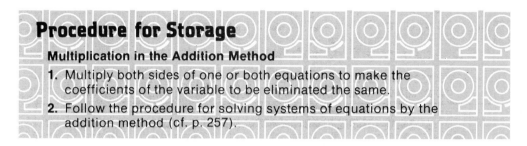

Multiplication in the Addition Method

1. Multiply both sides of one or both equations to make the coefficients of the variable to be eliminated the same.

2. Follow the procedure for solving systems of equations by the addition method (cf. p. 257).

EXAMPLE

Example 2.   Solve $2x + 3y = 6$
$3x - 2y = 8$

Solution.

$2x + 3y = 6$ $3x - 2y = 8$
$2(2x + 3y) = 2(6)$ $3(3x - 2y) = 3(8)$
$4x + 6y = 12$ $9x - 6y = 24$

1. Before you can eliminate the *y* terms, you must multiply the first equation by 2 and the second equation by 3 to obtain a numerical coefficient of 6 for both *y* terms. Then add these equations and solve for *x*.

$$4x + 6y = 12$$
$$+ \ 9x - 6y = 24$$
$$\overline{13x \qquad = 36}$$

$$x = \frac{36}{13}$$

$$2x + 3y = 6$$
$$2\left(\frac{36}{13}\right) + 3y = 6$$
$$\frac{72}{13} + 3y = 6$$
$$3y = 6 - \frac{72}{13}$$
$$3y = \frac{78 - 72}{13}$$
$$3y = \frac{6}{13}$$
$$y = \frac{6}{13} \cdot \frac{1}{3}$$
$$y = \frac{2}{13}$$

2. Find *y* by substituting $\frac{36}{13}$ for *x* in one of the original equations.

The solution is $(\frac{36}{13}, \frac{2}{13})$. This system is consistent and independent.

When you solve systems of equations (whether they are linear or nonlinear systems), you can use one of three methods: the graphing method, the substitution method, or the addition method. Each method will yield the same solution. Though it may be easier to identify inconsistent and consistent systems with the graphing method, you can determine whether a system is inconsistent or consistent when you solve either of the other two methods algebraically. You can also use any method to determine whether a consistent system is dependent or independent.

graphic solution	lines coincide	lines parallel	lines intersect
algebraic solution	true statement (e.g., 0 = 0)	false statement (e.g., 0 = 5)	statement containing a variable and its value (e.g., $x = 6$)
type of system	consistent and dependent	inconsistent	consistent and independent

Exercises

Solve each system of equations by eliminating a variable. Tell whether the system is consistent or inconsistent. If it is consistent, tell whether it is dependent or independent.

1. $3x + 2y = 18$
$5x - 3y = 11$

2. $x - 3y = 8$
$x + y = -4$

3. $2x - 7y = 3$
$-4x + 14y = -6$

4. $x + y = 10$
$2y = 20 - 2x$

5. $5x - 4y = 7$
$7x - 3y = 2$

6. $x + y = 18$
$2x + 2y = 10$

7. $x + y = 14$
$2x - 3y = -17$

8. $x + 2y = 9$
$3x + y = 16$

9. $2x + y = 15$
$x + 2y = 18$

10. $2x + 4y = 5$
$3x - 2y = 7$

11. $5x - 4y = 3$
$2x + 3y = 17$

12. $5x - y = -42$
$-44 + y = 5x$

13. $6x - 11y = -26$
$x + 3y = -14$

14. $3x - 2y = 5$
$4x + 3y = 8$

15. $\frac{x}{2} + y = 9$
$x + y = 14$

16. The difference of two numbers is 62, and the sum of twice the larger and 3 times the smaller is 304. Find the numbers.

17. The sum of two numbers is 621, and their difference is 109. Find the two numbers.

MOTION PROBLEMS

In Chapter 3 you worked motion problems with only one variable. Now that you can solve a system of equations containing two variables, you should be able to solve motion problems containing two variables by either the substitution method or the addition method. Sometimes a problem in two variables is easier to solve than one in one variable. Remember, the basic formula for solving motion problems is $rt = d$.

EXAMPLES

Example 1. Two cars start toward each other at the same time from towns 612 miles apart. They meet in 6 hours. One travels 2 mph faster than the other. How fast is each car traveling?

Solution. Let x = rate of faster car
y = rate of slower car

1. Determine the variables.

	r $\cdot$	t =	d
faster car	x	6	$6x$
slower car	y	6	$6y$

2. Make a drawing and a chart. Fill in the chart with information in the problem. Remember to fill in two columns first; then fill in the third column by using the formula $rt = d$.

3. Now set up a system of equations derived from the chart and the information in the problem.

$x = y + 2$ The rate of the faster car is 2 mph faster than the rate of the slower car.

$6x + 6y = 612$ The total distance traveled in 6 hours is 612 miles.

$$6x + 6y = 612$$
$$6(y + 2) + 6y = 612$$
$$12y = 600$$
$$y = 50$$

4. Solve this system by substituting $y + 2$ for x.

$$x = y + 2$$
$$x = 52$$

The faster car is traveling 52 mph, and the slower car is traveling 50 mph.

Example 2. When his Sunday school class went canoeing, Bill canoed 12 miles down the river in 3 hours. After paddling back upstream for 2 hours, he had traveled 4 miles. How fast does Bill paddle in still water? What is the rate of the current of the river?

Solution. The two unknowns are the rate of the river and the rate Bill is rowing.

Let x = Bill's paddling rate
y = rate of the current of the river

	r	$\cdot$	t	=	d
traveling upstream	$x - y$		2		$2(x - y)$
traveling downstream	$x + y$		3		$3(x + y)$

1. Because the current works with Bill as he travels downstream, Bill's overall downstream rate will be the sum of his paddling rate and the current's rate $(x + y)$. Bill's upstream rate, however, will be his paddling rate less the current rate $(x - y)$. Fill in two columns in the chart; then complete the third column by using the motion formula $rt = d$.

$$3(x + y) = 12$$
$$2(x - y) = 4$$

2. Use the information in the third column and in the original problem to set up a system of equations.

$$(x + y) = 4$$
$$(x - y) = 2$$

3. Instead of multiplying the variables in parentheses by the coefficient, you can divide both sides of the equation by the coefficients.

$$
\begin{array}{r}
x + y = 4 \\
\underline{x - y = 2} \\
2x = 6 \\
x = 3
\end{array}
$$

$$x + y = 4$$
$$3 + y = 4$$
$$y = 1$$

4. Substituting 3 for x, find y.

So Bill paddles his canoe 3 mph, and the current moves 1 mph.

Exercises

Use systems of equations to solve these word problems.

1. The Holiday Hiking Club went on a hike one Saturday. In the morning they walked at an average speed of 3 mph; in the afternoon they walked at an average speed of 2 mph for 1 hour more than the number of hours they had walked in the morning. How many hours did they walk in the morning if they walked a total of 22 miles?

2. Find the rate of two cars traveling in the same direction if they leave the same place at the same time. The rate of one is twice as fast as the other, and after 4 hours the faster car is 80 miles farther than the slower car.

3. Bill Jenkins leaves Centerville at 11:00 A.M. and travels west at 45 mph. Lane Fitzgerald leaves Centerville at 1:00 P.M. the same day and travels east at 50 mph. At what time will the two men be 375 miles apart?

4. Flying with the wind, a plane travels 1200 miles in 4 hours. Flying against the wind, it travels 500 miles in 2 hours. What is the speed of the plane and the speed of the wind?

5. Grandma Vaughn and her son John live 184 miles apart. If they leave their homes at the same time and head towards each other they will meet in 2 hours. John travels 12 mph faster than Grandma. How fast does each travel?

6. A southbound train travels for 2 hours and meets a northbound train that has been traveling for 4 hours. The trains started from cities 350 miles apart. What is the speed of each train if the northbound train travels 10 mph slower than the southbound?

7. In 1898 Alberto Satos-Dumont, an aviation pioneer, ventured a flight in a small oblong bag called a dirigible. It had one propeller powered by two small engines. If on one flight he traveled 8 mph faster than the wind speed and the distance traveled with the wind in 2 hours was 4 miles more than the distance traveled against the wind in 3 hours, find the speed of the wind and the speed of the dirigible.

8. A plane leaves Littleton Airport and travels east at 230 mph. A second plane leaves 3 hours later and travels west at 215 mph. How

long has each plane flown when the two planes are 1135 miles apart?

9. A car leaves Middletown and heads toward Rochester 258 miles away at the same time a car leaves Rochester and heads toward Middletown. If the rate of the first car is 12 mph faster than the rate of the second car and if the cars meet in 3 hours, how fast is each car traveling?

10. A train leaves City View at 11:00 A.M. and heads east at 38 mph. At 2:00 P.M. another train leaves, traveling east at 53 mph. How long will it take the second train to come within 54 miles of the first train?

11. In 3 hours scouts raft 15 miles downstream from one camp to another, but they take 5 hours to paddle back to their camp upstream. What is the scouts' paddling rate in still water? What is the rate of the current in the stream?

12. Two trains leave the station at the same time, one traveling north and the other traveling south. The express travels 14 mph faster than the local. After 3 hours they are 315 miles apart. What is the rate of each train?

13. Mr. Brannon took his Sunday school boys on an overnight camping trip. They rode bicycles to the edge of the forest preserve and then hiked into the forest to set up camp. They rode at an average speed of 9 mph and walked at a speed of 2 mph in the 6 hours they traveled. How long did they walk in the forest if they traveled a total distance of 40 miles?

14. Young salmon hatch in freshwater streams and then migrate downstream to the ocean at the rate of 70 miles in 8 hours. There they live until they reach spawning age. Then they return upstream to fresh water to spawn and usually die soon after spawning. On the upstream trip, the salmon travel about 58 miles in 8 hours. Find the rate of the salmon swimming in still water and the rate of the current.

15. On his recent business trip, Mr. Modem left General Airport and took a flight to Scottsdale Airport, where he changed planes and continued to Calls Airport. The first plane traveled 376 mph and the second one 510 mph. How much time did he spend on each plane if he traveled 1463 miles and was on the planes 3 hours? How many miles did he travel on each plane?

INVESTMENT PROBLEMS

Investment problems, like motion problems, can be solved by using systems of equations. The basic formula used in interest or investment problems is $prt = i$; p (the principal or amount invested), r (the rate of interest), and t (the amount of time in years) are multiplied together to produce the interest gained.

EXAMPLE

Example 1.   Mr. Bland has $25,000 that he wants to invest at 8% and 10% interest. If his annual interest income is to be $2220, how much should he invest at each interest rate?

Solution.
Let x = amount to be invested at 8%
y = amount to be invested at 10%

1. Make a chart to help you determine what you are trying to find. Let the variables x and y stand for the unknowns, the two amounts to be invested. Fill in the rest of the chart from information in the problem. Notice that the rate of interest is recorded in decimal form. (Always change the rate to decimal form by dividing by 100.) Since annual interest means interest for one year, the number in the time column will be 1. Fill in the interest column by multiplying across the row.

	p	r	t	=	i
8% investment	x	.08	1		.08x
10% investment	y	.10	1		.10y

2. Now you must set up two equations to solve. Is there any information in the problem that you have not used yet? What about the $25,000 and the $2220? The $25,000 is principal, so using the principal column, you get the equation $x + y = 25,000$. $2220 is the interest, so using the interest column, you get the equation $0.08x + 0.10y = 2220$. Solve this system.

$x + y = 25,000$
$0.08x + 0.10y = 2220$

$x + y = 25,000$
$8x + 10y = 222,000$

$$-10x - 10y = -250{,}000$$
$$\underline{8x + 10y = 222{,}000}$$
$$-2x = -28{,}000$$
$$x = 14{,}000$$

$$14{,}000 + y = 25{,}000$$
$$y = 11{,}000$$

3. To solve this system by the addition method, multiply the top equation by -10 and the bottom equation by 100. Then solve for x.

4. Substitute 14,000 for x and solve for y.

Mr. Bland should invest $14,000 at 8% interest and $11,000 at 10% interest to make $2220 interest in one year.

As you study the next two problems, think of the reasoning behind the computations.

EXAMPLES

Example 2. The six-month interest check from a 11% investment was $95 more than a six-month interest check from a 9% investment. If $5000 was invested, how much was invested at each rate?

Solution. Let x = amount invested at 11%
y = amount invested at 9%

	p	r	t	=	i
1st investment	x	0.11	0.5		(0.11)(0.5)x = 0.055x
2nd investment	y	0.09	0.5		(0.09)(0.5)y = 0.045y

six months = 0.5 of a year
$$x + y = 5000$$
$$0.055x = 0.045y + 95$$

$$x + y = 5000 \rightarrow y = 5000 - x$$
$$1000\,(0.055x) = 1000\,(0.045y + 95)$$
$$55x = 45y + 95{,}000$$
By substitution, $55x = 45(5000 - x) + 95{,}000$
$$55x = 225{,}000 - 45x + 95{,}000$$
$$100x = 320{,}000$$
$$x = 3200$$

$$y = 5000 - 3200$$
$$y = 1800$$
So $3200 was invested at 11%, and $1800 was invested at 9% interest.

Example 3. Mike Davis is going to make two investments, and he knows that he will receive $770 in interest in a year. The sum of the interest rates is 17%. If he invests $4000 in one account and $5000 in the other account, what is the interest rate of each investment?

Solution. **1.** Assign variables.

Let x = the interest rate on the first investment
y = the interest rate on the second investment

2. Fill in the chart and set up a system of equations.

	p	r	t	$=$	i
first investment	4000	x	1		4000x
second investment	5000	y	1		5000y

$$4000x + 5000y = 770$$
$$x + y = 0.17$$
$$y = 0.17 - x$$

$$4000x + 5000(0.17 - x) = 770$$
$$4000x + 850 - 5000x = 770$$
$$-1000x = -80$$
$$x = 0.08$$

3. Solve this system by substitution.

$$y = .17 - .08$$
$$y = 0.09$$

The interest rate of the $4000 investment is 8%. The interest rate of the $5000 investment is 9%.

Exercises

Solve.

1. Mr. Hunter invested $10,000 in two different accounts. One account yields 10% interest while the other yields 9.5% interest. How much did he invest in each account if his total annual interest was $971?

2. A total of $6200 is invested in stock. The preferred stock yields 7% interest while the common stock yields 5.5% interest. How much is invested in each type of stock if the total investment brings in $389 per year?

3. Mark invests $8000 into an account that pays 12% interest and $2000 into an account that pays 8% interest. If he leaves the money in the accounts for the same length of time, how long must he leave it to gain $5600 in interest?

4. Mr. Cocran can invest one sum of money at 7% and a second sum at 10% and get $640 per year. If he invests his first sum at 10% and his second sum at 7%, he will make $550 per year. How much is he going to invest in the separate accounts? Which method of investment would be wiser?

5. Dr. Taylor invested $12,500, part at 9% and part at 7.5%. If the annual income from the investments is $1004.70, what was the amount of each investment?

6. Mary plans to invest a total of $7500 in two types of stocks, one paying 6% interest and the other paying 15% interest. How much does she invest into each type of stock if the total interest gained annually is $585?

7. Scott borrowed money from two different low-interest lending institutions. The total amount that he borrowed was $1200. He pays 7% annual interest on one loan and 8.5% annual interest on the other loan. The total amount of interest he pays annually is $89.25. How much did he borrow at each interest rate?

8. Miss Bunker invested one amount of money at 9.2% interest and another amount $700 more than the first at 10.4% interest. If the total amount of interest is $425.60 annually, how much money is in each investment?

9. Mr. Herbster invests a total of $15,000 in two different accounts. One of the accounts yields an interest rate of 8% and the other account pays 10%. The total amount of interest paid him is $1330 annually. What is the amount invested at each rate?

10. Paul Wilt is going to borrow $2000 for a computer. He cannot borrow it all from the same lending institution so he plans to get two loans. He can borrow from Federal Savings and Loan at a rate of 11% and at First Bank at the rate of 13%. How much does he borrow from each institution if he has to pay $232 in interest for the year?

11. Diane Ward invested $8000 into two separate accounts, but she can't remember the interest rate that she is being paid. She invested $2200 in one account and $5800 in the other account. What interest rate is she paid on each account if the rate on the $5800 investment pays 3 percentage points more than the other investment and her total interest was $734 for the year?

12. The Green Publishing Company invests a total of $27,000 into two new businesses. It expects a return of 14% on one business and 25% on the other business. How much did it invest in each business if it received $5540 in one year?

13. Gene receive an allowance of $1.00 per week. He has saved his money for three weeks and now wants to make an investment. His mother promises to pay him 30% interest if he leaves the money for a year. His father promises to pay him 25% interest for a year. If Gene makes an investment in each of his parents offers and receives 85¢ interest at the end of the year, how much did he invest in each parent's offer?

14. A businessman wants to invest some money in a branch business. He invests $20,000 in a dry cleaning establishment and $30,000 in a restaurant. What is his expected rate of return of profit, or rate of interest, on each investment if he expects a total of $4600 annually and the average of the two rates is 9%?

15. Miss Gresham plans to deposit $1200 into one account and $900 into another account. The rate of interest paid on the first account is two percentage points more than the second. If the total annual income from the two investments is $223.50, what is the interest rate of each investment?

16. Bob invests $8000 in one account and $3000 in a different account. The account in which he invested $8000 pays an interest rate 2 percentage points higher than that of the other account. What are the interest rates if the total amount of interest paid after 2 years is $1860?

MIXTURE PROBLEMS

Do you remember how to solve mixture problems with one variable? Look at example 1 to refresh your memory.

EXAMPLE

Example 1. The Nut Shop in the new mall sells roasted cashews for $5.50 a pound and roasted pecans for $4.00 a pound. The manager wants to make 75 pounds of a cashew and pecan party mix that sells for $4.40 a pound. How many pounds of each nut should he put in the mix?

Solution. (one variable)

Let x = pounds of cashews
      $75 - x$ = pounds of pecans

	number of pounds	price per pound	total price
cashews	x	5.50	5.50x
pecans	75 - x	4.00	4.00(75 - x)
mix	75	4.40	330.00

1. Set up a chart and fill in the information. The product of the number of pounds and the price per pound is the total price.
2. Set up an equation and solve.

$$5.50x + 4.00(75 - x) = 330.00$$
$$5.50x + 300 - 4.00x = 330.00$$
$$1.5x = 30$$
$$x = 20 \qquad 75 - x = 55$$

So the mix should contain 20 pounds of cashews and 55 pounds of pecans.

This problem can be solved just as easily by using two variables and by forming two equations from the information in the problem and from the chart.

Solution. (two variables)

Let x = pounds of cashews
y = pounds of pecans

1. Determine what the two variables will be and make a chart.

	numbers of pounds	price per pound	total price
cashews	x	5.50	5.50x
pecans	y	4.00	4.00y
mix	75	4.40	330.00

$x + y = 75$
total pounds of nut mixture

$5.50x + 4.00y = 330.00$
total price of nut mixture

2. Next set up two equations.

$$x + y = 75$$
$$550x + 400y = 33{,}000$$

3. Solve these equations simultaneously. First eliminate the decimals in the second equation by multiplying both sides by 100.

$$550x + 400(75 - x) = 33{,}000$$
$$550x + 30{,}000 - 400x = 33{,}000$$
$$150x = 3000$$
$$x = 20$$

$$y = 75 - x$$
$$y = 75 - 20$$
$$y = 55$$

4. Choose either the substitution method or the addition method for solving the system. The substitution method is illustrated here.

The mix contains 20 pounds of cashews and 55 pounds of pecans.

Study the solution using two equations and make sure you understand the procedures. Always make a chart and fill in each column.

Procedure for Storage

Solving Word Problems with Two Variables

1. Read the problem carefully and look for unknown quantities.
2. Let one variable represent one unknown and another variable represent the other unknown.
3. Make a chart and fill in as much information as possible from the problem.
4. Set up a system of equations from information in the chart and in the problem.
5. Solve the system.
6. Check the results in the original problem.

Look at examples 2 and 3. Think of each step as you go along.

EXAMPLES

Example 2. Emmanuel Christian School sent out 150 pieces of mail. Some of the letters required 20 cents postage while others required 32 cents postage. If the total postage bill was $35.52, how many pieces of each type were mailed?

Solution. Let x = number of letters with 20¢ postage
y = number of letters with 32¢ postage

	number of pieces	cost per piece	total price
20¢	x	0.20	$0.20x$
32¢	y	0.32	$0.32y$

$$x + y = 150$$
$$0.20x + 0.32y = 35.52$$

$$x + y = 150$$
$$20x + 32y = 3552$$

$$-20x - 20y = -3000$$
$$\underline{20x + 32y = 3552}$$
$$12y = 552$$
$$y = 46$$

$$x + y = 150$$
$$x + 46 = 150$$
$$x = 104$$

Emmanuel Christian School sent 104 letters with 20¢ postage and 46 letters with 32¢ postage.

Example 3. A dairy farmer is going to mix cream that is 30% fat with water that is 0% fat to make 60 gallons of milk that is 10% fat. How many gallons of cream and water should he mix together?

Solution.

Let x = number of gallons of cream   **1.** Assign variables and make chart.
y = number of gallons of water

	gal. of liquid	% of fat	gal. of fat
cream	x	0.30	$0.30x$
water	y	0.00	$0y$
mixture	60	0.10	$(0.10)60$

The liquid equation is
$x + y = 60$.

The fat equation is
$0.30x + 0y = (0.10)60$.

2. Make two equations, one for gallons of liquid and one for gallons of fat.

$$x + y = 60$$
$$0.30x = 6$$

3. Simplify both equations.

$$3x = 60$$
$$x = 20$$

4. Solve for x in the second equation. Eliminate the decimal by multiplying by 10.

$$20 + y = 60$$
$$y = 40$$

5. Substitute 20 for x in the first equation and solve for y.

Therefore, the farmer should mix 20 gallons of cream with 40 gallons of water.

Exercises

Use systems of equations to solve each word problem.

1. A butcher wants to grind round steak and sirloin steak together to make a deluxe ground beef. The round steak sells for $2.99 per pound and the sirloin sells for $3.89 per pound. How many pounds of each should he grind together to make 45 pounds of deluxe ground beef that will sell for $3.15 per pound?

2. Karen wants to make a mix of nuts and raisins for a party. Nuts cost 20¢ per ounce and raisins cost 12¢ per ounce. How many ounces of each should she buy if she wants 48 ounces of a mix that costs 15¢ per ounce?

3. At the local dairy two farmers bring in milk that are different percentages of fat. The first farmer has milk that is 15% fat, and the second farmer has milk that is 5% fat. If the standard fat content of milk that the dairy distributes is 11%, how many gallons of each farmer's milk should be mixed into 100-gallon cans?

4. A grocer wants to mix oranges and bananas to make a 10-pound fruit basket. The oranges cost 30¢ per pound and the bananas cost 35¢ per pound. How many pounds of each fruit should he use if the fruit basket is to cost $3.20?

5. The florist advertises a special on roses and carnations. Roses cost 85¢ a bud and carnations cost 55¢ a flower. If John pays $10.10, excluding tax, for a bouquet of 14 flowers for Teresa, how many of each flower is in the bouquet?

6. The pharmacist at Sam Will's Drugstore is making an antiseptic of iodine and alcohol. The iodine/alcohol mixture that he now has is only 5% iodine. He wants a mixture that contains 6% iodine. How much of a 10% iodine solution and how much of his original antiseptic should he mix to make 50 ml of the new antiseptic?

7. Bill Ramsey made a salt water solution that is 30% salt. How many gallons of pure water (0% salt) and salt water solution should he mix to make 40 gallons of a diluted solution that is 9% salt?

8. Grandma Lee mixes corn syrup and molasses together to make a special syrup that she uses on pancakes. If she can afford to pay 11¢ per ounce for the mix and corn syrup costs 6¢ per ounce and molasses costs 12¢ per ounce, how many ounces of each should she mix together to make 12 ounces of the mix?

9. Caramels cost 7¢ apiece, and butterscotches cost 3¢ apiece. Joy wants to buy a mixture of the two candies so that each candy will cost 5¢ apiece. If she buys a total of 20 pieces, how many of each kind of candy will she buy?

10. Raisin Rich breakfast cereal is 10% protein. A dietician wants to raise the percentage of protein served in a bowl of cereal to 20%. The high-protein grain that will be mixed with Raisin Rich is 40% protein. How many grams of each cereal should be mixed together to make a 12-gram serving of cereal with the proper percentage of protein?

11. Max Biggs, the gardener, plans to seed the front lawn with a new mix of grass seed. He has a mix that is 80% bluegrass and 15% clover. How much pure bluegrass and how much of his previous mix should he blend together to form 50 pounds of an 86% bluegrass mixture?

12. A grain farmer can sell 50 bushels of beans and 100 bushels of corn for $832.50, or he can sell 20 bushels of beans and 205 bushels of corn for $968.25. What is the selling price of beans and corn per bushel?

13. Concrete is made up of cement and an aggregate such as sand. Aggregates should make up 75% of the total mass of concrete. If the S. J. Concrete Company has a concrete mixture that is 60% aggregate, how many kilograms of this mix and how many kilograms of pure sand should be combined to form 48 kilograms of the concrete mix with the proper percentage of sand?

14. Mr. Lucas, the owner of a local pet store, wants to mix two different kinds of seed together to form a high-grade birdseed. Seed A sells for $1.17 per pound, seed B sells for $2.09 per pound, and the mixture will sell for $1.72 per pound. If Mr. Lucas wants to make 85 pounds of the seed mixture, how much of each seed (to the nearest tenth of a pound) should he mix together?

15. In ordinary ocean water, sodium chloride (the chemical name for ordinary table salt) represents 2.8% by mass. The Dead Sea, which lies between Israel and Jordan, is about 12% sodium chloride. If a chemist takes a sample of water from the Dead Sea and wants to dilute it with ordinary ocean water, how much ocean water and how much water from the Dead Sea (to the nearest tenth of a liter) should he combine to form 12 liters of a 10% sodium chloride solution?

16. Chemist John Wetzel has two HNO_3 acid and water solutions. John knows that the percentage of acid in solution I is 20 percentage points less than the percentage of acid in solution II. If he mixes 40 ml of solution I with 60 ml of solution II and obtains a mixture that is 27% acid, what percentage of acid is in each solution?

17. Betty Lou makes a homemade antiseptic that is a mixture of alcohol and water. If she buys a mixture that is 40% alcohol to make a 12.5% alcohol solution, how much water and alcohol should she mix to obtain 128 ml of homemade antiseptic?

18. How many pounds of $1.89 per pound coffee and $1.27 per pound grain must be mixed in order to make 86 pounds of a mixture that will sell for $1.55 per pound? (Round to the nearest tenth.)

19. Bill's Gas Station sells two types of bulk antifreeze mix. Type A is 40% ethylene glycol, and type B is 52% ethylene glycol. A customer wants ten quarts of antifreeze that would protect his radiator to -25°. To protect to -25°, the mix must be 45% ethylene glycol. How many quarts (to the nearest tenth of a quart) should Bill mix together to get the correct strength of ethylene glycol?

20. In District 12, 85% of the voters voted for Mr. Johnson for mayor. In District 13, 43% of the voters voted for Mr. Johnson. From the two districts 10,253 voters cast votes for Mr. Johnson. How many people voted for Mr. Johnson in each district if a total of 16,460 people voted in the districts?

MIND OVER MATH

Identify the next five numbers in each sequence and explain the progression.

1. 2, 4, 6, 8, . . .

2. 3, 6, 9, 15, 24, . . .

3. 1, 1, 2, 3, 5, 8, 13, . . .

4. 1, 3, 6, 10, 15, 21, . . .

5. 1, 4, 9, 16, 25, . . .

Identify the next group of letters in each sequence.

1. ABC, FGH, KLM, . . .

2. AZ, BY, CX, DW, . . .

3. AAB, ABB, BBC, BCC, . . .

4. ZX, ZV, ZT, . . .

5. AB, BD, DG, GK, . . .

Dynamic Mathematician

Leonhard Euler
(1707-1783)

Leonhard Euler was a unique individual. As one of the important men in the history of mathematics, he also had strong biblical convictions. It is encouraging to study the example of a man of such brilliance who also had a saving knowledge of Jesus Christ and a good testimony to those around him.

Leonhard was born to Paul and Marguerite Brucker Euler on April 15, 1707, in Basel, Switzerland. The family soon moved to Riechens, a small village where his father was the Calvinist pastor of the village church. Though Paul Euler, also an accomplished mathematician, introduced his young son to mathematics, he wanted Leonhard to follow in his footsteps as a preacher. Therefore, young Leonhard entered the University of Basel to study theology and Hebrew. Because he loved mathematics, he continued taking private math lessons each week from Johann (I) Bernoulli. At age seventeen, Leonhard had to give up temporarily his study of mathematics for theology. Finally Bernoulli convinced Leonhard's father that Leonhard was destined to be a great mathematician.

Then, with his father's approval, Leonhard turned his full attention to mathematics. His early training in theology served him well, however, and he never renounced one tenet of the Calvinist faith. As an old man, Leonhard conducted family prayers for his whole household, usually ending devotions with a sermon.

In 1727 at the age of twenty, Euler became chairman of mathematics at the New St. Petersburg Academy, founded by Peter the Great. Euler lived in Russia most of his life and gained his livelihood as a professor of math. In 1741 he moved to Berlin to head the Prussian Academy, where he served for almost twenty-five years. He was not very happy in Berlin, however, so he moved back to Russia.

In 1735 Euler lost the sight in his right eye because of an illness brought on by eyestrain he suffered when he solved a very difficult math problem in only three days. It had taken other prominent mathematicians several months to solve this same problem. Because of a cataract on his left eye, Euler was completely blind by 1766.

Despite his blindness Euler continued working for over fifteen years. He had a remarkable memory and the ability to concentrate amid loud disturbances. Perhaps he developed this ability because he was accustomed to working with his thirteen children gathered around him. During his lifetime he published 530 books and papers and wrote enough to fill 73 large volumes, which were published after his death.

Euler's mathematical achievements include classical research in algebra, trigonometry, analytical geometry, and calculus. He extended methods of analysis and greatly improved mathematical notation. He introduced the following notations: $f(x)$ for functional notation; $a, b, c,$ for the sides of a triangle ABC; and i for the imaginary number $\sqrt{-1}$. Leonhard lived a long, fruitful Christian life, and he should be remembered as one of the great mathematicians of the eighteenth century.

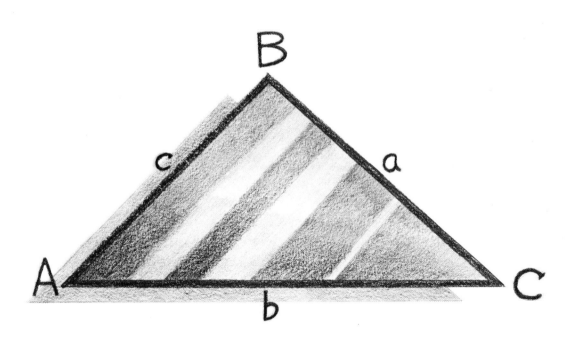

DIGIT PROBLEMS

The number system that we use today is based on the number 10 and is called the *decimal system.* Look up *decimal* in your dictionary. What does it mean? Where did the word come from? The word *decimal* comes from the Latin *decimalis,* meaning "tithe." You have probably heard the word *tithe* many times. What does it mean? What is a tithe?

Several Scripture passages such as Genesis 14:18-20; 28:22 and Leviticus 27:30-34 show that the Israelites, God's chosen people, gave a tenth (tithe) of everything they owned—not just their money—as part of their worship. Christians today are not bound by the Old Testament law, but they should recognize that a tenth is the bare minimum of what rightfully belongs to God. Actually, everything a Christian has belongs to God. So the Christian should cheerfully give to God (cf. II Cor. 9:7 and Rom. 12:1). Do you give to God because you love Him and want to do His will?

The decimal system consists of only ten digits, but all numbers can be represented by these ten digits. Each digit has its own value; its position in a number also indicates its value. For example, the numbers 38 and 83 contain the same digits. But do they represent the same value? No, the value is not the same. In the number 38, the digit 3 is in the tens place and has the value $3 \cdot 10$. The digit 8 is in the units place and has the value $8 \cdot 1$. So 38 can be expressed $3 \cdot 10 + 8 \cdot 1$. In 83, the digits have been reversed. The 8, in the units place in the original number, is now in the tens place and has the value $8 \cdot 10$. The 3, originally in the tens place, is now in the units place and has the value $3 \cdot 1$. So 83 can be expressed $8 \cdot 10 + 3 \cdot 1$.

Digit problems give you information usually about the digits in a number. Then you must solve a system of equations to find the two digits. Where do the equations come from? If you let t equal the tens digit and u equal the units digit, you can write $10t + u$ to represent any two-digit number. Then $10u + t$ represents the number with the digits reversed. $t + u$ represents the sum of the digits.

EXAMPLE

Example 1.   The sum of the digits of a two-digit number is 10. If you reverse the digits, the new number is 54 less than the original number. Find the original number.

Solution.   Let
$$t = \text{the tens digit}$$
$$u = \text{the units digit}$$
$$10t + u = \text{the original number}$$
$$10u + t = \text{the number with the digits reversed}$$
$$t + u = \text{the sum of the digits}$$

original number new number	**1.** Use the information given in the problem to set up a system of equations.

$$(10t + u) - 54 = (10u + t)$$

$$t + u = 10 \text{ the sum of the digits}$$

1. Use the information given in the problem to set up a system of equations.

$$10t + u - 10u - t = 54$$
$$9t - 9u = 54$$
$$t - u = 6$$

2. To solve this system, first simplify the first equation. Divide both sides by 9.

$$
\begin{aligned}
t - u &= 6 \\
\underline{t + u} &= \underline{10} \\
2t &= 16 \\
t &= 8
\end{aligned}
$$

3. Solve, using the addition method.

$$
\begin{aligned}
t - u &= 6 \\
8 - u &= 6 \\
-u &= -2 \\
u &= 2
\end{aligned}
$$

4. Substitute 8 for t into one of the equations.

The original number is $10 \cdot 8 + 2 = 82$

Procedure for Storage

Solving Digit Problems

1. Read the problem carefully and determine the necessary facts.
2. Set up a system of equations from the problem.
3. Solve the system.
4. Check the solution.

In the next example see if you can provide the reasons in the solution.

EXAMPLE

Example 2. The units digit of a two-digit number is one more than three times the tens digit. The sum of the digits is 9. Find the number.

Solution. Let

$$
\begin{aligned}
t &= \text{the tens digit} \\
u &= \text{the units digit} \\
10t + u &= \text{the number} \\
t + u &= \text{the sum of the digits}
\end{aligned}
$$

$$
\begin{aligned}
u &= 3t + 1 \\
t + u &= 9
\end{aligned}
$$

$$t + (3t + 1) = 9$$
$$4t + 1 = 9$$
$$4t = 8$$
$$t = 2$$

$$u = 3t + 1$$
$$u = 3 \cdot 2 + 1$$
$$u = 6 + 1$$
$$u = 7$$

The number is 27.

Exercises

Solve.

1. The sum of the digits of a number is 9, which is also one-third of the same two-digit number. What is the number?

2. The sum of the two digits of a number is 12, and the tens digit is twice the ones digit. What is the number?

3. The sum of the digits of a number is 10. The number is 36 less than the reversal of its digits. Find the number.

4. The tens digit of a certain two-digit number is 5 less than the units digit. When the digits are reversed, the sum of the two numbers is 121. Find the original number.

5. The sum of the two digits of a number is 10. When the digits are reversed, the original number is 72 less than the new number. What is the original number?

6. The tens digit of a number is 3 more than the units digit. If the digits are reversed and the original tens digit is added to this new number, the sum is 66. Find the original number.

7. The tens digit is 4 times the ones digit in a two-digit number. The original number minus the number when the digits are reversed is 54. Find the original number.

8. The sum of a two-digit number and the number represented by the reversal of the digits of that number is 88. The sum of the original number and its units digit is 24. Find the original number.

9. There is a certain two-digit number whose tens digit is equal to $1\frac{1}{2}$ times the units digit. The sum of the two digits is 15. What is the original number?

10. The difference of a two-digit number and the number with its digits reversed is 9. The sum of the digits is 7. What is the original number?

SYSTEMS OF INEQUALITIES

In Chapter 5 you learned how to graph an inequality with two unknowns. A system of inequalities generally has an infinite number of solutions. The solution to a system of inequalities can be determined by graphing each inequality on the same pair of axes and identifying the intersection of all the graphs.

EXAMPLE

Example 1.   Solve $3x + y > 4$
$x - y \leq 8$

Solution. $3x + y > 4$
$y > -3x + 4$
$x - y \leq 8$
$y \geq x - 8$

Why did the inequality sign change here?

1. Place both inequalities in slope-intercept form for easy graphing.

2. Graph the inequalities on the same set of axes.

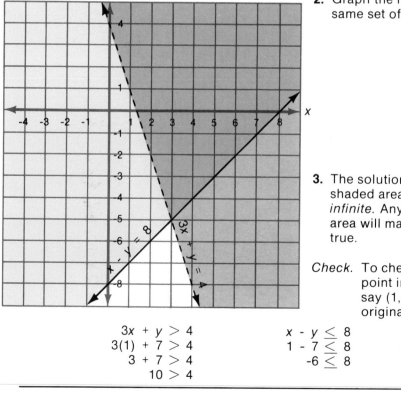

3. The solution is the darkest shaded area. This solution is *infinite.* Any point in this shaded area will make both inequalities true.

Check.   To check, choose any point in the shaded area, say (1,7), and try it in the original inequalities.

$3x + y > 4$
$3(1) + 7 > 4$
$3 + 7 > 4$
$10 > 4$

$x - y \leq 8$
$1 - 7 \leq 8$
$-6 \leq 8$

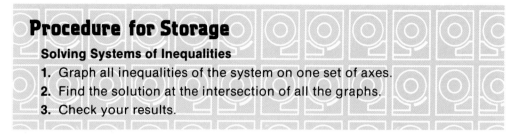

Procedure for Storage

Solving Systems of Inequalities

1. Graph all inequalities of the system on one set of axes.
2. Find the solution at the intersection of all the graphs.
3. Check your results.

EXAMPLE

Example 2.   Solve
$$x \geq 0$$
$$y \geq 0$$
$$2x + y \leq 4$$
$$3x + 2y \leq 6$$

Solution.
$$x \geq 0$$
$$y \geq 0$$

$$2x + y \leq 4$$
$$y \leq -2x + 4$$

$$3x + 2y \leq 6$$
$$2y \leq -3x + 6$$
$$y \leq \frac{-3x}{2} + 3$$

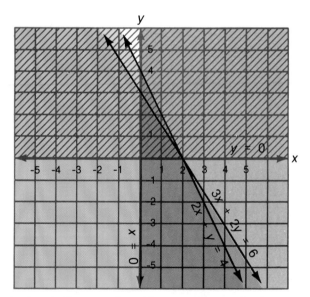

The solution is all the points in the darkest region. How could you find the ordered pairs for the three corner points in this shaded region?

Exercises

Graph each system of inequalities.

1. $x + y \geq 2$
$x - y < 4$

2. $3x + y > 9$
$2x + y \geq 6$

3. $5x + y > 2$
$2x + y \leq 1$

4. $3x - 2y \geq 6$
$x + y \leq 3$

5. $2x - y < 5$
$3x + y \geq 4$

6. $x + 5y < 15$
$3x + 2y \leq 8$

7. $x \geq 0$
$y \geq 0$
$2x + y \leq 4$
$x + y \geq 2$

8. $x \geq 0$
$y \geq 0$
$x + 4y \leq 8$
$2x + y \leq 4$

9. $x \geq 0$
$y \geq 0$
$3x + y \leq 8$
$x + 2y \leq 6$

10. $x \geq 0$
$y \leq 2$
$x + y > 1$

LINEAR PROGRAMMING

From the things you have learned in this chapter and a few more ideas presented in this section, you will be able to solve a linear program. A *linear program* is a method of solving problems that contain several conditions. Since linear programs are always concerned with finding the maximum or minimum value of an objective function, which determines the cost or profit of producing certain items, linear programs are an important part of a business company's work. Study the following examples to familiarize yourself with linear program problems.

EXAMPLES

Example 1. Maximize $z = x + 4y$ with the given set of constraints.

$$x \geq 0$$
$$y \geq 0$$
$$x + y \leq 4$$
$$2x + y \leq 6$$

Solution.

1. Graph the set of inequalities.

$$x \geq 0$$
$$y \geq 0$$
$$y \leq -x + 4$$
$$y \leq -2x + 6$$

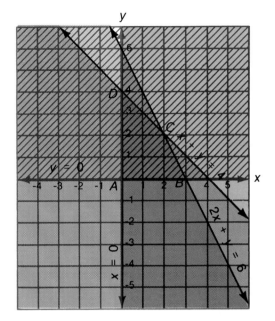

2. Find all the corner points of the shaded region on the graph (figure $ABCD$) by finding the intersection of the lines that produced the points. Point A is the origin $(0,0)$. Point B is on both the x-axis (the line $y = 0$) and the line defined by $2x + y = 6$. Solve this system to find the point B.

Substitute.

$$y = 0 \qquad 2x + 0 = 6$$
$$2x + y = 6 \qquad 2x = 6$$
$$x = 3$$

So point B is $(3,0)$.

Point C is the intersection of $x + y = 4$ and $2x + y = 6$. Subtract and solve these equations simultaneously to find C.

$$\begin{array}{r} x + y = 4 \\ - \quad 2x + y = 6 \\ \hline -x \quad\;\; = -2 \\ x = 2 \end{array} \qquad \begin{array}{l} x + y = 4 \\ 2 + y = 4 \\ y = 2 \end{array}$$

So point C is $(2,2)$.

Point D is the y-intercept of the line $x + y = 4$. So D is $(0,4)$.

	(x, y)	$z = x + 4y$
A	$(0,0)$	$z = 0 + 4(0) = 0$
B	$(3,0)$	$z = 3 + 4(0) = 3$
C	$(2,2)$	$z = 2 + 4(2) = 10$
D	$(0,4)$	$z = 0 + 4(4) = 16$

3. Since the problem says to maximize z, the ordered pair $(0,4)$ is the solution because it gives the largest value of z (16). So z is greatest at $(0,4)$.

The corner points of the shaded region are the only points that need to be checked to find the optimal solution.

Example 2. A manufacturing company has only 150 pounds of aluminum and 80 pounds of rubber from which to make softball bats and tennis rackets. Each softball bat requires 28 oz. of aluminum and 3 oz. of rubber. Each tennis racket requires 16 oz. of aluminum and 2 oz. of rubber. If the company makes $3 on each bat and $5 on each racket, how many of each piece of equipment should the company manufacture to make the most profit?

Solution.

1. Read the problem carefully and identify the important things to look for.
   a. Assign the variables x and y to the articles manufactured.
      Let x = the number of bats
         y = the number of rackets
   b. Since aluminum and rubber are important items in this problem, how much of each is required for each product? How many ounces of each raw material does the plant have on hand? Consolidate the information from the problem into a chart.

	oz. of Al	oz. of rubber	profit
bats	28	3	3
rackets	16	2	5
supply	2400	1280	

2. Determine the inequalities.
   Since x represents the number of bats and y represents the number of rackets, both x and y must be greater than or equal to 0.

   $$x \geq 0$$
   $$y \geq 0$$

   The total amount of aluminum and rubber to be used must be less than or equal to the quantities available.

   $$28x + 16y \leq 2400$$
   $$3x + 2y \leq 1280$$

   The set of inequalities (constraints) for this problem is this:

   $$x \geq 0$$
   $$y \geq 0$$
   $$28x + 16y \leq 2400$$
   $$3x + 2y \leq 1280$$

3. Place the inequalities in slope-intercept form and graph them on the same set of axes.

$$x \geq 0$$
$$y \geq 0$$

$$28x + 16y \leq 2400$$
$$7x + 4y \leq 600$$
$$4y \leq -7x + 600$$
$$y \leq \frac{-7x}{4} + 150$$

$$3x + 2y \leq 1280$$
$$2y \leq -3x + 1280$$
$$y \leq \frac{-3x}{2} + 640$$

The solution to the system of inequalities is the small shaded area. But the problem is not solved yet. You still have to find out how many of each piece of equipment the company should manufacture to make the most profit.

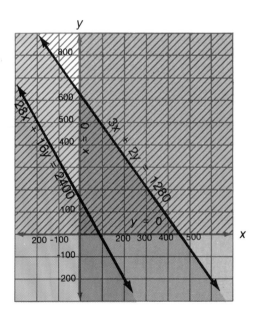

4. What does the problem say about profit? On each bat $3 is made; on each racket $5 is made. So to find the profit function (objective function) z, use the equation $z = 3x + 5y$.

5. To solve this equation, substitute values for x and y, which are determined by finding the corner points of the solution to the inequalities. It can be proved that the corner points are the only possible solutions. How can you find these corner points? Aren't they the intersection points of two lines?

corner point (x, y)	objective function z = 3x + 5y
(0, 0)	z = 3(0) + 5(0) = 0
(0, 150)	z = 3(0) + 5(150) = 750 maximum
(85.7, 0)	z = 3(85.7) + 5(0) = 257.1

Since we are maximizing the profit, we must choose the ordered pair that makes z the largest, which is (0, 150). Therefore the company should manufacture 0 bats and 150 rackets to make $750 profit.

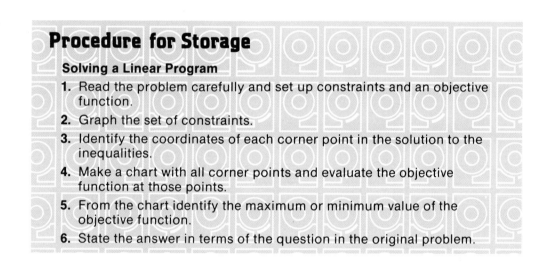

Procedure for Storage

Solving a Linear Program

1. Read the problem carefully and set up constraints and an objective function.
2. Graph the set of constraints.
3. Identify the coordinates of each corner point in the solution to the inequalities.
4. Make a chart with all corner points and evaluate the objective function at those points.
5. From the chart identify the maximum or minimum value of the objective function.
6. State the answer in terms of the question in the original problem.

EXAMPLE

Example 3.　Maximize $z = 2x + y$, subject to the following constraints.

$$x \geq 0$$
$$y \geq 0$$
$$x + y \leq 2$$
$$3x + y \leq 5$$

Solution.

$$x \geq 0$$
$$y \geq 0$$
$$y \leq -x + 2$$
$$y \leq -3x + 5$$

Find the corner points. One of them is (0, 0).

$3x + y = 5$ $y = 0$	$x + y = 2$ $- \ 3x + y = 5$	$x + y = 2$ $x = 0$
	$\overline{-2x \qquad = -3}$	
$3x + 0 = 5$ $3x = 5$	$x = \dfrac{3}{2}$	$0 + y = 2$ $y = 2$
$x = \dfrac{5}{3}$	$x + y = 2$ $\dfrac{3}{2} + y = 2$	$(0, 2)$
$\left(\dfrac{5}{3},\ 0 \right)$	$y = \dfrac{1}{2}$ $\left(\dfrac{3}{2},\ \dfrac{1}{2} \right)$	

Make a chart.

(x, y)	$z = 2x + y$
$\left(\dfrac{5}{3},\ 0 \right)$	$z = 2\left(\dfrac{5}{3} \right) + 0 = \dfrac{10}{3}$
$\left(\dfrac{3}{2},\ \dfrac{1}{2} \right)$	$z = 2\left(\dfrac{3}{2} \right) + \dfrac{1}{2} = \dfrac{7}{2}$
$(0, 2)$	$z = 2(0) + 2 = 2$
$(0, 0)$	$z = 2(0) + 0 = 0$

The maximum value of z is $3\frac{1}{2}$ at $\left(\dfrac{3}{2},\ \dfrac{1}{2} \right)$

Exercises

Solve each linear program.

1. Maximize $z = 2x + 6y$

subject to $x \geq 0$
$y \geq 0$
$x + y \leq 6$

2. Maximize $z = x + 10y$

subject to $x \geq 0$
$y \geq 0$
$2x - y \leq 6$
$x + y \leq 3$

3. Maximize $z = 3x - 2y$

subject to $x \geq 0$
$y \geq 0$
$4x + y \leq 5$
$x + 2y \leq 4$

4. Maximize $z = 5x + y$

subject to $x \geq 0$
$y \geq 0$
$3x + y \leq 13$
$x + y \leq 9$

5. The manager of Big Burger must decide how many of two kinds of burgers to prepare for the after-ball-game crowd. A regular burger requires $\frac{1}{4}$ lb. of hamburger, $\frac{1}{2}$ oz. of catsup, and 3 pickle slices. A superburger requires $\frac{1}{2}$ lb. of hamburger, 1 oz. of catsup, and 5 pickle slices. If the profit is 35¢ per regular burger and 50¢ per superburger and the stand has 20 lbs. of hamburger, 50 oz. of catsup, and 300 pickle slices, how many of each burger should the manager prepare to maximize profit? (Assume that all the hamburgers will be purchased.)

COMPUTER GRAPHICS

Computer graphics (using computers to create pictures) is an exciting and fairly new application of computers. Complex mathematical equations describe the surfaces of the objects shown on the facing page. Such a picture requires hundreds of millions of calculations. Computers that could handle those calculations at a reasonable cost were not designed until the late 1970s. These powerful but relatively inexpensive computers opened up the fledgling field of computer graphics and allowed it to grow rapidly.

Computer graphics allow engineers to design many different products without ever touching pen to paper. Mechanical engineers design mechanical parts and let the computers produce the drawings they need. Electronic engineers use computers to design every conceivable electronic device from transistor radios to computers on chips. Yet these are just the beginning of the possible applications of computer graphics.

Since computers have become easier to use, increasing numbers of nontechnical people have used them for artistic endeavors.

Artists who use computers can produce almost any type of image they can think of. Working from scratch and using the computer as a type of erasable canvas, an artist can create an image like the one with the "glass spheres" floating above the red and yellow checkerboard. Mathematical equations describe the textures and the reflections the artist wanted in the picture. Geometric shapes are especially easy to create.

Another growing use of computer graphics is in the field of medicine. Doctors can use special x-ray machines, called CAT (computerized axial tomography) scanners, to examine internal organs without

performing an operation. These computer-controlled instruments have taken their place alongside the doctor's stethoscope and scalpel.

In the future we will depend more and more on computerized information networks to keep in touch with the world around us. These networks will form the basis of our communications, and therefore will determine how we interact with society. Computer graphics will be a vital part of that information system. They could become as necessary as electricity and cars for our function in the modern world.

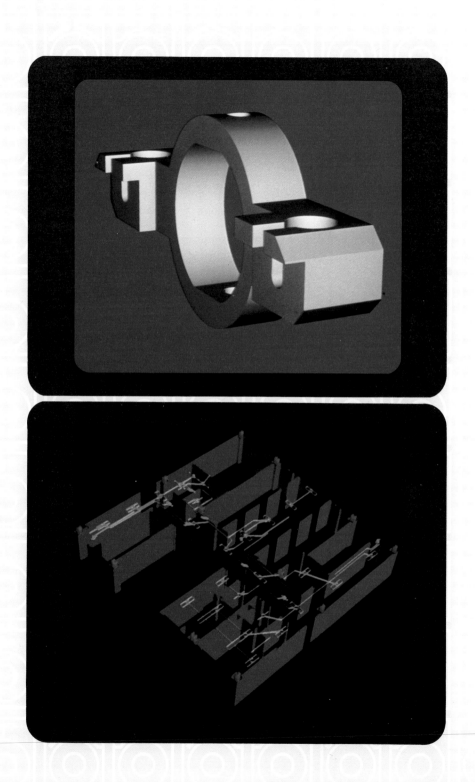

SYSTEMS WITH THREE VARIABLES

Find three numbers such that the sum of the first two is 39, the sum of the second two is 30, and the sum of the first and the third is 15.

To solve a problem like this, you need to know how to solve a system of three equations in three unknowns carefully and systematically so that you do not make mistakes.

As with systems of two equations, you must eliminate variables one at a time. To solve these systems, you need to combine the substitution and addition methods.

EXAMPLE

Example 1.   Solve
$$2x + y + z = 8$$
$$x - y + z = 6$$
$$3x + 2y + z = 15$$

Solution. You are trying to find an ordered triple (x, y, z) that will make all three equations true. To solve this system, choose a variable to eliminate by the addition method. Since z has the same coefficient in each equation, it is the easiest to eliminate.

$$
\begin{array}{r}
2x + y + z = 8 \\
- \quad x - y + z = 6 \\
\hline
x + 2y \quad\quad = 2
\end{array}
$$

1. Subtract to eliminate the z terms in the first and second equations.

$$
\begin{array}{r}
x - y + z = 6 \\
- \quad 3x + 2y + z = 15 \\
\hline
-2x - 3y \quad\quad = -9
\end{array}
$$

2. Next eliminate the z terms in the second and third equations.

$$2x + 4y = 4$$
$$+ \; \underline{-2x - 3y = -9}$$
$$y = -5$$

3. Now you have two equations in two unknowns. Solve them as a system.

$$x + 2y = 2$$
$$x + 2(-5) = 2$$
$$x - 10 = 2$$
$$x = 12$$

4. Substitute $y = -5$ into one of these equations to find x.

$$x - y + z = 6$$
$$12 - (-5) + z = 6$$
$$12 + 5 + z = 6$$
$$17 + z = 6$$
$$z = -11$$

5. Substitute $x = 12$ and $y = -5$ into one of the original equations.

So the ordered triple that will make all three equations true is (12, -5, -11).

Procedure for Storage

Solving a System in Three Unknowns

1. Use one or two steps to eliminate one variable and obtain a system of two equations with the same two unknowns.

2. Solve the resulting system.

3. Substitute results in one of the original equations to find the third unknown.

EXAMPLE

Example 2.   Find three numbers such that the sum of the first and the second is 39, the sum of the second and the third is 30, and the sum of the first and the third is 15.

Solution.   1. Assign variables and make a system of the equations.

Let x = the first number $x + y = 39$
y = the second number $y + z = 30$
z = the third number $x + z = 15$

$$x + y = 39$$
$$- y + z = 30$$
$$\overline{x - z = 9}$$

2. Use the first two equations to eliminate the y terms.

$$x + z = 15$$
$$+ x - z = 9$$
$$\overline{2x = 24}$$
$$x = 12$$

3. Now you have two equations in x and z. Solve this system.

$$x + z = 15$$
$$12 + z = 15$$
$$z = 3$$

4. Substitute to find the value of each of the other variables.

$$y + z = 30$$
$$y + 3 = 30$$
$$y = 27$$

The solution is (12, 27, 3).

Exercises

Solve each system of equations.

1. $2x + y + z = 8$
$x + y - z = 4$
$x + z = 6$

2. $x + z = 0$
$y = 3x - 6$
$x + y + z = 9$

3. $x - y = 4$
$y - z = 8$
$x + z = 12$

4. $2x + y - z = 12$
$x - y + z = -3$
$x + y + 3z = 17$

5. $3x - y + 2z = -5$
$x + y + 4z = -3$
$8x + 2y - z = 18$

6. $x - 2y + 3z = 20$
$3x + 4y - z = -20$
$x + y - 7z = -53$

7. $x - 3y + 5z = 33$
$2x - y + 4z = 32$
$x - 2y - z = -17$

8. $3x + y - z = 16$
$x + y + 2z = 12$
$x - y + z = 8$

9. $x + y = 8$
$x + z = 2$
$y + z = 11$

10. $2x + 3y - z = 21$
$x + y + 2z = 18$
$x - 3y + 2z = 12$

11. The sum of the digits of a certain three-digit number is 12. The units digit is one more than the hundreds digit. If the tens digit and the units digit are reversed, the number is 36 smaller than the original number. What is the number?

Here is a 3 x 3 magic square. Use the numbers 1 through 9 to fill in the square so that the sum of each row, column, and diagonal is equal to $\frac{n^3 + n}{2}$.

(n = the length of one side of the square)

You can make a magic square for any odd number by following the instructions given here. Try a 5 x 5 square.

1. Place 1 in the center square in the top row.

2. Move up diagonally to the right. Since you have moved out of the top of the square, put 2 in the square at the bottom of that column.

3. Move up diagonally to the right from 2 and put 3 in the square.

4. Move up diagonally to the right again. Since you have moved out of the right side of the square, put 4 in the square at the left end of that row.

5. Move up diagonally to the right and put 5 in the square.

6. Since you cannot move up diagonally to the right from 5, put 6 in the square below 5. Then proceed with the steps as given above.

Can you finish this magic square? Can you make a 7 x 7 magic square? What is the sum of each row? column? diagonal? What is the sum of the four corners and the center square?

If you move out of the top of the square, put the next number in the empty square closest to the bottom of the column.

If you move out of the right side of the square, put the next number in the empty square closest to the left end of that row.

If you cannot move up diagonally to the right within the square, put the next number below the previous number.

If you always begin your magic square with 1, you can use the formula $\frac{n^3 + n}{2}$ to find the sum of the rows, columns, and diagonals.

MEMORY RECALL

Identify.
consistent system   inconsistent system
decimal system   independent system
dependent system   substitution method
eliminating a variable   system of equations

You should be able to do the following:

1. Solve a system of linear equations by using three different methods: graphing, substitution, and addition.
2. Tell if a system of equations is consistent or inconsistent.
3. Tell if a consistent system is independent or dependent.
4. Solve various applied problems.
5. Solve a given system of inequalities.
6. Solve a system of three equations in three unknowns.

You should be able to solve these problems:

1. Use the graphing method to solve each system. Label the system inconsistent or consistent. Label the consistent systems independent or dependent.

   a. $x + y = 11$ **b.** $3x - y = 14$ **c.** $x + y = -2$
       $2x - y = -5$ $x + 3y = -12$ $3x + y = -10$

2. Use the substitution method to solve each system. Label the system inconsistent or consistent. Label the consistent systems independent or dependent.

   a. $2x + 3y = 8$ **c.** $4x + 3y = -20$
       $x + 2y = 4$ $5x - 2y = -2$
   b. $5x - 3y = 12$ **d.** $5x + y = 8$
       $3x + y = -2$ $-10x - 2y = -3$

3. Use the addition method to solve each system. Label the system inconsistent or consistent. Label the consistent systems independent or dependent.

   a. $x - 2y = -11$ **c.** $5x - 3y = -25$
       $3x + y = 16$ $6x + 2y = -2$
   b. $2x + 3y = 9$ **d.** $x + y = -2$
       $4x - y = 2$ $2x + 2y = -4$

4. Sugar Tooth Candy Company needs 300 gallons of a 32% sucrose solution for a certain kind of candy. The company has a solution that is 60% sucrose and a solution that is 25% sucrose. How many gallons of each should the company mix together to obtain the desired solution?

5. Mr. Arnold is going to invest $1550 in two separate accounts. One account pays 7.5%, and the other account pays 8.25%. How much should he invest in each account so that his annual return on his investment will be $121.20?

6. Two fishing boats leave Sandy Cove at the same time traveling in the same direction. One boat is traveling three times as fast as the other boat. After five hours the faster boat is 80 miles ahead of the slower boat. What is the speed of each boat?

7. The sum of the digits of a certain two-digit number is 12. If the digits are reversed the difference between the original number and the new number is 18. What is the original number?

8. Graph each system of inequalities.

   a. $2x + y < 6$ **b.** $5x + 2y \leq 8$ **c.** $3x + 5y \geq 12$

       $3x - y \geq 4$ $x + y > -5$ $2x - 3y < -6$

9. Solve the following linear programming problem.

$$x \geq 0$$
$$y \geq 0$$
$$x + 2y \leq 8$$
$$4x - y \leq 12$$
$$\text{Maximize } z = 3x + 2y$$

10. Find the value of x, y, and z.

$$x + 3y - 2z = 5$$
$$2x + y + 3z = -7$$
$$3x - y + 6z = -17$$

CHAPTER 7

RADICALS

A tsunami is a large, deadly ocean wave that is produced by an earthquake in the ocean floor. The water waves are deadly because they can reach fantastic speeds as they roll along the ocean's surface. Some tsunamis have been clocked as high as 600 mph out in deep water. They produce dangerous tidal waves when they get close to shore and often kill many people when they hit the shore.

The speed of the waves can be calculated according to the formula $V = \sqrt{gh}$, in which V represents the speed, or velocity, of the ocean wave; g is gravitational acceleration of 32 ft./sec.^{2}; and h is the depth of the water in feet. What is the velocity of the tsunami in water that is 60 feet deep? 800 feet deep? 1800 feet deep?

When an earthquake of a magnitude greater than 6.5 on the Richter scale occurs on the ocean floor, computers quickly go to work figuring the speed of the waves and the place that the killer wave will hit. This technology is saving many lives, for people can be warned to go inland to avoid the tsunami.

The formula that describes the velocity of the wave is a radical equation. You can find radicals in many practical problems and frequently in physics and other scientific problems. At this point you may not know how to solve this problem or any like it, but by the end of this chapter you will be able to tell how fast the waves are moving at the given depths.

APPROXIMATING SQUARE ROOTS

When you studied square roots in Chapter 1, the radicands you looked at were perfect squares. Since you memorized the squares of the first twenty integers, you should be able to easily identify the positive (principal) root when you see one of those numbers squared. All of the roots of perfect squares are rational numbers. You will now study radicals whose roots are irrational numbers. Do you remember what irrational numbers are? Irrational numbers cannot be expressed as fractions but are frequently expressed as nonterminating, nonrepeating decimals. Irrational numbers in decimal form are only approximations of the real number defined by the radical. The square root sign and π are used to symbolize certain irrational numbers because it is impossible to write them in precise decimal form.

An approximation is an act or process of drawing near or together. Christian education should help Christian young people come closer to the image of God. If you have accepted Jesus Christ as your personal Saviour, James 4:7-8 commands you to draw near to God and promises that He will draw near to you. What a blessed promise that Christians can claim! Can you claim this promise? Do you know Christ as your Saviour? Can you find some other verses about the nearness of God?

What does $\sqrt{8}$ equal? God is the only one who knows the exact decimal value of $\sqrt{8}$. In most of your algebraic work you will want to leave the answer in square root form without finding the approximation. Sometimes you will need to know a close approximation to the square root of a number.

To find the whole number approximation of any radicand greater than 0, think of the largest perfect square less than the radicand and the smallest perfect square greater than the radicand. For $\sqrt{8}$, 4 is the largest perfect square less than 8, and 9 is the smallest perfect square greater than 8. Since $4 < 8 < 9$, then $\sqrt{4} < \sqrt{8} < \sqrt{9}$, which can be simplified to $2 < \sqrt{8} < 3$. So the $\sqrt{8}$ is between 2 and 3. If you are asked to find a more exact approximation to the radical, say, for example, $\sqrt{8}$ rounded to tenths, you can use any one of the three following methods.

1. Use a calculator with a square root button. Round the solution to the nearest tenth.

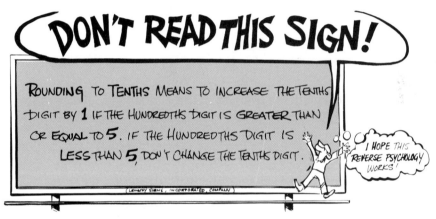

2. Look for the number on a square root table. (See page 564.) Become familiar with the table and learn how to use it.

3. When you do not have access to a calculator or a table, or when the number is so large that it is not listed on the table, you will need to use the successive approximation method, which yields the square root of a number through a series of approximations, divisions, and averages.

EXAMPLE

Example 1.   Find $\sqrt{8}$ to the nearest tenth.

Solution.   Method 1.
A calculator giving square roots will give 2.8284271 for $\sqrt{8}$. Rounded to the nearest tenth, $\sqrt{8}$ is 2.8 .

Method 2.
The square root table on page 564 gives $\sqrt{8}$ as 2.828 .
Rounded to the nearest tenth, $\sqrt{8}$ is 2.8 .

Method 3.

1. Determine the whole number whose square is less than 8. That number, 2, is the first approximation.

2. Divide the radicand, 8, by the first approximation, 2.

$$8 \div 2 = 4$$

3. Calculate the average of the quotient, 4, and the first approximation, 2, to get the second approximation.

$$\frac{4 + 2}{2} = \frac{6}{2} = 3$$

4. Divide the radicand by the second approximation.

$$8 \div 3 = 2.66$$

5. Calculate the average of the quotient and the second approximation to get the third approximation.

$$\frac{2.66 + 3}{2} = \frac{5.66}{2} = 2.83$$

6. Divide the radicand by the third approximation.

$$8 \div 2.83 = 2.827 = 2.83$$

Using this method, you find that $\sqrt{8} = 2.8$.

Procedure for Storage

Approximating Square Roots by Successive Approximation

1. Find a whole number whose square is less than the given radicand.

2. Divide the radicand by the approximation.

3. Calculate the average of the quotient and the approximation to obtain a new approximation.

4. Repeat steps 2 and 3 until two successive approximations are equal at the desired degree of accuracy.

EXAMPLES

Example 2. Using the successive approximation method, find $\sqrt{132}$ to the nearest hundredth.

Solution.

$$11 < \sqrt{132} < 12$$

1. Determine the whole number approximation. Choose the number whose square is less than the radicand.

$$132 \div 11 = 12$$

2. Divide the radicand by the approximation.

$$\frac{12 + 11}{2} = 11.5 \text{ second}$$
approximation

3. Calculate the average to get the second approximation.

$$132 \div 11.5 = 11.478$$

4. Divide.

$$\frac{11.478 + 11.5}{2} = 11.489 \text{ third}$$
approximation

5. Average.

$$132 \div 11.489 = 11.489$$

6. Divide. Since the third approximation and this quotient are the same at the desired degree of accuracy, round for the final solution.

Therefore, $\sqrt{132} = 11.49$ to the nearest hundredth.

Example 3. Find $\sqrt{0.54}$ to the nearest hundredth.

Solution. $0 < \sqrt{0.54} < 1$

IF THE RADICAND IS BETWEEN 0 AND 1, LET 1 BE YOUR FIRST APPROXIMATION

$$0.54 \div 1 = 0.54$$ 1 is the first approximation.

$$\frac{0.54 + 1}{2} = 0.77$$ second approximation

$$0.54 \div 0.77 = 0.701$$ rounded to thousandths

$$\frac{0.701 + 0.77}{2} = 0.736$$ third approximation

$$0.54 \div 0.736 = 0.734$$ rounded to thousandths

$$\frac{0.734 + 0.736}{2} = 0.735$$ fourth approximation

$$0.54 \div 0.735 = 0.735$$ rounded to thousandths

So $\sqrt{0.54} = 0.74$ rounded to the nearest hundredth.

Exercises

Use either a calculator or the table on page 564 to find the approximate value of each square root. Try at least three problems with each method. Round to the nearest tenth.

1. $\sqrt{43}$
2. $\sqrt{25}$
3. $\sqrt{141}$
4. $\sqrt{95}$
5. $\sqrt{56}$
6. $\sqrt{23}$
7. $\sqrt{12}$
8. $\sqrt{3}$

9. $\sqrt{148}$
10. $\sqrt{111}$
11. $\sqrt{72}$
12. $\sqrt{121}$
13. $\sqrt{687}$
14. $\sqrt{19600}$
15. $\sqrt{1296}$
16. $\sqrt{13456}$

Use the successive approximation method to find the approximate value of each square root. Round to the nearest tenth.

17. $\sqrt{30}$
18. $\sqrt{1.58}$
19. $\sqrt{106}$
20. $\sqrt{1592}$
21. $\sqrt{92.84}$

22. $\sqrt{103}$
23. $\sqrt{17}$
24. $\sqrt{0.382}$
25. $\sqrt{67}$
26. $\sqrt{128}$

RADICAL AND EXPONENTIAL EQUIVALENTS

Square roots, or any root for that matter, can be written in exponential form. In the radical $\sqrt[3]{4^2}$ the index is 3, the radicand is 4 and the exponent is 2. In general, we could write every radical in the form $\sqrt[b]{x^a}$ where the index is b, the radicand is x, and the exponent on the radicand is a. In some cases the exponent 1 is understood, such as in $\sqrt[3]{8}$. In some cases the index 2 is understood, such as in $\sqrt{3^4}$.

Comparing the following computations will show a pattern for changing radicals to their exponential equivalents. Consider these two facts.

1. $\sqrt{4} \cdot \sqrt{4} = \sqrt{4^2}$ and   **2.** $4^{\frac{1}{2}} \cdot 4^{\frac{1}{2}} = 4^{(\frac{1}{2} + \frac{1}{2})}$

$$= \sqrt{16} \qquad\qquad = 4^1$$
$$= 4 \qquad\qquad\quad = 4$$

Since $4 = 4$,

Then $\sqrt{4} \cdot \sqrt{4} = 4^{\frac{1}{2}} \cdot 4^{\frac{1}{2}}$

$$(\sqrt{4})^2 = (4^{\frac{1}{2}})^2$$

$$\sqrt{4} = 4^{\frac{1}{2}}$$

You can change any radical to exponential form by following the pattern. $\sqrt[b]{x^a} = x^{\frac{a}{b}}$

THEY SURE MAKE THESE THINGS HARD TO PUT UP!

HC RRRRRRATTLE!

WHEN YOU CHANGE A RADICAL TO EXPONENTIAL FORM, BE SURE YOU CHANGE EVERY MEMBER OF THE RADICAL

Earlier you were introduced to some roots other than square roots, such as $\sqrt[3]{8}$, read "the cube root of 8." Recall that you are trying to find three equal factors whose product is 8.

$$\sqrt[3]{8} = 2$$

Notice that this radical can be expressed in exponential form.

$$\sqrt[3]{8} = 8^{\frac{1}{3}} = 2$$

EXAMPLES

Example 1. Change $\sqrt[5]{4x^3y^2}$ to exponential form.

Solution. $\sqrt[5]{4x^3y^2} = (4^1x^3y^2)^{\frac{1}{5}} = 4^{\frac{1}{5}}x^{\frac{3}{5}}y^{\frac{2}{5}}$

Example 2. Change $3^{\frac{1}{3}}x^{\frac{2}{3}}$ to a radical form.

Solution. $3^{\frac{1}{3}}x^{\frac{2}{3}} = (3^1x^2)^{\frac{1}{3}} = \sqrt[3]{3x^2}$

You should be able to give a whole number approximation for roots other than square roots, but you will not be required to find their approximation any more accurately.

Exercises

Change each radical to exponential form.

1. $\sqrt{5}$ **6.** $\sqrt[4]{x^3y^2z}$

2. $\sqrt{3x}$ **7.** $\sqrt[10]{8^3xy^4}$

3. $\sqrt[3]{2x^2}$ **8.** $\sqrt{2^2x^2}$

4. $\sqrt{127}$ **9.** $\sqrt[7]{9^2a^5}$

5. $\sqrt[5]{3x^2t}$ **10.** $\sqrt[8]{2^{16}a^8}$

Change each exponential expression to radical form.

11. $5^{\frac{1}{2}}a^{\frac{1}{2}}$

12. $7^{\frac{2}{3}}b^{\frac{1}{3}}c^{\frac{4}{3}}$

13. $2^{\frac{4}{7}}x^{\frac{1}{7}}y^{\frac{3}{7}}$

14. $5^{\frac{1}{9}}a^{\frac{2}{9}}b^{\frac{5}{9}}$

15. $3^{\frac{3}{8}}5^{\frac{1}{4}}x^{\frac{5}{8}}$

Give a whole number approximation for each radical.

16. $\sqrt[3]{9}$

17. $\sqrt[4]{15}$

18. $\sqrt{18}$

19. $\sqrt[5]{38}$

20. $\sqrt[3]{29}$

Place the numbers 1 through 11 in the circles below so that any three circles in a straight line make the same sum.

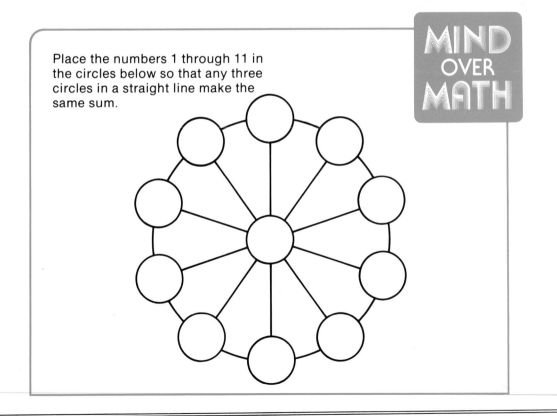

Making Math Work

Karl Friedrich Gauss
(1777-1855)

Karl Friedrich Gauss was born in a duchy of West Germany. His father was a bricklayer. His mother and father were common people who did not see the value of an education for their son but thought he should work as a common laborer to help them financially. Johann Martin Bartels, a professor of math at Dorpat, observed Gauss's unique aptitude for calculation. Professor Bartel told Charles William, Duke of Brunswick, about the boy, and the duke decided to educate Karl himself.

In 1792 at age fifteen, Gauss was sent to Caroline College to study. Three years later he knew everything the professors there could teach him. While attending Caroline College, Gauss studied two advanced concepts of mathematics: the methods of least squares, and the proof of the law of quadratic reciprocity. He did all of this before he reached age nineteen. In 1796

Gauss found a way to construct a seventeen-sided regular polygon using only a compass and a straightedge.

By 1798 Gauss earned a living by being a private tutor in Brunswick. In 1799 he published a proof of the fundamental theorem of algebra, which states that every algebraic equation has at least one root (solution).

Gauss's studies were not limited to mathematics. He was the first theoretical astronomer; he calculated the orbits of the asteroids between Mars and Jupiter. Because of his study of math and astronomy, Gauss became the director of the Gottingen Observatory and a professor of astronomy there in 1807. From 1830 to 1840 he did research on electricity and magnetism. In 1840 he published his research on optics and systems of lenses. However, his most famous work, *Disquisitiones Arithmeticae,* was a paper dealing with his research in number theory.

One of Gauss's most distinguishing characteristics was that he was one of the last men to have a diversified field of study. He studied not only mathematics but also many math-related fields, such as astronomy, electricity, and optics. Many students today need to become more diversified and be able to apply the mathematical knowledge they have obtained to different areas of study.

SIMPLIFYING RADICALS

Do you remember that fractional answers are always given in simplest form? Each time you have a radical in the solution to a problem, that radical must be expressed in simplified form. A radical is in simplified form when the radicand has no perfect power factors, no radicals in the denominator, and no fractions under the radical sign. A basic property of radicals that is used when simplifying radicals is the *product property*, which states that for real numbers x and y greater than or equal to 0,

$$\sqrt[n]{xy} = \sqrt[n]{x} \cdot \sqrt[n]{y}.$$

Because approximations are not completely accurate, mathematicians usually use simplified radicals to express a completely accurate solution. One way to simplify radicals is to factor the radicand so that one factor is a perfect power (a power that is divisible by the index).

EXAMPLES

Example 1.   Simplify $\sqrt{24}$.

$$\sqrt{24} = \sqrt{4} \cdot \sqrt{6} = \sqrt{2^2} \cdot \sqrt{6} = 2\sqrt{6}$$

Example 2.   Simplify $\sqrt{75}$.

$$\sqrt{75} = \sqrt{25} \cdot \sqrt{3} = \sqrt{5^2} \cdot \sqrt{3} = 5\sqrt{3}$$

Example 3.   Simplify $\sqrt[3]{40}$.

$$\sqrt[3]{40} = \sqrt[3]{8} \cdot \sqrt[3]{5} = \sqrt[3]{2^3} \cdot \sqrt[3]{5} = 2\sqrt[3]{5}$$

Procedure for Storage

General Method of Simplifying Radicals
1. Prime factor the radicand.
2. Divide the exponent on each prime factor by the index.
3. The quotient becomes the exponent on the prime factor outside the radical sign, and the remainder becomes the exponent on the prime factor inside the radical sign.

EXAMPLES

Example 4. Simplify $\sqrt{16}$.

Solution.

1. Prime factor 16.

$$16 = 2^4$$

2. Divide the exponent by the index.

$$2^2\sqrt{2^0}$$
$$2^2\sqrt{1}$$

$$2^2 \cdot 1 = 4$$

So $\sqrt{16} = 4$

3. The quotient, 2, becomes the exponent on the prime factor, 2, outside the radical sign; the remainder, 0, becomes the exponent on the prime factor, 2, inside the radical sign. Simplify.

Example 5. Simplify $\sqrt[3]{648}$.

Solution.

1. Prime factor 648.

$$\sqrt[3]{648} = \sqrt[3]{2^3 \cdot 3^4}$$

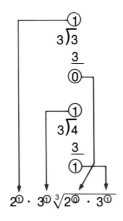

2. Divide the exponent on each prime factor by the index.

   a. The exponent on 2 is 3, so divide 3 by the index 3.

   b. The exponent on 3 is 4, so divide 4 by the index 3.

3. Determine the exponents of the factors.

   a. The exponent on the factor 2 outside the radical is the quotient 1, and the exponent on the factor 2 inside the radical is the remainder 0.

   b. The exponent on the factor 3 outside the radical is the quotient 1, and the exponent on the factor 3 inside the radical is the remainder 1.

4. Simplify.

$$2 \cdot 3 \sqrt[3]{1 \cdot 3}$$

$$6 \sqrt[3]{3}$$

Therefore $\sqrt[3]{648} = 6\sqrt[3]{3}$

Example 6. Simplify $\sqrt{76}$.

   Solution. $76 = 2^2 \cdot 19^1$ So $\sqrt{76} = \sqrt{2^2 \cdot 19^1}$

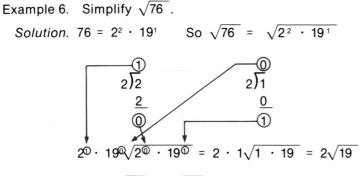

$$2^① \cdot 19^⓪\sqrt{2^⓪ \cdot 19^①} = 2 \cdot 1\sqrt{1 \cdot 19} = 2\sqrt{19}$$

Therefore $\sqrt{76} = 2\sqrt{19}$

Example 7.   Simplify $\sqrt[5]{14580}$

Solution. $14580 = 2^2 \cdot 3^6 \cdot 5^1$

$$\sqrt[5]{14580} = \sqrt[5]{2^2 \cdot 3^6 \cdot 5^1}$$

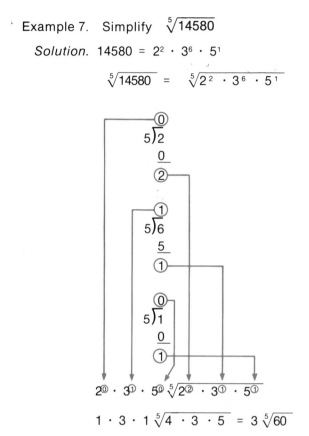

$$2^{⓪} \cdot 3^{①} \cdot 5^{⓪} \sqrt[5]{2^{②} \cdot 3^{①} \cdot 5^{①}}$$

$$1 \cdot 3 \cdot 1 \sqrt[5]{4 \cdot 3 \cdot 5} = 3 \sqrt[5]{60}$$

$$\sqrt[5]{14580} = 3 \sqrt[5]{60} \ .$$

Always leave your answers to problems with radicals in the solutions in simplest form. If you simplify your answers, you and others will be able to work with your solutions more easily.

Another thing that you shouldn't complicate but should communicate in the simplest form possible is the gospel message. Read I Corinthians 15:1-4 and notice that Paul made the gospel message very simple to the Corinthians. When you witness to others, you should present the plan of salvation simply and clearly.

Exercises

Simplify each radical that can be simplified.

1.	$\sqrt{32}$	**11.**	$\sqrt[5]{1025}$
2.	$\sqrt{18}$	**12.**	$\sqrt[7]{1792}$
3.	$\sqrt[3]{54}$	**13.**	$\sqrt[3]{14000}$
4.	$\sqrt[3]{116}$	**14.**	$\sqrt{694575}$
5.	$\sqrt[4]{244}$	**15.**	$\sqrt{44100}$
6.	$\sqrt[5]{32}$	**16.**	$\sqrt{4704}$
7.	$\sqrt{12}$	**17.**	$\sqrt[3]{70875}$
8.	$\sqrt{182}$	**18.**	$\sqrt[3]{160}$
9.	$\sqrt{98}$	**19.**	$\sqrt[4]{729}$
10.	$\sqrt[3]{98}$	**20.**	$\sqrt[3]{18900}$

MULTIPLYING RADICALS

Radicals must have the same index before they can be multiplied. When you multiply radicals, perform the product rule in reverse.

$$\sqrt[n]{x} \cdot \sqrt[n]{y} = \sqrt[n]{xy}$$

You can either multiply and then simplify, or you can simplify and then multiply. If you simplify first, you may have to simplify again after you multiply. If the radicals have coefficients, you must multiply the coefficients together too.

EXAMPLES

Example 1.   Multiply $\sqrt{2} \cdot \sqrt{3}$.

Solution.

$$\sqrt{2} \cdot \sqrt{3} = \sqrt{2 \cdot 3} = \sqrt{6}$$ Since both of the original factors are in simplest form and have the same index, simply multiply the factors.

Example 2.   Multiply $3\sqrt{2} \cdot 4\sqrt{5}$.

Solution. $3\sqrt{2} \cdot 4\sqrt{5}$

$(3 \cdot 4)(\sqrt{2} \cdot \sqrt{5})$

1. Following the commutative property, you can arrange this multiplication problem in a different order.

$12(\sqrt{2 \cdot 5})$

2. Multiply the coefficients; then multiply the radicands.

$12\sqrt{10}$

Can you simplify this radical?

Example 3.   Multiply $\sqrt{12} \cdot \sqrt{4}$.

Solution. $\sqrt{12} = \sqrt{2^2 \cdot 3} = 2\sqrt{3}$

1. Simplify each factor.

$\sqrt{4} = 2$

$\sqrt{12} \cdot \sqrt{4} = 2\sqrt{3} \cdot 2$

2. Multiply.

$= 4\sqrt{3}$

Example 4.   Multiply $\sqrt{10} \cdot \sqrt{8}$.

Solution. $\sqrt{10} = \sqrt{2 \cdot 5}$

$\sqrt{8} = \sqrt{2^3} = 2\sqrt{2}$

1. If possible, simplify each factor first. $\sqrt{10}$ cannot be simplified.

$\sqrt{10} \cdot \sqrt{8} = \sqrt{2 \cdot 5} \cdot 2\sqrt{2}$

2. Multiply. (Remember, when multiplying like bases, add the exponents.)

$= 2\sqrt{2^2 \cdot 5}$

3. Simplify this radical.

$= 2 \cdot 2\sqrt{5}$

$= 4\sqrt{5}$

Therefore $\sqrt{10} \cdot \sqrt{8} = 4\sqrt{5}$.

Example 5. Multiply $\sqrt[3]{1125} \cdot \sqrt[3]{63}$.

Solution. $\sqrt[3]{1125} = \sqrt[3]{3^2 \cdot 5^3} = 5\sqrt[3]{3^2}$ **1.** Simplify each factor.

$\qquad\sqrt[3]{63} = \sqrt[3]{3^2 \cdot 7}$

$\sqrt[3]{1125} \cdot \sqrt[3]{63} = 5\sqrt[3]{3^2} \cdot \sqrt[3]{3^2 \cdot 7}$ **2.** Multiply, observing the properties of exponents.

$\qquad\qquad = 5\sqrt[3]{3^4 \cdot 7}$ **3.** Simplify again.

$\qquad\qquad = 5 \cdot 3\sqrt[3]{3 \cdot 7}$

$\qquad\qquad = 15\sqrt[3]{21}$

Procedure for Storage

Multiplying Radicals
1. Simplify each radical.
2. Multiply coefficients together. Then multiply radicals together, observing the properties of exponents.
3. Simplify the solution.

EXAMPLE

Example 6. Multiply $\sqrt[5]{2240} \cdot \sqrt[5]{151875}$.

Solution. $\sqrt[5]{2240} = \sqrt[5]{2^6 \cdot 5 \cdot 7}$

$\qquad\qquad = 2\sqrt[5]{2 \cdot 5 \cdot 7}$

$\qquad\sqrt[5]{151875} = \sqrt[5]{3^5 \cdot 5^4}$

$\qquad\qquad = 3\sqrt[5]{5^4}$

$\sqrt[5]{2240} \cdot \sqrt[5]{151875} = 2\sqrt[5]{2 \cdot 5 \cdot 7} \cdot 3\sqrt[5]{5^4}$

$\qquad\qquad = 2 \cdot 3\sqrt[5]{2 \cdot 5^5 \cdot 7}$

$\qquad\qquad = 2 \cdot 3 \cdot 5\sqrt[5]{2 \cdot 7}$

$\qquad\qquad = 30\sqrt[5]{14}$

Exercises

Multiply the radicals. State the product in simplest form.

1. $\sqrt{5} \cdot \sqrt{3}$

2. $\sqrt{8} \cdot \sqrt{3}$

3. $\sqrt{7} \cdot \sqrt{5}$

4. $\sqrt{3} \cdot \sqrt{6}$

5. $\sqrt{18} \cdot \sqrt{3}$

6. $\sqrt{12} \cdot \sqrt{5}$

7. $\sqrt{9} \cdot \sqrt{7}$

8. $\sqrt{126} \cdot \sqrt{3}$

9. $\sqrt{5} \cdot \sqrt{118}$

10. $\sqrt{34} \cdot \sqrt{36}$

11. $\sqrt{28} \cdot \sqrt{35}$

12. $\sqrt{42} \cdot \sqrt{16}$

13. $\sqrt{180} \cdot \sqrt{588}$

14. $\sqrt[5]{32} \cdot \sqrt[5]{64}$

15. $\sqrt[3]{136} \cdot \sqrt[3]{42}$

16. $\sqrt[3]{40} \cdot \sqrt[3]{54}$

17. $\sqrt{539} \cdot \sqrt{242}$

18. $\sqrt[4]{30625} \cdot \sqrt[4]{49}$

19. $\sqrt[3]{81} \cdot \sqrt[3]{64}$

20. $\sqrt{4000} \cdot \sqrt{324}$

DIVIDING RADICALS AND RATIONALIZING DENOMINATORS

You have learned the product property of radicals, $\sqrt[n]{x} \cdot \sqrt[n]{y} = \sqrt[n]{xy}$, which helps you simplify radicals when you multiply them. Now you will see another rule that will aid in division and in another form of simplification called *rationalizing the denominator*. A common practice in mathematics is to never leave a radical in the denominator of a fraction. The basic rule, called the *division property*, is

$$\sqrt[n]{\frac{x}{y}} = \frac{\sqrt[n]{x}}{\sqrt[n]{y}}$$

Look at this numerical example of the division property.

$$\sqrt{\frac{16}{25}} = \frac{4}{5}$$

$$\frac{\sqrt{16}}{\sqrt{25}} = \frac{4}{5}$$

By the substitution principle, $\sqrt{\frac{16}{25}} = \frac{\sqrt{16}}{\sqrt{25}}$

Do you remember that a division problem can be written in fractional form? So $3 \div 4$ is the same as $\frac{3}{4}$. Therefore, you can express the division of radicals as fractions. Thus $\sqrt{5} \div \sqrt{7}$ is the same as $\frac{\sqrt{5}}{\sqrt{7}}$.

Notice that this fraction has a radical in the denominator. Since you must never leave a radical in the denominator, you must rationalize the denominator.

EXAMPLES

Example 1. Simplify $\dfrac{\sqrt{5}}{\sqrt{7}}$.

Solution. $\dfrac{\sqrt{5}}{\sqrt{7}}$

1. Simplify the numerator and the denominator as far as possible. Neither $\sqrt{5}$ nor $\sqrt{7}$ can be simplified.

$$\frac{\sqrt{5}}{\sqrt{7}} \cdot \frac{\sqrt{7}}{\sqrt{7}} = \frac{\sqrt{5 \cdot 7}}{\sqrt{7 \cdot 7}}$$

2. To eliminate $\sqrt{7}$ from the denominator, multiply the fraction by a radical form of 1 to produce a perfect square in the denominator. Here we can multiply by $\dfrac{\sqrt{7}}{\sqrt{7}}$.

$$= \frac{\sqrt{35}}{\sqrt{7^2}}$$

3. Simplify the resulting expression.

$$= \frac{\sqrt{35}}{\sqrt{49}}$$

$$= \frac{\sqrt{35}}{7}$$

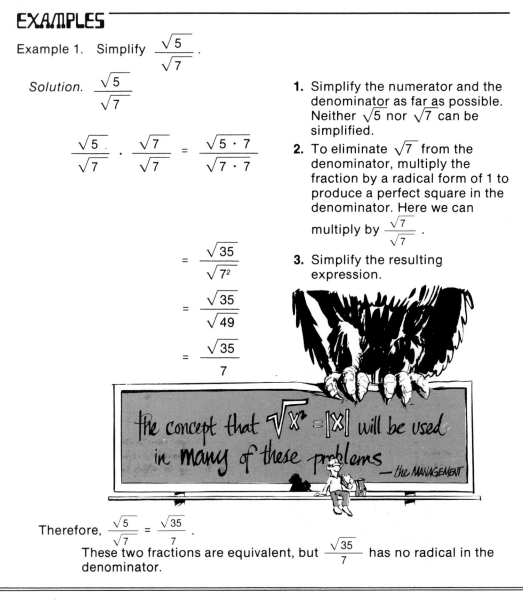

The concept that $\sqrt{x^2} = |x|$ will be used in many of these problems
— *the MANAGEMENT*

Therefore, $\dfrac{\sqrt{5}}{\sqrt{7}} = \dfrac{\sqrt{35}}{7}$.

These two fractions are equivalent, but $\dfrac{\sqrt{35}}{7}$ has no radical in the denominator.

Example 2. $\sqrt{3} \div \sqrt{6}$.

Solution. $\dfrac{\sqrt{3}}{\sqrt{6}} = \sqrt{\dfrac{3}{6}}$

1. Use the division property and simplify.

$= \sqrt{\dfrac{1}{2}}$

2. Simplify the fraction and use the division property again.

$= \dfrac{\sqrt{1}}{\sqrt{2}}$

$= \dfrac{1}{\sqrt{2}}$

3. Now you must rationalize the denominator by multiplying the numerator and the denominator by $\sqrt{2}$.

$= \dfrac{1}{\sqrt{2}} \cdot \dfrac{\sqrt{2}}{\sqrt{2}}$

$= \dfrac{\sqrt{2}}{\sqrt{2^2}}$

$= \dfrac{\sqrt{2}}{2}$

Therefore, $\sqrt{3} \div \sqrt{6} = \dfrac{\sqrt{2}}{2}$ This fraction is in simplest form.

Example 3. Simplify $\dfrac{\sqrt{3}}{\sqrt{12}}$

Solution. $\dfrac{\sqrt{3}}{\sqrt{12}} = \sqrt{\dfrac{3}{12}}$

1. Use the division property.

$= \sqrt{\dfrac{1}{4}}$

2. Simplify.

$= \dfrac{1}{2}$

Therefore, $\dfrac{\sqrt{3}}{\sqrt{12}} = \dfrac{1}{2}$

Example 4.   Simplify $\dfrac{\sqrt{2}}{\sqrt{75}}$.

Solution. $\sqrt{2}$ cannot be simplified.

$$\sqrt{75} = \sqrt{3 \cdot 5^2} = 5\sqrt{3}$$

$$\frac{\sqrt{2}}{\sqrt{75}} = \frac{\sqrt{2}}{5\sqrt{3}}$$

$$= \frac{\sqrt{2}}{5\sqrt{3}} \cdot \frac{\sqrt{3}}{\sqrt{3}}$$

$$= \frac{\sqrt{2 \cdot 3}}{5\sqrt{3^2}}$$

$$= \frac{\sqrt{6}}{5 \cdot 3}$$

$$= \frac{\sqrt{6}}{15}$$

Therefore, $\dfrac{\sqrt{2}}{\sqrt{75}} = \dfrac{\sqrt{6}}{15}$

YOU CANNOT CANCEL ANY FACTORS UNLESS BOTH ARE UNDER THE RADICAL SIGN OR BOTH ARE OUTSIDE THE RADICAL SIGN

THAT LIFT DEFINITELY NEEDS WORK!

Procedure for Storage

Rationalizing the Denominator

1. Place the radicals in fractional form by using the division property.
2. Simplify the numerator and the denominator as much as possible.
3. If a radical is left in the denominator, find the prime factorization of the radicand of the denominator. Then multiply the numerator and the denominator by a radical that will make the radicand in the denominator a perfect power.
4. Simplify both numerator and denominator to obtain the final answer.

This method of rationalizing the denominator works not only with square roots but also with other roots.

EXAMPLE

Example 5. Simplify $\dfrac{\sqrt[3]{8}}{\sqrt[3]{16}}$.

Solution.

$$\frac{\sqrt[3]{8}}{\sqrt[3]{16}} = \sqrt[3]{\frac{8}{16}}$$

   1. Use the division property.

$$= \sqrt[3]{\frac{1}{2}}$$

   2. Simplify.

$$= \frac{\sqrt[3]{1}}{\sqrt[3]{2}}$$

   3. Use the division property.

$$= \frac{1}{\sqrt[3]{2}}$$

   4. Simplify.

$$= \frac{1}{\sqrt[3]{2}} \cdot \frac{\sqrt[3]{2^2}}{\sqrt[3]{2^2}}$$

   5. Rationalize. To make the denominator a perfect cube, multiply by the power that will produce a perfect cube.

$$= \frac{\sqrt[3]{2^2}}{\sqrt[3]{2^3}}$$

$$= \frac{\sqrt[3]{4}}{2}$$

   6. Simplify.

Therefore, $\dfrac{\sqrt[3]{8}}{\sqrt[3]{16}} = \dfrac{\sqrt[3]{4}}{2}$.

Exercises

Simplify.

1. $\dfrac{2}{\sqrt{13}}$

2. $\dfrac{2\sqrt{3}}{\sqrt{9}}$

3. $\dfrac{3}{\sqrt{5}}$

4. $\dfrac{3\sqrt{5}}{\sqrt{15}}$

5. $\dfrac{\sqrt{4}}{\sqrt{25}}$

6. $\dfrac{1}{\sqrt{6}}$

7. $\dfrac{3}{4\sqrt{2}}$

8. $\sqrt{3} \div \sqrt{2}$

9. $\sqrt{5} \div \sqrt{4}$

10. $3\sqrt{7} \div \sqrt{12}$

11. $\dfrac{\sqrt{14}}{\sqrt{21}}$

12. $\dfrac{\sqrt{8}}{\sqrt{4}}$

13. $\dfrac{\sqrt{3}}{\sqrt{9}}$

14. $\dfrac{\sqrt{5}}{\sqrt{25}}$

15. $\dfrac{\sqrt{3}}{\sqrt{27}}$

16. $\dfrac{\sqrt{72}}{\sqrt{18}}$

17. $\dfrac{\sqrt{114}}{\sqrt{32}}$

18. $\dfrac{\sqrt{10}}{3\sqrt{5}}$

19. $\dfrac{\sqrt{86}}{4\sqrt{20}}$

20. $\dfrac{\sqrt{15}}{\sqrt{5}}$

Simplify.

21. $\dfrac{\sqrt[3]{9}}{\sqrt[3]{36}}$

22. $\dfrac{\sqrt[3]{16}}{\sqrt[3]{4}}$

23. $\sqrt[3]{\dfrac{1}{8}}$

24. $\dfrac{\sqrt[3]{5}}{\sqrt[3]{25}}$

25. $\dfrac{\sqrt[3]{7}}{2\sqrt[3]{21}}$

26. Give the steps for rationalizing a cube root in the denominator.

Solve each equation for the variable. Write the solution in the appropriate squares in the grid.

MIND OVER MATH

ACROSS

1. $5x + 35 = 3160$
4. $3y - 105 = 342$
7. $6x^2 - 672 = x^2 + 32(979)$
8. $3x - (8 - x) = 2x(5) - 242$
10. $9x - 16 = 227$
12. $\frac{x}{33} + \frac{x}{9} = 42$
13. $x - 100 = -30$
14. $\frac{x}{28} = 157$
16. $\frac{x}{6} + 27x = 263,245$
18. $\frac{x}{2} + 10(x - 3) = 568.5$
19. $x^2 = 144$
20. $13x - 15,079 = 52,755$
22. $2y - 583 = 4293$
24. $\sqrt{4} - 222 = -5x$
25. $\frac{x}{5} + \frac{x}{25} = 54$
26. $z = \sqrt{625} + 2\sqrt{100}$
27. $2^7 = k + 29$
28. $x^2 - 168 = 3313$
30. $16(2\sqrt[3]{27}) = x - 28$
31. $x = 8(100) + 3$

4. $10\sqrt{4900} = x - (26^2) - 3$
5. $x - 1 = \sqrt{64} \cdot 6$
6. $25^2 - x = 1$
9. $x^2 = 160,000$
11. $x \cdot 56^0 = 73,524$
13. $40^3 + 25^3 = x + 19^2 + 30$
15. $3x = 2913$
17. $\frac{1}{4}x = \frac{921}{6}$
20. $24^2 = x + 3^3$
21. $t - 669 = 85^2 + 20^2$
22. $50^2 = g - 58$
23. $\frac{6}{z} = \frac{1}{71} \cdot \frac{1}{2}$
27. $10^2 - 2^3 = e$
29. $2 \cdot 3^2 \cdot 5 = z$

DOWN

2. $2x = 7 \cdot 8$
3. $x + 599 = 75^2$

COMPUTERS IN THE HOME

Bill looked up from the living-room computer keyboard. "Hey, Dad, how do you spell *denouement*? I'm finishing my essay for English, and I'm not sure I spelled this word right."

"Why don't you just have the spelling checker scan the whole paper?" Mr. Rogers answered from the sofa. "That way you'll be sure to have everything right."

"Okay, but it seems like a lot of trouble. It's easier just to ask you."

"A lot of trouble?" Mr. Rogers laughed. "All you have to do is press a few buttons. I used to need a dictionary to check my spelling when I was in school. Computers were too expensive then to use for writing English papers. Oh, when you finish, will you punch in the command

that starts the sprinklers? The lawn looks a little dry."

"Sure, Dad."

"Bill," Mrs. Rogers called from the kitchen, "As soon as you've proofed your paper with the computer, I need it to retrieve my recipe for Cantonese chicken. I'll also need it to make sure I have all the ingredients. The Burkes' flight arrives at six o'clock, and I want to have supper ready to serve when they get here."

"Okay, Mom. I'm finished for now. I even spelled *denouement* right."

"I'll get the recipe for you, Mom," Jessica offered. "I need the practice."

"Thanks, Jessica." Mrs. Rogers went back to peeling vegetables.

Jessica leaned over the keyboard, punched in the request for the recipe, and watched as the printer began to print it out.

Mr. Rogers looked up from his newspaper. "Are you sure their flight comes in at six, dear?" he asked. "I thought it was due at five."

Mrs. Rogers appeared in the kitchen doorway and looked at her watch. "Five o'clock? And it's already quarter after four? I'd better check to make sure."

Mrs. Rogers hurried to the computer. Her fingers flew over the keyboard as she punched in her request for the airline schedule. The screen in front of her lit up with flight arrival and departure times. "Oh, no," she groaned. "It really is five o'clock. I'll never be able to fix supper before they get here. Now what am I going to do?"

"How about taking the Burkes out to eat?" Bill suggested. "They probably like Mexican food. We could go to the Electronic Tortilla!"

"Looks like we might have to," Mr. Rogers said. "But I heard that the Electronic Tortilla raised all their prices after they remodeled."

Still sitting at the keyboard, Mrs. Rogers typed out another command. This time the screen lit up with the latest menu and prices from the restaurant. "The prices are higher now," she noted, "but they're still not unreasonable."

"Then it's settled," her husband answered. "As soon as our company comes we'll all go out to eat."

"Great!" Jessica exclaimed. "They have a new computer quiz game there, and this time Bill isn't going to beat me!"

This narrative may seem like a glimpse of life in the near future, but it is not. Computers are already being used in the home as the Rogers family used theirs. As time passes, new technology allows what was once science fiction to become present-day reality.

ROOTS CONTAINING VARIABLES

So far you have learned to multiply, divide, and simplify radicals that involve only numerical radicands. Sometimes a radical expression will contain one or more variables. You can simplify those variables by following the same rules for simplifying numerical radicals. Here is a brief summary of those rules.

Simplify the expression if the radicand

1. is a perfect power.

2. has a perfect power factor that can be removed from the radical.

3. is a fraction or is in the denominator of a fraction.

EXAMPLES

Example 1. Simplify $\sqrt{32x^3y^2}$.

Solution.

1. Find the prime factorization of all the numbers. $\sqrt{32x^3y^2} = \sqrt{2^5x^3y^2}$

2. Simplify each number by dividing the exponent by the index.

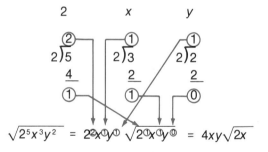

$$\sqrt{2^5x^3y^2} = 2^2x^1y^1\sqrt{2^1x^1y^0} = 4xy\sqrt{2x}$$

Therefore, $\sqrt{32x^3y^2} = 4xy\sqrt{2x}$.

SIMPLIFY THE VARIABLES, AS IF THEY WERE POSITIVE NUMBERS

Example 2. Solve $\sqrt[3]{4x^2y^5z} \cdot \sqrt[3]{8xy}$.

Solution.

1. Prime factor the numbers.

2. Multiply, observing the properties of exponents.

$$\sqrt[3]{2^2x^2y^5z} \cdot \sqrt[3]{2^3xy} = \sqrt[3]{2^5x^3y^6z}$$

3. Simplify.

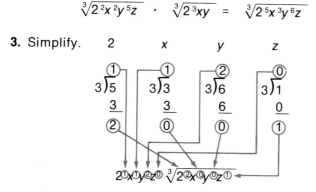

Therefore, $\sqrt[3]{4x^2y^5z} \cdot \sqrt[3]{8xy} = 2xy^2\sqrt[3]{4z}$.

Example 3. Solve $\sqrt{18a^2bc^3} \div \sqrt{9ab^3c^2}$.

Solution. $\sqrt{18a^2bc^3} \div \sqrt{9ab^3c^2} = \sqrt{\dfrac{18a^2bc^3}{9ab^3c^2}}$ Simplify under the radical sign.

$$= \sqrt{\dfrac{18a^2bc^3}{9ab^3c^2}}$$

$$= \sqrt{\dfrac{2ac}{b^2}}$$

$$= \dfrac{\sqrt{2ac}}{\sqrt{b^2}}$$

$$= \dfrac{\sqrt{2ac}}{b}$$

Example 4. Simplify $\dfrac{\sqrt{3x^3}}{4\sqrt{x^5y}}$.

Solution.

1. Simplify the numerator and the denominator as much as possible. Do you know why these simplifications are true?

$$\sqrt{3x^3} \;=\; x\sqrt{3x}$$

$$4\sqrt{x^5y} \;=\; 4x^2\sqrt{xy}$$

2. Simplify.

$$\dfrac{\sqrt{3x^3}}{4\sqrt{x^5y}} \;=\; \dfrac{x\sqrt{3x}}{4x^2\sqrt{xy}}$$

$$=\; \dfrac{\cancel{x}\sqrt{3\cancel{x}}}{4\cancel{x^2}\sqrt{\cancel{x}y}}$$

3. Now you must rationalize the denominator by multiplying the numerator and the denominator by $\sqrt{y}$.

$$=\; \dfrac{\sqrt{3}}{4x\sqrt{y}} \cdot \dfrac{\sqrt{y}}{\sqrt{y}}$$

4. Simplify.

$$=\; \dfrac{\sqrt{3y}}{4x\sqrt{y^2}}$$

$$=\; \dfrac{\sqrt{3y}}{4xy}$$

Make sure you understand each step. If you do not, go back through the example and study it again very carefully.

Exercises

Perform the indicated operation and give each answer in simplest form.

1. $\sqrt{3x^2y^3} \cdot \sqrt{2xy}$

2. $\sqrt[3]{4x^5y^7} \cdot \sqrt[3]{2x^6y}$

3. $\sqrt{5xy} \div \sqrt{10x^2y^3}$

4. $\sqrt{14x^3t^2z^5} \div \sqrt{7xtz}$

5. $\sqrt[3]{25a^4bc^6} \cdot \sqrt[3]{8abc^3}$

6. $\sqrt{15x^4y^2} \div \sqrt{3xy^3z}$

7. $\sqrt[3]{27a^3bc^2} \cdot \sqrt[3]{3abc^4}$

8. $\sqrt{82x^4y^3} \div \sqrt{14x^3y^5}$

9. $\sqrt[3]{12x^5y^3z^2} \div \sqrt[3]{4xyz^4}$

10. $\sqrt{2a^{15}b^3} \cdot \sqrt{8ab}$

ADDING AND SUBTRACTING RADICALS

When you add and subtract terms that contain radicals, you must be sure that the radicals are alike. Adding and subtracting radicals is much like adding and subtracting terms containing variables. You will recall from Chapter 2 that terms have to be similar before you can add or subtract them. Radicals, too, must be similar in order to be combined. When you add and subtract similar radicals, treat the radical as though it were a variable and combine the coefficients. Adding and subtracting radicals is very easy if you follow some simple steps.

DEFINITION

≫**Similar radicals:** radicals that have the
same radicand and the same index.

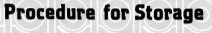

Procedure for Storage

Adding and Subtracting Radicals

1. Simplify each radical.
2. Combine like radicals by adding or subtracting the coefficients of
   the radicals.

EXAMPLES

Example 1.   Solve $4\sqrt{3} + 2\sqrt{3}$.

Solution.

   1. Both terms are already simplified.
   2. Combine these terms, considering $\sqrt{3}$ similar to a variable such as x.

   Therefore $4\sqrt{3} + 2\sqrt{3} = 6\sqrt{3}$.

Example 2.   Solve $\sqrt{5} + 9\sqrt{5} + \sqrt{2}$.

Solution.

   1. All terms are in simplest form.
   2. Combine similar radicals. Only $\sqrt{5}$ terms are similar.

   Therefore $\sqrt{5} + 9\sqrt{5} + \sqrt{2} = 10\sqrt{5} + \sqrt{2}$.

Did you try to combine $\sqrt{5}$ and $\sqrt{2}$? Are they like terms? Observe the
following procedure.

$$\text{Does } \sqrt{9} + \sqrt{16} = \sqrt{25} ?$$
$$3 + 4 = 5$$
$$7 = 5 \quad \text{No!}$$

You can see from this illustration that you cannot combine unlike radicals.

EXAMPLE

Example 3. Solve $\sqrt{12} - \sqrt{3}$.

Solution. $\sqrt{12} = \sqrt{2^2 \cdot 3} = 2\sqrt{3}$

1. Simplify each term.
   $\sqrt{3}$ is already in simplest form.

$$\sqrt{12} - \sqrt{3} = 2\sqrt{3} - \sqrt{3}$$

2. Combine like terms.

$$= \sqrt{3}$$

A definition of *radical* that you might be more familiar with is "one who is marked by considerable departure from the usual or traditional." When the unsaved man looks at a born-again believer, he might consider the Christian a radical. A Christian should be noticeably different from an unsaved man. I Peter 2:9 says, "But ye are a chosen generation, a royal priesthood, an holy nation, a peculiar people; that ye should shew forth the praises of him who hath called you out of darkness into his marvellous light." He should strive to be radical in that he is separated from the world. A Christian must be different and out of the ordinary so that nonbelievers can see Christ through him and thereby can be drawn to salvation in Jesus Christ. Though a Christian may appear radical in the eyes of the unsaved world, he must strive to be a "rational radical" in the eyes of God.

EXAMPLES

Example 4. Solve $2\sqrt{50} - 5\sqrt{8}$.

Solution. 1. Simplify each term.

$$2\sqrt{50} = 2\sqrt{5^2 \cdot 2} = 2 \cdot 5\sqrt{2} = 10\sqrt{2}$$
$$5\sqrt{8} = 5\sqrt{2^3} = 5 \cdot 2\sqrt{2} = 10\sqrt{2}$$

2. Combine. $2\sqrt{50} - 5\sqrt{8} = 10\sqrt{2} - 10\sqrt{2} = 0$

Example 5. Solve $-8\sqrt{5} + 9\sqrt{20} - 6\sqrt{5}$

Solution. **1.** Simplify each term.

$-8\sqrt{5}$ is simplified.

$9\sqrt{20} = 9\sqrt{2^2 \cdot 5} = 9 \cdot 2\sqrt{5} = 18\sqrt{5}$

$6\sqrt{5}$ is simplifed.

2. Combine. $-8\sqrt{5} + 18\sqrt{5} - 6\sqrt{5} = 4\sqrt{5}$

Exercises

Solve and simplify.

1. $\sqrt{3} + 5\sqrt{3}$
2. $2\sqrt{6} + 3\sqrt{6}$
3. $\sqrt{3} + 4\sqrt{2} + \sqrt{3}$
4. $2\sqrt{5} - 6\sqrt{5} + 3\sqrt{5}$
5. $\sqrt{8} + 3\sqrt{2} - 4\sqrt{2}$
6. $8\sqrt{7} - 3\sqrt{7}$
7. $\sqrt{20} + 4\sqrt{5}$
8. $5\sqrt{12} - 6\sqrt{3}$
9. $\sqrt{12} - \sqrt{48}$
10. $3\sqrt{8} + 2\sqrt{2}$

11. $-3\sqrt{3} + \sqrt{18} + \sqrt{27}$
12. $4\sqrt{x} + 3\sqrt{y} - 2\sqrt{x}$
13. $a\sqrt{3} - 3a\sqrt{3} + \sqrt{2}$
14. $\sqrt{5} + \sqrt{20} - \sqrt{72}$
15. $\sqrt{32a^3} + \sqrt{2a} - 5\sqrt{6}$
16. $\sqrt{x^2y} - x\sqrt{y}$
17. $\sqrt{75} - \sqrt{18}$
18. $3\sqrt{ab} + 4\sqrt{a} - 5\sqrt{b} + 5\sqrt{b}$
19. $\sqrt{x} + 3\sqrt{xy} + 5\sqrt{x}$
20. $2\sqrt{18} + 3\sqrt{12} - 4\sqrt{32}$

THE PYTHAGOREAN THEOREM

Ancient Egyptian farmers divided their farmlands into plots with square corners. Each year when the Nile River flooded, new boundary lines had to be marked and square corners had to be found again. (A square corner is a right angle, which is equal to 90°.) The Egyptians found that they could form a right angle by making a triangle whose sides measured 3, 4, and 5 units. The angle opposite the side 5 units long (the hypotenuse) was always a right angle.

DEFINITIONS

≫**Right angle:** an angle whose measure is 90°.

≫**Right triangle:** a triangle that contains a right angle.

≫**Hypotenuse:** the side of the right triangle opposite the right angle.

A group of Greek philosophers and mathematicians led by Pythagoras began to study the Egyptian's use of triangles. Pythagoras and his followers believed that every right triangle possessed a property such that the sum of the squares of the lengths of the legs was equal to the square of the length of the hypotenuse. Given any right triangle ABC with c the hypotenuse, $a^2 + b^2 = c^2$. To check this property, substitute the values in the equation.

$$3^2 + 4^2 = 5^2$$
$$9 + 16 = 25$$
$$25 = 25$$

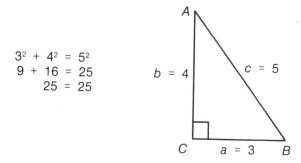

Before a mathematical observation can be called a theorem, it has to be proven, or shown to be true in all cases. Because Pythagoras may have been the first to prove this property of right triangles, this theorem is called the Pythagorean theorem.

DEFINITIONS

≫**Theorem:** a proven statement that is always true.

≫**Pythagorean theorem:** the sum of the squares of the lengths of the legs of a right triangle is equal to the square of the length of the hypotenuse.

$$a^2 + b^2 = c^2$$

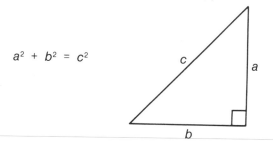

EXAMPLE

Example 1.   Find the value of x in the right triangle ABC.

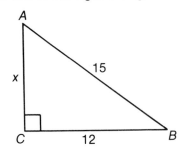

Solution.

Let c = 15, the hypotenuse
  a = 12
  b = x

1. Substitute the lengths of the sides in the Pythagorean theorem.

$a^2 + b^2 = c^2$
$12^2 + x^2 = 15^2$
$144 + x^2 = 225$
  $x^2 = 81$

$\sqrt{x^2} = \sqrt{81}$
  $x = \pm 9$

2. Solve for x by isolating x^2 on one side of the equals sign. Then take the square root of both sides.

Since you are looking for a length, use only the positive solution.

Therefore, side b = 9 units.

Data Base

To prove the Pythagorean theorem, let *a* and *b* denote the legs and *c* the hypotenuse of a given right triangle. Consider the following two squares, each with *a* + *b* as a side.

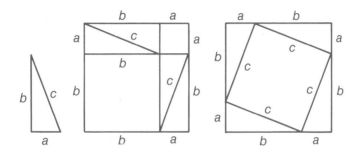

What is the area of each large square above? Are the areas equal? Each triangle in the above two figures is congruent to the given triangle. By subtracting equal triangles from each square, the figures that are left look like this.

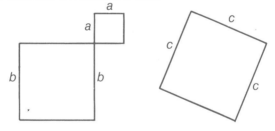

Since the original squares were the same size and equal triangles were subtracted, the sum of the areas of the squares on the left equals the area of the square on the right. So $a^2 + b^2 = c^2$.

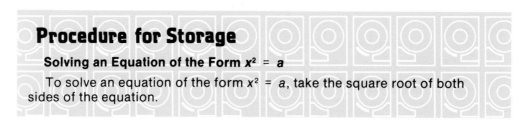

Procedure for Storage

Solving an Equation of the Form $x^2 = a$

To solve an equation of the form $x^2 = a$, take the square root of both sides of the equation.

EXAMPLE

Example 2.   Find the hypotenuse in the right triangle ABC.

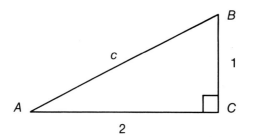

Solution.

$$\text{Let } a = 1$$
$$b = 2$$

1. Assign variables.

$$1^2 + 2^2 = c^2$$
$$1 + 4 = c^2$$
$$5 = c^2$$

2. Substitute values into the equation $a^2 + b^2 = c^2$.

$$\sqrt{5} = c$$

3. To find the value of c, take the square root of both sides.

Exercises

Find the length of the unknown side of the right triangle.

	a	b	c
1.	4	5	?
2.	3	3	?
3.	2	?	8
4.	1	9	?
5.	3	?	14
6.	2	5	?
7.	?	6	12
8.	?	8	10
9.	7	?	9
10.	?	2	5

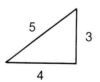

If the sum of the squares of the legs of a triangle equals the square of the hypotenuse, the triangle is a right triangle. Indicate each right triangle by using the Pythagorean theorem.

11.

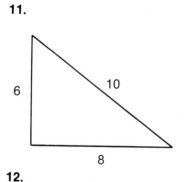

13.

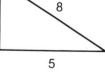

12.

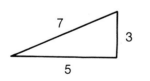

14.

15. An engineer in charge of designing a bridge to cross a lake from *A* to *B* needs to know the distance across the lake at that location. He knows that *A* to *C* is 5 miles and *C* to *B* is 9 miles. He also knows that AC and CB form a right angle. What is the distance from *A* to *B*?

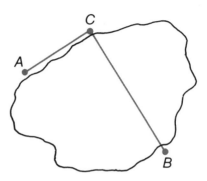

16. The bottom of a ladder is placed against the side of a house 6 feet from the house. If the ladder is 25 feet long, how high does the ladder reach?

17. The M.T. Container Manufacturing Company is planning to make a new line of boxes 3 inches high and 10 inches long. If the M.T. box measures 14 inches diagonally across the bottom, what is the width of the box?

THE DISTANCE FORMULA

Airlines plan their routes so that the planes can fly in a straight line to the next stop because a straight line is the shortest distance between two points. Can you find the distance from Washington, D.C., to Jackson, Mississippi? Is the distance from Washington to Jackson the same as the distance from Jackson to Washington? Yes, the distance is the same whichever direction you're headed. So always think of distance as a positive number. Finding the distance between two points on a graph is quite simple if the points are in a horizontal or vertical line.

EXAMPLES

Example 1. Find the distance between P_1 (read "P sub 1") and P_2.

Solution.

To find this horizontal distance, you can either (1) count the number of squares between the points or (2) subtract the values of the x-coordinates and find the absolute value of the difference. Counting the number of squares gives an answer of 4. Subtracting the values of the x-coordinates of the points and finding the absolute value of that number also give 4. You will come out with the same value no matter which point you choose first.

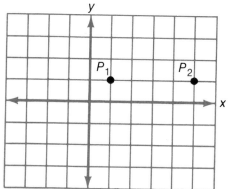

$$|5 - 1| = |4| = 4$$
$$|1 - 5| = |-4| = 4$$

Example 2. Find the vertical distance between P_1 and P_2.

Solution.

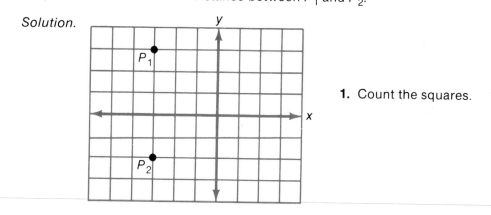

1. Count the squares.

$$|3 - -2| = |3 + 2|$$
$$= |5|$$
$$= 5$$

2. Find the absolute value of the difference between the y-coordinates of the two points.

The distance between P_1 and P_2 is 5.

By counting squares, you can easily find horizontal and vertical distances. But can you see any problem with counting squares? Counting squares between (-5, -127) and (-5, 318) would take a lot of time. You can find the distances much more quickly with the subtraction method.

What should you do to find the distance between two points not in a horizontal or vertical line? Can you count the squares between points? No, you cannot count the number of squares between the two points. You cannot just subtract x values or y values. To find the distance between any two points, you must first locate a third point that is on the same horizontal line as one point and on the same vertical line as the other point. This point will be the vertex of a right angle. By forming a right triangle, you can now use the Pythagorean theorem to find the distance between any two points.

EXAMPLE

Example 3.   Find the distance between P_1 (-3, 1) and P_2 (5, 4).

Solution.

1. Graph the points and label them P_1 and P_2.

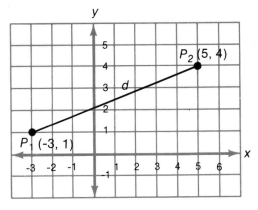

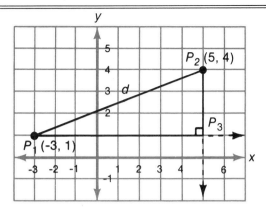

2. Form a right triangle by dropping a vertical from P_2 and drawing a horizontal from P_1 to intersect at P_3. The two lines form a right angle at P_3.

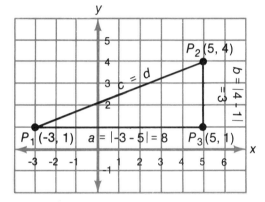

3. Label P_3 (5,1). The x value is the same as the x value in P_2. The y value is the same as the y value in P_1.

4. Determine the horizontal distance (a) between P_1 and P_3 and the vertical distance (b) between P_2 and P_3. Let c represent the hypotenuse (d) of the right triangle.

$$\text{So } a = 8$$
$$b = 3$$
$$c = d.$$

$$
\begin{array}{rcl}
a^2 + b^2 & = & c^2 \\
(P_3P_1)^2 + (P_3P_2)^2 & = & d^2 \\
8^2 + 3^2 & = & d^2 \\
64 + 9 & = & d^2 \\
73 & = & d^2 \\
\sqrt{73} & = & d
\end{array}
$$

5. Substitute values into the equation $a^2 + b^2 = c^2$ and solve for d.

So the distance between P_1 and P_2 is $\sqrt{73}$, which is approximately equal to 8.5.

The distance formula was developed from a procedure similar to the one you just followed. Study the following proof.

Consider points $P(x_1, y_1)$ and $Q(x_2, y_2)$ in the plane. Find the distance between these two points.

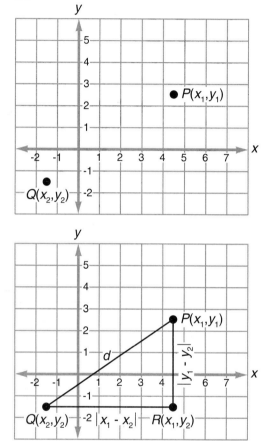

Form a right triangle and label the vertex of the right angle R. The coordinates of R must be (x_1, y_2). The vertical distance between P and R is $|y_1 - y_2|$ (vertical change); the horizontal distance between Q and R is $|x_1 - x_2|$ (horizontal change). Let d be the distance between P and Q. Using the Pythagorean theorem, you get

$$d^2 = (|x_1 - x_2|)^2 + (|y_1 - y_2|)^2 .$$

You can drop the absolute value signs since you are squaring the absolute value.

$$d^2 = (x_1 - x_2)^2 + (y_1 - y_2)^2$$

To solve for d, find the square root of both sides.

$$d = \sqrt{(x_1 - x_2)^2 + (y_1 - y_2)^2}$$

Since you can use this formula to find the distance between any two points in a plane, memorize it so that you can use it when you need it.

EXAMPLES

Example 4.   Find the distance between (1,1) and (5,1).

Solution.

Let $(x_1, y_1) = (1, 1)$
$(x_2, y_2) = (5, 1)$

$d = \sqrt{(x_1 - x_2)^2 + (y_1 - y_2)^2}$
$= \sqrt{(1 - 5)^2 + (1 - 1)^2}$
$= \sqrt{(-4)^2 + 0^2}$
$= \sqrt{4^2}$
$= 4$

The distance is 4 units.

Example 5.   Find the distance between (-2, 9) and (7, 5).

Solution.

Let $(x_1, y_1) = (-2, 9)$
$(x_2, y_2) = (7, 5)$

$d = \sqrt{(x_1 - x_2)^2 + (y_1 - y_2)^2}$
$= \sqrt{(-2 - 7)^2 + (9 - 5)^2}$
$= \sqrt{(-9)^2 + 4^2}$
$= \sqrt{81 + 16}$
$= \sqrt{97}$

The distance is $\sqrt{97}$, or approximately 9.8.

EITHER GIVEN POINT CAN BE
(x_1, y_1)

Suppose that Washington, D.C., and Jackson have the ordered pair relationship given here. Use the distance formula to find the flight distance.

$$d = \sqrt{(x_1 - x_2)^2 + (y_1 - y_2)^2}$$
$$= \sqrt{(-350 - 400)^2 + (100 - 500)^2}$$
$$= \sqrt{(-750)^2 + (-400)^2}$$
$$= \sqrt{562500 + 160000}$$
$$= \sqrt{722500}$$
$$= 850$$

So the air distance between Washington, D.C., and Jackson, Mississippi, is 850 miles.

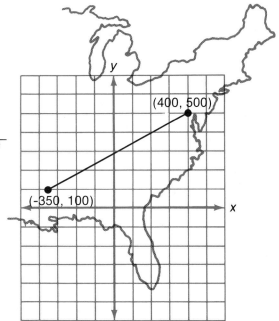

Exercises

Find the distance between the following pairs of points.

1. (2, 7) and (-3, 5)

2. (8, 4) and (-1, -4)

3. (2, 6) and (-4, 5)

4. (-3, -1) and (2, 3)

5. (1, 0) and (4, 2)

6. (3, 4) and (0, 0)

7. (1, 8) and (-2, -5)

8. (-7, 3) and (1, 8)

9. (-2, -6) and (2, 1)

10. (4, 7) and (1, 5)

Find the perimeter of each figure.

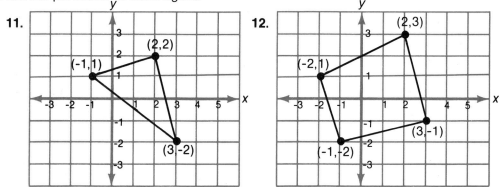

11.

12.

13.

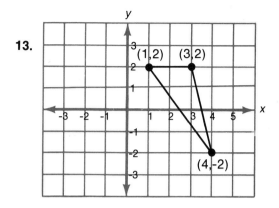

14. If the locations of two cities on a map are indicated by the ordered pairs (73, 132) and (3, -146), what is the distance in air miles between these two cities?

15. A submarine is located at point (4, 9), and a ship is at position (15, 3). What is the distance in nautical miles between the two vessels?

Data Base

Certain triples of numbers in the natural number system have a special property used for studying right triangles. For example, the ordered triple (2, 0, 2) and the ordered triple (4, 3, 5), when put into $a^2 + b^2 = c^2$, reveal that the sum of the squares of the first two numbers is equal to the square of the third.

$$2^2 + 0^2 = 2^2 \qquad\qquad 4^2 + 3^2 = 5^2$$
$$4 + 0 = 4 \qquad\qquad 16 + 9 = 25$$
$$4 = 4 \qquad\qquad 25 = 25$$

Here are a few Pythagorean triples.

	a	b	c
(1)	2	0	2
(2)	4	3	5
(3)	6	8	10
(4)	8	15	17

Notice that the numbers in the first column are two times the line number. The numbers in the middle column equal the line number squared less one. The numbers in the third column equal the line number squared plus one. For example, in the third line you can see that $a = 2 \cdot 3 = 6$, $b = 3^2 - 1 = 8$, and $c = 3^2 + 1 = 10$. Following this method, find the ninth line of triples.

$$(9) \quad ? \quad ? \quad ?$$

$a = 2 \cdot 9 = 18$
$b = 9^2 - 1 = 81 - 1 = 80$
$c = 9^2 + 1 = 81 + 1 = 82$

The ninth Pythagorean triple is (18, 80, 82).

RADICAL EQUATIONS

Equations such as $\sqrt{x} = 10$, $3 + \sqrt{x} = 24$, and $6\sqrt{x} = 9$ are called radical equations because they contain a variable in the radical. Equations such as $x + \sqrt{3} = 0$ and $5x - \sqrt{25} = 25$ are not radical equations because the variable is not in the radical. You can easily solve radical equations, but you must be sure to check all solutions in the original equation. A solution that does not check is called an *extraneous root*.

DEFINITION

≫**Radical equation:** an equation that contains a variable in a radical.

EXAMPLE

Example 1. Solve $\sqrt{x} = 10$.

Solution. To eliminate the square root sign, square both sides of the equation. When you square a square root, you get the radicand.
So $(\sqrt{x})^2 = x$

$$\sqrt{x} = 10$$
$$(\sqrt{x})^2 = (10)^2$$
$$x = 100$$

Check. Does $\sqrt{100} = 10$?

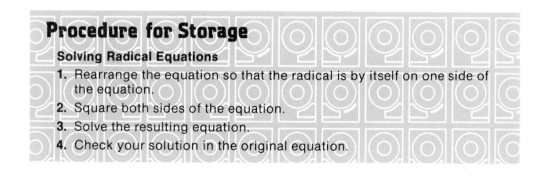

Procedure for Storage

Solving Radical Equations

1. Rearrange the equation so that the radical is by itself on one side of the equation.
2. Square both sides of the equation.
3. Solve the resulting equation.
4. Check your solution in the original equation.

EXAMPLES

Example 2. Solve $8 + \sqrt{x - 3} = 4$.

Solution.

$$8 + \sqrt{x - 3} = 4$$

$$\sqrt{x - 3} = -4$$ Isolate the radical on one side of the equation.

$$(\sqrt{x - 3})^2 = (-4)^2$$ Square both sides and solve.

$$x - 3 = 16$$

$$x = 19$$

Check.

$$8 + \sqrt{19 - 3} = 4$$

$$8 + \sqrt{16} = 4$$

$$8 + 4 = 4$$

$$12 = 4$$ This solution does not check. So 19 is an extraneous root, and there is no solution.

Example 3. Solve $\sqrt{2x + 5} = 8$.

Solution.

$$(\sqrt{2x + 5})^2 = 8^2$$ Since the radical is alone on one side, square both sides.

$$2x + 5 = 64$$

$$2x = 59$$

$$x = \frac{59}{2}$$

Check.

$$\sqrt{2\left(\frac{59}{2}\right) + 5} = 8$$

$$\sqrt{59 + 5} = 8$$

$$\sqrt{64} = 8$$

$$8 = 8$$

So $\frac{59}{2}$ is the solution.

Example 4.   Solve $10 - 2\sqrt{x} = 0$.

Solution.

$$10 - 2\sqrt{x} = 0$$
$$-2\sqrt{x} = -10$$
$$\sqrt{x} = 5$$
$$(\sqrt{x})^2 = 5^2$$
$$x = 25$$

Get the radical alone on one side and solve for *x*.

Check.

$$10 - 2\sqrt{x} = 0$$
$$10 - 2\sqrt{25} = 0$$
$$10 - 2 \cdot 5 = 0$$
$$10 - 10 = 0$$
$$0 = 0$$

So 25 is the solution.

Exercises

Solve each radical equation and check your solution.

1. $\sqrt{x} = 4$

2. $\sqrt{y} = 5$

3. $\sqrt{x + 2} = 8$

4. $\sqrt{y - 5} = 2$

5. $3 + \sqrt{x} = 9$

6. $2 - \sqrt{x} = -8$

7. $5 + \sqrt{x + 1} = 7$

8. $14 - \sqrt{x - 3} = 10$

9. $5 + 3\sqrt{x} = 14$

10. $8 + 2\sqrt{x} = 18$

11. $7 + 3\sqrt{x - 3} = -14$

12. $3 + 4\sqrt{x + 3} = 11$

13. $5 + 2\sqrt{y - 3} = 27$

14. $\sqrt{x} = 3.2$

15. $\sqrt{x + 5} = 0$

MEMORY RECALL

Identify.

distance formula	rationalizing the denominator
extraneous root	similar radicals
hypotenuse	simplified form
product property	square root
Pythagorean theorem	successive approximation method
radical equation	

You should be able to do the following:

1. Approximate the square root of any number by using several methods.
2. Change radical form to exponential form and change exponential form to radical form.
3. Simplify any radical.
4. Multiply and divide radicals.
5. Rationalize the denominator of a fraction when necessary.
6. Add and subtract radicals.
7. Solve problems using the Pythagorean theorem.
8. Develop and use the distance formula.
9. Solve a given radical equation.

You should be able to solve these problems:

1. Find the approximate value of each of the following square roots.

   a. $\sqrt{127}$

   b. $\sqrt{0.63}$

   c. $\sqrt{243}$

   d. $\sqrt{619}$

2. Change each radical to exponential form.

   a. $\sqrt{2x^3}$

   c. $\sqrt[3]{24a^5b^2}$

   b. $\sqrt[4]{3y^2}$

   d. $\sqrt[4]{16x^5y}$

3. Change each expression to radical form.

    a. $3^{\frac{2}{3}} a^{\frac{5}{3}}$

    b. $(2xy)^{\frac{1}{3}} z^{\frac{4}{3}}$

    c. $7^{\frac{1}{2}} x^{\frac{1}{2}} y^{\frac{1}{2}}$

4. Simplify each radical.

    a. $\sqrt{84}$

    b. $\sqrt[3]{216}$

    c. $\sqrt[3]{504}$

    d. $\sqrt[5]{1632}$

5. Find each product.

    a. $\sqrt{8} \cdot \sqrt{2}$

    b. $\sqrt[3]{21} \cdot \sqrt[3]{9}$

    c. $\sqrt{20} \cdot \sqrt{63}$

6. Divide and simplify.

    a. $\dfrac{5}{\sqrt{6}}$ **c.** $\dfrac{\sqrt[3]{3}}{\sqrt[3]{27}}$

    b. $\dfrac{\sqrt{5}}{\sqrt{15}}$ **d.** $\dfrac{17}{\sqrt{3}}$

7. Perform the indicated operation and simplify.

    a. $\sqrt{5x^3 y^4} \cdot \sqrt{15xy^5}$

    b. $\sqrt[3]{9a^5 b^2} \cdot \sqrt[3]{3ab^4}$

    c. $\sqrt{2x^{12} y^3} \div \sqrt{8x^4 y^9}$

8. Simplify each expression.

   a. $\sqrt{2} + 5\sqrt{2} + \sqrt{8}$

   b. $\sqrt[3]{7} + \sqrt[3]{56} - \sqrt[3]{189}$

   c. $\sqrt{6} - \sqrt{24} + 5\sqrt{6}$

9. If the two legs of a right triangle measure 4″ and 6″, what is the length of the hypotenuse?

10. A straight palm tree fell against another tree, forming a right triangle. The trunks of the two trees were 8 feet apart. A monkey climbs 53 feet up the leaning tree trunk and then comes down the standing tree trunk. How many feet does the monkey climb down to get to the ground?

11. Find the distance between each pair of points.

   a. (1, 7) (2, 9)

   b. (-3, 2) (-1, -5)

   c. (4, 3) (-5, 4)

   d. (1, 4) (-2, -9)

12. Solve each radical equation.

   a. $\sqrt{x} = 16$

   b. $\sqrt{x+5} = 25$

   c. $\sqrt{x-2} + 8 = 57$

13. A grandfather clock has a long pendulum. The time it takes for a pendulum to swing from one side to the other side and back again, a period, is described by the formula $T = 2\pi \sqrt{\frac{l}{g}}$, where T is in seconds if l is in cm and $g = 980$ cm/second². How long does it take a pendulum in a grandfather clock to go through one period if the pendulum is 98 cm long?

CHAPTER 8

POLYNOMIALS

The Sims family, vacationing in Arizona, visits the Grand Canyon. The canyon is a marvelous example of the beautiful colors God has painted in our world. As the family views this wonder, they remind themselves that the God who created such immense beauty is also interested in and loves each individual in their family. Though the colors of the Grand Canyon change hour by hour, moment by moment, God never changes.

Far below them the Colorado River winds its way 217 miles through the Grand Canyon Gorge. The width of the canyon from the plateaus varies from four to eighteen miles, and the height varies also, reaching a maximum of 5700 feet. While visiting the Grand Canyon, the family decides to backpack down the Kaibab Trail to the bottom of the canyon, cross the river, and backpack up the other side. As the family stops to rest on their way down, Bill, the oldest son in the Sims family, wonders how far it is to the bottom of the canyon from the point where the family is resting. Bill remembers from physical science class that distance can be found by using the formula $d = \frac{1}{2}gt^2$, where g is the gravitational acceleration of 32 ft./sec.^{2} and t is the amount of time in seconds that an object falls. Bill thinks that if he had something that he could drop from where he is standing and watch it fall to the bottom of the canyon, he could find the height of the canyon at that point. Mr. Sims suggests using a flare from the emergency kit. Bill gets one of the flares, lights it, and throws it over the cliff. Watching the flare fall, Bill sees it disappear into the river below in 6 seconds. Can you figure out how far above the river the family is at this point?

The formula that Bill is using has a polynomial in it. In this chapter you will learn how to add, subtract, multiply, and divide polynomials. You are probably able to find the solution to Bill's problem right now, but by the end of this chapter you should be able to do more extensive work with polynomials.

CLASSIFYING AND EVALUATING POLYNOMIALS

Do you remember what terms are? They are the parts of an algebraic expression that are separated by + or - signs. Like terms have the same variables with the same exponents. Remember that you can add and subtract only like terms. The algebraic expression $2x^2 + 3x + 5y - 4x$ contains four terms: $2x^2$, $3x$, $5y$, and $4x$. The like terms in this example are $3x$ and $4x$. The entire algebraic expression is called a polynomial.

DEFINITIONS

≫**Polynomial:** an algebraic expression of one or more terms.

≫**Monomial:** a polynomial with only one term.

≫**Binomial:** a polynomial with exactly two terms.

≫**Trinomial:** a polynomial with exactly three terms.

examples			
	monomial	binomial	trinomial	polynomial
one variable	$4y^3$	$2x^2 + 3x$	$5x^2 + 2x - 6$	$x^4 + 2x^3 - x^2 + 9$
two variables	$3x^2y$	$5x^2 + y^3$	$3x^2 + 6xy + 7y^2$	$x^3y + 5xy^2 + 3xy - 7y^5$
three variables	$8ab^2c$	$7a^2b + 5c^5$	$2a^2b^5 + 8c^4 - 2a^5$	$3c^2 + 4c - 8d + 2e - e^2$

Data Base

The study of words and their origins is fascinating. Often you can determine the definition of a word if you know what the parts of the word mean. Most words in the English language came from words in other languages. Consider the definitions given on page 358.

Each of these terms consists of two parts: a root and a prefix. Notice that the root word for each of these terms is *nomial*, which comes from the Greek word *nomos*, meaning "part." The prefixes indicate numerical values. Can you guess the value of each one?

The prefix *poly-* comes from Greek and means "much" or "many." Read the definition of *polynomial* again. Does the definition adhere to the meaning of the original parts of the word? Can you see that *polynomial* is made up of *poly* + *nomos*? How many other words with the prefix *poly-* can you think of?

The prefix *mono-* is also from Greek and means "one." Do you see that *mono* + *nomos* makes *monomial*? How many parts does a monomial have? Can you define any of the following words by looking at the parts of the words?

monotone	monoacid
monochrome	monorail

You have seen the Latin prefixes *bi-*, meaning "two," and *tri-*, meaning "three," on many words you know: *bicycle* and *tricycle*; *bicentennial* and *tricentennial*; *bicep* and *tricep*; *bimonthly* and *trimonthly*. Can you tell what each of these words means? Make a list of words that begin with these prefixes.

When you come across new words that you do not know the meaning of, look for any parts that you may know the meaning of. You will be surprised at how many new words you can learn by studying their etymologies.

Another way to classify polynomials is by the degree of the polynomial.

>**Degree of a term:** the sum of the exponents on the variables.

The degree of the term $5x^3y^2z^4$ is 9, and the degree of the term $4x^2y$ is 3. Remember, a variable without a written exponent has the exponent 1. The degree of the term 8 is 0 because the exponent on the variable is 0. But there is no variable, you may say. Observe the following:

$$8 = 8 \cdot 1$$
$$= 8 \cdot x^0$$

So the exponent on the variable is 0.

>**Degree of a polynomial:** the degree of the highest-degree term in the polynomial.

To find the degree of the polynomial $3x^3y + 2x + 4xy^2$, find the degree of each term: $3x^3y$ is 4; $2x$ is 1; $4xy^2$ is 3. Since the highest degree is 4, the degree of the trinomial is also 4.

Polynomials are easy to evaluate if you follow the substitution principle and the order of operations.

EXAMPLES

Example 1. Evaluate $2x^2 - 5x + 6$ when $x = 3$.

Solution. $2x^2 - 5x + 6$

$2(3)^2 - 5(3) + 6$

1. Substitute 3 for x in the trinomial.

$2 \cdot 9 - 5 \cdot 3 + 6$

$18 \quad - \quad 15 \quad + \ 6$

$3 \quad + \quad 6$

9

2. Follow the order of operations to evaluate this expression.

Example 2.   Evaluate $5x^3y + 2x - 3y + 5$ when $x = -2$ and $y = 1$.

Solution.

$$5x^3y + 2x - 3y + 5$$

$$5(-2)^3(1) + 2(-2) - 3(1) + 5 \qquad \text{Substitute.}$$

$$5(-8)(1) + 2(-2) - 3(1) + 5$$

$$-40 \quad - \quad 4 \quad - \quad 3 \quad + 5$$

$$-47 \qquad\qquad + 5$$

$$-42$$

Exercises

Classify each polynomial as a monomial, binomial, trinomial, or simply a polynomial. Give the degree of each.

1. $2x^2 + 3x + 5$

2. $-4x^2y + 5xy + y - 8$

3. $3x^2$

4. $5x^3y + k$

5. $2x^2 + 3x^3y - 5$

6. $4x^3y^5 + 2xy$

7. $-5xy^3z^2$

8. $3x + 4y - 8z + 9$

9. $4x^5y^2 + 2x^3y - 5x$

10. $8x^3 - 2xyz$

Evaluate each polynomial if $x = 3$, $y = -4$, and $z = 2$.

11. $3x^2 + 4z - 8$

12. $5x^2 - 3y^2 - 4z$

13. $x^2y + 2x^3y - 5xyz$

14. $8x^2y + 5x^3y^2$

15. $5x^4y^2z^5$

ADDING POLYNOMIALS

When you add polynomials, simply find the like terms and combine them. To add polynomials that contain parentheses, remove the parentheses by applying the distributive property.

EXAMPLES

Example 1. Add $3x^2 + 2x - 5$ and $8x^2 - 7x - 10$.

Solution. $(3x^2 + 2x - 5) + (8x^2 - 7x - 10)$

$\qquad\qquad 3x^2 + 2x - 5 + 8x^2 - 7x - 10$ **1.** Remove parentheses by applying the distributive property.

$\qquad\qquad\qquad 11x^2 - 5x - 15$ **2.** Combine like terms.

Example 2. Add $15a^2 - 7ab + 3c^2 - 12b$ and $8ab + 12c^2 - 3b$.

Solution. $(15a^2 - 7ab + 3c^2 - 12b) + (8ab + 12c^2 - 3b)$
$\qquad\qquad 15a^2 - 7ab + 3c^2 - 12b + 8ab + 12c^2 - 3b$
$\qquad\qquad\qquad 15a^2 + ab + 15c^2 - 15b$

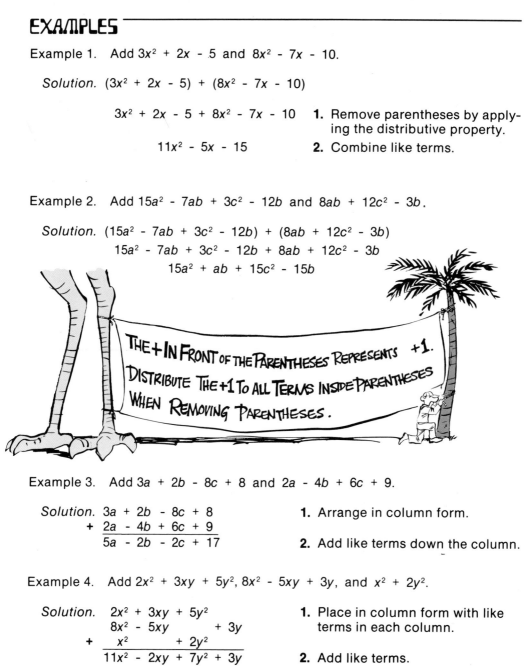

THE + IN FRONT OF THE PARENTHESES REPRESENTS +1.
DISTRIBUTE THE +1 TO ALL TERMS INSIDE PARENTHESES
WHEN REMOVING PARENTHESES.

Example 3. Add $3a + 2b - 8c + 8$ and $2a - 4b + 6c + 9$.

Solution.
$\qquad\;\; 3a + 2b - 8c + 8$ **1.** Arrange in column form.
$\underline{+\;\; 2a - 4b + 6c + 9}$
$\qquad\;\; 5a - 2b - 2c + 17$ **2.** Add like terms down the column.

Example 4. Add $2x^2 + 3xy + 5y^2$, $8x^2 - 5xy + 3y$, and $x^2 + 2y^2$.

Solution.
$\qquad\;\; 2x^2 + 3xy + 5y^2$ **1.** Place in column form with like
$\qquad\;\; 8x^2 - 5xy \qquad\;\; + 3y$ terms in each column.
$\underline{+\qquad x^2 \qquad\quad + 2y^2}$
$\qquad 11x^2 - 2xy + 7y^2 + 3y$ **2.** Add like terms.

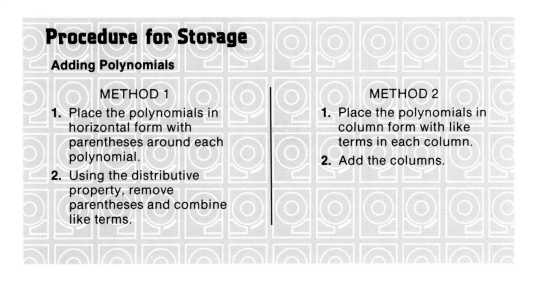

Procedure for Storage

Adding Polynomials

METHOD 1

1. Place the polynomials in horizontal form with parentheses around each polynomial.
2. Using the distributive property, remove parentheses and combine like terms.

METHOD 2

1. Place the polynomials in column form with like terms in each column.
2. Add the columns.

EXAMPLE

Example 5.   Add $-5x + 3xy + 7y + 9$, $5x^2 + 3xy + 8y^2$, and 10.

Solution.

$$
\begin{array}{r}
-5x + 3xy + 7y \quad\quad + 9 \\
5x^2 \quad\quad + 3xy \quad\quad + 8y^2 \\
+ \quad\quad\quad\quad\quad\quad\quad\quad\quad\quad + 10 \\
\hline
5x^2 - 5x + 6xy + 7y + 8y^2 + 19
\end{array}
$$

If possible, arrange the terms of a polynomial first in alphabetical order and then in order of descending powers of the variable. If two variables are present, arrange the terms so that powers of the first variable descend and powers of the second variable ascend. Place the constants at the end.

Exercises

Add.

1.
$$
\begin{array}{r}
3m + 4 \\
7m + 2 \\
9m - 12 \\
\hline
\end{array}
$$

2.
$$
\begin{array}{r}
x^4 - 3x^3 \\
- 4x^3 + x^2 \\
5x^3 \quad\quad + x - 3 \\
\hline
\end{array}
$$

3.
$$
\begin{array}{r}
4m^2 + 2m \\
8m - 9 \\
3m^2 \quad\quad + 4 \\
\hline
\end{array}
$$

4. $5k^2 - 3k + 2$
   $8k^2 + 9k - 8$

5. $-m + n - p$
   $m + n + p$
   $2m - n + p$

6. $3ay + 4y - 5z$
   $3y + 10z$
   $7ay - 5y$

7. $3x^3 + 4x - y$, $9x^2 - 5x + 7$, and $2x^3 + 3x + 8$

8. $4a + 9b - 10d$, $5a - 3b + 6d$, and $18a - 2c$

9. $3x^2 - 10xy + 7y^2$, $2x^2 + 8xy + 8y^2$, and $-9x^2 + 3y^2$

10. $12a^2 - 23ab - 6b^2$, $4a^2 - b^2$, $3a^2 + 2ab + b^2$, and $a^2 + ab + b^2$

11. $-4x^3 + 3x^2 - 5x + 10$, $-6x^2 + 3x + 9$, and $5x^2 - 10$

12. $8k^2 + 3km - 8m^2$, $3k^2 + 5m^2$, and $2k^2 - 4km$

13. $\frac{1}{2}x^2 + \frac{1}{3}xy + \frac{1}{4}y^2$, $\frac{1}{6}x^2 + \frac{1}{8}y^2$, and $\frac{1}{2}x^2 + \frac{3}{2}xy$

14. $0.82a + 0.19b - 0.84$, $1.23a + 11.2b + 4.2$, and $6.71a - 3.8b + 5.2$

15. $\frac{1}{2}x + \frac{1}{5}y$, $\frac{3}{2}x + \frac{8}{7}$, and $\frac{1}{3}x - \frac{4}{5}y$

16. Bill is x years old, Sue is 5 years older than Bill, and Jane is 3 years younger than Bill. What is their combined age?

17. The length of a rectangle is $5n + 3$ and the width is $2n - 6$. What is the perimeter of the rectangle?

Find the perimeter of each figure.

18.

19.

20.

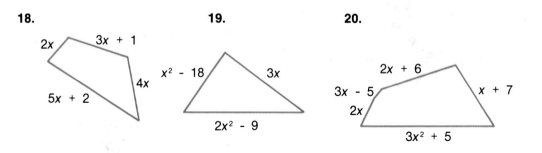

SUBTRACTING POLYNOMIALS

Can you change a subtraction problem to an addition problem? You should be able to because you learned in Chapter 1 that subtraction is the same as adding the opposite. When you subtract polynomials, you will follow the very same procedure: to subtract, add the opposite.

EXAMPLE

Example 1. Simplify $(3x^2 + 2x - 5) - (4x^2 - 5x + 2)$.

Solution.

$(3x^2 + 2x - 5) - (4x^2 - 5x + 2)$

$(3x^2 + 2x - 5) + (-4x^2 + 5x - 2)$

Solution.

1. To transform the problem to an addition problem, change the second polynomial to the opposite by reversing each sign inside the parentheses. The minus sign between the polynomials can be thought of as a -1. To find the opposite, simply distribute the -1 to each term of the second polynomial.

$3x^2 + 2x - 5 + -4x^2 + 5x - 2$
$-x^2 + 7x - 7$

2. Now remove the parentheses and combine like terms.

Polynomials can also be subtracted in column form. Make sure you place like terms in the same column.

EXAMPLES

Example 2. Simplify $(5a - 7b + 6c + 10) - (3a + 4b - 8c - 9)$.

Solution.

$$\begin{array}{r} 5a - 7b + 6c + 10 \\ + \quad -3a - 4b + 8c + 9 \\ \hline 2a - 11b + 14c + 19 \end{array}$$

1. Change the problem to an addition problem by reversing the signs of the second polynomial.

2. Add the polynomials.

Example 3. Simplify $(4x^2 + 3xy - y^2) - (5x^2 - 8xy + 4y^2)$.

Solution.

$$
\begin{array}{r}
4x^2 + 3xy - y^2 \\
+ \ -5x^2 + 8xy - 4y^2 \\
\hline
-x^2 + 11xy - 5y^2
\end{array}
$$

Add the opposite.

Exercises

Subtract.

1. $\begin{array}{r} 5a + 3 \\ 2a - 5 \end{array}$

2. $\begin{array}{r} 3a^2 + 2a - 4 \\ a^2 \quad\ \ - 6 \end{array}$

3. $\begin{array}{r} x + 2y - 3 \\ 4x - 8y + 3 \end{array}$

4. $\begin{array}{r} x^2 + 4xy - 10y^2 \\ 4x^2 - 8xy + 3y^2 \end{array}$

5. $\begin{array}{r} a^3 + 3a^2 - \quad 4a \\ 8a^3 - 9a^2 + 10a + 7 \end{array}$

6. $\begin{array}{r} 4x^2 - 3xy + 9y^2 \\ 2xy - \quad y^2 \end{array}$

Simplify.

7. Subtract $2x + 9$ from $3x - 7$.

8. Subtract $8a - 4$ from $3a$.

9. Subtract $4x - 7y - 9$ from 0.

10. $(2x + 3y) + (5x - 10) - (2x + y - 3)$

11. $(4x - 2y + 8) + (3x + 9y - 4) - (2x - y + 4)$

12. $(a^3 + 4b^2 - 3c) - (2a^3 - 12c)$

13. $(x^5 - x^4 + 8x - 7) - (x^4 + 2x - 2)$

14. $(y^2 + 3y + 8) - (9y^2 - 4y - 3)$

15. $(5x + 2y + 9) - (7x - 3y - 7)$

16. $(3a - 14b + c) - (6a + 21b - 5c)$

17. $(-x^3 + x^2y + xy^2 + y^4) - (5x^3 + 2x^2y - y^3 + 3y^4)$

18. $(a^3b + a^2b^3 - 4ab) - (12a^2b^3 + 9)$

19. $7x^5y - 3xy^2 + 12xy^4 - (8x^5y + 9xy^2 + 15xy^4)$

20. The perimeter of a rectangle is $3x + 10$ and the width of the rectangle is $x + 2$. Find the sum of the two lengths.

MULTIPLYING MONOMIALS

Too often young people, as well as adults, fail to transfer their learning to all areas of their lives. The Christian must live by biblical principles every day, not just on Sunday. God's Word is "profitable . . . for instruction in righteousness" (II Tim. 3:16d). The Christian young person must learn, memorize, review, and apply biblical principles throughout his life (cf. Ps. 119:9-11). Many algebraic principles and properties apply to more than one specific operation. For example, the operational sign rules that you learned in Chapter 1 apply to all operations whether they be operations with rational numbers, radicals, or polynomials. Here are the sign rules for multiplication for you to review.

1. If the factors have like signs, the product is positive.

2. If the factors have unlike signs, the product is negative.

Procedure for Storage

Multiplying Monomials

1. Multiply the numerical coefficients.

2. Multiply like variables by adding exponents on like-based terms.

3. Multiply the product of the coefficients with the product of the variables.

EXAMPLE

Example 1. Simplify $3x^2 \cdot 5x$.

Solution.

$3 \cdot 5 = 15$ **1.** Multiply the coefficients.

$x^2 \cdot x = x^3$ **2.** Multiply the variables.

$15 \cdot x^3 = 15x^3$ **3.** Multiply the coefficient product by the variable product.

Therefore $3x^2 \cdot 5x = 15x^3$.

Can you recall the associative and commutative properties of multiplication? Do you see where these properties apply in the multiplication of monomials? If you expand the terms first, you get $(3 \cdot x \cdot x) \cdot (5 \cdot x)$. By applying the associative and commutative properties, you get $(3 \cdot 5)(x \cdot x \cdot x)$, which equals $15x^3$.

EXAMPLES

IF THERE IS NO COEFFICIENT WRITTEN, THE COEFFICIENT IS ONE (1)

Example 2. Simplify $8x^2yz^3 \cdot xyz^2$.

Solution. $(8 \cdot 1) (x^2yz^3) (xyz^2)$	**1.** Multiply coefficients.
$8(x^3y^2z^5)$	**2.** Multiply variables.
$8x^3y^2z^5$	**3.** Multiply coefficients with variables.

Example 3. Simplify $(-4a^2b) (3a^3bc) (-5ab^2)$.

Solution. $(-4) (3) (-5) (a^2b) (a^3bc) (ab^2)$	
$60 (a^2b) (a^3bc) (ab^2)$	**1.** Multiply coefficients.
$60a^6b^4c$	**2.** Multiply variables.

Example 4. Simplify $(-9xy^2)^2$.

Solution. Remember that $(-9xy^2)^2$ means $(-9xy^2) (-9xy^2)$.
So $(-9xy^2)^2 = 81x^2y^4$.

WHEN YOU RAISE A NUMBER TO A POWER, MULTIPLY EXPONENTS

ANOTHER GOOD JOB DUSTED OFF

Exercises

Simplify.

1. $(8x^2y)(4xy^2z)$

2. $(3x^3y^2z)(18x)$

3. $(-4a^2b)(3ab^2)$

4. $(2abc)(-3a^3b)$

5. $(9x)(10y)$

6. $(\frac{1}{2}a^3b)(4b)$

7. $(-\frac{1}{4}mn)(\frac{1}{3}m^2)$

8. $(0.82ab^2)(0.3a^4)$

9. $(128x^2y)(-2xz)$

10. $(36m^2n^5)(-3mn^7)$

11. $(5a)(-6b^2)(3ab)$

12. $(10a^3)(-b^2c^5)(-8b^3c)$

13. $(4x^3y^2)(8xy)(-2x^5y)$

14. $(-4xy)^2$

15. $(3a^3)^3$

16. $(2a^2)(-5b^3)$

17. $(4abc)(-3a^3bc)$

18. $(-2a^2b)^2$

19. $(a^4b^5c^8)^4$

20. $(3ab^2c)^3$

Three computer programmers stopped at the Nite-E-Nite Motel on their way to a computer exhibition. The night clerk charged them $30 for the room so each man paid $10. In the morning the men did some minor repairs on the manager's computer, which had broken down during the night, so the manager decided to knock $5 off their room rate. While the men were at breakfast, the waiter came to them and gave each man $1, keeping the other $2 for himself. Thus the men now actually paid only $9 apiece, or a total of $27, for the room; the waiter kept $2, making a total of $29. What happened to the other $1?

MULTIPLYING MONOMIALS WITH POLYNOMIALS

What different meanings of *multiplication* does your dictionary give? Is one meaning "to increase in number or value"? Before Jesus Christ returned to heaven, He told His followers to spread the gospel to every creature so that anyone who believed could be saved. (See Matt. 28:19-20.) If Christians properly fulfilled the commission God gave them, the body of believers would greatly multiply as did the early church (cf. Acts 2:41-47). In just a few months after Christ's ascension, the church multiplied from a small number to thousands. Acts 9:31 reports that the church multiplied because the people were walking in the fear of the Lord. Do you want to be a multiplier of souls? Do you walk in the fear of the Lord so that you can be a good witness to your unsaved friends? Each Christian should strive to be a multiplier so that the number of souls in heaven will be greatly increased because of his testimony.

Look at the diagram. How many rectangles do you see? What is the area of each one? What formula do you use to find the area of a rectangle?

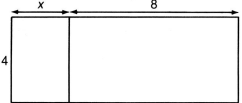

The length of the small rectangle on the left is x, and the width is 4. Therefore the area of the smaller rectangle is $4x$. What is the area of the rectangle on the right? The sum of the areas of the two rectangles is $4x + 32$. If you consider the entire large rectangle, the length is $x + 8$, and the width is 4. So $4(x + 8) = 4x + 32$. What property does this equation illustrate?

You can multiply a monomial by a polynomial, either horizontally or vertically. Set up vertically, the problem is quite similar to the usual multiplication of whole numbers.

$$
\begin{array}{r} x + 8 \\ 4 \\ \hline 4x + 32 \end{array}
\qquad
\begin{array}{r} 12 \\ 4 \\ \hline 48 \end{array}
$$

Procedure for Storage

Multiplying Polynomials by Monomials

1. Multiply each term of the polynomial by the monomial.
2. Combine any like terms.

EXAMPLES

Example 1.   Multiply $2x(4x + 5)$.

Solution. horizontal method, using the distributive property
$$2x(4x + 5) = 8x^2 + 10x$$

vertical method
$$
\begin{array}{r}
4x \;+\; 5 \\
2x \\
\hline
8x^2 \;+\; 10x
\end{array}
$$

Example 2.   Multiply $3x(x^2 - 7x + 8)$.

Solution. horizontal method
$$3x(x^2 - 7x + 8) = 3x^3 - 21x^2 + 24x$$

vertical method
$$
\begin{array}{r}
x^2 \;-\; 7x \;+\; 8 \\
3x \\
\hline
3x^3 \;-\; 21x^2 \;+\; 24x
\end{array}
$$

Example 3.   Multiply $8x^2(2x + 4y + 6z)$.

Solution. horizontal method
$$8x^2(2x + 4y + 6z) = 16x^3 + 32x^2y + 48x^2z$$

Example 4.   Multiply $2xy^2(3x - 8xy + 5y + 3z)$.

Solution. $2xy^2(3x - 8xy + 5y + 3z) = 6x^2y^2 - 16x^2y^3 + 10xy^3 + 6xy^2z$

Exercises

Multiply.

1. $2x^2 + 3x - 8$
$$\underline{7x}$$

2. $5a + 10b$
$$\underline{-4b}$$

3. $4m^2 - 3mn - 10$
$$\underline{6m}$$

4. $8k^2 + 9k + 6$
$$\underline{-7k}$$

5. $k + m - p$
$$\underline{3a}$$

6. $x^2 + 5x - 7$
$$\underline{-10x}$$

7. $3a^2(4a^4 + 5a - 18)$

8. $2k(k^3 + 6k^2 + 3k - 9)$

9. $4b^2(8a - 2b^2 + 6b)$

10. $-3x^2(4x^3y - 4xy + 3y^2)$

11. $\frac{1}{5}a^2(25a^3 + 15a^2 - 50)$

12. $-3xy^2(4x^2 - 8xy + 9z)$

13. $16x\left(\frac{1}{4}x^2 + \frac{1}{8}xy + \frac{1}{2}\right)$

14. $-ab(3a^2 - 6ab^2 + 4b^3)$

15. $-8x^3y(3x^2 + 7xy + 10)$

16. Find the area of a rectangle $5x$ long and $x - 9$ wide.

17. Using the formula $A = \frac{1}{2}bh,$ find the area of a triangle if the base is $x^2 + 12$ and the height is $7x$.

MULTIPLYING BINOMIALS

Because the procedure for multiplying binomials is very similar to the procedure for multiplying numbers, review thoroughly the process of multiplying two-digit numbers.

Notice that in this familiar process each digit of one factor is multiplied by the other factor to obtain the partial products. Then the 46 and the 1840 are added to obtain the product 1886.

23	multiplicand
82	multiplier
46	
1840	
1886	product

Binomials are like two-digit numbers in that binomials have two terms, so the multiplication process is exactly the same.

EXAMPLES

Example 1. Multiply $(2x + 5)(3x + 2)$.

Solution.

$$
\begin{array}{r}
2x + 5 \\
3x + 2 \\
\hline
4x + 10 \\
6x^2 + 15x \\
\hline
6x^2 + 19x + 10
\end{array}
$$

1. Multiply $+2$ with $+5$ to get $+10$ and with $2x$ to get $4x$.

2. Next multiply $3x$ with $+5$ to get $+15x$. Place the product below $4x$. (Keep like terms in the same column.) Then multiply $3x$ with $2x$ and write the product to the left of $15x$.

3. Add the two partial products by combining like terms.

Therefore $(2x + 5)(3x + 2) = 6x^2 + 19x + 10$.

Example 2. Multiply $(x - 9)(4x + 6)$.

Solution.

$$
\begin{array}{r}
x - 9 \\
4x + 6 \\
\hline
6x - 54 \\
4x^2 - 36x \\
\hline
4x^2 - 30x - 54
\end{array}
$$

WHEN MULTIPLYING, MAKE SURE YOU USE THE SIGN PRECEDING THE TERM, AS $+6 \cdot -9$

THIS IS A NICE SPOT FOR A SIGN!

Procedure for Storage

Multiplying Binomials Vertically

1. Multiply each term of one binomial with both terms in the other binomial.
2. Add like terms to obtain the final product.

EXAMPLES

Example 3.   Multiply $(a - b)(a + b)$.

Solution.

$$
\begin{array}{r}
a - b \\
a + b \\
\hline
ab - b^2 \\
a^2 - ab \\
\hline
a^2 \qquad - b^2
\end{array}
$$

Notice that the ab term is eliminated because ab and $-ab$ are additive inverses.

The vertical method of multiplication is fine to start with, but it is quite time-consuming and cumbersome. You must learn to multiply binomials quickly and accurately in your head because multiplication of binomials is a very important part of algebra. The process used to multiply binomials mentally is called the *FOIL method*. FOIL stands for **F**irst, **O**uter, **I**nner, **L**ast and relates to the terms of the binomials.

To solve, multiply the first terms, then the outer terms, then the inner terms, and then the last terms. Combine like terms and arrange variables to get the product.

First

Outer

$(x + 7) (x + 2)$

Inner

Last

$x^2 + 2x + 7x + 14$

$x^2 + 9x + 14$

First = x^2

Outer = $2x$

Inner = $7x$

Last = 14

Example 4.   Multiply $(4x - 5)(x + 3)$.

Solution.

$(4x - 5)(x + 3)$

$(4x - 5)(x + 3)$

$(4x - 5)(x + 3)$

$(4x - 5)(x + 3)$

$4x^2 + 12x + -5x + -15$

$4x^2 + 7x - 15$

1. Multiply by the FOIL method.
   product of first terms = $4x^2$
   product of outer terms = $12x$
   product of inner terms = $-5x$
   product of last terms = -15

2. Find the sum of the four products.

3. Combine like terms.

Procedure for Storage

Multiplying Binomials Mentally

1. Find the product of the first, outer, inner, and last terms.
2. Combine like terms.

EXAMPLE

Example 5.   Multiply $(2x - 5)(3x - 2)$.

Solution.

$F = 6x^2$
$O = -4x$
$I = -15x$
$L = 10$
$6x^2 - 4x - 15x + 10$
$6x^2 - 19x + 10$

Compare this answer with Example 1.

Exercises

Multiply the binomials vertically.

1. $(x + 5)(x + 2)$
2. $(x - 7)(x + 9)$
3. $(x + 6)(x - 4)$
4. $(x + 2)(x + 1)$
5. $(x - 3)(x - 4)$

6. $(x - 6)(x + 8)$
7. $(x + 1)(x - 5)$
8. $(x - 3)(x - 8)$
9. $(2x + 4)(3x - 6)$
10. $(5x + 6)(x - 4)$

Use the FOIL method to multiply these binomials.

11. $(x - 6)(x + 2)$
12. $(x + 3)(x + 8)$
13. $(x - 6)(x - 7)$
14. $(x - 7)(x - 9)$
15. $(x + 9)(x - 8)$

16. $(3x + 2)(x + 4)$
17. $(2x - 6)(4x + 1)$
18. $(x + 7)(3x - 4)$
19. $(5x + 6)(2x - 7)$
20. $(3x + 8)(2x - 3)$

21. $(x + 4)(2x - 9)$	**36.** $(x - 5)(x + 5)$
22. $(3x + 6)(x - 1)$	**37.** $(x + 3)(x - 3)$
23. $(2x + 14)(3x - 7)$	**38.** $(x - 7)(x + 7)$
24. $(x + 4)(2x - 11)$	**39.** $(x - 10)(x + 10)$
25. $(9x + 4)(4x - 8)$	**40.** $(a - b)(a + b)$
26. $(8x + 3)(3x - 2)$	**41.** $(3x + 4)(3x - 4)$
27. $(-2x - 5)(x - 12)$	**42.** $(2x - 13)(2x + 13)$
28. $(x + 9)(x - 7)$	**43.** $(x - 3)(x - 3)$
29. $(5x - 6)(3x + 2)$	**44.** $(x - 4)(x - 4)$
30. $(2x - 9)(4x - 11)$	**45.** $(x - 8)(x - 8)$
31. $(x + 6)^2$	**46.** $(a - b)(a - b)$
32. $(3x - 2)^2$	**47.** $(x + 1)(x + 1)$
33. $(-7x - 10)^2$	**48.** $(x + 9)(x + 9)$
34. $(11x + 12)^2$	**49.** $(x + 3)(x + 3)$
35. $(8x + 3)^2$	**50.** $(a + b)(a + b)$

MULTIPLYING POLYNOMIALS

The vertical method is the easiest method for multiplying polynomials with either factor larger than a binomial. Simply follow the procedure you learned for multiplying binomials vertically.

EXAMPLES

Example 1.   Multiply $(3x^2 - 4x + 9)(x + 2)$.

Solution.

$$
\begin{array}{r}
3x^2 - 4x + 9 \\
x + 2 \\
\hline
6x^2 - 8x + 18 \\
3x^3 + -4x^2 + 9x \\
\hline
3x^3 + 2x^2 + x + 18
\end{array}
$$

1. Arrange the terms in both polynomial factors in descending powers of the same variable. These polynomials are arranged in descending powers of x.

2. Write the problem out vertically.

3. Multiply each term in the multiplier by each term in the multiplicand. Be sure to use the sign in front of the term. Keep like terms in the same column and add.

This process illustrates an application of the distributive property.

Example 2. Multiply $(7a + 4b - 5c)(2a + b)$.

Solution.

$$
\begin{array}{r}
7a + 4b - 5c \\
2a + b \\
\hline
7ab + 4b^2 - 5bc \\
14a^2 + 8ab \qquad\qquad - 10ac \\
\hline
14a^2 + 15ab + 4b^2 - 5bc - 10ac
\end{array}
$$

Arrange in vertical form and multiply, placing only like terms in the same column.

Arrange the final answer in the order $14a^2 + 15ab - 10ac -5bc + 4b^2$.

Procedure for Storage

Multiplying Polynomials
1. Arrange both factors in descending powers of the same variable.
2. Place the factors in vertical form.
3. Multiply each term of the multiplier by each term of the multiplicand and place like terms in the same column.
4. Add like terms to obtain the final product.

EXAMPLE

Example 3. Multiply $(4x^3 + 5x^2 - 10x + 6)(3x^2 + 7x - 8)$.

Solution.

$$
\begin{array}{r}
4x^3 + 5x^2 - 10x + 6 \\
3x^2 + 7x - 8 \\
\hline
-32x^3 - 40x^2 + 80x - 48 \\
28x^4 + 35x^3 - 70x^2 + 42x \\
12x^5 + 15x^4 - 30x^3 + 18x^2 \\
\hline
12x^5 + 43x^4 - 27x^3 - 92x^2 + 122x - 48
\end{array}
$$

1. Terms are arranged in descending powers of x.
2. Place the problem in vertical form.
3. Multiply.
4. Combine like terms.

Exercises

Multiply the polynomials.

1. $(x^2 + xy + y^2)(x + y)$
2. $(3a^2 - 2a - 4)(a - 7)$
3. $(6x^2 + 3xy - 9y^2)(2x + y)$
4. $(7a + 3b - 9c + d)(a + b)$
5. $(2x^2 - x + 4)(3x - 7)$
6. $(a^2 - 3a - 9)(a + 2)$
7. $(2a + 4b)(3a - 9)$
8. $(4x^2 - 3x - 6)(x + 2)$

9. $(x^2 - 3x - 9)(x^2 + 4x - 6)$
10. $(2x^2 - 5x + 8)(3x + 6)$
11. $(8x^2 + 3x + 4)(x - 6)$
12. $(2x^2 + 5x + 10)(x + 4)$
13. $(5x^2 - 7x + 4)(x - 3)$
14. $(3x - 6)(3x + 5)$
15. $(8x^2 - 2x + 6)(3x + 4)$

SPECIAL PRODUCTS AND SHORT CUTS

You need to be familiar with two special products that occur when you multiply binomials. First, observe the process of squaring a binomial such as $x + 2$.

EXAMPLES

Example 1. Simplify $(x + 2)^2$.

Solution.

$$(x + 2)^2 = (x + 2)(x + 2)$$
$$= x^2 + 2x + 2x + 4$$
$$= x^2 + 4x + 4$$

Example 2. Simplify $(3x - 4)^2$.

Solution.

$$(3x - 4)^2 = (3x - 4)(3x - 4)$$
$$= 9x^2 - 12x - 12x + 16$$
$$= 9x^2 - 24x + 16$$

Example 3. Simplify $(x + y)^2$.

Solution.

$$(x + y)^2 = (x + y)(x + y)$$
$$= x^2 + xy + xy + y^2$$
$$= x^2 + 2xy + y^2$$

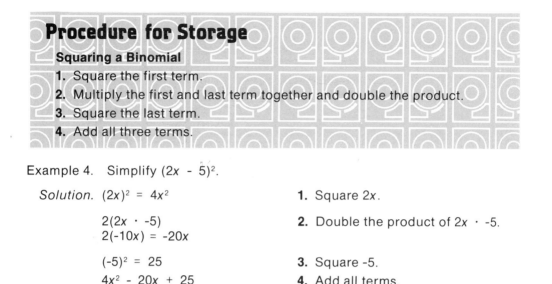

Procedure for Storage

Squaring a Binomial

1. Square the first term.
2. Multiply the first and last term together and double the product.
3. Square the last term.
4. Add all three terms.

Example 4.   Simplify $(2x - 5)^2$.

Solution. $(2x)^2 = 4x^2$ **1.** Square $2x$.

$2(2x \cdot -5)$ **2.** Double the product of $2x \cdot -5$.
$2(-10x) = -20x$

$(-5)^2 = 25$ **3.** Square -5.
$4x^2 - 20x + 25$ **4.** Add all terms.

Now consider the product of two binomials, one indicating the sum and the other indicating the difference of the same terms.

EXAMPLES

Example 5.   Multiply $(x - 4)(x + 4)$.

Solution. $(x - 4)(x + 4) = x^2 + 4x - 4x - 16$
$= x^2 - 16$

Example 6.   Multiply $(3x + 5)(3x - 5)$.

Solution. $(3x + 5)(3x - 5) = 9x^2 - 15x + 15x - 25$
$= 9x^2 - 25$

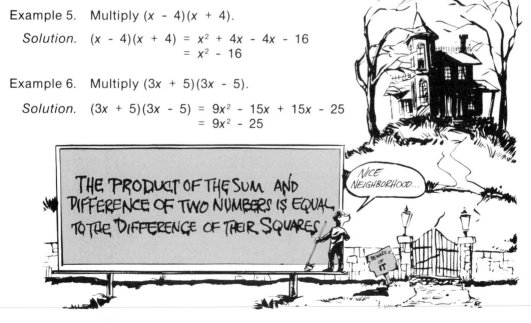

THE PRODUCT OF THE SUM AND DIFFERENCE OF TWO NUMBERS IS EQUAL TO THE DIFFERENCE OF THEIR SQUARES

Example 7.   Multiply $(x + y)(x - y)$.

Solution.
$$(x + y)(x - y) = x^2 - xy + xy - y^2$$
$$= x^2 - y^2$$

Notice that the middle terms are eliminated when finding the product of the sum and the difference.

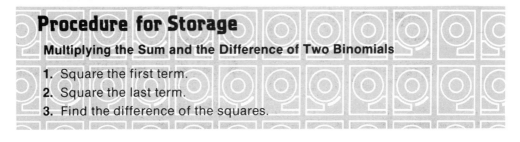

Procedure for Storage

Multiplying the Sum and the Difference of Two Binomials

1. Square the first term.
2. Square the last term.
3. Find the difference of the squares.

EXAMPLE

Example 8.   Multiply $(3x + 7)(3x - 7)$.

Solution.

$(3x)^2 = 9x^2$	**1.** Square $3x$.
$7^2 = 49$	**2.** Square 7.
$9x^2 - 49$	**3.** Write as the difference of the squares.

Exercises

Multiply.

1. $(x + 3y)^2$

2. $(5x - 3)(5x + 3)$

3. $(x^2 - 8)(x^2 + 8)$

4. $(3x + 4)(3x - 4)$

5. $(x - 6)^2$

6. $(2x + 3)^2$

7. $(x - 9y)^2$

8. $(x + 2y)(x - 2y)$

9. $(2x + 11)(2x - 11)$

10. $(6x - 12)^2$

Perform the indicated operation and simplify.

11. $(2x^2 + 3x - 5)(x + 3) + (x - 6)(x + 6)$

12. $(x + 3)(x - 3) - (x + 2)^2$

13. $(x + 5)(x + 6) + (x - 2)^2$

14. $(x^2 - 5x)(x + 2) + (3x - 6)(x + 2)$

15. $(x - 6)(x + 2)(x + 6)$

DIVIDING MONOMIALS

The Word of God divides (cf. Hebrews 4:12-13). It divides right from wrong, good from bad, light from dark, spiritual from unspiritual. The Holy Spirit speaks to the Christian to reveal sin in the Christian's life and to provide guidance and security. If a Christian does not read the Bible regularly and systematically, he cannot maintain fellowship with God as he should. He must read and study the Word of God every day so that he can rightly divide the word of truth to the unsaved world (cf. II Timothy 2:15).

Dividing monomials is really a review of several concepts that you have already learned. First, you must remember the sign rules for division. In Chapter 1 you learned that dividing two numbers with like signs yields a positive answer and dividing two numbers with unlike signs yields a negative answer. Second, you need to keep in mind the division properties of exponents. When dividing like bases, what do you do with the exponents? Third, you need to remember that a division problem can be written in the form of a fraction. With these things in mind, you should be able to divide monomials.

EXAMPLES

Example 1.   Simplify $27x^3y \div 3x$.

Solution.

$$\frac{27x^3y}{3x}$$

1. Change the problem to fractional form.

$$\frac{3^3x^3y}{3x}$$

2. Prime factor the numerical coefficients.

$$\frac{\overset{3^2\,x^2}{\cancel{3^3}\cancel{x^3}y}}{\underset{1\ 1}{\cancel{3x}}} = \frac{3^2x^2y}{1} = 9x^2y$$

3. Rename the fraction to lowest terms by reducing the numerical coefficients and the variables by using the properties of exponents.

Example 2.   Simplify $\dfrac{32xyz}{4x}$.

Solution.

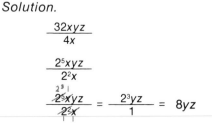

$$\frac{32xyz}{4x}$$

$$\frac{2^5xyz}{2^2x}$$

$$\frac{\overset{2^3\ 1}{\cancel{2^5}xyz}}{\underset{1\ 1}{\cancel{2^2}x}} = \frac{2^3yz}{1} = 8yz$$

Example 3.   Simplify $\dfrac{21a^3b}{7b}$

Solution.

$$\dfrac{21a^3b}{7b}$$

$$\dfrac{7 \cdot 3a^3b}{7b}$$

$$\dfrac{\cancel{7} \cdot 3a^3\cancel{b}}{\cancel{7}\cancel{b}} = 3a^3$$

Procedure for Storage

Dividing Monomials

1. Place in fractional form if necessary.
2. Prime factor all numerical coefficients.
3. Use the sign rules and the properties of exponents to cancel and simplify the expression.
4. Multiply the remaining coefficients.

EXAMPLES

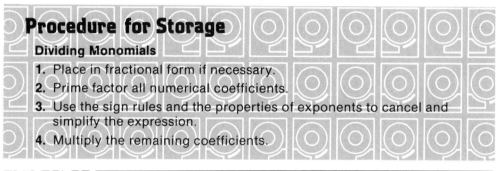

Example 4.   Simplify $\dfrac{-18a^2b}{9a}$.

Solution. $\dfrac{-18a^2b}{9a} = \dfrac{-2 \cdot \cancel{3^2} \cdot \cancel{a}a b}{\cancel{3^2}\cancel{a}}$

$$= -2ab$$

Example 5.   Simplify $\dfrac{54x^2yz^3}{3xyz^2}$.

Solution. $\dfrac{54x^2yz^3}{3xyz^2} = \dfrac{\cancel{3^3} \cdot 2\cancel{x^2}\cancel{y}\cancel{z^3}}{\cancel{3xyz^2}}$

$$= 18xz$$

Exercises

Divide.

1. $\dfrac{x^4}{x}$

2. $\dfrac{3x^2}{3}$

3. $\dfrac{25ab^3}{5a}$

4. $\dfrac{16x^5y}{8xy}$

5. $\dfrac{-74a^3bc^4}{-2abc^2}$

6. $\dfrac{-x^8}{x^2}$

7. $\dfrac{-108a^3b}{4a^3}$

8. $\dfrac{x^4y^5z^3}{xy^2z}$

9. $\dfrac{12z^9}{4z^5}$

10. $\dfrac{x^4y^3z^2}{-xy^2z}$

11. $\dfrac{1}{2}x^3y \div x$

12. $3x^3yz \div \dfrac{1}{2}$

13. $\dfrac{a^4b^3c}{ab^2}$

14. $\dfrac{-42x^5y^4z^{10}}{-6xz^3}$

15. $\dfrac{28a^4bc^5}{-4ac^2}$

DIVIDING POLYNOMIALS BY MONOMIALS

The principles for dividing polynomials are exactly the same as the principles for dividing numbers. So review the basic steps in division before you begin dividing polynomials.

EXAMPLE

Example 1. Simplify $(15 + 27) \div 3$.

Solution.

$\dfrac{15 + 27}{3}$ **1.** Place the problem in fractional form.

$\dfrac{15}{3} + \dfrac{27}{3}$ **2.** Separate addends.

$5 + 9$ **3.** Simplify.

14

Notice that the numerator was separated to form two addends with the same denominator. Do you remember from Chapter 1 that $\dfrac{a + b}{c} = \dfrac{a}{c} + \dfrac{b}{c}$? To check this property, add the numerator before you divide.

$$\frac{15 + 27}{3} = \frac{42}{3} = 14$$

You get the same answer by either method. If you cannot combine the numerator into one term, you must separate the addends before you divide.

EXAMPLES

Example 2. Simplify $(12x^2 + 20x) \div 4x$.

Solution.

$\dfrac{12x^2 + 20x}{4x}$ **1.** Place the problem in fractional form.

$\dfrac{12x^2}{4x} + \dfrac{20x}{4x}$ **2.** Separate into two addends.

$\dfrac{\overset{3}{\cancel{12}}\overset{x}{\cancel{x^2}}}{\cancel{4x}} + \dfrac{\overset{5}{\cancel{20}}\overset{1}{\cancel{x}}}{\cancel{4x}} = 3x + 5$ **3.** Simplify the addends.

Therefore $(12x^2 + 20x) \div 4x = 3x + 5$

Check your solution by multiplying the quotient that you obtained by the divisor. You should get the dividend. Does $4x(3x + 5) = 12x^2 + 20x$?

Example 3. Simplify $\dfrac{18a^2 + 3a - 27}{-3}$.

Solution.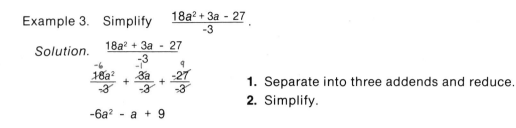

$\dfrac{18a^2 + 3a - 27}{-3}$

$\dfrac{\overset{-6}{\cancel{18a^2}}}{\cancel{-3}} + \dfrac{\overset{-1}{\cancel{3a}}}{\cancel{-3}} + \dfrac{\overset{9}{\cancel{-27}}}{\cancel{-3}}$

1. Separate into three addends and reduce.
2. Simplify.

$-6a^2 - a + 9$

Procedure for Storage

Dividing Polynomials by Monomials

1. Place the problem in fractional form.
2. Separate the expression into monomial addends.
3. Simplify each addend as much as possible.
4. Check the solution by multiplying the quotient by the divisor to get the dividend.

EXAMPLES

Example 4. Simplify $\dfrac{8x^3 + 16x^2 - 4x}{-4x}$.

Solution.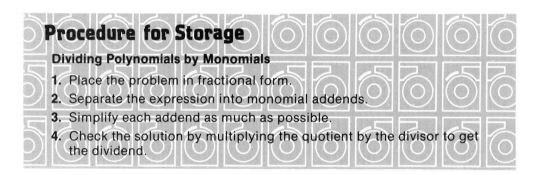

$\dfrac{8x^3 + 16x^2 - 4x}{-4x}$

$\dfrac{8x^3}{-4x} + \dfrac{16x^2}{-4x} + \dfrac{-4x}{-4x}$

$\dfrac{\overset{-2x^2}{\cancel{8x^3}}}{\cancel{-4x}} + \dfrac{\overset{-4x}{\cancel{16x^2}}}{\cancel{-4x}} + \dfrac{\cancel{-4x}}{\cancel{-4x}}$

$-2x^2 - 4x + 1$

Check. Does $-4x(-2x^2 - 4x + 1) = 8x^3 + 16x^2 - 4x$?

Example 5. Simplify $(a^3b^2 + a^2b^3 - ab^4) \div ab$.

Solution. $\dfrac{a^3b^2 + a^2b^3 - ab^4}{ab} = \dfrac{a^3b^2}{ab} + \dfrac{a^2b^3}{ab} + \dfrac{-ab^4}{ab}$

$$= \dfrac{\overset{a^2b}{\cancel{a^3b^2}}}{\underset{\shortmid\shortmid}{\cancel{ab}}} + \dfrac{\overset{ab^2}{\cancel{a^2b^3}}}{\underset{\shortmid\shortmid}{\cancel{ab}}} + \dfrac{\overset{-1b^3}{\cancel{-ab^4}}}{\underset{\shortmid\shortmid}{\cancel{ab}}}$$

$$= a^2b + ab^2 - b^3$$

Check. Does $ab(a^2b + ab^2 - b^3) = a^3b^2 + a^2b^3 - ab^4$?

ALWAYS SEPARATE THE EXPRESSION INTO MONOMIAL ADDENDS BEFORE CANCELLING

WHA?

SKI JUMP FINALS

Exercises

Divide as indicated.

1. $(5x^2 + 25x) \div 5x$

2. $(a + 5b - 3c) \div -1$

3. $(x^3 + x^2 - x) \div x$

4. $(24a^2b - 12ab + 9b^2) \div 3b$

5. $(abc + bcd) \div bc$

6. $(8x^3 - 2x) \div 2x$

7. $(7x^2 - 4x) \div x$

8. $(a^2bc + ab^3c^2 - b^2c^5) \div bc$

9. $(81x^3 - 27x^2y + 9xy^3) \div 3x$

10. $(-4a^3b^2 + 32ab^3 - 18b^5) \div -2b^2$

11. $(15x^2 - 3x + 27) \div -3$

12. $(-48a^4 + 36b^5) \div 6$

13. $(17a^3b^2 - 5a^2b^3 + 2ab^5) \div ab$

14. $(3n^4 - n^2) \div n^2$

15. $(3n^3 - 33) \div -3$

16. $(9x^2 + 54x + 3) \div 3$

17. $(17a^3b - 34ab^2) \div 17a$

18. $(22x^2y + 16xy - 8y) \div 2y$

19. $(15a^2bc^3 - 5ab^3c) \div 5abc$

20. $(6x^4y^3 - 26x^2y^2 - 18xy) \div 2xy$

DIVIDING POLYNOMIALS

Dividing with monomials is fairly simple, as you have seen. When the divisor is a binomial, the process becomes more complicated but is still much like dividing by a two-digit number. Divide 1634 by 32.

$$
\begin{array}{r}
51 \\
32\overline{)1634} \\
-160 \\
\hline
34 \\
-32 \\
\hline
2
\end{array}
$$

To check, multiply the quotient by the divisor. Then add the remainder. If you calculated correctly, you should obtain the original dividend.

$$51 \cdot 32 + 2 = 1632 + 2 = 1634$$

Now observe a polynomial division. Look for the similarities.

EXAMPLE

Example 1.   Compute $(x^2 + 4x - 9) \div (x + 2)$.

Solution. $x + 2\overline{)x^2 + 4x - 9}$

$$
\begin{array}{r}
x \\
x + 2\overline{)x^2 + 4x - 9} \\
\underline{x^2 + 2x} \\
2x - 9
\end{array}
$$

1. First, write the problem in long-division form. If necessary, arrange the terms of the dividend and the divisor so that they are in descending powers of one variable.

2. Look at the divisor and the first term of the dividend. Divide the first term of the dividend (x^2) by the first term of the divisor (x). You get x. Place x in the quotient.

3. Now multiply x by the whole divisor ($x + 2$) and place the products under the dividend in the proper columns.

4. Subtract to obtain a new dividend.

$$\begin{array}{r} x + 2 \\ x + 2 \overline{\smash{)}x^2 + 4x - 9} \\ \underline{x^2 + 2x} \\ 2x - 9 \\ \underline{2x + 4} \\ -13 \end{array}$$

So the answer is $x + 2$, R-13.

5. Divide the divisor into the new dividend.

6. Continue dividing and subtracting until the degree of the new dividend is less than the degree of the divisor.

HERE THE R STANDS FOR REMAINDER, NOT A VARIABLE.

Check. Does $(x + 2)(x + 2) - 13 = x^2 + 4x - 9$?

Procedure for Storage

Dividing Polynomials

1. Arrange both the dividend and the divisor in descending powers of the same variable.
2. Divide the first term of the dividend by the first term of the divisor to obtain the first term of the quotient.
3. Multiply this term by the whole divisor and place the product under the dividend.
4. Subtract this product from the dividend to obtain a new dividend.
5. Go back to step 2 unless the degree of the new dividend is less than the degree of the divisor.
6. Check your results by multiplying the quotient with the divisor and adding the remainder.

EXAMPLES

Example 2. Compute $(2x^4 - x^3 + 5x^2 + 9x - 6) \div (x - 1)$.

Solution. Follow the steps for solving.

$$
\begin{array}{r}
2x^3 + x^2 + 6x + 15 \\
x - 1 \overline{)2x^4 - x^3 + 5x^2 + 9x - 6} \\
\underline{2x^4 - 2x^3} \\
x^3 + 5x^2 + 9x - 6 \\
\underline{x^3 - x^2} \\
6x^2 + 9x - 6 \\
\underline{6x^2 - 6x} \\
15x - 6 \\
\underline{15x - 15} \\
9
\end{array}
$$

The solution is $2x^3 + x^2 + 6x + 15, R9$.

Check. Does $(x - 1)(2x^3 + x^2 + 6x + 15) + 9 = 2x^4 - x^3 + 5x^2 + 9x - 6$?

WHEN A POLYNOMIAL IS DIVIDED EVENLY, AS IN EXAMPLE 3, BOTH THE DIVISOR AND THE QUOTIENT ARE CALLED FACTORS OF THE POLYNOMIAL

A MASTERPIECE!

Example 3. Compute $(x^3 - 8) \div (x - 2)$.

Solution. Since the x^2 and x terms are missing from the dividend and you are putting the problem in long-division form, leave some space in the dividend and mentally insert 0's as coefficients of the missing variables.

$$\begin{array}{r}
x^2 + 2x + 4 \\
x - 2\overline{)x^3 + 0x^2 + 0x - 8} \\
\underline{x^3 - 2x^2} \\
2x^2 + 0x - 8 \\
\underline{2x^2 - 4x} \\
4x - 8 \\
\underline{4x - 8} \\
0
\end{array}$$

The solution is $x^2 + 2x + 4$

Example 4. Compute $(3a^3 + 4ab^2 - 5a^2b + 2b^3) \div (a + b)$

Solution.

$$\begin{array}{r}
3a^2 - 8ab + 12b^2 \\
a + b\overline{)3a^3 - 5a^2b + 4ab^2 + 2b^3} \\
\underline{3a^3 + 3a^2b} \\
-8a^2b + 4ab^2 \\
\underline{-8a^2b - 8ab^2} \\
12ab^2 + 2b^3 \\
\underline{12ab^2 + 12b^3} \\
-10b^3
\end{array}$$

1. First, arrange the polynomial in descending powers of a.
2. Divide.

The quotient is $3a^2 - 8ab + 12b^2$, R-$10b^3$.

Exercises

Divide.

1. $(x^3 - 2x^2 + 3x) \div (x - 4)$

2. $(4x^2 - 16) \div (x - 2)$

3. $(a^3b - 3a^2b^2 - 4b^3) \div (a + b)$

4. $(a^2 - 3b^2) \div (a - b)$

5. $(5x^2 - 2x + 9) \div (x + 1)$

6. $(12m^2 - 3m^3 + 4m) \div (3m - 2)$

7. $(24x^2 + 13x - 9) \div (x + 3)$

8. $(7x^2 + 8 - 3x) \div (x + 4)$

9. $(x^2 - 16) \div (x + 4)$

10. $(x^3 - 27) \div (x - 3)$

11. $(x^3 + 3x - 9) \div (x^2 + 2x - 6)$

12. $(x^4 - 8x^2 + 16) \div (x^2 + 4)$

13. $(a^5 + 3a) \div (a^2 - 2)$

14. $(x^3 + 2x - 8) \div (x + 3)$

15. $(a^2 + 4a + 12) \div (a - 6)$

COMPUTER LANGUAGES

Computers cannot directly understand human languages. A computer perceives all information only as a series of 0s and 1s. Mathematicians call groups of these numbers *binary numbers*, with each 0 and 1 known as a binary digit (or bit). Programs that are written in binary numbers are called machine-language programs.

Humans find machine-language programs extremely difficult to read. Consequently, men have devised other methods for communicating with computers. The first of these methods is called hexadecimal programming. Groups of four bits are converted into base 16 equivalent numbers (see the table) called hexadecimal numbers. Although these numbers are easier to read than binary numbers, they are still confusing for humans to use.

Assembly languages are one step further away from the machine-language level. Each microprocessor has its own assembly language. In these languages, easy-to-remember letter groupings (called mnemonics) replace one or more hexadecimal numbers. For example, the code that the Motorola 6809 microprocessor uses to tell the processor to store a number is 1010 0111 in binary, A7 in hexadecimal, and STA (store accumulator) in assembly language.

Assembly-language programming, though easier than machine-language programming, is still difficult to use. Consequently, programmers have designed languages that are even further removed from the computer level. These languages are called high-level languages.

High-level languages allow a programmer to design programs without worrying about what kind of computer the program will be run on. High-level languages translate the human-readable form of a language into machine language for the programmer. The programmer does not have to remember all the assembly- or machine-language instructions. This approach to programming saves much time.

The programming language BASIC (*B*eginner's *A*ll-Purpose *S*ymbolic *I*nstruction *C*ode) is one of the most popular high-level languages available today. BASIC exists on many different machines from

---

The Decimal Addition of Two Numbers

Machine Language Listing		Assembly Language	BASIC Language
Binary	**Hexidecimal**		
11010110	D6	LDB $40	T=A1+A2
01000000	40		
10111110	BE	LDX #$51	
00000000	00		
01000001	41		
00010000	10	LDY #$51	
10001110	8E		
00000000	00		
01010001	51		
00011100	1C	ANDC #%11111110	
11111110	FE		
10100110	A6	ADDIGS LDA .X	
10000100	84		
10101001	A9	ADCA .Y+	
10100000	AO		
00011001	19	DAA	
10100111	**A7**	**STA .X+**	
10000000	80		
01011010	5A	DECB	
00100110	26		
11110110	F6	BNE ADDIGS	
00111111	3F	SWI	

micros to mainframes. BASIC is an easy-to-learn high-level language.

In the late '70s and early '80s, two other high-level languages became popular. The first of these, Pascal, overcomes some of the deficiencies of BASIC. Programs that would require many instructions in BASIC are stated simply in one or two Pascal statements.

Pascal can be easily understood by those learning to program.

Another newer language is called C. Although C is quite cryptic, it is an extremely useful computer language. Many complex programs have been written in it. Programs written in C run quite quickly, and many programmers like to use it.

New computer languages, like computers themselves, are continually being created. Each new language performs some tasks better than others. So far, attempts to design a universal computer language have failed. Therefore, the programmer needs to know the strengths and weaknesses of all the languages he uses.

Table of common computer language terms in Pascal, BASIC, and C

BASIC	Pascal	C	Approximate Meaning
INPUT	readln	scanf	Read data from keyboard
PRINT	write or writeln	printf	Output data to screen
a ↑ 2	sqr(a)	a * a	Square the value of a
SQR(c2)	sqrt(c2)	sqrt(c2)	Square root of a number
REM	(* ... *)	/* ... */	Indicates a comment which the computer ignores

MULTIPLYING RADICAL EXPRESSIONS

In the last chapter you learned how to multiply and divide radicals and then simplify them. Now you will learn how to multiply and divide radical expressions.

> **Radical expression:** an algebraic expression containing at least one radical, such as $\sqrt{3} + 4$, $\sqrt{6} - \sqrt{3}$, and $5 + \sqrt{7}$.

Radical expressions are not polynomials, but to multiply them, you follow the same rules that you follow to multiply polynomials.

EXAMPLES

Example 1.   Multiply $\sqrt{5}\,(\sqrt{3} - 2)$.

Solution.   Apply the distributive property.

$$\sqrt{5}\,(\sqrt{3} - 2) = \sqrt{15} - 2\sqrt{5}$$

Example 2.   Multiply $(\sqrt{7} + \sqrt{2})\,(\sqrt{3} - 6)$.

Solution.   Use the FOIL method to multiply.

$$(\sqrt{7} + \sqrt{2})\,(\sqrt{3} - 6) = \sqrt{7} \cdot \sqrt{3} + (-6)(\sqrt{7}) + \sqrt{2} \cdot \sqrt{3} + (-6)\,\sqrt{2}$$
$$= \sqrt{21} - 6\sqrt{7} + \sqrt{6} - 6\sqrt{2}$$

Can any terms in this radical expression be simplified or combined? If not, this is the final answer.

Once again you recognize that you must apply principles you have learned earlier. Because mathematics constantly builds on previously learned material, a strong foundation is essential. The wise man's house withstood the storm because it was built upon a rock (cf. Matt. 7:24-25). The Christian's foundation is Christ Jesus. Paul wrote to carnal Christians at Corinth and told them that they needed to grow up (cf. I Cor. 3:1-15). Spiritual maturity comes only as the Christian applies the biblical truths that he already knows. God will not reveal more truth to the one who refuses to do what God has already revealed. Are you a growing Christian? Or have you refused to obey the truths that God has revealed in His Word?

The special products that you observed in the section on multiplying polynomials also apply to radical expressions. Learning to recognize these special cases quickly will aid you in the next chapter when you proceed one step higher to the factoring of polynomials.

EXAMPLES

Example 3. Multiply $(\sqrt{5} - \sqrt{7})(\sqrt{5} + \sqrt{7})$.

Solution. Since this is the product of the sum and the difference of two numbers, you can apply the short cut you learned on page 380. Otherwise, you could use the FOIL method to multiply.

$$(\sqrt{5} - \sqrt{7})(\sqrt{5} + \sqrt{7}) = (\sqrt{5})^2 - (\sqrt{7})^2$$
$$= 5 - 7$$
$$= -2$$

Example 4. Simplify $(\sqrt{3} - 2)^2$.

Solution.

$(\sqrt{3} - 2)^2 = (\sqrt{3})^2 + (2 \cdot -2\sqrt{3}) + 2^2$ **1.** If you use the short cut, you get this.

$\qquad = 3 - 4\sqrt{3} + 4$ **2.** Combine like terms.

$\qquad = 7 - 4\sqrt{3}$

How would you find a decimal approximation of the solution to example 4? Find the solution accurate to the nearest hundredth.

1. Find the value of $\sqrt{3}$. $\sqrt{3} \doteq 1.732$

2. Substitute that value for $\sqrt{3}$ $7 - 4\sqrt{3}$
in the expression. Compute. $7 - 4(1.732)$
$\qquad\qquad\qquad\qquad\qquad\qquad 7 - 6.928$
$\qquad\qquad\qquad\qquad\qquad\qquad\quad 0.072$

To the nearest hundredth, the solution is 0.07.

Procedure for Storage

Multiplying Radical Expressions

1. Follow the same rules that you follow for multiplying polynomials.

2. After multiplying, simplify radicals and combine like terms.

EXAMPLES

Example 5. Multiply $(\sqrt{3} - \sqrt{2})(\sqrt{3} + \sqrt{2})(\sqrt{6} - 4)$.

Solution. Multiply the first and second radical expressions. (They represent a special product.) Then multiply that product with the third factor.

$$(\sqrt{3} - \sqrt{2})(\sqrt{3} + \sqrt{2}) = (\sqrt{3})^2 - (\sqrt{2})^2$$
$$= 3 - 2$$
$$= 1$$

$$1(\sqrt{6} - 4) = \sqrt{6} - 4$$

The solution is $\sqrt{6} - 4$.

Example 6. Multiply $(\sqrt{3} - \sqrt{8})(\sqrt{9} - 3)$.

Solution. $(\sqrt{3} - \sqrt{8})(\sqrt{9} - 3)$

$$\sqrt{27} - 3\sqrt{3} - \sqrt{72} + 3\sqrt{8}$$

$$3\sqrt{3} - 3\sqrt{3} - 6\sqrt{2} + 6\sqrt{2}$$

1. Multiply by the FOIL method.
2. Simplify.
3. Combine like terms.

Therefore $(\sqrt{3} - \sqrt{8})(\sqrt{9} - 3) = 0$

Exercises

Multiply.

1. $\sqrt{3}\ (\sqrt{2} - 1)$
2. $\sqrt{5}\ (5 + \sqrt{3})$
3. $\sqrt{7}\ (\sqrt{21} + \sqrt{2})$
4. $\sqrt{4}\ (\sqrt{8} + \sqrt{2})$
5. $(\sqrt{3} - \sqrt{11})(\sqrt{3} + \sqrt{11})$
6. $(\sqrt{6} + \sqrt{2})(3 - \sqrt{2})$
7. $(\sqrt{12} - \sqrt{3})(\sqrt{5} + \sqrt{2})$
8. $(\sqrt{8} + 3)(\sqrt{7} + 5)$
9. $(x\sqrt{3} - 5)(x\sqrt{6} - 3)$
10. $(\sqrt{5} - \sqrt{3})^2$
11. $(7 + \sqrt{3})(4 - \sqrt{11})$
12. $(\sqrt{7} + 8)^2$
13. $\sqrt{5}\ (\sqrt{3} - \sqrt{2})(\sqrt{5} - 6)$

14. $(\sqrt{6} - \sqrt{2})(\sqrt{8} + 4)$
15. $\sqrt{7}\ (\sqrt{3} + \sqrt{21})^2$
16. $(\sqrt{5} - 3)(\sqrt{2} + 1)(\sqrt{5} + 3)$
17. $(3 - \sqrt{2})^2(\sqrt{5} + 3)$
18. $\sqrt{5}\ (\sqrt{35} + 5)(\sqrt{15} + 2)$
19. $(4 - \sqrt{2})^2$
20. $\sqrt{x}\ (\sqrt{3} - 5)(\sqrt{x^3} + 2)$
21. $\sqrt{xy^2}\ (\sqrt{x} - \sqrt{y})(\sqrt{x} + \sqrt{y})$
22. $(3 - \sqrt{10})(4 + \sqrt{20})$
23. $\sqrt{x}\ (x + \sqrt{8})^2$
24. $3\sqrt{5}\ (\sqrt{7} - \sqrt{3})(\sqrt{7} + \sqrt{3})$
25. $(\sqrt{7} - \sqrt{10})^2$

DIVIDING RADICAL EXPRESSIONS

As you recall from Chapter 7, you can never leave radicals in the denominator of an algebraic expression. So you learned how to eliminate a radical in the denominator. What did you do to eliminate the radical in the denominator of a problem like $\dfrac{3}{\sqrt{2}}$? To eliminate the $\sqrt{2}$, you multiplied the numerator and the denominator by 1 in the form $\dfrac{\sqrt{2}}{\sqrt{2}}$.

$$\frac{3}{\sqrt{2}} \cdot \frac{\sqrt{2}}{\sqrt{2}} = \frac{3\sqrt{2}}{2}$$

When a radical expression appears in the denominator of a fraction, as in $\dfrac{4}{\sqrt{2}-1}$, you must still eliminate the radical from the denominator. However, simply multiplying by the radical will not eliminate the radical from the denominator. To eliminate the radical, you must use another radical expression called the conjugate. So to eliminate $\sqrt{2}$ - 1 from the denominator, multiply the numerator and the denominator by the conjugate of $\sqrt{2}$ - 1, which is $\sqrt{2}$ + 1. Multiplication by a conjugate fits the special case of the product of the sum and difference of two numbers. Thus the middle terms will be eliminated.

DEFINITION

≫**Conjugate of a radical expression:** the radical expression with the opposite sign between the terms.

EXAMPLE

Example 1.   Simplify $\dfrac{4}{\sqrt{2}-1}$.

Solution. Rationalize the denominator by multiplying the numerator and the denominator by the conjugate of the denominator.

$$\frac{4}{\sqrt{2}-1} \cdot \frac{\sqrt{2}+1}{\sqrt{2}+1} = \frac{4(\sqrt{2}+1)}{(\sqrt{2})^2 - 1^2}$$

$$= \frac{4(\sqrt{2}+1)}{2-1}$$

$$= \frac{4\sqrt{2}+4)}{1}$$

$$= 4\sqrt{2}+4$$

Be sure to use this method only when there is a radical expression in the denominator. When the radical in the denominator is not a radical expression, you should use the method in Chapter 7.

EXAMPLES

Example 2. Simplify $\dfrac{3\sqrt{2} + 4}{\sqrt{5} + \sqrt{3}}$.

Solution.

$$\frac{3\sqrt{2} + 4}{\sqrt{5} + \sqrt{3}} = \frac{3\sqrt{2} + 4}{\sqrt{5} + \sqrt{3}} \cdot \frac{\sqrt{5} - \sqrt{3}}{\sqrt{5} - \sqrt{3}}$$

$$= \frac{(3\sqrt{2} + 4)(\sqrt{5} - \sqrt{3})}{(\sqrt{5})^2 - (\sqrt{3})^2}$$

$$= \frac{3\sqrt{10} - 3\sqrt{6} + 4\sqrt{5} - 4\sqrt{3}}{5 - 3}$$

$$= \frac{3\sqrt{10} - 3\sqrt{6} + 4\sqrt{5} - 4\sqrt{3}}{2}$$

1. Find the conjugate of the denominator and multiply the numerator and the denominator by this conjugate. The conjugate of $\sqrt{5} + \sqrt{3}$ is $\sqrt{5} - \sqrt{3}$.

2. Multiply the numerator by the FOIL method.

The solution is in its simplest form and the denominator is rational.

Example 3. Simplify $\dfrac{\sqrt{m} - \sqrt{n}}{\sqrt{m} + \sqrt{n}}$.

Solution.

Both the numerator and the denominator are special cases. The conjugate of the denominator is $\sqrt{m} - \sqrt{n}$. Multiply the numerator and the denominator by this conjugate.

$$\frac{\sqrt{m} - \sqrt{n}}{\sqrt{m} + \sqrt{n}} \cdot \frac{\sqrt{m} - \sqrt{n}}{\sqrt{m} - \sqrt{n}} = \frac{(\sqrt{m} - \sqrt{n})^2}{(\sqrt{m})^2 - (\sqrt{n})^2}$$

$$= \frac{(\sqrt{m})^2 - 2(\sqrt{m})(\sqrt{n}) + (\sqrt{n})^2}{m - n}$$

$$= \frac{m - 2\sqrt{mn} + n}{m - n}$$

Procedure for Storage

Dividing Radical Expressions

1. Find the conjugate of the denominator.
2. Multiply the numerator and the denominator by the conjugate.
3. Simplify.

   Mathematicians always rationalize the denominator to make radical expressions consistent. Thus anyone solving problems containing radicals can understand the answers because they are in a consistent form and are easier to work with. Consistency is important in daily living. The Christian's life must be consistent with God's Word. The Christian can know that his life is consistent with the Word of God only if he is reading and studying it.

Exercises

Simplify.

1. $\dfrac{2}{\sqrt{3} - 1}$

2. $\dfrac{\sqrt{5} - 3}{\sqrt{5} + 3}$

3. $\dfrac{\sqrt{2} + \sqrt{5}}{\sqrt{3} - \sqrt{10}}$

4. $\dfrac{5}{\sqrt{2} - \sqrt{6}}$

5. $\dfrac{\sqrt{5} + 1}{\sqrt{7} - 2}$

6. $\dfrac{\sqrt{11}}{\sqrt{3} + \sqrt{2}}$

7. $\dfrac{\sqrt{13}}{\sqrt{6}}$

8. $\dfrac{9}{3 + \sqrt{2}}$

9. $\dfrac{7\sqrt{3}}{2\sqrt{4} + 1}$

10. $\dfrac{3\sqrt{2} - 8\sqrt{7}}{4\sqrt{3} + \sqrt{5}}$

MEMORY RECALL

Identify.
>   binomial
>   conjugate
>   degree of a polynomial
>   degree of a term
>   FOIL method
>   monomial
>   polynomial
>   radical expression
>   trinomial

You should be able to do the following:

1. Classify and evaluate any given polynomial.
2. Add and subtract given polynomials.
3. Multiply monomials.
4. Multiply monomials and polynomials.
5. Multiply binomials.
6. Multiply polynomials.
7. Recognize special cases and learn short cuts for multiplying them.
8. Divide monomials.
9. Divide polynomials by monomials.
10. Divide polynomials.
11. Multiply radical expressions.
12. Divide radical expressions.

You should be able to do the following problems:

Classify each polynomial, give its degree, and evaluate the polynomial if $x = 2, y = -1$, and $z = 0$.

1. $4x^3 + 2x - 5z$
2. $8y^4 + 7y^2 + 3y + 9$
3. $3x^2 - 5xz$

Do the indicated operation and simplify.

4. $(2x^2 + 3x - 5) + (7x^2 - 9)$
5. $(5a^2 - ab - 3b^2) - (6a^2 - 7ab + 10b^2)$
6. $(x^2 + y^2) - (x + y^2) + (12x^2 + y)$

7. $(r^2 + 2t) + (r^2 + 6rt - 9t)$

8. $(5x^2y^3)(16xy^4)$

9. $(12ab^5)(-4a^4b)$

10. $(a^5ab^3)^4$

11. $7xy^2(3x - 5xy^4)$

12. $-3a^4bc^2(2a^3b + 7abc^5)$

13. $(x + 4)(x - 6)$

14. $(a + 5)(a + 7)$

15. $(y - 6)(y + 6)$

16. $(x + 3)^2$

17. $(x - 9)(x - 11)$

18. $(a + 3b)(a - 7b)$

19. $(x^2 + 3x + 5)(x + 2)$

20. $(x - 2y)^2$

21. $(x + 3)(x - 3)(x - 3)$

22. $\dfrac{x^5}{x^2}$

23. $8x^2y^3z \div 2xy^2$

24. $\dfrac{7x^2y + 21x^3y^4}{7xy}$

25. $(6x^2 + 21x + 9) \div (x + 3)$

26. $\sqrt{5}\ (\sqrt{7} + 3)$

27. $\sqrt{11}\ (\sqrt{2} - \sqrt{13}\,)$

28. $(\sqrt{2} + \sqrt{3}\,)(\sqrt{2} - \sqrt{3}\,)$

29. $\dfrac{\sqrt{7}}{\sqrt{27}}$

30. $\dfrac{\sqrt{6}}{3 + \sqrt{2}}$

CHAPTER 9

FACTORING POLYNOMIALS

The Cascade Mountain Range, a line of mountains 700 miles long, extends from northern California through Oregon into British Columbia. These volcanic mountains are among the highest in the United States and include Mt. Rainier in Washington.

At the tops of many of these mountain peaks lie great glaciers, which are easily identified in infrared photographs such as this one of a mountain peak in the Cascade Range. Notice also the glacier-fed lake in the upper left-hand corner.

Infrared photography is often used in making maps, discovering drought areas, locating oil fields, and even developing defense projects, because it detects light rays that are not visible to the human eye. The radiation that an object emits is a function of that object's temperature. The more heat an object emits, the darker red that object appears in the infrared photograph. The dark red at the bottom of the photo indicates the abundant plant life at the lower elevations of the mountain, where there are large numbers of ponderosa pines and Douglas firs. The cooler areas, such as the glacier and snow-capped peaks, have little color. Can you find the glacier, rivers, lakes, and timberline? Where are the warmest areas? the coolest areas?

The white mass at the top of the photo indicates the glacier, which is emitting virtually no infrared radiation. Its height is 10,568 feet, and its surface area in square yards is given by the formula $A = x^2 + 5720x$, where x is the width of the glacier. If the width of the glacier measures 1320 yards, can you find the number of square yards that the glacier covers? Although you can master this problem, you may not know how to factor the polynomial in the formula. In this chapter you will learn to factor many different forms of polynomials in order to solve quadratic equations, which will come in a later chapter.

FACTORING COMMON MONOMIALS

What is a factor? What is factoring? A factor, as you have already learned, is a quantity (known or unknown) that can be multiplied with another quantity to yield a product. When you learned to find the greatest common divisor (GCD) and the least common multiple (LCM) of two numbers, you factored each number to its prime factors. Prime factoring is the process of determining the two or more prime quantities that have been multiplied to produce the stated product. Multiplication begins with the factors and finds the product. Factoring, the opposite of multiplication, begins with the product and finds the factors. In the last chapter you learned to multiply a monomial with a polynomial. In this section you will learn to find a common monomial factor in a polynomial by applying the distributive property in reverse.

DEFINITION

≫**Common monomial factor:** a factor of a polynomial common to all terms in the polynomial.

EXAMPLES

Example 1. Factor $8x^2 - 16$.

Solution.

$$8x^2 = 2^3x^2$$
$$16 = 2^4$$

1. Find the prime factorization of the terms. Then find the GCD of the terms. This is also the greatest factor common to both terms.

2. The greatest common monomial factor is 8.

$$8x^2 - 16 = 8(x^2 - 2)$$

3. Factor 8 out of each term of the polynomial.

Factored, $8x^2 - 16 = 8(x^2 - 2)$.

Example 2. Factor $3x^2y - 27xy + 9xy^3$.

Solution.

$3x^2y - 3^3xy + 3^2xy^3$ **1.** Find the prime factorization of each term.

$3xy = $ GCD   **2.** Identify the factors common to the three terms. Then find the highest power of each factor that all the terms have in common. This is the GCD of the terms in the polynomial.

$3xy(x - 9 + 3y^2)$ **3.** Factor the GCD from each term of the polynomial by dividing the GCD into each term of the polynomial.

Factored, $3x^2y - 27xy + 9xy^3 = 3xy(x - 9 + 3y^2)$.

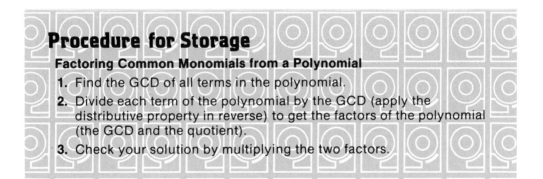

Procedure for Storage

Factoring Common Monomials from a Polynomial

1. Find the GCD of all terms in the polynomial.

2. Divide each term of the polynomial by the GCD (apply the distributive property in reverse) to get the factors of the polynomial (the GCD and the quotient).

3. Check your solution by multiplying the two factors.

EXAMPLES

Example 3.   Factor $14a^3 + 21a$.

Solution.

$$14a^3 = 7 \cdot 2 \cdot a^3$$
$$21a = 7 \cdot 3 \cdot a$$

1. By factoring, you can see that the GCD is $7a$.

$$2a^2 + 3$$

2. Dividing $14a^3$ by $7a$ gives $2a^2$. Dividing $21a$ by $7a$ gives 3.

$$7a(2a^2 + 3)$$

3. The factorization is $7a(2a^2 + 3)$.

Check. Does $7a(2a^2 + 3) = 14a^3 + 21a$?

Example 4.   Factor $xa^2 + xy - x$.

Solution.

The common monomial here is x. By factoring x out of the trinomial, you obtain $x(a^2 + y - 1)$.

Check. Does $x(a^2 + y - 1) = xa^2 + xy - x$?

Exercises

Factor.

1. $6a^2b + 3ab^2$

2. $300x^2 - 100x$

3. $10a^2bc^3 + 5ab^2c$

4. $7x^2 - 49xy + 28y^2$

5. $a^2 - a$

6. $45a^3 - 40a$

7. $8x - 32y$

8. $2\pi x - 4\pi r$

9. $12x^3 - 16xy^2$

10. $ax + ay$

11. $21x^3 - 6x^2 - 3$

12. $3x + 3y$

13. $20a^3x + 50ax + 10x$

14. $15x + 30$

15. $7a^5 - 84a^3 + 21a$

16. $x^2 - 3x$

17. $6a^2 + 48a - 24$

18. $x^5 + x^3 - x^2 + x$

19. $10 - 50x$

20. $x^2 - xyz$

FACTORING THE DIFFERENCE OF TWO SQUARES

In Chapter 8 you learned how to multiply binomials, including the sum and difference of two numbers. Don't forget that the product of the sum $(x + y)$ and the difference $(x - y)$ of two numbers is equal to the difference of their squares $(x^2 - y^2)$.

$$(x + y)(x - y) = x^2 - y^2$$

Since factoring is the opposite of multiplication, you will get the binomial sum $(x + y)$ and the binomial difference $(x - y)$ as factors when you factor any binomial that is the difference of two squares.

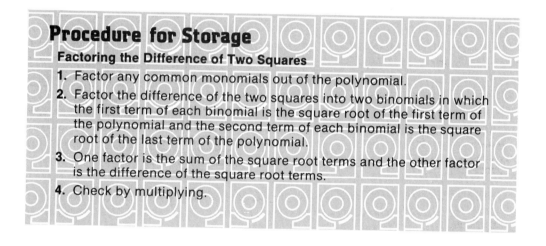

Procedure for Storage

Factoring the Difference of Two Squares

1. Factor any common monomials out of the polynomial.
2. Factor the difference of the two squares into two binomials in which the first term of each binomial is the square root of the first term of the polynomial and the second term of each binomial is the square root of the last term of the polynomial.
3. One factor is the sum of the square root terms and the other factor is the difference of the square root terms.
4. Check by multiplying.

EXAMPLES

Example 1.   Factor $x^2 - 49$.

Solution.

Do you recognize this binomial as the difference of two squares? Find the square root of each term. Then express the roots as two binomials, one of the sum of the roots and the other of the difference of the roots.
The factorization is $(x + 7)(x - 7)$.

Example 2.   Factor $5a^2 - 125x^2$.

Solution.

$5(a^2 - 25x^2)$

1. Factor out the common monomial factor 5, leaving the difference of two squares.

$a^2 - 25x^2 = (a + 5x)(a - 5x)$

2. Factor the difference of two squares.

So $5a^2 - 125x^2 = 5(a + 5x)(a - 5x)$.

Check. Does $5(a + 5x)(a - 5x) = 5a^2 - 125x^2$?

Example 3.   Factor $1 - 64y^2$.

Solution.

$(1 + 8y)(1 - 8y)$

Exercises

Factor.

1. $4x^2 - 16$

2. $x^2 - y^2$

3. $2a^2 - 242$

4. $25 - 100y^2$

5. $a^2x^2 - 16x^2$

6. $63x^2 - 175$

7. $y^2 - 144$

8. $3x^2 - 108y^2$

9. $a^2 - 225b^2$

10. $a^2x^2 - y^2$

11. $36a^2 - 49$

12. $25x^2 - 49$

13. $147a^2 - 507$

14. $a^4 - a^2b^2$

15. $9x^2 - 100$

16. $392a^5 - 200a^3$

17. $16x^2 - 4$

18. $x^7 - x^5$

19. $81a^2 - 9$

20. $49x^2 - 4$

FACTORING PERFECT SQUARE TRINOMIALS

When factoring polynomials, you can save yourself a lot of time if you recognize the special cases when you see them. Can you identify a polynomial that is the difference of two squares? What characteristics should you look for?

Can you recognize the characteristics of sin? In someone else's life you probably can identify sin quickly and easily. But can you recognize sin in your own life? How can you know what is sin and what is not sin? If you consistently read the Word of God, the Holy Spirit will identify sin, such as rebellion (cf. I Sam. 15:23a). When the Holy Spirit does direct your attention to sin in your life, you should immediately confess the sin and forsake it so that God can forgive and cleanse you from the sin (cf. I John 1:9). If you do not confess and forsake the sin, you will become insensitive toward sin and enslaved to it. Don't allow sin to creep into your life (cf. Rom. 6:12-14).

One special product you learned about in Chapter 8 was the square of a binomial. Review the squaring process and look for characteristics of the product that will identify it as the square of a binomial.

$$(x + y)^2 = (x + y)(x + y)$$
$$= x^2 + 2xy + y^2$$

$$(y + 4)^2 = (y + 4)(y + 4)$$
$$= y^2 + 8y + 16$$

$$(x + 3)^2 = x^2 + 6x + 9$$

$$(x - 1)^2 = x^2 - 2x + 1$$

Can you see anything that these four trinomials have in common? First, each product is a trinomial. Next, the first and last terms of each trinomial is a perfect square. The middle term is twice the product of the square roots of the first and last terms of the trinomial. Notice that all four trinomials follow the same pattern. Anytime you see a trinomial in this pattern, you should recognize it as a perfect square trinomial.

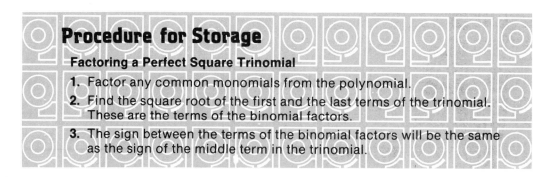

Procedure for Storage

Factoring a Perfect Square Trinomial

1. Factor any common monomials from the polynomial.
2. Find the square root of the first and the last terms of the trinomial. These are the terms of the binomial factors.
3. The sign between the terms of the binomial factors will be the same as the sign of the middle term in the trinomial.

EXAMPLES

Example 1. Factor $x^2 + 10x + 25$.

Solution. $x^2 + 10x + 25$

1. Is the first term a perfect square? Is the last term a perfect square? Is the middle term twice the product of the square roots of the first and last terms of the trinomial? Is this a perfect square trinomial?

$$\sqrt{x^2} = x$$

$$\sqrt{25} = 5$$

$$(x + 5)^2$$

2. Factor by finding the square root of x^2 and of 25. So the binomial factor has the terms x and 5.

3. Place the sign of the middle term of the trinomial between the terms of the factor.

So the factorization of $x^2 + 10x + 25$ is $(x + 5)^2$.

Check. Does $(x + 5)^2 = x^2 + 10x + 25$?

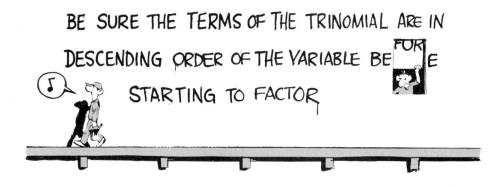

BE SURE THE TERMS OF THE TRINOMIAL ARE IN DESCENDING ORDER OF THE VARIABLE BEFORE STARTING TO FACTOR

Example 2.   Factor $4x^2 + 12x + 9$.

Solution. $\sqrt{4x^2} = 2x$ The sign of the middle term is $+$.

$\sqrt{9} = 3$

The factorization is $(2x + 3)^2$.

Check.   Does $(2x + 3)^2 = 4x^2 + 12x + 9$?

Example 3.   Factor $x^2y^2 - 8xyz + 16z^2$.

Solution.   Is this a perfect square trinomial?

$\sqrt{x^2y^2} = xy$ The sign of the middle term is $-$.

$\sqrt{16z^2} = 4z$

The factorization is $(xy - 4z)^2$.

Check.   Does $(xy - 4z)^2 = x^2y^2 - 8xyz + 16z^2$?

Example 4.   Factor $x^2 - 4x + 4y^2$.

Solution.   Is this a perfect square trinomial? No, the middle term is not twice the product of the square roots of the other terms.

Exercises

Identify the perfect square trinomials.

1. $x^2 + 6x + 9$

2. $x^2y - 8xy + 16y^2$

3. $x^2 + 14x + 49$

4. $a^2b^2 - 12abc + 36c^2$

5. $4x^2 - 10x + 25$

6. $a^2b^4 + 24ab^2 + 144$

7. $81x^2y^4 + 9xy^2z + z^2$

8. $x^6y^2 - 4x^3yz + 4z^2$

9. $a^2 - 4ab - 4b^2$

10. $16x^2y^8 + 16xy^4 + 4$

Factor.

11. $x^2 - 6x + 9$

12. $16a^2 + 8a + 1$

13. $x^2 - 16x + 64$

14. $9x^2 + 12x + 4$

15. $\frac{1}{16} y^2 - 2y + 16$

16. $x^2 + .6x + .09$

17. $9x^2 + 30xz + 25z^2$

18. $m^2 + 24m + 144$

19. $4x^4y^2 - 24x^2yz^3 + 36z^6$

20. $x^8 + 26x^4 + 169$

21. $a^2 - 10ab + 25b^2$

22. $x^2t^4 - 20xt^2 + 100$

23. $x^2 + 2x + 1$

24. $a^2 - 14a + 49$

25. $36x^2 + 12x + 1$

FACTORING TRINOMIALS OF THE FORM $x^2 + bx + c$

Most polynomials are neither the difference of two squares nor perfect square trinomials. When you factor a trinomial that is not a perfect square, you must use a trial-and-error method of factoring until you gain enough experience to factor trinomials easily. Just remember that factoring is the opposite of multiplying.

EXAMPLE

Example 1. Factor $x^2 + 7x + 12$.

Solution. $x^2 + 7x + 12$.

$x^2 = x \cdot x$

or

$x^2 = x^2 \cdot 1$

$(x \qquad)(x \qquad)$

1. To begin factoring this trinomial, find all possible factors of x^2, the first term. Because this trinomial form requires an x in each factor, you will use $x \cdot x$. Place each x in parentheses, leaving space for the other term.

$12 = 12 \cdot 1$
$12 = -12 \cdot -1$
$12 = 6 \cdot 2$
$12 = -6 \cdot -2$
$12 = 4 \cdot 3$
$12 = -4 \cdot -3$

2. To find the second number in these binomial factors, list all the factors of 12, the last term.

$(x \quad 3)(x \quad 4)$

3. Choose the factors whose sum equals 7, the coefficient of the middle term. Since $3 \cdot 4 = 12$ (the last term) and $3 + 4 = 7$ (the coefficient of the middle term), place 3 in one set of parentheses and 4 in the other.

$(x + 3)(x + 4)$

4. Determine the signs of the binomial factors by observing the signs in the trinomial. All signs in this trinomial are positive; therefore, all signs in the factorization will also be positive.

Check. Does $(x + 3)(x + 4)$
$= x^2 + 7x + 12$?

Procedure for Storage

Factoring $x^2 + bx + c$ Trinomials

1. Factor the first term. Use the factors as the first term in the binomial factors.
2. Factor c, the last term.
3. Choose the factors of c whose sum is b and place these factors in the factorization as the last terms in the binomial factors.
4. Insert the correct operational signs.
5. Check the results by multiplying the factors.

EXAMPLE

Example 2.   Factor $x^2 + 9x + 8$.

Solution. $x^2 + 9x + 8$.

$(x \quad)(x \quad)$ **1.** Factor the first term.

$8 = 1 \cdot 8$ **2.** Factor the last term.
$8 = -1 \cdot -8$
$8 = 2 \cdot 4$
$8 = -2 \cdot -4$

$8 + 1 = 9$ **3.** Choose the factors whose sum equals the coefficient of the middle term.

$(x \quad 1)(x \quad 8)$

$(x + 1)(x + 8)$ **4.** Since all signs in the product are positive, all signs in the factorization will be positive.

Check.   Does $(x + 1)(x + 8) = x^2 + 9x + 8$?

YOU CAN DO ALL OF THE STEPS SHOWN HERE IN YOUR HEAD TO SAVE YOURSELF TIME.

Energy Matters

Albert Einstein
(1879-1955)

Albert Einstein was born of Jewish parents on March 14, 1879, in Ulm, a city in southwestern Germany where Albert's father ran a small electrochemical factory. His mother was an accomplished musician who encouraged her son to play the violin. He loved classical music and played the violin very well.

While a youngster Albert did not like formal education. One day his Uncle Jakob introduced him to algebra and the Pythagorean theorem. "Algebra is a merry science," his uncle told him. "We go hunting for a little animal whose name we don't know, so we call it x. When we bag our game, we pounce on it and give it its right name." From then on Albert enjoyed pouncing on simple algebraic and geometric problems on his own.

Albert became interested in physics, and at age sixteen he sought admission to the Swiss Polytechnic Institute in Zurich. He had to take the entrance exams twice before he passed them, but he was finally admitted. He graduated from the Institute in 1900 after studying math and physics.

Einstein is best known for his theory of relativity and the formula $E=mc^2$, which he developed in 1905 at the age of twenty-six. That same year he also developed the study of photoelectric effect, called the quantum theory, for which he received the Nobel Prize in physics in 1921. From 1909 to 1933 he was a professor at several European universities and began lecturing abroad. In 1933 Einstein was lecturing in California when Hitler came to power in Germany. Because Einstein was a Jew, the Nazi government confiscated his property and deprived him of his citizenship. He took refuge in the United States and became a professor at the Institute for Advanced Study in Princeton, New Jersey. Einstein became an American citizen in 1940.

Einstein's scientific work laid the foundation for splitting the atom. He is one of the fathers of the atomic age. He arrived at his theories by means of intricate mathematical calculations and equations. But he always insisted that anyone who understood the intricacies of higher math could easily understand his theory. If you continue your study of mathematics, perhaps someday you will be able to study the theories that Einstein developed.

Procedure for Storage

Determining Signs When Factoring

1. If the sign of the last term is positive and the sign of the middle term is positive, the signs between terms in the binomial factors will be positive.
2. If the sign of the last term is positive and the sign of the middle term is negative, the signs between terms will be negative.
3. If the sign of the last term is negative, the sign of one factor will be positive and the other will be negative.

EXAMPLES

Example 3. Factor $x^2 + x - 72$.

Solution. $x^2 + x - 72$.

$(x \quad)(x \quad)$ 1. Factor the first term.

$-72 = -1 \cdot 72$ 2. Factor the second term.

$-72 = 1 \cdot -72$

$-72 = -2 \cdot 36$

$-72 = 2 \cdot -36$

$-72 = 4 \cdot -18$

$-72 = -4 \cdot 18$

$-72 = 6 \cdot -12$

$-72 = -6 \cdot 12$

$-72 = -8 \cdot 9$

$-72 = 8 \cdot -9$

$-8 + 9 = 1$ 3. Choose the factors whose sum is 1 and place them in the parentheses.

$(x - 8)(x + 9)$ 4. Notice that the factors determined the signs.

Check. Does $(x - 8)(x + 9) = x^2 + x - 72$?

WHENEVER POSSIBLE FACTOR OUT COMMON MONOMIALS BEFORE DOING ANY OTHER FACTORING

Example 4.   Factor $2x^2 + 22x + 48$.

Solution. $2x^2 + 22x + 48$ **1.** Since this polynomial contains the common monomial factor 2, factor it out first. The remaining trinomial, $x^2 + 11x + 24$, now fits the form $x^2 + bx + c$. Factor the polynomial in parentheses as usual.

$2(x^2 + 11x + 24)$

$2(x \quad)(x \quad)$ **2.** Factor the first term.
$24 = 1 \cdot 24$ **3.** Factor the last term.
$24 = -1 \cdot -24$
$24 = 2 \cdot 12$
$24 = -2 \cdot -12$
$24 = 3 \cdot 8$
$24 = -3 \cdot -8$
$24 = 4 \cdot 6$
$24 = -4 \cdot -6$

$3 + 8 = 11$ **4.** Choose the pair whose sum is 11.

$2(x + 3)(x + 8)$

Check.   Does $2(x + 3)(x + 8) = 2x^2 + 22x + 48$?

Example 5.   Factor $a^2 - 5a - 14$.

Solution. $a^2 - 5a - 14$

$(a \quad)(a \quad)$
$-7 \cdot 2 = -14$
$-7 + 2 = -5$

$(a - 7)(a + 2)$

Check.   Does $(a - 7)(a + 2) = a^2 - 5a - 14$?

Exercises

Factor.

1. $x^2 + 4x - 32$
2. $a^2 + 8a + 15$
3. $x^2 - 2x - 3$
4. $a^2 + 2a - 8$
5. $b^2 + b - 20$
6. $x^2 + 15x + 54$
7. $a^2 - 6a + 5$
8. $x^2 - x - 30$
9. $y^2 + 7y + 10$
10. $x^2 + 5x + 4$
11. $4x^2 + 28x + 24$
12. $3x^2 + 24x + 36$
13. $a^2 + 3a - 28$

14. $x^2 - 9x + 20$
15. $6b^2 - 42b + 72$
16. $a^2 - 4a + 3$
17. $x^2 - 8x + 12$
18. $x^2 + 20x + 100$
19. $x^2 - 16$
20. $x^2 + 6x + 9$
21. $a^2 - 5a - 14$
22. $x^2 - 25$
23. $x^2 + 7x + 12$
24. $x^2 + 8x + 16$
25. $2x^2 - 20x + 48$

FACTORING TRINOMIALS OF THE FORM $ax^2 + bx + c$

To learn how to factor a trinomial of this form, just observe the multiplication of two binomials to produce a trinomial of this form. Multiply the binomials $(3x + 2)(x - 5)$ by the FOIL method and you get $3x^2 - 13x - 10$. The product of the outside terms is called the outer product. The product of the inside terms is called the inner product. When factoring a trinomial of the form $ax^2 + bx + c$, you must factor it into two binomials such that the sum of the outer and inner products equals bx. What is the product of $(3x - 2)(x + 5)$?

The polynomials in this section differ from those in the last section in that these have a coefficient other than 1 on the x^2 term. The coefficient must be factored with the variable. Study the following examples and notice how to factor a trinomial of this form.

EXAMPLE

Example 1.   Factor $3x^2 + 5x + 2$.

Solution. $3x^2 + 5x + 2$

$3x^2 = x \cdot 3x$
$3x^2 = -x \cdot -3x$

$(3x \quad)(x \quad)$

$2 = 1 \cdot 2$
$2 = -1 \cdot -2$

$(3x + 1)(x + 2)$ or $(3x + 2)(x + 1)$

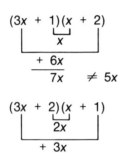

$7x \;\neq\; 5x$

$5x \;=\; 5x$

The solution is $(3x + 2)(x + 1)$.

Check.   Does $(3x + 2)(x + 1) = 3x^2 + 5x + 2$?

1. Look for a common monomial factor. This polynomial has none.
2. Factor $3x^2$. Use the positive factors unless the negative ones are needed to produce the correct middle term. Place these factors in parentheses.
3. Factor 2. Since the sign of the middle term is positive, you must use the positive factors. They can be combined with the other terms in two ways.
4. Choose the combination of binomials that makes the sum of the outer and inner products equal to $5x$.

Procedure for Storage

Factoring $ax^2 + bx + c$ Trinomials

1. Factor any common monomials from the trinomial.
2. Check to see if the trinomial is a perfect square trinomial. If so, factor by the short cut. If not, factor the first term of the trinomial and place the factors in parentheses.
3. Factor the last term of the polynomial. Choose the binomial factor combination that makes the sum of the outer and inner products equal to the middle term.
4. Check your factorization by multiplying the factors.

Example 2.   Factor $2x^2 - 9x + 4$.

Solution. $2x^2 - 9x + 4$

1. No common monomials can be factored out.

$2x^2 = x \cdot 2x$
$2x^2 = -x \cdot -2x$
$(x\quad)(2x\quad)$

2. Factor the first term. Use positive factors.

$4 = 1 \cdot 4$
$4 = -1 \cdot -4$
$4 = 2 \cdot 2$
$4 = -2 \cdot -2$

3. Factor the last term. Since the sign of the middle term is negative, you must use the negative factors and combine them with the first terms of the binomial factors. From the three combinations, choose the one whose sum of the outer and inner products equals $-9x$. The first factorization produces the middle term $-6x$. The second factorization produces the middle term $-9x$, the correct middle term. So $(x - 4)(2x - 1)$ is the factorization. You do not need to check the third combination.

$(x - 1)(2x - 4) \quad \rightarrow -6x$
$(x - 4)(2x - 1) \quad \rightarrow -9x$
$(x - 2)(2x - 2) \quad \rightarrow$

Therefore $2x^2 - 9x + 4 = (x - 4)(2x - 1)$.

Check.   Does $(x - 4)(2x - 1) = 2x^2 - 9x + 4$?

As you become more proficient in factoring, you will not need to write down all factors because you can figure the sums mentally. If you understand the procedures to follow, you can increase your speed with practice.

EXAMPLE

Example 3.   Factor $6x^2 - 14x - 40$.

Solution. $6x^2 - 14x - 40$

$2(3x^2 - 7x - 20)$ **1.** Remove the monomial factor 2.
$3x^2 = 3x \cdot x$ **2.** Factor the first term.
$2(3x\quad)(x\quad)$

$-20 = -1 \cdot 20$ $-20 = -2 \cdot 10$ **3.** Factor the last term.
$-20 = 1 \cdot -20$ $-20 = 4 \cdot -5$
$-20 = 2 \cdot -10$ $-20 = -4 \cdot 5$

$2(3x - 1)(x + 20)$ $\rightarrow 59x$ no   **4.** Then find the combination of
$2(3x - 2)(x + 10)$ $\rightarrow 28x$ no   outer and inner products that
$2(3x - 4)(x + 5)$ $\rightarrow 11x$ no   produces $-7x$. You may have to
$2(3x + 5)(x - 4)$ $\rightarrow -7x$ yes   try each pair of factors before
                                          you find the correct combination.

The factorization of $6x^2 - 14x - 40$ is $2(3x + 5)(x - 4)$.

Exercises

Factor.

1. $3x^2 - 18x + 27$

2. $12x^2 - 8x - 20$

3. $3x^2 + 5x - 28$

4. $9x^2 - 30x + 25$

5. $4x^2 - 16$

6. $8a^2 - 104a - 112$

7. $2x^2 + 9x + 4$

8. $a^2 - 9$

9. $x^2 - 18x + 81$

10. $6a^2 - 5a - 4$

11. $9x^2 + 3x - 2$

12. $x^2 - 4x - 32$

13. $18x^2 + 54x + 36$

14. $16a^2 + 40a - 24$

15. $9x^2 - 576$

16. $2x^2 + x - 21$

17. $30x^2 - 100x - 250$

18. $5x^2 + 8x - 21$

19. $6x^2 + 5x - 4$

20. $3a^2 + 13a - 10$

FACTORING TRINOMIALS
OF THE FORM $ax^2 + bxy + cy^2$

What is different about this form of the trinomial compared to the previous forms you have studied? Did you notice that variables accompany all the terms? To factor a trinomial of this form, follow the same steps you have used, remembering also to factor the variable in the last term.

EXAMPLES

Example 1. Factor $2x^2 - 3xy - 14y^2$.

Solution. $2x^2 - 3xy - 14y^2$ **1.** No monomials can be factored out.

$(2x \quad)(x \quad)$ **2.** Factor the first term as usual.

$-14y^2 = -14y \cdot y$
$-14y^2 = 14y \cdot -y$
$-14y^2 = -7y \cdot 2y$
$-14y^2 = 7y \cdot -2y$

3. Factor the last term, including the variable. There are eight possible combinations. Try different ones until you find the one that yields the correct middle term.

$(2x - y)(x + 14y) \rightarrow 27xy$ no
$(2x + 14y)(x - y) \rightarrow 12xy$ no
$(2x - 2y)(x + 7y) \rightarrow 12xy$ no
$(2x + 7y)(x - 2y) \rightarrow 3xy$ no
$(2x - 7y)(x + 2y) \rightarrow -3xy$ yes

$2x^2 - 3xy - 14y^2$ factored is $(2x - 7y)(x + 2y)$.

Check. Does $(2x - 7y)(x + 2y) = 2x^2 - 3xy - 14y^2$?

Example 2. Factor $18a^2 - 57ab + 35b^2$.

Solution. $18a^2 - 57ab + 35b^2$ **1.** No monomial can be factored out.

$18a^2 = a \cdot 18a$
$18a^2 = 2a \cdot 9a$
$18a^2 = 3a \cdot 6a$

2. Factor the first term of the trinomial. The first terms of the binomial factors will be $(a \quad)(18a \quad)$, $(2a \quad)(9a \quad)$, or $(3a \quad)(6a \quad)$.

$$35b^2 = b \cdot 35b$$
$$35b^2 = -b \cdot -35b$$
$$35b^2 = 5b \cdot 7b$$
$$35b^2 = -5b \cdot -7b$$

$(a - b)(18a - 35b) \rightarrow -53ab$ no
$(2a - b)(9a - 35b) \rightarrow -79ab$ no
$(a - 5b)(18a - 7b) \rightarrow -97ab$ no
$(2a - 5b)(9a - 7b) \rightarrow -59ab$ no
$(3a - 5b)(6a - 7b) \rightarrow -51ab$ no
$(3a - 7b)(6a - 5b) \rightarrow -57ab$ yes

3. Factor the last term. Since the sign before the last term is positive and the sign before the middle term is negative, only the negative factors $-b \cdot -35b$ or $-5b \cdot -7b$ are possible. Try different combinations of factors until you find the one combination that produces $-57ab$.

Finally, after many tries, you have found the correct factorization. Sometimes you have to try several combinations before you find the correct factorization. If you do this figuring mentally instead of writing it all down, you can save yourself a lot of time.

Check. Does $(3a - 7b)(6a - 5b) = 18a^2 - 57ab + 35b^2$?

Exercises

Factor.

1. $x^2 + 4xy - 60y^2$

2. $a^2 + 4ab - 12b^2$

3. $y^2 - 6yz + 9z^2$

4. $a^2 - b^2$

5. $6x^2 + xy - 5y^2$

6. $8a^2 - 26ac - 7c^2$

7. $9x^2 + 6xy - 8y^2$

8. $a^2 - 4ab - 32b^2$

9. $6x^2 - 17xy + 12y^2$

10. $21a^2 + 5af - 6f^2$

11. $3x^2 - 14xy - 5y^2$

12. $3a^2 + 12ab - 36b^2$

13. $18c^2 + 9cd - 6d^2$

14. $a^2 + 3ab - 28b^2$

15. $5x^2 - 125y^2$

16. $2y^2 - 3yz + z^2$

17. $m^2 - mn - 20n^2$

18. $3a^2 - 11ac + 6c^2$

19. $8p^2 - 35pq + 12q^2$

20. $x^2 - xy - 56y^2$

DESIGNING A COMPUTER PROGRAM

What is programming? In fact, what is a computer program? Without first answering these two questions, you will not be able to understand how man uses computers to manipulate information and solve problems.

Computers are stupid. Without a computer program, a computer is useless. A computer program is a collection of instructions in a computer's memory that directs the operation of the computer. If the program is wrong, the computer will not function properly.

Computer programming is the process that a human programmer uses to design and write computer programs. Many programmers accomplish this task by using the Programming Cycle. This method breaks the programming job into five different steps:

1. Defining the problem
2. Designing the program
3. Coding the program
4. Testing the program
5. Documenting the program

This section explores only the first two of these steps.

Defining the Problem

In order for a programmer to write a program, he must know what it is for. It would be silly for him to write an accounting program if what is actually needed is an inventory program. The first step of the Programming Cycle takes care of this.

A person wanting a program written defines for the programmer what he wants. For instance, a teacher might ask you for a program to compute the hypotenuse of a right triangle, given the length of the two sides. Accordingly,

1. Defining the problem   2.   3.   4.   5.

WELL, THERE'S THE PROBLEM.

PRETTY HARD TO DEFINE, ISN'T IT?

LET'S SEE NOW–ITS...

HMMM

this defining step specifies the fact that the side lengths will be inputs and the hypotenuse will be the output. Of course, this is only a simple example. Writing complex computer applications requires vast amounts of time in this part of the program-writing process.

Designing the Program

If a programmer sits down and haphazardly writes a computer program, he will make mistakes. To avoid errors, a programmer ought to spend time considering how the program should be put together. To accomplish this task, many programmers use what is known as the "top-down approach."

Following the top-down approach, the programmer breaks a problem up into smaller problems, each of which is easier to handle. For example, to find the hypotenuse of the triangle, we need to do the following:

1. Input the length of the two sides.
2. Compute the hypotenuse.
3. Output the length of the hypotenuse.

From this meager beginning we would take each of those steps and examine them even more carefully.

We need to break the step of computing the hypotenuse into even smaller steps. We would want to use the Pythagorean theorem for this step.

The expanded Step 2 might look like this:

2a. Square the length of side *A*.
2b. Square the length of side *B*.
2c. Add the results of 2a and 2b.
2d. Take the square root of the result of 2c.

Although it may seem trivial for our hypotenuse-calculation program, the top-down approach helps the programmer organize his thoughts, resulting in fewer program errors.

1. Defining the problem   2. Designing the program   3.   4.   5.

FACTORING COMPLETELY

You should realize that every polynomial can be factored. All of the factoring you have done has been done over the set of integers. If a polynomial cannot be factored over the set of integers, it can be factored over the set of real numbers or over the complex number system. You will learn to factor over the complex number system in a subsequent mathematics course. Sometimes after you factor a polynomial, you can factor the resulting polynomial. In Algebra I, we will consider a polynomial completely factored when it cannot be factored further over the set of integers. From this point on *factor* means "factor completely over the set of integers."

Procedure for Storage

Factoring Completely over the Set of Integers

1. Factor out any common monomial terms.
2. If the remaining polynomial is a special product, factor by the short cut learned for that special product. If it isn't a special product, factor by trial and error.
3. Continue factoring until each factor is no longer factorable over the set of integers.
4. Check by multiplying the factors.

EXAMPLE

Example 1. Factor $5ax^5 - 5axy^4$.

Solution. $5ax^5 - 5axy^4$

1. $5ax$ is a common monomial. Factor it out of the polynomial.

$5ax(x^4 - y^4)$

2. Now the polynomial in parentheses is the difference of two squares. Factor it.

$$5ax(x^2 + y^2)(x^2 - y^2)$$

3. Check each new factor. Can any of them be factored over the set of integers? Yes, $x^2 - y^2$ can be factored because it is the difference of two squares. Factor it.

$$5ax(x^2 + y^2)(x - y)(x + y)$$

4. None of these factors can be factored over the set of integers.

Check. Does $5ax(x^2 + y^2)(x - y)(x + y) = 5ax^5 - 5axy^4$?

Sometimes a polynomial contains common binomial factors, such as $x + y$ in $3(x + y) - y(x + y)$. Considering $(x + y)$ as one variable and applying the distributive property, you can factor out the whole binomial from the polynomial.

$$3(x + y) - y(x + y) = (x + y)(3 - y)$$

Look at this process another way.

Let $z = x + y$ in $3(x + y) - y(x + y)$.

So $3(x + y) - y(x + y) = 3z - yz$.

Now can you factor $3z - yz$? Sure, it has a common monomial z.

So $3z - yz = z(3 - y)$. But what does z equal? Since we let $z = x + y$, we can now substitute $x + y$ back into the factorization in place of z. Therefore, $z(3 - y) = (x + y)(3 - y)$, the very same factorization that we obtained earlier.

EXAMPLES

Example 2. Factor $(am - an) - (pm - pn)$.

Solution. $(am - an) - (pm - pn)$.

$$a(m - n) - p(m - n)$$

1. Factor the common monomials from each binomial.

$$(m - n)(a - p)$$

2. Now you can see that the polynomial has the common binomial factor $m - n$. Factor it from the polynomial.

Example 3.   Factor $x^4 - 9x^2 + 8$.

Solution. $x^4 - 9x^2 + 8$

$(x^2 \quad)(x^2 \quad)$

$(x^2 - 1)(x^2 - 8)$

$(x - 1)(x + 1)(x^2 - 8)$

1. Since there are no common monomials and no special cases, begin factoring by trial and error.

2. You can factor the first binomial again because it is the difference of two squares.

3. This is the complete factorization over the set of integers.

Exercises

Factor completely.

1. $a^2 + 2a + 1$

2. $x^3 + x^2 - x$

3. $100 - a^2$

4. $12a^8 - 10a^6$

5. $8a^2 - 48ab^2 + 72b^4$

6. $a^4x^4 - 81$

7. $3a^5 - 4a^3$

8. $x^2 - 14x + 49$

9. $(2ax^2 + bx^2) - (2ay^2 + by^2)$

10. $3x^3 - 33x^2 + 84x$

11. $10x^2 + 50x + 70$

12. $ax^2 - 6ax + 9a$

13. $m^{10} + 2m^5 + 1$

14. $3x^2 - 21x - 180$

15. $25x^2 - 1$

16. $2m^2 - 2m - 112$

17. $5a + 35$

18. $pqx + p$

19. $x^2 - 6x + 8$

20. $a^2 + 16a$

21. $a(b + c) - m(b + c)$

22. $a(m + n) + b(m + n) - c(m + n)$

23. $(at - aw) + (bt - bw)$

24. $xy + xz + wy + wz$

25. $(x + y)^2 + 2(x + y) + 1$

One purpose for studying mathematics is to teach our-
selves how to reason correctly. Read the following
proofs. Can you detect the faulty reasoning?

MIND OVER MATH

Proof that 1 = 2

Let $a = b$.	$a = b$
Multiply both sides by b.	$ab = b^2$
Subtract a^2 from both sides.	$ab - a^2 = b^2 - a^2$
Factor both sides.	$a(b - a) = (b + a)(b - a)$
Divide both sides by $(b - a)$.	$a = b + a$
Substitute 1 for a.	$1 = b + 1$
Since $a = b$, substitute 1 for b.	$1 = 1 + 1$
Add.	$1 = 2$

Proof that 4 = 8

The equation is balanced since both
sides equal -32. Add 36 to both sides
and then factor the perfect square
trinomials.

$$16 - 48 = 64 - 96$$
$$16 - 48 + 36 = 64 - 96 + 36$$
$$(4 - 6)^2 = (8 - 6)^2$$

Take the square root of both sides.

$$4 - 6 = 8 - 6$$

Since 6 is subtracted from both sides,
4 = 8

$$4 = 8$$

MEMORY RECALL

Identify.
> common monomial factor
> difference of two squares
> perfect square trinomials

You should now be able to do the following:

1. Factor common monomials from polynomials.
2. Factor the difference of two squares.
3. Factor perfect square trinomials.
4. Factor any trinomials of the forms $x^2 + bx + c$, $ax^2 + bx + c$, and $ax^2 + bxy + cy^2$.
5. Factor completely a given polynomial over the set of integers.

You should be able to do these problems:

Factor completely.

1. $8x^2y^3 + 5xy^2 - 2x$

2. $3r^2 + 5r$

3. $x^4 + 3x^3y + 7x^2$

4. $a^2 - 9b^2$

5. $25x^2 - 144y^2$

6. $24x^2 - 96y^2$

7. $a^2 + 14a + 49$

8. $5b^2 - 50b + 125$

9. $4x^2 - 12xy + 9y^2$

10. $x^2 + 5x - 14$

11. $2x^2 - 30x + 108$

12. $2a^2 + 9a - 18$

13. $6a^2 - 20a + 14$

14. $15x^2 - x - 6$

15. $x^2 - 5x - 84$

16. $15x^2 + xy - 2y^2$

17. $12x^2 + 78xy + 90y^2$

18. $x^2y + xy - 56y$

19. $12x^2 + 22x - 70$

20. $(x + y)^2 - 9$

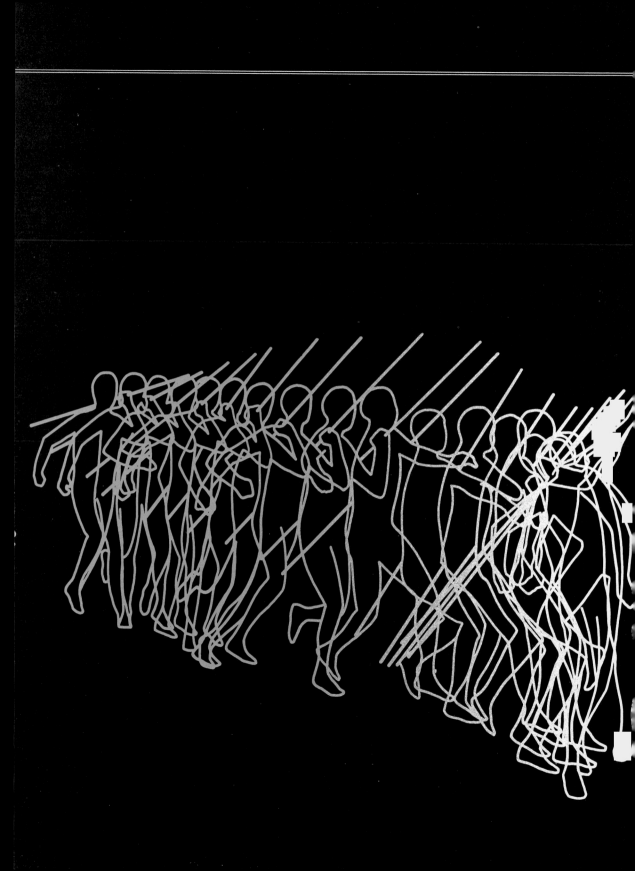

CHAPTER 10

QUADRATIC EQUATIONS

Karen was determined to place first in the girl's softball toss during her Christian school's field-day activities. As she practiced for the event, she found that the ball traveled different distances for different angles of release. By experimenting, she found that the best angle of release was halfway between straight up and straight out. Although she trusted her evaluation of these experiments, she wondered why her observation was true.

Doing some library research, Karen found that many athletes work with biomechanics laboratories to learn more about the motions of life. The athletes realize that once a projectile (e.g., baseball, softball, discus) leaves their hands, they can no longer control that object. Biomechanics laboratories use a complex series of equations to analyze the bodily movements of athletes. Using this information, physical education specialists can tell the athletes how to position their bodies for the best angles of release.

The equations that describe the motion of a softball or discus are much simpler. After talking with her physics teacher, Karen found that the following equations approximately describe her softball throw:

$$x = 40t$$

$$0 = 40t - 16t^2$$

The first equation tells how far the ball moves in a given amount of time; the second equation gives enough information to find how long the ball remains in the air. Using the result of the second equation, Karen could determine how far she usually throws the ball.

The second equation is a quadratic equation. You will learn methods for solving Karen's problem and other projectile problems when you learn the material in this chapter.

THE ZERO PRODUCT PROPERTY AND QUADRATIC EQUATIONS

All of the equations that you have solved so far have been linear equations, equations of the first degree. Now you will increase your mathematical knowledge and learn how to solve second-degree equations such as quadratic equations. Do you remember how to determine the degree of an equation?

≫**Quadratic equation:** an equation of the second degree, of the form $ax^2 + bx + c = 0$, where a, b, and c are real numbers and $a \neq 0$.

When solving quadratic equations by factoring, you must first understand the zero product property.

Zero Product Property

If the product of two or more factors is 0, at least one of the factors is 0.

What is the value of x in the equation $3x = 0$? of y in $-8y = 0$? of x or y in $xy = 0$? In the equation $xy = 0$, either $x = 0$ or $y = 0$ or $x = 0$ and $y = 0$. Now in $(x - 1)(x + 3) = 0$, either $x - 1 = 0$ or $x + 3 = 0$. These separate equations are linear, and you already know how to solve linear equations. The zero product property is the key to solving quadratic equations by factoring.

EXAMPLE

Example 1.   Solve $x^2 - 3x - 10 = 0$.

Solution. $x^2 - 3x - 10 = 0$
$(x - 5)(x + 2) = 0$
$x - 5 = 0$ or $x + 2 = 0$
$x = 5$ or $x = -2$

1. Factor the polynomial on the left.

2. Set each factor equal to 0.

3. Solve each linear equation.

You can see that this quadratic equation has two solutions: 5 or -2.

Does the word *or* mean intersection or union? Most quadratic equations will have two solutions.

EXAMPLE

Example 2.   Solve $8x^2 - 16x = 0$.

Solution. $8x^2 - 16x = 0$
$8x(x - 2) = 0$
$8x = 0$ $x - 2 = 0$
$x = 0$ $x = 2$

1. Factor the polynomial.

2. Set each factor equal to 0 and solve.

The two solutions are 0 or 2.

Check. $8 \cdot 0^2 - 16 \cdot 0 = 0$ $8(2)^2 - 16 \cdot 2 = 0$
$0 - 0 = 0$ $8 \cdot 4 - 16 \cdot 2 = 0$
$0 = 0$ $0 = 0$

Exercises

Solve.

1. $5x = 0$

2. $(x - 2)(x + 4) = 0$

3. $(y + 5)(y + 2) = 0$

4. $(x - 3)(x - 1) = 0$

5. $2x(x + 7) = 0$

6. $(x + 2)(x + 6) = 0$

7. $(y - 3)(y - 8) = 0$

8. $(x - 2)(x + 1)(x - 6) = 0$

9. $3x(x + 12) = 0$

10. $-5x(x - 1)(3x + 2) = 0$

11. $(x - 7)(x + 4)(x - 6) = 0$

12. $8x(x + 1)(x - 10) = 0$

13. $(x - 2)(x - 2) = 0$

14. $x^2 + 5x - 36 = 0$

15. $x^2 - x - 56 = 0$

SOLVING QUADRATIC EQUATIONS BY FACTORING

In the last section you learned the basic property for solving quadratic equations by factoring. You will get more practice in this section, thus expanding your knowledge of solving quadratic equations.

Procedure for Storage

Solving Quadratic Equations by Factoring

1. Place all terms on one side of the equation in descending powers of the variable and 0 on the other side. Factor the polynomial side of the equation.
2. Set each factor that contains a variable equal to 0. Solve the resulting equations.
3. Check your solutions in the original equation.

Some of the quadratic equations that you see will not be factorable over the set of integers. You will learn another method for solving these quadratic equations later in this chapter. Whenever possible, use the factoring method, because it is usually the easiest method to use.

EXAMPLES

Example 1. Solve $x^2 + 2x - 63 = 0$.

Solution. $x^2 + 2x - 63 = 0$ 1. No rearrangement of terms is
$(x + 9)(x - 7) = 0$ necessary. Factor the left side.

$x + 9 = 0 \qquad x - 7 = 0$ 2. Set each factor equal to 0 and solve.
$\quad x = -9 \qquad\quad x = 7$

Often the solutions are expressed as a set, called the solution set. The solution set is $\{-9, 7\}$.

Check. $(-9)^2 + 2(-9) - 63 = 0 \qquad 7^2 + 2 \cdot 7 - 63 = 0$
$81 - 18 - 63 = 0 \qquad\quad 49 + 14 - 63 = 0$
$0 = 0 \qquad\qquad\qquad 0 = 0$

Example 2. Solve $x^2 - 49 = 0$.

Solution.
$$x^2 - 49 = 0$$
$$(x - 7)(x + 7) = 0$$

1. Factor the left side.

$$x - 7 = 0 \qquad x + 7 = 0$$
$$x = 7 \qquad\quad x = -7$$

2. Set each factor equal to 0 and solve.

The solution set is {7, -7}.

Check.
$$7^2 - 49 = 0 \qquad (-7)^2 - 49 = 0$$
$$49 - 49 = 0 \qquad\quad 49 - 49 = 0$$
$$0 = 0 \qquad\qquad\quad 0 = 0$$

Example 3. Solve $x^2 = 3x + 4$.

Solution.
$$x^2 - 3x - 4 = 0$$
$$(x - 4)(x + 1) = 0$$

1. Place all terms on the left side of the equation and 0 on the right side. Factor the left side.

$$x - 4 = 0 \qquad x + 1 = 0$$
$$x = 4 \qquad\quad x = -1$$

2. Set each factor equal to 0 and solve the linear equation.

The solution set is {4, -1}.

Check.
$$4^2 = 3 \cdot 4 + 4 \qquad (-1)^2 = 3 \cdot -1 + 4$$
$$16 = 12 + 4 \qquad\qquad 1 = -3 + 4$$
$$16 = 16 \qquad\qquad\quad 1 = 1$$

Sometimes a word problem results in a quadratic equation.

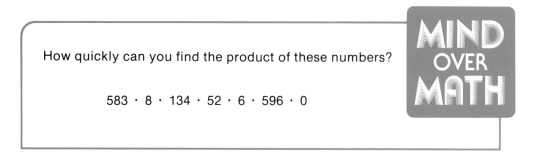

How quickly can you find the product of these numbers?

$$583 \cdot 8 \cdot 134 \cdot 52 \cdot 6 \cdot 596 \cdot 0$$

MIND OVER MATH

EXAMPLE

Example 4.   Find the dimensions of a rectangular living room 5 feet longer than wide, requiring 204 square feet of carpet.

Solution.

Let $\quad x$ = the width
$x + 5$ = the length

1. Identify what you are asked to find. In this problem you are asked to find the dimensions of the living room.

2. Draw a picture.

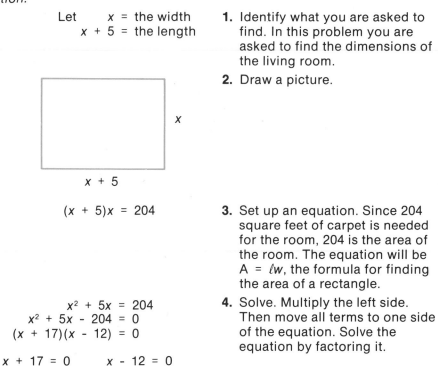

$(x + 5)x = 204$

3. Set up an equation. Since 204 square feet of carpet is needed for the room, 204 is the area of the room. The equation will be $A = \ell w$, the formula for finding the area of a rectangle.

$$x^2 + 5x = 204$$
$$x^2 + 5x - 204 = 0$$
$$(x + 17)(x - 12) = 0$$

$x + 17 = 0 \qquad x - 12 = 0$
$\qquad x = -17 \qquad\qquad x = 12$

4. Solve. Multiply the left side. Then move all terms to one side of the equation. Solve the equation by factoring it.

Since you are dealing with dimensions, neither the length nor the width can be negative. Consequently, 12 is the only possible solution. Therefore, the width (x) is 12, and the length ($x + 5$) is 17. Is this a reasonable solution? Does it work in the problem?

Quadratic equations are easy and fun to solve if you understand factoring well.

Exercises

Solve each quadratic equation by factoring it.

1. $x^2 + 6x + 9 = 0$
2. $a^2 + 2a - 15 = 0$
3. $x^2 - 9 = 0$
4. $p^2 = 2p + 24$
5. $x^2 + 3x = 0$
6. $m^2 - 2m = 35$
7. $4x^2 = 9$
8. $x^2 - 7x = 0$
9. $a^2 - 4a + 4 = 0$
10. $x^2 = 5x$

11. $x^2 - 10x = -16$
12. $x^2 - 7x = 8$
13. $30 = a^2 + 13a$
14. $8x^2 + 10x = -3$
15. $x^2 + 8 = -6x$
16. $a^2 + 15a = -50$
17. $x^2 - 12 = -4x$
18. $a^2 = 169$
19. $16a^2 = 9$
20. $2r - r^2 = 0$

21. The difference of two numbers is 6 and the difference of their squares is 60. Find the two numbers.
22. A farmer planted 168 tomato plants. If he had 2 more plants in a row than the number of rows, how many rows did he have?
23. Find two consecutive odd numbers whose sum of their squares is 202.
24. Joe said, "If five times my age in 8 years is subtracted from the square of my present age, the result is 86." Find Joe's present age.
25. Mr. Brady wants to build a sidewalk around his flower garden that is 52 feet long by 44 feet wide. How wide should the sidewalk be if the flower garden will cover only 1748 square feet?

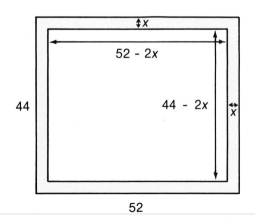

SOLVING EQUATIONS OF THE FORM $x^2 - c = 0$

Example 2 in the last section showed you how to solve equations of the form $x^2 - c = 0$. The two solutions to the quadratic equation in Example 2 are 7 and -7, or ± 7. Review that example; then you will be ready to learn another method of solving these equations.

The second method for solving equations of this form depends upon the following general principle: the nth roots of equals are equal.

$$\text{If } x^2 = 36$$
$$\text{then } \sqrt{x^2} = \sqrt{36}$$
$$\sqrt[3]{x^2} = \sqrt[3]{36} \quad \text{etc.}$$

In more specific terms, the square roots of both sides of an equation make an equivalent equation.

Procedure for Storage

Solving Equations of the Form $x^2 - c = 0$

1. Place the constant opposite x^2.
2. Find the square root of both sides.

EXAMPLE

Example 1. Solve $x^2 - 49 = 0$.

Solution. $x^2 - 49 = 0$

$$x^2 = 49 \qquad \text{1. Place 49 on the right side of the equal sign.}$$
$$\sqrt{x^2} = \pm \sqrt{49} \qquad \text{2. Find the square root of both sides.}$$
$$x = \pm 7$$

Compare this answer with the previous answer. Notice that when you take the square root of both sides you get $\pm x = \pm 7$, or the four equations $x = 7$, $x = -7$, $-x = 7$, $-x = -7$. These four equations simplify to $x = \pm 7$.

EXAMPLES

Example 2. Solve $x^2 - 3 = 0$.

Solution.

$x^2 - 3 = 0$ **1.** Place in the proper form.

$x^2 = 3$

$\sqrt{x^2} = \pm\sqrt{3}$ **2.** Find the square root of both sides.

$x = \pm\sqrt{3}$

Check. Check the solution by substituting $\sqrt{3}$ and $-\sqrt{3}$ in the original equation.

$(\sqrt{3})^2 - 3 = 0$ $(-\sqrt{3})^2 - 3 = 0$

$\quad\quad 3 - 3 = 0$ $3 - 3 = 0$

$\quad\quad\quad 0 = 0$ $0 = 0$

Example 3. Solve $(x + 2)^2 = 36$.

Solution.

$(x + 2)^2 = 36$

$\sqrt{(x + 2)^2} = \pm\sqrt{36}$ **1.** Find the square root of both sides.

$x + 2 = \pm 6$

$x + 2 = 6 \quad\quad x + 2 = -6$ **2.** Solve these two linear equations.

$x = 4 \quad\quad\quad\quad x = -8$

Check.

$(4 + 2)^2 = 36$ $(-8 + 2)^2 = 36$

$\quad\quad 6^2 = 36$ $(-6)^2 = 36$

$\quad\quad 36 = 36$ $36 = 36$

AT LEAST IT'S WELL SHADED UP HERE!

Exercises

1. $x^2 - 100 = 0$
2. $x^2 - 64 = 0$
3. $x^2 = 25$
4. $x^2 - 5 = 31$
5. $x^2 = 6$
6. $x^2 - 5 = 0$
7. $x^2 = 7$
8. $2x^2 - 17 = x^2 + 3$

9. $4x^2 - 16 = 3x^2 + 9$
10. $3x^2 + 10 = x^2 + 24$
11. $(x + 4)^2 = 25$
12. $(x - 6)^2 = 13$
13. $(x + 3)^2 = 121$
14. $(x - 5)^2 - 17 = 0$
15. $(x + 2)^2 = 18$

COMPLETING THE SQUARE

Many times you will find that a quadratic equation is difficult to solve by factoring. So you must use another method of solving a quadratic equation called *completing the square.* Completing the square involves changing the polynomial to a perfect square trinomial. What is a perfect square trinomial? What are its characteristics? What is always true about the last term of a perfect square trinomial? about the middle term? The last term is a perfect square, and the middle term is twice the product of the square roots of the first and last terms.

If you are asked to complete the square of $x^2 + 10x$, you need to find the perfect square to add to the expression to make it a perfect square trinomial. You can find that perfect square by dividing the numerical coefficient of x by 2 and squaring the results. Dividing 10 by 2, you get 5, and $5^2 = 25$. You must add 25 to $x^2 + 10x$ to get the perfect square trinomial $x^2 + 10x + 25$. Now you can factor the perfect square trinomial and get $(x + 5)^2$.

Procedure for Storage

Completing the Square

1. Find half of the numerical coefficient of x (or the variable to the first power).
2. Square the result of step 1 and add the square to the given expression.

EXAMPLES

Example 1. Complete the square of $a^2 - 16a$. Then factor the perfect square trinomial.

Solution.

$16 \div 2 = 8$ **1.** Divide the coefficient of a by 2.

$8^2 = 64$ **2.** Square the result.

$a^2 - 16a + 64$ **3.** Add the result to the other terms.

So $a^2 - 16a + 64$ is the completed square. Its factorization is $(a - 8)^2$.

Example 2. Complete the square of $x^2 - \frac{3}{5}x$. Then factor the perfect square trinomial.

Solution.

$$\frac{3}{5} \div 2 = \frac{3}{5} \cdot \frac{1}{2}$$

$$= \frac{3}{10}$$

$$\left(\frac{3}{10}\right)^2 = \frac{9}{100}$$

The completed square is $x^2 - \frac{3}{5}x + \frac{9}{100}$. The factorization is $(x - \frac{3}{10})^2$.

You can use this method to solve any quadratic equation, especially one that is difficult to factor. You must remember, however, that if you add a number to one side of the equation you must add the same number to the other side of the equation.

EXAMPLE

Example 3. Solve $x^2 + 8x = 9$.

Solution.

$$x^2 + 8x = 9$$

1. Complete the square. Think $8 \div 2 = 4$ and $4^2 = 16$.

$$x^2 + 8x + 16 = 9 + 16$$

$$(x + 4)^2 = 25$$

2. Factor the left.

$$\sqrt{(x + 4)^2} = \pm\sqrt{25}$$

3. Since this equation is like the equations in the last section, simply find the square root of both sides and solve.

$$x + 4 = \pm 5$$

$$x + 4 = 5 \qquad x + 4 = -5$$

$$x = 1 \qquad\qquad x = -9$$

The solution set is $\{ 1, -9 \}$.

Check. $\quad 1^2 + 8 \cdot 1 = 9 \qquad\qquad -9^2 + 8 \cdot -9 = 9$

$$1 + 8 = 9 \qquad\qquad 81 - 72 = 9$$

$$9 = 9 \qquad\qquad\qquad 9 = 9$$

Example 4. Solve $a^2 - 8a - 40 = 0$.

Solution. $\quad a^2 - 8a - 40 = 0$

$$a^2 - 8a = 40$$

1. Move the 40 to the other side so that you can find the perfect square term.

$$a^2 - 8a + 16 = 40 + 16$$

2. Complete the square.

$$(a - 4)^2 = 56$$

3. Solve.

$$\sqrt{(a - 4)^2} = \pm\sqrt{56}$$

$$a - 4 = \pm 2\sqrt{14}$$

$$a - 4 = 2\sqrt{14} \qquad a - 4 = -2\sqrt{14}$$

$$a = 4 + 2\sqrt{14} \qquad 2 = 4 - 2\sqrt{14}$$

The solution set is $\{ 4 + 2\sqrt{14}, 4 - 2\sqrt{14} \}$.

Check.

$$(4 + 2\sqrt{14})^2 - 8(4 + 2\sqrt{14}) - 40 = 0$$

$$[16 + 8(2\sqrt{14}) + 56] - 8(4 + 2\sqrt{14}) - 40 = 0$$

$$16 + 16\sqrt{14} + 56 - 32 - 16\sqrt{14} - 40 = 0$$

$$0 = 0$$

$$(4 - 2\sqrt{14})^2 - 8(4 - 2\sqrt{14}) - 40 = 0$$

$$[16 - 8(2\sqrt{14}) + 56] - 8(4 - 2\sqrt{14}) - 40 = 0$$

$$16 - 16\sqrt{14} + 56 - 32 + 16\sqrt{14} - 40 = 0$$

$$0 = 0$$

Procedure for Storage

Solving Quadratic Equations by Completing the Square

1. Rearrange terms so that the constant is on one side of the equation and all terms containing variables are on the other side of the equation.
2. Complete the square on the side containing the variable, making sure the same operation is performed on both sides of the equation.
3. Factor the side containing the variable.
4. Find the square root of both sides and solve each equation.
5. Check the solutions in the original equation.

Exercises

Complete each square.

1. $x^2 + 8x$

2. $x^2 - 5x$

3. $x^2 + 16x$

4. $x^2 - 10x$

5. $x^2 + 52x$

6. $x^2 - 2x$

7. $x^2 + 3x$

8. $x^2 - 12x$

9. $x^2 - 7x$

10. $x^2 - 24x$

Solve each quadratic equation by completing the square.

11. $x^2 + 4x - 5 = 0$

12. $a^2 - 7a = -10$

13. $m^2 - 14m + 40 = 0$

14. $x^2 + 6x + 5 = 0$

15. $a^2 + 2a = 15$

16. $m^2 - \dfrac{4}{3}m = 0$

17. $x^2 + x = 2$

18. $x^2 + 4x = 5$

19. $x^2 - 10x = 24$

20. $a^2 + 6a = 55$

21. $x^2 - 2x - 99 = 0$

LEADING COEFFICIENTS AND COMPLETING THE SQUARE

In all of the problems in the preceding section, the numerical coefficient of the squared variable was 1. Completing the square works only if the coefficient of the second-degree variable (x^2) is 1. If it is not 1, you will need to factor the term so that the coefficient becomes 1. You must factor the numerical coefficient of the second-degree variable from both the squared variable and the first-degree variable. You do not, however, factor the constant term.

EXAMPLE

Example 1. Solve $3x^2 - 2x - 1 = 0$ by completing the square.

Solution. $3x^2 - 2x - 1 = 0$

$$3x^2 - 2x = 1$$

1. Place the 1 on the right side of the equation.

$$3\left(x^2 - \frac{2}{3}x\right) = 1$$

2. Factor the 3 from the terms on the left.

3. Complete the square of the polynomial inside the parentheses.

$$\frac{2}{3} \cdot \frac{1}{2} = \frac{1}{3}$$

$$\left(\frac{1}{3}\right)^2 = \frac{1}{9}$$

$$3\left(x^2 - \frac{2}{3}x + \frac{1}{9}\right) = 1 + \frac{1}{3}$$

$$3\left(x - \frac{1}{3}\right)^2 = \frac{4}{3}$$

4. Why is $\frac{1}{3}$ added to the right? Remember the 3 outside the parentheses? What is $3 \cdot \frac{1}{9}$? You really added $\frac{3}{9}$ to the left of the equation, so you must add the same thing to the right side of the equation. Now factor the left side and combine like terms on the right side.

$$\frac{1}{3} \cdot 3(x - \frac{1}{3})^2 = \frac{4}{3} \cdot \frac{1}{3}$$

$$(x - \frac{1}{3})^2 = \frac{4}{9}$$

$$\sqrt{(x - \frac{1}{3})^2} = \sqrt{\frac{4}{9}}$$

$$x - \frac{1}{3} = \pm \frac{2}{3}$$

5. Solve this equation. First, multiply both sides by $\frac{1}{3}$ to clear the left side of the constant 3.

6. Find the square root of both sides and solve the linear equations.

$$x - \frac{1}{3} = \frac{2}{3} \qquad\qquad x - \frac{1}{3} = \frac{-2}{3}$$

$$x = 1 \qquad\qquad\qquad x = \frac{-1}{3}$$

Check.

$$3 \cdot 1^2 - 2 \cdot 1 - 1 = 0 \qquad 3\left(\frac{-1}{3}\right)^2 - 2 \cdot \left(\frac{-1}{3}\right) - 1 = 0$$

$$3 - 2 - 1 = 0 \qquad\qquad 3\left(\frac{1}{9}\right) + \frac{2}{3} - 1 = 0$$

$$0 = 0 \qquad\qquad\qquad\qquad 0 = 0$$

Procedure for Storage

Solving Quadratic Equations of the Form $ax^2 + bx + c = 0$ by Completing the Square

1. Place the constant term opposite the variable terms.
2. Factor a from the variable terms.
3. Complete the square inside parentheses. To the constant term, add the product of the number used to complete the square and the factor a.
4. Factor the completed square.
5. Solve the resulting equation.
6. Check the results in the original equation.

EXAMPLE

Example 2. Solve $-4 - 17x = 4x^2$ by completing the square.

Solution. $-4 - 17x = 4x^2$

$$-4 = 4x^2 + 17x$$

$$-4 = 4\left(x^2 + \frac{17}{4}x\right)$$

$$-4 + \frac{289}{16} = 4\left(x^2 + \frac{17}{4}x + \frac{289}{64}\right)$$

$$\frac{-64}{16} + \frac{289}{16} = 4\left(x + \frac{17}{8}\right)^2$$

$$\frac{225}{16} = 4\left(x + \frac{17}{8}\right)^2$$

$$\frac{1}{4} \cdot \frac{225}{16} = \frac{1}{4} \cdot 4\left(x + \frac{17}{8}\right)^2$$

$$\frac{225}{64} = \left(x + \frac{17}{8}\right)^2$$

$$\pm\sqrt{\frac{225}{64}} = \sqrt{\left(x + \frac{17}{8}\right)^2}$$

$$\pm\frac{15}{8} = x + \frac{17}{8}$$

1. Place the constant opposite the variables.

2. Factor 4 from the variable terms.

3. Complete the square on the right. Remember to multiply $\frac{289}{64}$ with 4 to find the number to add to the left side.

4. Factor the right side.

5. Solve.

$$\frac{15}{8} = x + \frac{17}{8} \qquad\qquad \frac{-15}{8} = x + \frac{17}{8}$$

$$\frac{-2}{8} = x \qquad\qquad\qquad \frac{-32}{8} = x$$

$$\frac{-1}{4} = x \qquad\qquad\qquad\quad -4 = x$$

Check.

$$-4 - 17\left(\frac{-1}{4}\right) = 4\left(\frac{-1}{4}\right)^2 \qquad\qquad -4 - 17(-4) = 4(-4)^2$$

$$-4 + \frac{17}{4} = 4\left(\frac{1}{16}\right) \qquad\qquad\qquad -4 + 68 = 4(16)$$

$$\frac{-16}{4} + \frac{17}{4} = \frac{1}{4} \qquad\qquad\qquad\qquad 64 = 64$$

$$\frac{1}{4} = \frac{1}{4}$$

Example 3. Solve $0 = 5x^2 - 40x - 25$ by completing the square.

Solution.
$$5x^2 - 40x = 25$$
$$5(x^2 - 8x) = 25$$
$$5(x^2 - 8x + 16) = 25 + 80$$
$$5(x - 4)^2 = 105$$
$$(x - 4)^2 = 21$$
$$\sqrt{(x - 4)^2} = \pm\sqrt{21}$$
$$x - 4 = \pm\sqrt{21}$$
$$x = 4 \pm\sqrt{21}$$

Can you explain the steps in this example?

Check.
$$5(4 + \sqrt{21})^2 - 40(4 + \sqrt{21}) - 25 = 0$$
$$5(16 + 8\sqrt{21} + 21) - 40(4 + \sqrt{21}) - 25 = 0$$
$$80 + 40\sqrt{21} + 105 - 160 - 40\sqrt{21} - 25 = 0$$
$$0 = 0$$

$$5(4 - \sqrt{21})^2 - 40(4 - \sqrt{21}) - 25 = 0$$
$$5(16 - 8\sqrt{21} + 21) - 160 + 40\sqrt{21} - 25 = 0$$
$$80 - 40\sqrt{21} + 105 - 160 + 40\sqrt{21} - 25 = 0$$
$$0 = 0$$

Exercises

Solve each quadratic equation by completing the square.

1. $2x^2 + x = 3$

2. $4x^2 - 4x = 11$

3. $2x^2 - x = 1$

4. $2a^2 = -3a - 1$

5. $6x^2 = 9x + 27$

6. $2x^2 - 6x = -1$

7. $2a^2 - a - 3 = 0$

8. $3x^2 - 2x - 8 = 0$

9. $2x^2 = 3x + 35$

10. $3x^2 = -8x - 5$

CODING A COMPUTER PROGRAM

The last three steps of the Programming Cycle are usually the easiest if a programmer has been faithful to do his job in the first two steps.

Coding the Program

"Coding a program" means taking the program the programmer has designed and translating it into the proper computer language. The programmer's choice of language depends on what he wants to do. For simple programs, BASIC is fairly easy to use. More complex programs may need some of the capabilities of the more advanced languages, like Pascal and C.

In the figures in this section you can see how the programmer's design has been converted into the three above-mentioned languages:

Testing the Program

After the program has been coded, a programmer must test it to see if it works correctly. For example, if the programmer types a letter instead of a number in any of these programs, it will cause an error, stopping the program.

A programmer must determine what does and does not constitute an error. If an error is found, the programmer must go back to the coding step, or

sometimes even to the definition step. Reconsider the example above. If the programmer and his employer decide that they want to keep the program from stopping when it is given letters, the programmer must change the design of the program to account for this procedure.

An error may be caused by a syntax problem. Syntax is the set of rules a language follows for accepting computer commands. For example, if the programmer incorrectly types IMPUT instead of INPUT, the computer will signal that he has made a syntax error. In this case the programmer needs only to recode a small portion of the program.

Documenting the Program

One step of the Programming Cycle that many programmers fail to

| 1 | 2 | 3 Coding the program | 4 Testing the program | 5 |

accomplish is the documentation step. Documentation specifies to a computer user how a program can and should be used.

Documentation usually includes sample inputs and sample outputs from the program as well as examples of how the program should be used. For example, if the programmer decided not to bother with the alphabetic entry errors, he could specify that the user should never enter letters in his hypotenuse program.

A programmer also includes internal documentation in his program. He should leave comments in his program to tell another programmer what he has done. If another programmer needed to correct an error in the program but the original programmer did not document his work, the error would be almost impossible to correct.

Documentation is a vital part of the Programming Cycle. Even a good program is nearly useless if the user cannot understand how to run the program.

```pascal
(* Hypotenuse program in Pascal *)
program hypotenuse;
var
   a, b, c, a2, b2, c2: real;
begin
   write ('Enter the length of side A:');          Input
   readln (a);                                      lengths
   write ('Enter the length of side B:');
   readln (b);
      a2: = sqr(a);              |Square the length of side A|
      b2: = sqr(b);              |Square the length of side B|
      c2: = a2 + b2;            |Add the lengths squared together|
      c: = sqrt(c2);             |Take the square root of the sum|
   writeln ('The hypotenuse of a right triangle with
      sides of length ',a,' and ',b,' is ',c).
   end.
```

Input lengths

Calculate hypotenuse

Output

```basic
10    REM Hypotenuse Program in BASIC
20    INPUT "Enter the length of side A: "; a
30    INPUT "Enter the length of side B: "; b
40    a2 = a↑2                     ' Square the length of A
50    b2 = b↑2                     ' Square the length of B
60    c2 = a2 + b2                 ' Add the squares
70    c = SQR (c2)                 ' Find the square root
80    PRINT "The hypotenuse of a right triangle with
      sides of length" ;a; " and" ;b; "is" ; c
```

Input lengths

Calculate hypotenuse

Output

```c
# include < stdio.h >
main ( ) /* Hypotenuse program in C */
|float a, a2, b, b2, c, c2;
   printf ( " Enter length of side A: ");
   scanf (" %f " , &a);
   printf ("\n Enter length of side B: " );
   scanf (" %f", &b);
      a2 = a * a;
      b2 = b * b;
      c2 = a2 + b2;
      c = sqrt (c2);
   printf ("\n The hypotenuse of a right triangle with sides
   of length %f and %f is %f." , a , b , c);
|
```

Input lengths

Calculate hypotenuse

Output

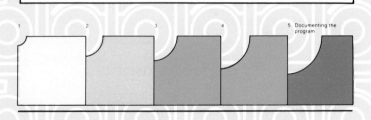

5. Documenting the program

WELL, ZIRCON'S PROGRAM TESTS OUT OK ON THE COMPUTER.— NOW I JUST HAVE TO WRITE HIS USER'S MANUAL.

NOW WHAT IS IT, ZIRCON?

OH, ALL RIGHT, I'LL WRITE IN SOMETHING ABOUT YOUR TEDDY BEAR FRIEND.

THE QUADRATIC FORMULA

You have learned to solve quadratic equations by factoring and by completing the square; however, not all quadratic equations can be easily solved by either of these methods. For some, you will find that the quadratic formula, developed below, is a much easier way to solve a quadratic equation than either factoring or completing the square. You can use this formula to solve all quadratic equations, including those you encounter in business and applied science. Carefully read through the development of the formula, making sure you thoroughly understand each step.

Consider a quadratic equation of the form $ax^2 + bx + c = 0$, in which a, b, and c are numerical coefficients and constant terms, and you are to solve for x by completing the square.

1. First move the constant term c to the right side.

$$ax^2 + bx + c = 0$$
$$ax^2 + bx = -c$$

2. Factor the a from the variable terms.

$$a\left(x^2 + \frac{bx}{a}\right) = -c$$

3. Complete the square. Think $\frac{1}{2} \cdot \frac{b}{a} = \frac{b}{2a}$ and $\left(\frac{b}{2a}\right)^2 = \frac{b^2}{4a^2}$.

$$a\left(x^2 + \frac{bx}{a} + \frac{b^2}{4a^2}\right) = -c + \frac{b^2}{4a}$$

4. Factor the perfect square on the left. Combine terms on the right using the common denominator $4a$.

$$a\left(x + \frac{b}{2a}\right)^2 = \frac{-4ac + b^2}{4a}$$

5. Rearrange the terms in the numerator so the positive term appears first.

$$a\left(x + \frac{b}{2a}\right)^2 = \frac{b^2 - 4ac}{4a}$$

6. Multiply both sides by $\frac{1}{a}$ to eliminate the a on the left side outside the parentheses.

$$\frac{1}{a} \cdot a\left(x + \frac{b}{2a}\right)^2 = \frac{1}{a} \cdot \frac{b^2 - 4ac}{4a}$$

7. Simplify.

$$\left(x + \frac{b}{2a}\right)^2 = \frac{b^2 - 4ac}{4a^2}$$

8. Find the square root of both sides. Since the denominator on the right is a perfect square, it can be removed from the radical sign.

$$\sqrt{\left(x + \frac{b}{2a}\right)^2} = \pm\sqrt{\frac{b^2 - 4ac}{4a^2}}$$

$$\sqrt{\left(x + \frac{b}{2a}\right)^2} = \frac{\pm\sqrt{b^2 - 4ac}}{2a}$$

9. The square root and square on the left side cancel each other.

To solve for x, subtract $\frac{b}{2a}$ from both sides.

$$x + \frac{b}{2a} = \frac{\pm\sqrt{b^2 - 4ac}}{2a}$$

$$x = \frac{\pm\sqrt{b^2 - 4ac}}{2a} - \frac{b}{2a}$$

10. Since the fractions have like denominators, combine them and rearrange terms.

$$x = \frac{-b \pm\sqrt{b^2 - 4ac}}{2a}$$

 ≫**Quadratic formula:** $\quad x = \dfrac{-b \pm\sqrt{b^2 - 4ac}}{2a}$

Notice that the quadratic formula describes two answers because the root of a radical can be either positive or negative. Be sure to memorize this formula so you can use it quickly to solve quadratic equations.

EXAMPLE

Example 1.   Use the quadratic formula to solve $x^2 - 5x - 6 = 0$.

Solution.

$a = 1$
$b = -5$
$c = -6$

1. Assign the numerical coefficients in this equation to the corresponding letters in the general quadratic equation form $ax^2 + bx + c = 0$. Notice that each coefficient takes the sign preceding it.

$$x = \frac{-b \pm \sqrt{b^2 - 4ac}}{2a}$$

$$x = \frac{-(-5) \pm \sqrt{(-5)^2 - 4(1)(-6)}}{2(1)}$$

2. Substitute these values in the quadratic formula.

$$x = \frac{5 \pm \sqrt{25 + 24}}{2}$$

3. Simplify.

$$x = \frac{5 \pm \sqrt{49}}{2}$$

$$x = \frac{5 \pm 7}{2}$$

$$x = \frac{5 - 7}{2} \qquad\qquad x = \frac{5 + 7}{2}$$

$$x = \frac{-2}{2} \qquad\qquad x = \frac{12}{2}$$

$$x = -1 \qquad\qquad x = 6$$

If you solved this equation by completing the square, you would get the same solution set. For the remainder of this section, however, use the quadratic formula to solve the quadratic equations. Later you can choose the method that you want to use. With practice you will learn to recognize those equations that can be quickly factored, those that can easily be made into perfect square trinomials, and those that must be solved by the quadratic formula.

EXAMPLE

Example 2.   Use the quadratic formula to solve $3x^2 + 4x - 8 = 0$.

Solution.

$a = 3$
$b = 4$
$c = -8$

1. Identify coefficients by letter.

$x = \dfrac{-b \pm \sqrt{b^2 - 4ac}}{2a}$

2. Substitute values in the quadratic formula and solve.

$x = \dfrac{-4 \pm \sqrt{4^2 - 4(3)(-8)}}{2(3)}$

$x = \dfrac{-4 \pm \sqrt{16 + 96}}{6}$

$x = \dfrac{-4 \pm \sqrt{112}}{6}$

3. Simplify the radical.

$x = \dfrac{-4 \pm 4\sqrt{7}}{6}$

4. Factor 4 from the numerator.

$x = \dfrac{4(-1 \pm \sqrt{7})}{6}$

$x = \dfrac{2(-1 \pm \sqrt{7})}{3}$

5. Reduce $\dfrac{4}{6}$ to $\dfrac{2}{3}$.

The solution set is $\left\{ \dfrac{2(-1 + \sqrt{7})}{3}, \ \dfrac{2(-1 - \sqrt{7})}{3} \right\}$.

Procedure for Storage

Solving Quadratic Equations by the Quadratic Formula

1. Arrange the equation in the form $ax^2 + bx + c = 0$.
2. Identify the values of a, b, and c from the equation.
3. Place these values in the quadratic formula and simplify.

Example 3. Use the quadratic formula to solve $5x^2 + 3x = 2$.

Solution. $5x^2 + 3x = 2$
$5x^2 + 3x - 2 = 0$

1. Write the equation in the form $ax^2 + bx + c = 0$.

$a = 5$
$b = 3$
$c = -2$

2. Identify the values of a, b, and c.

$$x = \frac{-b \pm \sqrt{b^2 - 4ac}}{2a}$$

3. Substitute values in the quadratic formula and simplify.

$$x = \frac{-3 \pm \sqrt{3^2 - 4(5)(-2)}}{2(5)}$$

$$x = \frac{-3 \pm \sqrt{9 + 40}}{10}$$

$$x = \frac{-3 \pm \sqrt{49}}{10}$$

$$x = \frac{-3 \pm 7}{10}$$

$$x = \frac{-3 + 7}{10} \quad \text{or} \quad x = \frac{-3 - 7}{10}$$

$$= \frac{4}{10} \qquad\qquad\qquad = \frac{-10}{10}$$

$$= \frac{2}{5} \qquad\qquad\qquad = -1$$

The solution set to this quadratic equation is $\{\frac{2}{5}, -1\}$.

A formula expresses a fundamental truth. It is very important that you, as a teen-ager, use the Bible as the formula book for your life. The Bible is full of fundamental truths. Jesus expressed one to Nicodemus in John 3:3. Read John 3:15-18. What fundamental truth is given in this passage? Find three more passages that give fundamental Bible truths.

Exercises

Use the quadratic formula to solve each quadratic equation.

1. $x^2 + 6x + 8 = 0$

2. $x^2 + 4x = -3$

3. $x^2 + 8x + 15 = 0$

4. $x^2 - 9x + 20 = 0$

5. $7x^2 + 9x = -2$

6. $15x^2 + 22x + 8 = 0$

7. $2x^2 = x + 3$

8. $x^2 + 3x = 28$

9. $x^2 - 6x = -9$

10. $8x^2 = 26x + 7$

11. $2x^2 - 9x + 4 = 0$

12. $3x^2 - 2x - 5 = 0$

13. $2x^2 - 5x - 10 = 0$

14. $4x^2 - 3x = 8$

15. $x^2 - 9 = 0$

16. $4x^2 - 5x - 9 = 0$

17. $-3x^2 + 2x + 10 = 0$

18. $4x^2 + 4x - 3 = 0$

19. $x^2 - 9x = -8$

20. $5x^2 - 2x - 7 = 0$

THE DISCRIMINANT
OF QUADRATIC EQUATIONS

Does every quadratic equation have a solution? What about the one given here?

EXAMPLE

Example 1. Use the quadratic formula to solve $x^2 + 2x + 5 = 0$.

Solution. $a = 1$
$b = 2$
$c = 5$

$$x = \frac{-b \pm \sqrt{b^2 - 4ac}}{2a}$$

$$x = \frac{-2 \pm \sqrt{2^2 - 4(1)(5)}}{2(1)}$$

$$x = \frac{-2 \pm \sqrt{4 - 20}}{2}$$

$$x = \frac{-2 \pm \sqrt{-16}}{2}$$

So far you have never taken the square root of a negative number. What is $\sqrt{-16}$? Do negative numbers have square roots? You do not know how to find $\sqrt{-16}$ because $\sqrt{-16}$ is an imaginary number, or complex number, not a real number. Therefore, you must say that in the set of real numbers there is no solution to this equation. But there is a solution to every quadratic equation although it may not be in the set of real numbers.

From example 1, you have learned that quadratic equations sometimes have imaginary numbers for solutions. If you knew that the solution was going to be imaginary, you would not have had to take time to solve the whole problem. To identify the nature of the solution of a quadratic equation, you need only analyze the discriminant. The discriminant is the part of the quadratic formula under the radical sign, the radicand $b^2 - 4ac$. The following chart summarizes the nature of solutions to quadratic equations.

DEFINITION ≫**Discriminant:** the radicand in the quadratic formula.

discriminant $(b^2 - 4ac)$	number of distinct real solutions	nature of the solutions
$b^2 - 4ac > 0$	2	rational or irrational
$b^2 - 4ac = 0$	1	rational
$b^2 - 4ac < 0$	0	complex

Remember that even if there are no solutions in the set of real numbers there are complex solutions.

EXAMPLES

Example 2.   Tell the number and nature of the real solutions for each equation by evaluating the discriminant.

a. $x^2 + 3x + 5 = 0$ **b.** $x^2 + 4x - 9 = 0$

Solution.

$a = 1$ $a = 1$
$b = 3$ $b = 4$
$c = 5$ $c = -9$

$b^2 - 4ac$ $b^2 - 4ac$
$3^2 - 4(1)(5)$ $4^2 - 4(1)(-9)$
$9 - 20$ $16 + 36$
$-11 < 0$ $52 > 0$

This equation has no solutions in the set of real numbers.

This equation has two solutions in the set of real numbers. Since $\sqrt{52} = 2\sqrt{13}$ is irrational, both solutions to the quadratic equation are irrational.

Exercises

Evaluate the discriminant for each equation. Tell whether the solution is real or imaginary. If the solution is real, tell whether it is rational or irrational. Solve the equation.

1. $x^2 + 3x - 5 = 0$

2. $4x^2 + 2x + 3 = 0$

3. $x^2 - 5x + 9 = 0$

4. $x^2 - 2x - 15 = 0$

5. $x^2 - 3x - 8 = 0$

6. $3x^2 - 19x - 14 = 0$

7. $2x^2 - 5x + 7 = 0$

8. $4x^2 - 9x - 6 = 0$

9. $x^2 + 14x + 40 = 0$

10. $8x^2 + x - 4 = 0$

11. $2x^2 - 3x - 10 = 0$

12. $3x^2 + 2x = 5$

13. $8x^2 + x + 3 = 0$

14. $x^2 - 4x + 7 = 0$

15. $4x^2 - 3x - 9 = 0$

SOLVING QUADRATIC EQUATIONS

Data Base

The first record of anyone's solving quadratic equations is from around A.D. 200. At that time the Greek mathematician Diophantus used quadratic equations and symbols to solve problems. Diophantus solved quadratic equations using a method similar to the completing the square method.

When you work a quadratic equation, choose the method of solving that is most appropriate and easiest for you to work with for that particular problem.

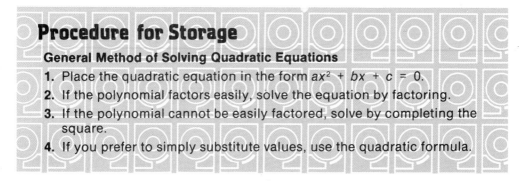

Procedure for Storage

General Method of Solving Quadratic Equations

1. Place the quadratic equation in the form $ax^2 + bx + c = 0$.
2. If the polynomial factors easily, solve the equation by factoring.
3. If the polynomial cannot be easily factored, solve by completing the square.
4. If you prefer to simply substitute values, use the quadratic formula.

These are only three methods of solving quadratic equations. In other math classes you may learn some of the other ways to solve these second-degree equations.

Exercises

Use any method to solve each quadratic equation.

1. $2x^2 - 7x + 2 = 0$
2. $(3x + 4)(2x - 5) = 4$
3. $a^2 - 2a - 8 = 0$
4. $6x^2 = 13x - 2$
5. $(x + 5)(2x - 7) = 9$
6. $3a^2 - 5 = -2a$
7. $(3x - 1)^2 + 6 = 0$
8. $x^2 - 3x - 5 = 0$
9. $x(5x - 9) + 6 = 0$
10. $a^2 + 3a = -1$
11. $x^2 - 2x - 8 = 0$
12. $(x + 4)^2 - x(x + 2) = 9$
13. $4x^2 - 5x - 9 = 0$
14. $(x - 2)^2 + (x - 5) + 1 = 0$
15. $x^2 + 8x - 2 = 0$

16. $-x^2 + 4 = 0$
17. $3a^2 + 13a = -4$
18. $a^2 + 44a + 2 = 0$
19. $x^2 + 12x - 45 = 0$
20. $a^2 + 9a - 4 = 0$
21. $(2x + 4)^2 - (3x - 6) = 0$
22. $4x^2 - 5 = x$
23. $x^2 + x = 2$
24. $2x^2 + 4x - 6 = 0$
25. $x^2 + 3x - 2 = 0$
26. $(x - 1)^2 - (3x + 2)(x - 5) = 0$
27. $x^2 - 15x + 54 = 0$
28. $x^2 - 21 = 4x$
29. $(x - 6)(x + 2) - (x - 6) = 9$
30. $x^2 - 4x + 2 = 0$

RADICAL EQUATIONS

You learned in Chapter 7 to solve radical equations by isolating a radical on one side of the equation, squaring both sides of the equation, solving the resulting equation, and checking solutions for extraneous roots. You can solve the radical equations in this section by repeating the same processes until all the radicals have been removed.

EXAMPLE

Example 1. Solve $\sqrt{2a - 1} - \sqrt{a - 1} = 1$.

Solution. $\sqrt{2a - 1} - \sqrt{a - 1} = 1$ **1.** Isolate one of the radicals. Square terms and simplify.

$$\sqrt{2a - 1} = 1 + \sqrt{a - 1}$$

$$(\sqrt{2a - 1})^2 = (1 + \sqrt{a - 1})^2$$

$$2a - 1 = 1 + 2\sqrt{a - 1} + a - 1$$

$$2a - 1 - a = 2\sqrt{a - 1}$$ **2.** Since a radical remains in the equation, isolate it. Square terms again and simplify.

$$a - 1 = 2\sqrt{a - 1}$$

$$(a - 1)^2 = (2\sqrt{a - 1})^2$$

$$a^2 - 2a + 1 = 4(a - 1)$$

$$a^2 - 2a + 1 = 4a - 4$$

$$a^2 - 6a + 5 = 0$$ **3.** Solve the quadratic equation.

$$(a - 5)(a - 1) = 0$$

$$a - 5 = 0 \qquad a - 1 = 0$$

$$a = 5 \qquad\quad a = 1$$

Check. $\sqrt{2 \cdot 5 - 1} - \sqrt{5 - 1} = 1$ $\sqrt{2 \cdot 1 - 1} - \sqrt{1 - 1} = 1$

$$\sqrt{10 - 1} - \sqrt{5 - 1} = 1 \qquad\qquad \sqrt{2 - 1} - \sqrt{1 - 1} = 1$$

$$\sqrt{9} - \sqrt{4} = 1 \qquad\qquad\qquad \sqrt{1} - \sqrt{0} = 1$$

$$3 - 2 = 1 \qquad\qquad\qquad\qquad 1 - 0 = 1$$

$$1 = 1 \qquad\qquad\qquad\qquad\qquad 1 = 1$$

Procedure for Storage

Solving Radical Equations

1. Isolate a radical on one side of the equation.
2. Square both sides.
3. Simplify as much as possible.
4. If a radical remains in the equation, repeat steps 1 to 3 until you have eliminated all radicals.
5. Solve the resulting equation.
6. Check for extraneous roots.

EXAMPLES

Example 2.   Solve $-7 - \sqrt{2m^2 - 3m + 5} = -3m$.

Solution. $-7 - \sqrt{2m^2 - 3m + 5} = -3m$

$-\sqrt{2m^2 - 3m + 5} = 7 - 3m$ **1.** Isolate the radical.

$(-\sqrt{2m^2 - 3m + 5})^2 = (7 - 3m)^2$ **2.** Square both sides.

$2m^2 - 3m + 5 = 49 - 42m + 9m^2$ **3.** Simplify.

$0 = 7m^2 - 39m + 44$ **4.** Solve the quadratic equation.

$0 = (7m - 11)(m - 4)$

$7m - 11 = 0 \qquad\qquad m - 4 = 0$

$7m = 11 \qquad\qquad\qquad m = 4$

$m = \dfrac{11}{7}$

Check. $-7 - \sqrt{2\left(\frac{11}{7}\right)^2 - 3\left(\frac{11}{7}\right) + 5} = -3\left(\frac{11}{7}\right)$

$$-7 - \sqrt{2\left(\frac{121}{49}\right) - \frac{33}{7} + 5} = \frac{-33}{7}$$

$$-7 - \sqrt{\frac{242}{49} - \frac{231}{49} + \frac{245}{49}} = \frac{-33}{7}$$

$$-7 - \sqrt{\frac{256}{49}} = \frac{-33}{7}$$

$$-7 - \frac{16}{7} = \frac{-33}{7}$$

$$\frac{-49}{7} - \frac{16}{7} = \frac{-33}{7}$$

$$\frac{-65}{7} \neq \frac{-33}{7}$$

Since this solution does not check, $\frac{11}{7}$ is an extraneous root.

$$-7 - \sqrt{2(4)^2 - 3(4) + 5} = -3(4)$$

$$-7 - \sqrt{2 \cdot 16 - 12 + 5} = -12$$

$$-7 - \sqrt{32 - 12 + 5} = -12$$

$$-7 - \sqrt{25} = -12$$

$$-7 - 5 = -12$$

$$-12 = -12$$

So 4 is a real solution.

Example 3. Solve $\sqrt{x + 20} - \sqrt{x} = 10$.

Solution. $\sqrt{x + 20} - \sqrt{x} = 10$.

$\sqrt{x + 20} = \sqrt{x} + 10$	**1.** Isolate a radical.
$(\sqrt{x + 20})^2 = (\sqrt{x} + 10)^2$	**2.** Square both sides.
$x + 20 = x + 20\sqrt{x} + 100$	**3.** Simplify.
$-80 = 20\sqrt{x}$	
$\dfrac{-80}{20} = \dfrac{20\sqrt{x}}{20}$	
$-4 = \sqrt{x}$	**4.** Isolate and square again.
$(-4)^2 = (\sqrt{x})^2$	
$16 = x$	

Check. $\sqrt{16 + 20} - \sqrt{16} = 10$

$\sqrt{36} - \sqrt{16} = 10$

$6 - 4 = 10$

$2 \neq 10$

Since this solution does not check, 16 is an extraneous root. There is no real solution.

Exercises

Solve each radical equation.

1. $\sqrt{2a^2 + 5a + 1} = \sqrt{2a + 6}$

2. $x - 1 = \sqrt{x + 1}$

3. $0 = \sqrt{2a^2 - 3a + 1} - 2a + 4$

4. $x + 3 = \sqrt{x + 3}$

5. $\sqrt{8m - 1} = \sqrt{4m + 1}$

6. $\sqrt{2a + 2} = \sqrt{6a + 7} - \sqrt{2a - 5}$

7. $x + 2 = \sqrt{3x^2 + 3x - 2}$

8. $\sqrt{2x - 7} = \sqrt{x + 4}$

9. $\sqrt{x + 8} - x = 2$

10. $\sqrt{8x - 5} = \sqrt{3x + 20}$

WORD PROBLEMS USING QUADRATIC EQUATIONS

A carpenter wants to fit three boards together to form a right triangle to use as a brace. The hypotenuse must be 3 feet longer than one leg and 5 feet longer than the other leg. Use the Pythagorean theorem to find the measurements of the sides of the triangle. Approximate your answer to the nearest hundredth.

You can solve the above problem quite easily with the methods you have learned in this chapter. First, review how to attack word problems. (See page 112.)

Read the problem again. Since the carpenter wants to make a right triangle, he must use the Pythagorean theorem, which is $a^2 + b^2 = c^2$. Sketch a right triangle and label the legs a and b. Label the hypotenuse c.

Now introduce the variables.

$$\text{Let } x = \text{the hypotenuse}$$
$$x - 3 = \text{one leg}$$
$$x - 5 = \text{the other leg}$$

Substitute these variables in the Pythagorean theorem and solve the resulting quadratic equation.

$$(x - 5)^2 + (x - 3)^2 = x^2$$
$$x^2 - 10x + 25 + x^2 - 6x + 9 = x^2$$
$$x^2 - 16x + 34 = 0$$

$$x = \frac{-b \pm \sqrt{b^2 - 4ac}}{2a}$$

Now substitute values in the quadratic formula and evaluate.

$$x = \frac{16 \pm \sqrt{(-16)^2 - 4(1)(34)}}{2(1)}$$

$$x = \frac{16 \pm \sqrt{256 - 136}}{2}$$

$$x = \frac{16 \pm \sqrt{120}}{2}$$

$$x = \frac{16 + 2\sqrt{30}}{2}$$

$$x = 8 \pm \sqrt{30}$$

$$x \doteq 8 \pm 5.477$$

Approximate $\sqrt{30}$ so a value for the hypotenuse can be determined.

$x \doteq 8 + 5.477$	$x \doteq 8 - 5.477$
$x \doteq 13.477$	$x \doteq 2.523$
$x - 3 \doteq 10.477$	$x - 3 \doteq -0.477$
$x - 5 \doteq 8.477$	$x - 5 \doteq -2.477$

The only sensible solution for the hypotenuse is 13.477 feet because 2.523 feet would give both legs negative values, which is impossible. So 13.48 feet is the length of the hypotenuse, 10.48 feet is the length of one leg, and 8.48 feet is the length of the other leg.

Look again at this problem, this time considering the processes you had to learn in order to solve this problem. Here are just a few.

1. the Pythagorean theorem
2. the quadratic formula
3. how to approximate square roots

Of course, many other facts you have learned so far had to be used to solve this particular problem. Much of what you learn this year you can apply to practical problems that you encounter each day. The foundation that you are now building will help you not only in your math classes throughout high school and college but also in your future career. But what good are all these rules and facts if you don't apply them? In Proverbs, Solomon wrote several times, "Apply thine heart . . ." (2:2; 22:17; 23:12). In the New Testament, James commanded believers to "be doers of the word, and not hearers only" (cf. James 1:22). He told them to listen to the Word and to apply it to their lives. That a Christian go to church and participate in other Christian activities is important, but that he apply the truths of God's Word and let them change his life is more important. If he doesn't apply the Word, he deceives himself. Do you let the Word of God mold your life, or do you deceive yourself?

EXAMPLE

Example 1. Your Dad asks you to paint one side of the rectangular fence in the back yard. He gives you $30 to buy Cover-All paint, which costs $10.49 per gallon, and says that you can have any money left over as your pay for painting the fence. You know that the length of the fence is 5 feet greater than 5 times the height and that each gallon of Cover-All paint will cover 275 square feet. You also remember that exactly two gallons of paint were used the last time the fence was painted. What are the height and length of the fence? If there is 5% sales tax in your state, how much money will you get for painting the fence?

Solution. The total area of the fence must be 2 · 275, or 550 square feet. Why? The first question asks you to find the height and length of the fence. Since you know that the area is 550 square feet, you can set up an equation using the formula $A = lw$. Substitute height for w.

Let $x =$ the height
$5x + 5 =$ the length

$$x(5x + 5) = 550 \qquad \text{Set up the equation and solve.}$$
$$5x^2 + 5x - 550 = 0$$
$$5(x^2 + x - 110) = 0$$
$$5(x + 11)(x - 10) = 0$$
$$x = -11, 10$$

So the height is 10 feet, and the length is 55 feet. The second question can be handled completely arithmetically. Two gallons of paint at $10.49 cost $20.98, to which 5% sales tax of $1.05 is added, making the total bill $22.03. Subtract $22.03 from the $30 your Dad gave you, and you have $7.97 as payment for doing a good job.

Exercises

Solve, using a quadratic equation.

1. The difference of two numbers is 6, and their product is 216. Find the two numbers.

2. The width of a rectangular flower bed is 4 feet less than the length. What are the dimensions if the area is 96 square feet?

3. What are the dimensions of a rectangle whose perimeter is 54 inches and area 180 square inches?

4. One integer is 2 less than eight times another. The difference of their squares is 884. Find the integers.

5. If one side of a square is increased by 3 inches and the adjacent side is decreased by 1 inch, the rectangle formed has an area of 77 square inches. Find the length of the side of the square.

6. The area of a rectangular garden is 270 square feet, and the perimeter is 66 feet. Find its dimensions.

7. The hypotenuse of a right triangle is 8 inches more than one leg and 3 inches more than the other leg. To the nearest tenth, find the dimensions of the triangle.

8. A rectangular piece of cardboard is made into a box by cutting 3-inch squares from each corner and then folding the cardboard up. The cardboard is 3 inches longer than the width. If the volume ($V = lwh$) of the box is 540 cubic inches, what are the dimensions of the original cardboard?

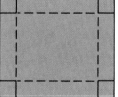

9. Mr. Smith is taking the scouts on a camping trip, and he has a rope to reach from a stake in the ground to the top of the tent pole. If the pole is 8 feet high and the rope is 12 feet long, how far from the pole should he place the stake to make the rope taut?

10. A baseball diamond is a square with an area of 8100 square feet. How far does a catcher have to throw the ball to second base to get a runner out who is trying to steal second?

MEMORY RECALL

Identify.
> completing the square
> discriminant
> quadratic equation
> quadratic formula
> zero product property

You should be able to do the following:

1. Apply the zero product property to solve quadratic equations.

2. Solve quadratic equations by factoring.

3. Solve quadratic equations of the form $x^2 - c = 0$.

4. Complete the square for a polynomial.

5. Solve quadratic equations by completing the square.

6. Use the quadratic formula.

7. Identify the number and nature of the solutions of a quadratic equation by evaluating the discriminant.

8. Solve radical equations.

9. Solve word problems that involve the quadratic equation.

You should be able to solve the following problems:

1. $(x - 7)(x + 2) = 0$

2. $x(5x - 8) = 0$

3. $x^2 - 5x - 24 = 0$

4. $x^2 - 9 = 0$

5. $2x^2 + 9x - 56 = 0$

6. $a^2 = 16$

7. $y^2 = 17$

8. $x^2 + 6x + 9 = 0$

9. $a^2 + 7a - 12 = 0$

10. $2x^2 + 8x + 9 = 0$

11. $5a^2 + 3a = -6$

12. $x^2 - 14x - 8 = 0$

13. $a + 3 = a^2 - 2$

14. $x + 8 = x^2 - 3$

15. $\sqrt{x + 7} - x = 5$

Tell the number of solutions in the set of real numbers for each equation. If the solution is a real number, tell whether it is rational or irrational.

16. $x^2 + 7x + 9 = 0$

17. $3a^2 - 9a + 2 = 0$

18. $3y^2 - 2y + 8 = 0$

19. The difference of two numbers is 19; their product is -84. Find the two numbers.

20. The area of a rectangular piece of concrete is 120 square feet, and its perimeter is 46 feet. What are the dimensions of the rectangle?

CHAPTER 11

RATIONAL EXPRESSIONS

The sleek red train filled with twenty-four squirming, excited people anticipating the 87-foot drop just ahead creeps up the 105-foot hill. Then the last car breaks loose from the lift chain, and the train hurtles down the hill at a speed of 84 feet per second. At the bottom of the dip, the riders feel the force of gravity pressing twice as hard as usual. No wonder then that they also feel a sinking feeling. Recovering from the first dip, the train speeds on, zipping up hills, careening around corners, and plunging down less frightening dips, while the jostled riders scream with delight (or perhaps fright) for less than two minutes.

Have you ever ridden a roller coaster and wondered if the track would hold up under the weight of a 4800-pound train containing twenty-four passengers? With all the squeaks and creaks and clicks and clacks, the track certainly doesn't sound like it will last much longer. When you board a coaster, you may not consider whether the track will hold up under the stress, but the designers of the ride had to. They know that a force of 2 g is obtained at the bottom of that first dip. In other words, the acceleration at that point is twice the acceleration caused by the pull of gravity and is represented by the formula $a = 2g$. This g force causes the riders to feel the sinking sensation at the bottom of the first drop. Thus a 100-pound person is pressed against the seat of the car with a force of 200 pounds, or 2 g. The designers had to calculate the maximum weight of each rider in addition to the weight of the train to find the force that will be applied to the track at the bottom of that first breathtaking dip. The formula for finding force is $f = \left(\frac{w}{g}\right) a$, where f is the force in pounds, w is the weight in pounds, g is the acceleration caused by gravitational pull in feet per second, and a is the acceleration of the moving body in feet per second. If the designers design a coaster that can withstand 20,400 pounds of force at the bottom of that first dip, what is the average maximum weight per person that they are allowing for the train?

The force equation contains a rational expression, which you will learn about in this chapter. Do you know how to simplify the rational expression and solve the force equation? If you don't know now, you will know by the end of the ride, uh, chapter. So hang on. Here we go!

RATIONAL EXPRESSIONS

What is a rational number? Are all numbers rational? In what form do rational numbers usually appear? A rational expression is an expression in the form $\frac{P_1}{P_2}$, in which P_1 and P_2 are polynomials and P_2 is not equal to 0.

➤**Rational expression:** an algebraic expression that is a ratio of two polynomials, with the polynomial in the denominator not equal to 0.

Look at the rational expressions given below. Notice that the numerators and the denominators are polynomials. Can you identify the parts of a polynomial? What are the terms of each polynomial in the rational expressiohs below? What are the factors? What is the difference between terms and factors?

1. $\dfrac{x}{x + 2}$

2. $\dfrac{3x^2 + 4x - 5}{x}$

3. $\dfrac{x + 6}{x - 9}$

4. $\dfrac{2x^2 + 3x + 6}{x^2 - 4x + 7}$

5. $\dfrac{4}{5}$

6. $\dfrac{x + 7}{x^2 + 3x - 9}$

What would happen in problem 1 if $x = -2$? Substituting -2 for x, you get $\frac{-2}{-2+2}$ simplified to $\frac{-2}{0}$. But you have already learned that division by 0 is undefined. Notice that the variable could equal 0, but the polynomial cannot equal 0. To determine when a rational expression is undefined, you must determine what values of x will make the denominator equal 0.

EXAMPLE

Example 1.   Determine when $\dfrac{x^2 + 3x + 6}{x^2 + 5x + 6}$ is undefined.

Solution. To find when the rational expression is undefined, set the denominator equal to 0 and solve.

$$x^2 + 5x + 6 = 0$$
$$(x + 2)(x + 3) = 0$$

$$x + 2 = 0 \qquad\qquad x + 3 = 0$$
$$x = -2 \qquad\qquad\quad x = -3$$

So x can take any value other than -2 or -3.

To operate with rational expressions, you must know how to find the greatest common factor (GCF) of two polynomials and the least common multiple (LCM) of two polynomials. The processes are the same as finding the greatest common divisor and least common multiple of rational numbers.

To find the GCF of two or more polynomials, factor them completely. Then identify the common factors.

EXAMPLE

Example 2.   Find the common factors of $2x^2 + 12x + 18$ and $6x^2 - 6x - 72$.

Solution.   Factor both polynomials completely. Then identify common factors.

$$2x^2 + 12x + 18 \qquad\qquad 6x^2 - 6x - 72$$
$$2(x^2 + 6x + 9) \qquad\qquad 6(x^2 - x - 12)$$
$$2(x + 3)^2 \qquad\qquad 6(x - 4)(x + 3)$$
$$\qquad\qquad\qquad 3 \cdot 2(x - 4)(x + 3)$$

The common factors are 2 and $(x + 3)$.

To find the LCM of two or more polynomials, factor them completely. Then find the product of the highest power of each factor. You must be able to find the GCF and LCM of radical expressions in order to add, subtract, and simplify them.

EXAMPLE

Example 3.   Find the LCM of $x^4 - 3x^3 - 10x^2$ and $3x^2 - 30x + 75$.

Solution.

$$x^4 - 3x^3 - 10x^2 \qquad 3x^2 - 30x + 75 \qquad \textbf{1. Factor each polynomial.}$$
$$x^2(x^2 - 3x - 10) \qquad 3(x^2 - 10x + 25)$$
$$x^2(x - 5)(x + 2) \qquad 3(x - 5)^2$$

The factors are x^2, $(x - 5)$, $(x + 2)$, and 3.

LCM $= 3x^2(x - 5)^2(x + 2)$ **2.** The LCM is the product of the highest power of each factor.

Exercises

State the value or values that would make the rational expression undefined.

1. $\dfrac{3x + 4}{x}$

2. $\dfrac{x^2 - 3}{x + 4}$

3. $\dfrac{x - 7}{x + 2}$

4. $\dfrac{x + 8}{x - 5}$

5. $\dfrac{x^2 + 3x - 2}{x^2 + 5x - 24}$

6. $\dfrac{x - 5}{x^3 - 3x^2 - 4x}$

7. $\dfrac{x - 7}{x^2 + 7x - 18}$

8. $\dfrac{x + 4}{x^2 - 5x - 24}$

Find the GCF for each pair of polynomials.

9. $x^2 - 4x - 12$ $x^2 - 9x + 18$

10. $x^2 - 2x - 15$ $x^3 - 25x$

11. $x^2 - 2x + 1$ $x^2 - 5x + 4$

12. $x^3 + 7x^2 - 30x$ $x^2 + 3x - 18$

13. $3x^3 - 54x^2 + 240x$ $6x^2 - 54x - 60$

14. $4x^2 + 32x + 60$ $8x^2 + 8x - 160$

15. $x^2 + 3x - 4$ $x^2 + x - 12$

Find the LCM for each pair of polynomials.

16. $8x^2 + 16x + 8$ $3x^3 + 8x^2 + 5x$

17. $x^2 - 4$ $x^2 + 4x + 4$

18. $x^4 - 16$ $x^2 + 4x + 4$

19. $6x^2 - 15x - 36$ $2x^2 + 5x + 3$

20. $12x^3 - 4x^2 - 16x$ $x^2 - 5x - 6$

21. $2x^2 - 13x + 15$ $16x^2 + 24x - 72$

22. $x^2 + x - 72$ $x^2 - 16x + 64$

SIMPLIFYING RATIONAL EXPRESSIONS

Do you recall how to reduce a fraction such as $\frac{12}{15}$ to lowest terms? First, find the prime factors of both the numerator and the denominator. Then cancel any common factors. When you cancel, you are actually dividing both the numerator and the denominator by the same number. Simplifying is based on the fundamental principle of fractions that you learned in Chapter 1. That principle states that if a is an integer and b and c are nonzero integers, $\frac{a}{b} = \frac{ac}{bc}$.

EXAMPLES

Example 1. Simplify $\dfrac{4a^3}{8a}$.

Solution. Factor to primes and cancel like factors.

$$\frac{2^2 a^3}{2^3 a} = \frac{2^2 a \cdot a^2}{2^2 a \cdot 2} = \frac{a^2}{2}$$

Example 2. Simplify $\dfrac{180m^3 n^2}{27mn}$.

Solution. Factor to primes and cancel common factors.

$$\frac{180m^3 n^2}{27mn} = \frac{2^2 \cdot 3^2 \cdot 5m^3 n^2}{3^3 mn} = \frac{2^2 \cdot 5m^2 n}{3} = \frac{20m^2 n}{3}$$

Remember, you cancel factors, not terms.

Example 3. Simplify $\dfrac{4x^2 + 4x - 48}{x - 3}$.

Solution. Factor each polynomial completely. Cancel common factors.

$$\frac{4(x^2 + x - 12)}{x - 3} = \frac{2^2(x + 4)(x - 3)}{x - 3} = 4(x + 4)$$

Example 4. Simplify $\dfrac{x^2 - 4}{x^2 + 4x + 4}$.

Solution. After factoring both numerator and denominator, simplify.

$$\begin{aligned}
\frac{x^2 - 4}{x^2 + 4x + 4} &= \frac{(x - 2)(x + 2)}{(x + 2)^2} \\
&= \frac{(x - 2)(x + 2)}{(x + 2)(x + 2)} \\
&= \frac{x - 2}{x + 2}
\end{aligned}$$

Exercises

Simplify each rational expression.

1. $\dfrac{3x^2}{15x}$

2. $\dfrac{24x^2y^3}{8xy}$

3. $\dfrac{15a^3bc^2}{27abc^4}$

4. $\dfrac{x^3 - 3x^2 - 10x}{x^3 + 2x^2}$

5. $\dfrac{5xyz + 5z}{10x^2y^2 - 10}$

6. $\dfrac{2xy^2 - xy - 6x}{4y^2 - 2y - 12}$

7. $\dfrac{3xy^2}{3x^2 + 12xy + 9y^2}$

8. $\dfrac{3x^2 + 3xy}{x^2 - y^2}$

9. $\dfrac{15x^2 - 100x + 60}{3x^2 + x - 2}$

10. $\dfrac{3x^5y - 3x^4y - 60x^3y}{9x^4 + 36x^3}$

11. $\dfrac{2x^2 + x - 45}{9 - 11x + 2x^2}$

12. $\dfrac{x^7y^2 + x^6y^2 - 6x^5y^2}{x^5 - 9x^3}$

MULTIPLYING RATIONAL EXPRESSIONS

The basic rule for the multiplication of rationals is to multiply the numerators and divide the product by the product of the denominators. You can multiply first and then simplify or you can simplify first and then multiply.

EXAMPLES

Example 1.   Compute $\dfrac{5}{9} \cdot \dfrac{27}{40}$

Solution. Multiply first; then simplify.

$$\frac{5}{9} \cdot \frac{27}{40} = \frac{135}{360}$$

$$= \frac{5 \cdot 3^3}{5 \cdot 3^2 \cdot 2^3}$$

$$= \frac{\overset{1}{\cancel{5}} \cdot \overset{3}{\cancel{3^3}}}{\underset{1}{\cancel{5}} \cdot \underset{1}{\cancel{3^2}} \cdot 2^3}$$

$$= \frac{3}{2^3}$$

$$= \frac{3}{8}$$

Or simplify first, and then multiply.

Prime factor all numerators and denominators and simplify.

$$\frac{5}{9} \cdot \frac{27}{40} = \frac{5}{3^2} \cdot \frac{3^3}{2^3 \cdot 5}$$

$$= \frac{\cancel{5}}{\cancel{3^2}} \cdot \frac{\overset{3}{\cancel{3^3}}}{2^3 \cdot \cancel{5}}$$

$$= \frac{3}{2^3}$$

$$= \frac{3}{8}$$

Which method do you prefer? It is easier to simplify rational expressions before multiplying them.

Example 2. Compute $\dfrac{3a}{2ab} \cdot \dfrac{12a}{18bc}$.

Solution.

$$\frac{3a}{2ab} \cdot \frac{12a}{18bc} = \frac{3a}{2ab} \cdot \frac{2^2 \cdot 3a}{3^2 \cdot 2bc}$$ **1.** Prime factor each numerator and denominator.

$$= \frac{\cancel{3a}}{\cancel{2ab}} \cdot \frac{\overset{2}{\cancel{2^2}} \cdot \cancel{3a}}{\cancel{3^2} \cdot 2bc}$$ **2.** Simplify.

$$= \frac{a}{b^2c}$$

Example 3. Compute $\dfrac{5x^2y}{2x^3yz} \cdot \dfrac{24xy^2z^5}{10xy}$.

Solution. Prime factor each numerator and denominator, multiply, and simplify.

$$\frac{5x^2y}{2x^3yz} \cdot \frac{24xy^2z^5}{10xy} = \frac{5x^2y}{2x^3yz} \cdot \frac{2^3 \cdot 3xy^2z^5}{2 \cdot 5xy}$$

$$= \frac{5 \cdot 2^3 \cdot 3x^3y^3z^5}{5 \cdot 2^2x^4y^2z}$$

$$= \frac{\cancel{5} \cdot \overset{2}{\cancel{2^3}} \cdot 3\cancel{x^3}\overset{y}{\cancel{y^3}}\overset{z^4}{\cancel{z^5}}}{\cancel{5} \cdot \cancel{2^2}\cancel{x^4}\cancel{y^2}\cancel{z}}$$

$$= \frac{2 \cdot 3yz^4}{x}$$

$$= \frac{6yz^4}{x}$$

Procedure for Storage

Multiplying Rational Expressions

1. Prime factor all numerators and denominators.
2. Simplify the expressions by dividing (canceling) common factors that appear in both the numerators and the denominators.
3. Multiply the numerators and divide by the product of the denominators.

EXAMPLES

Example 4. Compute $\dfrac{x + y}{9} \cdot \dfrac{18}{x^2 - y^2}$.

Solution. $\dfrac{x + y}{9} \cdot \dfrac{18}{x^2 - y^2}$

$$\dfrac{x + y}{3^2} \cdot \dfrac{3^2 \cdot 2}{(x-y)(x+y)}$$

1. Factor the numerators and the denominators.

$$\dfrac{\cancel{x+y}}{\cancel{3^2}} \cdot \dfrac{\cancel{3^2} \cdot 2}{(x-y)\cancel{(x+y)}}$$

2. Simplify by canceling common factors.

$$\dfrac{2}{x - y}$$

Make sure you cancel only common factors.

Example 5. Compute $(x^3 - x^2 - 72x) \cdot \dfrac{3}{x^2 + x - 56}$.

Solution. $(x^3 - x^2 - 72x) \cdot \dfrac{3}{x^2 + x - 56}$.

$$x(x^2 - x - 72) \cdot \dfrac{3}{(x+8)(x-7)}$$

Factor the numerators and denominators; then simplify.

$$\dfrac{x(x+8)(x-9)}{1} \cdot \dfrac{3}{(x+8)(x-7)}$$

$$\dfrac{x\cancel{(x+8)}(x-9)}{1} \cdot \dfrac{3}{\cancel{(x+8)}(x-7)}$$

$$\dfrac{3x(x-9)}{x - 7}$$

Exercises

Multiply.

1. $\dfrac{2}{5} \cdot \dfrac{19}{28}$

2. $\dfrac{16}{9} \cdot \dfrac{27}{8}$

3. $\dfrac{4}{11} \cdot \dfrac{33}{32}$

4. $\dfrac{2a}{3} \cdot \dfrac{9}{16}$

5. $\dfrac{3a^2}{17b} \cdot \dfrac{34b^2}{6ab}$

6. $\dfrac{5x^2y}{18xy} \cdot \dfrac{3y^3}{9y}$

7. $\dfrac{x^3yz^2}{xy} \cdot \dfrac{x^4y}{x^9y^2z}$

8. $\dfrac{32a^2b}{xy^3} \cdot \dfrac{2xy}{8a^2}$

9. $\dfrac{(x+2)}{5} \cdot \dfrac{25}{(x+2)}$

10. $\dfrac{(x-3)(x+4)}{(x-1)} \cdot \dfrac{(x+3)}{(x-4)(x-3)}$

11. $\dfrac{3x^3y(x-1)}{8x} \cdot \dfrac{18xy^2}{27(x-1)}$

12. $\dfrac{x^2 - 5x - 14}{8} \cdot \dfrac{4}{x - 7}$

13. $\dfrac{x^2 + 3x - 18}{x^2 - x} \cdot \dfrac{x^3y}{xy - 3y}$

14. $\dfrac{x^2 + 10x + 16}{x - 4} \cdot \dfrac{x^2 - x - 12}{x + 2}$

15. $\dfrac{x^2 - x - 20}{x^2 - 6x + 5} \cdot \dfrac{x + 3}{x^2 + 7x + 12}$

16. $\dfrac{2x^2 - xy - y^2}{x^2 - y^2} \cdot \dfrac{x^2 + 2xy + y^2}{3x^2 - xy - 4y^2}$

17. $\dfrac{x - 2}{x^3 - 5x^2 + 6x} \cdot \dfrac{xy^2}{xy + 4y}$

18. $\dfrac{a^2 + ab - 2b^2}{a^2 - b^2} \cdot \dfrac{a^2 - 2ab - 3b^2}{a^2 - 3ab}$

19. $\dfrac{2m^2 - mn - 3n^2}{m - n} \cdot \dfrac{m^2 - n^2}{2m^2 - 5mn + 3n^2}$

20. $\dfrac{3x^2 - 19xy + 20y^2}{x + y} \cdot \dfrac{y + x}{2x^2 - 11xy + 5y^2}$

21. $\dfrac{x^3y^2 - 2x^2y^2 - 15xy^2}{x^2 - 12x + 35} \cdot \dfrac{x^2 - 4x - 21}{x^2y^3 + 6xy^3 + 9y^3}$

22. $\dfrac{3x^2 - 11xy - 4y^2}{x^3y - 4x^2y^2} \cdot \dfrac{x^2y - 3xy^2}{3x + y}$

23. $\dfrac{3x^2 + xy - 2y^2}{2x^2 - 3xy + y^2} \cdot \dfrac{2x^2 + xy - y^2}{x^2 + 2xy + y^2}$

24. $\dfrac{a^2 + 7ab + 10b^2}{a^2 + ab - 2b^2} \cdot \dfrac{3a^2 - 7ab + 4b^2}{3a^2 + 11ab - 20b^2}$

25. $\dfrac{(x+3)(x-2)}{x^2y} \cdot \dfrac{xy}{(x-2)(x+5)} \cdot \dfrac{x(x+5)}{(x+3)}$

26. $\dfrac{x^2 - 7x - 18}{x + 4} \cdot \dfrac{x^2 - 5x + 6}{x - 9} \cdot \dfrac{x + 4}{x - 3}$

27. $\dfrac{x^4 + x^3 - 6x^2}{xy^3 - 2y^3} \cdot \dfrac{x^2 + 2x - 15}{x^2 + 8x + 15} \cdot \dfrac{y^2}{x^3}$

28. $\dfrac{a^2 + 2ab - 3b^2}{a^2b^3} \cdot \dfrac{4ab^4}{a^2 + 8ab + 15b^2} \cdot \dfrac{a^2 + 3ab - 10b^2}{a + 7b}$

MICROCOMPUTERS

When the first electronic computers were designed, engineers had only bulky, power-hungry vacuum tubes to work with. Later, designers replaced the tubes with transistors. Transistorized computers used less power and were much more reliable.

During the early 1960s, America launched its program to land men on the moon. Since spacecraft

need to be as light as possible, engineers sought methods of reducing the size and the power requirements of the onboard electronics. Out of this research came devices known as integrated circuits: many different electronic elements combined into a single unit. These units are often called chips. Computers have been growing smaller ever since.

Near the end of the 1960s, an engineer experimented with reducing the complete central processing unit of a computer to the size of one integrated circuit. His idea worked! The microprocessor became the foundation of a new generation of computers.

Microprocessors are not microcomputers. A microprocessor is only a central processing unit, the heart of both minicomputers and microcomputers. The microprocessor needs memory and I/O (input/output) circuits in order for it to function as a computer.

The microcomputer age dawned when one company began marketing a small kit from which a hobbyist could build a fully functional computer. Several other companies soon duplicated this idea. Before long, one competitor released a computer kit that had four times the memory capacity of the original machine. This development immediately pressured all competitors in the field to improve their own products.

This back-and-forth process of microcomputer development continues today. More powerful computers with lower prices and greater reliability are being introduced all the

time. A healthy environment of competition and free enterprise has given birth to many microcomputer companies and encouraged manufacturers of mainframes and minicomputers to develop even smaller computers. Some microcomputers available are Apple, Radio Shack, Commodore, Gimix, Texas Instruments, and IBM.

Many companies offer computers in various price ranges. This variety makes it possible for clients ranging from young children to major businesses to own computers. With the low prices of many microcomputers, almost anyone can afford to purchase one and to become familiar with its uses.

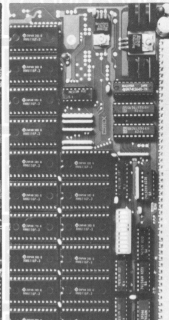

DIVIDING RATIONAL EXPRESSIONS

What operation is the opposite of multiplication? What does *opposite* mean? According to the dictionary, one meaning of opposite is "natures or characters that are diametrically different." The Bible tells of two opposite natures: man in his sin nature before salvation and man in his regenerated nature after salvation. II Corinthians 5:17 says that when a man is "in Christ" his old ways pass away and he gets new ways. Can people tell that you are a new creation? When the Apostle Paul got saved, people noticed a change. His conversion is recorded in Acts 9:1-20. Read verses 1 and 2. Then read verse 20. Do you see the opposite nature he had after salvation? Shouldn't all Christians show a nature opposite the sinful nature of this world?

When you divide rational numbers, such as $\frac{1}{2} \div \frac{7}{4}$, find the reciprocal of the second fraction (the divisor) and multiply. So $\frac{1}{2} \div \frac{7}{4} = \frac{1}{2} \cdot \frac{4}{7} = \frac{2}{7}$. Follow this same procedure when you divide rational expressions.

EXAMPLES

Example 1.   Compute $\dfrac{x^2}{3y^2} \div \dfrac{x}{9y}$.

Solution. Invert the divisor and multiply.

$$\frac{x^2}{3y^2} \div \frac{x}{9y} = \frac{x^2}{3y^2} \cdot \frac{9y}{x}$$
$$= \frac{x^2}{3y^2} \cdot \frac{3^2 9y}{x}$$
$$= \frac{3x}{y}$$

Example 2.   Compute $\dfrac{(x+y)^2}{x^2 - 4xy + 4y^2} \div \dfrac{9}{x^2 - xy - 2y^2}$.

Solution. Invert the divisor and multiply.

$$\frac{(x+y)^2}{x^2 - 4xy + 4y^2} \div \frac{9}{x^2 - xy - 2y^2} = \frac{(x+y)^2}{(x-2y)^2} \cdot \frac{(x-2y)(x+y)}{9}$$
$$= \frac{(x+y)^2}{(x-2y)^2} \cdot \frac{(x-2y)(x+y)}{9}$$
$$= \frac{(x+y)^3}{9(x-2y)}$$

Procedure for Storage

Dividing Rational Expressions

1. Invert the divisor.
2. Factor.
3. Multiply.
4. Simplify.

EXAMPLE

Example 3.   Divide $\dfrac{x^2 + 3xy + 2y^2}{x^2 + xy - 2y^2} \div \dfrac{x^2 + 4xy + 3y^2}{x^2 - y^2}$.

Solution.

$$\frac{x^2 + 3xy + 2y^2}{x^2 + xy - 2y^2} \cdot \frac{x^2 - y^2}{x^2 + 4xy + 3y^2}$$

$$\frac{x^2 + 3xy + 2y^2}{x^2 + xy - 2y^2} \cdot \frac{x^2 - y^2}{x^2 + 4xy + 3y^2}$$

$$\frac{(x+2y)(x+y)}{(x+2y)(x-y)} \cdot \frac{(x-y)(x+y)}{(x+3y)(x+y)}$$

$$\frac{x+y}{x+3y}$$

Exercises

Divide.

1. $\dfrac{4}{5} \div \dfrac{8}{35}$

2. $\dfrac{14}{9} \div \dfrac{28}{27}$

3. $\dfrac{1}{3} \div \dfrac{2}{3}$

4. $\dfrac{3x^3}{5} \div \dfrac{6x^2y}{25}$

5. $\dfrac{8x^4y^2}{x^3y} \div \dfrac{24x}{7y}$

6. $\dfrac{a^2b^3}{x^5y^2} \div \dfrac{a^4b}{xy^3}$

7. $\dfrac{(x+y)^2}{x - y} \div \dfrac{(x+y)(x-y)}{(x-y)^2}$

8. $\dfrac{x^2 - y^2}{(x-y)^2} \div \dfrac{x^2 - 2xy + y^2}{x - y}$

9. $\dfrac{4x + 4}{5x - 25} \div \dfrac{3x + 3}{x - 5}$

10. $\dfrac{x^2 + 2x}{3x - 9} \div \dfrac{x^3 - 9x}{x - 3}$

11. $(x+1) \div \dfrac{x^2 + 2x + 1}{x}$

12. $\dfrac{x^2 - 11x + 18}{x - 3} \div \dfrac{x^2 + 6x + 8}{x + 2}$

13. $\dfrac{x^2 - xy - 2y^2}{x^2 - y^2} \div \dfrac{x^2 - 3xy + 2y^2}{3x^2 + 4xy + y^2}$

14. $1 \div \dfrac{x^3 - x^2 + y}{x^5 + xy}$

15. $\dfrac{x^2 + 3x - 54}{x^2 + 5x + 6} \div \dfrac{x^2 - 12x + 36}{x^2 - 3x - 18}$

16. $\dfrac{x^4y - 3x^3y - 10x^2y}{x^2 + 4x + 3} \div \dfrac{x^2y^4 - xy^4 - 2y^4}{x^2 + 7x + 12}$

17. $\dfrac{1}{2x^2 + xy - y^2} \div \dfrac{x^2 + 2xy + y^2}{2x^2 - 3xy + y^2}$

18. $\dfrac{3a^2 - 6a}{7a^3} \div \dfrac{a^2 - 4}{14}$

19. $\dfrac{3m^2 - 2mn - n^2}{m^3n^2} \div (m^2 - 2mn + n^2)$

20. $\dfrac{12x^2 - 29xy + 14y^2}{x^2 - xy - 12y^2} \div \dfrac{3x^2 + xy - 2y^2}{x^2 - 2xy - 8y^2}$

ADDING RATIONAL EXPRESSIONS

Have you had any problem operating with rational expressions? If you have followed the rules you learned for operating with rational numbers, you should be progressing through this chapter with few problems, because the same rules apply here. Now it is time to add rational expressions. If two rational numbers have to have a common denominator in order to be combined, do rational expressions have to have a common denominator as well? Of course they do. But you will learn how to find a common denominator for two or more rational expressions in another section. This section will be easy because the addends in each problem will have a common denominator.

EXAMPLE

Example 1. $\dfrac{4}{x} + \dfrac{9}{x} = ?$

Solution. $\dfrac{4}{x} + \dfrac{9}{x} = \dfrac{13}{x}$

Procedure for Storage

Adding Rational Expressions with a Common Denominator

1. Add the numerators.
2. Simplify the rational expression.

EXAMPLES

Example 2. $\dfrac{a}{x} + \dfrac{b}{x} + \dfrac{3}{x} = ?$

Solution. $\dfrac{a}{x} + \dfrac{b}{x} + \dfrac{3}{x} = \dfrac{a + b + 3}{x}$

Example 3. $\dfrac{3x^2 + 4x - 8}{x + 2} + \dfrac{x^2 - 3x - 6}{x + 2} = ?$

Solution. $\dfrac{3x^2 + 4x - 8}{x + 2} + \dfrac{x^2 - 3x - 6}{x + 2}$

$\dfrac{3x^2 + 4x - 8 + x^2 - 3x - 6}{x + 2}$ **1.** Add the numerators.

$\dfrac{4x^2 + x - 14}{x + 2}$ **2.** Combine like terms.

$\dfrac{(4x - 7)(x + 2)}{x + 2}$ **3.** Factor and simplify.

$4x - 7$

Example 4. $\dfrac{2x + 9}{x - 4} + \dfrac{3x + 2}{x - 4} = ?$

Solution. $\dfrac{2x + 9}{x - 4} + \dfrac{3x + 2}{x - 4} = \dfrac{2x + 9 + 3x + 2}{x - 4}$ **1.** Add the numerators.

                         2. Combine like terms.

$= \dfrac{5x + 11}{x - 4}$ This rational cannot be simplified.

A rational number has three signs: one in the numerator, one in the denominator, and one preceding the fraction. The rational $-\frac{4}{5}$ could be expressed as follows:

$$+ \ \frac{-4}{+5} \qquad\qquad + \ \frac{+4}{-5} \qquad\qquad - \ \frac{-4}{-5}$$

All of these different forms are equivalent expressions. Sometimes it is easier to simplify a problem like $\frac{3}{5} + \frac{2}{-5}$ if you use another form of the rational. To add $\frac{3}{5}$ and $\frac{2}{-5}$, change $\frac{2}{-5}$ to $-\frac{2}{5}$ and then add. You should be able to change any rational or rational expression to another form by changing the positions of the signs to yield equivalent expressions. Can you give the three equivalent forms of $\frac{3}{7}$?

Exercises

Add and simplify.

1. $\dfrac{1}{4} + \dfrac{3}{4}$

2. $\dfrac{5}{13} + \dfrac{2}{13}$

3. $\dfrac{7}{8} + \dfrac{9}{8}$

4. $\dfrac{3}{7} + \dfrac{5}{7}$

5. $\dfrac{2}{x} + \dfrac{5}{x}$

6. $\dfrac{8}{x} + \dfrac{6}{x}$

7. $\dfrac{3x}{8} + \dfrac{5x}{8}$

8. $\dfrac{a}{b} + \dfrac{c}{b}$

9. $\dfrac{7}{2c} + \dfrac{-9}{2c}$

10. $\dfrac{4c}{d} + \dfrac{5c}{d}$

11. $\dfrac{5}{x+2} + \dfrac{7}{x+2}$

12. $\dfrac{6}{a+b} + \dfrac{-3a}{a+b}$

13. $\dfrac{4}{x+y} + \dfrac{9}{x+y}$

14. $\dfrac{2x}{x-7} + \dfrac{-14}{x-7}$

15. $\dfrac{3a}{a+b} + \dfrac{3b}{a+b}$

16. $\dfrac{3\sqrt{5}}{x-7} + \dfrac{4\sqrt{5}}{x-7}$

17. $\dfrac{2\sqrt{8}}{a-c} + \dfrac{5\sqrt{8}}{a-c}$

18. $\dfrac{x+2}{x^2-4x-7} + \dfrac{x-9}{x^2-4x-7}$

19. $\dfrac{3+\sqrt{7}}{a-4} + \dfrac{3-\sqrt{7}}{a-4}$

20. $\dfrac{a-2}{a^2-3a+9} + \dfrac{a+4}{a^2-3a+9}$

21. $\dfrac{2x^2+3x}{x+3} + \dfrac{2x-3}{x+3}$

22. $\dfrac{2x^2-6x+4}{x^2-8x+15} + \dfrac{x^2-5x-19}{x^2-8x+15}$

23. $\dfrac{a}{x} + \dfrac{b}{x} + \dfrac{3}{x}$

24. $\dfrac{5x^2+3x-9}{x^2+7x+10} + \dfrac{2x^2+8x+3}{x^2+7x+10}$

25. $\dfrac{10a^2 + 4a - 3}{6a^2 + 7a - 5} + \dfrac{-4a^2 + 3a - 2}{6a^2 + 7a - 5}$

26. $\dfrac{m^2 + 3m - 6}{m^2 - 5m - 36} + \dfrac{2m^2 + 7m - 2}{m^2 - 5m - 36}$

27. $\dfrac{3x^2 - xy + 4y^2}{x^2 + xy - 2y^2} + \dfrac{x^2 - 2xy + 5y^2}{x^2 + xy - 2y^2}$

28. $\dfrac{2x^2 - xy + 8y^2}{x^2 - y^2} + \dfrac{x^2 - xy - 9y^2}{x^2 - y^2}$

29. $\dfrac{6a^2 - 3a - 9}{a^3 - a^2 - 12a} + \dfrac{-5a^2 + 2a - 3}{a^3 - a^2 - 12a}$

30. $\dfrac{2m^2 + 4mn + n^2}{m^2 + mn - 2n^2} + \dfrac{m^2 + 3mn + n^2}{m^2 + mn - 2n^2}$

Write three equivalent forms for each rational.

31. $\dfrac{5}{-7}$

32. $\dfrac{3}{4}$

33. $\dfrac{7}{-12}$

34. $\dfrac{-8}{9}$

35. $\dfrac{-2}{-7}$

SUBTRACTING RATIONAL EXPRESSIONS

To subtract rational expressions, follow the procedure for subtracting rational numbers. If the rationals have a common denominator, combine like terms in the numerator and place them over the common denominator. Then simplify.

EXAMPLES

Example 1. $\dfrac{5}{9} - \dfrac{2}{9} = ?$

Solution. $\dfrac{5}{9} - \dfrac{2}{9} = \dfrac{3}{9}$

1. Subtract numerators.

$= \dfrac{1}{3}$

2. Simplify.

Example 2. $\dfrac{4}{x} - \dfrac{8}{x} = ?$

Solution. $\dfrac{4}{x} - \dfrac{8}{x} = \dfrac{-4}{x}$

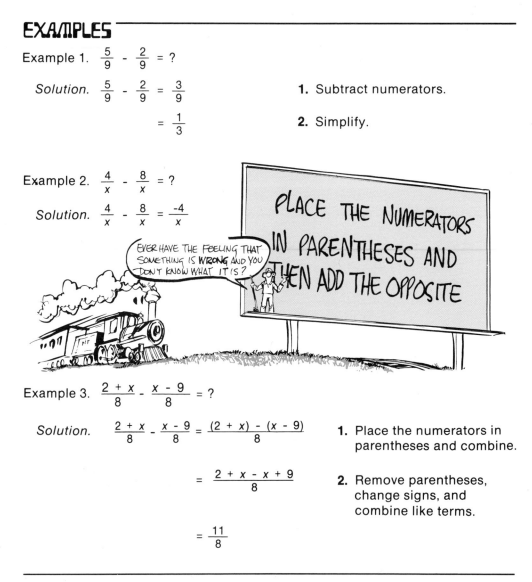

Example 3. $\dfrac{2 + x}{8} - \dfrac{x - 9}{8} = ?$

Solution. $\dfrac{2 + x}{8} - \dfrac{x - 9}{8} = \dfrac{(2 + x) - (x - 9)}{8}$

1. Place the numerators in parentheses and combine.

$= \dfrac{2 + x - x + 9}{8}$

2. Remove parentheses, change signs, and combine like terms.

$= \dfrac{11}{8}$

Procedure for Storage

Subtracting Rational Expressions with a Common Denominator

1. Subtract the numerators.
2. Simplify the resulting rational expression.

EXAMPLE

Example 4. $\dfrac{3x^2 + 31x + 18}{x^2 + 5x - 36} - \dfrac{x^2 + 10x - 9}{x^2 + 5x - 36} = ?$

Solution. $\dfrac{3x^2 + 31x + 18}{x^2 + 5x - 36} - \dfrac{x^2 + 10x - 9}{x^2 + 5x - 36}$

$\dfrac{(3x^2 + 31x + 18) - (x^2 + 10x - 9)}{x^2 + 5x - 36}$ **1.** Subtract.

$\dfrac{3x^2 + 31x + 18 - x^2 - 10x + 9}{x^2 + 5x - 36}$ **2.** Simplify.

$\dfrac{2x^2 + 21x + 27}{x^2 + 5x - 36}$

$\dfrac{(2x + 3)(x + 9)}{(x + 9)(x - 4)}$ **3.** Factor.

$\dfrac{(2x + 3)(x + 9)}{(x + 9)(x - 4)}$ **4.** Reduce.

$\dfrac{2x + 3}{x - 4}$

What happens to a binomial such as $x - 4$ when you multiply it by -1?
$$-1(x - 4) = -x + 4 = 4 - x.$$
Has the value of the expression changed? Yes, it has, because $x - 4 \neq 4 - x$.
Sometimes you may need to change the form of a denominator so that
you have a common denominator. But you must change the form without
changing the value of the rational expression.

EXAMPLES

Example 5. $\dfrac{4x}{x - 7} - \dfrac{3x}{7 - x}$

Solution.

$$-1(7 - x) = -7 + x$$
$$= x - 7$$

1. Notice that the denominators differ only in their order. If one of the denominators were turned around, it would match the other. You can change the order of one of the denominators if you multiply by -1. Try 7 - x.

$$\dfrac{-1}{-1} \cdot \dfrac{3x}{7 - x} = \dfrac{-3x}{x - 7}$$

2. But the value of the expression also changes if you multiply the denominator by -1. Since 1 is the identity element, you can multiply the whole rational by $\frac{-1}{-1}$ to change the form of the denominator without changing the value of the rational expression.

$$\dfrac{4x}{x - 7} - \dfrac{3x}{7 - x} = \dfrac{4x}{x - 7} - \dfrac{-3x}{x - 7}$$
$$= \dfrac{(4x) - (-3x)}{x - 7}$$
$$= \dfrac{4x + 3x}{x - 7}$$
$$= \dfrac{7x}{x - 7}$$

3. Substitute the new form for the old form. Now you can easily subtract the rational expressions.

Example 6. $\dfrac{x^2 + x - 9}{(x + 2)(x - 5)} - \dfrac{2x^2 + x + 1}{(x + 2)(5 - x)}$

Solution. $\dfrac{x^2 + x - 9}{(x + 2)(x - 5)} - \dfrac{2x^2 + x + 1}{(x + 2)(5 - x)}$

$$\dfrac{2x^2 + x + 1}{(x + 2)(5 - x)} = \dfrac{-1}{-1} \cdot \dfrac{(2x^2 + x + 1)}{(x + 2)(5 - x)}$$
$$= \dfrac{-2x^2 - x - 1}{(x + 2)(x - 5)}$$

1. Change 5 - x to x - 5 by multiplying the second rational expression by $\frac{-1}{-1}$.

$$\frac{x^2 + x - 9}{(x + 2)(x - 5)} - \frac{2x^2 + x + 1}{(x + 2)(5 - x)}$$

$$\frac{x^2 + x - 9}{(x + 2)(x - 5)} - \frac{-2x^2 - x - 1}{(x + 2)(x - 5)}$$

2. Combine and simplify.

$$\frac{(x^2 + x - 9) - (-2x^2 - x - 1)}{(x + 2)(x - 5)}$$

$$\frac{x^2 + x - 9 + 2x^2 + x + 1}{(x + 2)(x - 5)}$$

$$= \frac{3x^2 + 2x - 8}{(x + 2)(x - 5)}$$

$$= \frac{(3x - 4)\,\cancel{(x + 2)}}{\cancel{(x + 2)}\,(x - 5)}$$

$$\frac{3x - 4}{x - 5}$$

Exercises

Subtract and simplify.

1. $\dfrac{2}{5} - \dfrac{9}{5}$

2. $\dfrac{3}{7} - \dfrac{2}{7}$

3. $\dfrac{1}{9} - \dfrac{8}{9}$

4. $\dfrac{7}{12} - \dfrac{5}{12}$

5. $\dfrac{11}{a} - \dfrac{7}{a}$

6. $\dfrac{4}{x} - \dfrac{9}{x}$

7. $\dfrac{a}{c} - \dfrac{b}{c}$

8. $\dfrac{5}{y} - \dfrac{b}{y}$

9. $\dfrac{3x}{y^2} - \dfrac{5x}{y^2}$

10. $\dfrac{9x}{yz} - \dfrac{3y}{yz}$

11. $\dfrac{2x}{x + y} - \dfrac{2y}{x + y}$

12. $\dfrac{4a}{a - b} - \dfrac{4b}{a - b}$

13. $\dfrac{5x}{x^2 + y} - \dfrac{4x}{x^2 + y}$

14. $\dfrac{3a}{a^2 - b^2} - \dfrac{3b}{a^2 - b^2}$

15. $\dfrac{x + 4}{9} - \dfrac{x + 7}{9}$

16. $\dfrac{x - 6}{19} - \dfrac{x + 8}{19}$

17. $\dfrac{x + 4}{7} - \dfrac{x - 3}{7}$

18. $\dfrac{x - 5}{x + 2} - \dfrac{x + 7}{x + 2}$

19. $\dfrac{a+7}{a^2} - \dfrac{a-9}{a^2}$

20. $\dfrac{m-3}{n} - \dfrac{6}{n}$

21. $\dfrac{x^2+3}{x^2} - \dfrac{3}{x^2}$

22. $\dfrac{5}{a^2+3a-2} - \dfrac{7}{a^2+3a-2}$

23. $\dfrac{(x+2)}{x^2-3x-9} - \dfrac{(x-4)}{x^2-3x-9}$

24. $\dfrac{x^2-8x+13}{x^2-4x-12} - \dfrac{-x^2-4x-1}{x^2-4x-12}$

25. $\dfrac{4}{x-2} - \dfrac{10}{2-x}$

26. $\dfrac{a^3}{a-b} - \dfrac{a}{a-b}$

27. $\dfrac{x-3}{(x+2)\,(4-x)} - \dfrac{x+9}{(x+2)\,(x-4)}$

28. $\dfrac{3x^2+4x+12}{(x+9)\,(x-3)} - \dfrac{-2x^2+8x+15}{(x+9)\,(3-x)}$

29. $\dfrac{3a^2+2ab+2b^2}{(a+2b)\,(a-b)} - \dfrac{-2a^2+3ab+4b^2}{(a+2b)\,(b-a)}$

30. $\dfrac{3x^2+4x-10}{x^2+5x-36} - \dfrac{2x^2+x+18}{x^2+5x-36}$

ADDING AND SUBTRACTING RATIONAL EXPRESSIONS WITH DIFFERENT DENOMINATORS

Before you add or subtract rational numbers that have different denominators, you must change each rational into an equivalent rational expression that has the same denominator that the other rationals have. You might want to review pages 39-40, which explain how to find the LCM of two numbers. Here you will learn how to find the LCM of rational expressions.

EXAMPLES

Example 1. Compute $\dfrac{3}{2a} + \dfrac{5}{8a}$.

Solution. $\dfrac{3}{2a} + \dfrac{5}{8a}$

$2a \quad 8a \;=\; 2^3a$

1. To find the common denominator, determine what the LCM of $2a$ and $8a$ is. Find the prime factors of each denominator, and use the product of the highest power of each factor as the LCM. The highest power of 2 is 2^3, and the highest power of a is a. So the LCM is 2^3a, or $8a$.

$$\frac{3}{2a} \cdot \frac{4}{4} = \frac{12}{8a}$$

2. Now you must make equivalent rational expressions with the denominator 8*a*. What should you multiply with 2*a* to get the common denominator 8*a*? Since 4 · 2*a* = 8*a*, multiply the numerator and the denominator by 4.

$$\frac{3}{2a} + \frac{5}{8a} = \frac{12}{8a} + \frac{5}{8a}$$

3. Add.

$$= \frac{17}{8a}$$

Example 2. Simplify $\dfrac{2x - 5}{3x} - \dfrac{x - 1}{2x} + \dfrac{5x + 6}{12x^2}$.

Solution. $3x = 3 \cdot x$

$2x = 2 \cdot x$

$12x^2 = 2^2 \cdot 3 \cdot x^2$

1. Find the common denominator by prime factoring each denominator and finding the product of the highest powers of each factor.
$2^2 \cdot 3x^2 = 12x^2$, the LCM.

$$\frac{2x - 5}{3x} \cdot \frac{4x}{4x} = \frac{8x^2 - 20x}{12x^2}$$

$$\frac{x - 1}{2x} \cdot \frac{6x}{6x} = \frac{6x^2 - 6x}{12x^2}$$

2. Make equivalent rational expressions using $12x^2$ as the denominator.

$$\frac{2x - 5}{3x} - \frac{x - 1}{2x} + \frac{5x + 6}{12x^2}$$

$$\frac{(8x^2 - 20x)}{12x^2} - \frac{(6x^2 - 6x)}{12x^2} + \frac{(5x + 6)}{12x^2}$$

$$\frac{(8x^2 - 20x) - (6x^2 - 6x) + (5x + 6)}{12x^2}$$

3. Add numerators, remove parentheses, and combine like terms.

$$\frac{8x^2 - 20x - 6x^2 + 6x + 5x + 6}{12x^2}$$

$$\frac{2x^2 - 9x + 6}{12x^2}$$

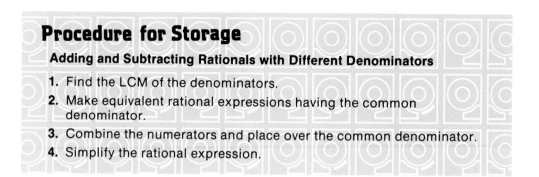

Procedure for Storage

Adding and Subtracting Rationals with Different Denominators

1. Find the LCM of the denominators.
2. Make equivalent rational expressions having the common denominator.
3. Combine the numerators and place over the common denominator.
4. Simplify the rational expression.

EXAMPLE

Example 3. Simplify. $\dfrac{y}{x^2 + xy} - \dfrac{x}{xy + y^2}$.

Solution.
$$\dfrac{y}{x^2 + xy} - \dfrac{x}{xy + y^2}$$

$$x^2 + xy = x(x + y)$$
$$xy + y^2 = y(x + y)$$

1. The LCM is $xy(x + y)$.

$$\dfrac{y}{x^2 + xy} = \dfrac{y}{x(x + y)} \cdot \dfrac{y}{y}$$

$$= \dfrac{y^2}{xy(x + y)}$$

$$\dfrac{x}{xy + y^2} = \dfrac{x}{y(x + y)} \cdot \dfrac{x}{x}$$

$$= \dfrac{x^2}{xy(x + y)}$$

2. Make equivalent rational expressions having the common denominator $xy(x + y)$.

$$\dfrac{y}{x^2 + xy} - \dfrac{x}{xy + y^2} = \dfrac{y^2}{xy(x + y)} - \dfrac{x^2}{xy(x + y)}$$

3. Subtract and simplify.

$$= \dfrac{y^2 - x^2}{xy(x + y)}$$

$$= \dfrac{(y - x)(y + x)}{xy(x + y)}$$

$$= \dfrac{(y - x)(x + y)}{xy(x + y)}$$

$$= \dfrac{(y - x)(x + y)}{xy(x + y)}$$

$$= \dfrac{y - x}{xy}$$

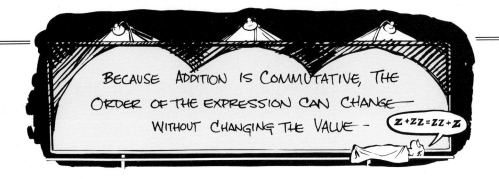

BECAUSE ADDITION IS COMMUTATIVE, THE ORDER OF THE EXPRESSION CAN CHANGE WITHOUT CHANGING THE VALUE — $z + zz = zz + z$

Exercises

Perform the indicated operations and simplify.

1. $\dfrac{3x}{4} + \dfrac{9}{16}$

2. $\dfrac{x}{9} - \dfrac{4x}{7}$

3. $\dfrac{a + b}{12} + \dfrac{a}{26}$

4. $\dfrac{x - 3}{18} + \dfrac{x + 7}{4}$

5. $\dfrac{x + y}{125} - \dfrac{x}{15}$

6. $\dfrac{a^2 + 3a}{52} + \dfrac{a^2 - 9}{28}$

7. $\dfrac{4}{3x} - \dfrac{7}{21x^3}$

8. $\dfrac{9}{3m^3} - \dfrac{14}{8m^2}$

9. $\dfrac{5}{2x^3y^2} + \dfrac{10}{xy}$

10. $\dfrac{3x}{9yz^3} - \dfrac{4x^2}{6y^3z}$

11. $\dfrac{14x^3y^2}{9z^5} + \dfrac{12xy}{4x^3z}$

12. $\dfrac{x + y}{3x} - \dfrac{x}{27y^2}$

13. $\dfrac{x^2 + y^3}{4xy} - \dfrac{x^2 + y}{9x^3}$

14. $\dfrac{x^2 + xy - y^2}{8x^4} - \dfrac{2x^2 + 3xy - 5y^2}{28x^3y}$

15. $\dfrac{3}{x^2 - y^2} + \dfrac{5}{x + y}$

16. $\dfrac{7}{(x + 2)(x - 5)} - \dfrac{9}{(x + 2)^2(x + 3)}$

17. $\dfrac{10}{x^2 - 6x - 27} + \dfrac{8}{x^2 - 3x - 18}$

18. $\dfrac{2x}{(x - 7)(x + 4)} - \dfrac{9}{(x - 7)^2}$

19. $\dfrac{3y}{y^2 + 7y + 10} - \dfrac{2y}{y^2 + 10y + 25}$

20. $\dfrac{x^2 - 4}{x^2} + \dfrac{x - y}{x}$

21. $\dfrac{5x}{x - 1} - \dfrac{6x^2}{x^2 - 1}$

22. $\dfrac{3x^2 - 7x + 3}{x^2 - 8x + 15} + \dfrac{-2x^2 + 2x + 3}{x^2 - 6x + 9}$

23. $\dfrac{5x^2 + 3x - 7}{x^2 + 2x - 63} - \dfrac{4x^2 + 8x + 7}{x^2 - 16x + 63}$

24. $\dfrac{1}{3x - 9} + \dfrac{1}{x} + \dfrac{1}{4x + 16}$

25. $\dfrac{2x}{x + 4} - \dfrac{3x}{x^2 - 5x - 36}$

26. $\dfrac{a + 3}{a + 5} - \dfrac{a + 2}{a - 5} + \dfrac{a}{a^2 - 25}$

27. $\dfrac{2x^2 + 3x}{2x + 8} + \dfrac{x^2 + 2x - 28}{3x - 12}$

28. $\dfrac{x^4}{x^2 + 12x + 32} - \dfrac{8x^3}{x^4 - 4x^3 - 32x^2}$

29. $\dfrac{a + b}{a - b} - \dfrac{4}{a + b} + \dfrac{a^2 + 3a - 10}{a^2 - b^2}$

30. $\dfrac{x}{x + 3} + x - \dfrac{x}{x + 5}$

COMPLEX RATIONAL EXPRESSIONS

 DEFINITION

≫**Complex rational expression:** an algebraic expression of the form $\frac{c}{d}$ where either c or d or c and d are rational expressions.

The first complex rational expression below has a rational expression in the numerator; the second has one in the numerator and another in the denominator; the third has one in the denominator.

$$\frac{\dfrac{x}{y}}{4} \qquad\qquad \frac{\dfrac{x+2}{x^2}}{\dfrac{x+2}{x}} \qquad\qquad \frac{x^2+3x-9}{\dfrac{x+2}{x^3}}$$

You should always simplify a complex expression. The examples in this section show two methods you can use. Choose the method that seems easier to you.

EXAMPLES

Example 1.   Simplify $\dfrac{\dfrac{x}{y}}{4}$.

Solution.

Method 1

Multiply the numerator and the denominator by the common denominator of the rationals in the numerator and the denominator. The LCM of y and 1 is y.

Remember

$$\frac{y}{y} = 1$$

$$\frac{\dfrac{x}{y}}{4} = \frac{\dfrac{x}{y} \cdot y}{4 \cdot y}$$

Simplify if possible

$$= \frac{\dfrac{x}{y} \cdot y}{4 \cdot y}$$

$$= \frac{x}{4y}$$

Method 2

Since the fraction sign also means "divided by", change the expression to a divison problem. Then multiply the numerator by the reciprocal of the denominator.

$$\frac{\dfrac{x}{y}}{4} = \frac{x}{y} \div \frac{4}{1}$$

$$= \frac{x}{y} \cdot \frac{1}{4}$$

$$= \frac{x}{4y}$$

Example 2.   Simplify $\dfrac{\dfrac{x+2}{x^2}}{\dfrac{x+2}{x}}$

Solution.

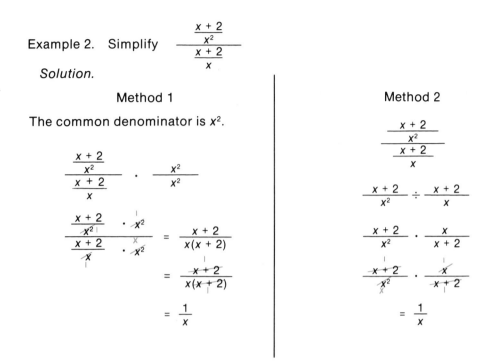

Method 1

The common denominator is x^2.

$$\dfrac{\dfrac{x+2}{x^2}}{\dfrac{x+2}{x}} \cdot \dfrac{x^2}{x^2}$$

$$\dfrac{\dfrac{x+2}{x^2} \cdot x^2}{\dfrac{x+2}{x} \cdot x^2} = \dfrac{x+2}{x(x+2)}$$

$$= \dfrac{x+2}{x(x+2)}$$

$$= \dfrac{1}{x}$$

Method 2

$$\dfrac{\dfrac{x+2}{x^2}}{\dfrac{x+2}{x}}$$

$$\dfrac{x+2}{x^2} \div \dfrac{x+2}{x}$$

$$\dfrac{x+2}{x^2} \cdot \dfrac{x}{x+2}$$

$$\dfrac{x+2}{x^2} \cdot \dfrac{x}{x+2}$$

$$= \dfrac{1}{x}$$

Procedure for Storage

Simplifying Complex Rational Expressions

Method 1

1. Find the common denominator of the rational expression in the numerator and the denominator.
2. Multiply the numerator and the denominator by the common denominator found in step 1.
3. Simplify.

Method 2

1. If possible, simplify the numerator and the denominator separately.
2. Divide as indicated.
3. Simplify.

EXAMPLES

Example 3. Simplify $\dfrac{1 + \dfrac{a^2}{b^2}}{1 - \dfrac{a}{b}}$

Solution.

Method 1

The common denominator is b^2.

$$\dfrac{1 + \dfrac{a^2}{b^2}}{1 - \dfrac{a}{b}} \cdot \dfrac{b^2}{b^2}$$

$$\dfrac{b^2 + a^2}{b^2 - ab}$$

Method 2

Simplify both the numerator and the denominator.

$$1 + \dfrac{a^2}{b^2} = \dfrac{b^2}{b^2} + \dfrac{a^2}{b^2}$$

$$= \dfrac{b^2 + a^2}{b^2}$$

$$1 - \dfrac{a}{b} = \dfrac{b}{b} - \dfrac{a}{b}$$

$$= \dfrac{b - a}{b}$$

Divide as indicated.

$$\dfrac{1 + \dfrac{a^2}{b^2}}{1 - \dfrac{a}{b}} = \dfrac{\dfrac{b^2 + a^2}{b^2}}{\dfrac{b - a}{b}}$$

$$= \dfrac{b^2 + a^2}{b^2} \div \dfrac{b - a}{b}$$

Simplify.

$$= \dfrac{b^2 + a^2}{b^2} \cdot \dfrac{b}{b - a}$$

$$= \dfrac{b^2 + a^2}{\cancel{b^2}} \cdot \dfrac{\cancel{b}}{b - a}$$

$$= \dfrac{b^2 + a^2}{b^2 - ab}$$

Example 4.   Simplify $\dfrac{\dfrac{x^2 - 9}{4x}}{\dfrac{x + 3}{8x^2}}$.

Solution.   Method 1

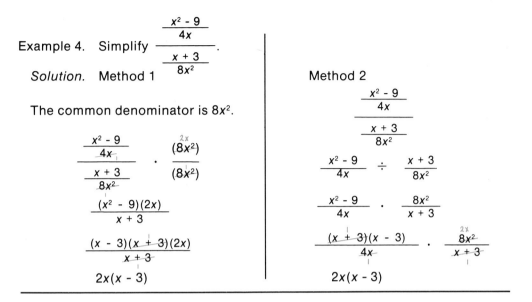

The common denominator is $8x^2$.

$$\dfrac{\dfrac{x^2 - 9}{4x}}{\dfrac{x + 3}{8x^2}} \cdot \dfrac{(8x^2)}{(8x^2)}$$

$$\dfrac{(x^2 - 9)(2x)}{x + 3}$$

$$\dfrac{(x - 3)(x + 3)(2x)}{x + 3}$$

$$2x(x - 3)$$

Method 2

$$\dfrac{\dfrac{x^2 - 9}{4x}}{\dfrac{x + 3}{8x^2}}$$

$$\dfrac{x^2 - 9}{4x} \div \dfrac{x + 3}{8x^2}$$

$$\dfrac{x^2 - 9}{4x} \cdot \dfrac{8x^2}{x + 3}$$

$$\dfrac{(x + 3)(x - 3)}{4x} \cdot \dfrac{8x^2}{x + 3}$$

$$2x(x - 3)$$

Exercises

Simplify each complex rational expression.

1. $\dfrac{\dfrac{1}{4}}{\dfrac{5}{8}}$

2. $\dfrac{\dfrac{1}{a + b}}{\dfrac{a + b}{a^2 - b^2}}$

3. $\dfrac{\dfrac{9}{5}}{\dfrac{3}{7}}$

4. $\dfrac{\dfrac{x + y}{x - y}}{x^2 - y^2}$

5. $\dfrac{x^2 + 2xy + y^2}{\dfrac{x + y}{x - y}}$

6. $\dfrac{3 - \dfrac{2}{3}}{2 + \dfrac{5}{6}}$

7. $\dfrac{\dfrac{x}{y} + 1}{\dfrac{x}{y} - \dfrac{y}{x}}$

8. $\dfrac{\dfrac{5}{x + y}}{x - y}$

9. $\dfrac{\dfrac{m + n}{m - n}}{m^2 - n^2}$

10. $\dfrac{\dfrac{1}{m} + m}{\dfrac{1}{m} - m}$

11. $\dfrac{\dfrac{3a}{2a^2 + 4a}}{\dfrac{6a}{a^2 + 2a}}$

12. $\dfrac{x}{1 + \dfrac{1}{x}}$

MEMORY RECALL

Identify.
  complex rational expression
  rational expression

You should be able to do the following:
  1. Identify the terms of a rational expression.
  2. Tell when a rational expression will be undefined.
  3. Simplify rational expressions.
  4. Multiply and divide rational expressions.
  5. Add and subtract rational expressions with and without common denominators.
  6. Simplify complex rational expressions.

You should be able to solve the following problems:
Give the values for x that make each rational expression undefined.

1. $\dfrac{2x + 1}{x^2 + 5x}$

2. $\dfrac{x - 8}{x^2 - 4x - 12}$

3. $\dfrac{x - 9}{3x^2 + 16x + 21}$

Find the LCM for each pair of polynomials.

4. $x^2 - 2x - 63$ $x^2 - 3x - 54$
5. $2x^2 + 11x + 5$ $2x^2 - 15x - 8$
6. $x^2 + 14x + 24$ $x^3 + 20x^2 + 96x$

Simplify each rational expression.

7. $\dfrac{x^4 - 10x^3}{x^6 + 8x^5 + 15x^4}$

8. $\dfrac{2x - 14}{2x^2 - 22x + 56}$

9. $\dfrac{3x + 4}{6x^2 - 7x - 20}$

Perform the indicated operation and simplify.

10. $\dfrac{x^2 - 5x - 14}{2x + 3} \cdot \dfrac{2x^2 + x - 3}{x^2 - 7x}$

11. $\dfrac{x^2 + 13x + 22}{3} \cdot \dfrac{9}{x + 2}$

12. $\dfrac{2x^2 + 10x - 28}{x - 6} \cdot \dfrac{2x^2 - 21x + 54}{3x^3 - 5x^2} \cdot \dfrac{x^4}{2x^2 - 5x - 18}$

13. $\dfrac{x - 1}{x^2 + 9x + 18} \div \dfrac{x^2}{x^2 + x - 30}$

14. $\dfrac{5x^3}{3x^2 + x - 10} \div \dfrac{15x}{6x^2 + 13x + 2}$

15. $\dfrac{x}{x^2 - y^2} + \dfrac{y}{x^2 - y^2}$

16. $\dfrac{x + 1}{x^2 + 2x - 5} - \dfrac{x - 7}{x^2 + 2x - 5}$

17. $\dfrac{x + 2y}{27y} + \dfrac{x}{3}$

18. $\dfrac{x^2 + 2x + 5}{x^2 - 2x - 24} + \dfrac{-5x - 23}{x^2 - 7x + 6}$

19. $\dfrac{x + y}{x^2 + 2xy + y^2} + \dfrac{3x}{x - y} - \dfrac{2x + 3y}{x + y}$

20. $\dfrac{\dfrac{2x}{y} + 1}{\dfrac{2x + y}{y^3}}$

CHAPTER 12

RATIONAL EQUATIONS

Looking out across the shimmering lake, Glenn Osborne marveled at the beauty that God created. Glenn's work as a freshwater zoologist for the National Park Service keeps him in close contact with God's wonderful world as he studies different types of animal life in the many lakes and ponds. In this particular lake, Glenn is studying tiny swimming and drifting animals, one of which is the phantom midge larva, a stage in the life of the Clear Lake gnat. Unlike most zooplankton, which are usually microscopic aquatic organisms, the phantom midge sometimes measures half an inch long. It is called "phantom" because of the ghostly appearance created by its transparent body and two silvery air sacs. These two air bladders expand (inflate), allowing the midge to rise to the surface of the lake at night. Then the air sacs deflate, allowing the midge to descend to the bottom of the lake during the day.

This small creation of God fascinated Glenn so much that he decided to study the midge larva in greater detail. But Glenn realized that he had to do some study of water pressures at various depths in the lake to determine how the pressure would affect the midge in its daily migrations. So he rigged up an apparatus to lower into the lake. Using the readings from the apparatus, he can determine the water pressure at a certain depth by substituting the values into the equation

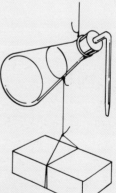

$$P_2 = \left(\frac{P_1 V}{T_1} \right) \left(\frac{T_2}{V - W} \right),$$

in which the letters have the following meanings:

P_1 = atmospheric pressure

P_2 = water pressure at a given depth

V = volume of air in the container before submersion

T_1 = temperature of the air in the container before submersion

T_2 = temperature of the air in the container after submersion

W = volume of water in the container after submersion

This equation is a rational equation. Glenn frequently uses equations like this one to determine the information he needs to study the effects of water pressure on the phantom midge larva and other aquatic animals. Can you solve a rational equation like the one Glenn is working with? By the time you finish this chapter, you will be able to.

NUMERICAL DENOMINATORS

In Chapter 3 you learned to solve equations containing fractions with variables in the numerators. The denominators were always constant. To solve these equations, you cleared them of the fractions by multiplying both sides of each equation by the common denominator. Then you solved the resulting equations.

EXAMPLES

Example 1. Solve $\dfrac{x}{5} = 7$

Solution.

$\dfrac{x}{5} = 7$ **1.** Determine the common denominator which is 5.

$5\dfrac{x}{5} = 7 \cdot 5$ **2.** Multiply both sides by the common denominator.

$x = 35$ **3.** Solve and check.

Check. Does $\dfrac{35}{5} = 7$?

Example 2. Solve $\dfrac{x + 4}{2} + \dfrac{x - 6}{3} = \dfrac{1}{6}$

Solution. $6\left(\dfrac{x + 4}{2} + \dfrac{x - 6}{3} \right) = 6\left(\dfrac{1}{6} \right)$ The common denominator is 6. Multiply both sides by 6 and solve.

$6\left(\dfrac{x + 4}{2} \right) + 6\left(\dfrac{x - 6}{3} \right) = 6\left(\dfrac{1}{6} \right)$

$\overset{3}{6}\left(\dfrac{x + 4}{\underset{1}{2}} \right) + \overset{2}{6}\left(\dfrac{x - 6}{\underset{1}{3}} \right) = 1$

$3(x + 4) + 2(x - 6) = 1$

$3x + 12 + 2x - 12 = 1$

$5x = 1$

$x = \dfrac{1}{5}$

Example 3. Solve $\dfrac{x - 7}{7} - \dfrac{x + 2}{3} = 1$

Solution. $21 \left(\dfrac{x - 7}{7} - \dfrac{x + 2}{3} \right) = 21 \cdot 1$ The common denominator is 21. Multiply both sides of the equation by 21.

$$21 \left(\dfrac{x - 7}{7} \right) - 21 \left(\dfrac{x + 2}{3} \right) = 21 \qquad \text{What property is used in this step?}$$

$$\overset{3}{\cancel{21}} \left(\dfrac{x - 7}{\underset{1}{\cancel{7}}} \right) - \overset{7}{\cancel{21}} \left(\dfrac{x + 2}{\underset{1}{\cancel{3}}} \right) = 21$$

$$3(x - 7) - 7(x + 2) = 21$$

$$3x - 21 - 7x - 14 = 21$$

$$-4x - 35 = 21$$

$$-4x = 56$$

$$x = -14$$

Check $\dfrac{-14 - 7}{7} - \dfrac{-14 + 2}{3} = 1$

$$\dfrac{-21}{7} - \dfrac{-12}{3} = 1$$

$$-3 + 4 = 1$$

$$1 = 1$$

Exercises

Solve.

1. $\dfrac{x}{4} = 10$

2. $\dfrac{x}{9} = \dfrac{1}{8}$

3. $\dfrac{m}{3} = 9$

4. $\dfrac{a}{6} = \dfrac{1}{3}$

5. $\dfrac{x + 1}{3} = 4$

6. $\dfrac{x - 9}{7} = \dfrac{1}{14}$

7. $\dfrac{a + 3}{5} = \dfrac{a - 2}{10}$

8. $\dfrac{x - 7}{2} = \dfrac{x - 3}{4}$

9. $\dfrac{a - 9}{15} = \dfrac{a - 6}{5}$

10. $\dfrac{x + 2}{3} = \dfrac{x + 9}{2}$

11. $\dfrac{a + 4}{11} - \dfrac{a + 2}{3} = 7$

12. $\dfrac{x - 12}{2} + \dfrac{x + 7}{5} = \dfrac{1}{10}$

13. $\dfrac{m + 5}{7} - \dfrac{m - 3}{6} = \dfrac{m + 3}{2}$

14. $\dfrac{y - 5}{12} + \dfrac{y + 3}{3} = \dfrac{2}{24}$

15. $\dfrac{x+4}{9} - \dfrac{x-7}{3} = 2$

16. $\dfrac{a-3}{2} = \dfrac{a+4}{3} - 7$

17. $\dfrac{x+5}{9} = \dfrac{x-8}{3} + 2$

18. $\dfrac{m^2}{5} = \dfrac{m}{10}$

19. $\dfrac{x^2}{9} = \dfrac{x}{3} + 4$

20. $\dfrac{x^2}{4} - \dfrac{29x}{8} = 3$

FIRST AND SECOND DEGREE DENOMINATORS

Although you are solving rational equations in this section, you apply the rules that you have already learned for solving an equation containing fractions. The denominator in each rational expression will be either a first or a second degree polynomial.

DEFINITION

≫**Rational equation:** an equation containing a rational expression with a variable in the denominator.

EXAMPLE

Example 1. $\dfrac{9}{x+3} = 9$.

Solution. The common denominator is $x + 3$. Multiply both sides of the equation by the common denominator and solve.

$$(x + 3)\left(\dfrac{9}{x+3}\right) = 9\,(x + 3)$$

$$9 = 9x + 27$$

$$-18 = 9x$$

$$-2 = x$$

Check.

$$\dfrac{9}{-2 + 3} = 9$$

$$\dfrac{9}{1} = 9$$

$$9 = 9$$

The steps for solving rational equations and fractional equations are the same. You must always check your solutions in the original equation, though, for you might introduce new roots into the equation whenever you multiply an equation by an expression containing a variable. Remember that any solution that does not check is an extraneous root.

EXAMPLES

Example 2. Solve $\dfrac{5}{x + 1} = \dfrac{-2}{x - 6}$.

Solution. The common denominator is $(x + 1)(x - 6)$. Multiply both sides of the equation by the common denominator and solve.

$$\frac{5}{x + 1} = \frac{-2}{x - 6}$$

$$(x + 1)(x - 6)\left(\frac{5}{x + 1}\right) = (x + 1)(x - 6)\left(\frac{-2}{x - 6}\right)$$

$$5(x - 6) = -2(x + 1)$$

$$5x - 30 = -2x - 2$$

$$7x = 28$$

$$x = 4$$

Check.

$$\frac{5}{4 + 1} = \frac{-2}{4 - 6}$$

$$\frac{5}{5} = \frac{-2}{-2}$$

$$1 = 1 \qquad\qquad \text{There are no extraneous roots.}$$

Example 3. Solve $\dfrac{x - 12}{x - 10} = \dfrac{2}{x} - \dfrac{20}{x^2 - 10x}$

Solution. Multiply both sides by the common denominator, which is $x(x - 10)$.

$$\frac{x - 12}{x - 10} = \frac{2}{x} - \frac{20}{x^2 - 10x}$$

$$x(x - 10)\left(\frac{x - 12}{x - 10}\right) = \left(\frac{2}{x} - \frac{20}{x^2 - 10x}\right)x(x - 10)$$

$$x(x - 10)\left(\frac{x - 12}{x - 10}\right) = \left(\frac{2}{x}\right)x(x - 10) - \left(\frac{20}{x(x - 10)}\right)x(x - 10)$$

$$x(x - 12) = 2(x - 10) - 20$$

$$x(x - 12) = 2(x - 10) - 20 \qquad \text{Solve as a quadratic equation.}$$

$$x^2 - 12x = 2x - 20 - 20$$

$$x^2 - 12x = 2x - 40$$

$$x^2 - 14x + 40 = 0$$

$$(x - 10)(x - 4) = 0$$

$$x - 10 = 0 \quad \text{or} \quad x - 4 = 0$$

$$x = 10 \qquad\qquad x = 4$$

Check.

$$\frac{10 - 12}{10 - 10} = \frac{2}{10} - \frac{20}{10^2 - 10 \cdot 10}$$

$$\frac{-2}{0} = \frac{2}{10} - \frac{20}{0}$$

Since division by 0 is undefined, 10 is an extraneous root.

$$\frac{4 - 12}{4 - 10} = \frac{2}{4} - \frac{20}{4^2 - 10 \cdot 4}$$

$$\frac{-8}{-6} = \frac{1}{2} - \frac{20}{16 - 40}$$

$$\frac{4}{3} = \frac{1}{2} - \frac{20}{-24}$$

$$\frac{4}{3} = \frac{1}{2} + \frac{20}{24}$$

$$\frac{4}{3} = \frac{8}{6}$$

$$\frac{4}{3} = \frac{4}{3} \qquad \text{So 4 is a real root.}$$

Example 4. $\dfrac{a + 4}{a - 6} - \dfrac{5}{a} = 1$

Solution. The common denominator is $a(a - 6)$.

$$\frac{a + 4}{a - 6} - \frac{5}{a} = 1$$

$$a(a - 6)\left(\frac{a + 4}{a - 6} - \frac{5}{a}\right) = 1 \cdot a(a - 6)$$

$$a(a - 6)\left(\frac{a + 4}{a - 6}\right) - \left[a(a - 6)\left(\frac{5}{a}\right)\right] = a^2 - 6a$$

$$a(a - 6)\left(\frac{a + 4}{a - 6}\right) - \left[a(a - 6)\left(\frac{5}{a}\right)\right] = a^2 - 6a$$

$$a(a + 4) - 5(a - 6) = a^2 - 6a$$

$$a^2 + 4a - 5a + 30 = a^2 - 6a$$

$$30 = -5a$$

$$-6 = a$$

Exercises

Solve each rational equation.

1. $\dfrac{2}{x} = 8$

2. $\dfrac{9}{x} = 3$

3. $\dfrac{8}{y} = 16$

4. $\dfrac{20}{m} = 4$

5. $\dfrac{8}{x + 2} = 3$

6. $\dfrac{10}{a - 5} = 7$

7. $\dfrac{36}{a + 5} = 6$

8. $\dfrac{x + 3}{x - 2} = 1$

9. $\dfrac{x - 5}{x - 4} = 2$

10. $\dfrac{m + 4}{m - 9} = 2$

11. $\dfrac{5}{x + 9} = \dfrac{7}{x - 8}$

12. $\dfrac{6}{x + 3} = \dfrac{2}{x}$

13. $\dfrac{2}{a - 7} = \dfrac{9}{a + 3}$

14. $\dfrac{4}{3x} + 7 = \dfrac{1}{6x}$

15. $\dfrac{6x + 5}{2x} - \dfrac{8x + 3}{9x} = \dfrac{5}{18}$

16. $\dfrac{x + 8}{x - 9} = 18$

17. $\dfrac{a - 3}{4} - \dfrac{5}{a + 2} = 1$

18. $\dfrac{x + 3}{x - 4} = \dfrac{4}{x} + \dfrac{28}{x^2 - 4x}$

19. $\dfrac{m + 4}{m - 9} = \dfrac{m - 3}{m - 6}$

20. $\dfrac{x}{x + 2} = \dfrac{x + 5}{x - 4}$

21. $\dfrac{a - 5}{a + 3} = \dfrac{a + 3}{a + 4}$

22. $\dfrac{x + 12}{x - 2} - \dfrac{4}{x} = \dfrac{-4}{x^2 - 2x}$

23. $\dfrac{4}{x^2 - 8x + 15} = \dfrac{1}{x^2 - 3x - 10}$

24. $\dfrac{3}{x^2 + 6x + 5} = \dfrac{-5}{x^2 + x - 20}$

25. $\dfrac{1}{x^2 - 2x - 8} - \dfrac{4}{x^2 - x - 12} = \dfrac{2}{x^2 - 2x - 8}$

26. $\dfrac{5}{x^2 - 2x - 15} + \dfrac{3}{x^2 - 3x - 10} = \dfrac{-2}{x^2 - 2x - 15}$

LIMITATIONS OF COMPUTERS

The computer is an essential tool to modern man. Everywhere one goes he finds some form of a computer in action. Whether the computer is a machine-programmed to fly spacecraft or a small pocket calculator to help with math homework, computers are now as common as hammers and screwdrivers. Despite the fact that computers have so many uses, they also have limitations.

A computer can make no judgments because it is not human and cannot think for itself. It cannot decide whether or not a thing is wrong or right. A computer can do no more than a person programs it to do. A programmer may program a computer to "believe" certain things, but the programmer is actually making the decisions for the computer. Sometimes people use computers to help them

make judgments. For example, a computer might be used to compile, list, and categorize clues that will aid police in solving a crime; but the computer cannot find the motive behind the crime.

Because a computer is unable to think for itself, it is absolutely helpless without a program. If a programmer writes a program incorrectly, the computer will process the data incor-

rectly. A programmer may write a program that repeats errors thousands and even millions of times, thus causing much needless work. The computer cannot recognize the mistake or correct the error. It cannot change the instructions it is given.

Computers cannot solve all types of problems. For example, many unknown variables affect weather. A computer used to predict the weather will not be able to take these variables into account. A human working on the problem could make an educated guess; the computer would be virtually useless.

Another problem with computers is that they are mechanical devices that are often subject to failure. The failure may occur because of faulty equipment or an interruption in the power supply. Because we depend so heavily on computers today, a computer that has "gone down" (stopped functioning efficiently) can cause many problems. Perhaps you have had to stand in line and wait at the bank because the computer went down.

The purchase and upkeep of a computer system can cost thousands and even millions of dollars, depending on the type of system. Although the cost of computer equipment steadily declines, it still limits the availability of computers for many people.

A list of their limitations tends to make computers sound useless. They are not! They are a tool essential to modern society. But their usefulness depends on man's recognizing the limits of their talents and making the most of what they can accomplish.

PROBLEM SOLVING

Do you think word problems are difficult? If you have kept up with your work, you should find them quite simple—particularly investment and mixture problems, since you have had them before.

Have you remembered to ask God to help you study carefully and thoughtfully? He is willing, ready, and able to help; but don't expect God to help you understand the lessons if you don't spend the necessary amount of time studying on your own.

In II Samuel 22 you can read one of David's psalms of thanksgiving. He tells how God protected him from his enemies and comforted him in trouble. Do you trust in God for your strength? Only He can bring peace and stability to your life.

You now have a strong foundation in algebraic concepts. It is up to you to build on this foundation and to practice and expand your knowledge of mathematics.

What are the steps to solving a word problem? Write them down so you will remember them. If you have already forgotten them, look back to page 112. You have learned two ways to solve word problems: with one variable and one equation or with two variables and two equations. Choose the method that you like best.

EXAMPLES

Example 1. What number added to both the numerator and the denominator of $\frac{3}{5}$ makes a fraction equal to $\frac{6}{7}$?

Solution.

$$\frac{3 + x}{5 + x} = \frac{6}{7}$$

1. Let $x =$ the number to be added to the numerator and the denominator. Write the appropriate equation.

$$7(5 + x)\left(\frac{3 + x}{5 + x}\right) = \frac{6}{7} \cdot 7(5 + x)$$

$$7(5 + x)\left(\frac{3 + x}{5 + x}\right) = \frac{6}{7} \cdot 7(5 + x)$$

$$7(3 + x) = 6(5 + x)$$

$$21 + 7x = 30 + 6x$$

$$7x - 6x = 30 - 21$$

$$x = 9$$

2. Multiply both sides of the equation by the common denominator $7(5 + x)$ and solve.
Check your solution.

Example 2. Find the number whose reciprocal, when subtracted from $\frac{8}{7}$, gives $\frac{17}{21}$.

Solution.

$$\text{Let } x = \text{ the number}$$

$$\frac{1}{x} = \text{ the reciprocal}$$

$$\frac{8}{7} - \frac{1}{x} = \frac{17}{21}$$

$$21x \left(\frac{8}{7} - \frac{1}{x} \right) = \frac{17}{21} (21x) \qquad \begin{array}{l}\text{The common denominator} \\ \text{is } 21x.\end{array}$$

$$\overset{3}{21}x \left(\frac{8}{\underset{1}{7}} \right) - 21x \left(\frac{1}{x} \right) = \frac{17}{\underset{1}{21}} (21x)$$

$$24x - 21 = 17x$$

$$24x - 17x = 21$$

$$7x = 21$$

$$x = 3 \qquad \qquad \text{The number is 3.}$$

Check. Does $\frac{8}{7} - \frac{1}{3} = \frac{17}{21}$?

You could solve this problem with two variables.

$$\text{Let } x = \text{ the number}$$
$$y = \text{ the reciprocal of the number.}$$

$$xy = 1$$

$$\frac{8}{7} - y = \frac{17}{21}$$

$$-y = \frac{17}{21} - \frac{8}{7}$$

$$-y = \frac{17}{21} - \frac{24}{21}$$

$$-y = \frac{-7}{21}$$

$$y = \frac{1}{3}$$

$$xy = 1$$

$$x \cdot \frac{1}{3} = 1$$

$$x = 3$$

1. Form two equations from the information in the problem. Remember that the product of a number and its reciprocal is 1.

2. Solve the system of equations.

3. Substitute this value of y in the first equation and find x.

The number is 3.

Example 3. Find three consecutive integers such that $\frac{1}{5}$ of the first plus $\frac{3}{4}$ of the second less the third is -2.

Solution.   Let x = the first integer
$$x + 1 = \text{the second integer}$$
$$x + 2 = \text{the third integer}$$

$$\frac{x}{5} + \frac{3(x + 1)}{4} - (x + 2) = -2$$

$$20\left(\frac{x}{5} + \frac{3(x + 1)}{4} - (x + 2)\right) = -2(20)$$

$$4x + 15(x + 1) - 20x - 40 = -40$$

$$4x + 15x + 15 - 20x - 40 = -40$$

$$x = 15$$

So the integers are 15, 16, and 17.

Check. Does $\frac{1}{5}(15) + \frac{3}{4}(16) - 17 = -2$?

Exercises

Solve.

1. What number must be added to the numerator and the denominator of $\frac{5}{11}$ to make a rational number equivalent to $\frac{3}{4}$?

2. What number must be subtracted from the numerator and the denominator of $\frac{7}{12}$ to make a rational number equivalent to $\frac{3}{8}$?

3. What number must be added to the numerator and subtracted from the denominator of $\frac{1}{2}$ to make a rational number equivalent to $-\frac{8}{7}$?

4. One number is six less than another number. The quotient of the larger divided by the smaller is $\frac{5}{2}$. What are the two numbers?

5. The sum of two numbers is 7. If 1 is added to seven times the smaller and then divided by the larger, the result is 3. Find the two numbers.

6. The width of a rectangle is one-half the length. If the area is 648 square inches, what are the dimensions of the rectangle?

7. When Jack and Emily went to the state fair, they paid $10 for parking, admission to the fair, and food. In addition they spent $\frac{1}{4}$ of the money they had taken with them for rides. How much did they start out with that day if they returned home with $\frac{4}{7}$ of their money?

8. Divide 84 into two parts so that the smaller part divided by the larger part is equal to $\frac{3}{4}$.

9. The sum of a number and the reciprocal of twice the number equals $\frac{41}{24}$. Find the number.

10. Find three consecutive odd integers such that the sum of $\frac{1}{7}$ of the first, $\frac{1}{5}$ of the third, and three times the second is 77.

INVESTMENT PROBLEMS

In Luke 19:11-27 Jesus told a parable about a nobleman who gave each of his ten servants a certain amount of money to manage. Two of the servants increased the amount given them. The third servant, afraid that he would lose what he had, hid the money. When the nobleman returned, he was very angry with the third servant because the servant could at least have invested the money and gotten interest from it. But he had done nothing.

What do you think the spiritual application of this parable is? Are you investing all that God has given you?

The main formula that you must remember when solving investment problems is $i = prt$, where i stands for the interest gained on an investment, p is the principal amount invested, r is the interest rate in decimal form, and t is the time of the investment in years.

EXAMPLES

Example 1. For $2\frac{1}{2}$ years Mr. Williams invested $5000 in a bank paying 8% simple interest. How much interest did he gain?

Solution. Using the formula $i = prt$, substitute values for p, r, and t.

$r = .08$ (notice 8% is changed to decimal form)

$t = \dfrac{5}{2}$

$i = p \ r \ t$

$i = (5000) \ (.08) \ \dfrac{5}{2}$

$i = 400 \ (\dfrac{5}{2})$

$i = \dfrac{2000}{2}$

$i = 1000$

Example 2. The freshmen saved money for their senior trip. At the end of their freshman year, they invested one-third of their money in a savings account yielding $5\frac{1}{2}$% interest and one-half of their money in an account yielding 8% interest. The rest was put in a checking account, yielding 5% interest. If the total interest per year from all three accounts is $40, how much money did the freshman class invest?

Solution.

1. Let x represent the total amount of money the freshman class invested. Use a chart for simplification.

	p	r	t	$=$	i
first investment	$\frac{x}{3}$	0.055	1		$\frac{x}{3}(0.055)$
second investment	$\frac{x}{2}$	0.08	1		$\frac{x}{2}(0.08)$
third investment	$\frac{x}{6}$	0.05	1		$\frac{x}{6}(0.05)$

2. Since the total interest is $40, you can set up an equation.
$$\left(\frac{x}{3}\right)(0.055) + \left(\frac{x}{2}\right)(0.08) + \left(\frac{x}{6}\right)(0.05) = 40$$

3. This equation has fractions and decimals. We will eliminate the fractions first. The common denominator is 6.
$$6\left[\left(\frac{x}{3}\right)(0.055) + \left(\frac{x}{2}\right)(0.08) + \left(\frac{x}{6}\right)(0.05)\right] = 6(40)$$
$$2x(0.055) + 3x(0.08) + x(0.05) = 240$$

4. To eliminate the decimals, multiply both sides by 1000. Do you know why?
$$1000[2x(0.055) + 3x(0.08) + x(0.05)] = 1000(240)$$
$$110x + 240x + 50x = 240,000$$
$$400x = 240,000$$
$$x = 600$$

Therefore, the freshman class invested $600 for that year.

Exercises

1. Mr. Willis has one-fifth of his savings invested at 6%, three-fifths at 8%, and the rest at 10%. His total interest from his savings is $1078.00 annually. How much does he have invested at each rate?

2. Mary Sue invested $2000, part at $5\frac{1}{2}$% and part at 7%. If the total yearly income from the two investments is $115.22, how much is invested in each account?

3. Mrs. Weber has a sum of money invested at 9% and another sum equalling one-third of the first sum invested at $5\frac{3}{4}$%. The yearly income from the 9% investment exceeds the interest of the $5\frac{3}{4}$% investment by $425.00. How much is invested at each rate?

4. Grace Gordon plans to invest her $10,000 in three kinds of stock. She will invest half as much in stock A as B and the rest in stock C, which yield 4%, 7%, and 11% respectively. If her total interest for a year is $830.00, how much will she invest in stocks A, B, and C?

5. The yearly interest income from two investments is $1050.00. If $3000 is invested at a rate two percentage points higher than an $8000 investment, what are the interest rates for the two investments?

6. Mr. and Mrs. Stees plan to invest $8500 in two accounts, the first paying 8% interest and the second paying $6\frac{1}{2}$% interest. How much should they invest in each account in order to gain $3302.50 in 5 years?

7. Paul plans to buy some stocks in a new computer company. He can buy preferred stock, which yields an average of 11% interest, and he can buy common stock, which yields an average of 9% interest. If he invests three-fourths of his money in preferred stock and one-fourth in common stock, he will gain $1312.50 in $2\frac{1}{2}$ years. How much must Paul invest?

8. Mr. Young will make two $8000 investments. If one account yields 11%, what should the interest rate be on the other account to make a yearly total of $1720.00 in interest?

9. Mr. and Mrs. Beach opened a retirement account that will yield $9\frac{1}{2}$% interest annually. They also invested a certain amount in a passbook savings account that pays $5\frac{3}{4}$% interest. If their total investment is $2200 and they gain a total of $171.50 annually in interest, how much did they invest in each account?

10. The H. Finn Realty Company makes two investments in different companies. They invest $17,000 in one company and $12,000 in the other, whose rate of interest is four-fifths the rate of the first investment. They expect to make $3990 in interest income each year from these investments. What is the rate of return (interest) on each investment?

MIXTURE PROBLEMS

Mixture problems appear most extensively in chemistry and in business applications. Your mother works with mixtures in her baking (or kitchen chemistry) and even in her routine housework. For example, she has to dilute a cleaning solution instead of using it full strength. When solving mixture problems, use a chart to organize the information and make the problem much easier to solve.

EXAMPLE

Example 1. Dr. Walters instructed the head nurse at the hospital to increase the concentration of a patient's medicinal solution from 18% to 42%. How much pure medicine to the nearest tenth of a ml should she add to 9 ml of the solution?

Solution.   **1.** Make a chart.

	number of ml	percentage of medicine	number of ml of medicine
solution	9	0.18	1.62
pure medicine	x	1	x
stronger solution	$x + 9$	0.42	$0.42(x + 9)$

$1.62 + x = 0.42(x + 9)$

$1.62 + x = 0.42x + 3.78$

$0.58x = 2.16$

$x = 3.7$

2. Make an equation from the last column. Do you understand why this equation is true? The 1.62 ml is the amount of pure medicine in the 9 ml of solution, x represents the number of ml of medicine to be added, and $0.42 (x + 9)$ represents the number of ml of pure medicine in the new mix.

So the nurse should add 3.7 ml of pure medicine to the solution to make it a 42% solution.

Exercises

Solve.

1. Carbon steel is an alloy that ranges from 0.08% to 0.60% in carbon content. Low-carbon steel is used in items such as tin cans, auto bodies, and home appliances. High-carbon steel is used mainly for railroad-car wheels and rails. A company has low-carbon steel and receives an order to make some replacement rails for a railroad. The low-carbon steel is 0.15% carbon, and the high-carbon steel needed is 0.52%. If the company has 8-ton ingots of low-carbon steel, how many pounds of carbon per ingot should be added to fill the rail order?

2. A jeweler has 32 ounces of 24-carat gold (100% pure) from which to make 18-carat gold rings. If 18-carat gold is 75% pure gold, how many ounces of copper should be added to the gold to make the rings?

3. A chemist wants to dilute 6 ℓ of an 85% sulfuric acid mixture to a 59% sulfuric acid mixture. How much water should he add?

4. Mark has 12 quarts of paint that is 8% paint thinner. If he wants the paint to be 14% paint thinner, how many quarts of thinner to the nearest hundredth should he add to the paint?

5. Mr. Fuqua prepares anhydrous ammonia to fertilize his field. He has 86 gallons of a mixture that is 28% ammonia, and he wants a mixture that is 53% ammonia. To the nearest tenth, how many gallons of pure ammonia should he add to produce the correct percentage?

6. A researcher is studying the effect of various concentrations of a new drug upon the growth of laboratory mice when the drug is administered in their drinking water. He has prepared two stock solutions: solution A containing 0.5% of the drug and solution B containing 1%. How many ml of solution A and solution B does he need to mix in order to obtain 25 ml of an 0.8% solution for one of his test animals?

7. A gardener has 80 pounds of a lime/fertilizer mixture that is 25% fertilizer. How much lime should he add to produce a mixture that is 20% fertilizer?

8. Mr. Leity wanted to prepare a batch of mortar to repair a brick wall. The instructions on the bag of mortar called for a mixture of 25% mortar and 75% additional sand before the addition of water. After adding sand to his 100-pound bag of mortar, he realized that by mistake he had made a mixture containing 80% sand. How many additional pounds of mortar must he add to his mixture in order to have the correct proportions?

9. A chemist wanted to prepare a solution of potassium iodide for an experiment in order to use up some previously prepared solutions of different concentrations. How many grams of a 28% solution and how many grams of a 60% solution must he mix in order to prepare 800 grams of a 40% solution?

10. Mr. Brown placed 6 quarts of antifreeze in his truck's 10-quart radiator and finished filling it with water, providing protection against freezing down to a temperature of -52° C. Water without antifreeze freezes at 0° C (32° F). Some time later he discovered a leak in his radiator and added 1 quart of antifreeze and 3 quarts of water to replace the lost fluid. What is the percentage of antifreeze in his system now? To what minimum temperature (in ° C) will the adjusted antifreeze mixture in his car provide protection, assuming a direct proportionality between the percentage of antifreeze and the drop in temperature at which the fluid would freeze?

WORK PROBLEMS

In an age of welfare and social programs, the word *work* has been struck from many people's vocabularies. But the Bible frequently comments on the attitude that a Christian should have toward work. In II Thessalonians 3, Paul reminds the Thessalonians that he and those with him worked "night and day, that we might not be chargeable to any of you." He said that he worked hard for his room and board as an example of his teaching to them "that if any would not work, neither should he eat." He goes on to reprimand some who, as a result of not working, had become busybodies and had caused division in the church.

The Christian, whether he is a student or someone's employee, has a responsibility to do his work to the very best of his ability because he serves not just a teacher, employer, or parent, but the Lord Jesus Himself (cf. Rom. 12:11). "Whatsoever thy hand findeth to do, do it with thy might" (Eccles. 9:10a), Solomon wrote.

Business managers are constantly interested in getting a job done as quickly and as efficiently as possible. Management supervisors realize that a job can sometimes be done faster if more than one machine or person is working on the project. Periodically a supervisor will analyze the work output of the employees and make personnel changes based on the results of the studies. The work problems in this section can help you analyze some of the everyday jobs you might be involved in. These problems are relatively easy to solve if you follow certain procedures and make charts.

For instance, the production manager knows that Kena can type fifteen pages for a book in 60 minutes. Shawn can type the same amount in 75 minutes. If a fifteen-page chapter needs to be typed, how long will it take the girls to finish the project if they work together?

To solve a problem such as this, you must first decide what you are looking for. You are looking for the number of minutes it will take Kena and Shawn to do the job together. So let x = the number of minutes required to do the job together.

Next, make a chart that indicates the amount of work each girl does in one minute as well as the time it takes each girl to do all the work. If Kena can do the job in 60 minutes, she does $\frac{1}{60}$ of the job in 1 minute. Do you understand why? If Shawn can do the job in 75 minutes, she does $\frac{1}{75}$ of the job in 1 minute. Since the girls can do the job together in x minutes, they can do $\frac{1}{x}$ of the job in 1 minute.

	minutes to do all the work	part of work done in one minute
Kena	60	$\frac{1}{60}$
Shawn	75	$\frac{1}{75}$
together	x	$\frac{1}{x}$

Once the chart is complete, you can set up an equation. What does $\frac{1}{60}$ + $\frac{1}{75}$ equal? It equals the part of work the girls do together in one minute, or $\frac{1}{x}$ of the total work. So the equation is

$$\frac{1}{60} + \frac{1}{75} = \frac{1}{x}$$

Now can you solve this equation? What is the common denominator? The common denominator is 300x.

$$300x\left(\frac{1}{60} + \frac{1}{75}\right) = \frac{1}{x}(300x)$$

$$\overset{5}{\cancel{300}}x\left(\frac{1}{60}\right) + \overset{4}{\cancel{300}}x\left(\frac{1}{75}\right) = \frac{\overset{1}{\cancel{300x}}}{\cancel{x}}$$

$$5x + 4x = 300$$
$$9x = 300$$
$$x = 33\frac{1}{3}$$

Since the girls, working together, can complete the project in $33\frac{1}{3}$ minutes, the production manager can get the project done sooner by having both girls work on the project.

Can you see how knowing the time it will take for workers to finish a project would be helpful to a company or business trying to get a particular job done? When the labor cost can be estimated, the marketing manager can determine how to price and promote the products.

EXAMPLE

Bill and Jim, who mow yards in the summer, have a big mowing job coming up. Bill figures that doing the job by himself will take 10 hours, but doing the job with Jim will take only 4 hours. How long would it take Jim to mow the whole lawn by himself?

Solution.

Let x = the amount of time it takes Jim by himself

1. What are you looking for? Making a chart will aid in solving this problem.

	hours for whole job	part of work done in 1 hour
Bill	10	$\frac{1}{10}$
Jim	x	$\frac{1}{x}$
together	4	$\frac{1}{4}$

$$\frac{1}{10} + \frac{1}{x} = \frac{1}{4}$$

$$20x\left(\frac{1}{10} + \frac{1}{x}\right) = \frac{1}{4}(20x)$$

$$20x\left(\frac{1}{10}\right) + 20x\left(\frac{1}{x}\right) = \frac{1}{4}(20x)$$

$$\overset{2}{\cancel{20}}x\left(\frac{1}{\cancel{10}}\right) + 20\cancel{x}\left(\frac{1}{\cancel{x}}\right) = \frac{1}{\cancel{4}}(\overset{5}{\cancel{20}}x)$$

$$2x + 20 = 5x$$

$$20 = 3x$$

$$6\frac{2}{3} = x$$

So it takes Jim $6\frac{2}{3}$ hours to mow the whole lawn.

2. Form the equation from the information in the right-hand column. Solve this equation.

Exercises

Solve to the nearest tenth.

1. If Jim, who takes twice as long as Brent to detassle an acre of corn, works with Brent, he and Brent can detassle an acre in 50 minutes. How long does it take each fellow to do the job alone?

2. Frank, Mike, and Tim are going to paint a house together. Frank can paint 2000 square feet of the house in 6 hours. To paint an equal area Mike takes only 3 hours and Tim 2 hours. If the boys work together, how long will it take them to paint 2000 square feet of the house?

3. Joan can wallpaper a living room in 9 hours. Kelly is inexperienced at wallpapering, but she wants to learn. If Kelly and Joan work together on wallpapering the living room, it takes 6 hours. How long would it take Kelly to wallpaper the living room by herself?

4. It takes 9 hours for one water pipe to fill a swimming pool. If another pipe is added and both pipes work together, the pool fills in only three hours. How long would it take the second pipe to fill the pool if it were the only one used?

5. The junior class is getting ready for the spring play, and Larry is in charge of painting the sets, which will take 52 hours if Larry paints them by himself. Larry knows that John is a good artist and could paint the sets in 36 hours. If Larry decides to ask John to help him, how long will it take the two boys to paint the sets?

6. Darlene figured that making puppets for Vacation Bible School would take her 4 hours. If she worked with her sister, who would take 6 hours for the job, she could get finished faster. If the girls work together, how long will it take them to finish the puppets?

7. If the weather is just right, Farmer Green can plant his acreage in 74 hours. His neighbor can do the same amount of acreage with his larger tractor in 50 hours. How long will it take to plant Mr. Green's field if they work together on the acreage?

8. A certain computer can grade 2000 objective-answer exams in 10 minutes. A new computer can grade the 2000 exams in less time. If the two computers together can grade 2000 exams in 3 minutes, how long does it take the new computer to grade the 2000 exams?

9. Joy takes 3 hours longer than Frances to clean the house. If the girls work together, they can get the work done in 4 hours. How long does it take each girl working alone to clean the house?

10. A machine at a light-bulb factory produces metal bases for light bulbs. The company has a rush order that needs to be filled in 24 hours. After 7 hours the machine breaks down, and another machine completes the job in 5 hours. It would have taken the first machine 15 hours to do the whole job. How long would it have taken the second machine to do the whole job by itself?

MOTION PROBLEMS

Do you remember the basic equation that you used to solve the motion problems in Chapters 3 and 6? Remember to always make a chart and fill in two columns, using variables and information from the problem. Fill in the third column from the information in the other two columns; then make an equation using the last column you filled in and any unused information from the problem.

EXAMPLE

Example 1. If Lois flies home for vacation, she will arrive $12\frac{1}{2}$ hours earlier than if she drives the 780 miles. Find the average speed of the airplane if it is six times the speed that the car could travel.

Solution.

Let x = the speed of the plane

$\frac{x}{6}$ = the speed of the car

	r	t	= d
by car	$\frac{x}{6}$		780
by plane	x		780

	r	t	= d
by car	$\frac{x}{6}$	$\frac{780}{\frac{x}{6}}$	780
by plane	x	$\frac{780}{x}$	780

$$\frac{780}{\frac{x}{6}} = \frac{780}{x} + 12\frac{1}{2}$$

$$\frac{4680}{x} = \frac{780}{x} + \frac{25}{2}$$

$$2x\left(\frac{4680}{x}\right) = \left(\frac{780}{x} + \frac{25}{2}\right)2x$$

$$2x\left(\frac{4680}{x}\right) = \left(\frac{780}{x}\right)2x + \left(\frac{25}{2}\right)2x$$

$$9360 = 1560 + 25x$$

$$7800 = 25x$$

$$312 = x$$

So the plane travels 312 mph.

1. Determine what you are looking for in this problem.
2. Make a chart to aid in the solution of this problem. Fill in two columns of the chart.
3. When two columns are full, fill in the third column without looking at the problem.
4. Now reread the problem to find any information about the time column, since it was the last one filled in. The problem says that flying is $12\frac{1}{2}$ hours shorter than driving. So you can make an equation from this information.
5. Simplify all terms in the equation.
6. Multiply both sides of the equation by the common denominator and solve.

Did you follow all of the processes involved in solving that problem? If not, go back and read the example again. These problems are different from those you worked earlier only in the fact that these often contain rational expressions. If you set up the chart correctly, you will be able to solve the problems with little difficulty.

Example 2. A Thursday canoe race at summer church camp requires each team of canoers to paddle down the river, which flows at the rate of 3 mph, to a certain marker and then come back. The winning team, paddling at a rate of 5 mph, made the trip from the starting line to the marker and back in 5 hours. How far down the river is the marker?

Solution.

1. What are you looking for? You are looking for distance, so the variable should be in the distance column of the chart. Is the distance going to the marker the same as the distance from the marker?

	r	t	$= d$
downstream	5 + 3		x
upstream	5 - 3		x

2. Fill in the third column from the chart.

	r	t	$= d$
downstream	8	$\dfrac{x}{8}$	x
upstream	2	$\dfrac{x}{2}$	x

3. Does the problem contain any information about time that has not been used yet? Yes, the total time is 5 hours.

$$\frac{x}{8} + \frac{x}{2} = 5$$

$$8\left(\frac{x}{8} + \frac{x}{2}\right) = 5 \cdot 8$$

$$\overset{1}{8}\left(\frac{x}{8}\right) + \overset{4}{8}\left(\frac{x}{2}\right) = 40$$

$$x + 4x = 40$$

$$5x = 40$$

$$x = 8$$

So the distance from the starting line to the marker is 8 miles.

Exercises

Solve.

1. A bicyclist club took a weekend trip to a national forest and rode 60 miles at a certain average rate. On their return trip over the same route, they traveled 4 mph faster and took 4 hours less. How fast did they ride their bicycles going and coming?

2. Les walks $\frac{1}{6}$ as fast as a freight train travels. It takes 4 hours longer for Les to walk 30 miles than for the train to travel 60 miles. Find the speed of each.

3. Two flights left Karr Airport at the same time. One plane flew 250 mph. The other plane flew 375 mph. The faster plane went 750 miles farther than the slower plane and traveled one hour longer. How far did each plane travel?

4. At 7:00 A.M. Joey started walking to school at a rate of 5 mph. At 7:30 his brother Tommy started riding a bicycle. If Tommy rode his bicycle at a rate of 10 mph, how far did Joey walk before Tommy caught up with him?

5. The girls' bus for the senior trip left the school $\frac{1}{2}$ hour later than the boys' bus, which traveled at an average speed of 45 mph. When it finally got going, the girls' bus sped along at 50 mph. How far from home were the seniors when the girls' bus caught the boys' bus? How long had each group traveled?

6. An airplane flew 700 miles with the wind in the same amount of time that it flew 625 miles against the wind. The average speed of the plane with no wind is 265 mph. What was the wind speed?

7. A touring bus travels 200 miles to a historical site and back in $4\frac{1}{2}$ hours. If the rate returning was 10 mph faster than the rate going, find the rate each way.

8. Mr. Truman drove to his cottage in the mountains at a rate of 45 mph. On the way back from the cottage he drove at a speed of 50 mph but took a route 15 miles shorter than the route he traveled to the cottage. How many total miles did he travel on this trip if it took him $\frac{1}{2}$ hour longer to go than to return?

9. Jim and Mike walked 45 minutes to the bicycle repair shop. Their ride home took an hour, but it was 3 miles longer than their walk. If their riding rate was 2 mph faster than their walking rate, how fast did they walk and ride?

10. Mr. Johnson drives a semitrailer truck. On one trip to a city 275 miles from his home, he traveled $\frac{1}{2}$ hour longer going than he did coming along the same route. How long did it take him to make the trip each way if his rate going was 5 mph slower than his rate returning?

LITERAL EQUATIONS

What does *literal* mean? Look up the word in a dictionary and read all the definitions. Does *literal* mean what you thought it meant?

Did you know that the Bible teaches that there is a literal heaven and a literal hell? What does *literal* mean when used in this way? Do you believe that there is a literal heaven and a literal hell? What are you doing about that fact? Christians should develop their lives according to the literal principles of God's Word. Do you take time each day to delve into the literal Word of God and gain Bible truths?

You have used literal equations for a long time; in fact, you may remember being introduced to them in Chapter 3. What definition of *literal* applies to equations?

≫**Literal equation:** any equation with two or more letters in it.

Formulas, such as those you used in earlier chapters, are a common type of literal equation usually containing three or four letters. Can you identify these familiar literal equations?

$$A = \tfrac{1}{2}bh \qquad V = lwh \qquad i = prt \qquad P = 2(l + w)$$

$$d = rt \qquad a^2 + b^2 = c^2 \qquad A = lw \qquad e = mc^2$$

EXAMPLES

Example 1. Solve $F = \dfrac{WH}{L}$ for H.

Solution. $F = \dfrac{WH}{L}$

$L \cdot F = \dfrac{WH}{L} \cdot L$ **1.** The common denominator is L. Multiply both sides by L.

$LF = WH$ **2.** Now divide both sides by W.

$\dfrac{LF}{W} = H$

Example 2. Solve $d = 0.07v^2$ for v.

Solution. $d = 0.07v^2$

$\dfrac{d}{0.07} = v^2$ **1.** Divide both sides by 0.07.

$\pm\sqrt{\dfrac{d}{0.07}} = v$ **2.** To find v, you must take the square root of each side.

$\dfrac{\pm\sqrt{0.07d}}{0.07} = v$ **3.** Simplify the answer to eliminate the radical in the denominator.

Example 3. Solve $3a + bx = \dfrac{4x}{5}$ for x.

Solution. $3a + bx = \dfrac{4x}{5}$

$5(3a + bx) = \dfrac{4x}{5} \cdot 5$ **1.** Multiply by the common denominator.

$15a + 5bx = 4x$ **2.** Get all terms that contain x on one side of the

$15a = 4x - 5bx$ equation.

$15a = x(4 - 5b)$ **3.** Factor the unknown variable from the right side.

$\dfrac{15a}{4 - 5b} = x$ **4.** Divide both sides by the coefficient of x.

You have completely solved a literal equation only when the variable is on one side and the other terms are on the other side. The variable cannot appear on both sides in the final solution.

Procedure for Storage

Solving a Literal Equation

1. Eliminate fractions from the equation.
2. Perform any indicated operations and combine like terms.
3. Place all terms containing the variable on one side of the equation and all other terms on the other side.
4. If the variable is in more than one term, factor it from those terms. If the variable is raised to a power, take the proper root, or power, to solve.
5. Divide both sides by the coefficient of the variable.

EXAMPLE

Example 4. Solve $v = e^3$ for e.

Solution. Find the cube root of both sides.

$$v = e^3$$

$$\sqrt[3]{v} = \sqrt[3]{e^3}$$

$$\sqrt[3]{v} = e$$

Exercises

Solve for the stated variable.

1. $e = mc^2$ for c

2. $s = 16t^2$ for t

3. $p = .433h$ for h

4. $i = prt$ for r

5. $d = rt$ for t

6. $w = \dfrac{11(h - 40)}{2}$ for h

7. $c = 2\pi r$ for r

8. $w = s + cp$ for p

9. $P = 3s$ for s

10. $V = \pi r^2 h$ for h

11. $A = \pi r^2$ for r

12. $V = \dfrac{4}{3}\pi r^3$ for r

13. $P = 2b + 2h$ for b

14. $v + 10 = \dfrac{t}{v} - \dfrac{25}{v}$ for t

15. $P = \dfrac{d^2 n}{2.5}$ for d

16. $\dfrac{nx}{b} - n = x$ for x

17. $\dfrac{3a}{x - a} = y$ for x

18. $\dfrac{a}{3 + z} = \dfrac{b}{3 - z}$ for z

19. $2y - 3x = ay - 2x$ for y

20. $\dfrac{x}{b} - \dfrac{x}{c} = x$ for b

MEMORY RECALL

Identify.
    literal equations
    rational equations

You should be able to do the following:

1. Identify the difference between a rational equation and an equation containing fractions.
2. Solve equations containing fractions.
3. Solve rational equations.
4. Solve a variety of applied word problems that involve rational equations.
5. Solve literal equations.

You should be able to solve the following problems:

1. $\dfrac{x + 8}{6} + \dfrac{x - 6}{2} = 1$

2. $\dfrac{x^2}{4} = \dfrac{13x}{8} + 3$

3. $\dfrac{5}{x} = 25$

4. $\dfrac{6}{x - 3} = 3$

5. $\dfrac{x + 8}{2x - 6} = \dfrac{17}{23}$

6. $\dfrac{12x - 3}{x^2 + 4x - 5} - \dfrac{5}{x + 5} = \dfrac{6}{x - 1}$

7. What number must be added to both the numerator and the denominator of $\frac{7}{8}$ to produce a fraction equivalent to $\frac{12}{13}$?

8. Sonya invested one-fourth of her savings at 7%, two-thirds of her savings at 8%, and the rest at 9%. Her total interest income from the savings was $846 annually. How much did she invest at each rate?

9. Jim wants to solder two pieces of metal together with solder that is 62% tin and 38% lead, but his solder is 50% tin and 50% lead. How much pure tin and solder should he melt together to make $2\frac{1}{2}$ ounces of the solder that he wants?

10. Sue and Janet are washing dishes after the class reunion banquet. In one hour Sue can wash 200 plates, and Janet can wash 100 plates. If Sue and Janet work together on the 600 plates they have to wash, how many hours will they spend washing the plates?

11. Two trains left the same depot and traveled in opposite directions. The train traveling 38 mph went 60 miles farther than the train traveling 65 mph. Though it left 3 hours earlier, the slower train reached its destination at the same time the faster train reached its destination. How far apart were the two trains when they arrived at their destinations?

12. $km + v = t$ for m

13. $3x + 4z = n$ for z

14. $\frac{ab}{c} + \frac{b}{d} = x$ for b

15. $\frac{y}{3} - \frac{2}{z} = 12$ for y

CHAPTER 13

QUADRATIC FUNCTIONS

One of the highest dams in the United States is Shasta Dam. This dam, which is in northern California at the northern end of the Sacramento River, is 602 feet high and 3460 feet across. Shasta Dam is considered one of the engineering wonders of the United States. This monstrous construction consists of 6.3 million cubic yards of concrete and weighs 15 million tons. The dam created a reservoir, Shasta Lake, containing 6.25 billion tons of water and providing recreational areas and a refuge for fish and wildlife. The base of the dam, to withstand the thousands of pounds of water pressure per square foot, is 883 feet wide.

Shasta Dam has seven hydroelectric generators that produce two billion kilowatt-hours of electricity annually. This electric plant supplies energy to residents of northern California. The electricity produced by the captured water is used to defer the original cost of the construction of the dam. The water that goes through the dam creates the highest manmade waterfall in the world. The water falls 487 feet, three times the height of Niagara Falls.

Before construction could begin on Shasta Dam, engineers had to make detailed topographical maps and perform extensive geological studies. Civil engineers (engineers who design bridges, dams, and other public structures) have to take many classes in higher mathematics. As one engineer has said, "Algebra seems like the *ABC*'s to us. Algebra seems so easy that we don't even think about what we're doing." You are not able to understand the complex equations that are used to design and construct a dam such as Shasta Dam. But you can learn the *ABC*'s of engineering now. Quadratic functions, such as $f(x) = 3x^2 + 2x - 5$, are used often in the engineering field. By the end of this chapter, you should be able to find the zeros of this function and graph the function. Both of these concepts are important in the mathematical field of calculus, which you will use if you pursue an engineering occupation.

QUADRATIC FUNCTIONS OF THE FORM $f(x) = ax^2$

When you studied linear equations in Chapter 5, you learned that a relation is any set of ordered pairs and a function is a special kind of relation. Therefore, any function, linear or quadratic, is a special set of ordered pairs. In a linear equation such as $y = x + 5$, you learned that the value of y depends upon the value of x. Thus y is called a function of x, abbreviated $f(x)$, and when described as a set is written $\{(x, y) | y = x + 5\}$, which reads "the set of ordered pairs (x, y) such that y equals x plus 5." To graph such a function, you first make a table of values.

x	y
0	5
1	6
2	7

A shorter way to express a function is to use functional notation. Thus $f = \{(x, y) | y = x + 5\}$ would be written $f(x) = x + 5$ and read "f of x is equal to x plus 5." Since y and $f(x)$ are the same, the table of a function in functional notation would look like this:

x	f(x)
0	5
1	6
2	7

To evaluate a function, simply substitute the value of x in $f(x)$ for x in the expression.

EXAMPLE

Example 1. Find $f(x) = x - 8$, when $x = 4$, $x = -2$, and $x = 6$.

Solution. Substitute values of x in the function to produce a set of ordered pairs.

$$f(x) = x - 8$$

$$f(4) = 4 - 8 = -4$$

$$f(-2) = -2 - 8 = -10$$

$$f(6) = 6 - 8 = -2$$

x	f(x)
4	-4
-2	-10
6	-2

Notice that the functional notation always produces a set of ordered pairs.

EXAMPLE

Example 2. Find $f(x) = x^2 + 8$, when $x = 2$, $x = -4$, and $x = 0$.

Solution.

$f(x) = x^2 + 8$

$f(2) = 2^2 + 8 = 4 + 8 = 12$

$f(-4) = (-4)^2 + 8 = 16 + 8 = 24$

$f(0) = 0^2 + 8 = 0 + 8 = 8$

x	$f(x)$
2	12
-4	24
0	8

You can easily graph a quadratic function if you use functional notation and then graph on a Cartesian plane using the y-axis as the $f(x)$ axis. Notice that a quadratic function, like a quadratic equation, involves a second-degree polynomial.

DEFINITION

≫**Quadratic function:** a function of the form $f(x) = ax^2 + bx + c$ where a, b, and c are real numbers and $a \neq 0$.

Consider now some quadratic functions of the form $f(x) = ax^2$.

EXAMPLE

Example 3. Graph $f(x) = 3x^2$.

Solution.

$f(0) = 3 \cdot 0^2 = 0$

$f(1) = 3 \cdot 1^2 = 3$

$f(2) = 3 \cdot 2^2 = 12$

$f(-1) = 3 \cdot (-1)^2 = 3$

$f(-2) = 3 \cdot (-2)^2 = 12$

1. Make a table of at least five ordered pairs, using positive and negative values for x.

x	$f(x)$
0	0
1	3
2	12
-1	3
-2	12

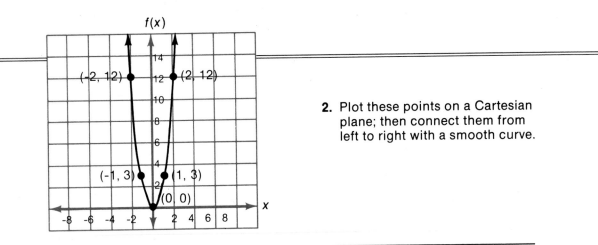

2. Plot these points on a Cartesian plane; then connect them from left to right with a smooth curve.

Notice the shape of this graph. It is not a straight line because the equation is not a linear equation. This figure is called a *parabola*. The graph of any quadratic function is a parabola.

EXAMPLE

Example 4. Graph $f(x) = -2x^2$.

Solution.

$$f(x) = -2x^2$$
$$f(0) = -2 \cdot 0^2 = 0$$
$$f(1) = -2 \cdot 1^2 = -2$$
$$f(2) = -2 \cdot 2^2 = -8$$
$$f(-1) = -2 \cdot (-1)^2 = -2$$
$$f(-2) = -2 \cdot (-2)^2 = -8$$

1. Make a table of ordered pairs.

x	$f(x)$
0	0
1	-2
2	-8
-1	-2
-2	-8

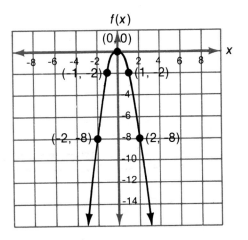

2. Graph and connect the points from left to right with a smooth curve.

The arrows at the ends of the parabola indicate that the parabola will extend without limit. The highest or lowest point of the parabola is called the *vertex* of the parabola. What is the vertex of each parabola in examples 3 and 4?

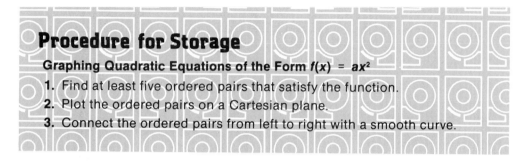

Procedure for Storage

Graphing Quadratic Equations of the Form $f(x) = ax^2$

1. Find at least five ordered pairs that satisfy the function.
2. Plot the ordered pairs on a Cartesian plane.
3. Connect the ordered pairs from left to right with a smooth curve.

Exercises

Find the value of each function when $x = 0$, $x = 2$, $x = -1$, and $x = 4$.

1. $f(x) = x + 3$

2. $f(x) = -x - 6$

3. $f(x) = 2x$

4. $f(x) = -2x + 6$

5. $f(x) = x^2$

6. $f(x) = x^2 - 4$

7. $f(x) = x^2 + 5$

8. $f(x) = 2x^2$

9. $f(x) = 3x^2 - 7$

10. $f(x) = 2x^2 - 8$

Graph each quadratic function.

11. $f(x) = x^2$

12. $f(x) = 2x^2$

13. $f(x) = 3x^2$

14. $f(x) = \frac{1}{2}x^2$

15. $f(x) = \frac{-1}{3}x^2$

16. $f(x) = -10x^2$

17. $f(x) = \frac{2}{3}x^2$

18. Where is the vertex in each graph? Where is the vertex of any quadratic function of the form $f(x) = ax^2$?

19. The line of symmetry of a parabola is the vertical line across which the parabola may be reflected. What is the line of symmetry in the equations you graphed?

20. Does the graph open upward or downward if $a > 0$?

QUADRATIC FUNCTIONS OF THE FORM $f(x) = ax^2 + k$

The algebraic principles and concepts you have learned this year are building blocks to further math studies. These principles will help you sharpen your reasoning and logical thinking processes as well as help you understand geometry, advanced algebra, and trigonometry.

In the last section you learned what functional notation is and what the graph of a quadratic function looks like. Now you can add another block to your foundation of knowledge. How does the quadratic function $f(x) = ax^2 + k$ differ from the one in the last section? How will the extra term affect the graph of the function? What is the vertex of each graph? What is the line of symmetry of the parabola? As you study the two examples, look for the answers to these questions. Remember, too, that mathematical concepts continually build on previous concepts.

EXAMPLES

Example 1. Graph $f(x) = 2x^2 + 4$.

Solution. Find at least five ordered pairs $(x, f(x))$. Then connect them from left to right with a smooth curve.

1. Choose any values for x and find $f(x)$ that corresponds to that x.

$f(x) = 2x^2 + 4$

			x	f(x)
$f(0)$	$= 2(0)^2 + 4 = 4$		0	4
$f(1)$	$= 2(1)^2 + 4 = 6$		1	6
$f(2)$	$= 2(2)^2 + 4 = 12$		2	12
$f(-1)$	$= 2(-1)^2 + 4 = 6$		-1	6
$f(-2)$	$= 2(-2)^2 + 4 = 12$		-2	12

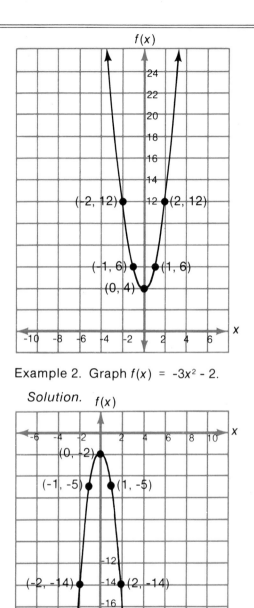

2. Graph the ordered pairs.

3. Connect the points with a smooth curve.

Example 2. Graph $f(x) = -3x^2 - 2$.

Solution.

$$f(0) = -3(0)^2 - 2$$
$$f(1) = -3(1)^2 - 2 \quad = -5$$
$$f(2) = -3(2)^2 - 2 \quad = -14$$
$$f(-1) = -3(-1)^2 - 2 = -5$$
$$f(-2) = -3(-2)^2 - 2 = -14$$
$$f(-3) = -3(-3)^2 - 2 = -29$$

x	$f(x)$
0	-2
1	-5
2	-14
-1	-5
-2	-14

Exercises

Graph each quadratic function.

1. $f(x) = x^2 + 2$

2. $f(x) = x^2 - 7$

3. $f(x) = 2x^2 - 3$

4. $f(x) = -5x^2 + 1$

5. $f(x) = 2x^2 + 4$

6. $f(x) = \frac{1}{2}x^2 + 5$

Graph each quadratic function without making a table of values.

7. $f(x) = 3x^2 - 9$

8. $f(x) = \frac{1}{4}x^2 + 2$

9. $f(x) = -3x^2 + 4$

10. $f(x) = \frac{2}{3}x^2 - 6$

11. $f(x) = -\frac{1}{5}x^2 + 4$

12. $f(x) = 7x^2 + -1$

QUADRATIC FUNCTIONS OF THE FORM $f(x) = a(x-h)^2 + k$

The final type of quadratic function is of the form $f(x) = a(x - h)^2 + k$. You learned in the last section that the k term in the function $f(x) = ax^2 + k$ moved the graph vertically. If $k > 0$, the parabola moved up k units; if $k < 0$, the parabola moved down k units. Another term has been added to the same basic function. What do you think the value h might do to the graph? Watch the examples to see what happens to the graph now.

EXAMPLE

Example 1. Graph $f(x) = (x - 2)^2 + 4$.

Solution.
$$a = 1$$
$$h = 2$$
$$k = 4$$

1. Determine the value of a, h, and k to find the maximum or minimum value of the parabola.

2. Choose some values for x and make a table of ordered pairs for this function.

$f(0) = (0 - 2)^2 + 4 = (-2)^2 + 4 = 4 + 4 = 8$
$f(1) = (1 - 2)^2 + 4 = (-1)^2 + 4 = 1 + 4 = 5$
$f(2) = (2 - 2)^2 + 4 = 0^2 + 4 = 0 + 4 = 4$
$f(3) = (3 - 2)^2 + 4 = 1^2 + 4 = 1 + 4 = 5$
$f(4) = (4 - 2)^2 + 4 = 2^2 + 4 = 4 + 4 = 8$
$f(5) = (5 - 2)^2 + 4 = 3^2 + 4 = 9 + 4 = 13$
$f(-1) = (-1 - 2)^2 + 4 = (-3)^2 + 4 = 9 + 4 = 13$

x	$f(x)$
0	8
1	5
2	4
3	5
4	8
5	13
-1	13

3. Graph these ordered pairs, and connect them with a smooth, curved line from left to right.

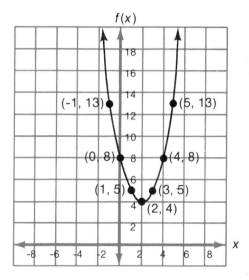

What happened to the parabola? How does this graph vary from the graph in the previous section? Remember that the k value moved the vertex vertically. How many units from the y-axis did the vertex move? What was the value of h? What is the line of symmetry for this parabola?

EXAMPLE

Example 2. Graph $f(x) = -2(x - 3)^2 + 1$.

Solution. Notice that $a = -2$, $h = 3$, and $k = 1$. Make a table of ordered pairs and graph them.

$f(1) = -2(1 - 3)^2 + 1 = -2(-2)^2 + 1 = -2 \cdot 4 + 1 = -8 + 1 = -7$
$f(2) = -2(2 - 3)^2 + 1 = -2(-1)^2 + 1 = -2 \cdot 1 + 1 = -2 + 1 = -1$
$f(3) = -2(3 - 3)^2 + 1 = -2(0)^2 + 1 = -2 \cdot 0 + 1 = 0 + 1 = 1$
$f(4) = -2(4 - 3)^2 + 1 = -2(1)^2 + 1 = -2 \cdot 1 + 1 = -2 + 1 = -1$
$f(5) = -2(5 - 3)^2 + 1 = -2(2)^2 + 1 = -2 \cdot 4 + 1 = -8 + 1 = -7$

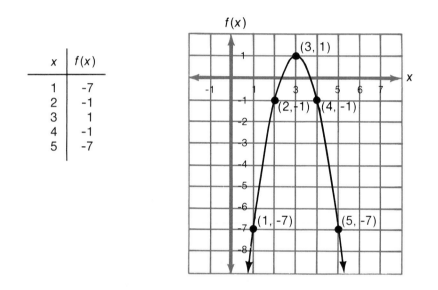

x	$f(x)$
1	-7
2	-1
3	1
4	-1
5	-7

How much did the graph move vertically? horizontally? What were the values of h and k? Is the vertex the ordered pair (h, k)?

Procedure for Storage

Graphing Quadratic Equations of the Form $f(x) = a(x - h)^2 + k$

1. Make a table of ordered pairs and graph the pairs. The vertex will be (h, k).

2. Connect the ordered pairs from left to right with a smooth curve.

If a quadratic function is not in the form $f(x) = a(x - h)^2 + k$, you can place it in the proper form by following a procedure very similar to the completing-the-square procedure that you learned in Chapter 10.

EXAMPLES

Example 3. Graph $f(x) = x^2 - 6x + 10$.

Solution. Since this quadratic function is not in any of the correct forms, you must place it in the correct form by completing the square on the right.

$$f(x) = (x^2 - 6x) + 10$$

1. Leave the last term on the outside of the parentheses.

$$\frac{1}{2} \cdot 6 = 3$$
$$3^2 = 9$$
$$f(x) = (x^2 - 6x + 9) + 10 - 9'$$

2. Complete the square of the terms inside the parentheses by taking $\frac{1}{2}$ of the coefficient of x and squaring it. Since you are adding 9 in the parentheses, you must subtract 9 from the outside of the parentheses.

$$f(x) = (x - 3)^2 + 1$$

3. Factor inside the parentheses and simplify as much as possible.

$$a = 1$$
$$h = 3$$
$$k = 1$$

4. Now the function is in the proper form and can be graphed easily. Identify a, h, and k. The vertex is (h, k), or $(3, 1)$, and the graph opens upward because $a > 0$. Find at least three more ordered pairs and graph them.

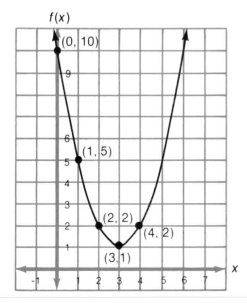

x	$f(x)$
0	10
1	5
2	2
3	1
4	2

Example 4. Graph $f(x) = -2x^2 - 12x - 19$.

Solution.

$f(x) = -2x^2 - 12x - 19$

1. This function must be placed in the form $f(x) = a(x - h)^2 + k$ by completing the square.

$f(x) = -2(x^2 + 6x) - 19$

2. Group the first two terms together. Then factor -2 from these two terms.

$f(x) = -2(x^2 + 6x + 9) - 19 + 18$

3. Complete the square by finding the square of half the coefficient of x. Be sure to keep the function equivalent by adding 18 outside the parentheses. Do you know why?

$f(x) = -2(x + 3)^2 - 1$

4. Simplify and factor to the form $f(x) = a(x - h)^2 + k$.

$a = -2$
$h = -3$
$k = -1$

5. The vertex is (h, k), or $(-3, -1)$, and the graph will open downward because $a < 0$.

6. Find three ordered pairs and graph.

x	$f(x)$
-3	-1
-2	-3
-4	-3

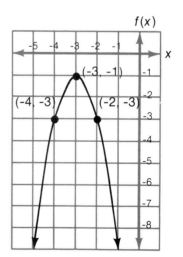

Exercises

Graph each quadratic function.

1. $f(x) = (x - 4)^2 + 2$
2. $f(x) = (x - 2)^2$
3. $f(x) = (x - 1)^2 - 3$
4. $f(x) = -2(x - 2)^2 + 5$
5. $f(x) = (x + 3)^2$
6. $f(x) = (x + 1)^2 - 2$
7. $f(x) = -(x + 4)^2 + 1$
8. $f(x) = (x - 3)^2 - 8$
9. $f(x) = 3(x + 1)^2 + 4$
10. $f(x) = -\dfrac{1}{2}(x - 2)^2 + 3$

Place each quadratic function in the form $f(x) = a(x - h)^2 + k$.

11. $f(x) = x^2 + 4x - 12$
12. $f(x) = x^2 - 6x + 8$
13. $f(x) = x^2 - 3x$
14. $f(x) = x^2 + 14x + 40$
15. $f(x) = x^2 - 8x + 15$
16. $f(x) = x^2 + 10x + 24$
17. $f(x) = x^2 + x - 6$
18. $f(x) = x^2 - x + 2$
19. $f(x) = x^2 - x - 12$
20. $f(x) = x^2 + 4x - 5$

Give the vertex and tell whether the graph opens upward or downward.

21. $f(x) = 3(x - 2)^2 + 4$
22. $f(x) = -4(x + 3)^2 - 2$
23. $f(x) = x^2 - x - 30$
24. $f(x) = 3x^2 - 2x - 8$
25. $f(x) = 5x^2 - 11x + 2$

ZEROS OF A FUNCTION

Do you remember what the y-intercept is? It is the point at which the graph crosses the y-axis. The value of x at this point is always 0. Likewise, the point at which the graph crosses the x-axis is called the x-intercept. The value of y at this point is always 0. Since the $f(x)$ in functional notation corresponds to y, the value of x at the point at which the graph crosses the x-axis is called the zero of the function.

DEFINITION ⟫**Zero of a function:** the value of x at the point at which the graph of the function crosses the x-axis.

The name *zeros of a function* is appropriate because the value of $f(x)$, or y, is 0 at this point. A linear function usually has one zero, but a quadratic function often has two zeros. To find zeros of a function that has been graphed, look at the graph and find the point or points at which the graph crosses the x-axis. The zeros of the function are the values of x at those points. To find zeros of a function algebraically, set the function equal to 0 and solve for x.

EXAMPLES

Example 1. Find the zeros of this quadratic function.

Solution. Since the graph crosses the x-axis at (1,0) and (4,0), the zeros of this function are $x = 1$ and $x = 4$.

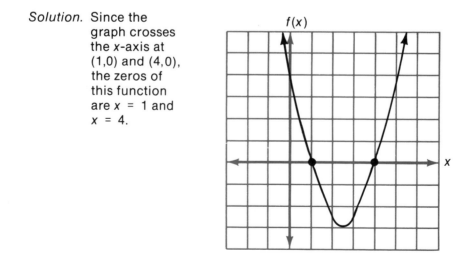

Example 2. Find the zeros of $f(x) = x^2 - 5x - 6$ algebraically.

Solution.

$$f(x) = x^2 - 5x - 6$$
$$0 = x^2 - 5x - 6$$

1. Set the function equal to zero and solve for x.

$$0 = (x - 6)(x + 1)$$
$$0 = x - 6 \qquad 0 = x + 1$$
$$6 = x \qquad\qquad -1 = x$$

2. Factor and set each factor equal to 0.

So the zeros of this function are
$x = 6$ and $x = -1$.

Exercises

Graph each function, and find the zeros of the function.

1. $f(x) = x^2 + 3$

2. $f(x) = (x - 3)^2$

3. $f(x) = 2(x - 6)^2 + 5$

4. $f(x) = -2(x + 3)^2 - 2$

5. $f(x) = x^2 - 7x + 12$

6. $f(x) = x^2 - 4x - 4$

Find the zeros of each function algebraically.

7. $f(x) = x^2 - 16$

8. $f(x) = x^2 - 2x - 8$

9. $f(x) = (x + 2)^2 - 3$

10. $f(x) = x^2 - 5x + 6$

11. $f(x) = x^2 + 3x$

12. $f(x) = x^2 - 6x + 9$

13. $f(x) = x^2 - 8x + 16$

14. $f(x) = x^2 - 6x - 7$

15. $f(x) = x^2 + 6x - 9$

WHY COMPUTERS?

The many benefits that computers offer have made them increasingly popular in various fields. Engineers use computers to sketch out many of their projects. Some of these computers are programmed to compare a sketch to certain requirements and then to correct it to fit those requirements. In science, computers retrieve information on research projects that have been performed in the past so that experiments will not be duplicated unnecessarily.

In all fields computers have three advantages that have led to their increasing popularity. Speed is an obvious advantage of a computer system. In just a few minutes a computer may complete equations that could take mathematicians hours to calculate.

Ratios, which often take days to analyze, may be figured out and printed in less than an hour. Thus, the company utilizing the computer realizes a savings because the cost of the computer system is not nearly so expensive as the total number of man-hours it would take people to do the same calculations. An inverse proportion exists between speed and cost in

the production of items; as speed increases, the production costs go down. At the same time, the products produced as a result of these calculations can be out on the market sooner, producing revenue for the company more quickly. Since profit is the major objective of most companies, computer systems appeal to them.

Another major benefit of a computer system is its accuracy. Although rounding errors often occur in computer computations, an error in the one-hundredth decimal place is minimal. People who work with numbers tend to make mistakes. Large numbers are virtually impossible to work with by hand or even with a calculator. A large computer, however, can deal with large numbers with great accuracy and no pain. A computer with a good program will be much less likely to make computational errors than the best mathematician in history. But the computer does not understand what it is doing; the programmer must have the understanding.

The third major benefit of a computer system is a computer's ability to do jobs repeatedly. A computer never gets tired or bored. Regardless of the assignment given to it, the computer never feels that its job is meaningless or insignificant. It is able to work during lunch, coffee breaks, and after hours. Many company computer systems never quit. They do their work around the clock. A computer never files insurance claims, never takes sick leave, never goes on a vacation, and retires only when its circuits are beyond repair.

SMEDLEY, HERE, IS GOING TO RUIN OUR REPUTATION.

APPLICATIONS OF QUADRATIC FUNCTIONS

Quadratic functions are often used to solve maximum or minimum problems. The maximum or minimum of a quadratic function is its vertex. If the parabola opens upward, the quadratic has a minimum point. If the parabola opens downward, the quadratic has a maximum point. Do you remember how to tell if a parabola opens upward or downward? When the quadratic function is of the form $f(x) = a(x - h)^2 + k$, the a will tell whether the vertex is the maximum or minimum point of the function. In summary,

if $a > 0$, $f(x)$ has a minimum point, and

if $a < 0$, $f(x)$ has a maximum point.

Remember, to graph a quadratic function, make sure that it is in the form $f(x) = a(x - h)^2 + k$.

Now you are ready to solve word problems involving quadratic functions. What are the steps to solving word problems? You should have these steps memorized. If you need to review them, turn to page 112.

> A farmer is going to fence in a rectangular pigpen along the bank of a stream, but he does not want to use any fencing on the stream bank. If he has 60 yards of fencing altogether, what should be the dimensions of the pen to allow for a maximum area?

Draw a picture to represent the problem. Notice that this is a maximum problem and should therefore turn into a quadratic function.

What are you looking for in this problem? You are looking for the dimensions of the pen so that a maximum area will be obtained. Let x represent the width of the pen. There are two widths, so these two sides together use $2x$ yards of the fencing. Therefore $60 - 2x$ yards are left for the one length opposite the stream side. Since both the length and the width are in terms of x, the area is a function of x. Next find the area of the rectangle by using the formula $A = lw$.

Let x = the width of the pen

$60 - 2x$ = the length of the pen

$f(x) = x(60 - 2x)$

$f(x) = 60x - 2x^2$

$f(x) = -2x^2 + 60x$

The quadratic function needs to be placed in the form $f(x) = a(x - h)^2 + k$ so you can find the vertex quickly and graph the function. To get this function in the proper form, you need to complete the square.

$f(x) = -2(x^2 - 30x)$

1. Factor -2 from the terms. Then complete the square.

$f(x) = -2(x^2 - 30x + 225) + 450$

$f(x) = -2(x - 15)^2 + 450$

2. Since you added 225 inside the parentheses and the quantity inside the parentheses is multiplied by -2, you are really adding a -450. To make an equivalent function, you must add 450 on the outside of the parentheses.

The value of $a = -2$, $h = 15$, and $k = 450$. Now graph the parabola. The vertex is (h, k), or $(15, 450)$. It is a maximum point because $a = -2$, which is less than 0.

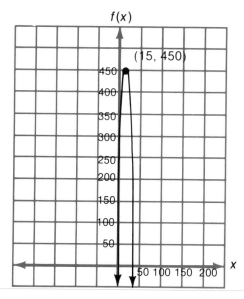

Since the area of the pen was to be maximized, you need to find the maximum point, which is (15,450). What do the values at this point represent? The first number in the ordered pair, 15, is x, the width of the pen. The second number, 450, is $f(x)$. What does $f(x)$ represent in this problem? To find the length of the pen, solve $60 - 2x$.

$$60 - 2(15)$$
$$60 - 30$$
$$30$$

For a maximum area of 450 square yards, the pen should be 15 yards wide and 30 yards long.

EXAMPLE

Example   The distance that a ball thrown into the air travels depends upon time, gravity, and velocity. The equation $f(t) = -16t^2 + 96t$ includes the factors of gravity and velocity and is written in terms of time, where $f(t)$ is the height the ball reaches at a particular time. Find the maximum height the ball reaches and the number of seconds it will take the ball to reach this height.

Solution.

$$f(t) = -16t^2 + 96t$$
$$= -16(t^2 - 6t)$$
$$= -16(t^2 - 6t + 9) + 144$$
$$= -16(t - 3)^2 + 144$$

To find this information, simply solve the quadratic function
$$f(t) = -16t^2 + 96t$$ by completing the square.

The vertex is (3, 144), and it is a maximum point because $a < 0$. Since the function is a function of t, the ordered pair (3, 144) is of the form $(t, f(t))$. So $t = 3$, and $f(t) = 144$. The ball will reach a maximum height of 144 feet in 3 seconds. Notice that if the quadratic function is in the form $f(x) = a(x - h)^2 + k$ you do not need to graph the parabola to find the maximum or minimum value.

Exercises

1. Find the dimensions of a rectangular rug that has a perimeter of 80 feet and has a maximum area.

2. Pastor Kliewer wants to fence in an area beside the pond on the church property to make a rectangular recreation area for the church family. If he has 50 yards of fencing to enclose an area bordering the pond and he wants to make sure he has a maximum area when finished, what should be the dimensions of the recreation area?

3. If the height a ball reaches when thrown into the air can be given by the equation $f(t) = -16t^2 + 64t$, where t is time in seconds, how long will it take the ball to reach its maximum height? What is the maximum height?

4. The cost equation used by the R & E Manufacturing Company is $C(x) = 2x^2 - 8x + 12$, where x represents the number of hours it takes to produce a particular product and $C(x)$ represents the cost of production in hundreds of dollars. What would be the minimum cost possible?

5. Of all the pairs of numbers whose difference is 8, only one pair has a product smaller than any other pair. Find this pair of numbers.

6. The difference of two numbers is 12, and their product is a minimum. What are the two numbers?

7. The accountants at the new microwave oven company have found that the equation $P(x) = -x^2 + 600x + 500$ relates the amount of profit that the company makes to the number of items made. How many ovens should the company produce to make a maximum profit? What will that profit be?

8. Julie wants to place 44 feet of picket fencing around a flower garden, to create the largest area possible. What dimensions should her garden be to have a maximum area?

9. The B & J Manufacturing Co. wants to produce items at a minimum cost to the company. If the cost of the items follows the equation $C(x) = x^2 - 140x + 5700$, where x is the number of items produced, how many items should they make to produce the minimum cost? What is the minimum cost?

10. Mr. Poss, the rancher, wants to create a rectangular pasture that has a maximum area and borders on a river, so that no fencing is required on that side of the pasture. What should the dimensions of the pasture and the maximum area of the pasture be if Mr. Poss has only 120 yards of fencing material available?

Get with the Program

John von Neumann
(1903-1957)

On December 28, 1903, John von Neumann was born in Budapest, Hungary, to Max and Gita von Neumann. John was to become one of the most important men in mathematics in the history of the United States and even of the world. Although most people today have never heard of him, his discoveries are important to our modern society.

John was born to wealthy parents who appreciated and encouraged their son in his endeavors in mathematics. By the time John was six, he could divide two eight-digit numbers in his head; by ten, he had completed college calculus. Needless to say, this boy was not the usual ten-year-old. He had a photographic memory that enabled him to look briefly at a page of numbers in a telephone book and then recall a whole column of names, addresses, and phone numbers. Despite his precocity John was not overly proud. He realized that God had given him a gift for obtaining knowledge. John was a considerate child who enjoyed playing with other children yet loved to carry on conversations with adults.

When von Neumann finished high school, his father thought he should enter into a field of study in which he could make more money than he could make in mathematics. It was thus decided that John would enter the University of Berlin to study chemistry. John submitted to his father's wishes although his real love was for mathematics. After receiving a degree in chemistry in 1925, he earned a Ph.D. in mathematics from the University of Budapest in just one year.

John von Neumann taught for several years at the universities of Berlin and Hamburg. In 1930 he came to the United States as a visiting professor at Princeton University and in

1933 became a professor at the newly established Institute for Advanced Study in Princeton, where Albert Einstein had just accepted a position as director of the school of mathematics. In 1937 von Neumann became an American citizen.

John loved to play with numbers in his spare time. He especially liked to search for prime numbers on car license plates. His wife, Klara von Neumann, became interested in programming computers. Soon John became interested in computers also.

During World War II, von Neumann was involved with the War Department of the U.S. government. His assignments included submarine warfare projects, economic intelligence projects, and ordnance problems. Each group that he worked with gave him the problems they could not solve. His most famous work came out of secret meetings at Los Alamos, New Mexico, where scientists and mathematicians were gathered to develop the atomic bomb. By creating a means of detonating a bomb by an inward burst, von Neumann expedited the development of the atomic bomb by one year.

When the war was over in 1945, John von Neumann became the director of Princeton Institute's Electronic Computer Project, which developed several electronic computers. One of these computers was called MANIAC (mathematical analyzer, numerical integrator and computer). Businesses and government were quick to take advantage of these new high-speed computers. Never satisfied, von Neumann constantly improved his computers. These improvements led to the computations necessary for the invention of the H- bomb, which in turn made the invention of intercontinental ballistic missiles (ICBMs) possible.

John von Neumann realized that man could make some amazing machinery that could find the answers to some difficult problems. But he believed that no machine that man could design or manufacture could compare to the intelligence God created in man. Von Neumann once said, "There is no comparison between the human nervous system and the most complicated machine that human intelligence has ever devised, or can devise. No man can tell me that behind the complications of the human nervous system there is no such thing as a greater intelligence. For me, that other intelligence is God." Von Neumann continued working with computers until his death February 8, 1957.

QUADRATIC INEQUALITIES

Quadratic inequalities, like linear inequalities, have an infinite number of ordered-pair solutions. Because quadratic inequalities are not functions, they cannot be put into the functional notation $f(x)$. Since quadratic inequalities do indicate sets of ordered pairs, they can be put into set notation. What is any set of ordered pairs called?

EXAMPLE

Example 1. Graph $\{(x, y) \mid y \geq 4(x - 2)^2 + 3\}$.

Solution.

$a = 4$
$h = 2$
$k = 3$

$f(x)$

x	y
3	7
1	7
$\frac{3}{2}$	4

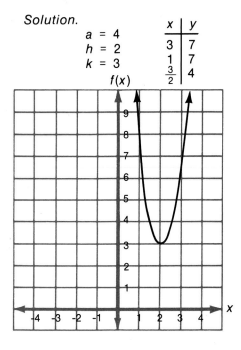

1. Graph the inequality as if it were the equation $y = 4(x - 2)^2 + 3$. Determine the values for a, h, and k. The graph opens upward and has a minimum vertex of $(2, 3)$. Solve for three more points of reference.

2. Graph the parabola with a solid line since the symbol $\geq$ is used.

3. Now decide where to shade for the solution. Choose some point inside or outside the parabola and substitute the coordinate values into the inequality to see if the point is a solution. Choose $(0, 0)$, as you did with linear inequalities.

$$y \geq 4(x - 2)^2 + 3$$
$$0 \geq 4(0 - 2)^2 + 3$$
$$0 \geq 4(-2)^2 + 3$$
$$0 \geq 4(4) + 3$$
$$0 \geq 16 + 3$$
$$0 \geq 19 \qquad \text{false}$$

The point (0,0) is usually easiest to check in the inequality, but any point can be used.

OK, WHO PUT THE SIGN ON BACKWARDS

This statement is false, so (0, 0) is not in the solution. Therefore the solution set is any point inside the parabola. Shade the area inside. Since the inequality indicates "greater than or equal to," the solution is any point inside or on the parabola.

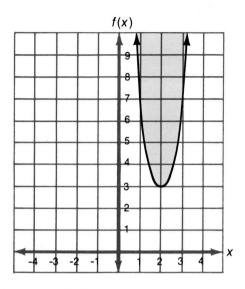

Check. Check a point inside the parabola, say (2, 5).

$$y \geq 4(x - 2)^2 + 3$$
$$5 \geq 4(2 - 2)^2 + 3$$
$$5 \geq 4(0) + 3$$
$$5 \geq 3$$

This statement is true, so (2, 5) is a solution.

Procedure for Storage

Graphing Quadratic Inequalities

1. Write the inequality as an equation in the form $y = a(x - h)^2 + k$.

2. Graph it as an equation, using a solid line if $\geq$ or $\leq$ is used and a dotted line if $>$ or $<$ is used.

3. Choose a point not on the parabola. If the ordered pair makes the inequality true, shade the area in which the point appears. If it makes the inequality false, shade the area in which the point does not appear.

EXAMPLE

Example 2. Graph $\{(x, y) \mid y < 2x^2 + 16x + 3\}$.

Solution.

$$y = 2x^2 + 16x + 3$$
$$y = 2(x^2 + 8x) + 3$$
$$y = 2(x^2 + 8x + 16) + 3 - 32$$
$$y = 2(x + 4)^2 - 29$$
$$y = 2(x - -4)^2 - 29$$

1. Place the inequality in proper equation form.

$$a = 2$$
$$h = -4$$
$$k = -29$$

2. Determine the values for a, h, and k.

x	y
0	3
-5	-27
-2	-21

3. Find at least three more ordered pairs. Connect them with a smooth, dotted curve because the inequality symbol is $<$.

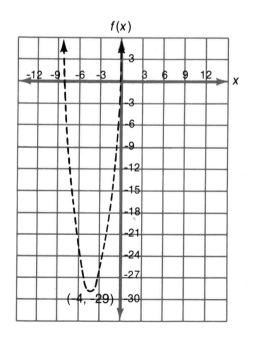

$(-4, -29)$

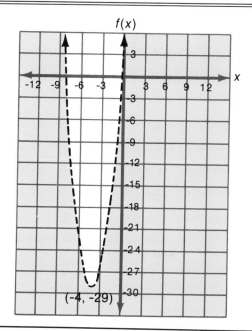

(-4, -29)

4. To determine the side of the parabola on which the solution lies, substitute (3, 0) (which is outside the parabola) in the inequality.

$$y < 2x^2 + 16x + 3$$
$$0 < 2(3)^2 + 16(3) + 3$$
$$0 < 69$$

This statement is true, so you should shade the area outside the parabola.

Exercises

Graph each inequality.

1. $\{(x, y) \mid y \leq x^2 - 4x\}$

2. $\{(x, y) \mid y > 2(x + 3)^2 - 5\}$

3. $\{(x, y) \mid y < -4(x - 2)^2 + 3\}$

4. $\{(x, y) \mid y \geq 3(x + 2)^2 - 5\}$

5. $\{(x, y) \mid y \leq x^2 - 4\}$

6. $\{(x, y) \mid y \geq x^2 + 4x + 4\}$

7. $\{(x, y) \mid y \leq 2x^2 - 3x + 1\}$

8. $\{(x, y) \mid y > 8x^2 + 16x\}$

9. $\{(x, y) \mid y < x^2 - 3x - 10\}$

10. $\{(x, y) \mid y \leq x^2 - 2x + 1\}$

11. $\{(x, y) \mid y > 3x^2 + 9x\}$

12. $\{(x, y) \mid y \leq 2x^2 - 10x + 12\}$

MEMORY RECALL

Identify.
> functional notation
> line of symmetry
> parabola
> quadratic function
> quadratic inequality
> vertex
> zeros of a function

You should be able to do the following:
1. Use functional notation.
2. Graph quadratic functions in three forms.
3. Place quadratic functions in the proper form for graphing.
4. Find the zeros of a quadratic function.
5. Apply procedures learned about quadratic functions to word problems.
6. Graph quadratic inequalities.

You should be able to solve the following problems:
1. Find the value of each function when $x = -5$, $x = 3$, and $x = 10$.

   a. $f(x) = 12x - 7$
   b. $f(x) = x^2 + 2x - 3$
   c. $f(x) = 2x^2 - 6x - 9$

Graph, giving the vertex and the zeros of each quadratic function.

2. $f(x) = 5x^2$

3. $f(x) = \frac{1}{3} x^2 + 6$

4. $f(x) = \frac{1}{4} x^2$

5. $f(x) = 3x^2 - 7$

6. $f(x) = -2x^2 + 12$

7. $f(x) = (x + 6)^2$

8. $f(x) = -3(x - 2)^2$

9. $f(x) = \frac{1}{2}(x + 4)^2$

10. $f(x) = -5(x - 7)^2 - 3$

11. $f(x) = \frac{2}{3}(x + 6)^2 + 2$

12. $f(x) = x^2 + 6x + 1$

13. $f(x) = x^2 - 14x + 37$

14. Frank Furter runs a hot dog distribution warehouse that distributes hot dogs to the local grocery stores. The amount of profit that he makes depends on the number of boxes of hot dogs he sells. The profit follows the equation $p(x) = -x^2 + 140x - 3940$. What is his maximum profit, and how many boxes must he sell to make the maximum profit?

Graph each quadratic inequality.

15. $y \geq 2x^2$

16. $y < -4(x + 5)^2$

17. $y > (x - 1)^2 + 6$

18. $y \leq x^2 + 10x + 15$

Table of Powers and Roots

No.	Sq.	Sq. Root	Cube	Cube Root	No.	Sq.	Sq. Root	Cube	Cube Root
1	1	1.000	1	1.000	51	2,601	7.141	132,651	3.708
2	4	1.414	8	1.260	52	2,704	7.211	140,608	3.733
3	9	1.732	27	1.442	53	2,809	7.280	148,877	3.756
4	16	2.000	64	1.587	54	2,916	7.348	157,464	3.780
5	25	2.236	125	1.710	55	3,025	7.416	166,375	3.803
6	36	2.449	216	1.817	56	3,136	7.483	175,616	3.826
7	49	2.646	343	1.913	57	3,249	7.550	185,193	3.848
8	64	2.828	512	2.000	58	3,364	7.616	195,112	3.871
9	81	3.000	729	2.080	59	3,481	7.681	205,379	3.893
10	100	3.162	1,000	2.154	60	3,600	7.746	216,000	3.915
11	121	3.317	1,331	2.224	61	3,721	7.810	226,981	3.936
12	144	3.464	1,728	2.289	62	3,844	7.874	238,328	3.958
13	169	3.606	2,197	2.351	63	3,969	7.937	250,047	3.979
14	196	3.742	2,744	2.410	64	4,096	8.000	262,144	4.000
15	225	3.873	3,375	2.466	65	4,225	8.062	274,625	4.021
16	256	4.000	4,096	2.520	66	4,356	8.124	287,496	4.041
17	289	4.123	4,913	2.571	67	4,489	8.185	300,763	4.062
18	324	4.243	5,832	2.621	68	4,624	8.246	314,432	4.082
19	361	4.359	6,859	2.668	69	4,761	8.307	328,509	4.102
20	400	4.472	8,000	2.714	70	4,900	8.367	343,000	4.121
21	441	4.583	9,261	2.759	71	5,041	8.426	357,911	4.141
22	484	4.690	10,648	2.802	72	5,184	8.485	373,248	4.160
23	529	4.796	12,167	2.844	73	5,329	8.544	389,017	4.179
24	576	4.899	13,824	2.884	74	5,476	8.602	405,224	4.198
25	625	5.000	15,625	2.924	75	5,625	8.660	421,875	4.217
26	676	5.099	17,576	2.962	76	5,776	8.718	438,976	4.236
27	729	5.196	19,683	3.000	77	5,929	8.775	456,533	4.254
28	784	5.292	21,952	3.037	78	6,084	8.832	474,552	4.273
29	841	5.385	24,389	3.072	79	6,241	8.888	493,039	4.291
30	900	5.477	27,000	3.107	80	6,400	8.944	512,000	4.309
31	961	5.568	29,791	3.141	81	6,561	9.000	531,441	4.327
32	1,024	5.657	32,768	3.175	82	6,724	9.055	551,368	4.344
33	1,089	5.745	35,937	3.208	83	6,889	9.110	571,787	4.362
34	1,156	5.831	39,304	3.240	84	7,056	9.165	592,704	4.380
35	1,225	5.916	42,875	3.271	85	7,225	9.220	614,125	4.397
36	1,296	6.000	46,656	3.302	86	7,396	9.274	636,056	4.414
37	1,369	6.083	50,653	3.332	87	7,569	9.327	658,503	4.431
38	1,444	6.164	54,872	3.362	88	7,744	9.381	681,472	4.448
39	1,521	6.245	59,319	3.391	89	7,921	9.434	704,969	4.465
40	1,600	6.325	64,000	3.420	90	8,100	9.487	729,000	4.481
41	1,681	6.403	68,921	3.448	91	8,281	9.539	753,571	4.498
42	1,764	6.481	74,088	3.476	92	8,464	9.592	778,688	4.514
43	1,849	6.557	79,507	3.503	93	8,649	9.644	804,357	4.531
44	1,936	6.633	85,184	3.530	94	8,836	9.695	830,584	4.547
45	2,025	6.708	91,125	3.557	95	9,025	9.747	857,375	4.563
46	2,116	6.782	97,336	3.583	96	9,216	9.798	884,736	4.579
47	2,209	6.856	103,823	3.609	97	9,409	9.849	912,673	4.595
48	2,304	6.928	110,592	3.634	98	9,604	9.899	941,192	4.610
49	2,401	7.000	117,649	3.659	99	9,801	9.950	970,299	4.626
50	2,500	7.071	125,000	3.684	100	10,000	10.000	1,000,000	4.642

Symbols

+	addition or positive
-	subtraction or negative
·	multiplication
÷	division
=	is equal to
±	positive or negative
$\sqrt{}$	principal square root
X	cross product
∈	an element of
{ }	set
∪	union
∩	intersection
V	or
Λ	and
≠	is not equal to
≥	greater than or equal to
≤	less than or equal to
>	greater than
<	less than
≐	approximately equal to
∅	empty set, null set
π	pi
$|x|$	absolute value of x
%	percent
$f(x)$	f of x, function of x
( )	parentheses
[ ]	brackets

GLOSSARY

A

abscissa The first element of an ordered pair; x-coordinate.

absolute value The number of units that a number is from 0 on the number line. More formally, the absolute value of a number is equal to that number if it is greater than or equal to 0 and is equal to the negative of that number if it is less than 0.

addition method A method of solving simultaneous equations by adding the equations to cause one of the variables to be eliminated.

addition property of inequality The principle that if a, b, and c are real numbers such that $a < b$, then $a + c < b + c$.

additive identity element The number 0; the value such that when added to another number yields the same number.

additive inverse property The principle that for any number a, $a + (-a) = 0$.

additive inverses Numbers that when located on a number line are the same distance from 0 but on opposite sides of it. Their sum is 0, the additive identity element.

algebraic expression A string of one or more variables and constants or products of variables and constants connected with + and - signs.

associative property of addition The principle that addends can be grouped in any order before they are added without affecting the sum. For any numbers a, b, and c, $a + (b + c) = (a + b) + c$.

associative property of multiplication The principle that factors can be grouped in any order before they are multiplied without affecting the product. For any numbers a, b, and c, $a(bc) = (ab)c$.

axis A reference line in a plane.

B

base A term that is raised to a power indicated by an exponent. In the expression a^3, the base a is raised to the third power.

binomial A polynomial with exactly two terms.

C

Cartesian plane The plane formed by a Cartesian product described by $\mathbb{R} \times \mathbb{R}$ on which algebraic equations are graphed.

Cartesian product The set of all possible ordered pairs in $A \times B$ where the first element of the ordered pairs comes from A and the second element comes from B.

coefficient *See* numerical coefficient.

common denominator The least common multiple of the denominators.

common monomial factor A factor of a polynomial common to all terms in the polynomial.

commutative property of addition The principle that addends can be arranged in any order without affecting the sum. For any numbers a and b, $a + b = b + a$.

commutative property of multiplication The principle that factors can be arranged in any order without affecting the product. For numbers a and b, $a \cdot b = b \cdot a$.

completing the square A method by which a polynomial can be changed to a perfect square trinomial.

complex rational expression An algebraic expression of the form $\frac{c}{d}$, where either c or d or c and d are rational expressions.

composite number A nonprime positive integer greater than 1.

compound sentence A mathematical relationship defined in terms of two or more equations or inequalities connected by *and* or *or*.

conjugate of a radical expression The radical expression with the opposite sign between the terms. For example, the conjugate of $\sqrt{2} - 1$ is $\sqrt{2} + 1$.

conjunction A compound sentence consisting of sentences connected by the word *and*, meaning intersection, and symbolized by $\wedge$.

consistent system of equations A system of equations that has a solution.

constant A symbol that represents a fixed number.

constant of variation The constant relating two variables in a direct variation. In the expression $y = kx$, k is the constant of variation.

coordinate The number that corresponds to a point on a number line.

coordinates An ordered pair of numbers that corresponds to the location of a point in a plane.

cube root One of a number's three equal factors.

D

degree of a polynomial The degree of the highest-degree term in a polynomial.

degree of a term The sum of the exponents on the variables.

dependent system of equations A consistent system of equations that has an infinite number of solutions.

direct variation A linear function in which one variable is a multiple of the other variable.

discriminant The radicand in the quadratic formula.

disjunction A compound sentence consisting of sentences connected by the word *or*, meaning union, and symbolized by V.

distance formula The formula $d = (x_1 - x_2)^2 + (y_1 - y_2)^2$, which is used to find the distance (d) between the two points (x_1, y_1) and (x_2, y_2).

distributive property The principle that the sum (or difference) of two numbers multiplied by a factor is equal to the two numbers individually multiplied by the factor and then added (or subtracted). For any numbers a, b, and c, $a(b + c) = ab + ac$ or $a(b - c) = ab - ac$.

division property of inequality The principle that if a, b, and c are real numbers such that $a < b$ and $c \neq 0$, then $\frac{a}{c} < \frac{b}{c}$ if $c > 0$ and $\frac{a}{c} > \frac{b}{c}$ if $c < 0$.

division property of radicals The principle that a radical having a fractional term in its radicand is equal to the numerator of the original radicand taken to the root indicated by its index divided by the denominator of the original radicand taken to the same root; for real numbers x and y with $y \neq 0$,

$$\sqrt[n]{\frac{x}{y}} = \frac{\sqrt[n]{x}}{\sqrt[n]{y}}$$

domain The set of first elements of the ordered pairs of a relation.

E

elements The components of a set.

empty set A set that has no elements.

equation A mathematical sentence stating that two expressions are equal.

equivalent inequalities Inequalities that have the same solution set.

evaluating the expression The process of calculating the numerical value of an expression.

exponent A superscript written to the right of a term (the base), indicating the number of times the base is to be multiplied by itself. In the expression a^3, 3 is the exponent of the base a.

exponential form A simplified form of writing repeated multiplication.

extraneous root An apparent solution to an equation, but one that does not check.

F

factor *n.* A number that when multiplied with another number gives a product.

v. To find the numbers that have been multiplied to give a product.

finite set A set in which the elements can be counted or listed.

FOIL method A quick method of mentally multiplying binomials by finding the products of the first, outer, inner, and last terms and then combining like terms.

formula An equation that describes a principle of nature or numbers.

function A relation in which each x-coordinate is paired with one and only one y-coordinate.

functional notation A means of expressing the dependence of one variable upon another. For example, $y = x + 5$ can be expressed in functional notation as $f(x) = x + 5$, indicating that the value of y depends upon the value assigned to x, and hence, is a "function of x."

G

graph of a number A dot placed at the indicated number on a number line.

greatest common divisor (GCD) The largest positive integer that divides evenly into two numbers.

H

hypotenuse The side of a right triangle opposite its right angle.

I

identity An equation or statement that is true for any value of the variable.

identity property of zero The principle that adding zero to a number gives the original number. For any number a, there is a number 0, such that $a + 0 = a$.

inconsistent system of equations A system of equations that has no solution.

independent system of equations A consistent system of equations that has only one solution.

index The small number above the radical sign that indicates the root to be taken.

inequality A mathematical sentence that states that two numbers or expressions are not always equal.

infinite set A set that is not finite.

integers The set of whole numbers and their opposites.

$$\{ \ldots, -4, -3, -2, -1, 0, 1, 2, 3, 4, \ldots \}$$

intersection of sets The set of all elements that appear in all of the sets.

irrational numbers Numbers that cannot be expressed in fractional form as one integer over another integer.

L

least common multiple (LCM) The smallest positive integer that is a multiple of two numbers.

like terms Terms that have the same variable (or variables) with the same exponents.

linear equation An equation that when graphed is a straight line.

linear function A function described by the equation $f(x) = ax + c$.

linear program A method of solving problems containing several conditions (constraints) involving inequalities and having the primary objective of finding the maximum or minimum value of an objective function.

literal equation An equation with two or more letters in it.

M

mathematical property An equation or statement that is true for any value of the variable. Properties are sometimes called identities.

monomial A polynomial with only one term.

multiplication property of inequality The principle that if a, b, and c are real numbers such that $a < b$, then $ac < bc$ if $c > 0$ and $ac > bc$ if $c < 0$.

multiplicative identity element The number 1; a value such that when multiplied by a number gives the number.

multiplicative inverse property The principle that for any number $b \neq 0$, $b \cdot \frac{1}{b} = 1$.

multiplicative inverses Numbers that when multiplied produce 1.

N

natural numbers The counting numbers beginning with 1 and continuing infinitely.

$$\{1, 2, 3, 4, \ldots\}$$

null set *See* empty set.

number line A graphical representation of numbers with positive numbers of increasing magnitude plotted successively at equal intervals along a line to the right of (or above) a zero point and with negative numbers plotted in the same manner to the left of (or below) the zero point.

numerical coefficient The numerical factor accompanying the variables in a term.

O

opposite numbers Numbers that when located on a number line are the same distance from 0 but on opposite sides of 0.

order of operations A method of evaluating from left to right a string of terms in which exponentials are evaluated first, multiplication and division operations are performed next, and addition and subtraction operations are done last.

ordered pair A pair of symbols in which the order of the symbols has meaning.

ordinate The second element of an ordered pair; y-coordinate.

origin The point at which the axes of a coordinate plane cross.

P

parabola The graph of a quadratic function.

perfect square trinomial The square of a binomial, characterized by three terms, the first and last, which are perfect squares, and the middle term, which is twice the product of the square roots of the first and last terms of the trinomial.

perimeter The sum of the lengths of the sides of a polygon.

plane A flat surface that extends infinitely and has an infinite number of points.

point-slope form a linear equation in the form $y - y_1 = m(x - x_1)$, where m is the slope of the line and (x_1, y_1) are the coordinates of a given point.

polynomial An algebraic expression with one or more terms.

prime factorization The expression of a number as the product of prime numbers.

prime number An integer greater than 1 whose only positive factors are 1 and itself.

product property of radicals The principle that the product of two radicals having the same index is equal to the product of their radicands taken to the root indicated by the index. For real numbers x and y,

$$\sqrt[n]{xy} = \sqrt[n]{x} \cdot \sqrt[n]{y}$$

Pythagorean theorem The statement that the sum of the squares of the lengths of the legs of a right triangle is equal to the square of the length of the hypotenuse.

Q

quadrant One of four sections into which two perpendicular lines divide a plane.

quadratic equation An equation of the second degree in the form $ax^2 + bx + c = 0$, where a, b, and c are real numbers and $a \neq 0$.

quadratic formula The formula

$$x = \frac{-b \pm \sqrt{b^2 - 4ac}}{2a},$$

used to solve quadratic equations in the form $ax^2 + bx + c = 0$, with $a \neq 0$.

quadratic function A function described by the equation $f(x) = ax^2 + bx + c$, with $a \neq 0$.

R

radical An expression in the form $\sqrt[n]{x}$.

radical equation An equation that contains a variable in a radical.

radical expresson An algebraic expression containing at least one radical.

radical sign The symbol ($\sqrt{\ }$) for the principal (positive) square root.

radicand The number in a radical whose root is to be found.

range The set of second elements of the ordered pairs of a relation.

ratio The comparison of two numbers by division.

rational equation An equation containing a rational expression with a variable in the denominator.

rational expression An algebraic expression that is a ratio of two polynomials, with the polynomial in the denominator not equal to zero.

rational number A number that can be expressed as a ratio of two integers, with the denominator not equal to zero.

rationalizing the denominator A procedure for removing a radical from the denominator of a fraction by multiplying both numerator and denominator by a radical that will cause the radicand in the denominator to become a perfect power.

real numbers Numbers from the set of rational and irrational numbers.

reciprocals Two numbers whose product is 1.

relation Any set of ordered pairs.

relatively prime numbers Two numbers whose greatest common divisor is 1.

right angle An angle whose measure is 90°.

right triangle A triangle that contains a right angle.

S

set A group or collection of objects or numbers.

square root One of a number's two equal factors.

substitution The process of replacing a variable with a value.

substitution method A method for solving simultaneous equations by solving one equation for one variable, substituting the solution into the other equation, and then solving for the other variable.

subtraction property of inequality The principle that if a, b, and c are real numbers such that $a < b$, then $a - c < b - c$.

successive approximation method A method of obtaining the square root of a number through a series of approximations, divisions, and averages.

system of equations Two or more equations in two or more variables to be solved simultaneously.

term A variable, number, product, or quotient of numbers and variables that is a part of an algebraic expression separated by + and - signs.

theorem A proven statement that is always true.

trinomial A polynomial with exactly three terms.

twin primes Prime numbers that differ in value by 2.

U

union of sets The set of all the elements that appear in any of the sets.

V

variable A symbol used to represent any number of a given set of numbers.

vertex of a parabola The point at which a parabola reaches its highest or lowest point; the point at which a parabola intersects its line of symmetry.

vertical line test The method of moving a vertical line across the graph of a relation to determine if the relation is also a function.

W

whole numbers The set of natural numbers with 0.

$$\{0, 1, 2, 3, \dots \}$$

X

***x*-axis** The horizontal reference line in a Cartesian plane.

***x*-coordinate** The first element of an ordered pair; the abscissa.

***x*-intercept** The point at which a graph of an equation crosses, or intersects, the *x*-axis.

Y

***y*-axis** The vertical reference line in a plane.

***y*-coordinate** The second element of an ordered pair; the ordinate.

***y*-intercept** The point at which a line crosses, or intersects, the *y*-axis.

Z

zero product property The principle that if the product of two or more factors is 0, at least one of the factors is 0.

zero property of multiplication The principle that whenever a number is multiplied by 0, the product will always be 0. For any number $a, a \cdot 0 = 0$.

zeros of a function The *x*-value (or values) of the point (or points) at which a graph of a function crosses the *x*-axis.

INDEX

To the Student

In I Thessalonians 4:11-12 Paul says to the believers at Thessalonica, "And that ye study to be quiet, and to do your own business, and to work with your own hands, as we commanded you; That ye may walk honestly toward them that are without, and that ye may have lack of nothing." It is the Christian student's duty to his Lord and Saviour Jesus Christ to act honestly in all things.

Answers to the odd-numbered problems in each exercise section are provided here for you to use as immediate individual feedback. Diligently and thoroughly do your daily assignments before you check your work against the answers. If any answer is incorrect, examine each step of your work to find your mistake. You need to understand how to arrive at the answer.

The author hopes that these answers will provide you with the immediate feedback necessary to help you gain a better understanding and thus a greater satisfaction and more enjoyment in your study of algebra. Use the answers to increase your knowledge, not just to get your homework done.

"The fear of the Lord is the beginning of knowledge; but fools despise wisdom and instruction." Proverbs 1:7

Chapter 1 Numbers and Their Operations

Page 5

1-13.

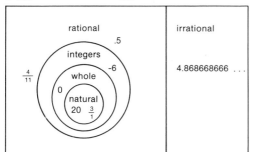

15. no; no **17.** yes, 1; no

Page 8

1.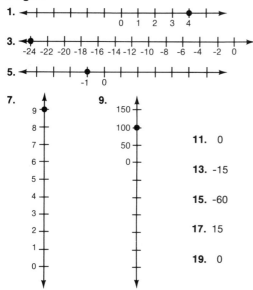

3.

5.

7.

9.

11. 0

13. -15

15. -60

17. 15

19. 0

Pages 12-13

1. -38 **3.** -42 **5.** -134 **7.** 412 **9.** 5 **11.** 8
13. 382 **15.** 0 **17.** 84 **19.** 74 **21.** 4 **23.** 307
25. 315 **27.** 857 **29.** 32 **31.** 13 **33.** 12
35. 63 **37.** 76 **39.** 85 **41.** They are the same.

Page 18

1. 24 **3.** -2 **5.** -91 **7.** 4 **9.** 55 **11.** 360 **13.** 0
15. -14 **17.** 1032 **19.** -4510 **21.** The addends have unlike signs. 1. Determine the absolute value of the addends. 2. Subtract the smaller absolute value from the larger. 3. Give the difference the sign of the number with the greater absolute value. The result is the sum.
23. Additive inverse **25.** 12 knots

Page 21

1. 5 **3.** 10 **5.** -2 **7.** -329 **9.** -17 **11.** -24
13. -130 **15.** 14 **17.** 414
19.

Page 24

1. -6 **3.** 24 **5.** 3 **7.** 36 **9.** 287 **11.** 125
13. -16,014 **15.** -17,112 **17.** 351,934
19. -38,920 **21.** $24

Page 26

1. 9 **3.** undefined **5.** -9 **7.** -63 **9.** 83 **11.** -8
13. -6 **15.** undefined **17.** -9 **19.** -56

Page 27

1. -48 **3.** -2214 **5.** -416 **7.** -140 **9.** 1992
11. -2756 **13.** -496 **15.** 1296 **17.** -403 **19.** 93
21. -193 **23.** -764 **25.** 57 **27.** -24 **29.** 134
31. -42 **33.** -2555 **35.** 76 **37.** 630 **39.** -5489
41. See chart on p. 26 for examples.

Pages 30-31

1. $4 \cdot 4 \cdot 4 = 64$ **3.** $5 \cdot 5 \cdot 5 = 125$
5. $(-2)(-2)(-2)(-2) = 16$ **7.** $1 \cdot 1 \cdot 1 \cdot 1 = 1$
9. $6 \cdot 6 \cdot 6 \cdot 6 = 1296$ **11.** 7^4 **13.** 5^6
15. 127^3 **17.** 7^{11} **19.** 8^4 **21.** 3^8 **23.** 28^8 **25.** 2^2
27. 12^9 **29.** 10^{50} **31.** $2^5 \cdot 3^4 \cdot 5^3$ **33.** negative
35. positive **37.** negative

Page 34

1. $2^4 \cdot 3$ **3.** $3^2 \cdot 97$ **5.** $2^2 \cdot 5 \cdot 41$ **7.** $2^3 \cdot 173$
9. $2 \cdot 47$ **11.** $7^3 \cdot 3^4$ **13.** $7 \cdot 5 \cdot 3^2 \cdot 2^6$
15. $7 \cdot 3 \cdot 2^7$

Page 40

1. 2 **3.** $2^3 = 8$ **5.** $7 \cdot 5 \cdot 3 \cdot 2^2 = 420$
7. $2^2 \cdot 7 \cdot 5 \cdot 17 = 2380$ **9.** $2 \cdot 19 \cdot 5 = 190$
11. $7 \cdot 3^2 \cdot 11 \cdot 2^5 = 22{,}176$

Page 45

1. $\frac{5}{7}$ **3.** $\frac{1}{3}$ **5.** $\frac{3}{5}$ **7.** 40 **9.** 42 **11.** $\frac{24}{48}$
13. $\frac{18}{48}$ **15.** $\frac{56}{48}$ **17.** -1 **19.** $\frac{5}{6}$ **21.** $\frac{82}{21}$
23. $\frac{103}{35}$ **25.** $\frac{-44}{189}$ **27.** 849.83 **29.** 617.1

Page 51

1. $\frac{5}{21}$ **3.** $\frac{49}{8}$ **5.** $\frac{12}{5}$ **7.** $\frac{4}{9}$ **9.** $\frac{1}{68}$

11. 78.96 **13.** 282 **15.** 0.87 **17.** $\frac{1}{2}$ gal.

19. 1; multiplicative identity

Pages 52-53

1. multiplicative identity **3.** commutative of addition **5.** commutative of multiplication
7. additive identity **9.** commutative of multiplication **11.** commutative of addition
13. See examples on page 52.

Page 55

1. 7 **3.** 9 **5.** 1 **7.** $\frac{9}{5}$ **9.** $\frac{3}{4}$ **11.** -15 **13.** 19
15. 6 **17.** -3 **19.** 7

Pages 58-59

1. {1, 3} **3.** {-1} **5.** {-1, 2, 5, 6} = C
7. {Ala., Ark., Fla., Ill., Iowa, Ky., La., Minn.,
Miss., Mo., Tenn., Tex., Wis.} **9.** {Minn., Mo.,
Miss.} **11.** {Miss., La.} **13.** {0, 1, 2, 3, ...}
15. A = {-5, -3, -1, 0, 1, 2, 3}
     B = {0, 2, 4, 6, 8, 10}

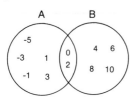

17. Answers will vary; ex. A = {2, 4, 6, 8, 10, ...}

Pages 61-63

1. Numerical examples will vary; natural, 3;
whole, 0; integer, -6; rational, $\frac{5}{2}$; and irrational, $\sqrt{2}$

3. a.

> -3 -2 -1 0

c.

> 0   6   12   18   24

5. a. 13   c. 249 **7.** a. -2   c. 4
e. 185   g. 20   i. 444   k. 180
m. -0.124   o. 4   **9.** a. $5^2 \cdot 3$
c. $2 \cdot 59$ **11.** a. $2^2 = 4$ **13.** a. 13
13. c. $\frac{1}{2}$ **15.** a. {2, 4, 6, 8, 10, 14, 20, 26, 32, ...}
c. {2, 4}   e. {0, 1, 2, 3, 4, 5, 6, 8, 10}

Chapter 2 The Language of Algebra

Page 68

1. 17 **3.** 11 **5.** 7 **7.** 8 **9.** 5 **11.** 9 **13.** 22
15. 0 **17.** 23 **19.** 14

Page 72

1. 45 **3.** 75 **5.** 126 $\frac{1}{2}$ **7.** 20 **9.** 1389 **11.** 30
13. -6 **15.** 9 **17.** 3 + 9 · (2 - 6)
19. 5 · [(6 -1) + 3] ÷ 20

Page 75

1. 8x **3.** 8s **5.** 325n **7.** 5n + 4 **9.** 5x + 25y
11. -8, -1, -3, 4 **13.** -12, 9, 3, 24 **15.** a. V—x;
C—3, 6 **17.** V—c, d; C—5 **19.** commutative
21. associative

Page 78

1. a^3 **3.** k^2 **5.** d^2p^4 **7.** v^7 **9.** rua^2 **11.** xxxxx
13. ccc **15.** tttttt **17.** $\frac{1}{x^5}$ **19.** $\frac{1}{y^2}$ **21.** $\frac{1}{4^3}$ **23.** 8^{-2}
25. x^{-2}, y^{-9} **27.** $x^{-2}y^{-1}z^{-3}$
29. 4^7 **31.** 9^2 **33.** $\frac{1}{4^3}$ **35.** 1 **37.** $\frac{1}{y^2}$ **39.** x^{10}

Page 80

1. a. -32   c. -2   e. -5   g. 37   i. -59

Pages 82-83

1. 12.56 ft. **3.** 180 ft. **5.** 87.92 sq. ft.
7. a. 40 cu. in.   c. 336 cu. in.

Page 88

1. 3x, 4x; 3, 4, 5 **3.** xy, 2xy, 9xy; 1, 2, 9
5. $2x^3$, $5x^3$; 2, 17, 5 **7.** 6k
9. 19b **11.** -3d + 10f **13.** -5.94m + 1.6n
15. 14ab **17.** $3y^2$ -8y **19.** Add $-a^2 + 3a + 4$
21. 3x + y; 3 **23.** cannot be simplified; -3
25. $1 + xy^2 + x$

Page 91

1. 6a + 9 **3.** 4x + 8y **5.** -2x + 23 **7.** -6a -8b
9. 5a - 4b **11.** b - 18 **13.** $15x^2$ - 40x + 85
15. $5x^2$ - 2x **17.** -9p - 17 **19.** $-a^2 + 3a + 5$

Page 93

1. add 5 **3.** add 2 **5.** multiply by 2
7. divide by 2 **9.** divide by 5
11. Answers will vary. See chart on page 92.

Pages 95-96

1. n - 17 **3.** 2x + 6 **5.** x + y **7.** n + 24
9. 126 - n(n - 1) **11.** n + 82n
13. a number + 4
15. The difference of a number and 9 **17.** The
quotient of 4 and a number **19.** 8 less than the
sum of a and b **21.** Answers will vary.
sum, more, added to, plus, combined, increased
difference, less, minus, decreased, less than
product, multiply, times, of, doubled
quotient, divided by, division, fraction, half

Pages 98-99

1. 12x = 780 **3.** $\frac{3x}{16}$ = 12 **5.** 3x - 2 + x = 26
7. x + 29 + x = 85 or x - 29 + x = 85
9. x + x + 1 = 175 **11.** 2(x + 7) + 2x = 74
13. 3x + x + x + 120 = 180
15. x + x + 7 = 31 or x + x - 7 = 31

Pages 100-103

1. a. 15   c. -3   e. 38
g. -281   i. 93   k. 294
3. a. {-6, -5, 0, - 12}   c. {8, 13, 38, -22}
5. a. $\frac{1}{5^3}$ c. $\frac{1}{x^8}$ **7.** a. $\frac{1}{3^{10}}$ c. $\frac{1}{7^6}$ e. 2^4
9. 64 cu. in. **11.** a. 5x - 5y
c. -3x + 6y + 15   e. $4a^2 + 6a - 4$
13. Answers will vary.
15. a. 2x + 8 = 24   c. x + x + 3 = 59

Chapter 3 Solving Equations

Pages 108-9

1. 9 **3.** -10 **5.** 8 **7.** -56 **9.** 41 **11.** 34
13. -28 **15.** -10 **17.** 0.49 **19.** $\frac{1}{4}$ **21.** 22
23. 68 **25.** 8 **27.** 16.12 **29.** 28 **31.** 21 **33.** $\frac{1}{2}$
35. 4 **37.** 125 **39.** 56.28 **41.** $c - a$ **43.** $\frac{d}{r}$

Pages 114-15

1. -41 **3.** 84 **5.** 17 ft. **7.** 7 in. **9.** 81 stamps
11. -83 **13.** 5¢ **15.** 13

Pages 117-18

1. 8 **3.** 5 **5.** -8 **7.** -355 **9.** 41 **11.** 14 **13.** $\frac{31}{3}$
15. 35 **17.** 23 pieces of furniture **19.** 110 newspapers

Page 121

1. 1 **3.** 2 **5.** 7 **7.** -3 **9.** -2 **11.** -7 **13.** -14
15. -6 **17.** 2 **19.** $\frac{-b}{2}$
21. $x + (x + 11) = 63$; 26 boys; 37 girls
23. $x + (x - 12) = 87$ or $x + (x + 12) = 87$;
$49.50 for the camera, $37.50 for the calculator
25. $2[x + (x + 5)] = 34$ or $2[x + (x - 5)] = 34$;
6 ft. wide and 11 ft. long

Page 124

1. 2 **3.** 3 **5.** 1 **7.** 4 **9.** $\frac{3}{2}$ **11.** $\frac{4}{3}$ **13.** 0 **15.** 1
17. 13 **19.** -9 **21.** $\frac{2n}{m}$ **23.** 10 and 12 **25.** -3
and -2 **27.** -34

Page 127

1. 16, -16 **3.** 35, -39 **5.** $\frac{5}{2}$, $\frac{1}{2}$ **7.** 6, -10 **9.** 2, $\frac{-7}{6}$
11. $\frac{-5}{7}$, $\frac{13}{7}$ **13.** 19, -14 **15.** $\frac{95}{12}$, $\frac{-85}{12}$

Page 132

1. 2 **3.** 21 **5.** $\frac{50}{3}$ **7.** -4 **9.** 12 **11.** -44 **13.** 22
15. 7 **17.** 1 **19.** 5

Pages 137-38

1. a. 54 **c.** $\frac{19}{x}$ **e.** $35(x + 2)$ **g.** 4
3. 700 mph **5.** 63 mph, 40 mph **7.** 4 hours
9. 12 hours **11.** uphill, 10 ft./ sec.;
downhill, 80 ft./sec. **13.** 2 hr.
15. Jay ran $7\frac{1}{3}$ yd./sec.; John ran 7 yd./sec.
for 31.4 sec.

Pages 142-43

1. $\frac{2}{15}$ liter **3.** 27 gal. cream **5.** 3 gal. **7.** 2.4 oz.
9. 5 gal. **11.** 18 lb. hamburger, 12 lb. sausage

Pages 146-47

1. 14 nickels, 26 pennies, 9 half dollars
3. 26 quarters, 208 pennies
5. 7 dimes, 27 nickels
7. 75 pennies, 114 nickels **9.** 28 nickels,
4 quarters **11.** 10, 8, 3 **13.** Jack, 10; Emily, 13
15. Jill, 24; Beth, 12 **17.** 18 years

Pages 148-49

1. 131 **3.** 152 **5.** 45 **7.** 24 **9.** -2 **11.** -1
13. 6 **15.** 1 **17.** $\frac{-10}{7}$ **19.** 6 **21.** $\frac{-18}{5}$, 0 **23.** ±5
25. 5 **27.** $\frac{3y + 2}{6}$ **29.** $\frac{H}{R}$ **31.** Bill, 15; Jim, 6
33. 24, 87 **35.** $1\frac{1}{2}$ hours **37.** Angie, 16;
Barb, 12

Chapter 4 Solving Inequalities

Pages 154-55

1. > **3.** ≠ **5.** = **7.** < **9.** <, <

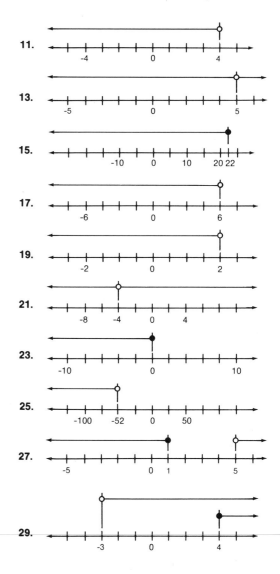

Page 159

1. $x > -12$

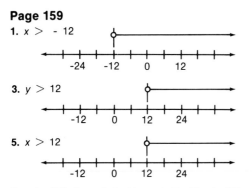

3. $y > 12$

5. $x > 12$

7. $y > 108$ **9.** $y \neq 8$ **11.** $x < 10$ **13.** $x \geq 155$
15. $z > 44$

Page 162

1. $x < 21$ **3.** $y \geq 32$ **5.** $x < 2$ **7.** $x \geq 7$ **9.** $x \geq \frac{-10}{7}$
11. $y \leq 96$ **13.** $x < -2$ **15.** $x < 26$

Page 164

1. $x \leq -2$

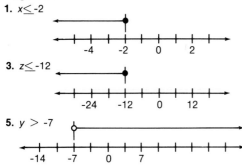

3. $z \leq -12$

5. $y > -7$

7. $x \leq -48$ **9.** $x > 0$ **11.** $z \geq \frac{-24}{11}$ **13.** $z < -130$
15. $z > -18$

Page 167

1. $x > 4$ **3.** $-3 < x \leq 1$ **5.** $x \geq 7$ **7.** $x < 4$
9. $x < -12$ **11.** $5 \leq x < 8$ **13.** $x > 7$

Page 170

1. $x =$ any real number **3.** $x =$ any real
number **5.** $x \leq 0$ or $x > 5$ **7.** $x > 3$ **9.** $x < 6$

Page 174

1. $x > -7$ and $x < 13$ **3.** $x \geq -6$ and $x \leq -2$
5. $x > \frac{1}{3}$ and $x < \frac{19}{3}$ **7.** $x \geq \frac{9}{2}$ and $x \leq \frac{33}{2}$
9. $x > -1$ and $x < 9$ **11.** $x > -1$ or $x < -3$
13. $x > -1$ or $x < -17$ **15.** $x > \frac{-9}{2}$ and $x < \frac{15}{2}$

Page 177

1. $x > 8$; $x + 4 > 12$ **3.** 3 cans **5.** at least
$80,000 **7.** 3 cars **9.** Naomi earns $\leq$ $80; Paul
earns $\leq$ $160; John earns $\leq$ $50.

Page 178-79

1. a.

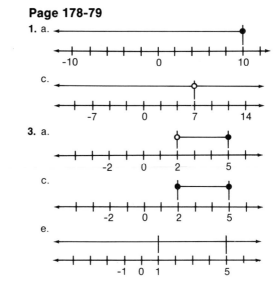

c.

3. a.

c.

e.

5. The number is greater than $\frac{7}{6}$; the integer is 2.

Chapter 5 Relations, Functions, and Graphs

Page 187

1. a. (-3, -1)
 c. (3, 5)
 e. (-4, 1)
 g. (-5, -4)
 i. (-1, 2)

15. The signs of
both coordinates
are positive; x is
negative; both
are negative;
y is negative.

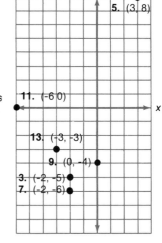

5. (3, 8)
11. (-6, 0)
13. (-3, -3)
9. (0, -4)
3. (-2, -5)
7. (-2, -6)

Page 193

1. is Relation,
Domain:{2, 5, 8},
Range: {4, 9, 2},
is function

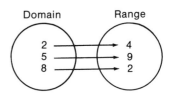

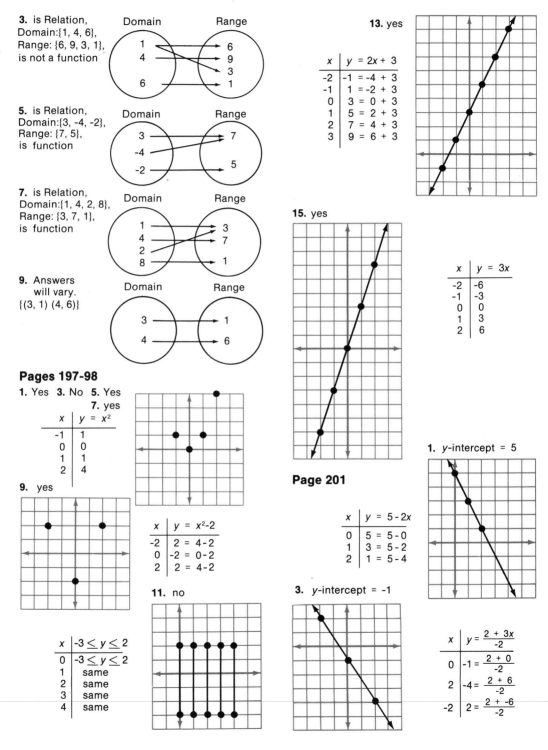

3. is Relation, Domain:{1, 4, 6}, Range: {6, 9, 3, 1}, is not a function

Domain Range

1 → 6
4 → 9
6 → 3
→ 1

5. is Relation, Domain:{3, -4, -2}, Range: {7, 5}, is function

Domain Range

3 → 7
-4 →
-2 → 5

7. is Relation, Domain:{1, 4, 2, 8}, Range: {3, 7, 1}, is function

Domain Range

1 → 3
4 → 7
2 →
8 → 1

9. Answers will vary. {(3, 1) (4, 6)}

Domain Range

3 → 1
4 → 6

Pages 197-98

1. Yes **3.** No **5.** Yes

7. yes

x	$y = x^2$
-1	1
0	0
1	1
2	4

9. yes

x	$y = x^2 - 2$
-2	2 = 4 - 2
0	-2 = 0 - 2
2	2 = 4 - 2

11. no

x	$-3 \leq y \leq 2$
0	$-3 \leq y \leq 2$
1	same
2	same
3	same
4	same

13. yes

x	$y = 2x + 3$
-2	-1 = -4 + 3
-1	1 = -2 + 3
0	3 = 0 + 3
1	5 = 2 + 3
2	7 = 4 + 3
3	9 = 6 + 3

15. yes

x	$y = 3x$
-2	-6
-1	-3
0	0
1	3
2	6

Page 201

x	$y = 5 - 2x$
0	5 = 5 - 0
1	3 = 5 - 2
2	1 = 5 - 4

3. y-intercept = -1

1. y-intercept = 5

x	$y = \frac{2 + 3x}{-2}$
0	-1 = $\frac{2 + 0}{-2}$
2	-4 = $\frac{2 + 6}{-2}$
-2	2 = $\frac{2 + -6}{-2}$

5. y-intercept = -3

x	$y = \frac{x-9}{3}$
0	$-3 = \frac{0-9}{3}$
3	$-2 = \frac{3-9}{3}$
6	$-1 = \frac{6-9}{3}$

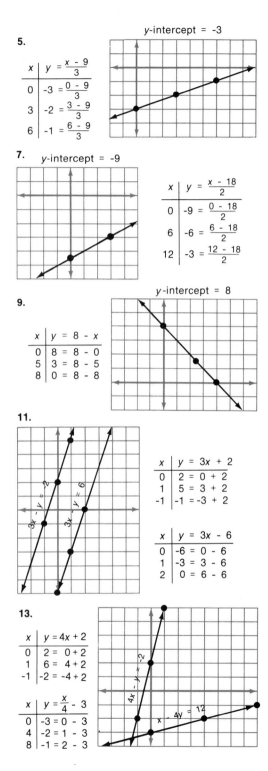

7. y-intercept = -9

x	$y = \frac{x-18}{2}$
0	$-9 = \frac{0-18}{2}$
6	$-6 = \frac{6-18}{2}$
12	$-3 = \frac{12-18}{2}$

9.

y-intercept = 8

x	$y = 8 - x$
0	$8 = 8 - 0$
5	$3 = 8 - 5$
8	$0 = 8 - 8$

11.

x	$y = 3x + 2$
0	$2 = 0 + 2$
1	$5 = 3 + 2$
-1	$-1 = -3 + 2$

x	$y = 3x - 6$
0	$-6 = 0 - 6$
1	$-3 = 3 - 6$
2	$0 = 6 - 6$

13.

x	$y = 4x + 2$
0	$2 = 0 + 2$
1	$6 = 4 + 2$
-1	$-2 = -4 + 2$

x	$y = \frac{x}{4} - 3$
0	$-3 = 0 - 3$
4	$-2 = 1 - 3$
8	$-1 = 2 - 3$

15.

x	$y = x + 1$
0	$1 = 0 + 1$
1	$2 = 1 + 1$
-1	$0 = -1 + 1$

x	$y = 2x + 1$
0	$1 = 0 + 1$
1	$3 = 2 + 1$
-1	$-1 = -2 + 1$

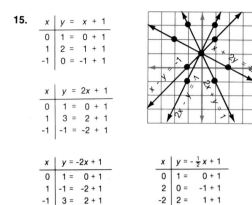

x	$y = -2x + 1$
0	$1 = 0 + 1$
1	$-1 = -2 + 1$
-1	$3 = 2 + 1$

x	$y = -\frac{1}{2}x + 1$
0	$1 = 0 + 1$
2	$0 = -1 + 1$
-2	$2 = 1 + 1$

All four equations have the same y-intercept.

Page 209

1. $m = -\frac{2}{3}$, $b = 1$ **3.** $m = \frac{1}{7}$, $b = 0$ **5.** 4 **7.** $\frac{5}{3}$

9. 0 **11.** no slope **13.** 2 **15.** $\frac{8}{3}$

Page 214

1. yes

$y = -3x + 5$
$m = -3$
$b = 5$

x	y
0	5
1	2
2	-1

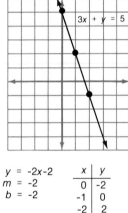

$3x + y = 5$

3. yes

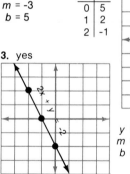

$y = -2x-2$
$m = -2$
$b = -2$

x	y
0	-2
-1	0
-2	2

5. none; vertical line at $x = 4$; no

7. yes

$y = -2x + \frac{9}{2}$
$m = -2$
$b = \frac{9}{2}$

x	y
0	$\frac{9}{2}$
1	$\frac{5}{2}$
2	$\frac{1}{2}$

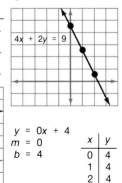

$4x + 2y = 9$

9. yes

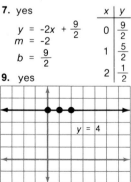

$y = 4$

$y = 0x + 4$
$m = 0$
$b = 4$

x	y
0	4
1	4
2	4

11. yes

$y = -x + 8$
$m = -1$
$b = 8$

x	y
0	8
2	6
4	4

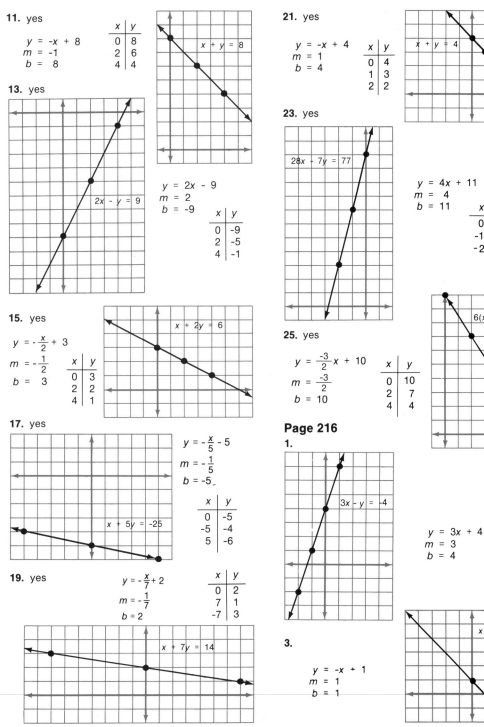

$x + y = 8$

13. yes

$2x - y = 9$

$y = 2x - 9$
$m = 2$
$b = -9$

x	y
0	-9
2	-5
4	-1

15. yes

$y = -\dfrac{x}{2} + 3$
$m = -\dfrac{1}{2}$
$b = 3$

x	y
0	3
2	2
4	1

$x + 2y = 6$

17. yes

$x + 5y = -25$

$y = -\dfrac{x}{5} - 5$
$m = -\dfrac{1}{5}$
$b = -5$

x	y
0	-5
-5	-4
5	-6

19. yes

$y = -\dfrac{x}{7} + 2$
$m = -\dfrac{1}{7}$
$b = 2$

x	y
0	2
7	1
-7	3

$x + 7y = 14$

21. yes

$y = -x + 4$
$m = 1$
$b = 4$

x	y
0	4
1	3
2	2

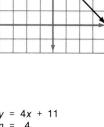

$x + y = 4$

23. yes

$28x - 7y = 77$

$y = 4x + 11$
$m = 4$
$b = 11$

x	y
0	11
-1	7
-2	3

25. yes

$y = \dfrac{-3}{2}x + 10$
$m = \dfrac{-3}{2}$
$b = 10$

x	y
0	10
2	7
4	4

$6(x - 10) + 4y = -20$

Page 216

1.

$3x - y = -4$

$y = 3x + 4$
$m = 3$
$b = 4$

3.

$y = -x + 1$
$m = 1$
$b = 1$

$x + y = 1$

5.

$y = \frac{1}{3}x + 2$

$m = \frac{1}{3}$

$b = 2$

x − 3y = −6

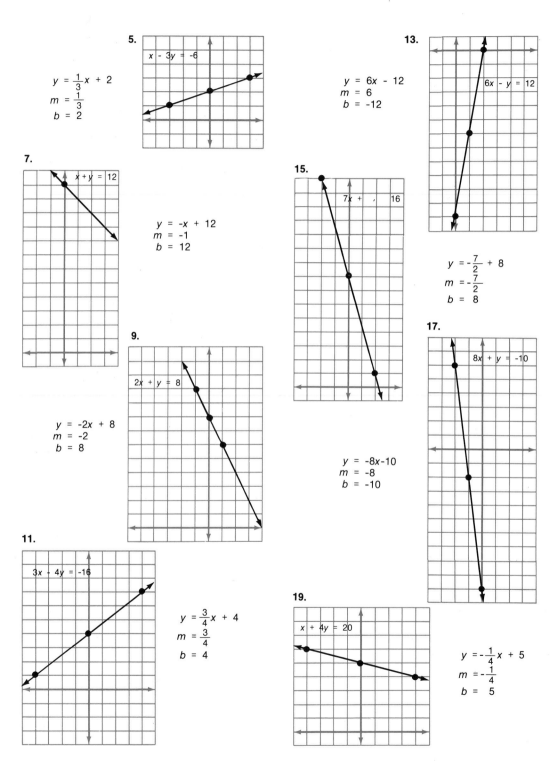

13.

$y = 6x - 12$

$m = 6$

$b = -12$

6x − y = 12

7.

x + y = 12

$y = -x + 12$

$m = -1$

$b = 12$

15.

7x + , 16

$y = -\frac{7}{2} + 8$

$m = -\frac{7}{2}$

$b = 8$

9.

2x + y = 8

$y = -2x + 8$

$m = -2$

$b = 8$

$y = -8x-10$

$m = -8$

$b = -10$

17.

8x + y = −10

11.

3x − 4y = −16

$y = \frac{3}{4}x + 4$

$m = \frac{3}{4}$

$b = 4$

19.

x + 4y = 20

$y = -\frac{1}{4}x + 5$

$m = -\frac{1}{4}$

$b = 5$

Page 221

1. $y = 3x + \frac{1}{4}$ **3.** $y = -5x + 10$ **5.** $y = 7$

7. $y = 9x - \frac{2}{3}$ **9.** $y = \frac{1}{4}x + 8$ **11.** $y = -\frac{1}{4}x + \frac{25}{4}$

13. $y = \frac{3}{5}x + 4$ **15.** $y = -\frac{1}{8}x - \frac{9}{8}$ **17.** $y = -4x - 15$

19. $y = \frac{4}{5}x + 6$

Page 224

1. $y = \frac{7}{5}x + \frac{26}{5}$ **3.** $y = \frac{13}{5}x - \frac{32}{5}$

5. $y = 4x + 0$ **7.** $y = \frac{1}{11}x + \frac{26}{11}$

9. $y = -\frac{8}{13}x + \frac{2}{13}$ **11.** $y = -x + 9$ **13.** $y = -4$

15. $y = \frac{12}{5}x + \frac{3}{5}$ **17.** $y = \frac{1}{4}x + \frac{23}{4}$

19. $y = -x + 6$

Page 230

1. $y = 6x$

3.

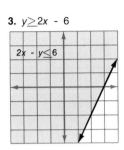

$y = 2x$

5. yes; k = 0.433

h	p
1	0.433
2	0.866
3	1.299

7. $k = 2, y = 2x$ **9.** $k = \frac{4}{7}, y = \frac{4}{7}x$ **11.** 40

13. 100

Page 233

3. $y \geq 2x - 6$

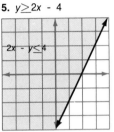

7. $y > -x - 2$

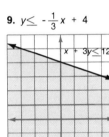

11. an infinite number

1. $y > 3x + 2$

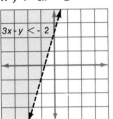

5. $y \geq 2x - 4$

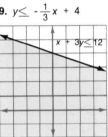

9. $y \leq -\frac{1}{3}x + 4$

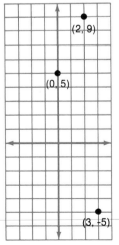

Page 235

1. a. IV c. I e. on y-axis

3. a. yes

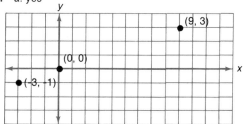

c. yes

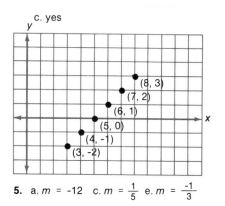

5. a. $m = -12$ c. $m = \frac{1}{5}$ e. $m = \frac{-1}{3}$

7 a.

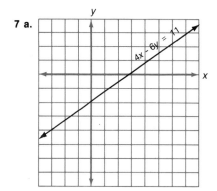

7 c.

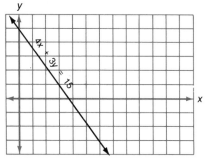

7 e.

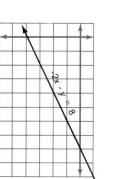

9. a. $\frac{1}{2}$ **c.** 3

11 a. $y \leq x + 7$

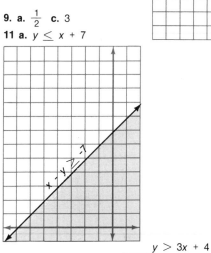

$y > 3x + 4$

11 c.

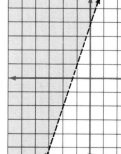

Chapter 6
Page 244

1.

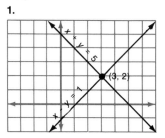

588

3.

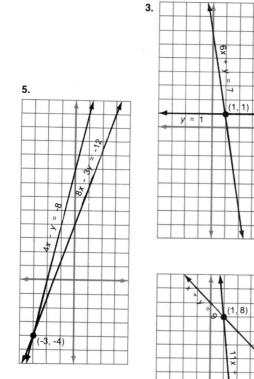

5.

11.

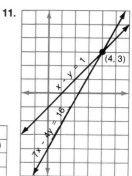

13.

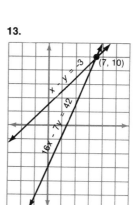

7.

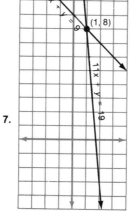

15.

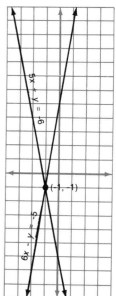

9.

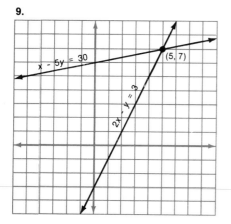

17.

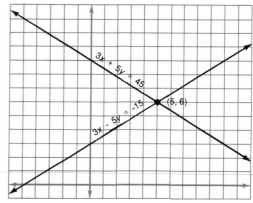

Page 247

19.

7. consistent, independent

1. consistent, independent

9. consistent, independent

3. consistent, dependent

11. consistent, independent

13. consistent, independent

5. consistent, independent

15. consistent, independent

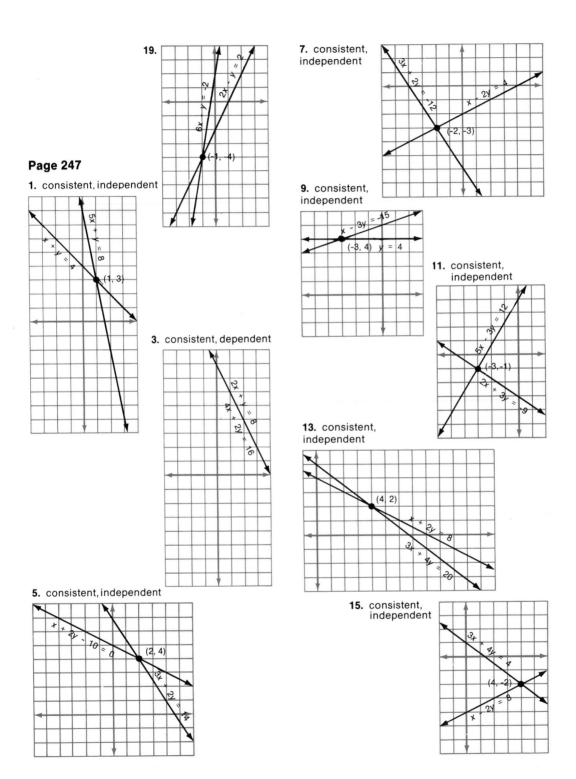

Pages 250-51

1. (-4, 24) **3.** $(\frac{10}{3}, \frac{20}{3})$ **5.** $(\frac{-10}{3}, \frac{-8}{3})$ **7.** (2, 7)
9. (-2, 1) **11.** (-1, -6) **13.** $(\frac{41}{7}, \frac{-3}{7})$ **15.** $(\frac{28}{5}, \frac{14}{5})$
17. (-1, 3) **19.** (3, 9)

Pages 254-55

1. (3, 11); consistent; independent **3.** (-3, -1); consistent; independent **5.** infinite number of solutions; consistent; dependent **7.** $(\frac{-9}{26}, \frac{-25}{26})$; consistent; independent **9.** (9, -1); consistent; independent **11.** consistent; dependent
13. (6, 5); consistent; independent **15.** $(\frac{67}{22}, \frac{-5}{22})$; consistent; independent **17.** 675 and 321

Page 258

1. (1, 4) **3.** (10, -11) **5.** $(-\frac{1}{2}, 1)$ **7.** (-3, -1)
9. $(4, \frac{5}{2})$ **11.** $(\frac{5}{2}, \frac{9}{2})$ **13.** (-6, 3) **15.** $(\frac{41}{7}, \frac{3}{35})$

Page 261

1. (4, 3); consistent; independent **3.** infinite number of solutions; consistent; dependent
5. (-1, -3); consistent; independent **7.** (5, 9); consistent; independent **9.** (4, 7); consistent; independent **11.** $(\frac{77}{23}, \frac{79}{23})$; consistent; independent **13.** (-8, -2); consistent; independent **15.** (10, 4); consistent; independent
17. 365 and 256

Pages 264-65

1. 4 hours **3.** 4 P.M. **5.** Grandma, 40 mph; John, 52 mph **7.** wind, 3 mph; dirigible, 11 mph
9. 49 mph, 37 mph **11.** scouts, 4 mph; stream, 1 mph **13.** 2 hours **15.** 1st plane, $\frac{1}{2}$ hour, 188 mi.; 2nd plane, $2\frac{1}{2}$ hours, 1275 mi.

Page 268

1. $4200 at 10%, $5800 at 9.5% **3.** 5 yrs.
5. $4480 at 9%, $8020 at 7.5% **7.** $850 at 7%, $350 at 8.5% **9.** $8500 at 8%, $6500 at 10%
11. 7% for $2200 account, 10% for $5800 account **13.** $2 in the mother's 30% offer, $1 in the father's 25% offer **15.** 11.5% for the $1200 account, 9.5% for the $900 account

Pages 274-77

1. 37 lb. round steak, 8 lb. sirloin steak **3.** 60 gal. 1st farmer, 40 gal. 2nd farmer **5.** 8 roses, 6 carnations **7.** 12 gal. of 30% salt solution, 28 gal. of pure water **9.** 10 of each **11.** 35 lb. mixture, 15 lb. bluegrass **13.** 30 kg of concrete mix, 18 kg of sand **15.** 2.6 ℓ ocean water, 9.4 ℓ Dead Sea water **17.** 40 ml of 40% alcohol, 88 ml of water **19.** 5.8 qt. of A, 4.2 qt. of B

Page 282

1. 27 **3.** 37 **5.** 19 **7.** 82 **9.** 96

Page 285

1.

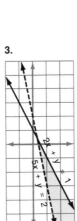

3.

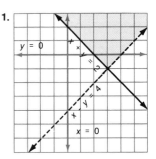

5.

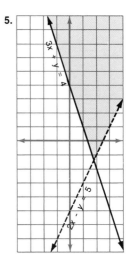

7.

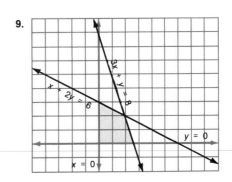

9.

Page 291

1. Maximum + 36 at (0, 6) **3.** Maximum + $\frac{15}{4}$ at$(\frac{5}{4}, 0)$ **5.** 80 regulars and no supers for a profit of $28.00

Page 296

1. (8, -6, -2) **3.** (12, 8, 0) **5.** (1, 4, -2) **7.** (0, 4, 9)
9. $(\frac{-1}{2}, \frac{17}{2}, \frac{5}{2})$ **11.** 273

Page 298-299

1 a.

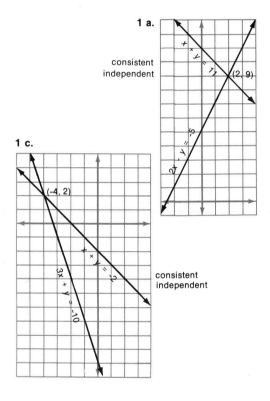

consistent independent

(2, 9)

1 c.

(-4, 2)

consistent independent

3. a. (3, 7) consistent, independent; c. (- 2, 5) consistent, independent **5.** $890 at 7.5%, $660 at 8.25% **7.** 75

9. Maximum = 15.1 at $(\frac{32}{9}, \frac{20}{9})$

x	y	z = 3x + 2y
(0, 0)		$3 \cdot 0 + 2 \cdot 0 = 0$
(3, 0)		$3 \cdot 3 + 2 \cdot 0 = 9$
$(\frac{32}{9}, \frac{20}{9})$		$3 \cdot \frac{32}{9} + 2 \cdot \frac{20}{9} = \frac{136}{9}$ (15.1)
(0, 4)		$3 \cdot 0 + 2 \cdot 4 = 8$

9.

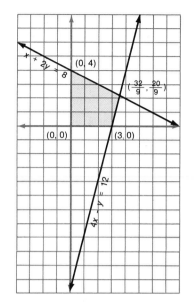

(0, 4)

$(\frac{32}{9}, \frac{20}{9})$

(0, 0)   (3, 0)

Chapter 7

Page 306

1. 6.6 **3.** 11.9 **5.** 7.5 **7.** 3.5 **9.** 12.2 **11.** 8.5
13. 26.2 **15.** 36 **17.** 5.5 **19.** 10.3 **21.** 9.6
23. 4.1 **25.** 8.2

Page 308

1. $5^{\frac{1}{2}}$ **3.** $2^{\frac{1}{3}} x^{\frac{2}{3}}$ **5.** $3^{\frac{1}{5}} x^{\frac{2}{5}} t^{\frac{1}{5}}$ **7.** $8^{\frac{3}{10}} x^{\frac{1}{10}} y^{\frac{2}{5}}$
9. $9^{\frac{2}{7}} a^{\frac{5}{7}}$ **11.** $\sqrt{5a}$ **13.** $\sqrt[7]{2^4 xy^3}$
15. $\sqrt[8]{3^3 5^2 x^5}$

17. between 1 and 2 **19.** between 2 and 3

Page 316

1. $4\sqrt{2}$ **3.** $3\sqrt[3]{2}$ **5.** cannot be simplified
7. $2\sqrt{3}$ **9.** $7\sqrt{2}$ **11.** cannot be
simplified **13.** $10\sqrt[3]{14}$ **15.** 210 **17.** $15\sqrt[3]{21}$
19. $3\sqrt[4]{9}$

Page 319

1. $\sqrt{15}$ **3.** $\sqrt{35}$ **5.** $3\sqrt{6}$ **7.** $3\sqrt{7}$
9. $\sqrt{590}$ **11.** $14\sqrt{5}$ **13.** $84\sqrt{15}$
15. $2\sqrt[3]{714}$ **17.** $77\sqrt{22}$ **19.** $12\sqrt[3]{3}$

Page 324

1. $\frac{2\sqrt{13}}{13}$ **3.** $\frac{3\sqrt{5}}{5}$ **5.** $\frac{2}{5}$

7. $\dfrac{3\sqrt{2}}{8}$ 9. $\dfrac{\sqrt{5}}{2}$ 11. $\dfrac{\sqrt{6}}{3}$

13. $\dfrac{\sqrt{3}}{3}$ 15. $\dfrac{1}{3}$ 17. $\dfrac{\sqrt{57}}{4}$

19. $\dfrac{\sqrt{430}}{40}$ 21. $\dfrac{\sqrt[3]{2}}{2}$ 23. $\dfrac{1}{2}$

25. $\dfrac{\sqrt[3]{9}}{6}$

Page 331
1. $xy^2\sqrt{6x}$ 3. $\dfrac{\sqrt{2x}}{2xy}$ 5. $2ac^3\sqrt[3]{25a^2b^2}$

7. $3ac^2\sqrt[3]{3ab^2}$ 9. $\dfrac{x\sqrt[3]{3xy^2z}}{z}$

Page 334
1. $6\sqrt{3}$ 3. $4\sqrt{2}+2\sqrt{3}$ 5. $\sqrt{2}$
7. $6\sqrt{5}$ 9. $-2\sqrt{3}$ 11. $3\sqrt{2}$
13. $-2a\sqrt{3}+\sqrt{2}$ 15. $4a\sqrt{2a}+\sqrt{2a}-5\sqrt{6}$
17. $5\sqrt{3}-3\sqrt{2}$ 19. $6\sqrt{x}+3\sqrt{xy}$

Pages 339-40
1. $\sqrt{41}$ 3. $2\sqrt{15}$ 5. $\sqrt{187}$ 7. $6\sqrt{3}$ 9. $4\sqrt{2}$
11. yes 13. no 15. $\sqrt{106}$ miles 17. $4\sqrt{6}$ in.

Page 346
1. $\sqrt{29}$ 3. $\sqrt{37}$ 5. $\sqrt{13}$ 7. $\sqrt{178}$ 9. $\sqrt{65}$
11. $\sqrt{10}+\sqrt{17}+5$ 13. $7+\sqrt{17}$
15. 12.5 nautical mi.

Page 351
1. 16 3. 62 5. 36 7. 3 9. 9 11. 52 is an extraneous root. 13. 124 15. -5

Pages 352-54
1. a. 11.3 c. 15.6 3. a. $\sqrt[3]{9a^5}$ c. $\sqrt{7xy}$ 5. a. 4 c. $6\sqrt{35}$ 7. a. $5x^2y^4\sqrt{3y}$ c. $\dfrac{x^4}{2y^3}$ 9. $\sqrt{52}$
11. a. $\sqrt{5}$ c. $\sqrt{82}$ 13. 2.0 sec.

Chapter 8
Page 361
1. trinomial; 2 3. monomial; 2 5. trinomial; 4
7. monomial; 6 9. trinomial; 7 11. 27 13. -132
15. 207,360

Pages 363-64
1. $19m-6$ 3. $7m^2+10m-5$ 5. $2m+n+p$
7. $5x^2+9x^2+2x-y+15$ 9. $-4x^2-2xy+18y^2$
11. $-4x^3+2x^2-2x+9$
13. $\dfrac{7x^2}{6}+\dfrac{11xy}{6}+\dfrac{3}{8}y^2$ 15. $\dfrac{7x}{3}-\dfrac{3y}{5}+\dfrac{8}{7}$
17. $14n-6$ 19. $3x^2+3x-27$

Page 366
1. $3a+8$ 3. $-3x+10y-6$ 5. $-7a^3+12a^2-14a-7$ 7. $x-16$ 9. $-4x+7y+9$
11. $5x+8y$ 13. x^5-2x^4+6x-5 15. $-2x+5y+16$ 17. $-6x^3-x^2y+xy^2+y^3-2y^4$
19. $-x^5y-12xy^2-3xy^4$

Page 369
1. $32x^3y^3z$ 3. $-12a^3b^3$ 5. $90xy$ 7. $\dfrac{-1}{12}m^3n$
9. $-256x^3yz$ 11. $-90a^2b^3$ 13. $-64x^9y^4$ 15. $27a^9$
17. $-12a^4b^2c^2$ 19. $a^{16}b^{20}c^{32}$

Pages 371-72
1. $14x^3+21x^2-56x$ 3. $24m^3-18m^2n-60m$
5. $3ak+3am-3ap$ 7. $12a^6+15a^3-54a^2$
9. $-8b^4+24b^3+32ab^2$ 11. $5a^5+3a^4-10a^2$
13. $4x^3+2x^2y+8x$ 15. $-24x^5y-56x^4y^2-80x^3y$
17. $\dfrac{7x^3}{2}+42x$

Pages 375-76
1. $x^2+7x+10$ 3. $x^2+2x-24$ 5. $x^2-7x+12$ 7. x^2-4x-5 9. $6x^2-24$ 11. $x^2-4x-12$ 13. $x^2-13x+42$ 15. x^2+x-72
17. $8x^2-22x-6$ 19. $10x^2-23x-42$
21. $2x^2-x-36$ 23. $6x^2+28x-98$
25. $36x^2-56x-32$ 27. $-2x^2+19x+60$
29. $15x^2-8x-12$ 31. $x^2+12x+36$
33. $49x^2+140x+100$ 35. $64x^2+48x+9$
37. x^2-9 39. x^2-100 41. $9x^2-16$ 43. x^2-6x+9 45. $x^2-16x+64$ 47. x^2+2x+1
49. x^2+6x+9

Page 378
1. $x^3+2x^2y+2xy^2+y^3$ 3. $12x^3+12x^2y-15xy^2-9y^3$ 5. $6x^3-17x^2+19x-28$ 7. $6a^2-18a+12ab-36b$ 9. $x^4+x^3-27x^2-18x+54$ 11. $8x^3-45x^2-14x-24$ 13. $5x^3-22x^2+25x-12$ 15. $24x^3+26x^2+10x+24$

Page 380
1. $x^2+6xy+9y^2$ 3. x^4-64 5. $x^2-12x+36$
7. $x^2-18xy+81y^2$ 9. $4x^2-121$
11. $2x^3+10x^2+4x-51$ 13. $2x^2+7x+34$
15. $x^3+2x^2-36x-72$

Page 382
1. x^3 3. $5b^3$ 5. $37a^2c^2$ 7. $-27b$ 9. $3z^4$
11. $\dfrac{1}{2}x^2y$ 13. a^3bc 15. $-7a^3bc^3$

Page 385
1. $x+5$ 3. x^2+x-1 5. $a+d$ 7. $7x-4$
9. $27x^2-9xy+3y^3$ 11. $-5x^2+x-9$
13. $17a^2b-5ab^2+2b^4$ 15. $-n^3+11$
17. a^2b-2b^2 19. $3ac^2-b^2$

Page 389
1. $x^2+2x+11$, R44 3. $a^2b-4ab^2+4b^3$ R $-4b^3-4b^4$ 5. $5x-7$, R 16 7. $24x-59$, R 168
9. $x-4$ 11. $x-2$, R $13x-21$ 13. a^3+2a, R 7a
15. $a+10$, R 72

Page 394

1. $\sqrt{6} - \sqrt{3}$ 3. $7\sqrt{3} + \sqrt{14}$ 5. -8
7. $\sqrt{15} + \sqrt{6}$ 9. $3x^2\sqrt{2} - 3x\sqrt{3} - 5x$
$\sqrt{6} + 15$ 11. $28 - 7\sqrt{11} + 4\sqrt{3} - \sqrt{33}$
13. $5\sqrt{3} - 6\sqrt{15} - 5\sqrt{2} + 6\sqrt{10}$
15. $24\sqrt{7} + 42$ 17. $11\sqrt{5} + 33 - 6\sqrt{10} - 18$
$\sqrt{2}$ 19. $18 - 8\sqrt{2}$ 21. $xy\sqrt{x} - y^2\sqrt{x}$
23. $x^2\sqrt{x} + 4x\sqrt{2x} + 8\sqrt{x}$
25. $3 - 2\sqrt{70}$

Page 397

1. $\dfrac{2\sqrt{3} + 2}{2} = \sqrt{3} + 1$

3. $\dfrac{\sqrt{6} + 2\sqrt{5} + \sqrt{15} + 5\sqrt{2}}{-7}$

5. $\dfrac{\sqrt{35} + 2\sqrt{5} + \sqrt{7} + 2}{3}$ 7. $\dfrac{\sqrt{78}}{6}$ 9. $\dfrac{7\sqrt{3}}{5}$

Page 398

1. trinomial; 3; 36 3. binomial; 2; 12
5. $-a^2 + 6ab - 13b^2$ 7. $2r^2 + 6rt - 7t$ 9. $-48a^5 b^6$
11. $21x^2y^2 - 35x^2y^6$ 13. $x^2 - 2x - 24$ 15. $y^2 - 36$
17. $x^2 - 20x + 99$ 19. $x^3 + 5x^2 + 11x + 10$
21. $x^3 - 3x^2 - 9x + 27$ 23. $4xyz$ 25. $6x + 3$
27. $\sqrt{22} - \sqrt{143}$ 29. $\dfrac{\sqrt{21}}{9}$

Chapter 9
Page 404

1. $3ab(2a + b)$ 3. $5abc(2ac^2 + b)$ 5. $a(a - 1)$
7. $8(x - 4y)$ 9. $4x(3x^2 - 4y^2)$ 11. $3(7x^3 - 2x^2 - 1)$
13. $10x(2a^3 + 5a + 1)$ 15. $7a(a^4 - 12a^2 + 3)$
17. $6(a^2 + 8a - 4)$ 19. $10(1 - 5x)$

Page 406

1. $4(x - 2)(x + 2)$ 3. $2(a - 11)(a + 11)$
5. $x^2(a - 4)(a + 4)$ 7. $(y - 12)(y + 12)$
9. $(a - 15b)(a + 15b)$ 11. $(6a - 7)(6a + 7)$
13. $3(7a - 13)(7a + 13)$ 15. $(3x - 10)$
$(3x + 10)$ 17. $4(2x - 1)(2x + 1)$ 19. $9(3a - 1)$
$(3a + 1)$

Page 409

1. yes 3. yes 5. no 7. no 9. no 11. $(x - 3)^2$
13. $(x - 8)^2$ 15. $(\frac{1}{4}y - 4)^2$ 17. $(3x + 5z)^2$
19. $4(x^2y - 3z^3)^2$ 21. $(a - 5b)^2$ 23. $(x + 1)^2$
25. $(6x + 1)^2$

Page 416

1. $(x + 8)(x - 4)$ 3. $(x + 1)(x - 3)$
5. $(b + 5)(b - 4)$ 7. $(a - 5)(a - 1)$
9. $(y + 5)(y + 2)$ 11. $4(x + 6)(x + 1)$
13. $(a + 7)(a - 4)$ 15. $6(b - 4)(b - 3)$
17. $(x - 6)(x - 2)$ 19. $(x + 4)(x - 4)$
21. $(a + 2)(a - 7)$ 23. $(x + 3)(x + 4)$
25. $2(x - 6)(x - 4)$

Page 419

1. $3(x - 3)^2$ 3. $(3x - 7)(x + 4)$ 5. $4(x - 2)$
$(x + 2)$ 7. $(2x + 1)(x + 4)$ 9. $(x - 9)^2$
11. $(3x - 1)(3x + 2)$ 13. $18(x + 1)(x + 2)$
15. $9(x - 8)(x + 8)$ 17. $10(3x + 5)(x - 5)$
19. $(3x + 4)(2x - 1)$

Page 421

1. $(x + 10y)(x - 6y)$ 3. $(y - 3z)^2$ 5. $(x + y)$
$(6x - 5y)$ 7. $(3x - 2y)(3x + 4y)$ 9. $(2x - 3y)$
$(3x - 4y)$ 11. $(3x + y)(x - 5y)$
13. $3(6c^2 + 3cd - 2d^2)$ 15. $5(x - 5y)(x + 5y)$
17. $(m - 5n)(m + 4n)$ 19. $(8p - 3q)(p - 4q)$

Page 426

1. $(a + 1)^2$ 3. $(10 - a)(10 + a)$ 5. $8(a - 3b^2)^2$
7. $a^3(3a^2 - 4)$ 9. $(2a + b)(x - y)(x + y)$
11. $10(x^2 + 5x + 7)$ 13. $(m^5 + 1)^2$ 15. $(5x - 1)$
$(5x + 1)$ 17. $5(a + 7)$ 19. $(x - 2)(x - 4)$
21. $(b + c)(a - m)$ 23. $(a + b)(t - w)$
25. $[(x + y) + 1]^2$

Pages 428-29

1. $x(8xy^3 + 5y^2 - 2)$ 3. $x^2(x^2 + 3xy + 7)$
5. $(5x - 12y)(5x + 12y)$ 7. $(a + 7)^2$ 9. $(2x - 3y)^2$
11. $2(x - 9)(x - 6)$ 13. $2(3a - 7)(a - 1)$
15. $(x - 12)(x + 7)$ 17. $6(2x + 3y)(x + 5y)$
19. $2(3x - 5)(2x + 7)$

Chapter 10
Page 433

1. 0 3. $^-5, ^-2$ 5. 0, -7 7. 3, 8 9. 0, -12 11. 7,
-4, 6 13. 2 15. -7, 8

Page 437

1. -3 3. 3, -3 5. 0, -3 7. $\dfrac{-3}{2}, \dfrac{3}{2}$ 9. 2 11. 8, 2
13. 2, -15 15. -2, -4 17. 2, -6 19. $\dfrac{-3}{4}, \dfrac{3}{4}$ 21. 2,
8 23. 9, 11 or -9, -11 25. 3 ft.

Page 440

1. ±10 3. ±5 5. $\pm\sqrt{6}$ 7. $\pm\sqrt{7}$ 9. ±5
11. 1, -9 13. 8, -14 15. $-2\pm3\sqrt{2}$

Pages 443-44

1. 16 3. 64 5. 676 7. $\dfrac{9}{4}$ 9. $\dfrac{49}{4}$ 11. 1, -5
13. 10, 4 15. 3, -5 17. 1, -2 19. 12, -2 21. 11, -9

Page 447

1. 1, $\dfrac{-3}{2}$ 3. 1, $\dfrac{-1}{2}$ 5. 3, $\dfrac{-3}{2}$ 7. $\dfrac{3}{2}$, -1 9. 5, $\dfrac{-7}{2}$

Page 455

1. -2, -4 3. -3, -5 5. -1, $\dfrac{-2}{7}$ 7. $\dfrac{3}{2}$, -1 9. 3
11. 4, $\dfrac{1}{2}$ 13. $\dfrac{5\pm\sqrt{105}}{4}$ 15. ±3 17. $\dfrac{1\pm\sqrt{31}}{3}$
19. 8, 1

Page 457

1. 29, real, irrational, $\dfrac{-3\pm\sqrt{29}}{2}$ 3. -11, imaginary
5. 41, real, irrational, $\dfrac{3\pm\sqrt{41}}{2}$ 7. -31, imaginary

9. 36, real, rational, -4, -10 **11.** 89, real, irrational, $\frac{3 \pm \sqrt{89}}{4}$ **13.** -95, imaginary **15.** 153, real, irrational, $\frac{3 \pm 3\sqrt{17}}{8}$

Page 459

1. $\frac{7 \pm \sqrt{33}}{4}$ **3.** 4, -2 **5.** $\frac{-11}{2}$, 4 **7.** imainary

9. imaginary **11.** 4, -2 **13.** $\frac{9}{4}$, -1

15. $-4 \pm 3\sqrt{2}$ **17.** $\frac{-1}{3}$, -4 **19.** -15, 3

21. imaginary **23.** -2, 1 **25.** $\frac{-3 \pm \sqrt{17}}{2}$

27. 6, 9 **29.** $\frac{5 \pm \sqrt{85}}{2}$

Page 463

1. 1, $\frac{-5}{2}$ **3.** 5 **5.** $\frac{1}{2}$ **7.** $\frac{-3}{2}$, 2 **9.** 1

Page 467

1. 12, 18 or -12, -18 **3.** 12 in. by 15 in.
5. 8 in. **7.** 17.9, 14.9, 9.9 in.
9. $4\sqrt{5} \doteq 8.9$ ft.

Pages 468-69

1. 7, -2 **3.** 8, -3 **5.** $\frac{7}{2}$, -8 **7.** $\pm \sqrt{17}$

9. $\frac{-7 \pm \sqrt{97}}{2}$ **11.** imaginary **13.** $\frac{1 \pm \sqrt{21}}{2}$

15. -3; -6 is an extraneous root. **17.** 2, real, irrational **19.** 12, -7 or 7, -12

Chapter 11
Page 474

1. 0 **3.** -2 **5.** 3, -8 **7.** -9, 2 **9.** $(x - 6)$
11. $(x - 1)$ **13.** $3(x - 10)$ **15.** $(x + 4)$
17. $(x - 2)(x + 2)^2$ **19.** $3(2x + 3)(x - 4)(x + 1)$
21. $8(2x - 3)(x - 5)(x + 3)$

Page 476

1. $\frac{x}{5}$ **3.** $\frac{5a^2}{9c^2}$ **5.** $\frac{z}{2(xy - 1)}$

7. $\frac{xy^2}{(x + y)(x + 3y)}$ **9.** $\frac{5(x - 6)}{x + 1}$ **11.** $\frac{x + 5}{x - 1}$

Page 479

1. $\frac{19}{70}$ **3.** $\frac{3}{8}$ **5.** a **7.** $\frac{z}{x^3y}$ **9.** 5

11. $\frac{x^3y^3}{4}$ **13.** $\frac{x^2(x + 6)}{x - 1}$ **15.** $\frac{1}{x - 1}$

17. $\frac{y}{(x - 3)(x + 4)}$ **19.** $\frac{(m + n)^2}{m - n}$ **21.** $\frac{x}{y}$

23. $\frac{3x - 2y}{x - y}$ **25.** 1 **27.** $\frac{x - 3}{xy}$

Pages 483-84

1. $\frac{7}{2}$ **3.** $\frac{1}{2}$ **5.** $\frac{7y^2}{3}$ **7.** $x + y$ **9.** $\frac{4}{15}$

11. $\frac{x}{x + 1}$ **13.** $\frac{(3x + y)(x + y)}{(x - y)^2}$ **15.** $\frac{x + 9}{x + 2}$

17. $\frac{(x - y)}{(x + y)^3}$ **19.** $\frac{3m + n}{m^3n^2(m - n)}$

Pages 486-87

1. 1 **3.** 2 **5.** $\frac{7}{x}$ **7.** x **9.** $\frac{-1}{c}$

11. $\frac{12}{x + 2}$ **13.** $\frac{13}{x + y}$ **15.** 3 **17.** $\frac{14\sqrt{2}}{a - c}$

19. $\frac{6}{a - 4}$ **21.** $2x - 1$ **23.** $\frac{a + b + 3}{x}$

25. 1 **27.** $\frac{4x^2 - 3xy + 9y^2}{(x + 2y)(x - y)}$ **29.** $\frac{1}{a}$

31. $\frac{-5}{7}$, $-\frac{5}{7}$, $-\frac{-5}{-7}$ **33.** $\frac{-7}{12}$, $-\frac{-7}{-12}$, $-\frac{7}{12}$

35. $-\frac{2}{7}$, $-\frac{2}{-7}$, $\frac{2}{7}$

Pages 491-92

1. $\frac{-7}{5}$ **3.** $\frac{-7}{9}$ **5.** $\frac{4}{a}$ **7.** $\frac{a - b}{c}$ **9.** $\frac{-2x}{y^2}$

11. $\frac{2(x - y)}{x + y}$ **13.** $\frac{x}{x^2 + y}$ **15.** $-\frac{1}{3}$ **17.** 1

19. $\frac{16}{a^2}$ **21.** 1 **23.** $\frac{6}{x^2 - 3x - 9}$ **25.** $\frac{14}{x - 2}$

27. $\frac{-2(x + 3)}{(x + 2)(x - 4)}$ **29.** $\frac{a + 3b}{a - b}$

Page 495

1. $\frac{12x + 9}{16}$ **3.** $\frac{19a + 13b}{156}$ **5.** $\frac{-22x + 3y}{375}$

7. $\frac{4x^2 - 1}{3x^3}$ **9.** $\frac{5 + 20x^2y}{2x^3y^2}$ **11.** $\frac{14x^3y^2 + 9yz^4}{9z^5}$

13. $\frac{9x^4 + 9x^2y^3 - 4x^2y - 4y^2}{36x^3y}$ **15.** $\frac{3 + 5x - 5y}{(x - y)(x + y)}$

17. $\frac{6(3x - 22)}{(x + 3)(x - 6)(x - 9)}$ **19.** $\frac{y(y + 11)}{(y + 2)(y + 5)^2}$

21. $\frac{-x^2 + 5x}{(x - 1)(x + 1)}$ **23.** $\frac{x^3 - 86x^2 - 113x}{(x - 7)(x + 9)(x - 9)}$

25. $\frac{2x^2 - 21x}{(x + 4)(x - 9)}$ **27.** $\frac{8x^3 - 3x^2 - 76x - 224}{6(x + 4)(x - 4)}$

29. $\frac{2a^2 - a + 2ab + 4b + b^2 - 10}{(a - b)(a + b)}$

Page 499

1. $\frac{2}{5}$ **3.** $\frac{21}{5}$ **5.** $(x + y)(x - y)$

7. $\frac{x}{x - y}$ **9.** $\frac{1}{(m - n)^2}$ **11.** $\frac{1}{4}$

Pages 500-1

1. -5, 0 **3.** $\frac{7}{-3}$, -3 **5.** $(2x + 1)(x + 5)$
$(x - 8)$ **7.** $\frac{x - 10}{x(x + 3)(x + 5)}$ **9.** $\frac{1}{2x - 5}$

11. $3(x + 11)$ **13.** $\frac{(x - 1)(x - 5)}{x^2(x + 3)}$ **15.** $\frac{1}{x - y}$

17. $\frac{x + 9xy + 2y}{27y}$ **19.** $\frac{x^3 + x^2 + 3x^2y + 5xy^2 - y^2 + 3y^3}{(x + y)^2(x - y)}$

Chapter 12
Pages 505-6

1. 40 **3.** 27 **5.** 11 **7.** -8 **9.** $\frac{9}{2}$ **11.** $\frac{-241}{8}$

13. $\frac{-6}{11}$ **15.** $\frac{7}{2}$ **17.** $\frac{11}{2}$ **19.** $\frac{3 \pm 3\sqrt{17}}{2}$

Page 509

1. $\frac{1}{4}$ **3.** $\frac{1}{2}$ **5.** $\frac{2}{3}$ **7.** 1 **9.** 3 **11.** $\frac{-103}{2}$ **13.** $\frac{69}{7}$
15. $\frac{-13}{11}$ **17.** $\frac{-5 \pm \sqrt{161}}{2}$ **19.** $\frac{51}{10}$ **21.** $\frac{-29}{7}$ **23.** $\frac{-11}{3}$
25. $\frac{-11}{5}$

Page 514

1. 13 **3.** 23 **5.** 2, 5 **7.** $56 **9.** $\frac{4}{3}, \frac{3}{8}$

Page 517

1. $2695 at 6%, $8085 at 8%, $2695 at 10%
3. $6000 at 9%, 2000 at $5\frac{3}{4}$% **5.** 11% for $3000
investment, 9% for $8000 investment
7. Preferred: $3750; Common: $1250; Total:
$5000 **9.** $1200 at $9\frac{1}{2}$%; $1000 at $5\frac{3}{4}$%

Pages 519-20

1. 59.5 lb. **3.** 2.64 ℓ **5.** 45.7 gal. **7.** 20 lb. of
lime **9.** 500 g of 28% solution, 300 g of 60%
solution

Pages 523-24

1. Brent, 75 min.; Jim, 150 min. **3.** 18 hrs.
5. 21.3 hrs. **7.** 29.8 hrs. **9.** Frances, 6.8 hrs.;
Joy, 9.8 hrs.

Page 527

1. 6 mph going, 10 mph returning **3.** slower
plane, 750 mi.; faster plane, 1500 mi. **5.** 225
mi.; boys, 5 hrs.; girls, $4\frac{1}{2}$ hrs. **7.** 40 mph
going, 5 mph returning **9.** 4 mph walking, 6 mph
riding

Page 531

1. $c = \frac{\pm \sqrt{em}}{m}$ **11.** $r = \frac{\pm \sqrt{A\pi}}{\pi}$

3. $h = \frac{p}{0.433}$ **13.** $b = \frac{p - 2h}{2}$

5. $t = \frac{d}{r}$ **15.** $d = \frac{\pm \sqrt{2.5\,nP}}{n}$

7. $r = \frac{c}{2\pi}$ **17.** $x = \frac{a(3 + y)}{y}$

9. $s = \frac{p}{3}$ **19.** $y = \frac{x}{2 - a}$

Page 532

1. 4 **3.** $\frac{1}{5}$ **5.** 26 **7.** 5 **9.** 1.9 oz. solder,
0.6 oz. tin **11.** 320 mi. apart **13.** $z = \frac{n - 3x}{4}$
15. $y = \frac{36z + 6}{z}$

Chapter 13
Page 539

1. 3, 5, 2, 7
3. 0, 4, -2, 8
5. 0, 4, 1, 16
7. 5, 9, 6, 21
9. -7, 5, -4, 41

11. $f(x) = x^2$

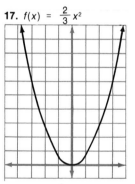

13. $f(x) = 3x^2$
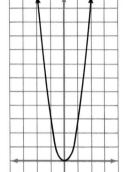

15. $f(x) = -\frac{1}{3} x^2$
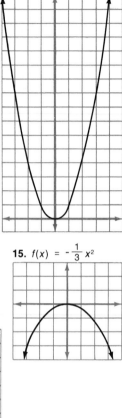

17. $f(x) = \frac{2}{3} x^2$

19. y-axis

Page 542

1. $f(x) = x^2 + 2$
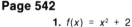
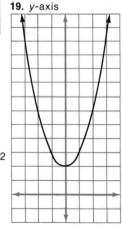

3. $f(x) = 2x^2 - 3$

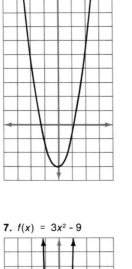

Page 547

1. $f(x) = (x - 4)^2 + 2$

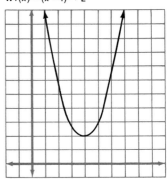

5. $f(x) = 2x^2 + 4$

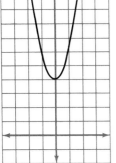

3. $f(x) = (x - 1)^2 - 3$

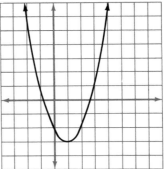

7. $f(x) = 3x^2 - 9$

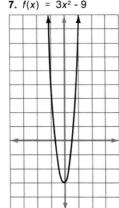

5. $f(x) = (x + 3)^2$

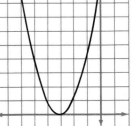

9. $f(x) = -3x^2 + 4$

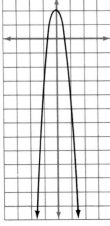

11. $f(x) = -\dfrac{1}{5} x^2 + 4$

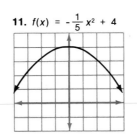

7. $f(x) = -(x + 4)^2 + 1$

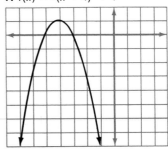

9. $f(x) = 3(x + 1)^2 + 4$

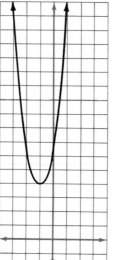

11. $(x + 2)^2 - 16$
13. $(x - \frac{3}{2})^2 - \frac{9}{4}$
15. $(x - 4)^2 - 1$
17. $(x + \frac{1}{2})^2 - \frac{25}{4}$
19. $(x - \frac{1}{2})^2 - \frac{49}{4}$
21. $(2, 4)$ up
23. $(\frac{1}{2}, -\frac{121}{4})$ up
25. $(\frac{11}{10}, \frac{-81}{20})$ up

Page 549

1. $f(x) = x^2 + 3$

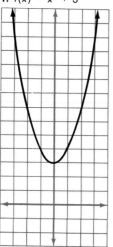

 No zeros
of the function

3. $f(x) = 2(x - 6)^2 + 5$

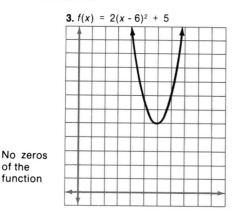

No zeros
of the
function

5. $f(x) = x^2 - 7x + 12$

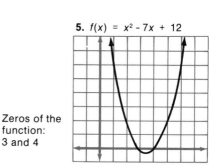

Zeros of the
function:
3 and 4

7. ±4 **9.** $-2 \pm \sqrt{3}$ **11.** $-3, 0$ **13.** 4 **15.** $-3 \pm 3\sqrt{2}$

Page 555

1. 20′ x 20′ **3.** time, 2 sec.; max. height, 64 ft.
5. -4, 4 **7.** 300 ovens; $90,500 profit
9. 70 items; $800

Page 561

3. $y < -4(x - 2)^2 + 3$

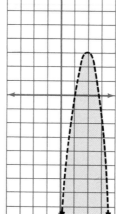

1. $y \leq x^2 - 4x$

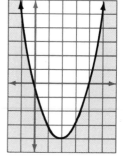

5. $y \leq x^2 - 4$

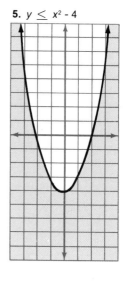

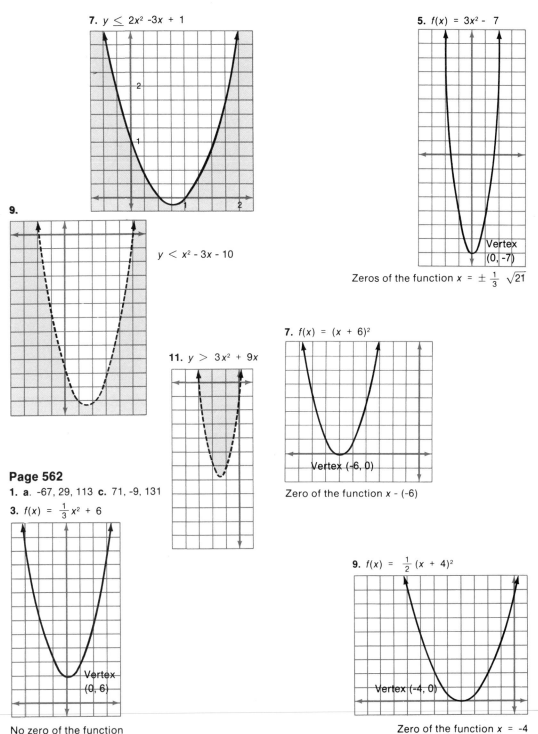

7. $y \leq 2x^2 - 3x + 1$

5. $f(x) = 3x^2 - 7$

Vertex
(0, -7)

Zeros of the function $x = \pm \frac{1}{3} \sqrt{21}$

9.

$y < x^2 - 3x - 10$

7. $f(x) = (x + 6)^2$

Vertex (-6, 0)

Zero of the function $x - (-6)$

11. $y > 3x^2 + 9x$

Page 562

1. a. -67, 29, 113 **c.** 71, -9, 131

3. $f(x) = \frac{1}{3}x^2 + 6$

Vertex
(0, 6)

No zero of the function

9. $f(x) = \frac{1}{2}(x + 4)^2$

Vertex (-4, 0)

Zero of the function $x = -4$

11. $f(x) = \frac{2}{3}(x + 6)^2 + 2$

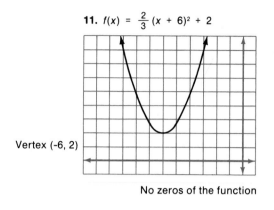

Vertex (-6, 2)

No zeros of the function

13. $f(x) = x^2 - 14x + 37$

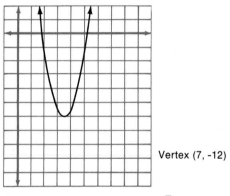

Vertex (7, -12)

Zeros of the function $x = 7 \pm 2\sqrt{3}$

15. $y \geq 2x^2$

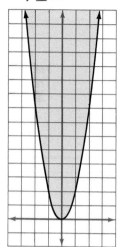

17. $y > (x - 1)^2 + 6$

PHOTO CREDITS